THE
RELUCTANT
REBELS

THE RELUCTANT REBELS

THE STORY OF THE CONTINENTAL CONGRESS

1774-1789

BY

LYNN MONTROSS

BARNES & NOBLE, Inc.

NEW YORK

PUBLISHERS & BOOKSELLERS SINCE 1873

Printed in the United States of America

TO

MY WIFE,

LOIS HARTZELL MONTROSS

Contents

Part One: 1774-1775—REBELLION
1. A Consistory of Kings   3
2. The Egg of Sedition   15
3. Doctor, Lawyer, Merchant, Chief   28
4. The Tolling of the Bells   43
5. Wardens of the Promised Land   58
6. Congress Declares War   74

Part Two: 1775-1776—INDEPENDENCE
7. The State of America   89
8. Every Wind from the North   102
9. The Committee of the Whole   116
10. The Hour of Decision   130
11. From this Time Forward   143

Part Three: 1776-1778—ALLIANCE
12. Embarrassment of Riches   161
13. The Flight to Baltimore   176
14. Year of the Hangman   193
15. Snow on Valley Forge   210
16. The Treaty with France   227

Part Four: 1778-1783—VICTORY
17. The Ailing Physician   247
18. That Froward Hussy, Maryland   262
19. Watchman, What of the Night?   276
20. Bricks Without Straw   291
21. The News from Yorktown   306
22. The Shadow and the Substance   324

Part Five: 1783-1789—UNION
23. Congress Takes to the Road   343

24. The Winning of the West   359
25. Through a Glass, Darkly   374
26. The Law of the Land   390
27. And On with the New   407

Appendix
  Presidents, Members and Seats of the Continental Congress   426

Sources and Acknowledgments   435

Chapter References   441

Index   453

List of Illustrations

*The following reproductions of portraits or
sketches will be found in a group facing page 214.*

The State House in Philadelphia, where the Continental Congress
met from 1775 to 1783, except for two interludes

George Washington, John Adams, Thomas Jefferson, James Madison,
James Monroe

John Jay, Benjamin Franklin, Henry Laurens

Edward Rutledge, Thomas McKean, Peyton Randolph

Benjamin Rush, David Ramsay, Oliver Wolcott

Lewis Morris, Carter Braxton, Arthur Middleton

John Hancock, Charles Carroll of Carrollton, Thomas Lynch, Jr.

Robert Morris, Alexander Hamilton, Gouverneur Morris

William Whipple, Philip Livingston, Francis Lewis

Thomas Mifflin, Philip Schuyler, John Sullivan

Thomas Paine, Charles Thomson, the Rev. Jacob Duché

John Dickinson, James Duane, James Wilson

Richard Henry Lee, Elbridge Gerry, Patrick Henry

Abraham Clark, William Ellery, Roger Sherman

Samuel Adams, Silas Deane, Arthur Lee

The City Hall of New York, eighth and final meeting place of the
Continental Congress, 1785 to 1789

PART ONE

Rebellion

The revolution was effected before the war commenced.
The revolution was in the minds and hearts of the
people.

— JOHN ADAMS

Chapter 1

A Consistory of Kings

THE temperature at Philadelphia was exactly 70 at six o'clock on the morning of July 2, 1776. During the next three hours it rose eight degrees, and the afternoon had turned hot and humid when the delegates gathered again in the State House.

These statistics were noted by a tall, redheaded Virginian who took readings thrice daily with the new thermometer he had purchased at a cost of three pounds and fifteen shillings. Thomas Jefferson also remembered to the end of his long life the bothersome horseflies which buzzed through the open windows from a near-by livery stable and hastened a vote on the issue:

> Resolved, That these United Colonies are, and, of right, ought to be, Free and Independent States; that they are absolved from all allegiance to the British crown, and that all political connexion between them, and the state of Great Britain, is, and ought to be, totally dissolved.

There was no doubt as to whether the resolution would pass. If there had been any misgivings, the experienced politicians of the Continental Congress would never have put them to a test. The only question was whether a unanimous vote of approval could be proclaimed from the twelve colonies empowered to decide. And that question depended on the arrival of a man slowly dying from cancer—a delegate making an eighty-mile ride to break the deadlock in his colony.

For months the great issue had been "independency." Only within the last few hours had the opposition of Pennsylvania and South Carolina been overcome. New York would be unable to vote until its delegates were instructed by a newly elected provincial convention meeting for the first time the following week. Approval had been indicated by all the other colonies save Delaware, where the opposite sides taken by McKean and Read put

3

the decision squarely up to their colleague, Caesar Rodney. As a militia colonel he had been investigating a reported Tory uprising on the shores of Chesapeake Bay when an express rider reached him with a message imploring his presence in Philadelphia.

Some of the silk-stockinged gentlemen slapping at horseflies in the State House were already assured of their page in history—Jefferson, Dr. Franklin, John and Samuel Adams, Dr. Witherspoon and Richard Henry Lee. In comparison, Caesar Rodney cut a small figure as a self-educated farmer and petty officeholder who had never climbed higher at the age of 48 than speaker in his provincial legislature. But Caesar Rodney had an appointment with destiny that hot Tuesday afternoon; and he staggered up to the door of the State House, booted and spurred, in time to cast his vote.

During the all-night ride through a thunderstorm he had worn out several horses. He was splashed with mud from head to foot, and on his haggard face could be seen the malignant growth which would bring him to a painful and lingering death a few months after the final victory. But there is no evidence that the other members of the Continental Congress indulged in any noisy demonstration. It was enough that with Rodney's vote the long and bitter struggle for independence had ended in a "unanimity" of approval which would be more authentic when New York signified its belated acceptance.

It may be, too, that some of the delegates were somberly reminded of another dying man in another assembly across the Atlantic, for the emotional ties with the mother country had not been broken even by separation. Nearly a year and a half had passed since a fierce, gaunt old statesman stood up before the peers on a January day in 1775 to save the Empire he had created. A recent peer himself, the Earl of Chatham still rejoiced in the name of the Great Commoner after exchanging the black velvet suit of Commons for the crimson robes of the House of Lords. All over the English-speaking world, however, men knew him simply as Mr. Pitt, the foremost parliamentarian of the generation.

At the age of 67 Mr. Pitt was dying from the most aristocratic of eighteenth-century ailments, and he seldom lost an opportunity to dramatize that fact. Ever theatrical, he made a point of appearing in flannel bandages and glaring reproachfully at the peers, as if blaming them for his gout in addition to their own ineptitude. But such gestures were permitted Mr. Pitt. It could not be forgotten that as prime minister he had conquered for England a world empire—not in an absent-minded moment, as has been more wittily than wisely said, but in a moment of prophetic illumination.

The phrases "lightning war" and "global warfare" had not been heard when Mr. Pitt smote the foe by land and sea on four continents. Yet it took him only a few months with the slow weapons of his age to win India and America. In a few more months, before the peace was signed, he had been reduced to a bystander and the ministers of the new king were enacting the first measures which would lead to dismemberment of the Empire.

Other men such as Burke, Fox and Wilkes could see the justice of the American cause, but Mr. Pitt loved America. He meant it when he said, "I rejoice that America has resisted!" He was equally sincere in declaring, "Were I but ten years younger I should spend the rest of my days in America, which has given the most brilliant proofs of its independent spirit." And on that January afternoon in 1775 Mr. Pitt believed that he had come before the House of Lords with an eleventh-hour solution which would be acceptable to both the colonies and the mother country.

It was statesmanship a century in advance of its day—a proposal to recognize the new Continental Congress by giving it the status of a dominion parliament in America without sacrificing the legitimate powers of England as the seat of empire. As a necessary preliminary, he pled that day for approval of a motion to remove the British troops occupying Boston.

Mr. Pitt knew, of course, that many of the peers had been bought, either directly or indirectly. But he hoped this time to overcome even the corruption of the reign. "I trust it is obvious to your Lordships," he said, after reviewing the accomplishments of the assembly in Philadelphia, "that all attempts to impose servitude on such men, to establish despotism over such a mighty continental nation, must be vain, must be fatal. We shall be *forced ultimately* to *retract*; let us retract when we can, not when we must." [1]

It was not Mr. Pitt's habit to plead with his inferiors. But even the rejection by a vote of 68 to 18 of his motion to withdraw the troops did not discourage him. The following month he was back before the House of Lords with his cherished bill which sought the key to reconciliation in the Continental Congress. And this time he met not only defeat but gross insult from such peers as Lord Gower and Lord Sandwich.

It was the sick old man's last appearance in Parliament until the spring of 1777, when the time had passed for keeping America in the Empire. But before leaving the House of Lords in the winter dusk, Mr. Pitt had a final fling with all of his old arrogance. The famous hooked nose and blazing eyes were never more scornful as he croaked in a voice trembling with fury, "You well know, if the present measure should prevail, that you must instantly relinquish your places. . . . Such then being your precarious situations, who should wonder that you can put a negative on any measure which must annihilate your power, deprive you of your emoluments, and at once reduce you to that state of insignificance for which God and nature designed you!"

Mr. Pitt had spoken for history and his words must have been recalled a year and a half later by at least one of the delegates who voted for independence. Dr. Franklin, the elder statesman of America, had been present in the House of Lords that afternoon. He himself had not been spared by the insults of the peers, for it was Dr. Franklin who served as Mr. Pitt's chief adviser in drawing up the bill recognizing the Continental Congress.

It is a credit to that Congress on July 2, 1776, that the members could take independence in stride as a means rather than an end. Even on the fourth— a date which had not yet attained to a capital letter—the committee of the whole did not approve the Declaration until it had disposed of a piece of routine business, "Resolved, That an application be made to the committee of safety for a supply of flints for the troops at New York. . . ." [2]

Only a few letters written by delegates on the first Independence Day appear to have been preserved. Caesar Rodney reported to his brother, "I arrived in Congress (tho detained by thunder and Rain) time enough to give my Voice to the matter of Independence." And he ended on a practical note, "Don't Neglect to Attend Closely and Carefully to my Harvest." [3]

Abraham Clark, the New Jersey surveyor and amateur lawyer, was another self-educated delegate whose modest record of achievement at the age of 50 included several terms as Essex County sheriff. His letter to a friend shows more of a feeling that posterity might be glancing over his shoulder: "I am among a Consistory of Kings as our Enemy says. I assure you, Sir, our Congress is an August Assembly, and can they Support the Declaration now on the Anvil, they will be the Greatest Assembly on Earth." But on August 6th, only four days after affixing his signature, Clark was neither so lyrical nor so confident. Writing to the same friend, he speculated, "As to my title, I know not yet whether it will be honourable or dishonourable; the issue of the war must settle it. Perhaps our Congress will be exalted on a high gallows." [4]

Caesar Rodney soon had other things than independence on his mind. The tall and lanky Delaware farmer had taken his long ride not only to vote but also to order new shoes in Philadelphia for his small nieces. On July 10th he wrote irritably to his brother that the cobbler had not yet finished. On August 3rd, the day after signing the Declaration, Rodney communicated with emotional spelling, "I believe I shall never be able to get that scoundrel to make Betsey's and Sally's Shooses." Not until the 28th was he able to announce that the shoes had been sent by post. "I know," he grumbled, "that they were very dear, to wit: 14 s. 6 d. a pair." [5]

Dr. Franklin, as was his habit in Congress, thought much and said little. Mr. Jefferson, whose feelings were smarting from the changes made in his final draft of the Declaration, recorded the purchase of seven pairs of gloves for his wife on July 4th at a cost of twenty-seven shillings. His new thermometer showed that the temperature had moderated to a reading of 76 degrees at 1:00 P.M.

All of the delegates, of either high or low estate, would doubtless have been disconcerted if they could have foreseen that posterity would place the fifty-six signers of the Declaration on a pedestal above other members of the Continental Congress. They could hardly have anticipated that Button Gwinnett, who contributed little except his signature, might someday wear a brighter halo than that great patriot John Dickinson, whose conscience did not permit him to sign. Even less could they have suspected that seven generations later the minor battles of the Revolution would be more celebrated than the decisions of the assembly which became the only substitute for a central government in America from 1774 to 1789.

Much as democracy has always been praised in the abstract by citizens of democratic nations, it is seldom that a legislator ever becomes a hero either to his constituents or to posterity. Generals and admirals have the surest claim to fame, particularly those warriors who strut or at least stride across the stage. Executives such as presidents and prime ministers also are considered fit subjects for sculpture, and some of the more forthright judges, diplomats and financiers may expect recognition. But there is little hope for a parliamentarian to be long remembered unless his career has been gilded by oratory.

It is a further irony that the Continental Congress might have had more appeal if it had been less successful. The tattered glory of a lost cause has a peculiar fascination for the English-speaking peoples, whose tears have kept green such melancholy fields as Worcester, Culloden, Appomattox and the Boyne. After being safely defeated, a cavalier is always a more romantic figure than a roundhead; and even that incredible gadfly Bonnie Prince Charlie has been preserved in the amber of plaintive ballads. There were times when it appeared that the Continental Congress might gain a like renown by ending in anarchy or surrender. There were blunders, squabbles, errors of omission, and dreary interludes of utility. But in its darkest hours the little parliament of provincial lawyers, merchants and planters never quite lost the brisk air of a going concern; and it ended by creating a new nation after winning a long war against the world's most powerful empire.

The very name "Congress," with its later connotations, brings up a picture of dignified senators exercising their authority according to the Constitution by passing laws and levying taxes. Present-day Americans are all too likely to forget that the Continental Congress came into being as a revolutionary body composed of rebels and traitors with their heads in a noose. It remains unique among the legislatures of history in that it had no authority to pass laws, no powers for enforcing the measures it did take, no means of raising money except printing, begging or borrowing. Such prerogatives as it seized were based upon broad interpretations of instructions from the provincial assemblies; and it could only suggest rather than dictate to constituents.

The Continental Congress, in short, was simply an advisory council which depended for its effectiveness on the good will of thirteen scattered colonies with conflicting interests. If it exceeded its authority and accomplished prodigies in spite of all, much of the credit is due to the co-operation of a people long trained in local self-government.

American loyalists accused "King Congress" of worse tyrannies than any committed by George III. They saw every delegate as an "independent incendiary" or a "lean and grinning Cassius." [6] Sometimes their vilification took the form of doggerel:

> Down at night a bricklayer or carpenter lies,
> Next sun a Lycurgus, a Solon doth arise!

But the historical evidence shows a conspicuous lack of sansculottes in the Continental Congress. During the fifteen years a large share of the 342 members were property owners in comfortable financial circumstances, professional men who had graduated from some American or European college. Despite the absence of Jacobinism, the historian Van Tyne has declared:

> The audacity of the second Continental Congress will ever be a matter of wonder. Without unity in instruction, with no power to form a government, without jurisdiction over an acre of territory, with no authority to administer government in an acre if they had it, with no money, no laws and no means to execute them, they entered upon the task of regulating a society in the state of revolution.[7]

The Declaration of Independence was not considered the greatest labor of Congress by many of the members themselves—the founding fathers who referred to one another by such malicious nicknames as Swivel-Eye and Bacon-Face. First, it was necessary to put the cart before the horse by organizing a war effort against an incomparably stronger foe; and John Adams tried to give an idea of these earlier problems in a letter to his wife:

"When fifty or sixty men have a Constitution to form for a great empire, at the same time that they have a country of fifteen hundred miles in extent to fortify, millions to arm and train, a naval power to begin, an extensive commerce to regulate, numerous tribes of Indians to negotiate with, a standing army of twenty-seven thousand men to raise, pay and victual, I shall really pity those fifty or sixty men." [8]

The rotund Braintree lawyer did not exaggerate the difficulties. They multiplied until the Continental Congress became perhaps the only parliament on earth to make a practice of deliberating before breakfast. From six in the morning until ten at night the delegates kept their noses to the grindstone. Adams himself served on ninety committees during his four years in the assembly and acted as chairman of twenty-five.

No business was too petty for King Congress. While the members were debating independence, planning confederation, publishing memorable state papers, conferring on strategy and seeking foreign alliances, several such decisions as the following were recorded every day in the *Journals*:

> *Resolved*, That the Secret Committee be directed to supply Captain Romans with 24 musquets for his company. [9]

Twelve of the colonies were invaded at various times by enemy forces which occupied the four largest cities. Yet if anyone had inquired as to the war, the members of Congress might well have asked, "Which war?" For they had not only a war with Great Britain on their hands, but also such sideshows as Indian massacres on the frontier and a bloody civil strife between rebels and loyalists. There were Tory plots to kidnap the delegates wholesale, and twice they had to take to their heels just ahead of an advancing foe. An even more humiliating scene ensued when King Congress was besieged for a few hours in the State House by unpaid American troops marching on Philadelphia in open mutiny.

The military effort culminated in the surrender of two British armies in the field. But victory did not bring surcease from strife, and the political struggle for power became more bitter after Yorktown. Then a beggared Congress was stripped of much of the power it had wielded by tacit consent during the emergency. The specter of states' rights had reared its head—never to be entirely downed until the day of Appomattox—and there was reason for Washington's warning in his circular letter of 1783: "It is yet to be decided whether the Revolution must ultimately be considered a blessing or a curse."

Congress itself had encouraged the new states to form governments of their own. Such able members as Jefferson, Patrick Henry and John Hancock resigned to become governors in their states. They were replaced by lesser men until Hamilton was moved to declare that "the road to popularity in each state is to inspire jealousy of the power of Congress."

A cynical contemporary put it more bluntly in a remark often quoted by exponents of the masochistic school of American historical writing. "What a lot of damned scoundrels we had in that second Congress!" commented Gouverneur Morris. But he tempered this verdict with an amendment which is not so well known: "The present Congress considered in the double sense of integrity and ability is at least as respectable as any. . . . And since the Deity chose one Judas among twelve disciples, it cannot be wondered at if among a much greater number a few should be charged with peculiar gravity." [10]

During the fifteen years there were opportunists, obstructionists, profiteers and at least one incipient traitor among the 342 delegates. Absenteeism had become such a curse by 1784 that the gains of the peace with England were endangered for lack of enough votes to ratify a favourable treaty before the appointed date. But even in its decline the assembly was saved from futility by a hard core of such able parliamentarians as Roger Sherman, Elbridge Gerry and Richard Henry Lee. They were reinforced now and then by some veteran of the great days who returned to serve another term, as did Jefferson in 1783. And as time went on, young men were elected who had been recent college students when Congress first met—Madison and Hamilton and Monroe.

Certainly the career of a delegate held forth few enough rewards or even compensations. Dr. Witherspoon, the president of Princeton, had to drop out for a year because he could not afford to serve. Gouverneur Morris found it impossible to support himself without practicing law on the side. Young Madison, after a twelve-day ride to Philadelphia over muddy roads, incurred a board bill of $21,373 for his first six months. During this period he also paid $1,176 for laundry, $6,511 for the care of his horse, and $2,495 for liquors, sugar and fruit.[11] Such prices, of course, reflected the cruel inflation of the Continental currency, for in "hard money" the board bill amounted to only about two specie dollars a day. Even so, Madison's funds from the state could not be stretched to cover personal expenses, and he had to borrow from a moneylender.*

Congress itself was bankrupt. In five years it issued a total of $200,000,000 in unbacked bills of credit, but the states would not levy taxes to redeem the federal currency or give Congress the power to do so. Contrary to a popular legend, the members of the assembly were never for a moment so simple as to trust that the printing press offered a sound solution of the financial problem. They were driven to desperate expedients in order to carry on from

---

* Although it is anticipating the practice of a later day to use the dollar sign in connection with Revolutionary finances, this liberty seems justified on grounds of familiarity and convenience. Americans of that age were accustomed to the Spanish milled dollar, worth about four shillings sixpence.

month to month, and only loans or gifts from France enabled them to limp
through the worst years.

Both as a parliamentarian and a scholar of history, Mr. Pitt must have
foreseen in 1775 the troubles awaiting any attempt to unite the thirteen
colonies under a strong central government. Although he flattered America
at this early date by referring to it as "a mighty continental nation," he
must have realized what a chasm lay between the ideal and the reality.

Nothing appears more easy to the casual reader of history than the
forming of a union by consent of the participating states, and yet the fingers
of one hand are enough to number the lasting examples. Only two precepts
offered much encouragement to the Americans of 1776—the Swiss Cantons
and the United Provinces of the Netherlands. In each case the threat of
being mastered by a common foe had supplied the incentive. But in Switzerland the blood of several civil wars was added to the political cement, and
it could not be forgotten that nine of the sixteen provinces of the Netherlands deserted the confederation within a few years and returned to the
rule of the oppressor.

The chronicles of the past furnished more object lessons than examples
in 1776, including the downfall of two of the most brilliant civilizations ever
known. After all efforts to unite the city-states of ancient Greece had failed,
they became the prey of the Macedonian conqueror. Eighteen centuries later
the tragedy was repeated in faithful detail when the disputing Italian city-
states of the Renaissance fell to Charles V. In both cases the advantages of
confederation were acknowledged in theory, but just as Athens and Sparta
and Thebes found it impossible to agree, so did Florence and Milan and
Naples. The political genius of Machiavelli was as powerless to save Italy
as the eloquence of Demosthenes had been to prevent the ruin of Greece.

It took the Continental Congress thirteen years to create a permanent
federal union on a much larger scale than the Dutch or Swiss confederation,
and this may be considered a remarkably brief period of gestation. The five
great documents of the revolutionary assembly represented the progressive
stages:

the Articles of Association, 1774;
the Declaration of Independence, 1776;
the Articles of Confederation, 1777-1781;
the Northwest Ordinance, 1787;
the Constitution of the United States, 1787-1788.

As the first practical instrument of American government, the Association
deserves more attention than it has received. On the surface, of course, it

appeared to be merely a nonimportation and nonexportation agreement. Actually it set up a simple but effective revolutionary administration in which the will of the assembly was executed by the countless committees of safety which sprang up everywhere to seize the reins of local power.

From the beginning the word "nation" frequently appeared in state papers, but it remained a symbol of wishful thinking until June 11, 1776. On that date, a few weeks before approving the Declaration of Independence, the Continental Congress appointed a committee to begin the labor of preparing a constitution.

The ensuing debates owed a great deal to a prejudice against oratory which has not been inherited by subsequent Congresses. Washington, Franklin and Jefferson set the tradition by seldom speaking at all, and even Patrick Henry kept within very moderate limits. Thus the early discussions of union were pitched in a conversational tone, which give them such an advantage that the first American constitution was adopted toward the end of 1777.

This document, so hopefully entitled the Articles of Confederation and Perpetual Union, belongs among the gallant failures of history. So many compromises were included, due to the fears and jealousies of the states, that Congress retained less actual power than it had been wielding by tacit consent. The Articles simply confirmed the worst weaknesses of the assembly, which still had no authority to pass laws, levy taxes, regulate commerce or enforce measures. Even these concessions did not overcome the distrust of the states; and it was not until 1781, a few months before Yorktown, that the Articles were ratified.

Generations of schoolboys have been given a vague impression that the Constitutional Convention somehow sprang full grown from the American soil. But it was the Continental Congress that retained enough influence in 1786 to call the representatives of twelve states together the following spring to frame a new constitution. In fact, the Convention was virtually a committee of Congress, since it consisted almost entirely of men who had been members—men of the stamp of Washington, Franklin, Madison, Hamilton, Randolph, King, Sherman, Gerry and Gouverneur Morris.

That is why there were no blithe optimists among the 55 delegates meeting in Independence Hall. The Continental Congress had been operating since 1774 as a laboratory of political science, and it had taught by painful experience that the creation of a new nation is a tremendous undertaking.

Some of the failures and frustrations experienced in that assembly could now be counted as blessings. With them in mind, the Convention began by scrapping the Articles of Confederation altogether. It was a new national constitution, from top to bottom, which evolved from the hard lessons learned in the Continental Congress. Even after its adoption, the founding fathers did not regard it as a sacred cow. All of them were frankly skeptical, and they might have been more dubious if they could have foreseen a day when worshipful praise would be paid by speakers addressing luncheon clubs over the chicken patties and peas. For the gloomy realists who created the Republic knew that no constitution is perfect, that no political rights can be guaranteed, that no people can afford to be complacent about their national institutions.

During the very summer when the Convention was meeting, the fourth great document of the Continental Congress came into being with the adoption of the act for the government of the western lands—usually known as the Northwest Ordinance. Thus did the assembly lay the foundation of a mighty future nation, after inducing the states to give up their claims to this vast area which would soon be made into new states. As an instrument of government, moreover, the Northwest Ordinance provided for individual liberties which were afterwards incorporated in the Constitution and the so-called Bill of Rights.

After the adoption of the Constitution two months later and its ratification in 1788, the Continental Congress slowly withered on the vine. It was then meeting in New York—the eighth seat of government for the migratory assembly—and days passed in the spring of 1789 without a single member showing up to relieve the loneliness of Secretary Charles Thomson. The little revolutionary parliament had outlived its usefulness, but it still had the greatest contribution of all to offer the new nation—the men it had trained.

The first five presidents of the United States were graduates of that school of practical politics. So were most of the governors of the new states and the members of the new Senate and House. For it was not until 1832, when knee breeches and cocked hats had long since disappeared, that the last of the old men of the Continental Congress vanished from the American scene.

Mr. Pitt, for all his prescience, could hardly have anticipated so much in 1775 when he urged that the assembly be made a dominion parliament within the British Empire. But after its day was done, the Continental Congress had not fallen too far short of deserving his famous tribute in the House of Lords:

"When your lordships look at the papers transmitted to us from America; when you consider their decency, firmness, and wisdom, you cannot but respect their cause and wish to make it your own. For myself, I must declare and avow, that in all my reading and observation . . . and I have studied and admired the master states of the world—that for solidity of reasoning, force of sagacity, and wisdom of conclusion, under such a complication of difficult circumstances, no nation, or body of men, can stand in preference to the general congress at Philadelphia." [12]

Chapter 2

The Egg of Sedition

B OSTON, the storm center of revolt, had its first revelation of the
Continental Congress on an August morning in 1774. The bells were
ringing and a great crowd had gathered on the Common.

All summer the beleaguered town had worn a heavy yoke for its sins.
Five regiments of red-coated British regulars were quartered on the inhabitants, enforcing the "Intolerable Acts" passed by Parliament to punish Boston for the Tea Party. The soldiers and camp followers outnumbered the
able-bodied citizens, and Sam Adams' old Newfoundland dog growled every
time it met one of the invaders. It was said that the animal could distinguish
without fail between a redcoat and a proper Bostonian.

The town lived by shipping, and all seaborne commerce had been throttled by the guns of the warships and the bayonets of the soldiers. For that
was the purpose of the Port Bill—to compel submission by cutting off trade
and even the main sources of food supplies. Idle vessels, their sails furled
like captive banners, were tied up at the Long Wharf and Hancock's
Wharf. Idle seamen and mechanics and cordwainers thronged the crooked
streets and exchanged gibes with the idle soldiers.

Only a single road across the narrow, tide-lapped Neck connected eighteenth-century Boston with the mainland, and communication had been reduced to a file of creaking carts bringing produce from the country. There
was no serious shortage of supplies, but the closing of the port had inflicted
a tedium of daily existence which hung over the town like a miasma. Any
new sight or sound brought people flocking into the streets, and the brave
spectacle of a coach-and-four attracted a "popular escort" on this August
morning.

It was no ordinary coach-and-four. Two mounted guards rode in front
and four blacks in livery brought up the rear. The passengers were well

15

known, at least by name, to every Bostonian and not a few of King George's officers. They were John Adams, Samuel Adams, Thomas Cushing and Robert Treat Paine; and they were setting off on the long journey to Philadelphia as the Massachusetts delegates to the first Continental Congress.

Every age coins words which are remembered as curiosities by later generations, and in 1774 the term "Continental" was as bright as a newly minted guinea. Even then, of course, such a designation must have seemed highflown when applied to a mere strip of Atlantic seaboard held by thirteen scattered colonies. But some word was needed to convey a daring hope that these colonies could and would unite in spite of differences which set them apart almost as widely as so many foreign nations. And since Americans of all ages have preferred a resounding word even at a discount in accuracy, what could be better than "Continental" to express the first vague aspirations toward nationalism?

The coach-and-four was Continental. It reminded Bostonians that all the other colonies from New Hampshire to the Carolinas were making the cause of Massachusetts their own. All of them, with the single exception of distant Georgia, which would come in later, were sending delegates to Philadelphia.

The British authorities did not regard the forthcoming assembly as cause for alarm. Revolutions which fail to begin with bloodshed are likely to be underrated. The flash of the assassin's dagger, the hoarse cries from the barricades, the shrieks of the wounded and dying—these are the customary preludes in Latin or Slavic lands. Calling a congress seems mild in comparison, and scarlet-coated officers watching the coach-and-four roll past the Common might have been pardoned for a disdainful smile.

If these officers had been at all familiar with the history of their own country (as so few gentlemen were in that day of classical education) they might have reflected that the English-speaking peoples have always shown a perverse distaste for violence in their revolutions. In 1215, to cite a famous example, the stout barons of Runnymead did not plot assassination. They conferred. They discussed their grievances. They drew up a charter. And not a drop of blood was shed by the "army of God" which challenged divine right by bringing King John to terms.

Four centuries later Parliament did not begin the Great Rebellion by chopping off the king's head. Parliament did its best to convert Charles I to reason before regretfully taking up arms and executing that obstinate monarch. The experience proved helpful in 1688 when another Stuart ruler was hustled off the throne with no more violence than if James II had been a butler discharged for unsatisfactory service.

It might even have been argued that Guy Fawkes became the villain of English folklore because of an excitability which his countrymen found alien and abhorrent. They realized that a true Englishman would never have plotted to blow up Parliament. That was the sort of idea which might have occurred to a foreigner, and Fawkes' blunder was commemorated in the lines:

> The fifth of November
> As you well remember
> Was gunpowder, treason and plot;
> I know of no reason
> Why the gunpowder treason
> Should ever be forgot.

Order, method and respectability—these have always been the best traditions of revolt in English-speaking lands, and it should have been interpreted as a warning that the passengers of the coach-and-four were not furtive and skulking figures. All of them were graduates of Harvard, citizens of sober years and habits, regular attendants of the Congregational church. The delegates elected by the other colonies to the Continental Congress were likewise men of position, education and substance.

Every revolution must have its revolutionist. But even Sam Adams, whose reputation had extended to London, had the air of a deacon rather than a terrorist. A calm, pipe-smoking man nearing his fifty-second birthday, he appeared to be made up of middling attributes—middling height, middling age, middling station in life. Overlooking his prematurely gray hair and the palsy which set his hands to trembling, he might have passed for a typical colonial petty officeholder. There was nothing ostentatious about the archrebel except his poverty, for his garments and his home on Purchase Street had always been more shabby than was strictly necessary. But respectability had conquered in the end, and on this August morning Boston was treated to the spectacle of Sam Adams attired in a handsome new wardrobe from head to foot. His friends had also presented him with a purse of gold, and some of the items of apparel are recorded in an old inventory:

> a new whig
> a new Hatt
> six pairs of the best silk hose
> six pairs of fine thread ditto.

Then, as now, it was customary to speak of "poor Adams" as a failure. This verdict was shrewdly encouraged by Adams himself, who took every advantage of protective coloring in his career. But if he had never achieved wealth or position, it was equally true that he had never aspired to any such rewards. Most of his adult life had been dedicated to the single-minded aim of undermining British authority in America, and by 1774 he had become a tremendous success according to his own lights.

. Like so many other great revolutionists of history, Adams was born in comfortable circumstances. His father, Deacon Samuel Adams, had been a prosperous merchant and brewer, a pillar of the Congregational church. Such was the family position that the boy entered Harvard as fifth in his class on a basis of social standing and lingered to take his degree as Master of Arts.

All his life he showed a sublime indifference to money, as Boston would learn to its sorrow. He failed both as merchant and as brewer, then after his father's death he scattered his remaining patrimony. He was not interested even in making a living for his wife and two small children, and at the age of 31 had advanced no further than being elected town scavenger.

As a first step, it was not contemptible in his own eyes. His interests lay in the field of practical politics, and he had received no more valuable inheritance than the example set by his father as a charter member of the Boston Caucus. This club is said to have derived its name from a corruption of the word "caulker," since its membership was made up largely of shipyard workers, mechanics and small merchants. In his day Deacon Adams had held such offices as constable and assessor. But these posts were not important as compared to the influence he wielded—it might even be said that holding office is very often a penalty which must be paid for holding power.

Sam Adams knew at a tender age that the decisions of Boston town meetings were not so spontaneous as they seemed. He knew that decisions could be shaped in advance for citizens who never suspected that they were doing the bidding of the Caucus. His distant cousin John Adams made a similar discovery, which he recorded in his diary as the first mention of the smoke-filled room in the annals of American politics, "This day learned that the Caucus Club meets, at certain times, in the garret of Tom Dawes. . . . There they smoke tobacco till you cannot see from one end of the garret to the other. There . . . selectmen, assessors, collectors, wardens, fire-wards, and representatives are regularly chosen before they are chosen in the town." [1]

It was as the most beloved of Boston's tax collectors that Sam Adams next appears. His circle of friends soon extended far beyond the Caucus Club when he demonstrated his leniency, but at last he could no longer maintain an apparent balance by combining one year's collections with the next. The total of his shortages amounted to some £7,000, and the ugly word "embezzler" was heard despite the admitted fact that he had not profited to any large extent himself. This exposure did not prejudice his loyal followers, who enthusiastically returned him to the office for another term.

Tories liked to point out that Adams had a prison term hanging over his head in 1760 when he first saw the possibilities of applying his political gifts to patriotism. During the next fourteen years he was to earn distinction as the one revolutionist of the American Revolution—the only man in the colonies who devoted all his time and energy to assembling the machinery of unrest.

Adams himself was not a creative political thinker. He made up for this deficiency by hitching his wagon to one of the most brilliant and tragic stars which ever blazed its way across the American sky. For it was James Otis who gave the Revolution its creed while Patrick Henry was an unknown country lawyer, while Thomas Jefferson was a college student, while Alexander Hamilton and James Monroe were still at the age of infancy.

James Otis lived his whole life so immoderately that it surprised nobody when he was removed from this earth by a bolt of lightning, as he had always predicted. Any other end would have been inappropriate. A "great Leviathan" of a man, moody and violent, consistent only in his inconsistencies, he added alcoholism to insanity and was periodically placed in a straitjacket for his own good. The Tories called him a rebel and the rebels accused him of Tory sympathies, for he wore the harness of no faction. But before his plunge into madness he formulated in a few lucid years the major principles of the American Revolution.

In 1760, at the age of 31, Otis was not only the foremost lawyer of the province but also a scholar who had just published his *Rudiments of Latin Prosody*. George III had begun his reign that year and his ministers supplied the first grievance by deciding to make the colonists bear a larger share of the financial burden of the current war. The new policy called for a strict enforcement of the Navigation Acts, which had long been disregarded. American shippers, having grown to think smuggling their tacit right, were horrified when a plague of upright customs officials descended upon them like locusts. Paradoxically, it seemed dishonest on the part of Parliament to withhold from Americans the benefits of governmental corruption which every privileged Englishman then enjoyed.

It was bad enough to be deprived of bribery, but the British made matters worse with their Writs of Assistance, empowering customs officers to search any man's home for smuggled goods. Otis, as advocate general, had the duty of representing the government. He resigned and championed the cause of the people with a four-hour oration so powerful that nobody ever forgot it. Young John Adams did remember to bring pen and paper to the State House but was too spellbound to make notes. Sixty years later, writing as a national patriarch, he recollected his impressions of that day:

"Otis was a flame of fire! . . . He burned everything before him. American independence was then and there born; the seeds of patriots and heroes were then and there sown." [2]

This oration, according to Adams, gave the Revolution its slogan: "Taxation without representation is tyranny." George III did not take the hint and Otis continued to oppose the administration. He also opposed rebels who dared to mention separation, for Otis wished to see the British Empire even stronger and more unified. These conflicting principles kept him constantly embroiled, and his very home life was made stormy by an adored but not adoring wife of high Tory ideals.

The man had a brain which consumed ideas like a furnace, melting them down into ringing phrases which became the catchwords of a revolt he never desired. His great bull-necked body burned up food and liquor with the same intensity. John Adams described him as "extremely quick and elastic, his apprehensions as quick as his temper. He springs and twitches his muscles about in thinking." Tory critics called him "rash, unguarded, foulmouthed" and "a filthy scunk." For Otis managed to offend with his drunken rages and Rabelaisian talk a great many people in both camps who might otherwise have respected him.

As early as 1760 he had been suspected of insanity, but a long enough period of grace was allowed him to publish pamphlets which made a great stir on both sides of the Atlantic. The end came with brutal suddenness one autumn evening in 1769. Otis hurled himself into the Royal Coffee House, loudly demanding an apology because he fancied that British officials had questioned his loyalty to the crown. The dispute turned into a blind, breathless struggle with swords and canes in the darkness after the tables were overturned. When the tapers were lighted again James Otis was stretched out insensible with a terrible gash laying his head open. His powerful body lived on until the last spring of the war, but the light of that brain had been extinguished like one of the candles during the brawl. Soon it was being noted by a Boston chronicler, "Mr. Otis got into a mad Freak tonight & broke a great many windows in the Town [State] House." Then a little later, "Mr. Otis behaved very madly, firing guns out of his Windows."

He was not even granted the boon of continuous insanity. Sometimes the darkness lifted for a while, and Otis even argued a few more cases in court. But as the years went by, Bostonians were to grow accustomed to seeing the wreck of a man bound hand and foot for an enforced journey to a retreat in the country.

Otis has been called the Luther of this period, Sam Adams the Calvin. It would be hard to imagine two less congenial personalities, but Adams had the adaptability of a master propagandist. He knew that revolutions are made and not born.

The contrasts worked to his advantage. For the blasphemies, the domineering ways, even the intellect of James Otis had disturbed people who were soothed by the gentle piety of Sam Adams. Surely there could be nothing to fear from this shabby and threadbare figure, slightly stooped from bending over an inkwell, who gave the effect of premature senility with his palsied hands. Sam Adams could quote Holy Writ like a Congregational parson, and he contrived to lend the same sanctity to his denunciations of taxation without representation. He made the most of all the other principles conceived by Otis, rehashing them again and again in the *Gazette* with that repetition which is the soul of propaganda.

Adams spoke and wrote well—but not well enough to offend better writers and speakers. Whenever possible, he was content to remain behind the scenes and whisper the cues to younger patriots on the stage. He was an organizer of men and events, an adroit manager who got his way with the arts of the politician.

Some of his first disciples were made among the small shopkeepers and artisans of Boston—such sturdy fellows as Paul Revere, whose skilled hands turned out silverware, copper-plate engravings, and the primitive false teeth of the age. The Caucus had long ago shown the possibilities, and Adams busily recruited his followers into clubs which met in taverns. He was no less successful at converting fashionable young men of family and education —such recent graduates of Harvard as John Hancock, Joseph Warren and Josiah Quincy. But his greatest triumph was undoubtedly the organization of a mob into a disciplined private army.

For years the water-front gangs of Boston had terrified honest citizens with riots which the authorities were helpless to curb. Only Sam Adams could have guessed that these bully boys hungered for respectability, yet the time came when he had them marching in orderly parades under their own officers. With such storm troopers at his disposal, "trained as regular as a military Corps," he had the means of plunging the town into a horror of bloodshed after the British occupation. But as a propagandist Adams preferred that the invaders take the responsibility for acts of violence. There were but four instances of tarring and feathering in Boston up to 1775, and it may be questioned if he sanctioned any of them. One of the victims, in fact, was a patriot mobbed by British regulars acting under orders from their colonel.

When the time came for bloodshed Sam Adams would be able to rejoice, "Oh, what a glorious morning is this!" Meanwhile he chose to paint a picture of a virtuous town writhing under a wicked and heartless tyranny. Tories accused the archrebel of the vilest hypocrisy, just as they persisted in the error that he could be bribed. The truth is that Sam Adams was a fanatic both as a political agitator and as a religious crusader. Liberty was to him only a means toward a greater end—the establishment of a stern Puritan theocracy governing from behind the façade of an American republic. Down to the end of the Revolution his models were Bradford and Winthrop, not Franklin and Washington. British tyranny seemed less odious to him than British "frippery"—a term which covered such sins as dancing, gaming, banqueting, horse racing and the theater. Virtue outshone freedom in his eyes; and if Sam Adams had got his way, Americans would probably have bent their heads under a heavier yoke than the rule of George III.

Art often came to the aid of circumstance in the causes of the Revolution; for Boston was not the only town with a patriotic organization, nor was Sam Adams the only organizer. Philadelphia had its Charles Thomson, New York its Alexander McDougall, Charleston its Christopher Gadsden, and Williamsburg its Patrick Henry.

A century of local self-government had given Americans an extensive experience in the nuances of practical politics. Bosses and demagogues were not unknown, and there was no lack of bargaining, wire-pulling and log-rolling in the provincial legislatures. On the brighter side, men of high estate felt it their duty to run for office even at the sacrifice of material interests.

Adam Smith, in his contemporary *Wealth of Nations,* deplored the "paltry rabble of colonial faction" in America. Unhappily for his own British countrymen, they were losing the art of practical politics under a Whig system prescribing that offices should be bought and not won. It put them at a disadvantage in dealing with America, which had developed a tougher breed of politicians in an arena where a long purse could not compensate for a short wit. The royal governors sent out from England were usually made to appear blockheads by the colonists, and at a later date the members of Parliament fared no better against the Continental Congress.

Incredible as it may seem, Parliament passed the Stamp Act without any intimation that it would offend Americans. The time could not have been chosen more ineptly, for in 1765 the colonists were in the midst of a postwar depression aggravated by a smallpox epidemic. Insult was added to injury when it became known that the measure would provide jobs for collectors—more sinecures for fat political cattle grazing in the lush pastures of Whig patronage. But most infuriating of all was the assumption that Americans had not been paying their fair share of the taxes of the recent war—the Americans who took pride in a record of having contributed more men and money in proportion to population than the mother country.

A century of political experience had at least given the colonists good noses for sniffing a rat, and mobs of howling Liberty Boys surged through the streets of every town in America. There was a great deal of spectacular hell-raising which reached a climax when forts occupied by British garrisons were attacked in New York and both Carolinas. But violence accomplished little in the most orderly of all great revolutions, and the episodes were so infrequent as to gain an undue prominence. Organization proved to be a far more effective weapon, and the obnoxious measure was hastily withdrawn after nine of the colonies sent delegates to the Stamp Act Congress to petition for redress. As an added protest, the merchants of America put pressure on the merchants of England, who in turn put pressure on Parliament. Trade with America was so profitable to the mother country that its exporters did not care to risk a general boycott.

The world's most liberal nation had an enlightened colonial policy for that day. But it was England's misfortune to be ruled by a stupid king, bent on personal power, who had surrounded himself with stupid advisers. James Otis, with his customary vigor, described the members of Commons as "a parcel of Button-Makers, Pin-Makers, Horse Jockeys, Gamesters, Pensioners, Pimps and Whore Masters." At any rate, few of them had ever visited the colonies or taken the trouble to inform themselves about colonial conditions. They paid no attention to Pitt's plea, "The Americans are the sons, not the bastards of England." [3]

It had been the money as well as the principle of the thing that made the Stamp Act so odious. England's new chancellor of the exchequer, "Champagne Charlie" Townshend, fancied in 1767 that he could escape his predecessor's troubles with internal taxation by levying small external duties on such products as paper, lead, tea and paint. The imposts were less irksome but Townshend planned to use most of the proceeds to pay judges and governors, thus making them independent of colonial legislatures. The Writs of Assistance were to be revived and stiffened, moreover, to aid in the enforcement.

Opposition to the Townshend Acts reached a climax early in 1770 after most of the colonies adopted nonimportation agreements, usually called associations, modeled after those enforced with no gentle methods in Massachusetts and Virginia. The merchants of England were dismayed by a loss of £900,000 in trade, and again Parliament beat an inglorious retreat by repealing the duties on March 5th—the day of the Boston Massacre.

It was still not too late for reconciliation. The controversy was threatened with malnutrition when the news came that Parliament had retained only a nominal duty on tea, though insisting on the principle of colonial taxation. The rebels had to cope with dissension and lethargy in their own ranks; and nonimportation agreements could not be enforced at a time when tea was actually cheaper in Boston, after paying the tax, than in London.

The patriotic cause might have collapsed if Sam Adams had not been inspired to organize his committees of correspondence in Massachusetts. Writing letters may not at first have seemed a threat to the Empire, but the Tories learned better after the Boston committee reached the point of indoctrinating more than three hundred towns in the province. Then, too late as usual, they perceived that Adams had "hatched the foulest, subtlest and most venomous serpent ever issued from the egg of sedition." [4]

All the archrebel's political gifts were needed to energize a movement which had been brought almost to a standstill. From 1770 to 1773 the American colonies were scarcely mentioned in Parliament, and the mother country seemed to have returned to the policy of "salutary neglect" which had resulted in friendly relations up to 1760. This new era of good will might have lasted indefinitely if Parliament had not come to Sam Adams' rescue with a sly attempt to save the East India Company from financial distress at the expense of the colonies.

The barb was thought to be hidden by the bait. When the tottering company gained a monopoly on the American market, so British politicans reasoned, it would be able to dump its surplus tea at prices undercutting smuggled teas even after a hidden duty had been paid in London to retain the principle of taxation. The scheme had the further merit, so dear to a politician's heart, of creating in the American consignees a new swarm of petty officeholders who would owe gratitude to the crown.

Unfortunately for the Tea Act of 1773, the provincials saw the hook and shunned the lure. They saw that like monopolies could be extended to other products, shoes or wine or clothing, so as to leave the colonial merchant out entirely. And it was this threat which united Americans in anger as they had never been united since the Stamp Act. All the colonies refused to accept the tea, but Boston's gesture of defiance was first and most dramatic.

The fine hand of Sam Adams can be seen in the stage management, for the Boston Massacre had taught the master propagandist how to whip the devil around a post. Ever since the creation of five martyrs by the redcoat volley in 1770, he had seen to it that anniversaries were observed with processions and inflammatory oratory. Again the enemy had presented Sam Adams with the opening for an "incident," and he stirred up a town meeting of seven thousand citizens to lend public sanction to a private riot. His signal sent a band of patriots rather sketchily disguised as Mohawks to board the British vessels in the December dusk and toss 342 chests of tea into the harbor.

Often in the past Adams had been disappointed by the mildness of British reactions and his cries of "Tyranny!" fell flat. But the Boston Tea Party had all the success he could have desired when Parliament passed the Intolerable Acts in the spring of 1774. The ancient Massachusetts charter was practically abrogated, with the right of appointing executive officers being transferred from the people to the royal governor. Town meetings of any importance could not be called without the governor's permission. A new Quartering Act required the inhabitants to provide food and lodging for British soldiers, and officers charged with murder in enforcing the measures were all but guaranteed immunity by being given the privilege of trial in England.

As if these regulations were not harsh enough, the Boston Port Bill closed the harbor even to fishing boats until the province should be starved into paying for the tea destroyed. Boston, in short, was to be treated by the mother country as a captured enemy city, and troops under the command of General Thomas Gage were being sent in such numbers as to constitute a small army of occupation.

The news reached Boston by a fast ship from England on May 10, 1774. Frequent changes of horses enabled Paul Revere to ride the 350 miles to Philadelphia in six days, and there were few villages in all the colonies which had not been informed before the end of the month.

Again Parliament had chosen an inopportune time to arouse the colonies. Within the past year the entire "Continent" had acquired the framework of a revolutionary machine such as the one built up by Sam Adams in Massachusetts. The incentive came from Virginia, where the radical group had maneuvered a resolution through the House of Burgesses establishing a committee of correspondence and urging the other provincial assemblies to do likewise. This proposal met with so much favor that the leaders of revolt in most of the colonies were soon exchanging ideas and composing differences.

It had not been long since a New York newspaper described Boston as "the Common Sewer of America" and the Boston *Gazette* referred to "the little, filthy, nasty, dirty colony of Rhode Island." But a new spirit of inter-colonial unity was demonstrated when food, money and messages of sympathy poured into beleaguered Boston from all sides. Only the recent committees of correspondence could have provided such a simple yet effective means of bridging the political and geographical gaps which had kept the colonies apart.

Six to nine days were required to send a letter from Boston to New York by ordinary postal service, and a citizen of Georgia could not expect to hear from New Hampshire in less than a month. This slow pace of colonial communication was overcome to an amazing extent by the express riders who pounded along country roads in the summer of 1774, bearing messages between the various committees of correspondence. In June the other little Americas agreed in theory to make the cause of Massachusetts their own. In July they responded to the practical suggestion of Virginia that a general assembly be called at Philadelphia. And by the first week of August, eleven of the colonies had already elected their delegates to the proposed Continental Congress.

The whole thing had occurred in no more time than was often taken by a storm-tossed sailing vessel in crossing the Atlantic with dispatches for England.

The political problems were even more formidable than the difficulties of communication. Naturally the royal governors and provincial assemblies were not eager to endorse decisions regarded by many loyalists as bordering on treason. The marvel is that four colonies really did manage to make use of the ordinary mechanism of administration.

There was no opposition worth mentioning in the "little Congregational republic" of Connecticut, which had fewer Tories than any other colony and boasted the only governor upholding the patriotic cause throughout the war. The House of Representatives left the choice to the committee of correspondence, which made the appointments. In Rhode Island and Pennsylvania the delegates were elected by the regularly constituted legislatures, though not without some political manipulation. And in Massachusetts the rebels "stole" the House of Representatives. Sam Adams and his lieutenants simply packed the assembly with their followers, locked the door to exclude Tories, and elected their delegates in defiance of General Gage.

The remaining colonies found it necessary to hold elections either directly or indirectly by means of revolutionary bodies. Provincial assemblies under various designations were called for that purpose in Maryland, Delaware, New Jersey, New Hampshire and North Carolina. Appointments in South Carolina were made at a "general meeting of the inhabitants" at Charleston, and in Virginia a "convention" was summoned by the radical group of the House of Burgesses.

Georgia, where the white population numbered only 17,000, had too many troubles of its own with Indians and Tories to send delegates at all. New York, ridden by the largest and most aggressive Tory faction in America, did not achieve enough unity for a central assembly. Delegates were chosen by the city and five counties in any manner which suited their convenience. So irregular were these elections, according to a Tory account, that the one in Kings County was held by Simon Boerum and a single other patriot, with Boerum being unanimously appointed.

Outside of Connecticut and Rhode Island, which enjoyed a higher degree of self-government than the other colonies, it is doubtful if any of the elections carried out the will of a popular majority. Neither the word nor the theory of democracy found much approval in that day, and it is the rule of history that revolutions in their early stages are imposed upon the bulk of a people by an organized and determined minority.

Sam Adams, if given his way, would probably never have endorsed a general congress in the first place. The archrebel did not trust legislative processes unless they were controlled by an inner circle, and he feared the influence that conservative delegates might have on the proceedings at Philadelphia.

Nobody foresaw more clearly than Sam Adams the opposition which awaited New England delegates suspected of radical principles. The conservatives of the middle and southern colonies had no intention of burning their fingers to pull Boston's chestnuts out of the fire. In fact, they had already made it plain through their committees of correspondence that colonial unity would never stand the strain of any proposal which threatened a break with the mother country.

Such tendencies, of course, were disturbing to a revolutionist who had decided in his own heart for independence even at the cost of war. But Sam Adams was too experienced a politician to fly signals of distress on the August morning of departure for Philadelphia. The coach-and-four with its mounted guards and blacks in livery was doubtless intended as a display of unfelt confidence. And though the new wardrobe may have embarrassed a man whose only pomp was poverty, it is a safe conjecture that nobody nodded more blandly than Sam Adams as he rode past the crowded Common, past his own shabby home on Purchase Street, past the enclosure where the town bull grazed, past the town gallows which awaited traitors—past the familiar limits of Boston and out on the long road leading toward some unknown destiny.

Chapter 3

Doctor, Lawyer, Merchant, Chief

NO American city of the twentieth century ever greeted a national
political convention with more cordiality than Philadelphia evinced
in welcoming the Continental Congress. The delegations from the various
colonies, arriving by coach or on horseback, were met several miles outside
the city by large groups of leading citizens and promptly invited to "mighty
feasts."

Even the banquets given by Quakers struck John Adams as being Babylonian in luxury, and he was soon scribbling in his diary: "Dined with Mr.
Miers Fisher. . . . But this plain Friend and his plain though pretty wife,
with her Thees and Thous, had provided us with the most costly entertainment: ducks, hams, chickens, beef, pig, tarts, creams, custards, jellies, fools,
trifles, beer, porter, wine, and a long &c." [1]

Philadelphia was not only hospitable but inquisitive. At this stage the
leaders of the colonies had learned just enough through the committees of
correspondence to whet their curiosity about one another. Already, if age
and property were to be taken as tests, it might have been supposed that the
assembly would be very conservative in tone. Of the 56 delegates who took
part in this first Congress, only two had not yet celebrated their thirtieth
birthdays, and five would never see sixty again. The others fell into these
age groups: from thirty to forty years, 13; from forty to fifty, 19; and from
fifty to sixty, 17.

It was decidedly a middle-aged assembly made up of property owners ranging from men of comfortable circumstances to several possessors of large
colonial fortunes. Sam Adams remained the sole delegate who insisted on

being poor, and during recent years he had been able to afford two family servants on his salary as clerk of the Massachusetts legislature.

A legal career was the surest road to political preferment, and no less than thirty of the delegates were lawyers or jurists. Three others could only have been described as officeholders; and there were nine planters or farmers, nine merchants, three millers, one surveyor and one carpenter.

The educational attainments were at least as high as those found at the time in the House of Commons. Twelve delegates, in fact, had received most of their schooling in the British Isles. Leading the list of colleges with seven graduates were the Inns of Court—those ancient London law schools which included the Middle and Inner Temples. Harvard was represented with five graduates, Yale with three, William and Mary with three, the College of Philadelphia (University of Pennsylvania) with two, and the College of New Jersey (Princeton), King's College (Columbia) and Edinburgh University with one each. Altogether, a third of the delegates had attended some college, and most of the others had acquired as good an education by means of private tutoring. Not even the roughest diamond of the Congress could be dismissed as ignorant, for Judge Roger Sherman of Connecticut was a shrewd, hardheaded character who had taught himself law at the cobbler's bench.

Only one of the 56, a native of Wales, had not been born in the colonies. Most of the others could trace their family history back through two or three generations to British grandsires, and it was not unusual for a young American to finish his education with a sentimental journey to England.

Such statistics, which might have been compiled at the time, were probably not so interesting to the delegates as their speculations. Already, if they had but suspected, the Judas of the assembly had made his appearance—the single member of the entire fifteen years who would be willing to betray his country for the king's gold. At this date he had an excellent reputation for patriotism as compared to two colleagues soon to have their property confiscated after being convicted of another kind of treason—the crime, from an American viewpoint, of remaining stubbornly loyal to the mother country. Nineteen future signers of a future Declaration of Independence were present, and as many more who would oppose that document to the last ditch. There were two men destined to be honored with the highest office of the new nation, and there were seventeen who would be in their graves before that nation ever came into being.

These were some of the straws in the wind which had not yet been revealed to the delegates straining their eyes across Philadelphia dinner tables. And meanwhile the menus continued to inspire exclamation points nearly every day in John Adams' diary: "Dined at Mr. Powell's . . . a most sinful feast again! everything which could delight the eye or allure the taste; curds and creams, jellies, sweetmeats of various sorts, twenty sorts of tarts, fools, trifles, floating islands, whipped sillabubs, &c. &c., a Parmesian cheese, punch, wine, porter, beer, &c." [2]

The visitors had not waited until they reached Philadelphia to take one another's measure. All of them had been surveying the political landscape from the moment they left their own doorsteps, but the only chroniclers of the journey happened to be New England delegates.

John and Samuel Adams held opposite views in regard to the written word. "I have seen him," John related of Sam, "at Mrs. Yard's in Philadelphia, when he was about to leave Congress, cut up with his scissors whole bundles of letters into atoms that could never be reunited, and throw them out of the window, to be scattered by the winds. This was in summer, when he had no fire; in winter he threw whole handfuls into the fire."

John himself, though he had as much reason to be prudent, displayed none of his remote cousin's caution. While Sam was destroying all evidence except letters filled with pious platitudes, John hoarded the comments which eventually went into the ten large volumes of his works. His jottings might have gained in polish if they had been written less hastily; but they might also have lost the candor, the malice, the irritability, the self-pity and indiscretion which makes them fascinating. For if the Braintree lawyer had left no other claim to fame, he would always be remembered as the greatest diarist of the Continental Congress.

The four Massachusetts delegates had a triumphant journey through Connecticut, where every village greeted them with pealing bells. No fault could be found with the warmth of New York's reception, yet a Bostonian soon felt that he was on alien soil. "With all the opulence and splendor of this city," reported Adams, "there is very little good breeding to be found. . . . At their entertainments there is no conversation that is agreeable; there is no modesty, no attention to one another. They talk very loud, very fast, and altogether. If they ask a question, before you can utter three words of your answer, they will break out upon you again, and talk away." [3]

Nothing would have annoyed Adams more than to be interrupted, but Silas Deane formed a better opinion of New York. The delegates from Connecticut, he wrote to his wife, met with such vigorous hospitality that they were hustled to a banquet "without allowing us time to shift our linen." Deane had the forethought to shift before arrival, so that he felt at ease upon meeting "the Boston delegates, two from S. Carolina, and all the gentlemen of considerable note in the city in a mercantile way. . . . We went the round of introduction and congratulation, and then took our seats. The glass had circulated just long enough to raise the spirits of every-one just to that nice point which is above disguise or suspicion, especially in persons any way generously disposed." [4]

Despite the convivial atmosphere, he gathered that "parties run exces-sively high in the city . . . yet I found many favorable to the cause we were upon, and willing to go to almost any length, while others were in reality against doing anything at all."

Adams had a confidential chat with Alexander McDougall, the leader of the local rebel faction—"a very sensible man and an open one." The son of a Scottish immigrant who became New York's milkman, he had the dis-tinction in 1770 of being the first American patriot imprisoned by the British authorities. The ordeal could not have been too severe, for ladies and gentlemen called at the jail in such numbers, bearing gifts, that he was obliged to announce visiting hours for public receptions. That same year, several weeks before the Boston Massacre, the first bloodshed of the Revo-lution occurred in New York when a patriot was slain and many others hurt in two days of street fighting between redcoats and citizens using clubs as weapons.

Significant as such episodes might seem, McDougall warned that New York's loyalists were powerful. Owing to their influence, five conservatives had been elected as delegates, and Adams had only faint praise for those he described. "Mr. Alsop is a soft, sweet man. Mr. Duane has a sly, surveying eye . . . a little squint-eyed . . . very sensible, I think, and very artful." Philip Livingston, the most reliable of all from a patriotic viewpoint, im-pressed Adams as "a great, rough, rapid mortal. There is no holding any conversation with him. He blusters away; says, if England should turn us adrift, we should instantly go into civil war among ourselves, to determine which colony should govern the rest; seems to dread the New England levelling spirit, &c." [5]

The feudal traditions still existing in New York could not have pleased a Yankee whose father had toiled a lifetime to acquire a few stony acres. Some of the baronial landowners of the Hudson valley numbered their ten-ants by villages and were entitled to a representative in the colonial assembly. Even when they leaned toward the patriotic cause, as did the Schuylers and Livingstons, their lordly doctrines were to be feared. And the clans which remained loyal, including the Van Courtlandts, De Peysters and De Lanceys, threatened to build New York into a Tory stronghold.

It was with apparent relief that the New Englanders shook the dust of this Gomorrah from their silver-buckled shoes and crossed into New Jersey. The next few nights were ruined for Deane by dysentery and the snoring of Judge Sherman. Not merely in a figurative sense did politics make strange bedfellows at a time when it was customary for inns to place two guests in a room. Nor had propinquity recommended the self-made jurist to the Yale graduate, for Deane sent home this supercilious sketch of his colleague: "Mr. Sherman is clever in private, but I will only say that he is as badly calculated to appear in such a Company as a chestnut-burr is for an eye-stone. He occasioned some shrewd countenances among the company, and not a few oaths, by the odd questions he asked, and the very odd and coun-trified cadence with which he speaks; but he was, and did, as well as I expected." [6]

At Princeton it reassured Adams to find Dr. John Witherspoon "as high a son of liberty as any in America." The Presbyterian scholar, who had been summoned from Scotland to the presidency of the struggling little college in 1768, also showed a lively sense of propaganda values. "He says it is necessary that the Congress should raise money and employ a number of writers in the newspapers in England, to explain to the public the American plea, and remove the prejudices of Britons." [7]

On the nineteenth day after leaving Boston, so leisured had been their progress, the Massachusetts men at last sighted Philadelphia. Hot, tired and dusty as they were, the delegates could not resist the importunity of a wel-coming committee which escorted them to a tavern. It was eleven that night before they crept into bed after "a supper as elegant as was ever laid upon a table."

The colonial metropolis, with about 38,000 inhabitants, far surpassed its two nearest rivals. New York could claim nearly 22,000, and the population of Boston had remained stationary for some years at 17,000. These figures did not seem insignificant in an age when London itself had only three-quarters of a million; for Philadelphia actually outranked Bristol and Dublin as the second city of the British Empire.

Most of the delegates were newcomers, and on a preliminary tour of inspection Colonel Eliphalet Dyer of Connecticut lost his way in the metro-politan surroundings. But it was not the size so much as the pattern of Philadelphia that most fascinated the visitors. Boston and to a lesser extent New York had retained many characteristics of Old World towns—narrow and winding streets huddled about a central green as if there were no room to expand. Philadelphia, in contrast, was the first truly American city; and its checkerboard plan moved John Adams to write a travelogue: "The regu-larity and elegance of this city are very striking. It is situated on a neck of land about two miles wide between the river Delaware and the river Schuyl-kill; the streets are all exactly straight and parallel to the river; Front Street is near the river, then 2nd Street, 3rd, 4th, 5th, 6th, 7th, 8th, 9th. The cross streets which intersect them are all equally wide, straight and parallel to each other, and are named from forest and fruit trees—Pear Street, Apple Street, Walnut Street, Chestnut Street, &c."

It might even be said that the Philadelphia of 1774 was the first American boom town. Not only had its growth been lusty during the past decade, but it lived by a brisk creed of progress which lacked only a Chamber of Commerce. As early as 1751 the city had instituted such unusual civic improvements as lighting its streets and replacing its volunteer night watch with paid constables. In 1768 a still more novel step was taken when Philadelphia let its first municipal garbage and street-cleaning contract at a time when London and Paris were putting up with medieval filth. Visitors from Europe were always impressed by the neatness of the tree-lined avenues, many of them paved in the middle and bordered by brick sidewalks. Neither slums nor poverty existed in this wealthy little city of fresh air and sunshine, and its commercial importance was attested by the streams of carts, carriages and sedan chairs.

Politics played second fiddle only to business in Philadelphia; and the New Englanders realized that their chief opponent would be Joseph Galloway, a prosperous local lawyer who aspired to the leadership of the conservatives in Congress. Forty-five years old, urbane and polished, he was not lacking in political experience as speaker of the Pennsylvania assembly. Nor did he lose any time in his efforts "to wait on, and endeavor to find out the Temper of the Delegates. Near two-Thirds of them are arrived," he wrote to another famous loyalist, Governor William Franklin of New Jersey, "and I conclude all will be ready to proceed to business on Monday. I have not had any great Opportunity of sounding them. But so far as I have, I think they will behave with Temper and Moderation."

The New England radicals were equally busy when it came to button-holing new delegates as they straggled in from Virginia, Maryland and New York those last few days before Congress met. Unhappily for Sam Adams, his fame as a revolutionist had preceded him; and Galloway probably summed up conservative opinion when he described him as "a man, who though by no means remarkable for brilliant abilities, yet is equal to most men in popular intrigue, and the management of a faction. He eats little, drinks little, sleeps little, thinks much, and is most indefatigable in the pursuit of his objectives."

The first test of strength developed before the opening day. "The City have offered us Carpenters Hall, so called, to meet in," Deane wrote to his wife, "and Mr. Galloway offers the State House and insists on our meeting there, which he says he had a right to offer as Speaker of that House. The last is evidently the best place, but as *he* offers, the other party oppose." [8]

As the radicals saw it, the selection of Carpenters' Hall would be interpreted as a democratic gesture setting the tone for future decisions of
Congress. For that new edifice was the pride of Philadelphia's skilled workmen, who had built it with their own labor and provided it with an excellent
library.

Another tug of war began as both factions reflected how helpful it would
be to have a sympathetic secretary of Congress installed. In line with good
political strategy, they raided each other's camps for acceptable candidates.
Galloway hoped to break the ranks of the New England phalanx by electing
Silas Deane, the 37-year-old Connecticut lawyer who had already shown
signs of being a trimmer. The choice of the left wing was hinted by a seemingly innocent entry in John Adams' diary: "Walked a little about town;
visited the Market, the State House, the Carpenters' Hall . . . then called
at Mr. Mifflin's; a grand, spacious and elegant house. Here we had much
conversation with Mr. Charles Thomson, who is, it seems, about marrying
a lady, a relation of Mr. Dickinson's, with five thousand pounds sterling.
This Charles Thomson is the Sam Adams of Philadelphia, the life of the
cause of liberty, they say." [9]

It was no coincidence that both these Philadelphians were opponents of
Galloway in local politics. Mifflin, a wealthy and handsome Quaker merchant just turned 30, could be reckoned an influence among the aggressive
younger members of his sect. Studious and reserved Charles Thomson,
though he might not have felt flattered by a comparison to Sam Adams, had
long been an inspiration to Pennsylvania's large Scotch-Irish population,
which backed the patriotic cause to a man.

The hardships endured by those early immigrants were appalling. Filth,
disease and brutality made life miserable on overcrowded sailing vessels
taking weeks for the voyage; and many of the newcomers had pledged themselves to years of servitude in payment for their passage. Thomson reached
America at the age of 10 as the son of a Scotch-Irish widower who died on
shipboard within sight of the promised land. The orphan and his five small
brothers and sisters were robbed of their little hoard by the captain and put
ashore in Delaware. After starting life as a "bound boy," the ambitious youth
managed to educate himself to the extent of becoming a schoolmaster.
Benjamin Franklin, who remained a lifelong friend, helped him to advance
to the position of Greek and Latin instructor at the Academy of Philadelphia.
But Thomson's interests were not all scholarly, and the success story took a
new turn when he resigned to make good as an importer and merchant. In
the late summer of 1774, at the age of 45, the prosperous business man and
widower was being accepted into one of Philadelphia's most aristocratic
families by his marriage to a cousin of John Dickinson.

Galloway could not forgive Thomson, Mifflin and Dickinson for their part in persuading Philadelphia "to return a friendly and affectionate answer to the people of Boston" after the enforcement of the Intolerable Acts. No sooner had Paul Revere galloped into town with the news than the local patriots called a mass meeting at the City Tavern. Thomson (as he recorded later, writing in the third person) "pressed for an immediate declaration in favor of Boston & making common cause with her. But being overcome with the heat of the room and fatigue, for he had scarce slept an hour for two nights past, he fainted & was carried out into an adjoining room. Great clamor was raised against the violence of the measure proposed. . . . As soon as T[homson] recovered he returned into the room. The tumult and disorder were past description. He had not strength to attempt opposing the gust of passion or to allay the heat by anything he could say. He therefore simply moved a question That an answer should be returned to the letter from Boston. Thus was put & carried." [10]

Trivial as the victory may seem, it proved to be a first wedge driven into the conservatism of a colony dominated by Quaker, German and proprietary influences. A few weeks later, after the governor refused to convene the assembly, John Dickinson presided at the State House over a meeting of 8,000 citizens addressed by Thomson. Resolutions were passed in favor of a committee of correspondence, a general congress, and plans to aid the sufferers from the Boston Port Bill. This day's work convinced Thomson "that although the people of Penna. are cautious & backward in entering into measures, yet when they engage, none are more firm, resolute & persevering."

Further proof was given on September 5th at the opening session of Congress when most of the Pennsylvania delegates, as well as those from other colonies, decided against Galloway in the two preliminary skirmishes. That Monday evening he had the melancholy duty of reporting to Dr. Franklin's son: "The Congress met this day at Carpenters' Hall, notwithstanding the Offer of the Assembly Room, a much more proper Place. They next proceeded to chuse a Secretary, and, to my Surprize, Charles Thomson was unanimously elected. The New Yorkers and myself and a few others, finding a great Majority did not think it prudent to oppose it. Both of these Measures, it seems, were privately settled by an Interest made out of Doors." [11]

The last three words were not meant to convey that the delegates had a passion for fresh air. Throughout the colonies the expression "out of doors" had long been current to signify political deals such as those remarked by John Adams when the Caucus Club met in a smoke-filled room of a Boston garret. And it may be that other measures had been passed unofficially before the delegates gathered at the City Tavern to march in a body to Carpenters' Hall with its neat rows of Windsor chairs.

The North Carolina contingent had not yet appeared, and a few delegates from other colonies remained to be seated. When these late arrivals took their places, the membership would be as follows:

CONNECTICUT—Silas Deane, Eliphalet Dyer, Roger Sherman;

DELAWARE—Thomas McKean, George Read, Caesar Rodney;

MARYLAND—Samuel Chase, Robert Goldsborough, Thomas Johnson, Jr., William Paca, Matthew Tilghman;

MASSACHUSETTS—John Adams, Samuel Adams, Thomas Cushing, Robert Treat Paine;

NEW HAMPSHIRE—Nathaniel Folsom, John Sullivan;

NEW JERSEY—Stephen Crane, John De Hart, James Kinsey, William Livingston, Richard Smith;

NEW YORK—John Alsop, Simon Boerum, James Duane, John Haring, John Jay, Francis Lewis, Philip Livingston, Isaac Low, Henry Wisner;

NORTH CAROLINA—Richard Caswell, Joseph Hewes, William Hooper;

PENNSYLVANIA—Edward Biddle, John Dickinson, Joseph Galloway, Charles Humphreys, Thomas Mifflin, John Morton, Samuel Rhoads, George Ross;

RHODE ISLAND—Stephen Hopkins, Samuel Ward;

SOUTH CAROLINA—Christopher Gadsden, Thomas Lynch, Henry Middleton, Edward Rutledge, John Rutledge;

VIRGINIA—Richard Bland, Benjamin Harrison, Patrick Henry, Richard Henry Lee, Edmund Pendleton, Peyton Randolph, George Washington.*

At this first meeting the delegates could not have realized that they were setting two traditions for a mighty future nation when they decided that the name of the assembly should be "the Congress" and that its presiding officer should be known as "the President." There were no familiar historical precedents in 1774 for either title; and as time went on, Congress named the nation itself by referring to it first as "the United Colonies" and later as "the United States."

The presidency was intended to be an honorary, nonexecutive office with the duties of chairman. Not a single member opposed the choice of Peyton Randolph, a 53-year-old, London-educated lawyer who had recently been speaker of the Virginia House of Burgesses. "Our President seems designed by nature for the business," wrote Deane. "Of an affable, open and majestic deportment—large in size, though not out of proportion, he commands

* A complete list of all the 342 delegates from 1774 to 1789, and the years of attendance, will be found in the Appendix.

respect and esteem by his very aspect, independent of the high character he sustains." [12]

For the sake of appearances a unanimous vote elected Thomson to the only paid office of Congress, though the result was "mortifying in the last degree to Mr. Galloway and his party." It would have been more distressing if they could have anticipated that the tall, thin, ascetic Philadelphian would be the only man to take part in every important session down the years to that March day in 1789 when he made his final entry in the *Journals*. Seventeen presidents were to preside over the assembly, but the secretary remained at his post even during inflation years when his modest salary did not begin to cover personal expenses.

The balance of the first day was taken up by the approval of credentials. All the delegations had brought written instructions from their colonies; but these authorizations dealt for the most part in mild generalities, and in no case did they include legislative, executive or money-raising powers.

Massachusetts, the storm center of revolt, expressed a hope of reconciliation by instructing its delegates "to consult upon the present state of the Colonies, and the miseries to which they are and must be reduced by the operation of certain acts of Parliament respecting America, and to deliberate and determine upon wise and proper measures, to be by them recommended to all the Colonies, for the recovery and establishment of their just rights & liberties, civil & religious, and the restoration of union & harmony between Great Britain and the Colonies, most ardently desired by all good men."

Connecticut, so united in patriotism, could have been expected to express strong sentiments. But the delegates were simply authorized "to consult and advise upon proper measures for advancing the best good of the Colonies." It might have been supposed that no differences of opinion existed between those colonies and the mother country.

South Carolina went further than all the rest when it empowered its delegates "to consider the acts lately passed, and bills depending in parliament with regard to the port of Boston and Colony of Massachusetts-Bay, which acts and bills in the precedent and consequences affect the whole Continent of America—also the grievances under which America labours, by reason of the several acts of parliament that impose taxes or duties for raising a revenue, and lay unnecessary burdens on Trade; and of the statutes, parliamentary acts and royal instructions, which made an invidious distinction between his majesty's subjects in Great-Britain and America, with full power and authority to concert, agree to, and effectually prosecute such legal measures, as in the opinion of said deputies . . . shall be most likely to obtain a repeal of the said acts, and a redress of these grievances. . . ." [13]

There was nothing in the American past to guide the delegates as to the authority they might assume. The Stamp Act Congress that met at New York in 1765 was the most notable precedent, and nine of its twenty-seven members were present in Carpenters' Hall. But it had contented itself with drawing up respectful protests; and the Congress of 1774, at the end of its second day's meeting, accepted a status as advisory council when the members

> Resolved, unan: That a Committee be appointed to State the rights of the colonies in general, the several instances in which these rights are violated or infringed, and the means most proper to be pursued for obtaining a restoration of them.[14]

The various delegations, as it proved, were to follow their own bent in the matter of reporting to colonial assemblies or conventions. Some of them sent home regular and detailed summaries, others thought it enough to write a chatty letter now and then. In any event, it was seldom that they had enough time to consult the wishes of their constituents before an issue came up for decision.

Officially, the members of Congress adopted a policy of secrecy at the outset by resolving "that the doors be kept shut during the time of business, and that the members consider themselves under the strongest obligations of honour, to keep the proceedings secret, untill the majority shall direct them to be made public."[15]

This was interpreted to mean that debates, arguments, statements from the floor, defeated measures, even the yeas and nays, were not to be recorded by the secretary. "What Congress adopted, I committed to writing," explained Thomson long afterwards. "With what they rejected, I had nothing further to do; and even this method led to some squabbles with the members who were desirous of having their speeches and resolutions, however put to rest by the majority, still preserved upon the Minutes."[16]

But if this first Congress had its limitations, the delegates were not lacking in an overwhelming sense of pride. Caesar Rodney considered it "the greatest assembly (in proportion to the members) that was ever collected in America." John Adams took in more territory when he wrote to a Massachusetts friend: "The Congress is such an assembly as never before came together, on a sudden, in any part of the world. Here are fortunes, abilities, learning, eloquence, acuteness, equal to any I have ever met with in my life. . . . Every question is discussed with a moderation, an acuteness, and a minuteness equal to that of Queen Elizabeth's privy council."[17]

Only one thing seemed to be lacking, but even at this early date a congressman's constituents were not backward about asking favors. Silas Deane scarcely had time to unpack his saddlebags before he received a request from a Connecticut acquaintance: "I am very desirous to put my son Giles (now fifteen years of age) to a merchant in Philadelphia. . . . I will be much obliged to you to get a good place for him."

The widows and spinsters of the city had not neglected their opportunity, and several of the boardinghouses for delegates were eventually to take on the atmosphere of salons. One of the most notable was Miss Jane Port's establishment at Arch near Second, where the Massachusetts members found lodgings. Mrs. Mary House, the motherly widow who provided for the South Carolina group at Fifth and Market, was to continue in business down to 1783, gaining the friendship of such later delegates as Jefferson and Madison.

Few of the visitors could have spent much time in their rooms, for the social whirl continued at such a pace that invitations to breakfast were not uncommon. Sometimes these occasions were obviously arranged for purposes of political guile, as when Joseph Galloway and Samuel Rhoads entertained several of the New England radicals. More often, however, the members of Congress were genuinely eager to break down the barriers of sectionalism.

As a sample of a delegate's activities just before Congress convened, John Adams dined on Friday "at Mr. Thomas Mifflin's, with Mr. Lynch, Mr. Middleton, and the two Rutledges and their ladies." On Saturday he "breakfasted at Dr. Shippen's . . . dined at Joseph Reed's . . . spent the evening with Lee and Harrison from Virginia, the two Rutledges, Dr. Witherspoon, Dr. Shippen, and other gentlemen; an elegant supper, and we drank sentiments till eleven o'clock. Lee and Harrison were very high. Lee had dined with Mr. Dickinson, and drank Burgundy the whole afternoon."

Many of the first impressions must have been embarrassing at a later date. Sam Adams, never dreaming that he was praising a future opponent, paid John Dickinson the ultimate tribute by referring to him as "a true Bostonian." And it might have astonished a quiet Virginia militia officer if he had suspected that he came to Congress with a reputation as an orator. For John Adams was informed "that Colonel Washington made the most eloquent speech at the Virginia convention that ever was made. Says he, 'I will raise one thousand men, subsist them at my own expense, and march myself at their head for the relief of Boston.'" [18]

Neither age nor wealth could always be trusted as an indication of a delegate's political views. Edward Rutledge and John Jay, the only members under thirty, were both conservatives. But Christopher Gadsden, who owned a 1,000-foot dock at Charleston for his mercantile operations, proved at the age of 51 to be the most fiery radical of Congress. "Mr. Gadsden leaves all

New England sons of liberty far behind," declared Deane. "He is for taking up his firelock and marching direct to Boston; nay, he affirmed this morning, that were his wife and all his children in Boston, and they were to perish by the sword, it would not alter his sentiment or proceeding for American Liberty. . . ." [19]

At times the spirit of cordiality at Philadelphia dinner tables seemed a little forced, as if the delegates were trying too hard to forget the differences that separated the colonies. Even the governments of the thirteen little Americas were of four different types. Massachusetts alone had its own charter combined with a governor representing the crown. Connecticut and Rhode Island, which came nearest to being republics, took pride in charters permitting them to control their own executive officers. Pennsylvania, Delaware and Maryland, the three proprietary provinces, were originally vast feudal domains owned by the Penn and Calvert families, which still claimed many rights and privileges in the executive administration. The remaining seven colonies had no charters and their assemblies were controlled to a large extent by crown-appointed governors.

Geographically the colonies were separated in their interests not only by distance but also by a diversity of products ranging from rice and indigo in the South to ship timbers in the forests of New England. The differences in population added to the estrangement; for the three smallest colonies, Delaware and Georgia and Rhode Island, had reason to be jealous of the three largest, Pennsylvania, Virginia and Massachusetts. Climate also played its part in shaping traditions for the northern provinces which were alien to those prevailing in the middle and southern areas.

Often the problems could not be contained within provincial borders. Immigration had created an early American melting pot which boiled with recent German and Scotch-Irish arrivals. Theology became a factor when the Congregationalists and Presbyterians took an active part in the revolt against England, while the Quakers, Episcopalians and German sects usually favored reconciliation. Even within the colonies themselves there were bitter factions. The small farmers of the frontier felt that they were being exploited by the tidewater merchants and planters; and in North Carolina this clash had already led to the pitched battle of the Alamance.

These were some of the specters that haunted Congress at the second day's meeting when the question arose as to how the colonies should vote. The arguments were not recorded in the minutes, but that tireless reporter John Adams took notes. [20]

Duane of New York opened the discussion by suggesting that a committee be appointed. "Mr. Henry then arose, and said this was the first General Congress which had ever happened . . . and therefore that a precedent ought to be established now; that it would be a great injustice if a little Colony should have the same weight in the councils of America as a great one, and therefore he was for a committee."

John Sullivan, the New Hampshire lawyer whose Scotch-Irish parents had come to this country as redemptioners, insisted that "a little Colony has its all at stake as well as a great one."

"This question is of great importance," declared John Adams. "If we vote by Colonies, this method will be liable to great inequality and injustice; for five small Colonies, with one hundred thousand people in each, may outvote four large ones, each of which has five hundred thousand inhabitants. If we vote by the poll, some Colonies have more than their proportion of members, and others have less. If we vote by interests, it will be attended with insuperable difficulties to ascertain the true importance of each Colony. Is the weight of a Colony to be ascertained by the number of inhabitants merely, or by the amount of their trade, the quantity of their exports and imports, or by any compound ratio of both? This will lead us into such a field of controversy as will greatly perplex us. Besides, I question whether it is possible to ascertain, at this time, the numbers of our people or the value of our trade."

The delegates might have had it out, hammer and tongs, if Patrick Henry had not saved the day with the first flight of eloquence heard on the floor of the Continental Congress. Thomson described him as "dressed in a suit of parson's gray, and from his appearance I took him for a Presbyterian clergyman, used to haranguing the people." He began, according to Adams, with three challenging words:

"Government is dissolved."

Here it may be assumed that he let a dramatic pause intervene before continuing: "Fleets and armies and the present state of things show that government is dissolved. Where are your landmarks, your boundaries of Colonies?" No doubt the orator paused again for emphasis, then answered his own rhetorical question: "We are in a state of nature, sir. . . . The distinctions between Virginians, Pennsylvanians, New Yorkers and New Englanders, are no more. I am not a Virginian, but an American."

Testimony as to the effect on the audience was offered by Deane, who assured his wife that "in a letter I can give you no idea of the music of his voice, or of the high-wrought yet natural elegance of his style."

Patrick Henry had shown Congress a glimpse of the promised land. But it is noteworthy that he continued to take the side of the larger colonies, which wished to vote according to population. And much as the delegates from smaller colonies may have esteemed his oratory, they stuck by their guns until they defeated him.

Thomas Lynch spoke for wealthy but not too populous South Carolina when he said, "I differ in one point from the gentleman from Virginia; that is, in thinking that numbers only ought to determine the weight of Colonies. I think that property ought to be considered, and that it ought to be a compound of numbers and property that should determine the weight of the Colonies."

Samuel Ward, a small-colony man from Rhode Island, reminded the orator that "there are a great many counties, in Virginia, very unequal in point of wealth and numbers, yet each has a right to send two members."

The limited powers of Congress were very sensibly pointed out by John Rutledge. "We have no legal authority; and obedience to our determination will only follow the reasonableness, the apparent utility and necessity of the measures we adopt. We have no coercive or legislative authority. Our constituents are bound only in honor to observe our determinations."

In the end it was agreed, for lack of a better solution, that each colony should have one vote. The compromise could not have pleased everybody, for the Connecticut delegates reported to Governor Trumbull, "As this was objected to as unequal, an entry was made on the journals to prevent it being drawn into precedent in the future."

At least, Congress had weathered its first sectional clash. But the more thoughtful members knew that the greatest problem before them was to create some unity out of the disunity of America. They knew that Patrick Henry had offered them the ideal and not the reality in his concluding statement:

"All distinctions are thrown down. All America is one mass."

Chapter 4

The Tolling of the Bells

TWO large committees were appointed this first week to grapple with the tasks which Congress deemed most important. The first, consisting of two members from each colony, had as its duty the drawing up of a statement of American rights, the violations of these rights, and the best means of securing a restoration of them. The second, limited to one member from each colony, was asked to examine the various statutes affecting trade and commerce, and to recommend the most practical methods of protecting American interests.

Nobody realized more clearly than the delegates themselves that some of their main arguments against England would not hold water from a strictly legal viewpoint. Lord Chatham, the foremost friend of America, had already pointed out the leaks in a favorite complaint; for many sections and interests of the mother country were also being taxed without representation. Actually, as the delegates well knew, their deepest grievances were emotional rather than constitutional—it enraged them no end to be treated as dull provincials by their inferiors in Parliament.

This was the sort of resentment which moved George Washington in a letter of 1765 to refer with heavy sarcasm to "our lordly masters." James Otis exploded more furiously in reply to a piece of British arrogance. "Colonies?" he roared. "Whose colonies can the creatures mean?"

Such grievances, much as they had to do with the revolt, could not of course be included among the violations of American rights. Nor was it safe for the large committee to confine itself entirely to constitutional grounds in drawing up a bill of complaints. The only way to avoid both horns of the dilemma, as the radicals plainly perceived, was to take the path of "natural law."

Here, again, is an expression, like "Continental," which needs translation

43

for following generations. Although the late eighteenth century saw the dawn of modern institutions, including the development of the steam engine which ushered in the Machine Age, the philosophers of that era preferred to think of it as old, corrupt and decadent. Diderot, the editor of the French *Encyclopédie*, summed up this attitude in terms more convincing to his contemporaries than to modern readers. "I am persuaded," he wrote, "that the industry of man has gone too far and that if it had stopped long ago and if it were possible to simplify the results, we should not be the worse. I believe there is a limit to civilization, a limit more conformable to the happiness of man in general than is imagined." And he concluded on a wistful note, "But how to return to it, having left it, or how to remain in it, if we were there, I know not."

The intellectuals of 1774, in short, believed that their own complex and overcivilized age had strayed far from the ideal of human felicity, as represented by some bygone Eden ruled by natural law. They believed in the pure, the simple, the innocent. They believed that man in a primitive state had governed himself with unerring wisdom until he was tempted to taste the apple of luxury; and they trusted that some of the principles of natural law could be restored.

The theory seems vague and sentimental in the present age. But before smiling at the foibles of the past, it might be well to consider a current doctrine. Not many moderns accustomed to the thought of this century would question the word "progress" as represented by the mechanical and scientific wonders of the day. It is a generally accepted theory that man has raised himself by his bootstraps and that he will continue to improve his lot. Yet the time may come when progress will seem as quaint as natural law to some future generation which has its own opinion of two horrible World Wars in a generation.

It might appear that eighteenth-century Americans could have sought guidance from the copper-colored primitives addicted to scalping settlers on the frontiers. But Jefferson held that Hengest and Horsa were the perfect models—"the Saxon chiefs from whom we claim the honor of being descended, and whose political principles we have assumed." He was willing to accept the English constitution when it seemed to follow the canons of natural law, but he believed that it had gone astray in many respects hurtful to America.

James Otis was probably the first patriot to grasp the practical advantages in the quarrel with England. He realized that when all other defenses fell, natural law was a citadel that could be held against all attacks of British legalists. For even when anybody could be sure just what was meant, the difficulties of rebuttal were obvious.

It would be unjust, however, to accuse the Americans of cynicism. Allowing for a few exceptions, most of the colonists were sincere in their conviction. Even Sam Adams, who seldom balked at any means to gain his end, trusted devoutly that natural law had been interpreted for America by such early Puritans as Bradford and Winthrop. As for the practical effects, any present-day skeptic who doubts the part played by the concept in the history of the United States needs only to supply the italics in the first paragraph of a famous national document:

"When in the course of human events, it becomes necessary for one people to dissolve the political bands which have connected them with another, and to assume among the powers of the earth the separate and equal station to which the *laws of Nature* and of *Nature's God* entitle them . . ."

There was no member of Congress less given to metaphysical flights than the 49-year-old politician and ex-governor of Rhode Island. But Samuel Ward did not think it a radical departure when he summed up, in order of importance, the codes claimed by the colonies as the basis of their liberties: "The Committee met, agreed to found our rights upon the laws of nature, the principles of the English constitution, and charters and compacts."

This stand was not reached without protests from conservative members of the committee, as John Adams reported in his notes. "Mr. Galloway and Mr. Duane were for excluding the law of nature. I was very strenuous for retaining and insisting upon it, as a resource to which we might be driven by Parliament much sooner than we were aware." [1]

Richard Henry Lee, of the already notable Virginia family, took a similar view. "The rights," he declared, "are built on a fourfold foundation; on nature, on the British constitution, on charters, and on immemorial usage." And he saw no good reason "why we should not lay our rights upon the broadest bottom, the ground of nature. Our ancestors found here no government."

The three leading conservatives of the committee objected. James Duane, whose "sly, surveying eye" will be recalled, advised "grounding our rights on the laws and constitution of the country from whence we sprung, and charters, without recurring to the law of nature; because this will be a feeble support."

"Our claims, I think, are well founded on the British constitution," said Edward Rutledge, "and not on the law of nature."

Galloway was equally positive. "I have looked for our rights in the law of nature, but could not find them in a state of nature, but always in a state of political society. I have looked for them in the constitution of the British government, and there found them. We may draw from this source securely."

The advocates of natural law prevailed, and Adams adds that "the other great question was, what authority we should concede to Parliament; whether we should deny the authority of Parliament in all cases. . . . These discussions spun into great length and nothing was determined."

The smaller committee, appointed to consider the statutes affecting American commerce, reached an early agreement advocating trade boycotts as the best means of bringing the mother country to terms. Experience seemed to recommend such a solution, for the "associations" of the various colonies in 1770 had cost English merchants such a pretty penny that Parliament was beseeched to repeal the Townshend Acts.

John Adams also served on this committee and took down statements which do not appear in the *Journals*. His account makes it apparent, in the light of later events, that the members had an exaggerated idea of the importance of American trade to England.[2]

Samuel Chase, the burly Annapolis lawyer who was nicknamed Bacon-Face because of his red countenance, voiced an optimism shared by his colleagues: "Force, I apprehend, is out of the question in our present inquiry. . . . The emigrations from Great Britain prove that they are taxed as far as they can bear. A total non-importation and non-exportation to Great Britain and the West Indies must produce a national bankruptcy in a very short space of time."

"We want not only redress, but speedy redress," said Lynch. "The mass can't live without government, I think, one year. . . . I believe that Parliament would grant us immediate relief. Bankruptcy would be the consequence if they did not."

Even the wildest radical of the Congress would never have spoken in favor of armed resistance. Yet it is significant that two members were already mentioning war as a possibility.

"I am for being ready," the fiery Gadsden declared, "but I am not for the sword. The only way to prevent the sword from being used, is to have it ready."

"Negotiation, suspension of commerce, and war, are the only three things," said John Jay. "War is, by general consent, to be waived at present. I am for negotiation and suspension of commerce."

So thoroughly were the other members of the committee in accord that they went ahead to frame nonimportation and nonexportation agreements in perfect confidence that such methods of passive resistance would wring concessions from Parliament. It was the greatest delusion of the first Continental Congress.

There were, as a matter of fact, two Congresses—the one which gathered each morning in Carpenters' Hall, and the other which held informal meetings "out of doors" as the opposing factions discussed their strategy.

From the beginning it had been no secret that Galloway and his cohorts intended to place some plan of reconciliation before the assembly. James Duane hinted as to its nature with the statement, "A firm union between the Parent State and her colonies ought to be the great object of this Congress."

The "violent party," as Galloway called it, was just as determined to widen the breach by persuading Congress to pass resolutions denouncing the Intolerable Acts and making the grievances of Massachusetts a common cause.

Circumstance came to the aid of the radicals the first week, and they were not slow to seize their advantage. On the afternoon of September 6th Congress was stunned by the news that Boston had been bombarded and burned by the redcoats—"a confused account but an alarming one indeed," John Adams wrote in his diary that evening. "God grant that it may not be found true."

But fresh reports the next morning only seemed to verify the rumor and multiply the horrors of the calamity. "An express arrived from N. York," wrote Deane to his wife, "confirming the acct. of a rupture at Boston. All is in confusion. I cannot say that all faces gather paleness, but they all gather indignation, and every tongue pronounces revenge. The bells toll muffled, and the people run as in a state of extremity, they know not where nor why." ³

The mood of Congress can be imagined. So far Sam Adams had been singing small, for he was aware that the other members suspected him of a Congregational bias as well as revolutionary ideas. But at this moment, according to John Adams, the archrebel rose and "said he was no bigot, and could hear a prayer from a gentleman of piety and virtue, who was at the same time a friend to his country. He was a stranger in Philadelphia, but had heard that Mr. Duché . . . deserved that character, and therefore he moved that Mr. Duché, an episcopal clergyman, might be desired to read prayers to the Congress tomorrow morning." ⁴

At the first meeting Cushing had moved that Congress be opened with prayer. Jay and Edward Rutledge opposed, according to the diarist, "because we were so divided in religious sentiments; some Episcopalians, some Quakers, some Anabaptists, some Presbyterians, and some Congregationalists, that we could not join in the same act of worship." This Wednesday morning, however, the occasion was so solemn that Sam Adams' resolution carried unanimously. And on Thursday, after all the bells of the city had been tolling for two days, the stage was set for drama as the Rev. Jacob Duché read the cadences of the Thirty-fifth Psalm:

"Plead my cause, O Lord, with them that strive against me: fight against them that fight against me. Take hold of shield and buckler, and stand up for mine help. . . ."

The Rev. Mr. Duché had a name as the city's most fashionable Church of England rector, renowned for his oratorical sermons. Wearing full canonicals, he concluded by praying "without book, about ten minutes, so pertinently, with such fervency, purity, and sublimity of style and sentiment, and with such an apparent sensibility of the scenes and business before us, that even the Quakers shed tears." [5]

All the members were so moved that the pastor was afterwards appointed chaplain of Congress. This was not the only effect of his prayer, for the strength of the radical faction had gained perceptibly. The rumor of Boston's destruction proved false, but it had left its effect on the minds of the delegates. Even though the bells were soon "ringing a peal of joy," Congress could not forget how dismally they had tolled for the death of an American city.

It was not the first time that piety had been summoned to the aid of patriotism. Only that spring Thomas Jefferson, Richard Henry Lee and Patrick Henry had used religion as a fulcrum for moving Virginia to elect delegates to this very Congress. As Jefferson rather flippantly recalled, they saw "the necessity for arousing our people from the lethargy into which they had fallen, as to passing events, and thought that the appointment of a day of general fasting and prayer would be most likely to call up and alarm their attention. . . . With the help, therefore, of Rushworth, whom we rummaged over for the revolutionary precedents and forms of the Puritans . . . we cooked up a resolution, somewhat modernizing their phrases, for appointing the 1st day of June, on which the port-bill was to commence, for a day of fasting, humiliation and prayer, to implore Heaven to avert from us the evils of civil war, to inspire us with firmness in support of our rights, and to turn the hearts of the King and Parliament to moderation and justice."

The conspirators persuaded Robert Carter Nicholas, one of the most grave and devout elderly members, to put the resolution through the House of Burgesses. He appears to have been pleased by such a sudden display of piety from a young man suspected of freethinking tendencies, but the crown authorities were not so credulous. "The Governor dissolved us, as usual," Jefferson added cheerfully. "We returned home, and in our several counties invited the clergy to meet assemblies of the people on the 1st of June . . . to address to them discourses suited to the occasion. The people met generally, with anxiety and alarm in their countenances, and the effect of that day, throughout the whole colony, was like a shock of electricity, arousing every man, and placing him erect and solidly on his center. They chose, universally, delegates for the convention." [6]

The conspicuous success of this maneuver set a precedent for many other days of fasting, humiliation and prayer to be proclaimed during the early years of the Revolution. It may be that Gouverneur Morris was recalling such occasions in his old age when he indulged in some somber speculations as to the nature of the hereafter. "There must be something more to hope," he mused, "than pleasure, wealth and power. Something more to fear than poverty and pain. Something after death more terrible than death: there must be religion."

But cynics, however brilliant, do not create nations; and the rebels of the first Continental Congress, almost to a man, were united in the firm persuasion of a righteous cause. They might use religion as the staff of patriotism, but their faith was strong enough to move mountains. Their deity was the Jehovah of the Old Testament, and sects could not divide them.

The bells were still tolling in their hearts for Boston when Paul Revere rode once more into Philadelphia on September 16th, this time with a copy of the famous Suffolk Resolves. The patriots of Boston, forbidden to meet in that city, had gone to a village in Suffolk County, under the leadership of Dr. Joseph Warren, to draw up a statement of rights and grievances. Nineteen articles listed "infractions of those rights to which we are justly entitled by the laws of nature, the British constitution and the charter of this province." And the signers agreed "that no obedience is due from this province to either or any part of the acts above-mentioned, but that they be rejected as the attempts of a wicked administration to enslave America." [7]

The day after the Suffolk Resolves arrived, as Sam Adams reported to Boston, they were "read with great applause" before Congress. Galloway at once scented a plot. In a pamphlet published six years later, when he was a loyalist refugee in England, he charged that "continual expresses were employed between Philadelphia and Boston. . . . Whatever these patriots in Congress wished to have done by their colleagues without, to induce General Gage, then at the head of his Majesty's army at Boston, to give them a pretext for violent opposition, or to promote their measure in Congress, Mr. Adams advised and directed to be done; and when done, it was dispatched by express to Congress. By one of these expresses came the inflammatory resolves of the county of Suffolk, which contained a complete declaration of war against Great Britain." [8]

This accusation is supported by the letters of Sam Adams, who had kept in constant touch with the Boston revolutionary machine. The radicals in

Congress knew their strength by this time, and on September 18th it was

> Resolved *unan,* That this assembly deeply feels the suffering of their
> countrymen in the Massachusetts-Bay, under the operation of the late unjust,
> cruel, and oppressive acts of the British Parliament—that they most thoroughly
> approve the wisdom and fortitude, with which opposition to these wicked
> ministerial measures has hitherto been conducted, and they earnestly recom-
> mend to their brethren, a perseverence in the same firm and temperate con-
> duct expressed in the resolutions . . . trusting that the effect of the united
> efforts of North America in their behalf, will carry such conviction to the
> British nation, of the unwise, unjust, and ruinous policy of the present ad-
> ministration, as quickly to introduce better men and wiser measures.[9]

A second article urged the colonies to continue sending supplies to the
beleaguered town. And as a final gesture of defiance, it was ordered "that
these resolutions, together with the resolutions of the county of Suffolk, be
published in the newspapers."

The "violent party" had drawn first blood. But Galloway and his faction
were not yet beaten, and on September 28th he made a speech introducing
his "plan of a proposed union between Great Britain and the Colonies."
John Adams, as usual taking notes, reported the climax of his plea:

> There must be a union of wills and strength, a distinction between a State
> and a multitude: a State is animated by one soul. . . . We want the aid and
> assistance and protection of our mother country. Protection and allegiance
> are reciprocal duties. Can we lay claim to the money and protection of Great
> Britain upon any principles of honor or conscience? Can we wish to become
> aliens to the mother state? We must come upon terms with Great Britain.[10]

There was nothing new about his idea of an American legislature inferior
to Parliament and supervised by a crown-appointed president-general with
strong executive powers. Several such proposals had been rejected in the
colonial past, for they contained the same defect which had led to constant
clashes between the provincial assemblies and crown-appointed governors.
After Duane had seconded the motion and expressed himself in favor,
Richard Henry Lee spoke in opposition: "This plan would make such
changes in the Legislature of the Colonies that I could not agree to it without
consulting my constituents."

"I am led to adopt this plan," said Jay. "Does this plan give up any one
liberty, or interfere with any one right?"

Edward Rutledge also ranged himself on Galloway's side. "I came with
the idea of getting a bill of rights and permanent relief. I think this plan may
be freed from almost every objection. I think it is almost a perfect plan."

"We shall liberate our constituents from a corrupt House of Commons," objected Patrick Henry, "but throw them into the arms of an American Legislature, that may be bribed by the nation which avows, in the face of the world, that bribery is a part of her system of government. Before we are obliged to pay taxes as they do, let us be as free as they; let us have our trade open with all the world."

Galloway himself had the last word: "In every government, patriarchal, monarchial, aristocratical, or democratical, there must be a supreme legislature. . . . There is a necessity that an American legislature should be set up, or else that we should give the power to Parliament or King."

From a radical point of view, the vote on the resolution was too close for comfort. Despite the rule of secrecy, it leaked out that Galloway had been defeated by six colonies to five. This narrow squeak appeared to have embarrassed the delegates afterwards, for great pains were taken to expunge all account of the proceedings from the record.

In further atonement for its lapse, Congress began mulling over the Suffolk Resolves again and concluded that it had not gone far enough in championing the cause of Massachusetts. But there could be no doubt on October 8th that the "violent party" was in the saddle after a majority of the delegates

> Resolved, That this Congress approve of the opposition by the Inhabitants of the Massachusetts-Bay, to the execution of the late acts of Parliament; and if the same shall be attempted to be carried into execution by force, in such case, all America ought to support them in their opposition.[11]

It was no wonder that Galloway and Duane endeavored to have their opposition entered upon the minutes. And when this privilege was denied, each supplied the other with a certificate attesting that he had given no support to such a seditious resolution.

Odd as it may appear, this same Duane had a great deal to do with composing the so-called Declaration of Rights in which Congress took such pride. The seeming inconsistency is explained by the fact that all the delegates were agreed as to the genuine grievances of the colonies. It was the question of what to do about it that caused the split between radicals and conservatives.

Oratory did not find much outlet in such an intimate little assembly, but a "strong pen" was esteemed when it came to drawing up state papers. From first to last the members of Congress reserved the privilege of editing these documents, and authors who did not please were likely to find their efforts rejected entirely. Duane's ideas and phraseology survived to such an extent that the Declaration of Independence later adapted with a few changes the paragraph in which the American colonies

Resolved, That they are entitled to life, liberty, & property, and they have never ceded to any sovereign power whatever, a right to dispose of either without their consent.

It was doubtless due to the New York lawyer's influence that the Declaration of Rights, approved by Congress on October 14th, showed an admirable restraint and moderation. The document included ten resolutions setting forth American rights based more often on the common law of England than natural law. The ancient rights of petition and assembly and "of being tried by their peers of the vicinage" were asserted, as well as the right of being free of a standing army in time of peace except by "the consent of the legislature of that colony, in which said army is kept." And though Duane himself had supported Galloway's plan, one of the resolutions stated in no uncertain terms that "a council appointed, during pleasure, by the crown, is unconstitutional, dangerous and destructive of the freedom of American legislation."

The most timeworn of colonial grievances was not forgotten, and the powers of Parliament were defined as being "restrained to the regulation of our external commerce, for the purpose of securing the commercial advantages of the whole empire to the mother country, and the commercial benefits of its respective members; excluding every idea of taxation, internal or external, for raising a revenue on the subjects in America, without their consent." [12]

The propaganda possibilities of the Address to the People of Great Britain appealed to Congress, and Richard Henry Lee was first nominated as author. His draft did not suit the committee, which turned the task over to John Jay. The change could not have been made without some jealousy and hurt feelings, as Thomas Jefferson learned to his embarrassment in 1775 when he committed the error of praising William Livingston for the composition.

"The next morning," related Jefferson, "walking into the hall of Congress . . . I observed Mr. Jay speaking to R. H. Lee and leading him by the button of the coat to me. 'I understand, sir,' said he to me, 'that this gentleman informed you, that Governor Livingston drew the Address to the people of Great Britain.' I assured him, at once that I had not received that information from Mr. Lee . . . and after some explanations the subject was dropped. These gentlemen had had some sparring in debate before, and continued ever very hostile to each other." [13]

In spite of young Jay's conservative views, the Address could hardly be called a model of tact and conciliation. The very first paragraph bristles with indignation: "When a nation, led to greatness by the hand of Liberty . . . descends to the ungrateful task of forging chains for her Friends and Children, and instead of giving support to Freedom, turns advocate for Slavery and Oppression, there is reason to suspect she has either ceased to be virtuous, or been extremely negligent in the appointment of her rulers."

After about 3,000 words in a similar tone, one of the concluding sentences leaves no doubt as to American sentiment: "But if you are determined that your ministers shall wantonly sport with the rights of Mankind—if neither the voice of justice, the dictates of the law, the principles of the constitution, or the suggestions of humanity can restrain your hands from shedding human blood in such an impious cause, we must then tell you, that we will never submit to be hewers of wood or drawers of water for any ministry or nation in the world." [14]

Patrick Henry had been assigned to drafting the petition to the king. But the spoken rather than the written word proved to be his medium; and the committee asked John Dickinson to wield a pen already famous for *The Letters of a Farmer in Pennsylvania*, published in 1768 to protest the Townshend Acts.

Up to this time the most outspoken complaints of the colonists had been careful to spare the monarch. The word "administration," often preceded by the adjective "wicked," was a favorite reliance of rebel pamphleteers who wished to toss a rhetorical bomb under the seats of the mighty in England. When the king was mentioned at all, it was usually with the intimation that he had been deceived by artful ministers. This style was faithfully followed by Dickinson, who declared that "as your majesty enjoys the signal distinction of reigning over freemen, we apprehend that the language of freemen cannot be displeasing. Your royal indignation, we hope, will rather fall upon those designing and dangerous men, who daringly interposing themselves between your royal person and your faithful subjects . . . by abusing your majesty's authority, misrepresenting your American subjects and prosecuting the most desperate and irritating projects of oppression, have at length compelled us, by the force of accumulated injuries too severe to be any longer tolerable, to disturb your majesty's repose by our complaints. These sentiments are extorted from hearts that much more willingly would bleed in your majesty's service. . . . Your royal authority over us and our connexion with Great Britain, we shall always carefully and zealously endeavor to support and maintain." [15]

Just as the petition to the king differed in tone from the address to the people of England, so the Address to the Inhabitants of the Province of Quebec was couched in still another style. It had long been a wishful conviction of the American colonists that French Canada, so recently conquered by Britain, would be fertile ground for propaganda. John Dickinson, who had murmured to the king in such respectful terms, gave proof of his adaptability by turning out staccato phrases peppered with exclamation points for Canadian consumption:

> Unhappy people! who are not only injured but insulted. Nay more!—With such a superlative contempt of your understanding and spirit, has an insolent Ministry presumed . . . to perswade themselves that your gratitude, for the injuries and insults they have recently offered to you, will engage you to take up arms and render yourselves the ridicule and detestation of the world, by becoming tools, in their hands, to assist them in taking that freedom from *us,* which they have treacherously denied to *you.*[16]

In their solicitations for Canadian sympathy the Americans had still another ax to grind. That spring, along with the Intolerable Acts, Parliament had passed the Quebec Act on the advice of a capable governor-general, Sir Guy Carleton. The measure, far from being repressive in purpose, was one of the few wise pieces of colonial legislation approved by Parliament in this era. Not only did it guarantee Britain's new Catholic subjects freedom of worship in an intolerant age, but it served a strategic purpose by extending Quebec Province westward and southward to include the French settlements of the Illinois country.

The members of Congress viewed the measure as an attempt to encircle the colonies. As aggressive Protestants they resented the religious clauses so much that one of the grievances of the Declaration of Rights was held to be the "establishing of the Roman Catholick Religion in the Province of Quebec." This fact did not embarrass John Dickinson, who asked the Canadians in his address, "What is offered to you by the late act of Parliament? . . . Liberty of conscience in your religion?" And he answered his own query with an unblushing "No."

The English-speaking colonies of Canada were not overlooked by Congress, which sent letters to St. Johns and Nova Scotia as well as East and West Florida. Nor were the American colonies themselves neglected; for a memorial of 5,000 words, after repeating the familiar lessons of indoctrination, ended by warning that if "the peaceable mode of opposition recommended by us, be broken and rendered ineffectual, as your cruel and haughty ministerial enemies, from a contemptuous opinion of your firmness, insolently predict will be the case, you must inevitably be reduced to chuse, either a more dangerous contest, or a final, ruinous and infamous subjection."[17]

The diarist of Congress continued to hop about Philadelphia like a plump New England robin, keeping a bright and inquisitive eye cocked for every development. "My time," he wrote, "is totally filled from the moment I get out of bed until I return to it. Visits, ceremonies, company, business, newspapers, pamphlets, &c, &c, &c."

A delegate's day usually began with an early awakening in one of the boardinghouses near Carpenters' Hall. Conferences before breakfast were not infrequent, then the time from nine to three was devoted to "debates upon the most abstruse mysteries of state." Four in the afternoon was the customary colonial dinner hour, followed by an evening of wine and talk leading up to a late supper and bedtime. That these occasions were not entirely social was hinted by Adams' comment: "We have been obliged to keep ourselves out of sight and to feel pulses and sound the depths; to insinuate our sentiments, designs, and desires, by means of other persons; sometimes of one Province, and sometimes of another." [18]

Philadelphia continued to be so hospitable that he sighed, "I shall be killed with kindness in this place." But he enjoyed his martyrdom, and it was rather grumpily one Saturday evening that he set down the unwonted item, "Dined at home . . . upon salt fish." The next week he was booked solidly by Philadelphia hostesses, and again the diary is filled with such notes as, "Dined with Mr. Charles Thomson, with only Mr. Dickinson, his lady and niece, in company. A most delightful afternoon we had; sweet communion indeed, we had."

The most voluptuous feast of all appears to have been the one given by Judge Samuel Chew for those close political allies, the Massachusetts and Virginia delegates. "We were shown into a grand entry and staircase," reported Adams, "and into an elegant and most magnificent chamber, until dinner. . . . The furniture was all rich. Turtle, and every other thing, flummery, jellies, sweetmeats of twenty sorts, trifles, whipped sillabubs, floating islands, fools, &c. and then a dessert of fruits, raisins, almonds, pears, peaches. Wines most excellent and admirable. I drank Madeira at a great rate and found no inconvenience in it."

All was not sweetness and light at Carpenters' Hall, however, when nerves were worn thin by the friction of committee duties. "I am wearied to death with the life I lead," Adams grumbled after a month of it. "The business of Congress is tedious beyond expression." As the session neared its end, he displayed even more irritation. "In Congress, nibbling and quibbling as usual. There is no greater mortification than to sit with half a dozen wits, deliberating upon a petition, address or memorial. These great wits, these subtle critics, these refined geniuses, these learned lawyers, these wise statesmen, are so fond of showing their parts and powers, as to make their consultations very tedious. Young Ned Rutledge is a perfect Bob-o-Lincoln—

a swallow, a sparrow, a peacock; excessively vain, excessively weak, and excessively variable and unsteady; jejune, inane, and puerile." [19]

It is likely that the Charleston delegate, only 24 years old and a recent bridegroom, annoyed Adams by his parochial opposition to two of the non-exportation clauses. All the other South Carolina members except Gadsden also threatened to withdraw unless rice and indigo, the chief products of the colony, were listed as exceptions. With unity at stake, Congress restored peace by a compromise allowing rice to be exported on condition that South Carolina yield in respect to indigo. There was nothing further to prevent the signing of the Articles of Association—the first of the five great documents of the Revolutionary era—which sets forth its purpose in an opening paragraph:

> To obtain redress of these grievances, which threaten destruction to the lives, liberty and property of his majesty's subjects, in North America, we are of the opinion that a non-importation, non-consumption, and non-exportation agreement, faithfully adhered to, will prove the most speedy, effectual, and peaceable measure.[20]

The economic causes of the Revolution had always been as vital as political grievances, even though they were not so stridently asserted. Such merchant princes as Gadsden, Hancock and Robert Morris did not risk their lives and fortunes without reason. They remembered that beaver hats, made of furs trapped in America, had been a thriving American industry until Parliament came to the rescue of English manufacturers by forbidding the colonists the right of exportation. A lusty young metal-working industry was likewise throttled when Parliament required the operators of American smelting furnaces to send their raw iron to the mother country—to be shipped back as finished products to the place of origin. American tobacco found one of its best markets in Holland, but Parliament demanded that it be sold first to English middlemen, unloaded and loaded again before being sold to Dutch distributors. Parliament passed the Navigation Acts for the purpose of crippling rather than taxing American manufacturers; and it will be recalled that the Tea Act of 1773 was resisted less as an impost than an entering wedge for commercial monopolies at the expense of America.

Regulations of this sort were not at all unusual in an age when all European nations held that colonies existed for the purpose of being milked. But Americans had long resented the prohibitions of their own manufactures which made it necessary for them to buy English goods at prices ranging from 25 to 40 per cent above those prevailing in a free market. After years of turning the other cheek, their representatives in Congress took great satisfaction in striking back with the nonintercourse provisions of the Association.

The document also seemed to them the foremost achievement of the assembly because it represented the promise if not actually the fulfillment of unity. After all, twelve colonies had demonstrated that they could reach an agreement based on sacrifices for a common cause; and the Association has every right to be considered the legitimate ancestor of the Declaration.

Most of the fourteen articles dealt with the terms of setting up and enforcing the boycotts. But Congress dreamed for a moment of a self-sufficient America when it pledged the colonies to "encourage frugality, economy, and industry, and promote agriculture, arts and the manufactures of this country, especially that of wool." Not even the morals of America were neglected, and it may be suspected that such pious Congregationalists as Sam Adams and Roger Sherman introduced this Puritanical note:

> We will, in·our several stations . . . discountenance and discourage every species of extravagance and dissipation, especially all horse-racing, and all kinds of gaming, cock-fighting, exhibitions of shews, plays, and other expensive diversions and entertainments. . . .

After the Association had been safely launched, the delegates elected Henry Middleton as their new president to replace the ailing Peyton Randolph. And having already written addresses to everyone else under the sun, Congress sent a bread-and-butter letter of formal thanks to its Pennsylvania hosts after partaking of a final banquet given at the City Tavern by the House of Representatives. "The whole House dined with us, making near one hundred guests on the whole; a most elegant entertainment," reported John Adams. "A sentiment was given: 'May the sword of the parent never be stained with the blood of her children.' "

On October 26th the session ended and the delegates began jogging homeward. It remained only for Secretary Charles Thomson to send the accumulation of documents to Benjamin Franklin in London, and he added a comment of his own: "I hope administration will see and be convinced that it is not a little faction but the whole body of American freeholders from Nova Scotia to Georgia that now complain & apply for redress; and who, I am sure, will resist rather than submit. . . . Even yet the wound may be healed & peace and love restored; But we are on the brink of a precipice." [21]

Chapter 5

Wardens of the Promised Land

NONE of the delegates seems to have doubted for a moment that the Association would solve most of the problems of America by compelling the mother country to choose between compromise and bankruptcy, even though nonimportation was not to go into effect until December 1, 1774, and nonexportation at the late date of September 10, 1775.

John Adams felt so certain that he indulged in a nostalgic farewell. Round of girth, with deceptively wide and trustful eyes, he may have reined in his horse for a last backward glance before composing this sentiment two days before his thirty-ninth birthday: "Took our departure, in a very great rain, from the happy, the peaceful, the elegant, the hospitable, and polite city of Philadelphia. It is not very likely that I shall ever see this part of the world again, but I shall ever retain a most grateful, pleasing sense of the many civilities I have received in it. . . ."

It had been decided that another general assembly of all the colonies should be convened in Philadelphia on May 10, 1775, if redress was not forthcoming before that date. But the delegates placed their confidence in Article XI of the Association, which is important enough to deserve special mention. Although Congress had neither any legislative nor any executive powers, it was actually taking a seven-league stride toward both with this provision:

> That a committee be chosen in every county, city or town . . . whose business it shall be attentively to observe the conduct of all persons touching this association; and when it shall be made to appear . . . that any person within the limits of their appointment has violated this association, that [they] do

forthwith cause the truth of the case to be published in the gazette; to the end, that all such foes to the rights of British-America may be publicly known, and universally contemned as the enemies of American liberty; and thenceforth we respectively will break off all dealings with him or her.[1]

At a glance it would merely appear that Congress did not propose to rely too much upon the frailty of human nature for the keeping of the covenant. But there was more to the Association than met the eye. The committees of correspondence, it will be recalled, also had seemed innocuous until they proved within a very few months to be the means of indoctrinating thirteen scattered colonies. The Association in its turn was to give the British and loyalists a more dismaying shock by setting up the administrative machinery of revolution. The Association, in short, was the first practical American system of government to be created after the break with the mother country— the crude political forerunner of the Confederation and the Constitution.

Congress could not legislate with the authority of Parliament, but it knew its constituents well enough to realize that Article XI was charged with high explosive. Within the next few months the fuse was lighted as riders pelted along country roads with copies of the Association. Hundreds of colonial villages had elected their committees of safety by the spring of 1775, and the Revolution entered upon a new militant stage.

As an example of the workings of this system of revolutionary government, Congress resolved on July 18th "that it be recommended to the inhabitants of all the united English colonies of North America, that all able bodied effective men, between sixteen and fifty years of age in each colony, immediately form themselves into regular companies of Militia." There is no slightest appearance of a law about a measure which merely recommends in an advisory tone. But it had the effect of an edict by the time it reached the committees of safety. They soon had militia companies drilling on every village green, and it took a great deal of explaining for a loyalist to be excused. Thus in reality King Congress had proclaimed a limited form of conscription with a stroke of the pen.

Soon the nonexportation and nonimportation features were subordinated as the Association proved its usefulness as a revolutionary system of government. King Congress had only to recommend, and hundreds of committees of safety would act, sometimes none too gently.

Naturally, this phase abounded in ugly incidents. At their worst the committees of safety were composed of petty tyrants, addicted to snooping, who made it their business to supervise the moral conduct as well as patriotism of their communities. Publicity and social ostracism were potent enough weapons, but too often the village Cromwells did not hesitate to sanction such reprisals as tarring and feathering a Tory or even burning his home. It was this sort of thing which caused Judge Samuel Seabury, a New York loyalist, to groan, "If I must be enslaved, let it be by a KING at least, and not by a parcel of upstart lawless Committee-men. If I must be devoured, let me be devoured by the jaws of a lion, and not gnawed to deth by rats and vermin." Another stout old loyalist, the Rev. Mather Byles of Boston, put it even more succinctly, "Which is better—to be ruled by one tyrant three thousand miles away or three thousand tyrants not a mile away?"

But there is another side to the story. For a century the colonists had been under the thumb of equally petty and annoying masters—the horde of office-holders made up of deserving native Americans as well as the scheming politicians or useless, impoverished members of the ruling class sent out from England. Owing their perquisites either directly or indirectly to the crown, these bureaucrats had often been tattlers who curried favor by spying on the colonists and making out derogatory secret reports about individuals or communities. Nor were such vexations any the less irksome because they had the authority of the mother country behind them.

It is understandable that as homesick exiles in Canada or England the losers of the American Revolution should have pictured themselves as fallen aristocrats overthrown by the mob—a legend which has been accepted at face value even by a few historians. The candid evidence, as represented by lists of the refugees who sailed from Boston and New York, does not uphold any such conclusion. Actually the American loyalists included a large proportion of mechanics, tradesmen, family servants and other folk of humble station as well as jurists, doctors and ministers of the gospel. If there was any predominant class, it consisted of the very officeholders who had lost their jobs after contributing so much to the causes of the insurrection.

The sudden transfer of power was bound to result in abuses. But after taking into account every episode of violence and injustice, the American Revolution remains unquestionably the most moderate of all the great polit-ical upheavals of world history. The word "liquidation" had no sinister meaning in 1775, and there were none of the mass slaughters which have been considered appropriate to prove the ideologies of other revolts.

The minor persecutions ordered by the committees of safety had their ridiculous as well as unpleasant side. Mather Byles, the outspoken Boston Tory, was considered dangerous enough to be placed under the surveillance of an armed militiaman. But the old pastor could not resist a pun, and he made the most solemn patriots chuckle by referring to the guard as "my observatory." The situation reached new heights of absurdity when the cap-tive obligingly held the musket of a captor fetching a bucket of water for the household.

In communities where the loyalists had the upper hand, they were no more gentle or considerate than the patriots. It may also be noted that thousands of them accepted the fortunes of war philosophically and lived out their lives on excellent terms with their republican neighbors. The royal governor of Maryland, in fact, was so well liked by the rebels of that colony that they kept him in office down to the very eve of the Declaration of Independence.

In his old age, looking back at this period, Thomas Jefferson took great pride in "the honor of having my name inserted in a long list of proscriptions, enrolled in a bill of attainder commenced in one of the Houses of Parliament, but suppressed in embryo by the hasty step of events, which warned them to be a little cautious. . . . The names, I think, were about twenty . . . but I recollect only those of Hancock, the two Adamses, Peyton Randolph . . . Patrick Henry and myself." [2]

Jefferson's good faith cannot be doubted, but no evidence of any such list has ever been found among British records. It may be seriously questioned, moreover, if the members of Parliament in 1775 could have named as many as twenty revolutionary leaders. For the besetting sin of Parliament was not tyranny so much as an incredible ignorance of American affairs, complicated by indifference and the misinformation sent home by crown-appointed office-holders.

This factor was to play its part in the forthcoming legislative duel between Parliament and the Continental Congress, with a continent at stake. All the advantages seemed at a glance to be on the side of an ancient assembly backed by the power, prestige and wealth of a great empire. But Congress was not striking out blindly in the dark. Congress had a detailed, accurate picture of conditions in the mother country, including some intimate character sketches supplied by Franklin, Arthur Lee and the many other Americans who had dwelt for long periods in London. On the other hand, it was almost unknown for an English parliamentarian of that day to visit America.

The colonists were aware that a revolution had also been brewing in England—which was much more in need of one—since the beginning of the reign. This insurrection might have gone further if it had found a more admirable popular champion than John Wilkes, whose private life was a scandal. The son of a wealthy merchant, he displayed an early interest in politics by attempting to buy his way into the House of Commons. Wilkes selected the corrupt borough of Berwick, near Newcastle, and launched his campaign by bribing a sea captain to land the hired opposition voters "by mistake" in Norway. In spite of such ingenious strategy and the £4,000 paid to purchase votes of his own, he did not bid high enough for the election. A few years later it cost him £7,000 in bribes to be sent to Commons from the seat of Aylesworth.

After this conventional start of a political career, the tall, homely, squint-eyed young parliamentarian showed a most unusual interest in popular rights. Other leaders such as Pitt and Burke had denounced colonial policies, but Wilkes concerned himself with home grievances far worse than any suffered in America. Nearly two hundred offenses at the time could be punished by the English law with death penalties, among them such crimes as stealing a sheep or cutting down a tree on a private estate. Long hours and starvation wages prevailed as a matter of upper-class principle for laboring folk who were often reduced to beggary or the workhouse by the time they were middle aged. But the most cruel and unforgivable oppression was the denying even of daylight to slum dwellers who huddled together like beasts crouching in dark, filthy dens. This was the result of a law passed by Parliament to tax buildings according to the number of windows, for the landlords of industrial towns found it cheaper to brick over such openings.

It was a genuine conviction on the part of most educated Englishmen that the victims of these conditions belonged to an inferior if not actually subhuman species. This belief seemed to be upheld by the universal drunkenness and sexual promiscuity in slum districts of London. On every street the gin houses offered the boon of oblivion for as little as twopence, with signs advertising "straw provided free" for those unable to stagger home. Suffrage, of course, was limited by property and other qualifications, so that the poor had no means of political protest except riots which terrified the entire kingdom on several historical occasions.

In contrast to these miseries, the ruling classes lived on a sybaritic scale. Most of the princely country houses of England were built during this era by aristocrats who thought nothing of spending many thousands of pounds annually for entertainment. Charles James Fox, one of America's best friends, gambled away £40,000 in a single night while sowing his wild oats, and the Duke of Devonshire lost Leicester Abbey on a wager. Wilkes himself was cited as an example of the loose morals of London's gallants, for he retained all his life the pruriency of a depraved schoolboy. The gentry of the realm were disgusted by accounts of the obscene black mass orgies celebrated by him with such boon companions as Lord Sandwich and Lord Orford. On one of these nights Wilkes frightened Orford nearly into insanity by producing a baboon disguised as the devil at the climax of a prayer addressed to Satan.

Benjamin Franklin is authority for the surmise that England might have had a cleansing revolution if the characters of the libidinous rebel and the decent, sober, hard-working young monarch had been reversed. Wilkes' enemies, who were legion, accused him of being an ambitious demagogue rather than a sincere reformer—a charge supported by many of his own cynicisms. At any rate he proved his courage as well as ability, and in 1763 the cry "Wilkes and liberty!" became the rallying call of the London mob.

For two generations a number had haunted the House of Hanover. George II's bloody repression of the Jacobite uprising of 1745 had been grimly known ever since in Scotland as "the Forty-Five." And it was the forty-fifth issue of Wilkes' newspaper *The North Briton* which enraged George III so much with its attacks that he had the printers arrested and the publisher imprisoned in the Tower. This martyrdom added to Wilkes' fame, and the two digits chalked on London walls served as a symbol of protest. Even in Boston a "45" was worn on the hats of Sam Adams' followers, and funds were sent to Wilkes from several of the colonies.

For a time it appeared that the English and American revolts might merge, but Wilkes went into a self-imposed European exile of four years as a consequence of publishing an indecent parody called *Essay on Woman*. After his homecoming he was sentenced to a year's imprisonment, and in 1769 England had its counterpart of the Boston Massacre when Scottish regulars fired into a crowd, killing one and wounding several. But instead of standing trial the soldiers of St. George's Fields were officially congratulated and rewarded.

Twice returned to Commons by honest majorities of Middlesex voters during the next few years, "that devil Wilkes" was twice expelled as a result of the king's opposition. In 1774 he fought through to being elected Lord Mayor of London, and in this position he worked fearlessly for the American cause as well as the reform of Parliament and the enfranchisement of England's "lower orders." But John Wilkes, rake and rebel, was already on his way to becoming the "spent volcano" of later years. Already the king had established his twelve-year period of personal rule, with the obedient Lord North as minister, which would witness the loss of America to the Empire.

Ironically, the American Revolution had a great deal to do with sidetracking the incipient English Revolution by diverting the attention of the kingdom to the colonies. In the role of "patriot king" George III used his power of patronage to make himself secure in Parliament. The Americans called themselves Whigs because most of their English friends belonged to that party, but the Tories of that day were actually more dynamic and progressive. It had been the Whigs under the practical politician Walpole who founded the system of open corruption used against them by George III; and the Whigs of 1775 still believed that the primary purpose of government was the protection of profits and property. Enough of these same Whigs joined the "king's friends," after he took advantage of divisions in the party, so that he could count on a safe majority.

The annual income of £800,000 voted the crown left a surplus which sufficed to buy many parliamentary seats at an average of about £5,000 each, and there were also royal gifts, honors and sinecures to be awarded the faithful. All England had only 174 peers at the accession of George III to the throne; but he busily conferred 388 more titles, most of them during his years of personal power.[3]

The old landowning nobility had been one of responsibility as well as privilege, while the new peerage brought to the front a crude new aristocracy of money—the models for the Lord Steyne and Lady Bareacres satirized by Thackeray in *Vanity Fair*. These were the members of the House of Lords who turned down Chatham's proposal to recognize the Continental Congress and voted overwhelmingly against withdrawing the British troops from Boston. The members of Commons were no more receptive when Edmund Burke delivered his famous speech on *Conciliation* in 1775, and the American colonies gave their answer with the shot heard round the world.

That memorable date of April 19th found some of the delegates already on their way to the second Continental Congress, for the American leaders had decided that no redress could be expected. The king had chosen instead to regard the Association as an act of sedition, and his attitude was anything but conciliatory. "The New England governments," he fumed, "are now in a state of rebellion; blows must decide whether they are to be subject to this country or independent."

This statement may have put dangerous notions into the heads of his American subjects, who had seldom been so bold as to mention war or independence up to this time. Sam Adams must have chuckled at receiving aid from such an unexpected quarter. For the archrebel, operating on the principle that enough negatives make an affirmative, had been denying any thought of separation so often and so piously as to implant that very idea in the New England mind.

Adams and the newly elected Massachusetts delegate, John Hancock, were informal representatives of Congress at Lexington. The expedition sent by General Gage to that village had as its object the capture of both men as well as the destruction of war materials. Later the two were excepted from the proclamation of pardon announced by the British commander, who deemed their offenses to be "of too flagitious a nature to admit of any other consideration than that of condign punishment."

The royal authorities found it especially hard to forgive the slender, nervous Hancock, whose inherited mercantile interests made him the wealthiest citizen of New England at the age of 38. With so much at stake, the man of property had been first in the colonies to defy the British in his own name. When customs officers boarded his new sloop *Liberty* in 1767, he had them clapped below decks while he landed a smuggled cargo of Madeira with forged papers. Actions brought against him for a total of £90,000 were still pending in a suit decided by the muskets of Lexington.

"Oh, what a glorious morning is this!" exulted Adams an hour after the minutemen made their brave but hopeless stand on the village green. The literal-minded Hancock, who thought that his colleague was referring to the weather, had shown the only enthusiasm for taking part in the fight. "This is not our business," Adams objected hastily. "We belong to the cabinet."

The fugitives, warned by Paul Revere at the end of his most famous ride, scrambled through the woods to a hiding place while the redcoats were making their disastrous retreat with losses of 273 killed, missing and wounded. As soon as Adams and Hancock dared to venture forth, they set out on their journey to Philadelphia. Some of the excitement of the occasion went into the jerky phrases scribbled by Hancock on April 24th to the Watertown committee of safety, inquiring about the other Massachusetts delegates:

"How are we to proceed? Where are our brethren? . . . Are our men in good spirits? For God's sake do not suffer the spirit to subside, until they have perfected the reduction of our enemies. . . . Where is Mr. Cushing? Are Mr. Paine and Mr. John Adams to be with us? What are we to depend upon? We travel rather as deserters, which I will not submit to. . . ."

The news of Lexington raced ahead of them at such a pace that it reached Charleston on May 8th and Savannah two days later. In every Connecticut village the Massachusetts delegates were greeted by crowds and wildly pealing bells. And at Hartford they became the first members of the Continental Congress to dabble in strategy when Governor Trumbull asked their advice about an expedition being sent to surprise the British garrison at Fort Ticonderoga.

The reception awaiting in New York surpassed anything ever known by the first Congress. Hancock tried to preserve the modesty becoming a hero while writing about it to his fiancée, Dorothy Quincy: "When we Arriv'd within three Miles of the City we were met by the Grenadier Company and Regiment of the City Militia under Arms, Gentlemen in Carriages and on Horseback, and many Thousands of Persons on Foot, the Roads fill'd with people, and the greatest Cloud of Dust I ever saw. In this Scituation we Entered the City, and passing thro' the Principal Streets of New York amidst the Acclamations of Thousands, were set down at Mr. Frances's. . . . My Carriage was stopt, and Persons appearing with proper Harnesses insisted on taking out my Horses and Dragging me into and through the city, a Circumstance I would not had taken place upon any consideration, not being fond of such parade." [4]

Silas Deane also commented on "the amazing concourse of people: I believe well nigh every open carriage in the city, and thousands on foot trudging and sweating thro' the dirt." That night he found it gratifying when "a Guard of Grenadiers was set at each door where we lodged, and relieved regularly, in the usual way. They are in a blue and scarlet uniform, and make a genteel appearance." [5]

Another great crowd escorted the three Connecticut and five Massachusetts men to the ferry a few days later to begin a triumphal march across New Jersey. At Newark a salute from four infantry companies welcomed them, and all the rest of the way to Trenton they were escorted along the road by relays of militiamen.

Before the little cavalcade reached Philadelphia, according to Deane, the New Jersey contingent had joined the other delegates who "were met at about six miles on this side the City by about two hundred of the principal gentlemen, on horseback, with their swords drawn; here we alighted, and baited. Thence began a most lengthy procession; half the gentlemen on horseback, in the van. . . . Our rear closed with the remainder of the gentlemen on horseback, with swords drawn, and then the carriages from the City. At about two miles distance, we were met by a Company on foot, and then by a Company of Riflemen in their uniform, which is very curious. Thus rolling and gathering like a snowball, we approached the City, which was full of people, and the crowd as great as at New York; the bells all ringing, and the air rent with shouts and huzzas." [6]

The forty-five delegates from eleven colonies who met on the morning of May 10th could hardly have imagined that the Continental Congress would remain in session, with only brief recesses, throughout the next fourteen years. Most of the former members had returned, and among the new arrivals were such well-known names as Franklin, Jefferson and Hancock. The two Rhode Islanders took their seats a few days later; and with the appearance of Lyman Hall, elected by a single parish in Georgia, all thirteen colonies were represented for the first time. Several delegates left for military duties before the last of the stragglers reached the city, but the following 65 members (with the new names in italics) served in the second Congress before the end of June:

CONNECTICUT—Silas Deane, Eliphalet Dyer, Roger Sherman;

DELAWARE—Thomas McKean, George Read, Caesar Rodney;

GEORGIA—*Lyman Hall;*

MARYLAND—Samuel Chase, Robert Goldsborough, *John Hall,* Thomas Johnson Jr., William Paca, *Thomas Stone,* Matthew Tilghman;

MASSACHUSETTS—John Adams, Samuel Adams, Thomas Cushing, *John Hancock,* Robert Treat Paine;

NEW HAMPSHIRE—*John Langdon,* John Sullivan;

NEW JERSEY—Stephen Crane, John De Hart, James Kinsey, William Livingston, Richard Smith;

NEW YORK—John Alsop, Simon Boerum, *George Clinton,* James Duane, *William Floyd,* John Jay, Francis Lewis, Philip Livingston, *Robert R. Livingston,* Lewis Morris, *Philip Schuyler,* Henry Wisner;

NORTH CAROLINA—Richard Caswell, Joseph Hewes, William Hooper;

PENNSYLVANIA—Edward Biddle, John Dickinson, *Benjamin Franklin,* Charles Humphreys, Thomas Mifflin, John Morton, George Ross, *Thomas Willing, James Wilson;*

RHODE ISLAND—Stephen Hopkins, Samuel Ward;

SOUTH CAROLINA—Christopher Gadsden, Thomas Lynch, Henry Middleton, Edward Rutledge, John Rutledge;

VIRGINIA—Richard Bland, Benjamin Harrison, Patrick Henry, *Thomas Jefferson,* Richard Henry Lee, Edmund Pendleton, Peyton Randolph, George Washington.

This second Congress met in the State House to be known later as Independence Hall, sharing that building with the Pennsylvania House of Representatives. In the council chamber with its high windows and white-paneled walls, the chairs of the delegates were drawn up in neat rows facing the low dais where the president and secretary sat. The bare State House yard, surrounded by seven-foot walls, played almost as much of a part in American history as the hall itself. For in clement weather a great many of the most confidential political bargains were made where the participants could be sure of privacy.

The Rev. Mr. Duché, as chaplain, opened the session with a solemn prayer for guidance. As soon as the credentials of the delegates had been approved, Congress resolved itself into a committee of the whole "to consider the state of America." An excerpt from the notes of James Duane gives an idea of the struggle of conflicting ideas in the hearts of many Americans after the news of Lexington:

The eyes of Europe and America are fixed on this Assembly, and the fate of one of the greatest empires on earth, in no small degree, depends on the issue of their deliberations. We are contending with the State from whence we spring, with those who were once our fathers, our guardians, our brethren, with those fleets and armies which were lately our protection. . . . Cemented by the ties of blood, religion and interest, victory itself however decided must be fatal: and whichever side prevails must weep over its conquests. . . . Let this ever be considered as a *family quarrel, disgraceful* and *ruinous* into which we are innocently plunged by intolerable oppression, and which we are sincerely disposed to appease and reconcile, whenever the good providence of God shall put it in our power, consistent with the preservation of our just rights.[7]

From the first day there could be little question about the stand that Congress would take. Fiery eloquence might have been expected from a Patrick Henry, but the British had more reason to be alarmed by the quiet defiance of John Morton. This Quaker delegate from Pennsylvania informed a friend in England that Congress was "preparing for the worst that can happen, viz. a Civil War. . . . Thou will hear before this reaches thee of the situation of General Gage. He is hem'd in by the Provincials on every side, and cannot penetrate 500 yards into the Country, were he supported by all the Troops now in England. You have declared the New England People Rebels, and the other Provinces Aiders and Abbettors. this is putting the Halter around our Necks, and we may as well die by the Sword as to be hang'd like Rebels."[8]

"The military spirit which runs through the continent is really amazing," John Adams wrote to Abigail. "Colonel Washington appears at Congress in his uniform, and by his great experience and abilities in military matters, is of much service to us."[9]

That there were also serious doubts and misgivings is evident from the message of Joseph Hewes to the president of the revolutionary convention in North Carolina: "I am exceedingly uneasy (so are my colleagues) not that I think we are doing any thing but what Necessity will Justify, but I fear we shall be obliged to promise for our Colony much more than it will perform and perhaps more than it is able to bear. When a large extensive Country Loses its Trade, when its Ports are all Shutt up and all exportation ceases, will there be Virtue enough found in that Country to bear heavy taxes with patience? suppose such a Country, no matter where, should be under such circumstances, and Necessity should oblige the inhabitants to raise a large Army for their defence, how is it to be paid? . . . I will not trouble you farther with imaginary Countries, but beg leave to call your attention to your Own, where I think it will be absolutely necessary to call a Provincial Convention immediately."[10]

Two of the five former delegates who did not serve in this Congress had already searched their souls and decided that they owed allegiance to the mother country. Within the next few months Joseph Galloway and Isaac Low would take refuge within the British lines, and both were eventually to be condemned as traitors by patriots who confiscated their property. No Patrick Henry ever spoke for such loyalists, but the fervent and even mystical spirit of their devotion was expressed by Ambrose Serle, who came to America as secretary for Lord Howe:

"Rebellion is indeed the Sin of Witchcraft, blinds the Eyes, and hardens the Heart against every sound principle of Religion and Duty. If such men in such a cause can prosper, it is only the prosperity of a Night, which the morning Cloud shall chase away." [11]

But it was not a fleeting night's prosperity which rejoiced Congress when an express told of the capture of the chief British post on Lake Champlain in the darkness of May 10th. The victor of the surprise was a Vermont border captain named Ethan Allen who had sent word to his Green Mountain Boys:

> To call them together to cross o'er the Lake,
> Then march from the shore and Fort Ti to take.

The whole affair had been highly irregular. The Hampshire Grants, as Vermont was then known, comprised territory disputed by New Hampshire and New York. Allen and his band were regarded as outlaws by New York, but Connecticut commissioned him to lead an expedition into that colony without asking anybody's leave. Massachusetts complicated the situation further by sending a Connecticut militia officer, Benedict Arnold, on the same mission. He reached the scene just in time to play a discordant second fiddle, but was first to claim the glory in a dispatch to Philadelphia.

"Last night," wrote George Read of Delaware on May 18th, "an express came to town from one Colonel Arnold, informing that, with a detachment of men from the colony of Connecticut, he had taken possession of the fort Ticonderoga, an important pass on Lake Champlain, which, if kept, will prevent any army from Canada." [12]

Equally doubtful, according to the purists of history, is the legend which has the real victor demanding the surrender of the post "in the name of the Great Jehovah and the Continental Congress." At least it was the sort of thundering challenge which Ethan Allen *would* have shouted if he had thought of it in time, and the truth of history is not compounded of fact alone. The name of no other deity could have been invoked with that of the Continental Congress, which had its first assurance of artillery in the cannon captured at Ticonderoga and the two other lake posts, Crown Point and

St. Johns. The next problem before the revolutionary assembly was the appointment of generals to command unorganized forces which lacked even a sufficiency of gunpowder.

There were other urgent matters to be decided, but the delegates knew that any day might bring an express telling of a bloody clash between General Gage's redcoats and the undisciplined militia forces encamped around Boston. So Congress put its house in order with a lick and a promise while concentrating on questions of defense. On June 3rd the members saw no inconsistency in naming one committee to draw up a respectful petition to the king, and a second committee to consider ways and means of borrowing six thousand pounds for buying gunpowder to fire at the king's troops. Both measures were put aside for the time being, though it was recommended to the colonies that saltpeter and brimstone be collected and sent to Philadelphia for the manufacture of gunpowder.

Washington, Schuyler, Deane, Cushing and Hewes were appointed on June 14th as a committee "to bring in a draft of Rules and regulations for the government of the army." And that same day Congress wrought a landmark of military history with the resolution:

"That six companies of expert rifflemen, be immediately raised in Pennsylvania, two in Maryland, and two in Virginia. . . . That each company, as soon as completed, shall march and join the army near Boston, to be there employed as light infantry, under the command of the chief officer in that army." [13]

The slow-paced tactics of eighteenth-century warfare, with Frederick the Great as their prophet, were adjusted to the uncertain aim and short range of smooth-bore flintlock muskets which had to be painstakingly charged with a ramrod by a soldier in a standing position. Only years of stern discipline could train men to march shoulder to shoulder in three ranks advancing with a stately parade step to fire at the word of command; and afterwards came the critical interval of reloading, when the soldier was prey for an enemy volley or bayonet attack. The human problem also entered into the equation, for the long-term "volunteers" of European nations were actually recruited from the lowest orders of society by means of press-gang methods.

Congress, if it had but known, was giving the first official sanction to the warfare of the future—the warfare of Grant and Lee. The American rifle, a weapon of precision as compared to its European counterpart, had several times the range and accuracy of the smooth-bore military musket. The American rifleman himself—the "timber beast" of the long frontier—was a freeman fighting for his own acres against dull European peasants or miserable slum dwellers forced into a harsh military bondage.

At least the civilians of Congress seem to have been aware that they were creating the *corps d'élite* of the new Continental army. In a letter Richard Henry Lee sang the praises of "Rifle Men that for their number make the most formidable light infantry in the world. The six frontier countries [of Virginia] can produce 6000 of these Men [with] their amazing hardihood, their method of living so long in the woods without carrying provisions with them, the exceeding quickness with which they can march to distant parts, and above all, the dexterity to which they have arrived in the use of the Rifle Gun. Their is not one of these Men who wish a distance less than 200 yards or a larger object than an Orange—Every shot is fatal." [14]

When it came to appointing generals for the new army, the give-and-take of practical politics might seem a poor means of selection as compared to choosing on a basis of military experience. Yet the evidence of history makes it plain that Congress succeeded with the first method and failed with the second.

If experience was to be the criterion, it would have been hard to find a better candidate for the post of commander in chief than Charles Lee, a half-pay British colonel and veteran of many a European field who had recently arrived in America and taken up the patriotic cause. He had a facile pen with which to advance his interests, and more than one delegate felt twinges of conscience because the demands of practical politics made it advisable to seek elsewhere.

New England had the first claim for consideration, since that region was the battleground and had raised most of the militiamen in active service. Congress had intended it as a concession to New England when John Hancock was elected its new president on May 24th. But there were sectional jealousies, John Adams realized, which would have been aroused by the nomination of the Boston merchant and militia officer as commander in chief.

"In canvassing this subject, out of doors, I found too that even among the delegates of Virginia there were difficulties," Adams noted. "In several conversations I found more than one very cool about the appointment of Washington. . . ."

The diarist brought the question into debate with a motion "that Congress would adopt the army at Cambridge, and appoint a General; that though this was not the proper time to nominate a General . . . I had no hesitation to declare that I had but one gentleman in mind for that important command, and that was a gentleman from Virginia who was among us and very well known to all of us, a gentleman whose skill and experience as an officer, whose independent fortune, great talents, and excellent universal character, would command the approbation of all America, and unite the cordial exertion of all the colonies better than any other person in the Union. Mr. Washington, who happened to sit near the door, as soon as he heard me allude to him, from his usual modesty, darted into the library-room. Mr. Hancock . . . heard me with visible pleasure; but when I came to describe Washington for the commander, I never remarked a more sudden and striking change of countenance. Mortification and resentment were expressed as forcibly as his face could exhibit them."

A few delegates spoke against Washington on sectional and political rather than personal grounds. "Mr. Pendleton of Virginia, Mr. Sherman of Connecticut, were very explicit in declaring this opinion; Mr. Cushing and several others more faintly expressed their opposition, and their fears of discontents in the army and in New England. . . . The subject was postponed to a future day. In the mean time, pains were taken out of doors to obtain a unanimity, and the voices were generally so clearly in favor of Washington, that the dissentient members were persuaded to withdraw their opposition, and Mr. Washington was nominated . . . and the army adopted." [15]

Artemas Ward, the popular Massachusetts militia officer, was appointed second in command to reward that colony for its aid in electing a Southerner as his superior in rank. Military experience finally got its recognition when the choice fell upon Charles Lee of Virginia as third major general, and an unhappy one it proved to be in the light of later events. Another Virginian and former British officer, Horatio Gates, won the post of adjutant general. The two remaining commissions as major general were frankly awarded on political grounds—one to Israel Putnam of Connecticut in appreciation of the large forces being raised by that colony; and the other to Philip Schuyler of New York "to sweeten and keep up the spirit in that province," as Eliphalet Dyer explained.

In the election of the eight brigadier generals the middle colonies had to be content with Richard Montgomery of New York, who soon justified all the hopes placed in him as a recent British officer. The three Massachusetts men, Seth Pomeroy, William Heath and John Thomas, turned out to be steady even if undistinguished soldiers, as did David Wooster and Joseph Spencer of Connecticut. New Hampshire had no reason to regret the choice of John Sullivan; but it was an unknown political appointee— "one Green of Rhode Island," as Sherman referred to Nathanael Greene— who would reveal military abilities entitling him to consideration as the foremost strategist of the war.

The problem of selecting regimental officers was dumped into the laps of the provincial assemblies and conventions, which were to submit their nominations to the commander in chief. They responded with such zest during coming months that the ranks of colonel and major soon lost most of their distinction.

So infectious was the warlike spirit of Congress that even John Adams had his dream of glory. "Oh that I were a soldier!" he confided to Abigail. "I will be. I am reading military books, Everybody must, and will, and shall be a soldier."

But the day when his four colleagues left for their new military duties, this bright vision was dimmed by self-pity. "I have this morning been out of town to accompany our generals, Washington, Lee and Schuyler, a little way on their journey to the American camp before Boston. The three generals were all mounted on horse-back, accompanied by Major Mifflin, who is gone in the character of aid-de-camp. All the delegates from the Massachusetts, with their servants and carriages attended; many others of the delegates from the Congress; a large troop of light horse in their uniforms; many officers of militia besides, in theirs; music playing, etc., etc. Such is the pride and pomp of war. I, poor creature, worn out with scribbling for my bread and my liberty, low in spirits and weak in health, must leave others to wear the laurels which I have sown; others to eat the bread which I have earned; a common case." [16]

As for the heroes of the hour, they were applauded in every village on the way to New York, where the most tremendous ovation of all awaited them. Martial music and deafening cheers welcomed the cavalcade, and General Washington found it hard to convince his hosts that he could tarry only a few hours on his journey to Boston. The city, however, was speedily consoled for his absence. That very same day Sir William Tryon, the royal governor of strong Tory convictions, arrived from London on the ship *Juliana*. And he too was welcomed by the martial music and deafening cheers of an equally tremendous ovation. New York, then as now, liked to greet distinguished guests.

Chapter 6

Congress Declares War

RUMORS of Bunker Hill reached Philadelphia five days after the event. The mood of Congress is evident from a dispatch hastily penned by President Hancock to General Artemas Ward: "We have just a report of a Battle. . . . We are anxious. No Express. God send us a good account."

Not until midnight of June 24th did the delegates have an official summary of the action fought on the 17th with such credit to American arms and heavy losses to British regiments twice repulsed before taking the position. One of the most dramatic descriptions was written by Abigail Adams to her husband:

"Charlestown is laid in ashes. The battle began upon our intrenchments upon Bunker's Hill, Saturday morning about three o'clock, and has not ceased yet, and it is now three o'clock Sabbath afternoon. It is expected they will come out over the Neck to-night, and a dreadful battle must ensue. How many have fallen, we know not. The constant roar of the cannon is so distressing that we cannot eat, drink or sleep." [1]

A second letter, dated four days later, revealed that Boston, like Philadelphia, nourished its anxiety with a diet of rumors. "We hear that the [British] troops destined for New York are all expected here; but we have got to that pass that a whole legion of them would not intimidate us. I think I am very brave, upon the whole. If danger comes near my dwelling, I suppose I shall shudder. We want powder, but, with the blessing of Heaven we fear them not." [2]

Among the fallen friends mourned by the Massachusetts delegates was Dr. Joseph Warren, who drew up the Suffolk Resolves. It might have been expected that this idealist would risk his life; but a ghost from the American

74

past also appeared at Bunker Hill when mad James Otis fought as a volunteer all that hot June afternoon without receiving a scratch.

The commander in chief had a full report of the battle before he reached New York. That he had no illusions as to the reasons influencing his appointment is indicated by a letter of June 20th to his half brother John Augustine: "I have been called upon by the unanimous Voice of the Colonies to take the Command of the Continental Army—an honour I neither sought after, nor desired, as I am thoroughly convinced that it requires greater abilities, and more experience, than I am Master of, to conduct a business so extensive in its nature, and arduous in the execution; but the partiality of the Congress, joined to a political motive, really left me without a choice. . . ." [3]

Most of the New England delegates seemed to feel it their duty to announce Washington with letters designed to soothe any jealousies or resentments. Typical of these communications is the one written by Hancock to Joseph Warren, who was lying dead on Bunker Hill even as the words were being penned:

"The Congress have appointed George Washington, Esqr., General and Commander in Chief of the Continental Army. He is a Gentleman you will all like. I submit to you the propriety of providing a suitable place for his Residence and the mode of his Reception." [4]

Eliphalet Dyer in his turn listed such negative virtues of the new leader as might appeal to Connecticut patriots. "He is a Gent. highly Esteemed by those acquainted with him tho I don't believe as to his Military for real service he knows more than some of ours but so it removes all jealousies, more firmly Cements the Southern to the Northern, and takes away the fear of the former lest an Enterprising eastern New England Genll. proving Successful, might with his Victorious Army give law to the Southern or Western Gentry. this made it absolutely Necessary in point of prudence, but he is Clever, and if any thing too modest. he seems discreet and Virtuous, no harum Starum ranting fellow but Sober, steady and Calm." [5]

It is noteworthy that the word "clever" in this letter was intended to convey the sense (still heard occasionally in New England rural communities) of simple and weak good nature. Within a few more years George Washington would achieve the rare distinction of being placed on a pedestal by his own generation. But at the outset he was introduced with an uneasy and almost apologetic air.

The atmosphere of this assembly was less convivial and more businesslike as compared to the first Congress. Tarts, trifles and whipped sillabubs are not mentioned as often in the pages of John Adams' diary these days as the

Spartan virtues of self-denial. "Let us eat potatoes and drink water," he counseled in one of these virtuous moods; "let us wear canvas, and undressed sheepskins, rather than submit to the unrighteous and ignominous domination that is prepared for us." [6]

Despite such protestations, silk stockings and velvet waistcoats continued to be the dress of delegates who put in heroically long working days.

"My time was never more fully employed," wrote Dr. Franklin to a friend in England. "In the morning at six, I am at the Committee of Safety, appointed by the Assembly to put the province in a state of defence; which committee holds till near nine, when I am at the Congress, and that sits till after four in the afternoon. . . . It will scarce be credited in Britain, that men can be as diligent with us from zeal in the public good, as with you for thousands per annum. Such is the difference between uncorrupted new states, and corrupted old ones." [7]

Early in the session George Read of Delaware had found it needful to apologize to his wife for lapses in writing letters. "I prepare in the morning for the meeting at nine o'clock, and often do not return to my lodgings till that time at night. We sit in Congress generally till half-past three o'clock, and once till five o'clock, and then I dine at the City Tavern. . . . Our daily table is formed by the following persons, to wit: Messrs. Randolph, Lee, Washington, and Harrison, of Virginia, Alsop of New York, Chase of Maryland, and Rodney and Read. A dinner is ordered for that number, eight, and whatever is deficient of that number is to be paid for at two shillings and sixpence a head, and each that attends pays only the expense of the day." [8]

The sober and industrious mood of Congress is understandable as that body tackled the problems of creating a Continental army where none had existed before. There is even an ironical note in the fact that the revolutionists of 1775 faced the danger of being hoist by two of their own favorite petards. For years they had inveighed against British imposts and British soldiers to such effect that Americans had acquired a prejudice against all taxes and all military establishments. Thus it remained a question whether Congress could persuade its constituents to dig into their pockets and submit to the sacrifices of personal liberty so necessary to the governing of an army.

The New Englanders, bearing more than their share of the war effort, were eager to distribute some of the burden among the other colonies. But it was this section which cherished the faith that undisciplined minutemen led by elected company officers could defeat highly trained regulars. It might have been a disguised blessing if the object lessons had come earlier in the war, but the Yankee military creed seemed only to be upheld by the results of Lexington, Ticonderoga and Bunker Hill.

On June 30th the delegates approved the sixty-nine articles of war drawn up by a committee for the regulation of the new "grand army of America." With the Great Jehovah as guidance, the Continental Congress showed a patriarchal concern in the moral welfare of the troops. It was "earnestly recommended to all officers and soldiers, diligently to attend Divine Service." Severe penalties were imposed for those who should "behave indecently or irreverently at any place of Divine Worship." Nor was there any leniency for men uttering "any profane oath or execration," and officers indulging in such blasphemies were "to forfeit and pay for each and every offence, the sum of Four Shillings, lawful money." [9]

But aside from the Puritanical codes, these first articles of war can hardly be described as forceful. So many concessions were made to the prejudices against military discipline that Congress would find it essential a few months later to try again. Even so, John Adams thought it prudent to write his Massachusetts constituents that the assembly had never considered "the most distant Intimation of any design to new model your Army."

Two words of this assurance provide a clue as to the fears which caused Congress to tread lightly. The phrase "new model" refers to the name of the disciplined standing army created by Cromwell for purposes of oppressing the English freemen he led to victory over Charles I. And the Americans rebelling against another king did not wish to take the risk of history repeating itself at the expense of their liberties.

After administering to the spiritual welfare of the new army, Congress realized that it must provide in material respects. Already, without a farthing of its own or any authority to raise funds directly, the assembly had fixed the pay of a major general at $166 a month and a brigadier at $125. Two more rifle companies were authorized, making ten in all, to be paid at monthly rates ranging from $20 for a captain and $13 1/3 for a lieutenant to $7 1/3 for a corporal and $6 2/3 for a private.

The idea of borrowing £6,000 on its own credit having been abandoned. the assembly gave thought to the possibilities of the printing press. Twenty days were spent in debating various plans, and on June 22nd the delegates passed two fateful measures:

> Resolved, That a sum not exceeding two million of Spanish milled dollars be emitted by the Congress in bills of credit, for the defence of America.
> Resolved, That the twelve confederated colonies be pledged for the redemption of the bills of credit, now directed to be emitted. [10]

These steps were not taken carelessly by dreamers so naïve as to suppose that paper currency had any miraculous worth of its own. The members of Congress were perfectly aware that the printing press could become a snare and delusion if the provincial assemblies did not redeem the bills of credit. But Congress had only this indirect means of raising funds, and it was plainly the duty of the colonies to impose the taxes, since they jealously guarded that power. It was even suggested that the currency would become a "new bond of union to the Associated Colonies, and every inhabitant thereof will be bound in interest to endeavor that ways and means be fallen upon for sinking it."

At this time, with patriotic zeal at high tide, there was no reason to doubt that the provincial assemblies would tap the financial resources at their disposal. Congress decided that 403,000 bills were to be issued in low denominations, and Dr. Franklin was appointed as chairman of a committee to get the copper plates engraved.

The assembly added another million dollars to the total on July 25th. A list of 28 authorized signers was approved in a resolution which confessed that "the signing of so great a number of bills as has been directed to be issued by this Congress, will take more time than the members can possibly devote to that business." [11]

Four days later Michael Hillegas and George Clymer were made "joint treasurers of the United Colonies." Congress put it squarely up to the provincial assemblies to raise the money when it resolved "that each colony provide ways and means to sink its proportion of the bills ordered to be emitted by this Congress in such manner as may be most effectual and best adapted to the condition, circumstances and usual mode of levying taxes in such colony." [12]

By way of a gentle hint, the delegates agreed as to the proportion of the three million dollars to be raised by each colony according to resources. New York, it will be noted, was so far from being the financial giant of America in 1775 that it stood in fifth place, tied with three other colonies:

Virginia	496,278	North Carolina	248,139
Massachusetts	434,244	South Carolina	248,139
Pennsylvania	372,208½	New Jersey	161,290½
Maryland	310,174½	New Hampshire	124,069½
Connecticut	248,139	Rhode Island	71,959½
New York	248,139	Delaware	37,219½

With funds in sight, Congress still had no prospect of meeting the urgent demands for gunpowder unless it violated some of the terms of the Association. Already the nonimportation features had resulted in shortages and mounting prices throughout the colonies. "The cry for pins is so great," wrote a thrifty Braintree housewife, "that what I used to buy for seven shillings and sixpence are now twenty shillings, and not to be had for that.'

In one of her next letters Abigail Adams commented, "We shall very soon have no coffee, nor sugar, nor pepper here; but whortleberries and milk we are not obliged to commerce for." [13]

Years of enforced dependence on British manufactures had left the colonists without experience or equipment when it came to shifting for themselves. Even the comparatively simple processes of manufacturing explosives seemed dismaying, and the needs of the Massachusetts troops were met at first by borrowing. The night when the report of Bunker Hill reached Philadelphia, with the news that the Americans had retreated for lack of ammunition, John Adams recorded that he and Hancock and Sam Adams "went out to enquire after the Committee of this City, in order to beg some Powder. We found Some of them, and these with great Politeness and Sympathy for their brave Brethren in the Mass. agreed to go out that night and send forward about Ninety Quarter Casks and before Morning it was in Motion. Between two and three o'Clock I got to bed." [14]

Congress did not shrink after it became apparent that the emergency could not wait for the development of home manufactures. Great Britain had prohibited the exportation of arms to America, but colonial shippers had long ago learned all the tricks of smuggling. On July 15th the assembly resolved to allow American vessels to export produce—"the non-exportation agreement notwithstanding"—in trade for gunpowder, saltpeter, sulphur, cannon, muskets and other munitions. This resolution was printed in the form of handbills and sent to ports of the West Indies, though Congress took pains to keep it out of the newspapers at home.

It was not to be expected that the assembly would neglect an opportunity to add more petitions and addresses to the formidable list approved at the last session. Lord North started the forensic springs gushing with his so-called plan of conciliation, passed by Parliament a few days after that body rejected Chatham's proposals. Americans were assured that no further duties, with the important exception of commercial imposts, would be laid upon them if they agreed to tax themselves to the satisfaction of the king and both houses of Parliament.

This offer, as colonial radicals interpreted it, simply meant that the mother country promised to cease some of her oppressions on condition that Americans become their own oppressors. Congress eventually disposed of the North plan on July 31st with a report, prepared by Jefferson, which condemned it as an attempt "to lull into fatal security our well-affected fellow subjects on the other side of the water, till time should be given for the operation of those arms, which a British minister pronounced would instantaneously reduce the 'cowardly' sons of America to unreserved submission." The report concluded by asserting that the world would not "hesitate to believe with us, that nothing but our own exertions may defeat the ministerial sentence of death or abject submission."[15]

Meanwhile Congress had been inspired to begin a task more to its taste—the drawing up of an address which became the nearest approach to a formal American declaration of war. Again the delegates proved to be exacting editors. The original committee consisted of Franklin, Jay, William Livingston, Thomas Johnson and John Rutledge; and it was intended that the address should be read by Washington to his troops. The first offering did not please Congress, which called upon Dickinson and Jefferson to prepare a document that the whole world might read. Before long the Virginian joined the other rejected authors because, as he supposed, his draft "was too strong for Mr. Dickinson. He was so honest a man, and so able a one, that he was greatly indulged even by those who could not feel his scruples."[16]

With the exception of a few paragraphs, the thoughts of the Pennsylvania lawyer went into the Declaration on Taking Arms adopted by Congress on July 6th. Jefferson's contribution, also included in the *Journals*, is so inferior in every respect that the editorial judgment of the delegates cannot be questioned. Nor does it appear that Dickinson was too soft and conciliatory in this challenge:

> We are reduced to the alternate of chusing between an unconditional submission to the tyranny of irritated ministers, or resistance by force. The latter is our choice. We have counted the cost of this contest, and find nothing so dreadful as voluntary slavery. . . . Our cause is just. Our union is perfect. Our internal resources are great, and, if necessary, foreign assistance is undoubtedly attainable. . . . With hearts fortified with these animating reflections, we most solemnly, before God and the world, declare, that . . . the arms we have been compelled by our enemies to assume, we will, in defiance of every hazard, with unabating firmness and perseverence, employ for the preservation of our liberties; being with one mind resolved to dye Free-men rather than live Slaves.[16]

Englishmen who read these words some weeks later may not have been much impressed by the boast of a perfect union. But they must have given thought to this first broad hint that the rebelling colonists would not stop short of seeking an alliance with a European nation.

Four days after approving the Declaration on Taking Arms, the delegates signed another document composed by the same pen. "Congress gave a signal proof of their indulgence to Mr. Dickinson," explained Jefferson, "and of their desire not to go too fast for any respectable part of our body, in permitting him to draw their second petition to the King according to his ideas, and passing it with scarcely any amendment."[17]

Again the monarch was assured in respectful terms that "notwithstanding the sufferings of your loyal colonists, during the course of the present controversy, our breasts retain too tender a regard for the kingdom from which we derive our origin, to request such a reconciliation as might in any manner be inconsistent with her dignity or her welfare. . . . And the apprehensions that now oppress our hearts with unspeakable grief, being once removed, your Majesty will find your faithful subjects on this continent ready and willing at all times, as they ever have been, with their lives and fortunes, to assert and maintain the rights and interests of your Majesty, and of our Mother country." [18]

Of all the documents approved by the delegates, the second petition to the king appears to have been the most controversial.

"The disgust against this humility was general," reported Jefferson; "and Mr. Dickinson's delight at its passage was the only circumstance which reconciled them to it. The vote being passed, although further observation on it was out of order, he could not refrain from rising and expressing his satisfaction, and concluded by saying, 'there is but one word, Mr. President, in the paper which I disapprove, and that is the word *Congress*;' on which Ben Harrison rose and said, 'There is but one word in the paper, Mr. President, of which I approve, and that is the word *Congress*.'" [19]

Dr. Franklin, the patriarch of the assembly at the age of 69, wrote to Joseph Priestley in England that "it has been with difficulty that we have carried another humble petition to the crown, to give Britain one more chance, one opportunity more, of recovering the friendship of the colonies; which, however, I think she has not sense enough to embrace, and so I conclude she has lost them for ever. . . . We have not yet applied to any foreign power for assistance, nor offered our commerce for their friendship. Perhaps we never may; yet it is natural to think of it, if we are pressed." [20]

But the opinions of Franklin and Jefferson tell only one side of the story, and there can be no doubt that "Farmer" Dickinson had strong support from the conservatives of Congress. Four years later, recalling the dispute in some observations intended for a history, Secretary Thomson came to his friend's defense:

> The subject of the Petition, as well as the Declaration, occasioned warm and long debates in Congress, in which D[ickinson] took a distinguished part, which was circulated to his disadvantage. However he maintained his ground among the generality of the people in his own Province, and particularly among those who still wished to see a Reconciliation take place; and it must be allowed that if his judgment had not quite approved the measure, yet on account of the people of Pennsylvania, it was both prudent and

politic to adopt it. . . . Whatever hand D[ickinson] had in the promoting, it ought to have redounded to his credit as a politician.[21]

Again following a precedent set by the first Congress, the assembly drew up a new Address to the Inhabitants of Great Britain which was stormily debated by paragraphs and approved on July 8th. Once more it was considered proper to approach the people as if they possessed a broader understanding than their king:

> Admit that your Fleets could destroy our Towns, and ravage our Sea-Coasts. . . . We can retire beyond the Reach of your Navy, and, without any sensible Diminunition of the Necessaries of Life, enjoy a Luxury, which from that period you will want—the Luxury of being Free. . . . Our Enemies charge us with Sedition. In what does it consist? In our refusal to submit to unwarrantable Acts of Injustice and Cruelty? If so, shew us a Period in your History, in which you have not been equally Seditious. . . . We have carried out dutiful Petitions to the Throne. We have applied to your Justice for Relief. . . . What has been the Success of our Endeavors? The Clemency of our Sovereign is unhappily diverted; our Petitions are treated with Indignity; our Prayers answered by insults. Our Application to you remained unnoticed and leaves us the melancholy Apprehension of your wanting either the Will, or the Power, to assist us.[22]

These sentiments should have been strong enough for the radicals of Congress, but John Adams was still disgusted. "Our address to the People of Great Britain," he declared, "will find many Admirers among the Ladies, and fine Gentlemen; but it is not to my Taste. Prettynesses, Juvenilities, and much less Puerilities become not a great assembly like this the Representative of a Great People." [23]

Letters to two previously neglected groups of fellow subjects, those of Ireland and Jamaica, also were approved. Most of the delegates believed at this time that the colonists of the British West Indies would eventually join in the revolt, and the address to Ireland was another blow aimed at a loose stone in the edifice of empire. Nor were the "oppressed inhabitants" of Canada overlooked by this Congress, which warned them that "the fruits of your labour and industry may be taken from you, whenever an avaritious governor and a rapacious council may incline to demand them. . . . Nay, the enjoyment of your very religion, on the present system, depends on a legislature in which you have no share, and over which you have no control, and your priests are exposed to expulsion, banishment, and ruin, whenever their wealth and possessions furnish sufficient temptation." The letter concludes with "hopes of your uniting with us in the defense of our common liberty." [24]

These hopes, it appears, were already of a strategic as well as political nature. For Congress committed itself more definitely a few weeks later with the resolution:

> That if General Schuyler finds it practicable, and that it will not be disagreeable to the Canadians, he do immediately take possession of St. John's, Montreal, and any other parts of the country, and pursue any other measures in Canada, which may have a tendency to promote the peace and security of those Colonies.[25]

Thoughts of Canada could not fail to remind the Americans of 1775 how often their frontier settlements had been terrorized during colonial wars by French and Indian raiders stealing silently down from the north. It was only natural to speculate whether the British might not also offer inducements to savage allies, and on July 12th Congress resolved:

> That the securing and preserving of the friendship of the Indian Nations, appears to be a subject of the utmost moment to these colonies. That there is too much reason to apprehend that Administration will spare no pains to excite the several Nations of Indians to take up arms against these colonies; and that it becomes us to be very active and vigilant in exerting every prudent means to strengthen and confirm the friendly disposition . . . which has long prevailed among the northern tribes, and which has lately been manifested by some of those to the southward.[26]

Three departments were created for the administration of Indian affairs: the northern, devoted to the Six Nations; the southern, with emphasis on the Cherokees; and the middle, including all tribes between those formidable groups. After the sum of $16,666 2/3 had been appropriated to buy rum and gifts, delegates acquainted with Indian customs were consulted in the preparation of an oration to be translated for the chiefs of the Six Nations. This effort, like all the other addresses of Congress, was drawn up in a style suited to its particular audience:

> Brothers and friends! . . . This is a family quarrel between us and Old England. You Indians are not concerned in it. We don't wish you to take up the hatchet against the king's troops. We desire you to remain at home, and not join on either side, but keep the hatchet buried deep. . . . Brothers, observe well! What is it we have asked of you? Nothing but peace . . . and if application should be made to you by any of the king's unwise and wicked ministers to join on their side, we only advise you to deliberate, with great caution, and in your wisdom look forward to the consequences of a compliance. For if the king's troops take away our property, and destroy us who are of the same blood as themselves, what can you, who are Indians, expect from them afterwards?[27]

In urging a policy of neutrality, Congress undoubtedly hoped to spare the frontier the horrors of warfare waged with tomahawk and scalping knife.

But it is also worth noting that after a century of border warfare, Americans had acquired a low opinion of the Indian as a fighting man—a lesson which the British would learn at a heavy cost in both money and prestige.

As the session neared the end of its third month, the heat of a Philadelphia summer turned the minds of the delegates to thoughts of adjournment. "The Congress has set much longer than I at first expected it would," grumbled Roger Sherman, "but I believe not longer than was needful. . . . It is very tedious Sitting here this hot season."

He and the other members from his colony had recently been engaged as peacemakers, trying to compose a petty civil war between Pennsylvanians dwelling in the Wyoming valley and settlers pouring in from Connecticut, which was one of the six provinces claiming the right of westward expansion to the "South Sea." Disturbances in this region had become so threatening that the Connecticut delegates appealed to the patriotism of their constituents:

> It has been represented to the Continental Congress that there is great danger of discord and Contention if not Hostility and bloodshed between the People setling under Connecticut Claim and those under Pensylvania, which would be attended with the most unhappy consequences at this time of general Calamity and when we want our whole United Strength against our Common Enemy. We are therefore desired by the Congress to write to you and press upon you the necessity of peace and good order not only among yourselves, but by no means to give the least disturbance or molestation to the persons, property or possessions of those setled under the Proprietaries of Pensylvania and especially to the family property or possessions of those who are gone as Riflers into the service of their Country and to join the Army near Boston.[28]

Other differences of opinion within Congress itself were fraught with more serious implications. The New York delegates, whose views caused that colony to be considered lukewarm, had received from their provincial assembly a plan for union within the Empire which differed in few essentials from the one proposed by Joseph Galloway at the last session. According to this design, the Continental Congress would be retained as an American legislature, subject to the negative of the sovereign as well as the supervision of a crown-appointed executive. And though the New Yorkers wanted some measures of Parliament repealed, they were willing to grant that body the right to decide questions of defense and commerce.

The representatives of the colony at Philadelphia judged the temper of Congress correctly when they thought it wise not to submit the plan. Another and vastly different instrument had meanwhile been circulating "out of doors"—a proposal drawn up by Benjamin Franklin which he called "Articles of Confederation and Perpetual Union." On July 21st he laid them before Congress to be considered not as a perfected plan but as the foundation for a future agreement to be worked out in detail. Copies found their way out into the colonies, one of them being seized by the British and published as an example of American sedition.

The shrewd old philosopher knew very well that his countrymen were not ready in the summer of 1775 for confederation, under either British or American auspices. On the contrary, some of the foremost colonial leaders still cherished the belief that they were fighting to smash the fetters of all central government, thus freeing each colony for local self-rule. Such men were willing to accept unity as a means, not as an end.

Any discussion of Franklin's plan belongs in a following chapter, since the name and many of the provisions were later adopted. At this time the conservatives of Congress recoiled from his calm suggestion that reparations be demanded from Great Britain for the burning of Charlestown and the injury done to Boston by the closing of the port. Jefferson, who favored the plan as a whole, recorded that "some of the members thought as I did; others were revolted at it. We found that it could not be passed, and the proposing it to Congress as the subject for any vote whatever would startle many members so much that they would suspect we had lost sight of reconciliation with Great Britain, and that we should lose more ground than we should gain by the proposition." [29]

On this same July day another proposal came up before Congress, which the conservatives also blocked. "We have had in Contemplation," wrote John Adams, "a resolution to invite all Nations to bring their Commodities to market here, and like Fools have lost it for the present." The suggestion to open American ports struck the majority as being too bold a gesture of defiance, and on July 31st the measure was again "postponed to be taken up at some future day." [30]

Two treasurers had already been employed at a salary of $500 for 1775, and on July 26th Congress added to its growing little bureaucracy another department which would eventually be included in the Cabinet. Dr. Franklin was appointed postmaster general for the colonies at $1,000 a year, and directed to set up a postal system extending from Falmouth to Savannah "for the speedy and secure conveyance of Intelligence from one end of the Continent to the other."

The next day Dr. Benjamin Church was named surgeon general, at $4 a day, and empowered to hire four surgeons at a third of that rate and other assistants to found a new hospital establishment intended for an army of

20,000. It is a comment on the times that these measures compared very well with the provisions made for taking care of the sick and wounded in European armies.

As an indication of its faith in reconciliation, the assembly again recommended that all able-bodied Americans between the ages of 16 and 50 form themselves into militia companies. And on August 1st, the last day of the session, another warlike resolution directed that "the sum of five hundred thousand dollars be immediately forwarded from the continental Treasury, to the paymaster general, to be applied to the use of the army in Massachusetts bay. . . ." [31]

None of the departing delegates paused this time to bid Philadelphia a nostalgic farewell, for Congress had decided as a matter of course to meet again on September 5th. Within a year the small revolutionary body had outgrown its original purposes and functions. It was no longer a temporary council of colonial leaders who contented themselves with discussing theories and drawing up petitions. The Association had changed all that. The Association had given half a hundred Americans more actual power than could be boasted by Parliament. Only in theory was the Continental Congress of 1775 a mere advisory council. In effect it had become the central government of a new nation which already existed in the hearts of its founders.

PART TWO

Independence

Our towns may be destroyed, but they will grow again. We compare them not with our rights and liberties.

— JOHN DICKINSON

Chapter 7

The State of America

M ORE than half the the delegates, instead of returning to their homes, took the long trip to Cambridge by coach or on horseback to see for themselves the new American army which had become their main preoccupation. They straggled back to Philadelphia so belatedly that it was not until the end of September that Congress resumed its consideration of questions relating to "the state of America."

If the delegates had been given to introspection, which they were not, they might have found some of the answers in a survey of Congress itself. What manner of men were these provincial lawyers, merchants and planters who went ahead so confidently to govern a nation which had no legal existence with powers which had never been authorized? That they were sober, honest and upright men in their private lives cannot be doubted. But the virtues of a statesman differ widely from those of a citizen, and in their official character the members of the Continental Congress could only have been described as bold, resourceful and unscrupulous men—dangerous men to have as foes or as allies. Richelieu or Mazarin would have understood them very well; and Machiavelli would doubtless have recommended that they "either be caressed or be destroyed."

George III, whose intellectual gifts were not remarkable, must at least be credited with perception in his estimate of the American rebels. He did his best to destroy them. Shunning half measures, he sent overseas the largest expeditionary force ever to sail from England up to that date. He hired German and Indian mercenaries to chastise his subjects in the New World, and he made an effort to employ Cossacks from the steppes of Russia. In an age of moderate warfare his troops burned a dozen American towns, sacked homes and plantations beyond number, and did not admit failure until after a second army had surrendered in the field.

89

Only a tough and resolute people could have withstood such an onslaught. It is not surprising that the Americans of 1775 preferred to think of themselves as excelling in milder virtues, since few peoples have any capacity for judging their national characterisitcs. Certain it is that they were already Americans with their own sharply defined traits, not transplanted Englishmen. Prominent among these traits was a ruthlessness of purpose which had not hesitated at the extermination of one "inferior" race and the enslavement of another. American legislators had offered bounties for Indian scalps, and American merchants had profited from a commerce in which rum was bartered for living cargoes of Africans.

It was not to be expected that such a determined people would let the mother country stand in the way of their destiny. As long ago as the last century several armed uprisings had been recorded—Bacon's Rebellion of 1676, and the Massachusetts revolt which overthrew Sir Edmund Andros in 1689. Americans had taken to smuggling to evade British imposts, and Americans had invented sharp political dodges to make a farce out of the authority of crown-appointed English governors.

The thought of this vigorous New World people had not found its expression in art. In all the America of 1775 there were only a few minor poets and several fairly good portrait painters. But in all the world there has never been a greater explosion of political genius than the one which supplied the motive force of the American Revolution. Any nation possessing a single first-rate political mind in an emergency may consider itself well endowed, but this narrow strip of Atlantic seacoast produced in the same generation such figures as Otis, Franklin, Washington, John Adams, Jefferson, Dickinson, Madison and Hamilton.

No demons of indecision or self-doubt ever weakened the purpose of these men. After it was all over, when John Adams went to London as minister of the new Republic, his official British hosts cut him dead with haughty contempt at a diplomatic ball. So far was the victim from being shaken that he commented pityingly in his diary:

"This people cannot look me in the face; there is conscious guilt and shame in their countenances when they look at me. They feel that they have behaved ill, and that I am sensible of it."

A great deal of the history of the American Revolution may be read in those lines. The founding fathers of 1775 did not think of themselves as unscrupulous or ruthless when they varied their petitions to the king with addresses stirring up sedition in every corner of the British Empire. They were upheld by a conviction of righteousness which has seldom been known in this world since the days of the Old Testament prophets. The spirit of the

Great Jehovah was hovering over the Continental Congress, and together they were invincible.

If some observer had been able to peer through the windows of the State House, he might easily have been mistaken in judgments based on the appearance of the delegates meeting in secret session during those autumn days of 1775.

In the foreground, facing the assembly, President Hancock would probably have been taken for a fop. So great was his vanity and love of display that a Philadelphia newspaper would soon be commenting, "John Hancock of Boston appears in public with all the state and pageantry of an Oriental prince; he rides in an elegant chariot . . . attended by four servants dressed in superb livery, mounted on fine horses richly caparisoned; and escorted by fifty horsemen with drawn sabres, the one half of which precedes and the other follow his carriage." [1]

Some of the most passionate lines ever penned by the wealthy merchant are to be found in orders for fine foods, wines, silks, and velvets. Yet Hancock presided so firmly and fairly over Congress that he won esteem as its most distinguished president. The slim, elegant gourmet had the heart of a lion when it came to personal peril, and he had the moral courage to oppose both of the Adamses at the height of their influence. It took John Adams many years to forgive this impertinence, but in his old age he rated Hancock as one of the indispensable men of the Revolution.

Secretary Thomson, seated opposite the president at the front of the room, affected a republican simplicity of attire. When not engaged in recording the minutes of Congress, he was poring over Greek and Hebrew texts for the translation of the Bible which he made his lifework. No hint of violence appeared in that thin, scholarly face; and yet it was Charles Thomson, with his hasty Scotch-Irish temper, who would figure in the two main physical encounters to mar the dignity of the assembly.

Among half a hundred delegates the patriarch was a benevolent old gentleman who had a habit of napping during afternoon meetings. "His conduct has been composed and grave, and, in the opinion of many gentlemen, very reserved. He has not assumed anything, nor affected to take the lead; but has seemed to choose that the Congress should pursue their own sentiments, and adopt their own plans. . . . He does not hesitate at our boldest measures, but rather seems to think us too irresolute and backward." [2]

This was Dr. Franklin. Soon he would be on his way to Paris at the age of 70 to begin a diplomatic career without an equal in American history. Meanwhile he dozed while others contended in wordy debate.

"Chase is violent and boisterous. . . . Rutledge is a very uncouth and ungraceful speaker; he shrugs his shoulders, distorts his body, nods and wriggles with his head, and looks about with his eyes from side to side, and speaks through his nose, as the Yankees sing. His brother John dodges his head too, rather disagreeably, and both of them spout out their language in a rough aind rapid torrent, but without much force or effect." [3]

The two South Carolina members, as conservatives, were frequently opposed on the floor by the New England delegates, who never fled from an argument. "Dyer is long-winded and roundabout, obscure and cloudy, very talkative and very tedious, yet an honest and worthy man, means and judges well. Sherman's air is the reverse of grace. . . . Generally he stands upright, with his hands before him, the fingers of his left hand clenched into a fist and the wrist of it grasped with his right. He has a clear head and judgment; but when he moves a hand in anything like action, Hogarth's genius could not have invented a motion more opposite to grace;—it is stiffness and awkwardness itself, rigid as starched linen or buckram; awkward as a junior bachelor or a sophomore." [4]

The pen portraits which John Adams entered in his diary varied according to his mood, but in the end he was usually just and often penetrating. Dr. Benjamin Rush, soon to be a Pennsylvania delegate, impressed him as "an elegant, ingenious body, a sprightly, pretty fellow. . . . But Rush, I think, is too much of a talker to be a deep thinker; elegant, not great." Arthur Middleton had "little information and less argument; in rudeness and sarcasm his forte lay, and he played off his artillery without reserve." Caesar Rodney was "the oddest looking man in the world; he is tall, thin and slender as a reed, pale; his face is not bigger than a large apple, yet there is sense and fire, spirit, wit and humor in his countenance."

The diarist neglected to give a description of himself or his distant cousin at this time, but it can be deduced that after a year Sam Adams had been relegated to a fairly unimportant status in the assembly. The surest yardstick of a delegate's influence could be found in the number and character of the committees on which he served. In the case of Sam Adams they were few and minor, while John Adams led Congress in both respects. For the archrebel was held in suspicion as a schemer by colleagues who recognized the integrity and fighting spirit of John Adams.

If ever the little Braintree lawyer left a self-portrait, it was in this account (written to Abigail) of a soulful moment: "Yesterday morning I took a walk into Arch Street to see Mr. Peale's painter's room. Peale is from Maryland, a tender, soft, affectionate creature. . . . He showed me one moving picture. His wife, all bathed in tears, with a child about six months old laid out upon her lap. This picture struck me prodigiously."

Congress also had its two jovial fat men—both of them Virginia delegates, Thomas Nelson and Ben Harrison. As the Falstaff of the assembly, Harrison was fond of telling broad jokes while his great girth shook with uninhibited laughter. These anecdotes offended some of the puritanical members, but one topic of conversation fascinated all alike—the symptoms discussed with such gusto by chronic invalids who managed to survive a daily schedule which would tax the strength of an athlete.

Gout led the list of ailments, with Franklin, Hancock and Dickinson being the principal sufferers. John Adams relates that after being introduced in 1774 Dickinson "gave us some account of his late ill health and his present gout. . . . Mr. Dickinson has been subject to hectic complaints. He is a shadow; tall, but slender as a reed, pale as ashes; one would not think at first sight that he could live a month; yet, upon a more attentive inspection, he looks as if the springs of life were strong enough to last many years." [5]

This proved indeed to be the case, for the 43-year-old Philadelphian cherished his ills until well into the next century. On first acquaintance he seemed "very modest, delicate, and timid" to Adams, who soon had reason to change his mind. For it was Dickinson who became floor leader of the conservatives and the most bitter personal opponent of Adams in the autumn of 1775. The two had not been on speaking terms since July, when one of the diarist's pen portraits got him into difficulties. So intense was his disgust at Dickinson's second petition to the king that he could not refrain from writing to a Boston friend:

"A certain great fortune and piddling genius, whose fame has been trumpeted so loudly, has given a silly cast to our whole doings. We are between hawk and buzzard."

Unfortunately for Adams, the letter fell into the hands of the British, who published it with glee. The consequences of the exposure were described by him in a diary entry: "Walking to the State House, this morning, I met Mr. Dickinson, on foot, in Chestnut Street. We met, and passed near enough to touch elbows. He passed without moving his hat or head or hand. I bowed, and pulled off my hat. He passed haughtily by. . . . I shall, for the future, pass him in the same manner; but I was determined to make my bow, that I might know his temper." [6]

Three new delegates arrived from Virginia—Thomas Nelson, George Wythe and Francis Lightfoot Lee, a brother of Richard Henry Lee. They were elected to take the places made vacant by Washington, Richard Bland and Patrick Henry.

New Hampshire elected a physician, Dr. Josiah Bartlett, to replace John Sullivan; and North Carolina sent John Penn to fill the shoes of Richard Caswell, who had declined. At last Georgia was represented with a full delegation—Archibald Bulloch, John Houstoun, Noble Wimberly Jones and the Rev. John Joachim Zubly as well as Lyman Hall, who had represented St. John's Parish at the last session.

Dr. Zubly, a Presbyterian pastor of Savannah, was one of the first ministers of the gospel to appear in Congress. As an added distinction, the recent immigrant from Switzerland, who still spoke with a German accent, remained the only member of the entire Continental Congress to have been born outside the British Empire.

Congress first gave thought to the military situation by naming a committee on September 29th to proceed immediately to Cambridge for conferences with Washington and the executive officers of all four New England colonies. Dr. Franklin, Benjamin Harrison and Thomas Lynch were appointed for the purpose of determining "the most effectual method of continuing, supporting, and regulating a continental army." [7]

There was more to this business than met the eye. Washington, who was soon to rise above sectional prejudices, started off on the wrong foot with some pointed remarks about the New England character, as revealed by the lax discipline he encountered at Cambridge. "I dare say the Men would fight very well (if properly Officered) although they are an exceedingly dirty and nasty people," he wrote in a letter of August 20th to his distant cousin, Lund Washington. The commander in chief may have been even less tactful in writing to a Virginian in Congress, judging by Ben Harrison's reply of July 21st: "Your fatigue and various kinds of trouble I dare say are great, but they are not more than I expected, knowing the people you have to deal with by the Sample we have here." [8]

Some of Washington's correspondents must have been given to gossiping, for it was not long until the New England delegates showed their resentment. After all, their section of the country had suffered the bloodshed and property damage of the war; and their troops had twice met the enemy in combat while the militiamen of other colonies were still drilling. As politicians, moreover, the New Englanders had not forgotten for a moment the leading part they took in electing the general.

On December 16th Eliphalet Dyer grumbled to Joseph Trumbull, "Indeed I think we have been Cooped up in this prison of a City long enough. Poor Connecticutt troops have lost (here) all their fame and glory. you will scarce hear anything but execrations against them." [9] Several months later John Adams spoke his mind even more bluntly in a letter to Henry Knox, the portly Boston bookshop proprietor who had turned artilleryman:

"Pray tell me, Colonel Knox, does every man to the southward of Hudson's River behave like a hero, and every man to the northward of it like a poltroon, or not? . . . I must say that your amiable general gives too much occasion for these reports by his letters, in which he often mentions things to the disadvantage of some part of New England, but seldom any thing of the kind about any other part of the continent." [10]

Such rebukes make it plain that Washington himself had to digest painful lessons in tact and discretion while his troops were acquiring the rudiments of arms. Both did learn in time, but the process was attended with thorny trials. The new army, hastily raised in the face of the foe, lacked all the traditions and methods gradually tested by long-established military organizations of old nations. It could only grope its way, and the articles of war recently passed by Congress had already proved inadequate. Franklin, Lynch and Harrison, after conferring for ten days in Cambridge, brought a recommendation of sweeping amendments on their return. They also proposed the re-enlistment of the existing New England militia forces for a year, and the recruiting of new companies to bring the strength of the Boston army up to a minimum of 20,372 men. The committee emphasized "that every moment's delay is big with danger."

Congress immediately stiffened the articles with sixteen "additions and alterations." The death penalty was prescribed for treason, mutiny, deserting to the enemy, or shamefully abandoning a post. Men found guilty of looting, drunkenness on duty, or stealing from army stores could be punished by flogging, to consist of from fifteen to thirty-nine lashes. Officers convicted of cowardice were to have an account of their shame "published in the newspapers, in and about the camp, and of that colony from which the offender came, or usually resides; after which it shall be deemed scandalous in any officer to associate with him."

All of Washington's suggestions were accepted by Congress, which further showed its confidence in him with the resolution "that General Washington may, if he thinks proper, for the encouragement of an Attack on Boston, promise, in case of success, a month's pay to the army and to the representatives of such of our brave countrymen as may chance to fall. . . ." [11]

Nothing is more exhilarating to military amateurs than dabbling in strategy; and Congress was poring over the map these autumn days, sending imaginary forces on far-flung marches into enemy territory. As early as September 15th an attempt to capture the British post at distant Detroit had been discussed. On that date President Hancock wrote to Lewis Morris and James Wilson that the delegates had taken "into consideration the proposed expedition against Detroit; and as the season is so far advanced, and the

Congress have not sufficient light to direct their judgment, they cannot undertake to give their countenance to the proposed enterprise; more especially, as an enterprise is now on foot, which, if successful, will necessarily draw that place after it." [12]

Hancock was referring to the two-headed invasion of Canada already being planned by Congress in combination with Washington and Schuyler. This strategic dream envisioned one force under General Montgomery proceeding from Ticonderoga to the capture of Montreal, while another under Colonel Benedict Arnold took the route from Boston through the Maine wilderness in an attempt on the great fortress of Quebec. It was an undertaking on a scale that would have worried the commanders of established armies, but the optimists at Philadelphia did not seem to think that they were expecting too much from ill-equipped recruits led by inexperienced officers.

As if the troubles of raising and directing an army were not enough, Congress was also toying with the happy idea of creating a navy as well. "What think you of an American Fleet?" John Adams inquired blithely of James Warren in a letter of October 19th. "I don't mean 100 ships of the Line, by a Fleet, but I suppose this Term may be applied to any naval force consisting of several Vessels, tho the Number, the Weight of Metal, or the Quantity of Tonnage may be small. The Expence would be very great—true. But the Expence might be born and perhaps the Profits and Benefits to be obtained by it, would be a Compensation. A naval Force might be created which would do something. It would destroy Single Cutters and Cruisers. It might destroy small Corvets. . . . It would oblige our Enemies to sail in Fleets." [13]

In his old age John Adams could look back to few honors which gave him as much pride as his undeniable right to be known as the father of the United States Navy. The fight began on the floor of Congress in October when he urged that small American vessels be armed to intercept two British ships known to be on their way to Canada with arms and powder. Even this reasonable proposal, Adams related, struck some of the delegates as "the most wild, visionary mad project that ever had been imagined. It was an infant, taking a mad bull by the horns; and what was more profound and remote, it was said it would ruin the character and corrupt the morals of all our seamen. It would make them selfish, piratical, mercenary, bent wholly upon plunder, &c. &c." [14]

By October 13th Congress had overcome its qualms to such an extent that two swift sailing craft, of ten small guns each, were authorized for preying upon enemy shipping in a cruise of three months. Two larger vessels were added in a resolution of the 30th, and Adams was appointed to a naval committee consisting also of Silas Deane, John Langdon, Christopher Gadsden, Stephen Hopkins, Joseph Hewes and Richard Henry Lee. The members rented a room at a water-front tavern and gathered each evening at six "in order to dispatch this business with all possible celerity."

It had been considered an amazing feat of organization when Colbert, the famous minister of Louis XIV, built a new French navy in ten years with the resources of Europe's largest kingdom at his disposal. The committee meeting at the Tun Tavern needed but two weeks to begin the task of fitting out the first four American warships, having been authorized "to draw upon the continental treasurers for the above purpose from time to time for as much cash as shall be necessary, not exceeding the sum of one hundred thousand dollars." Congress further recommended "that said committee have power to agree with such officers and seamen as are proper to man and command such vessels." On November 10th more history was made when the assembly passed the momentous resolution:

> That two battalions of marines be raised; . . . that particular care be taken that no persons be appointed to offices, or enlisted into said battalions, but such as are good seamen, or so acquainted with maritime affairs as to be able to serve to advantage by sea when required; that they be enlisted and commissioned to serve for and during the present war between Great Britain and the Colonies, unless dismissed by order of Congress. . . .[15]

On November 23rd, two weeks after the creation of a marine corps, Congress continued to put the cart before the horse by considering the committee's "draught of rules for the government of the American navy" before ever authorizing the navy itself. It was not until the 25th that the assembly passed the resolutions which "contain the true origin and foundation of the American navy."

Adams was justified in adding that he had "at least as great a share in producing them as any man living or dead." Glancing back over the years, he also recalled that some of the most pleasant hours of his life were spent with the committee in the Tun Tavern. "Mr. Lee, Mr. Gadsden, were sensible men, and very cheerful, but Governor Hopkins of Rhode Island, above seventy years of age, kept us all alive. Upon business, his experience and judgment were very useful. But when the business of the evening was over, he kept us in conversation till eleven, and sometimes twelve o'clock. His custom was to drink nothing all day, nor till eight o'clock in the evening, and then his beverage was Jamaica spirit and water. It gave him wit, humor, anecdotes, science and learning. He had read Greek, Roman, and British history, and was familiar with English poetry, particularly Pope, Thomson, and Milton, and the flow of his soul made all his reading our own, and seemed to bring to recollection in all of us, all we had ever read. . . . Hopkins never drank to excess, but all he drank was immediately not only converted into wit, sense, knowledge, and good humor, but inspired us with similar qualities." [16]

While Congress was planning invasions of Canada and creating a navy and marine corps, the legislative mills continued to grind out such small daily items as the approval of "the account of De Simitière, amounting to 8 dollars, for translating the Address of the united Col. to the Inhab. of Quebec" and John Thornton's "account of provisions for part of Captain Ross's company, and ferriage, amounting to 10 dollars."

Leaks of information occurred in spite of the best intentions. John Adams could not refrain at times from writing some bit of confidential news "under the rose" to Massachusetts, and other members were no more discreet. On November 9th, after rumors of naval preparations reached the public, the assembly renewed its pledge of secrecy with the resolution "that every member of this Congress consider himself under the ties of virtue, honor and love of his Country not to divulge directly or indirectly any matter or thing agitated or debated in Congress before the same shall have been determined, without leave of the Congress." It was further agreed that "if any member shall violate this agreement he shall be expelled this Congress and deemed an enemy to the liberties of America and liable to be treated as such, and that every member signify his consent . . . by signing his name."

Throughout the war the British seldom lacked for timely and reliable intelligence of rebel plans, including some of the most important measures debated in Congress. The possibility of treason had not been taken very seriously by the delegates until they had the shock of their lives, early in October, with the report that one of their own most trusted appointees had been caught redhanded as an enemy informer. A letter of the 11th written by Samuel Ward conveys some idea of the general reaction:

"Dr. Church, Who could have thought or even suspected it, a man who seemed to be all animation in the cause of his Country, highly caressed, employed in several very honorable and lucrative departments, and in full possession of the confidence of his country, what a complication of madness and wickedness must a soul be filled with to be capable of such Perfidy! What punishment can equal such horrid crimes?" [17]

It had been only a few months since Congress elected the supposed Boston patriot to the high office of director general and chief physician of its new army hospital establishment. As an associate of Hancock, Quincy, the Warrens and the Adamses, he was considered one of the inner circle; and in a grim mood the delegates resolved on November 4th:

That Dr. Church be close confined in some secure gaol in the colony of Connecticut, without the use of pen, ink, and paper, and that no person be allowed to converse with him, except in the presence and hearing of a Magistrate of the town, or the sheriff of the county where he shall be confined, and in the English language, until further orders from this or a future Congress.[18]

It was not a coincidence that this same day the assembly amended the articles of war to include more severe penalties. As a further effect of Benjamin Church's conviction, the delegates did not conclude that week's business until they had passed another resolution which was soon to transform colonies into states.

The incentive had come in October when New Hampshire informed her two members that the local government was in a "convuls'd state." The advice of Congress was asked "with respect to a method for our administering justice, and regulating our civil police."

A similar request, made earlier by Massachusetts, had not found the assembly ready to grapple with this problem. But now that treason had reared its head, Congress could no longer evade the fact that the colonies had been struggling along with local governments which consisted in effect of the old systems administered by new revolutionary officials who had seized illegal powers. The marvel is that widespread anarchy had not resulted, and yet the citizens of nearly every American community went about their daily lives with astonishingly little disorder. Already the Continental Congress and the committees of safety, without a scrap of authority except the Association, had been accepted by thousands of Americans as the successors to Parliament and the crown-appointed provincial executives.

But the time had come for a change. Even in Massachusetts it had been estimated by John Adams that the Tories were equal in numbers to the patriots, with the other third of the population remaining neutral or indifferent. The autumn of 1775 found the loyalists holding the balance of power in many communities of New York, Pennsylvania, New Jersey, Georgia and both Carolinas; and several of the royal governors were still making a pretense of ruling. Such a situation was fraught with too many perils of counterrevolution to be regarded lightly, and Congress realized that the colonies were not seeking advice as much as approval of a change in their governments. On November 3rd this approval was given in hearty measure with the resolution:

That it be recommended to the Provincial Convention of New Hampshire, to call a full and free representation of the people, and that the representatives, if they think it necessary, establish such a form of government as in their judgment will best produce the happiness of the people, and most effectually secure peace and good order in the Province, during the continuance of the present dispute between Great Britain and the Colonies.[19]

John Adams tried hard to win for the term "States" its first official sanction. "By this time I mortally hated the words, 'Province,' 'Colonies,' and 'Mother Country,' and strove to get them out of the report. The last was indeed left out, but the other two were retained. . . . Nevertheless, I thought this resolution a triumph, and a most important point gained." [20]

The two New Hampshire delegates were too jubilant to carp about such details when they announced the victory to their constituents. "The arguments on this matter . . . were truly Ciceronial," they reported. "The eminent Speakers did honor to themselves and the Continent. . . . We can't help rejoicing to see this as a ground work of our government, and hope by the Blessing of Divine Providence, never to return to our former despotick state." [21]

John Rutledge, the chairman of the committee which drew up the resolution, requested that the same counsel be offered to his own colony with the amendment ". . . if the Convention of South Carolina shall find it necessary."

Congress did not wait for Virginia to make application. On November 7th the royal governor, Lord Dunmore, invited reprisals when he "Erected his Standard" on board a British ship at Norfolk after decreeing martial law in the colony and offering Negro slaves their freedom if they would join him. At a time when there were still hundreds of household slaves in such northern cities as Boston and New York, this proclamation did great harm to the loyalist cause throughout America. While the iron was hot, Congress struck on December 2nd by urging Virginia to accept the advice sent to her two sister colonies.

The New Jersey assembly, influenced by the loyalist governor, William Franklin, had recently decided to draw up an humble petition to the king from that province. Congress, upon hearing the news, soon indicated that it was not giving its blessing to self-determination of this sort. A resolution warned that "it will be very dangerous to the liberties and welfare of America, if any Colony should separately petition the King or either house of Parliament." John Dickinson, George Wythe and John Jay were chosen as a committee to pay a visit to the assembly, which saw the error of its ways after hearing speeches from all three.

Loyalists looking back over the past eighteen months could only have been dazed by the acceleration of the revolt. Not until the early spring of 1774 did the rebel leaders establish a practical system of communication with their committees of correspondence. This led within a few months to the election of a revolutionary Congress which speedily won recognition as a functioning central government. By the following spring the last remnants of British power in the colonies were being seized by the committees of safety which the Association created. And it had taken only until the autumn of 1775 for the upstart provincial executives to begin the process of legalizing their authority by the drafting of state constitutions.

America had changed hands in a year and a half. The whole thing must have seemed as unreal as a nightmare to loyalists who foresaw that the next step would inevitably be a declaration of independence.

At the beginning of this period the loyalists had been fairly equal to the rebels in numbers and resources. Any analysis of their downfall must take into account the moderation of an uprising which brought about such swift transitions. Not a single man had been executed for his political beliefs, and there were surprisingly few instances of Tories being persecuted or imprisoned by overzealous committees of safety. Such restraints can scarcely be credited in a modern age when methods of torture and terrorism are taught in schools of revolutionary technique aiming at the creation of police states. The American Revolution seems a backward era in comparison, yet it is noteworthy that the very lack of bloodshed and violence had the effect of deluding the Tories into a false sense of security until the time had passed for effective political resistance.

Certainly it might have been supposed that Dr. Church would pay on the gallows for his crimes. But after a brief confinement in a Connecticut jail he was paroled on his promise to remain in Massachusetts. Interpreting this leniency as a tacit invitation to escape, he sailed for the West Indies the following spring in a vessel presumably lost at sea. The British government did not forget the traitor's services, and his widow and children were awarded a pension.

Chapter 8

Every Wind from the North

ACH province had its own idea as to the rate of compensation that
delegates should receive. The New York assembly, trying to fix an
amount covering "expenses and loss of time" of its representatives in Congress, was guided by their report of November 3rd, listing the provisions
made by ten other colonies:

> Georgia—£100 sterling to each delegate per month;
> South Carolina—£300 to each for the last Congress;
> North Carolina—£500 currency to each per year;
> Virginia—a half Johannes per day to each; *
> Maryland—40 shillings to each per day, Proclamation money;
> Pennsylvania—20 shillings to each per day, besides the allowance to such
> of the members as come from the counties;
> Connecticut—3 dollars to each per day for loss of time, besides all expenses,
> allowing each delegate a servant and two horses;
> Rhode Island—exactly the same as Maryland;
> Massachusetts—all expenses as above, and 2 dollars to each per day;
> New Hampshire—all expenses as above, and half a guinea per day to each.[1]

A rate of $4 a day was approved for the New York members. At this time,
generally speaking, delegates who lived on a modest scale had their actual
expenses defrayed. But after inflation set in, it grew to be a standing joke
that the morals of Congress were above suspicion, since it was obvious that
no member could afford to keep a mistress.

Idleness had never been a sin of Congress. But as more and more committees were created to take care of increasing business, the working day
came to be measured only by endurance.

* The Portuguese gold "Johannes," accepted everywhere in colonial America, was
worth about £3 12s.

102

"I rise at six," Silas Deane wrote to his wife, "write until seven, dress and breakfast by eight, go to the Committee of Claims until ten; then in Congress till half past three or perhaps four; dine by five, and then go either to the Committee of Secrecy or of Trade until nine; then sup and go to bed by eleven. This leaves little room for diversion or any thing else, and to tell you the truth I expect this kind of life must be my lot for some time." [2]

John Adams kept so busy that the stirring events of 1776 are covered by only two diary entries, though he made notes which later went into his autobiography. "The whole Congress is taken up, almost, in different committees from seven to ten in the morning," he informed Abigail in December, 1775. "From ten to four or sometimes five, we are in Congress, and from six to ten, in committees again. I don't mention this to make you think me a man of importance, because it is not I alone, but the whole Congress is thus employed, but to apologize for not writing to you oftener." [3]

The strain on the delegates is evident from a letter in which Joseph Hewes of North Carolina confessed that "we grow tired, indolent, Captious, Jealous, and want a recess. these only discover themselves now and then, in general we are pretty unanimous and friendly. . . . I am weary of politicks and wish I could retire to my former private Station." [4]

The time of the delegates was further taken up by an invasion of such crackpots as "Captain" John Macpherson, who had a mysterious scheme for destroying the entire British navy. Adams described him as an old privateersman, nine times wounded in sea battles of the last war. "He proposes great things; is sanguine, confident, positive, that he can take or burn every man-of-war in America. It is a secret, he says, but he will communicate it to any one member of Congress, upon condition that it be not divulged during his life at all, nor after his death, but for the service of this country. He says it is as certain as that he shall die, that he can burn any ship."

The plausible sea dog persuaded Congress to advance him $300 in a resolution of October 20th, but his scheme came to nothing. Another secret weapon, proposed by a young Connecticut inventor, had the encouragement of several delegates and reached the point of a test against the enemy the following year. David Bushnell's *American Turtle,* which made the first submarine attack of history, was described by a constituent in a letter to Silas Deane of the naval committee:

> The Body, when standing upright in the position in which it is navigated, has the nearest resemblance to the two upper shells of a Tortoise joined together. In length, it doth not exceed 7½ feet from the stem to the higher part of the rudder; the heighth not exceeding 6 feet. The person who navigates it enters at the top. It has a brass top or cover, which receives the person's head as he sits on a seat, and is fastened on the inside by screws. In this brass head

is fixed eight glasses, viz. two before, two on each side, one behind, and one to look out upwards. In the same brass head are fixed two brass tubes, to admit fresh air when requisite, and a ventilator at the side to free the machine from the air rendered unfit for consumption. On the inside is fixed a Barometer, by which he can tell the depth he is under water; a Compass, by which he knows the course he steers. In the barometer and on the needles of the compass is fixed *fox-fire*, i.e. wood that gives light in the dark. . . . He has a sounding lead fixed at the bow, by which he can take the depth of water under him; and to bring the machine into a perfect equilibrium with the water, he can admit so much water as is necessary, and has a forcing pump by which he can free the machine at pleasure, and can rise above water, and again immerge, as occasion requires.[5]

On his journey to Cambridge that fall Dr. Franklin had inspected the fantastic little craft, and at his suggestion Bushnell experimented to learn the effect of explosions under water.

In the bow [the description continues] he has a pair of oars fixed like the two opposite arms of a wind mill, by which he can row forward, and turning them the opposite way, row the machine backward; another pair . . . with which he can row the machine round, either to the right or left; and a third by which he can row the machine either up or down; all which are turned by foot, like a spinning wheel. The rudder with which he steers, he manages by hand, within board. All these shafts which pass through the machine are so curiously fix'd as not to admit any water to incommode the machine. The magazine for the powder is carried on the hinder part of the machine, without-board, and so contrived, that when he comes under the side of the Ship, he rubs down the side until he comes to the keel, and a hook so fix'd as that when it touches the keel it raises a spring which frees the magazine from the machine and fastens it to the side of the Ship; at the same time, it draws a pin, which sets the watch-work agoing, which, at a given time, springs the lock and the explosion ensues.

Deane's correspondent, Dr. Benjamin Gale, had a religious faith in the inventor and his submarine. "I do insist upon it, that I believe the inspiration of the Almighty has given him understanding for this very purpose and design. If he succeeds, a stipend for life, and if he fails, a reasonable compensation for time and expense is his due from the public."

In December the advice of Franklin was sought again after foxfire failed to illuminate the compass. Bushnell found that "the frost wholly destroys that quality in the wood. . . . He was detained near two months for want of money, and before he could obtain it the season was so far advanced that he was, in the manner I have now related, frustrated." Deane was requested "to enquire of Dr. Franklin whether he knows of any kind of phosphorus which will give light in the dark and not consume the air. He [Bushnell] has tried a candle but that destroys the air so fast that he cannot remain under water long enough to effect the thing."

Congress, having lost money on one pig in a poke, did not back the young inventor with anything more substantial than counsel and encouragement. He fared better with the governor and council of Connecticut, who urged him in February to "make every necessary preparation and experiment, with expectation of reward." The following summer, when the British fleet anchored off New York, Ezra Lee tried one night to blow up Admiral Howe's flagship *Eagle*. He submerged and made his way to the keel, but the attempt failed because he could not penetrate the copper sheathing to attach his bomb. The charge drifted away and exploded harmlessly after Bushnell's assistant rowed the *Turtle* to safety, and submarine warfare had to wait until a later period of history.

The new little navy, authorized in resolutions of November 25th, made such rapid progress that Congress elected officers less than a month later. Esek Hopkins of Rhode Island was chosen as commodore, and captains were appointed for the first four warships—Dudley Saltonstall, for the *Alfred;* Abraham Whipple, for the *Columbus;* Nicholas Biddle, for the *Andrea Doria;* and John Burrows Hopkins, for the *Cabot.*

It is hardly necessary to add that political considerations had much to do with the selections, though all the officers were men of maritime experience. Colonies which had been slighted in the appointment of captains were compensated with lesser honors; and Virginia had to be content with the naming of a recent arrival, John Paul Jones, as one of the first lieutenants. Joseph Hewes, a member of the marine committee, sponsored the Scottish seaman who had been recommended for zeal in the cause of his adopted country.

Articles of war, adapted and abridged from those of the British service, had already been approved for a navy which never at its peak reached a total of more than a fourth of the strength of the enemy fleet in American waters. It was enough of an achievement that the first four vessels actually had been manned and fitted out for active service in less than three months. The marine committee, one of the most successful of the standing committees, may be considered the ancestor of the modern Navy Department.

As the year drew toward a close, Washington's army before Boston was threatened with disintegration because the terms of thousands of militiamen were about to expire. The crisis was averted when volunteers or re-enlisted men kept the ranks filled, but the commander in chief had been obliged to take the risk of rebuilding his army within sight of a stronger foe. Congress has often been blamed by historians for the limited enlistments which handicapped the American cause, though the actual evidence is distinctly to the credit of that body. In its resolution authorizing the raising of rifle companies, the assembly specified a year's service instead of the three or six months usually demanded of colonial militiamen. When it created the Marine Corps Congress took another forward step by insisting on enlistments "for and during the present war." Curiously enough, it was Washington himself, the principal victim of the old system, who protested to Congress in a letter of November 28, 1775:

"From what I can collect, by my inquiries among the Officers, It will be impossible to get the men to inlist for the continuance of the War, which will be an insuperable Obstruction to the formation of the two Battalions of Marines on the plan resolved in Congress."

Responding to this well-meant advice, Congress beat a retreat on December 6th by resolving "that the seamen and marines be engaged for the first of January, 1777, unless sooner discharged." [6]

Within ten weeks the general repented the stand taken in his previous letter by recommending on February 7th a "bounty of twenty, thirty or more Dollars to engage the Men already Inlisted ('till January next) and such others as may be wanted to compleat to the Establishment, for and during the War."

After this game of blindman's buff, both Washington and Congress were consistent advocates of long enlistments, with the provincial assemblies just as stubbornly opposed. The century-old American tradition of short terms had been a natural growth, since the Indian wars of the past usually called for brief campaigns. When longer service became necessary, or military duty outside the colony, a cash bounty was offered less as a bribe than as provision for the support of a soldier's dependents. During the French and Indian War, the most severe test of this system, bounties as high as £14 had been paid for a year's enlistment.

Manpower was not lacking in a population of nearly three millions, and there is no doubt that America could have raised an army of at least 150,000 men for the duration of the war if numbers had been the only problem. The rub was how to arm, feed, pay and clothe even a fraction of that number for the next few months. Every theory was balked by the fact that thirteen colonies had accepted a conflict against the world's greatest empire before they had time to become a nation. As a consequence, their military effort had to live from hand to mouth for lack of organized resources.

The eager strategists of Congress were vouchsafed a single glimpse of glory in their Canadian campaign. On November 29th an express brought the news, seventeen days after the event, that General Montgomery had taken Montreal.

It was not a great military feat, since the town had few defenders; and the triumph was slightly tarnished by General Schuyler's threats of resigning. But Congress called upon three of its heaviest rhetorical guns, John Jay and James Wilson and William Livingston, to fire a verbal salute in the name of President Hancock. The congratulations sent to Schuyler, serving both to praise and to placate that thin-skinned warrior, were esteemed as a masterpiece:

> The Congress hear with Concern your Request for Leave to retire. . . . You have already reaped many Laurels, but a plentiful Harvest still invites you. Proceed, therefore, and let the Footsteps of Victory open a Way for the Blessings of Liberty, and the Happiness of well-ordered Government to visit that extensive Dominion. Consider that the road to glory is seldom strewed with Flowers, and that when the black and bloody Standard of Tyranny is erected in a Land possessed by Freemen, Patriots cease to remain inactive Spectators of their Country's Fall. Reflect, Sir, that the Happiness, or Misery, of Millions yet unborn is now to be determined; and remember that you will receive an honourable Compensation for all your Fatigues, in being able to leave the Memory of Illustrious Actions . . . as a fair, a splendid, and a valuable Inheritance, to your Posterity.[7]

Schuyler was sufficiently impressed to withdraw his request, and it may be supposed that Montgomery and Wooster were inspired by their letters of felicitation. In a final burst of optimism, Congress began counting its un-hatched chickens with the resolution "that the fortifications of Quebec, in case it comes into our hands, be repaired, and furnished with such pro-visions, arms, ammunition and artillery as may be necessary to its security."

There were signs, nevertheless, that the assembly had its doubts in more sober moments. A committee made up of John Langdon, Robert Treat Paine and Robert R. Livingston had already been sent to Ticonderoga to report on the state of the northern army. The members displayed an uncommon aptitude for digging up the facts. Congress was bluntly informed on their return that all but a handful of Montgomery's little army had melted away as a result of desertions and expired enlistments. His men had shown no enthusiasm for a winter campaign in an alien land, some of them "being half nacked" and others "haveing only a Coat, nearly worn out, and linnen under Cloaths."

The fault, it was intimated, lay with Congress for its lack of preparations. But the warlike ardor of the assembly was not chilled. That same week a secret resolution advised "that if General Washington and his council of war should be of opinion, that a successful attack may be made on the troops at Boston, he do it in any manner he may think expedient, notwithstanding the town and the property in it may thereby be destroyed." [8]

This broad hint might be interpreted as meddling with the prerogatives of the commander in chief. Fortunately for the cause, he decided not to risk an attack on regulars with green troops until he had the support of the heavy cannon of Ticonderoga, then being brought to Cambridge on ox-drawn sleds.

The first reports of Arnold left no doubt that he had emerged from the Maine wilderness with a force reduced by frightful hardships. But the army had its politicians as well as Congress, and on January 13th Silas Deane wrote to his wife: "I received a few days since, from before Quebec, two long letters from my brave friend, Col. Arnold, which I improved in his favor, and the other day he was unanimously chosen a Brigadier-General for the Army in Canada." [9]

On January 17th Congress had its first news of the disaster at Quebec. The two American columns had combined in a desperate attempt to storm the fortress during a snowfall on the last night of 1775. Montgomery was killed and Arnold wounded as their men met with a complete repulse. Captain Daniel Morgan of the riflemen won a foothold inside the walls for a short time, only to be captured with his detachment.

This was but the beginning. Every wind from the north seemed to bring more dismal tidings of the defeated force making a pretense of blockading Quebec. Freezing weather and smallpox were soon fighting on the side of the foe; and it was the further misfortune of the invaders to be opposed by the most able British soldier and administrator of the entire war, Sir Guy Carleton. The governor general, with few military resources at his command, had already earned the admiration of American officers by his humane treatment of prisoners as well as his resolute and energetic defense.

Congress was placed in the position of a gambler who must retire from the game or risk new losses. There was never for a moment any question as to the decision. Robert Morris, a recent delegate from Pennsylvania, echoed the opinion of his colleagues when he wrote to General Horatio Gates that Canada "must be ours at all events; shou'd it fall into the hands of the Enemy they will soon raise a Nest of Hornets at our backs that will sting us to the quick."

John Adams also tried to rationalize the attitude of Congress on strategic grounds. "The importance of Canada," he wrote to James Warren on February 18th, "arises from this and occasions our remarkable unanimity at present in deciding the Affairs of it: In the Hands of our Enemies it would enable them to inflame all the Indians upon the Continent, and perhaps induce them to take up the Hatchet and commit their Robberies and Murders upon the Frontiers of all the southern Colonies, as well to pour down Regulars, Canadians, and Indians, together upon the borders of the Northern." [10]

Plausible as such arguments were, they overlooked the obvious fact that the invaders did not have the military means to hold Canada even if they had captured Quebec. British sea power still had to be reckoned with; and in the last war it had been the decisive factor against French forces more powerful than any the Americans of 1776 could have raised and equipped. It was true that Canada offered a foe the bases for expeditions taking the route of Lake Champlain and the Hudson valley—the strategic backbone of America. This vital line had to be maintained if New York and New England were not to be detached from the other colonies. But the Americans of 1776 were beggars and not choosers when it came to war resources; they would have done better to invest their small means in posts defending the Hudson-Lake Champlain line.

The attitude of Congress, of course, was as much emotional as rational. All great revolutions are exported at the first opportunity, and Congress had set its heart on making Canada the fourteenth colony. Two days after learning of the repulse at Quebec, the delegates resolved "that the American army in Canada be reinforced with all possible dispatch, as well for the security and relief of our friends there, as for better securing the rights and liberties not only of that colony, but the other United Colonies." [11]

Only two of the many committees transacting the business of government were not closely tied to the apron strings of Congress. The importation of munitions was so necessary that the Secret Committee, composed of nine members, was allowed to export produce in payment. Later known as the Committee of Commerce, it took on such added executive powers in deciding questions of trade as to become the progenitor of the Department of Commerce.

Congress evidently put words in a class with gunpowder and bullets when it created another standing committee "for the sole purpose of corresponding with our friends in Great Britain, Ireland and other parts of the world." Benjamin Franklin, John Jay, Thomas Johnson, Benjamin Harrison and John Dickinson were the original five members of the Committee of Secret Correspondence, with Robert Morris being appointed early in 1775. From the outset they were given broad discretionary powers and required only to submit their correspondence when requested.

This was the beginning of the Department of State, for Congress gradually enlarged the province of the committee to include questions relating to foreign affairs. In the role of indulgent parent, the assembly offered to pay any expenses incurred, even to the employment of agents, and voted $3,000 for such purposes.

It was not to be supposed, however, that all addresses would be left to these specialists. In the late autumn of 1775 there were signs that Congress was about to become articulate again, and it needed only the behavior of the king to supply the incentive.

A semiofficial announcement in a Philadelphia newspaper made it known on November 10th that the "last dutiful petition to his majesty" had indeed been spurned, as its opponents had predicted. The same ship from England brought news of another affront—the monarch's proclamation of August 23rd, declaring the colonies in a state of rebellion and threatening the most severe punishments.

It was never the habit of Congress to receive a proclamation without giving a longer one in return, and George III had his answer on December 6th when the delegates approved a declaration "of the Thirteen United Colonies in North America." The purpose, as the first paragraph stated, was "to wipe off, in the name of the people of these United Colonies, the aspersions which it [the royal proclamation] is calculated to throw upon our cause; and to prevent, as far as possible, the undeserved punishments, which it is designed to prepare for our friends." [12]

As for the charge of forgetting the allegiance owed by colonial subjects, the declaration inquired:

> Allegiance to Parliament? We never owed—we never owned it. Allegiance to our King? Our words have ever avowed it,—our conduct has ever been consistent with it. We condemn, and with arms in our hands,—a resource which Freemen will never part with,—we oppose the claim and exercise of unconstitutional powers, to which neither the Crown nor Parliament were ever entitled. . . .
>
> It is alledged, that "we have proceeded to an open and avowed rebellion." In what does this rebellion consist? It is thus described—"Arraying ourselves in hostile manner, to withstand the execution of the law, and traitorously preparing, ordering and levying war against the King." We know of no laws binding upon us, but such as have been transmitted to us by our ancestors, and such as have been consented to by ourselves, or our representatives elected for that purpose.

The king had charged the rebel leaders with "traitorous designs" which were customarily punished by death. Congress, far from retreating an inch, ended its declaration on a note of defiance by countering with the first American threat of reprisals:

We, therefore, in the name of the people of these United Colonies, and by authority, according to the purest maxims of representation, derived from them, declare, that whatever punishment shall be inflicted upon any persons in the power of our enemies for favouring, aiding or abetting the cause of American liberty, shall be retaliated in the same kind, and in the same degree upon those in our power, who have favoured, aided, or abetted, or shall favour, aid and abet the system of ministerial oppression.

Lord Dunmore's proclamation, seeking to incite a loyalist uprising in Virginia, had not yet been answered. There were also reports of activity on the part of New York loyalists. Such provocations could not be ignored, and Congress fixed its righteous gaze on "all such unworthy Americans, as, regardless of their duty to their Creator, their country and their posterity, have taken part with our oppressors, and, influenced by the hope of possession of ignominous rewards, strive to recommend themselves to the bounty of administration, by misrepresenting and traducing the conduct and principles of the friends of American liberty."

Up to this time the assembly had not endorsed any stronger measures against American loyalists than publicity and ostracism. But on January 2nd the Revolution entered upon a stern new phase when the delegates resolved:

That it be recommended to the different assemblies, conventions and committees or councils of safety in the United Colonies, by the most speedy and effectual measures, to frustrate the mischievous machinations, and restrain the wicked practices of these men: And it is the opinion of this Congress, that they ought to be disarmed, and the more dangerous among them, either kept in safe custody, or bound with sufficient sureties as to their good behaviour.[13]

An accompanying resolution urged the committees of safety to call upon Continental troops, when they could be spared from war duties, if aid were needed in the work of disarming the Tory population.

That same day Congress gave its attention to the king's armed forces who had bombarded and burned Falmouth (Portland) in October, reducing to ashes the most important center in the district of Massachusetts which later became the State of Maine. If the delegates had known that during the past twenty-four hours British warships had destroyed Norfolk, the largest town in Virginia, they would have been even more wrathful in condemning "the execrable barbarity, with which this unhappy war has been conducted on the part of our enemies, such as burning our defenceless towns and villages, exposing their inhabitants, without regard to age and sex, to all the miseries which loss of property, the rigor of the season and inhuman devastation can inflict, exciting domestic insurrections and murders, bribing the savages, to

desolate our frontiers, and casting such of us as the fortune of war has put
into their power, into gaols, there to languish in irons and in want. . . ."
Some of these charges were a little farfetched, but in general the delegates stood on solid ground when they accused the invaders of violating the
accepted codes of humanity. Every age has its own standards, and the
eighteenth century held that the persons and property of enemy noncom-
batants were entitled to respect. There was no justification, according to
these principles, for the destruction of Falmouth and Norfolk, both of them
unfortified towns offering no armed resistance. Congress, with right on its
side, appealed to world opinion by recommending that Americans "continue
mindful that humanity ought to distinguish the brave, that cruelty should
find no admission among a free people, and to take care that no page in the
annals of America be stained by a recital of any action which justice or
Christianity may condemn, and to rest assured that whenever retaliation
may be necessary or tend to their security, this Congress will undertake the
disagreeable task." [14]

There would doubtless have been more declarations and addresses if the
delegates had followed their inclination. But while the publicists of Congress were lighting a candle in the hearts of their countrymen, an unknown
Philadelphia scribbler touched off a bonfire.

The strange and unpredictable factor of genius entered the equation on
January 8th with the appearance of an anonymous pamphlet called *Common
Sense*. Before the end of the year 120,000 copies had come off the presses,
establishing a record for a best seller which has never been equaled in the
history of American publishing. In order to reach the same proportion of the
total population in the middle of the twentieth century, it would be necessary
for a book to achieve a circulation of six million copies during its first year.
So obscure was the author that he remained the mystery of Philadelphia
taverns for a few days while gossip attributed his pamphlet to various members of Congress. Finally it became known that the work was written by one
Thomas Paine, who had been encouraged by Dr. Franklin to emigrate from
England in 1774 at the age of 39. A self-educated disciple of Wilkes in his
homeland, he had failed in turn as a staymaker, shopkeeper and petty excise
official. And though poverty had pursued him to his adopted country, he
spent the autumn of 1775 at revising the 25,000 words of *Common Sense*
with a view to turning over all profits to the American cause.
Neither Tom Paine's accent nor his linen was quite up to the standards
for an eighteenth-century gentleman. But it needed only a glance at his
pages for anyone to recognize that something new and tremendous had appeared in the field of American polemic writing. Even John Adams, one of

Paine's most spiteful critics, had to describe him as a "phenomenon" and a "meteor."

It might have been supposed that nothing original was left to be said on the old theme of natural law. But the first two paragraphs of *Common Sense* departed from the well-worn paths:

> Society is produced by our wants, and government by our wickedness; the former promotes our happiness *positively* by uniting our affections, the latter negatively by restraining our vices. The one encourages intercourse, the other creates distinctions. The first is a patron, the last is a punisher. Society in every state is a blessing, but Government, even in its best state, is but a necessary evil. . . . Government, like dress, is the badge of lost innocence; the palaces of kings are built upon the ruins of the bowers of paradise. For were the impulses of conscience clear, uniform and irresistibly obeyed, man would need no other lawgiver; but that not being the case, he finds it necessary to surrender up a part of his property to furnish means for the protection of the rest. . . .

Paine, like other writers of the age, could not resist the temptation to depict a primitive Eden in which natural law was gradually corrupted by political codes. With this formality out of the way, he got down to the main business of his pamphlet—the blasting away of the two main emotional obstacles which stood between the American people and independence.

Even in its recent bellicose declarations, Congress had not quite dared to lay rude hands on such sacred institutions as the monarchy and the English constitution. The last, Paine granted, had been "noble for the dark and slavish times in which it was erected. . . . But that it is imperfect, subject to convulsions, and incapable of producing what it seems to promise, is easily demonstrated." After several pages of demonstration, he reached a conclusion emphasized in italics:

> Wherefore, laying aside all national pride and prejudice in favor of modes and forms, the plain truth is that *it is wholly owing to the constitution of the people, and not to the constitution of the government* that the crown is not as oppressive in England as in Turkey.

Paine went back to Biblical times to begin his thundering attack on monarchy. "Government by kings," he declared, "was first introduced into the world by the Heathens, from whom the children of Israel copied the custom. It was the most prosperous invention the Devil ever set on foot for the promotion of idolatry."

Otis and Dickinson, the two best known pamphleteers of America up to this time, had been lawyers addressing men of education. But Tom Paine wrote in the language of the people.

"One of the strongest natural proofs of the folly of hereditary right in Kings," he chuckled, "is that nature disapproves it, otherwise she would not so frequently turn it into ridicule, by giving mankind an *Ass for a Lion.*" As for that other great prop of monarchy, the claim of divine right, he cited the case of William the Conqueror. "A French bastard landing with an armed Banditti and establishing himself king of England against the consent of the natives, is in plain terms a very paltry rascally original. It certainly hath no divinity in it."

With mockery and contempt Paine traced the institution of royalty down through the centuries to his own age. "In England a King hath little more to do than to make war and give away places; which, in plain terms, is to empoverish the nation and set it together by the ears. A pretty business indeed for a man to be allowed eight hundred thousand sterling a year for, and worshipped into the bargain. Of more worth is one honest man to society, and in the sight of God, than all the crowned ruffians that ever lived."

The last half of *Common Sense* was devoted to an appeal for independence and the establishment of a constitutional American republic. "No man was a warmer wisher for reconciliation than myself," wrote Paine, "before the fatal nineteenth of April, 1775, but the moment the event of that day was made known, I rejected the hardened, sullen-tempered Pharaoh of England for ever; and disdain the wretch, that with the pretended title of Father of his People can unfeelingly hear of their slaughter, and composedly sleep with their blood on his soul."

The author did not underrate the emotional hold of the monarchy on the loyalty of Americans who found it hard to imagine any other type of rule. "But where, some say, is the King of America? I'll tell you, friends, he reigns above and doth not make havoc of mankind like the Royal Brute of Great Britain."

The Continental Congress was obviously the model for the unicameral American legislature of 390 members proposed by Paine after independence had been declared. He suggested the election of a president from each province in rotation, and the framing "of a Continental Charter, or Charter of the United Colonies; (answering to what is called the Magna Charta of England) fixing the number and manner of choosing Members of Congress . . . always remembering, that our strength is Continental, not Provincial."

The effect of *Common Sense* on the America of 1776 can hardly be exaggerated. The very month of its publication Congress had assigned James Wilson of Pennsylvania the task of drawing up another "declaration to the inhabitants of America." This address, as he later explained, "was meant to lead the public mind into the idea of Independence, of which the necessity was plainly foreseen by Congress." But the 5,000-word document contained little that had not been said before, and it approached the subject of separation with obvious skittishness:

> Though an independent Empire is not our *Wish;* it may—let your Oppressors attend—it may be the fate of our Countrymen and ourselves. It is in the Power of your Enemies to render Independency or Slavery your and our Alternative. . . . We are *desirous* to continue Subjects: But we are *determined* to continue Freemen.[15]

Such sentiments, which might have seemed bold only a few weeks before, made tame reading for the delegates after *Common Sense* appeared with its challenge: "Everything that is right or reasonable pleads for separation. The blood of the slain, the weeping voice of nature cries, 'TIS TIME TO PART."

Congress quietly tabled its declaration. And while it fizzled out like a damp firecracker, Tom Paine's bomb was exploding in the imagination of every literate American:

> O ye that love mankind! Ye that dare oppose not only the tyranny, but also the tyrant, stand forth! Every spot of the old world is overrun with oppression. Freedom hath been hunted round the globe. Asia and Africa hath long expelled her. Europe regards her like a stranger, and England hath given her warning to depart. O receive the fugitive, and prepare in time an asylum for mankind!

Chapter 9

The Committee of the Whole

THE diplomatic ventures of the Continental Congress began in an atmosphere of mystery and intrigue which might have been created by a writer of historical novels. One December day in 1775 a personable French gentleman, M. Achard Bonvouloir, presented himself to Dr. Franklin and three other members of the Committee of Secret Correspondence. The visitor, who had just arrived from London after a rough voyage of a hundred days, let it be known that he took a warm personal interest in the fortunes of America.

He disclaimed, perhaps a little too hastily, any connection at all with the court of France. But Dr. Franklin drew his own inferences. He saw to it that the stranger was cordially welcomed and given all the information proper for him to receive.

As the conversations proceeded, M. Bonvouloir dropped a few hints. Although still protesting that he had no official status, he contrived to give that very impression. He offered no aid save his own friendly offices, but spoke in glowing terms of the private deals which might be arranged for European munitions of war. When members of the committee pressed him too hard, he parried all questions deftly.

The archives of France have long since established that Benjamin Franklin did not err in his assumption that the visitor was worth cultivating. Achard Bonvouloir, whose very name might have been mistaken for a pseudonym, actually had been employed by the Comte de Vergennes, foreign minister of Louis XVI, on the recommendation of the Comte de Guines, French ambassador to England. An adventurer who had traveled widely in America and the West Indies, the secret agent was instructed to gather information as to the progress of the American revolt while assuring the leaders of unofficial French sympathy.

His report of December 28th from Philadelphia could not have been dated at a more fortunate time. Montreal had just been taken, the British were besieged in Boston, and all indications then pointed to the capture of Quebec.

Bonvouloir's employment ended after this mission, but an idea had been implanted in the minds of Vergennes and his advisers. If a sham commercial firm could be set up to supply arms in exchange for American products, it might be possible for France to stir up trouble for her hereditary enemy across the Channel while still keeping up the role of good neighbor. The French court could make a show of stopping such shipments if necessary, for Vergennes did not have enough faith at this time in the prospects of American victory to take too many risks of exposure.

The members of the Committee of Secret Correspondence had meanwhile been endeavoring to learn just what aid might be expected from European powers. Only a few days before Bonvouloir's arrival, they had requested Arthur Lee, then living in London, to use "great circumspection and secrecy" in sounding out the attitude of foreign nations toward America.

The Secret Committee, which later became the Committee of Commerce, had also been making inquiries. Its main responsibility was the importation of munitions, and in January the members were visited in Philadelphia by two other mysterious Frenchmen named Penet and Pliarne. They too denied any official connection, but apparently they discussed quite frankly the possibilities of the French government in giving its secret sanction to some plan of exchanging arms for American produce.

On the strength of these intimations, the Secret Committee decided to send an agent to France. The choice fell upon Silas Deane, perhaps because he was free at the time, having been replaced by Dr. Oliver Wolcott as a Connecticut delegate. It might appear that a better selection could have been made, for Deane confessed in a letter to his wife that "people here, members of Congress and others, have unhappily and erroneously thought me a schemer." After failing of re-election, he wrote bitterly: "My enemies' designs have been, by superceding me in my absence, tacitly to censure me, and leave by implication a stigma on my character, which they know a public hearing must not only clear up, but tumble them into the pit they have (like moles as they are) been digging for me." [1]

John Adams also seems to have had his doubts of Deane. "He was a person of a plausible readiness and volubility with his tongue and pen, much addicted to ostentation and expense in dress and living, but without any deliberate forecast or reflection, solidity of judgment or real information."

Once the appointment had been made, the Committee of Secret Correspondence entrusted the Connecticut lawyer with the even more delicate mission of making contact with Vergennes himself and reporting on his intentions. "On your arrival in France you will, for some time, be engaged in the business of providing goods for the Indian trade," the instructions from the committee read. "This will give a good countenance to your appearing in the character of a merchant, which we wish you continually to retain among the French in general, it being probable that the court of France may not like it to be known publicly that any agent from the Colonies is in that country."

At his first good opportunity, Deane was to request an audience with the foreign minister, "acquainting him that you are in France upon the business of the American Congress, in the character of a merchant, having something to communicate to him that may be mutually beneficial to France and the North American Colonies." The benefits sought by the colonies were "clothing and arms for twenty-five thousand men, with a suitable supply of ammunition, and one hundred field pieces." The prospect of American independence was to be dangled before Vergennes as bait, with the explanation that "France has been pitched upon for the first application, from an opinion that if we should . . . come to a total separating from Great Britain, France would be looked upon as the power whose friendship it would be fittest to obtain and cultivate." [2]

Deane received these instructions the first week in March, but another month passed before he departed. Thus was launched the first frail craft sent out by Congress on the treacherous sea of foreign relations, though the fog of secrecy was not so impenetrable as the members of the two committees fondly imagined. Many a headache awaited Congress before its diplomatic problems would be even partially solved, and for Deane the end was to be poverty, disgrace and treason.

On Friday, February 16th, "the Congress resolved itself into a committee of the whole, to take into consideration the propriety of opening the ports, and of the restrictions and regulations of trade of these Colonies, after the first of March next."

Every delegate realized that this was the beginning of the fight for independence. The battle lines had been drawn "out of doors" and Congress formed itself into a committee of the whole only for the threshing out of the most controversial questions.

Next to independence itself, there could hardly have been a measure more calculated to burn the last bridges of reconciliation behind the American colonies. The right of Great Britain to administer trade and commerce for the Empire had generally been conceded even by the radicals of Congress, and a premature resolution to open the ports was tabled in July for lack of enough support to pass.

Obviously the issue was closely associated with the problems of foreign relations. During the debates of February 16th George Wythe of Virginia asked some of the questions which must have perplexed other members: "In what character shall we treat?—as subjects of Great Britain,—as rebels? Why should we be so fond of calling ourselves dutiful subjects? If we should offer our trade to the Court of France, would they take notice of it any more than if Bristol or Liverpool should offer theirs, while we profess to be subjects? . . . If we were to tell them that, after a season, we would return to our subjection to Great Britain, would not a foreign court wish something more permanent?" [3]

John Adams, who took notes, recorded that even such a stout radical as Roger Sherman was not unmindful of the risks. "I fear we shall maintain the armies of our enemies at our own expense with provisions," protested the member from Connecticut. "We can't carry on a beneficial trade, as our enemies will take our ships. A treaty with a foreign power is necessary, before we open our trade, to protect it."

"I think the merchants ought to judge for themselves of the danger and risk," said James Wilson. "We should be blamed if we did not leave it to them. . . . If we determine that our ports shall not be opened, our vessels abroad will not return. Our seamen are all abroad; will not return unless we open our trade. I am afraid it will be necessary to invite foreigners to trade with us, although we lose a great advantage, that of trading in our own bottoms."

Benjamin Harrison lamented the past dependence of the colonies on the mother country. "We have hobbled on under a fatal attachment to Great Britain. I felt it as much as any man, but I feel a stronger to my country."

"Americans will hardly live without trade," Wythe insisted. "It is said that our trade will be of no advantage to us, because our vessels will be taken, our enemies will be supplied, the West Indies will be supplied at our expense. This is too true unless we can provide a remedy. . . . If the inclination of our people should become universal to trade, we must open our ports."

It was plain by this time that the nonintercourse provisions of the Association would not bring the mother country to terms, as the delegates of the first Congress had so blithely anticipated in the autumn of 1774. They had made the historical mistake of underrating the determination of Great Britain in time of stress—an error which accounted for the downfall of more than one enemy nation in past wars. The merchants of the kingdom had suffered heavy losses, it was true, and there had been grievous unemployment as a result of the sudden decline in American trade. But privations only seemed to stiffen the will of Britons, so that the war with America was rapidly becoming a popular cause. Parliament had the support of the nation on December 22, 1775, when it passed an act removing the colonies from the protection of the crown, forbidding all trade with them, and authorizing the seizure and confiscation of American ships at sea.

An advance copy of this stern measure was smuggled across the ocean to Congress during the course of the February debates. About the same time there were rumors, too persistent to be discounted, that George III had arranged to hire European mercenary troops for the chastisement of his colonial subjects. Within a few months, it was reported, a mighty British expeditionary force would be on its way to America to stamp out the fires of rebellion.

These possibilities helped the radical faction in Congress to win converts among the moderates, who could tip the scale either way. But the conservatives, with John Dickinson as floor leader, managed to hold their ground. When John Adams likened him to a reed, he had not yet discovered that his adversary was neither frail nor readily shaken in debate. The two were still not on speaking terms, and their daily contests in the committee of the whole might have been compared to a duel with a rapier and bludgeon as weapons. Adams laid about him lustily, but the blade always flashed out in time to ward off his blows.

Dickinson's patriotism could not be challenged by his most bitter political foes. As the ranking colonel of the Pennsylvania militia, he had proved himself willing to risk his life as well as his fortune in the cause. He could even accept independence if it came to the worst, but the time did not seem ripe to him in the spring of 1776. Like a conscientious lawyer acting in the best interests of an impulsive client, he believed that he was saving America from reckless decisions which would later be regretted. He believed that all hopes for an honorable compromise and reconciliation were not yet dead, and he had the courage to put principle above popularity.

Many of the best minds of Congress agreed with him that independence was too grave a question to be decided emotionally. George Read, Robert Morris, John Alsop, James Duane, Robert R. Livingston and Edward Rutledge also argued that safety lay in caution; and John Jay saw the whole era in terms of "evolution, not revolution." Such conservatives distrusted the very eloquence of *Common Sense*, then at the height of its success, and sincerely held that it represented a danger to the patriotic cause.

Most of the delegations split on the rock of the dispute about opening the ports. Virginia, which usually took the radical side, had two members who could only have been called middle-of-the-road men, Carter Braxton and Benjamin Harrison. Even Massachusetts was divided, as John Adams recorded with prejudice:

> Mr. Harrison had courted Mr. Hancock, and Mr. Hancock had courted Mr. Duane, Mr. Dickinson and their party, and leaned so partially in their favor, that Mr. Samuel Adams had become very bitter against Mr. Hancock, and spoke of him with great asperity in private circles; and this alienation between them continued from this time till the year 1789, thirteen years, when they were again reconciled. . . . Although Harrison was another Sir John Falstaff, excepting in his larcenies and robberies, his conversation disgusting to every man of delicacy or decorum, yet, as I saw he was to be nominated with us in business, I took no notice of his vices or follies, but treated him, and Mr. Hancock, too, with uniform politeness. I was, however, too intimate with Mr. [Richard Henry] Lee, Mr. Adams, Mr. Ward, &c. to escape jealousy and malignity of their adversaries.[4]

Such judgments may be taken with a grain of salt, for John Adams was too resolute a fighter to be just in the heat of controversy. Hancock might more accurately have been described as a moderate who acquitted himself well in the difficult duty of acting as speaker of the opinionated assembly, for he seems to have given each faction its due share of time for presenting arguments.

Charles Thomson, who played no favorites, did not escape the criticism of contenders seeking every advantage. John Adams complained of "an extraordinary liberty taken by the secretary, I suppose, at the instigation of the party against independence, to suppress, by omitting on the Journals, the many motions that were made disagreeable to that set. These motions ought to have been inserted verbatim on the Journals, with the names of those who made them."[5]

The struggle in the committee of the whole continued day after day. Joseph Hewes put it mildly when he wrote to a friend in North Carolina: "We do not treat each other with that decency and respect that was observed heretofore. Jealousies, ill natured observations and recriminations take the place of reason and Argument. our Tempers are soured. some among us urge strongly for Independence and eternal separation, others wish to wait a little longer and to have the opinion of their Constituents on that subject."[6]

Rumors of the king's plan to hire European mercenaries were countered in Congress by equally persistent reports that the mother country had decided to send peace commissioners empowered to offer new terms of reconciliation. Dickinson and his faction urged that it would be only prudent to go slow, and the radicals were just as determined to commit America so far along the road to independence that there could be no retreat.

After a deadlock of nearly two weeks, it grew apparent to both sides that there was no hope of a decision before the first day of March, the date appointed in the motion for opening the ports. The conservatives had won the preliminary round in their fight for a delay, and Congress turned its attention to other problems, which were never lacking.

Late in 1775 a committee appointed to inquire into the condition of the treasury had recommended that no more paper money be issued. As an alternative, it was proposed that the assembly borrow such sums as it required on interest-bearing treasury notes. This suggestion was discussed on December 26th but "referred till Tomorrow."

The bleak fact remained that Congress had spent its first three million dollars in bills of credit payable in 1779, 1780, 1781 and 1782. More money had to be raised—at least three million dollars for immediate needs at the beginning of 1776. Authority for printing bills of credit to this amount was voted on the same terms as before, with the date of redemption being set at 1783-1786. Again the colonies were urged to stand back of the new issue by levying taxes in proportion to their resources.

Congress was already a victim of the vicious circle which has troubled all new governments depending on paper money—as more bills of credit were emitted, their value grew less in spending power. The first signs of pain were evinced on January 11th, when it was resolved:

> That if any person shall hereafter be so lost to all virtue and regard for his country, as to 'refuse to receive said bills in payment,' or obstruct or discourage the currency or circulation thereof, and shall be duly convicted by the committee of the city, county, or district, or in case of appeal from their decision, by the assembly, convention, council or committee of safety of the colony in which he shall reside, such person shall be deemed, published and treated as an enemy of his country, and precluded from all trade or intercourse with the inhabitants of these colonies.[7]

The assembly ordered that this resolution be published, and it appeared in the *Pennsylvania Gazette* of January 17, 1776.

Never in history has any government been able for very long to enforce laws compelling its citizens to accept a declining currency at face value, but this was a lesson which Congress in its turn would have to learn by experience. Meanwhile a new standing committee of five members was appointed on March 17th "to examine the accounts of the treasurers, and from time to time, report to Congress on the state of the treasury." The members were Thomas Nelson, James Duane, Richard Smith, Thomas Willing and the new delegate from Massachusetts, Elbridge Gerry.

Dismal news of the military situation in Canada continued to arrive with every express, and on February 14th Congress could only conclude that its propaganda campaign also was failing. The Committee of Secret Correspondence submitted a confidential report from one of its agents, a native Canadian, which disclosed "that when the Canadians first heard of the Dispute they were generally on the American side; but by the Influence of the Clergy and the Noblesse, who have been continually preaching and persuading them against us, they are now brought into a State of Suspence or Uncertainty which side to follow. . . . That the Letters we have address'd to them have made little Impression, the common People being generally unable to read, and the Priests and Gentry who read them to others, explain them in such a Manner as best answers their own purpose of prejudicing the People against us." [8]

The report ended with a recommendation that "it would be of great service if some Persons from the Congress were sent to Canada, to explain viva voce to the People there the Nature of our Dispute with England . . . and to satisfy the Gentry and Clergy that we have no intention against their interests, but mean to put Canada in full possession of Liberty, desiring only their Friendship and Union with us as good Neighbors and Brethren."

Congress decided the next day to send a committee to Canada. Dr. Franklin was selected, as John Adams explained, because of his "masterly acquaintance with the French language . . . his great Experience in Life, his Wisdom, Prudence, Caution; his engaging Address." Samuel Chase had zeal in his favor, and Congress went outside its own ranks for the third commissioner. The wealthiest man in the American colonies, who signed himself Charles Carroll of Carrollton, was obviously appointed because of his adherence to the Roman Catholic faith. Thirty-nine years of age, educated in French Jesuit colleges, he had a reputation as one of the leading patriots of Maryland. At the request of Congress he persuaded his brother John, a Catholic priest, to accompany him.

The first American diplomatic mission did not set out until March 25th. Even so, the season was early for pushing through the wilderness. Six inches of April snow imposed a week's delay at Saratoga, and Dr. Franklin wrote to Josiah Quincy: "I begin to apprehend that I have undertaken a fatigue that at my time of life may prove too much for me; so I sit down to write to a few friends by way of farewell." [9]

After an exhausting journey up the Hudson by sloop and rowboat, the travelers embarked with their own beds in open flatboats which had to battle ice floes in Lake George and Lake Champlain. The last frontier inn had been left behind, and they stopped occasionally on the shore to brew tea and warm themselves around a fire. At night they slept in the woods or under canvas awnings in the flatboats.

Calèches from Montreal met them at St. Johns, and the weary commissioners drove the rest of the way over muddy trails. Not until April 29th, the thirty-sixth day, did they arrive in Montreal and acknowledge a salute from the cannon of the American-held citadel to "the Committee of the Honourable Continental Congress."

Dr. Franklin must have realized from the beginning that the mission faced a hopeless task. In the entire province there were only 400 English Protestants, more than half of them opposed to the American cause. Nor had the behavior of the invading troops been such as to win friends among the French Catholic population. On April 23rd, a week before the committee reached Montreal, Congress adopted a recommendation which indicates that reports of American looting and disrespect to religion had aroused anxiety:

> Resolved, That the commissioners from Congress to Canada, be desired to publish an Address to the people of Canada, signifying, that Congress has been informed of injuries offered by our people to some of them: expressing our resentment at their misconduct; inviting them to state their grievances to our commissioners, and promising ample redress to them, and exemplary punishments to the offenders.[10]

At a later date Congress learned that every American shortcoming had been exploited by Sir Guy Carleton while defending Quebec with a handful of troops and awaiting the British reinforcements which arrived on May 6th. Long before that date the governor general had gained the sympathy of the French Catholics, though most of them stayed out of the fight altogether. They respected him for the principles of religious toleration he advocated in the Quebec Act, and Carleton displayed an unfailing tact in all his dealings with the clergy. He even managed to make friends among the American prisoners who had been so poorly clad and equipped for a winter campaign. In the role of friendly enemy, Carleton supplied these malcontents with warm clothing as well as loyalist indoctrination before they were exchanged.

"Since we have tried in vain to make them acknowledge us as brothers," he declared, "let us at least send them away disposed to regard us as first cousins."[11]

In spite of the discouraging results, Congress had no idea of abandoning its Canadian designs. General Charles Lee, who seemed qualified by long military experience as well as his knowledge of the French language, was transferred to the northern army and promised reinforcements for a vigorous spring campaign.

Although this officer's professional abilities were held in high esteem, he had only recently given Congress cause to make a public assertion of civil rights. The declaration appeared in the *Pennsylvania Gazette* of March 5, 1776:

> *Resolved,* That no oath by way of test be imposed upon, exacted, or required of any of the inhabitants of these colonies, by any military officers.[12]

The New York delegates, reporting to their provincial committee of safety, explained that General Lee "had imposed a Test upon the inhabitants of our Colony, in order to ascertain their political principles. However salutary such a measure might be, when grounded on a legal and constitutional basis, we were much alarmed that it should owe its authority to any military officer, however distinguished for his zeal, his rank, his accomplishments, and services. . . . There can be no liberty where the military is not subordinate to the civil power in everything not immediately concerned with their operations. . . . A similar effort in Rhode Island had passed over unnoticed; reiterated precedents must become dangerous; we therefore conceived it to be our unquestionable duty to assert the independence and superiority of the civil power, and to call the attention of Congress to this unwarrantable invasion of its rights by one of their officers." [13]

The same issue came up again the following week. Congress had appointed Edward Rutledge, Richard Henry Lee and William Whipple to confer with General Lee about the defenses of New York, where the next British attack was expected. Cries for vengeance had been heard throughout the colonies since the destruction of Falmouth and Norfolk, and feeling against American loyalists was bitter. The committee's report, in the handwriting of Whipple, the New Hampshire slave trader who had turned merchant, recommended on March 14th "that the inhabitants of Statten Island shou'd without loss of time be disarm'd and their arms delivered to some Regiment already raising but unfurnished with muskets. I do not imagine that the disarming the Tories will incapacitate them from acting against us, as they can easily be supplied by the Ships. I shou'd therefore think it prudent to secure their Children as Hostages. If a measure of this kind (hard as it may appear) is not adopted, the Childrens Children of america may rue the fatal omission." [14]

Congress seems to have concluded that posterity had better take its chances than be saved by such savage means. The committee's advice as to hostages was pointedly ignored, though the assembly voted another resolution, similar to the one passed in January, advocating that the Tories be disarmed.

In their letters the delegates continued to groan about long hours. There can be no doubt that they were overworked, but it was also plain in the spring of 1776 that they often had only themselves to blame. Although standing committees of members had been established, no attempt was made to assign some of the executive duties to departments made up of specialized employees.

Congress, in short, was diligent to the point of inefficiency, as Thomas Johnson of Maryland seems to have suspected. On March 19th this member, according to the diary of Richard Smith, "threw out for Consideration the Propriety of establishing a Board of Treasury, a War Office, a Board of Public Accounts, and other Boards to consist of Gent'n not Members of Congress."

These reforms had to wait until a later date. On April 1st, however, Congress approved instructions for setting up a treasury office of accounts under the supervision of the standing committee of finance. It was further resolved "that an auditor general, and a competent number of assistants or clerks, shall be appointed by Congress, and employed, for stating, arranging, and keeping the public accounts." [15]

The cluttered pages of the *Journals* testified as to the immediate need for a war office. Efforts which might have gone into the creation of a more effective military establishment were wasted day after day in the transaction of such typical petty business as the resolution "that four musquets and bayonets be lent to the delegates of Virginia, for the use of the guard that accompanies the powder going to Virginia."

An admirable tradition had been set when civil rights were protected against infringements excused on grounds of military expediency. But Congress sometimes flew to the opposite extreme by taking upon itself decisions which properly belonged in the military sphere. Not content with electing generals and shaping strategy as well as policy, the assembly did not hesitate to give orders for the smallest troop movements:

> Resolved, That Captain Nelson, with his riffle Company, be directed immediately to repair to New York.

Generals could only have been confused and frustrated by such meddling, but the watchful attitude of Congress was justified by Samuel Adams in a letter to James Warren: "A standing Army, however necessary it may be at some times, is always dangerous to the Liberties of the People. . . . I have a good opinion of the principal officers of our Army. I esteem them as Patriots as well as Soldiers. But if this war continues, as it may for years to come, we know not who may succeed them." [16]

The object lessons of the mismanaged Canadian campaign might perhaps have made more of an impression if Congress had not been cheered by news of victories in two other quarters. The little American fleet, which had sailed from Philadelphia in February to take the offensive in its first operation, raided Nassau in the Bahama Islands on March 3rd and captured valuable stores of British gunpowder. The report reached Congress late that month, and on the 25th a dispatch from General Washington announced that the enemy had been compelled to evacuate Boston.

There had been signs for some time that General Sir William Howe was planning to withdraw. This probability could not dim the glory of the greatest success won so far by American arms. For nearly ten months Washington's green troops had kept the British regulars blockaded in the overcrowded town filled with Tory refugees. The decision to evacuate was forced upon the foe when the Americans seized the commanding position of Dorchester heights in a brilliant night surprise. The next morning Howe found his army and ships exposed to bombardment from the heavy guns captured by the rebels at Ticonderoga. He could only choose between abandoning Boston and risking an attack which might prove more costly than Bunker Hill. The British commander wisely decided to give up a town which had small strategic worth, and on the 17th his troops and hundreds of American loyalists sailed for Halifax, leaving large military stores behind.

Congress had its faults but timidity and pessimism were not among them. On April 2nd the assembly approved an exultant letter of thanks to Washington and his "Band of Husbandmen." A gold medal was ordered to be struck in honor of the American triumph over "an Army of Veterans, commanded by the most experienced Generals, but employ'd by bad Men in the worst of Causes."

For the moment there was no formidable British force anywhere in the colonies. But the delegates realized that this interlude could only be compared to the dead center of a hurricane which would strike again with redoubled fury. Washington counseled that preparations be hastened for the defense of New York, where he predicted that the next enemy blow would fall.

On the floor of Congress the victory had the immediate effect of renewing the fight to open American ports. After failing to pass on March 1st, the measure had been brought up repeatedly in the committee of the whole, and John Adams concluded that "postponement was the object of our antagonists. . . . There was, however, still a majority of members who were either determined against all measures preparatory to independence, or yet too timorous and wavering to venture on any decisive steps. We therefore could do nothing but keep our eyes fixed on the great objects of free trade, new governments and independence . . . and seize every opportunity of advancing step by step in our progress. Our opponents were not less vigilant in seizing every opportunity for delay." [17]

Paragraphs which appear quite innocent in the pages of the *Journals* were regarded as the skirmishes of this struggle. Thus on March 20th the instructions for the commissioners to Canada were not passed without a wrangle in the committee of the whole. John Adams rejoiced that the radicals had "obtained one step more towards our great object" when they forced through a recommendation that the Canadians set up a government of their own and unite with the American colonies.

"It will readily be supposed," he commented, "that a great part of these instructions were opposed by our antagonists with great zeal; but they were supported on our side with equal ardor."

Even phrases were contested word by word. On March 19th the radicals could be sure of enough votes to pass a privateering act, yet four more days of argument were required before the committee of the whole managed to agree on a single sentence. Parliament had offered the provocation by legalizing the seizure of American ships on the high seas, and American privateering had been going on unofficially since the autumn of 1775. Although it remained only for Congress to sanction an existing condition, the resolution hung fire because Richard Henry Lee insisted on naming George III as "the Author of our Miseries." Dickinson and his faction stuck by their guns until the offending phrase was removed from a preamble which merely accused the monarch of treating petitions "with scorn and contempt." After this compromise had been accepted, Congress resolved on March 23rd:

> That the inhabitants of these Colonies be permitted to fit out armed vessels, to cruise on the enemies of these United Colonies.[18]

The deadlock in the committee of the whole lasted nearly two more weeks. Authentic reports had long since reached America that the very act of Parliament proclaiming the seizure of colonial ships carried a rider authorizing the sending of peace commissioners. It was plausibly argued by John Dickinson and his supporters that Congress ought not to make any such defiant gesture as opening the ports without at least considering the new terms of reconciliation.

Allowing for the slow communications of the day, enough time had elapsed since its decision for Parliament to offer some encouragement to the friends of reconciliation in America. They were left entirely in the dark as to British intentions, and on April 6th Robert Morris wrote irritably to General Gates:

"Where the plague are those Commissioners, if they are to come what is it that detains them: It is time we should be on a certainty and know positively whether the libertys of America can be established and secured by reconciliation, or whether we must totally renounce connection with Great Britain and fight our way to a total independence." [19]

Doubts such as these, which the British might have relieved, lost the conservatives their two-month fight in the committee of the whole. Men of good will, lacking any reassurance from the mother country, began to agree with Oliver Wolcott that "the ideal Phantom of Commissioners Comeing over to settle our Disputes has almost Vanished." It seemed futile to delay the opening of the ports any longer, and on April 6th Congress took a seven-league stride toward independence with the resolution:

> That any goods, wares, and merchandise, except such as are of the growth, production or manufacture of, or brought from any country under the dominion of the King of Great Britain, and except East India Tea, may be imported from any other parts of the world to the thirteen United Colonies, by the inhabitants thereof, and by the people of all such countries as are not subject to the said King. . . .[20]

Chapter 10

The Hour of Decision

O N the anniversary of Lexington it could safely have been said that there were no unalterable foes of independence left in the Continental Congress. One of the last had been Dr. Zubly, the studious Savannah pastor, who noted in his diary the convictions which led to his resignation at the end of 1775:

"I made it a point in every company to contradict and oppose every hint of a desire of independence or of breaking our connection with Great Britain. A separation from the Parent State I wd. dread as one of the greatest evils and should it ever be proposed I would write pray and fight against it. Some good men may desire it but good men do not always know what they are about." [1]

Such conservatives as John Dickinson, James Wilson, Edward Rutledge and Robert R. Livingston did not oppose independence and confederation in principle. Their resistance was based largely on the premise that these decisions were being crammed down the throats of an unready and unwilling people. Jefferson conceded that all four opposition leaders argued as "friends to the measures themselves, and saw the impossibility that we should ever again be united with Great Britain, yet they were against adopting them at this time." [2]

Other delegates of proved courage and patriotism, among them Robert Morris, John Jay, George Read, James Duane and Benjamin Harrison, also believed that independence was being advocated prematurely at America's peril. They agreed with Carter Braxton, who wrote to his friend Landon Carter on April 14th that independence "is in truth a delusive Bait which men inconsiderately catch at, without knowing the hook to which it is affixed.

"It is an object to be wished for by every American," he continued, "when it can be obtained with Safety and Honor. That this is not the moment I will prove by Arguments that to me are decisive, and which exist with certainty. Your refined notion of our publick honor being engaged to await the terms offered by [the British] Commissioners operates strongly with me and many others and makes the first reason I would offer. My next is that America is too defenceless a State for the declaration, having no alliance with a naval Power nor as yet any Fleet of consequence of her own to protect that trade which is so essential to the prosecution of the War, without which I know we cannot go on much longer."

Only a few months later the Virginia delegate signed the Declaration, as did Morris, Wilson, Harrison, Read and Rutledge. But in April he spoke for a decisive bloc in Congress when he declared that if independence "was to be now asserted, the Continent would be torn in pieces by Intestine Wars and Convulsions. Previous to Independence all disputes must be healed and Harmony prevail. A grand Continental league must be formed and a superintending Power also. When these necessary steps are taken and I see a Coalition formed sufficient to withstand the Power of Britain, or any other, then I am for an independent State and all its consequences, as then I think they will produce Happiness to America. It is a true saying of a Wit—We must hang together or separately." [3]

Congress had its stock jokes which improved with every telling, and hanging was the favorite theme of 1776. Ben Harrison, ponderous of humor as well as girth, chuckled that he had the advantage over pint-size Elbridge Gerry, who would suffer longer on a British gallows. Such exchanges of bravado were not without foundation. At this time the delegates had every reason to believe that they would be punished for treason if the rebellion failed. Already, as a foretaste of the wrath to come, the home of Josiah Bartlett, the New Hampshire physician, had been burned by Tories while he was serving in Congress. Before the war ended, more than half of the members were fated to have their property looted or destroyed. Others were to be imprisoned or driven into hiding by man hunts, and even their families would not escape persecution.

It took courage to debate independence at a moment when every delegate knew that Great Britain was sending the largest armada of her history to put down the rebellion. Yet there is no evidence that either the friends or the foes of the measure were much influenced by thoughts of personal peril. Just as Sam Adams defied the Tories to do their worst, John Dickinson did not flinch when the hatred of the Pennsylvania Whigs threatened him with disgrace if not violence.

It was a time for searching of hearts, and the answers were not always easy or apparent. Even Patrick Henry, whose radicalism was above suspicion, found his part not quite so simple as choosing between liberty and death. At the late date of May 7th the orator still had his doubts about independence, judging by these lines in a letter he received from General Charles Lee:

"The objection you made yesterday, if I understood you rightly, to an immediate declaration . . . is the only tolerable one that I have yet heard. You say, and with great justice, that we ought previously to have felt the pulse of *France* and *Spain*. I more than believe, I am almost confident that it has been done," declared Lee, who liked to hint that he knew all the secrets of the standing committees at Philadelphia.[4]

At least the pulse of America had been felt, and it did not beat so strongly for independence as the radicals of Congress might have wished. On the contrary, the delegates of six colonies—New York, New Jersey, Pennsylvania, Delaware, Maryland and South Carolina—were still under instructions in the early spring of 1776 to vote against separation.

Until the beginning of the year it had been possible for Americans of conflicting beliefs to dwell together in most communities without flying at one another's throats. The time had not yet come when a loyalist would be defined as "a thing whose head is in England, and its body in America, and its neck ought to be stretched."

The loyalists themselves were largely to blame for the sudden change in sentiment which caused them to be regarded as traitors rather than political opponents. Not until January 2nd and March 14th did Congress urge that they be disarmed, and both resolutions were passed as a result of Tory uprisings in which American blood was shed by Americans.

Up to this time the policy of the loyalists had been negative, if indeed it could be called a policy at all. The very conservatism which caused a man to uphold the existing order was likely to make him a passive opponent of revolt. He had only contempt in 1773 for the "noisy, blustering and bellowing patriots" who organized the revolution so effectively with their committees of correspondence. In 1774 he was still looking down his nose at the "pettyfogging lawyers, bankrupt shopkeepers and outlawed smugglers" of the Continental Congress. Even as late as 1775, when that assembly demonstrated that it could govern a people and direct a formidable war effort, few loyalists had progressed any further than empty denunciation.

If there had been more Tory leaders with the spunk of Joseph Galloway, who got himself elected to Congress in order to fight fire with fire, the story of the American Revolution might have had a different ending. It is even possible that the Pennsylvania lawyer might have won some measure of Washington's fame in the event of a British victory.

Certainly the loyalists did not lack courage or energy. They were willing, after it was too late, to make great personal sacrifices for the cause. It was snobbishness—plain, unvarnished snobbishness—which too often stultified their efforts. Since the last war a thriving commerce had been creating new British fortunes as fast as an indulgent monarch could create new titles and sinecures. The London of George III had become the center of a self-conscious plutocracy, lacking in tradition, lacking often in education and breeding, which supplied most of the governors and higher officials for the colonies. These appointments were prized by recent arrivals among the gentry and nobility, many of them making the awkward transition from a family background of trade. In some provincial capital, be it ever so petty, a royal governor could surround himself with his own retinue and live in princely style. Lord Botetourt made an overwhelming entry into Williamsburg in 1769 behind eight milk-white horses drawing a coach of state which had been presented to him by a brother of George III. His opening of the House of Burgesses was patterned after the ceremonial opening of Parliament by the king, and his entertainments reflected the glitter of court balls. Yet Botetourt was one of the best of the royal governors, respected by such Virginians as Jefferson and Washington. Most of the other governors believed that a colony, like a business enterprise, ought to show a profit. They gathered about them in every village capital a "herd of worthless parasites" who depended on their patronage—professional men, tradesmen, mechanics and servants as well as officeholders. These groups formed an American ruling class which became the backbone of the loyalist party in 1776.

It would be difficult to single out an "average loyalist" among the thousands of native Americans who upheld the king to the bitter end. There were brilliant, self-made men who had overcome poverty—John McAdam, inventor of the road-building process named after him; Benjamin Thompson, the scientist, better known as Count Rumford. There were true patricians, mellowed by time and tradition—William Byrd, the first gentleman of Virginia; Lord Halifax, proprietor of a vast estate. There were lackeys and hostlers, gentlemen and scholars, rascals and renegades. But if the loyalists of America had any one thing in common, it was the fatal conviction of superiority revealed by their writings. They candidly believed themselves to be a cut above the patriotic "rabble," despite a great deal of evidence to the contrary. And it was this delusion which ended in one of the most tragic chapters of history, comparable only to the expulsion of the Moors or the migration of the Huguenots—the exile of a hundred thousand heartsick Americans who left their own shores to begin a new life in Canada, England or the West Indies.

Abigail Adams saw the first of these refugees take their departure. On a

March day in 1776 she counted "upward of 170 sail" as the masts rose from Boston harbor "like a forest." These were the British vessels in which hundreds of Americans sailed away to Nova Scotia with their household goods—loyalists who believed, as one of them put it, that "neither Hell, Hull nor Halifax can afford any worse shelter than Boston." They remembered only too well the petty persecutions inflicted on the Whig residents when the British occupation seemed permanent. They could not forget that Old South Church had been turned into a stable, and Deacon Hubbard's pew used to build a pigsty. It had never occurred to them that Howe might be driven out by a ragtag rebel host, and the shock was terrible. Washington, who remained on friendly terms with several Tories throughout the war, had no pity for the Boston outcasts.

"One or two have done," he wrote, "what a great number ought to have done long ago, committed suicide."

In Virginia the influential Tory groups did little except frown and fume until the time passed for political resistance. Then they completed their own ruin by a premature resort to destruction and bloodshed. Lord Dunmore, the successor of Botetourt, made his name odious by arming a few bewildered slaves. On the first day of 1776, after taking refuge behind the guns of British warships, he bombarded Norfolk and applied the torch to water-front warehouses. The patriots retaliated by burning Tory dwellings, and as Virginia's largest town went up in flames the loyalist cause perished with it.

The following month North Carolina was lost to the Tories by another bootless uprising which culminated in the first civil war combat of the Revolution—the most important fight since Bunker Hill. Governor Josiah Martin conceived the idea of raising a force to unite with the British land and sea expedition being sent to the Carolinas under Sir Henry Clinton and Sir Peter Parker. The colony's strong loyalist faction included a settlement of Scottish Highlanders who had fought for Prince Charles Edward in "the Forty-Five" and found a refuge in the New World after their bloody defeat at Culloden. Although they had little love for the British royal family, the clansmen had still less for the rebels of North Carolina, many of whom were recent Lowland or Scotch-Irish immigrants. Besides, as Governor Martin pointedly reminded them, the Highlanders held their lands direct from the crown.

Twelve hundred strong, they marched to the screaming of the bagpipes, even though Admiral Parker's fleet had been delayed by storms. At Moore's Creek, when a thousand rebels under Colonel Richard Caswell barred the way on February 27th, the clansmen stormed across a narrow bridge with two-handed claymores, only to be cut down by the cool fire of Scotch-Irish woodsmen in hunting shirts. The action became another Culloden as the bright kilts of the slain filled the little stream, and hundreds of the survivors were taken prisoners in a well-timed counterattack.

Moore's Creek converted the colony to independence, just as the burning of Norfolk made the rebels supreme in Virginia. Not only had the North Carolina patriots won a decisive little victory; they proved that they knew how to use it politically. For their enemies might have profited from a study of the declaration issued by the provincial congress when the captive Highlanders were removed to other colonies for public safety:

> We have their security in contemplation, not to make them miserable. In our power, their errors claim our pity, their situation disarms our resentment. We shall hail their reformation with increasing pleasure, and receive them to us with open arms. . . . We war not with the helpless females which they left behind them; we sympathize in their sorrow. They are the rightful pensioners upon the charity and bounty of those who have aught to spare from their own necessities to the relief of their indigent fellow creatures; to such we recommend them.[5]

This proclamation, like most of the revolutionary documents, was obviously written with a view to propaganda values. But the clansmen actually were treated less as enemies than as erring brethren with political souls worth saving. Commissioners were appointed in six North Carolina counties to protect the property of the captives and see that their families did not want. Meanwhile their "reformation" was being earnestly sought not only by the North Carolina assembly but also the Continental Congress, which appropriated funds for the purpose. Missionaries of the rebel cause were sent to argue and plead with the beaten loyalists in the jails where they were confined; and though some of the elders could not be converted, Moore's Creek became a memorable victory of persuasion as well as arms.

Such episodes can only seem quaint and old-fashioned in the twentieth century, when trained German and Russian revolutionists have established an abattoir technique of torture, slavery and mass murder. These methods have even found apologists among present-day American observers—the beneficiaries of the only great revolution of history which managed from beginning to end to steer a middle course between anarchy and tyranny. The rebels of 1776 did not subscribe to the doctrine that terrorism is necessary and even desirable in the winning of great political reforms. They held that conversion could accomplish more in the long run than coercion, and it is worth repeating that the American Revolution achieved its main aims without the execution of a single man for his beliefs.

There were excesses, it is true, even though the worst examples of 1776 must seem mild in the present age. As the aggressors, the rebels were more often guilty during the early years than the loyalists, but violence on both sides was usually the result of passion rather than policy. At least the lawlessness stopped short of mass slaughter. Even the restrictions which most annoyed the loyalists were regarded as necessary wartime safeguards; and many Tory complaints of mob action had no justification except the fact that the rebel committees of safety were not sanctioned by the king.

The contest for independence in the Continental Congress had arrived at such a stalemate by the second quarter of 1776 that a bloody *coup d'état* might have been expected by anyone familiar with the repetitions of history. The hour would seem to have struck for the man on horseback, yet there is no evidence that any such ambition was ever cherished by an American of the day. On the contrary, Congress suffered from an obsession that another Cromwell might be hiding under some member's bed. The very name of the Lord Protector and his New Model was enough to arouse a shudder, and many blunders of the assembly can be charged to a fear of tyranny. The delegates did not even trust themselves with enough power to transact business with efficiency, preferring to limp along with the awkward system of standing committees.

In the fifth month of 1776 the struggle for independence reached the climax of an appeal to the people as the source of power. There was of course no possibility of holding a popular referendum, but Congress put the question squarely up to the provincial assemblies. Both the advocates and the opponents of immediate independence were confident of being upheld, and with "remarkable Unanimity" the resolution was adopted:

> That it be recommended to the various assemblies and conventions of the United Colonies, where no government sufficient to the exigencies of their affairs hath been hitherto established, to adopt such government as shall, in the opinion of the representatives of the people, best conduce to the happiness and safety of their constituents in particular, and America in general.[6]

At a glance this resolution seems to be more or less a repetition of those passed in November and December, when three colonies were advised to set an example by forming their own governments. On May 10th, however, the intention was to clear the way for a decision as to independence, and each of the opposing factions in Congress hoped to influence that verdict by the phrasing of the preamble.

Earlier in the week the radicals had won a minor victory when Washington asked for instructions in the event that British peace commissioners should land in Boston. On May 6th it was resolved "that Congress suppose, if commissioners are intended to be sent from Great Britain to treat of peace, that the practice usual in such cases will be observed, by making previous application for the necessary passports or safe conduct, and on such application being made, Congress will then direct the proper measures for the reception of such commissioners." [7]

This would not appear to be a controversial issue, but John Adams accused his opponents of an attempt to deceive the people and "turn their heads and thoughts from independence. They endeavored to insert in the resolution ideas of reconciliation; we carried our point for inserting peace. They wanted powers to be given to the General to receive the commissioners in ceremony; we ordered nothing to be done till we were solicited for passports. Upon the whole, we avoided the snare . . . but it will never be known how much labor it cost us to accomplish it." [8]

More travail awaited when the preamble to the resolution of May 10th was submitted. The debate raged for four days, with Duane and Wilson bearing the brunt of the opposition to Adams and Lee. Congress, said Duane, had no right to suggest that the colonies set up governments hostile to Great Britain. "Why all this haste?" he inquired; "why this urging? why this driving?" And Wilson asked the rhetorical question, "Before we are prepared to build the new house, why should we pull down the old one, and expose ourselves to the inclemencies of the season?"

On the 15th, after being hotly contested phrase by phrase, a preamble representing a radical victory was approved. It began with the customary recital of grievances against Great Britain, charging that

> the whole force of that kingdom, aided by foreign mercenaries, is to be exerted for the destruction of the good people of these colonies.
> And whereas, it appears absolutely irreconcilable to reason and good conscience, for the people of these colonies now to take the oaths and affirmations necessary for the support of any government under the crown of Great Britain, and it is necessary that the exercise of every kind of authority under the said crown should be totally suppressed, and all the powers of government exerted, under the authority of the people of the colonies, for the preservation of internal peace, virtue, and good order, as well as for the defense of their lives, liberties and properties, against the hostile invasions and cruel depredations of their enemies; therefore, resolved . . .[9]

This preamble struck Duane as "a machine for the fabrication of independence." John Adams replied with a smile that he "thought it was independence itself, but we must have it with more formality yet." [10]

The Massachusetts delegate termed it "the most important resolution that was ever taken in America" in a letter to James Warren. He wrote to Abigail that "Great Britain has at last driven America to the last step, a complete separation from her; a total absolute independence, not only of her Parliament, but of her crown, for such is the amount of the resolve of the 15th." [11]

The conservatives charged that King Congress was pushing the colonies into danger with tyrannical haste. As usual, however, the politicians of the assembly had a sensitive ear to the ground. Far from outdistancing popular opinion, Congress was now plodding a step or two behind. The preamble of May 15th, according to Braxton, passed by the narrow margin of six votes to four; and yet eight colonies had indicated by this date—half of them within the last few weeks—that they would join a majority in support of independence.

There had never for a moment been the slightest doubt about the four New England colonies. North Carolina needed only the Moore's Creek uprising as an incentive, and in April the provincial congress empowered the delegates at Philadelphia "to concur with the delegates of the other Colonies in declaring Independency and forming foreign alliances."

That same month the South Carolina assembly authorized its delegates to vote with the majority on any measure judged "necessary for the defence, security, or welfare of this colony in particular, and of America in general."

Before the end of April a new temporary constitution was adopted in Georgia. The following month Lyman Hall and Button Gwinnett, arriving to take their seats in Congress, brought a letter instructing the colony's delegates to exercise their own discretion in regard to independence.

This left only Virginia in the South, and since the burning of Norfolk that colony had been marching in the vanguard with Massachusetts. On the very day that saw the approval of the preamble, the Virginia convention voted unanimously that its delegates in Congress "be instructed to propose to that respectable body to declare the united Colonies free and independent States, absolved from all allegiance to, or dependence upon, the Crown or Parliament of Great Britain."

John Adams exulted in a letter of May 20th: "Every post and every Day rolls in upon Us, Independence like a Torrent. . . . Here are four colonies to the Southward who are perfectly agreed now with the four to the Northward. Five in the middle are not quite so ripe; but they are very near to it." [12]

His colleague Elbridge Gerry declared "that the eyes of every unbeliever are now open; that all are sensible of the perfidy of Great Britain, and are convinced that there is no medium between unqualified submission and actual independency. . . . A final declaration is approaching with great rapidity." [13]

Despite the optimism of the Massachusetts members, much spadework remained to be done in the southern as well as middle colonies before the dammed torrent of independence could flow freely. On the very day when Virginia advocated separation, the Maryland convention resolved without a dissenting vote:

> That as this Convention is firmly persuaded that a reunion with Great Britain on constitutional principles would most effectually secure the rights and liberties, and increase the strength and promote the happiness of the whole empire, objects which this Province has ever had in view, the said Deputies are bound and directed to govern themselves by the instructions given to them by this Convention in its session in December last. . . .

Nor were the delegates of the other four middle colonies at liberty to vote for separation at this time, whatever their personal convictions might be. Even among the radicals of Congress there was some difference of opinion. The New Englanders, generally speaking, left no doubt that they aspired to independence as an end in itself. Richard Henry Lee, for his part, regarded independence as a means toward the securing of foreign alliances. His colleague Thomas Jefferson, back in Congress after an absence of four and a half months, agreed that this prospect offered the only hope of importing essential supplies. But he feared that "several colonies, and some of them weighty, are not yet quite ripe."

In his old age John Adams recalled that the advocates of separation "could only now and then catch a transient glimpse of the promised land." These bright visions were obscured on May 18th by dark news from that region which Congress hoped would become the fourteenth state. "This day," Adams wrote to James Warren, "has brought us the Dismals from Canada— Defeated most ignominiously. Where shall we lay the blame?"

Any candid answer to this query would have indicated the door of the State House in Philadelphia. From first to last the invasion of Canada had been managed—or rather mismanaged—from the floor of Congress. A succinct summary of the consequences was contained in a letter written from the Onion River by one Colonel Wait:

> The Northern Army has been treated with the most cruel neglect or we might have been in possession of *Quebeck*. Sir, when I arrived here, I found Generals without men, and a small Artillery without supplies, and Commissaries without provisions, Paymasters without money, and Quartermasters without stores, and Physicians without medicine, and the small-pox very rife in our Army, which has been our destruction.[14]

After the repulse at Quebec the remnants of the battered little American force made a pretense of blockading the fortress. A smallpox epidemic became the last straw for discouraged troops who had endured a northern winter without adequate clothing or supplies. General Arnold left the army in April, and the following month the retreat might have been described as a rout.

The thirteen colonies themselves must soon prepare to resist a great British armada, and recent information had confirmed the rumors that German mercenaries would be employed. The British Ministry had first attempted to hire the Russian veterans who won Suvarov his first renown in bloody victories over the Turks. Catherine the Great refused bluntly, though she had no sympathy with Americans seeking to overthrow the sacred institution of monarchy. Finally the ministers of George III contracted for "German boars and vassals," as Burke scornfully put it. Altogether, during the course of the war, these mercenaries amounted to a total of 29,875 troops from six German principalities:

Anhalt-Zerbst, 1,160; Anspach-Bayreuth, 2,353; Brunswick, 5,723; Hesse-Cassel, 16,992; Hesse-Hanau, 2,492; Waldeck, 1,225.[15]

The Americans of 1776 were well aware that European nations thought nothing of hiring soldiers to supplement their own relatively small standing armies. At the outset of the last war England had even employed Germans for home defense until Pitt shamed his countrymen into volunteering. Still, the American Revolution up to this point had been strictly a family quarrel, not a foreign conflict. The idea of employing aliens to scourge one's own flesh and blood was repugnant to many Englishmen as well as Americans; and the propagandists of the Continental Congress made the best of an opportunity to shape world opinion.

England was particularly vulnerable at this time, having given the other European powers cause for jealousy and suspicion by her victories in the last war. The employment of German mercenaries might have been overlooked by nations tarred with the same brush; but there was also reason to suspect the British and Tories of preliminary efforts to arouse the Cherokees. And while it might be considered legitimate warfare to employ savages as auxiliaries under military discipline, a century of border strife had proved that Indians on the warpath could not be restrained from massacres of women and children.

A consistent policy of neutrality had been urged upon all tribes by the Continental Congress, even to the extent of appropriating funds for presents and bribes. Indian chiefs were brought to Philadelphia on several occasions for entertainment, and Joseph Hewes wrote to a friend on May 26th that "a deputation of the Six Nations . . . are to have an audience of Congress to-morrow, previous to which the city battallions are to be drawn out and reviewed by the Generals, in order to give these savages some idea of our strength and importance." [16]

The visiting redskins may have had similar ideas in mind, for Caesar Rodney noted three days later that "21 Indians of the Six Nations gave Congress a war dance yesterday."

Long experience had taught Americans that few Indians had any worth in civilized warfare save as scouts or woodsmen. But the menace of the tomahawk and scalping knife could terrorize the frontier, and hundreds of militiamen would be needed for defense. The Hessians, as all German mercenaries soon came to be called, represented a more formidable threat. Only thirteen years had passed since the victories which brought fame to Frederick the Great; and German troops trained according to his methods were reputed to be the world's best soldiers.

In an age of precise linear tactics, three to five years of intensive drill were held necessary to turn out a fit human instrument of battle. With all manufactures depending on hand labor, every item of a soldier's arms and equipment had an importance that is hard to realize in a day of mass production. The year 1776, in short, was one of the least propitious moments of history for rebels without armies and arsenals to challenge the world's greatest empire. The odds would have been stiff enough if the colonies had been threatened with the British army and navy alone, but the prospect of German hirelings in large numbers was dismaying.

Still, there was no flinching on the part of delegates who had every reason to believe that they were putting their heads in a noose. The financial problems had been discussed the first week in May, when Congress decided that ten million dollars would be needed for the current year. Half the amount was voted immediately, but it could hardly have been anticipated that the treasury would be as bare as Mother Hubbard's cupboard in a little more than two months.

The military problems came up for consideration the last week of the month, when Congress summoned General Washington to Philadelphia. A committee of fourteen members was appointed—two from Virginia and one from each of the other states—to confer with the commander and plan the strategy of the forthcoming campaign.

The news from Canada continued to be depressing; and Franklin, Chase and Carroll returned early in June from their mission with firsthand accounts of "shocking mismanagement." President Hancock reported to Washington that "our army in that quarter is almost ruined for Want of Discipline, and every Thing else necessary to constitute an Army, or to keep Troops together." [17]

The more candid members of Congress must have confessed to themselves that America's military resources of the first year had been largely frittered away in Canada—men, money and supplies needed so urgently in the spring of 1776 to defend the colonies themselves against the British invasion. There was not even the consolation that the northern campaign might serve as a diversion to draw off large enemy forces for the defense of Quebec. The American remnants were too weak even for this purpose; and it was already a probability that a second British invasion might be expected from the north before the end of the summer.

But Congress did not despair. The committee which conferred with Washington agreed that 6,000 militia must be sent as reinforcements to Canada while 13,000 were being raised for duty at New York. It was also decided to establish a flying camp of 10,000 militia, though Joseph Hewes appeared to have his doubts. In a letter he commented: "We resolve to raise regiments, resolve to make Cannon, resolve to make and import muskets, powder and cloathing, but it is a melancholly fact that near half of our men, Cannon, Muskets, powder, cloathes, etc., is to be found nowhere but on paper." Nevertheless, the North Carolina member was probably speaking for most of his fellow delegates when he added, "We are not discouraged at this; if our situation was ten times worse I could not agree to give up our cause."[18]

Chapter 11

From This Time Forward

O N the morning of June 7th, a tall, spare Virginian got to his feet to offer a resolution. It is a safe guess that a taut hush fell over Congress, for every delegate knew that the great issue was at last up for decision. The evening before, Sam Adams had written to Massachusetts that "tomorrow a Motion will be made, and a Question I hope decided, the most important that was ever agitated in America."

It was no secret why the radical faction had chosen Richard Henry Lee to present the resolution. Virginia had been boldest of all in demanding independence, and good political strategy made it desirable to have a Southerner as spokesman. Nobody had the confidence of the Yankee members to a greater extent than this wealthy planter, educated in England. As the closest friend of Sam Adams in Congress, he was accused by some of his constituents of representing Massachusetts rather than his own colony.

The resolution of the Virginia Convention on May 15th, calling for independence, had been tabled by general agreement until Congress could prepare to resist the British invasion. Inconsistent as it may seem, the members opposed to independence did not lag behind the warmest advocates when it came to approving warlike measures. Months before, when reminded that the American coastline was exposed to British naval attack, John Dickinson made the defiant reply which has been used as a quotation on the title page of this section: "Our towns may be destroyed, but they will grow again. We compare them not with our rights and liberties." [1]

Any prospect of commissioners being sent from England to offer acceptable terms had come to be regarded as a pipedream even by delegates who still hoped for an eleventh-hour compromise. They would doubtless have been astonished to know that on May 6th the king actually had placed his seal on the appointment of Lord Howe and his brother Sir William as

"Commissioners for restoring peace to his Majesty's Colonies and Plantations in North America, and for granting pardons to such of his Majesty's subjects there, now in rebellion, as shall deserve the Royal mercy."

The news of this boon, which reached America after independence had been declared, would have aided the king's cause immeasurably a few months earlier. But even if there had been no such delay, the friends of reconciliation might have deplored the appointment as peace commissioners of the admiral and general commanding the British expeditionary force. Such lapses in political tact caused Edmund Burke to declare that the ministers of George III "never had any kind of system, right or wrong; but only invented some miserable tale for the day, in order meanly to sneak out of difficulties into which they had proudly strutted." [2]

Unhappily for such great Englishmen as Burke and Pitt, most of the members of Congress were ready to agree with John Adams that "this story of commissioners is as arrant an illusion as ever was hatched in the brain of an enthusiast, a politician, or a maniac." Reports of British military preparations had reached America first, causing Richard Henry Lee to write on June 2nd to Landon Carter: "The infamous treaties with Hesse, Brunswick etc. of which we have authentic copies and the Ministerial reply to Graftons motion leaves not a doubt but that our enemies are determined upon the absolute conquest and subduction of N. America. *It is not choice then but necessity that calls for Independence, as the only means by which foreign Alliances can be obtained;* and a proper Confederation by which internal peace and union may be secured." [3]

This was the creed of the radicals of Congress on that Friday morning five days later when Lee offered his resolution:

> That these United Colonies are, and of right ought to be, free and independent States, that they are absolved from all allegiance to the British Crown, and that all political connection between them and the State of Great Britain is, and ought to be, totally dissolved.
>
> That it is expedient forthwith to take the most effectual measures for forming foreign Alliances.
>
> That a plan of confederation be prepared and transmitted to the respective Colonies for their consideration and approbation.

The fame won by the first of these three propositions has obscured the fact that Lee himself considered it a steppingstone to the other two. Even John Adams, whose eyes were fixed on independence with the fierce concentration of a fighter, wrote to Patrick Henry on June 3rd "that the natural course of things was this; for every colony to institute a government; for all the colonies to confederate, and define the limits of the continental Constitution; then to declare the colonies a sovereign state, or a number of confederated states; and last of all, to form treaties with foreign powers. But I fear we cannot proceed systematically," he added, "and that we shall be obliged to declare ourselves independent States, before we confederate, and indeed before all the colonies have established their governments." [4]

On June 7th the consideration of Lee's resolution was put off until the following morning. Congress then resolved itself into a committee of the whole and the two factions had it out, hammer and tongs, until seven that evening. A few hours later Ned Rutledge wrote to his friend John Jay (then surveying the political landscape in New York) a letter worth quoting at length for its presentation of the conservative viewpoint.

The South Carolina delegate reported that "the whole Argument was sustained on one side by R. Livingston, Wilson, Dickinson and myself, and by the power of all N. England, Virginia and Georgia at the other." He insisted that "the sensible part of the House opposed the Motion—they had no objection to forming a Scheme of a Treaty which they would send to France by proper Persons, and uniting this Continent by a Confederacy; they saw no Wisdom in a *Declaration* of Independence, nor any other Purpose to be enforced by it, but placing ourselves in the Power of those with whom we mean to treat, giving our Enemy notice of our Intentions before we had taken any steps to execute them and thereby enabling them to counteract us in our Intentions and rendering ourselves ridiculous in the Eyes of foreign powers by attempting to bring them into a Union with us before we had united with each other. For daily experience evinces that the Inhabitants of every Colony consider themselves at liberty to do as they please upon almost every occasion."

Young Rutledge concluded, not without prejudice, that "a Man must have the Impudence of a New Englander to propose in our present disjointed state any Treaty (honourable to us) to a Nation now at peace. No reason could be assigned for pressing us into this Measure, but the reason of every Madman, a shew of our spirit." [5]

On Monday, the 10th, when the question came up again in the committee of the whole, the conservatives felt that they had won a preliminary victory by passing a resolution to have the decision postponed until the first day of July. Their opponents, however, managed to include a provision that a committee be appointed to prepare a declaration of independence "in the mean while, that no time be lost, in case the Congress agree" to Lee's resolution. [6]

John Adams, Benjamin Franklin, Thomas Jefferson, Robert R. Livingston and Roger Sherman were elected next day to the committee for drawing up a document which might never be approved. Adams was not fond of playing second fiddle, and in a letter of 1822 he claimed the credit for

Jefferson's nomination as author. The Virginia member had been absent most of the year from Congress; and it could not be forgotten that his last attempt at writing a political address (the Declaration on Taking Arms of July, 1775) had been so weak that Congress turned the job over to Dickinson. According to Adams, he pointed out his own unworthiness to draft the Declaration of Independence as compared to Jefferson. "I am obnoxious, suspected, and unpopular. You are very much otherwise." As a clinching argument, Adams recalled that he said, "You can write ten times better than I can.." [7]

Such an outburst of unwonted modesty would be enough to hint that Adams' memory had tricked him nearly half a century later. There is better evidence that Jefferson was chosen as a result of a political deal made "out of doors." In fact, Adams himself recorded in his *Autobiography* that "Jefferson was chairman, because he had most votes; and he had most votes because we united in him to the exclusion of R. H. Lee, and to keep out Harrison." [8]

Virginia had to be represented on the committee; but Lee was distrusted because he had been too thick with Sam Adams, while both Harrison and Braxton were considered reactionaries. Jefferson seemed a safe even if unexciting choice—a retiring member, silent in debate, who had a scholarly reputation in Congress. Among the other traits which stamped him as being just a little odd, this bookworm liked to be alone in an age which did not esteem privacy. For 35 shillings a week—twice as much rent as a majority of the delegates paid—he had a suite in the new brick home of a young German bricklayer named Graaf. The house itself, one of a scattered few on the south side of Market Street between Seventh and Eighth, seemed to have withdrawn for privacy. There in his second-floor parlor, with a bedroom adjoining, the tall, redheaded Virginian composed the Declaration of Independence while taking his meals at a tavern where he shared a table with several colleagues.

After the debate of June 10th there is no mention of independence in the pages of the *Journals* for three weeks. Even the private letters of members do not refer to it as often as might be supposed. On the 12th, however, two closely related projects, regarded by some delegates as being more important to America's future, were given an impetus by the resolutions:

> That the committee to prepare and digest the form of a confederation, to be entered into between these Colonies, consist of a member from each Colony. The members appointed, Mr. Bartlett, Mr. S. Adams, Mr. Hopkins, Mr. Sherman, Mr. R. R. Livingston, Mr. Dickinson, Mr. McKean, Mr. Stone, Mr. Nelson, Mr. Hewes, Mr. E. Rutledge and Mr. Gwinnett.
> That the committee to prepare a plan of treaties to be proposed to foreign

powers consist of five. The members chosen, Mr. Dickinson, Mr. Franklin, Mr. J. Adams, Mr. Harrison and Mr. R. Morris.[9]

On this same busy Wednesday the assembly prescribed strong medicine for military ills, as revealed by the Canadian campaign, when it was resolved "that a committee of Congress be appointed, by the name of a board of war and ordnance, to consist of five members. . . ." John Adams, Edward Rutledge, Sherman, Harrison and Wilson were chosen, being authorized to hire a secretary and clerk.

This was one of the most ambitious attempts to delegate authority to committees of members, though experience had already taught the faults of such a system. Robert Morris, the Philadelphia merchant who had recently taken his seat, was enough of a businessman to perceive that Congress must eventually employ responsible specialists as the heads of departments. Meanwhile, throughout the next critical year, the Board of War and Ordnance can at least be credited with becoming one of the busiest and most energetic of the standing committees.

The news from Canada had been so grievous that Congress, in the manner of all legislatures, sought a scapegoat. The most logical victim was General David Wooster, whose recall in disgrace offered the further advantage of being a slap at the New England members. The 62-year-old Connecticut veteran, a hero of the last war, was cleared two months later of charges of incompetency and timidity. It came as a further reproach to Congress the following year when Wooster was killed in action at the head of his troops.

So far the assembly had tied the hands of every general in Canada, but on June 17th there seems to have been a change of policy. Horatio Gates was appointed to that thankless command with "the powers of a Roman dictator," as Chase phrased it in a letter. John Adams wrote to Gates in a similar tone: "We have ordered you to the Post of Honour, and made you Dictator in Canada for Six Months, or at least untill the first of October." Here the Braintree lawyer may have felt that he was being reckless, for he ended on a grimly playful note: "We don't choose to trust you Generals with too much Power, for too long Time." [10]

A glance at the resolution itself does not reveal that Congress had gone any further than relinquishing a few of the powers it had been unwisely trying to retain at long distance. Gates, far from being created into a dictator, was merely given the authority to appoint or fire his own subordinates without the meddling of legislators.

Naval affairs should have put Congress in a better mood, for the newly created little fleet won a triumph that week which remains one of the few humorous episodes in the chronicles of war. Sir William Howe's departure

from Boston had been so hasty that three British transports bringing the
71st Regiment of Highlanders were not warned. They reached the Massachusetts port after a long voyage only to be captured with all on board by
Captain Nicholas Biddle of the *Andrea Doria* and Captain Seth Harding of
the *Defence.*

Luck had favored the rebel cause, but Congress promptly demonstrated
that it knew how to use such fabulous good fortune. The six hundred kilted
warriors were divided among several colonies with a view to indoctrinating
the captives. In a letter of June 29th Richard Henry Lee commented that
"'the 217 that have fallen to our share are distributed thro' this Colony, a
few in each County, and permitted to hire themselves out to labour, thus
to become the Citizens of America instead of its enemies." [11]

In the same evangelical spirit Congress cast its net for the political souls
of the German hirelings before they ever reached these shores. The very
day that copies of the treaties were received, a committee of five was
appointed "to prepare an address to the foreign mercenaries who are coming
to invade America."

It seems a sharp departure from the wise statecraft of such measures to
one of those long-drawn sectional feuds in which the petty spite of the
motives only added to the fury. This squabble began on June 14th, when
President Hancock summoned Commodore Esek Hopkins to Philadelphia
for questioning:

> Notwithstanding the repeated Efforts and Solicitations of the Marine Board
> to put the Continental Ships upon a respectable Footing, and to have them
> employed in the Service for which they were originally designed, they are
> constrained to say that their Efforts and Solicitations have been frustrated
> and neglected in a Manner unaccountable to them; and in Support of their
> own Reputation they have been under the Necessity of representing the State
> of their Navy or Congress, and have informed them that there has been a
> great Neglect in the Execution of their Orders. . . .[12]

Of course, it was the right and duty of Congress to inquire into derelictions
of duty. But there is good evidence to support the charge of the New
England members that Hopkins was being pilloried rather than investigated.
John Adams, no man to pardon military inefficiency, concluded after the
hearing before the marine committee in August that the Rhode Island officer
"had done a great service and made an important beginning of naval operations. . . . It appeared to me that the Commodore was pursued and persecuted by that anti-New-England spirit which haunted Congress in many
other of their proceedings. . . . I saw nothing in the conduct of Hopkins
which indicated corruption or want of integrity." [13]

It is needless to add that the New England members were fully capable of holding their own or taking the aggressive in these disputes. The Hopkins affair dragged on for another year before the assembly dismissed him. But it was seldom throughout the proceedings of the Continental Congress that a similar quarrel was not being waged by bitter cliques. For factionalism might be described as an age-old occupational disease of all parliaments—a penalty that must be paid, as long as men are not divine, for the decencies of representative government.

During these three weeks when Congress seemed to have forgotten independence, the issue was never more alive. In fact, it was largely decided in the State House yard before ever coming up for formal debate on the first day of July.

Both sides realized that the ultimate decision lay with the colonies themselves. Hence the opponents of independence in Congress were striving for a negative victory with all the delaying tactics at their command. Dickinson and his supporters, according to Jefferson, argued that the middle colonies "had not yet accommodated their minds to a separation from the mother country." But it was conceded "that they were fast ripening, and, in a short time, would join in the general voice of America." When that hour struck, the conservatives of Congress intimated that they too would be ready for independence.

The advocates, reported Jefferson, made a great deal of the admitted fact "that no gentleman had argued against the right of separation from Great Britain, nor had supposed it possible we should ever renew our connection; but they had only opposed its being now declared." And since the two factions of Congress differed only as to *when* a declaration should come, Adams and Lee and Wythe urged that "we should declare a fact which already exists. . . . That it would be vain to wait either weeks or months for perfect unanimity, since it was impossible that all men should ever become of one sentiment on any question. . . . That a declaration of Independence alone could render it consistent with European delicacy, for European powers to treat with us. . . . That it is necessary to lose no time in opening a trade for our people." [14]

Such premises, set down at length by Jefferson in his *Autobiography* from notes made at the time, were the window dressing of the contest. But both sides knew very well that the issue would actually be decided by the give-and-take of practical politics. Not theories but hard political facts would be the weapons of the fight behind the scenes.

In June, 1776, it might truthfully have been said, "As Pennsylvania goes, so goes the nation." Without concerning themselves too much about ethics, the delegates of other colonies did not hesitate to dabble in the troubled waters of Pennsylvania politics. "Since my first arrival in this city," confessed Elbridge Gerry in a letter to James Warren, "the New England delegates have been in a continual war with the advocates of proprietary interest in Congress and this Colony. . . ."[15]

The result was a revolution within a revolution which at times boiled up almost to the point of violence. Sam Adams, an old hand at this sort of thing, was accused of trying to incite riots in Philadelphia. Greater results were accomplished for the radical cause by the influence of Dr. Franklin, then recuperating at his home from the Canadian mission.

For many years the colony had been the preserve of a compact governing class made up of proprietary, Quaker and German interests. The large Scotch-Irish population, solid for the rebel cause, had virtually no representation in a legislature which also took a dim view of the city workmen and petty tradesmen. On June 8th the Assembly, meeting in its own room of the State House, made a first concession. New instructions were adopted which wiped out the restrictions against the delegates in Congress voting for independence, though still not authorizing them to take such a step.

If the legislators fancied that they had found a safe position by straddling the fence, they were speedily disillusioned. The Pennsylvania radicals called a mass meeting and set up a revolutionary body of their own, known as the Provincial Conference, which seized control of the colonial government with the claim of representing the will of the people. On June 24th this Conference unanimously passed a declaration urging the delegates in Congress to concur with other colonies in voting for independence. Meanwhile the old Assembly was being virtually superseded as the county committees demanded a constitutional convention in July.

Delaware, the tail of the Pennsylvania kite, lost no time at passing similar instructions for its delegates in Congress. The House of Assembly also set aside the royal authority in a measure aiming toward establishing a colonial authority.

On June 15th the Provincial Congress of New Jersey ordered the arrest of William Franklin, the royal governor. Dr. Franklin had long ago given up any hope of converting his illegitimate son to his own political views. At the age of 45 William Franklin shared the leadership of the loyalist cause with Galloway, and after two years of confinement in rebel jails he became an exile in England. The long estrangement between father and son lasted until 1784, when they were reconciled to the extent of exchanging letters.

The New Jersey legislators did more than authorize their delegates in Congress to vote for independence; they made certain on June 21st by appointing new men whose radical views could not be doubted—Abraham Clark, John Hart, Richard Stockton, Francis Hopkinson and Dr. John Witherspoon.

New York's delegates at Philadelphia were anxiously awaiting instructions from home, having sent an express early in the month. This left among the middle colonies only Maryland, which already had a reputation as the most perverse of the thirteen wayward sisters—"so eccentric a Colony," grumbled John Adams, "sometimes so hot, sometimes so cold, now so high, then so low, that I know not what to say about it or to expect from it. I have often wished it could exchange places with Hallifax. When they get agoing I expect some wild extravagant Flight or other from it."

It was a scandal to prim patriots that Maryland could flirt so archly with the rebel cause before she divorced the royal governor, Sir Robert Eden. But the American Revolution might never have occurred in the first place if other British officeholders had been as able as this last representative of the crown in America. Liked by Whigs as well as Tories, he was permitted to remain until the very eve of the Declaration and sail for England in an atmosphere of mutual regrets.

The winning of Maryland to independence can still teach a lesson in applied politics. Samuel Chase and Charles Carroll of Carrollton, after their return from Canada, got down to the grassroots and rolled up a popular majority which overcame Tory wealth and influence. "I have appealed in *writing* to the people," Chase reported to John Adams in a letter of June 21st. "County after county is instructing." A week later, barely two days before the issue came up in Congress, the burly Annapolis lawyer sent a message of victory: "Fryday Evening at 9 o'Clock. I am this Moment from the House to procure an Express to follow the Post with an Unan: Vote of our Convention for Independence etc. etc.—see the glorious effects of County Instructions—our people have fire if not smothered." [16]

Feeling ran high these days in many communities of the middle colonies. Tories were coming to be regarded less as political opponents and more as incipient traitors who had sacrificed any claim to the protection of rights and property. Yet there was astonishingly little disorder; and it is a glorious page in the annals of the Continental Congress which records the appeal of June 18th, calling for law-abiding moderation at the very peak of the crisis:

> *Resolved,* That no man in these colonies, charged with being a tory, or unfriendly to the cause of American liberty, be injured in his person or his property, or in any manner whatever disturbed, unless the proceeding against him be founded on an order of this Congress, or the Assembly, convention, council or committee of safety of the colony, or committee of inspection and observation, of the district wherein he resides; provided, that this resolution

shall not prevent the apprehending of any person found in the commission of some act destructive of American liberty, or justly suspected of a design to commit such act, and intending to escape, and bringing such person before proper authorities for examination and trial.[17]

This resolution, ordered to be published in the *Pennsylvania Gazette* the next day, is worthy of being regarded as one of the memorable decisions of the Continental Congress. For the delegates who passed the measure knew that Tories were already arming here and there with a view to aiding the invaders of America.

When the debate opened on Monday, July 1st, both sides took it for granted that the question had been pretty well decided in advance. Maryland's resolution arrived that very morning; and the four New England colonies, never for an instant in doubt, had signified their approval of independence. The New York members, still awaiting instructions from a new convention called in that province, indicated that they would vote neither aye nor no. This neutral stand left twelve colonies to be claimed by the advocates of separation, who were due for a shock when the question came up for decision.

Oratory was held in low esteem by the gentlemen in cocked hats and white silk stockings who gathered that hot summer morning at the State House. Most of them agreed with John Adams that "eloquence in public assemblies is not the surest road to fame or preferment, at least, unless it be used with caution, very rarely, and with great reserve. The examples of Washington, Franklin, and Jefferson, are enough to show that silence and reserve in public, are more efficacious than argumentation or oratory. . . . Few persons can bear to be outdone in reasoning or declamation or wit or sarcasm or repartee or satire, and all these things are very apt to grow out of public debate. In this way, in a course of years, a nation becomes full of a man's enemies, or at least, of such as have been galled in some controversy, and take a secret pleasure in assisting to humble and mortify him." [18]

The floor leaders of the two factions addressed Congress on July 1st in the manner of lawyers summing up the cases for the prosecution and defense. Adams conceded in his *Autobiography* that John Dickinson, as befitted the master of Fairhill with its green acres and fine private library, was a worthy opponent:

"He had prepared himself apparently with great labor and ardent zeal, and in a speech of great length, and with all his eloquence, he combined together all that had before been written in pamphlets and newspapers, and all that had from time to time been said in Congress by himself and others.

He conducted the debate not only with great ingenuity and eloquence, but with equal politeness and candor, and was answered in the same spirit." [19]

Aggressiveness was John Adams' forte. The Massachusetts gamecock believed so wholeheartedly in his cause that he could not find enough superlatives in praise. "Objects of the most stupendous magnitude, and measures in which the lives and liberties of millions yet unborn are intimately interested," he had recently written to William Cushing, "are now before us. We are in the very midst of a revolution, the most complete, unexpected, and remarkable, of any in the history of nations."

By all accounts the debate of July 1st lasted the entire day. Adams had finished his speech in reply to Dickinson when the recently elected delegates from New Jersey entered. Hopkinson, Stockton and Dr. Witherspoon asked that the arguments be repeated, and after a show of reluctance the radical spokesman covered the ground again "till at length the Jersey gentlemen said they were fully satisfied and ready for the question."

As early as nine o'clock a thermometer just purchased by Thomas Jefferson registered 81½ degrees, and most of the delegates must have grown drowsy when not stung into irritability by the horseflies coming through the open windows. The speeches could hardly have made them forget the heat, for Adams admitted that evening in a disgruntled letter to Samuel Chase that "nothing was said but what had been repeated and hackneyed in that room before a hundred times for six months past."

Probably the vote brought the only surprise of the day. For it seems to have been an unexpected blow to the radical faction when Pennsylvania and South Carolina decided in the negative, while Delaware's two votes canceled each other.

The delegates from these colonies had interpreted their instructions to mean that they were free to record individual convictions. Edward Rutledge asked that the final determination be put off until the next day, and the radicals took encouragement from his hint that the South Carolina members might then concur for the sake of unanimity. Thomas McKean had meanwhile sent an express to summon his colleague Caesar Rodney, hoping that the two of them could swing Delaware to the affirmative side in spite of George Read's stubborn negative.

Accounts as to what took place on the 2nd and 4th of July are meager when not confused and contradictory. This is not surprising when it is considered that the main actors of the drama waited until the next century before ransacking their memories. Only a few of the participants were left alive by that time, and historians have had to depend largely on the recollections of Adams, McKean and Jefferson.

At least it seems certain that Congress formed itself again into a committee of the whole on Tuesday, and this time independence passed "without one dissenting vote," according to both John Adams and Henry Wisner. They meant, of course, that twelve of the colonies had declared in the affirmative, for New York was still holding aloof until the new convention sent instructions.

The express found Caesar Rodney in southern Delaware, where he had led his militiamen against a rumored Tory uprising. After an all-night gallop through thundershowers he reached the State House in good time. Still booted and spurred and mud spattered, wearing a green silk handkerchief tied about his face to hide the painful growth which was slowly killing him, the lanky farmer cast the vote which placed Delaware in the affirmative column.

On Monday, according to McKean's recollection, Morton, Wilson and Dr. Franklin voted aye for Pennsylvania, while Dickinson, Morris, Willing and Humphreys were opposed. The next day Dickinson and Morris reversed the verdict by voluntarily absenting themselves in preference to endorsing what they conceived to be a premature declaration. South Carolina, as Ned Rutledge had intimated, then agreed to make it a unanimous vote of the twelve colonies.

The author of America's most famous state document recalled in later life that he finished the first draft in two days and showed it to Adams and Franklin for their suggestions. Fifteen changes were made, most of them by Jefferson himself, before he submitted the Declaration of Independence to the committee of the whole on June 28th.

The sensitive and self-conscious author must have suffered pangs of anxiety during the next few days while his composition lay upon the table for the inspection of such unsympathetic critics as Dickinson, Morris and Rutledge. But the 34-year-old Virginia member did not lack for other interests during this period of waiting. Thrice daily he set down temperature readings from his new thermometer, and in an account book he kept a record of such purchases as the following:

pd for a comb	5/
pd for window shutter rings	25/2
pd dinner at Smith's	5/
pd for a straw hat	10/
pd Sparhawk for a pencil	1/6

Jefferson's ordeal began on July 3rd, when the committee of the whole was free to concentrate on the Declaration of Independence. He had learned from his rejected address in 1775 that the delegates could be stern editors; and on Wednesday and Thursday they made many minor changes in phraseology, while throwing out two long passages. As his production was being assailed, none too tactfully sometimes, Jefferson could only listen in an agony of silent embarrassment until Dr. Franklin took pity on him and told a comforting anecdote.

It was John Adams who fought tooth and nail for the document, leaping to his feet and defending every paragraph as if it were a redoubt to be held to the death. In his gratitude Jefferson never forgot that his tougher colleague was "the Colossus of the debate." Perhaps both of them were to recall this occasion as the last memory of their lives when they died on July 4, 1826, the fiftieth anniversary of independence.

From the viewpoint of the Continental Congress the document was strictly a polemic tract to be judged for its probable effect in justifying the American position to the rest of the world. The very first sentence made it plain that the creators of a new nation were resting their case on natural law—"the laws of Nature and of Nature's God"—as interpreted in the next paragraph:

> We hold these truths to be self-evident; that all men are created equal; that they are endowed by their creator with *inherent and* inalienable rights; that among these are life, liberty and the pursuit of happiness; that to secure these rights, governments are instituted among men, deriving their just powers from the consent of the governed; that whenever any form of government becomes destructive of these ends, it is the right of the people to alter or abolish it, and to institute new government . . .

From beginning to end the committee of the whole did not hesitate either to delete or to substitute. Thus in the above passage the two italicized words of Jefferson's version were rejected and the word *certain* inserted. In most instances the critics of Congress deserve praise for improving the document; and by killing the following accusation they saved the Declaration from a descent into the ridiculous:

> He [George III] has waged cruel war against human nature itself, violating its most sacred rights of life and liberty in the persons of a distant people who never offended him, captivating and carrying them into slavery in another hemisphere, or to incur miserable death in their transportation thither. This piratical warfare, the opprobrium of infidel powers, is the warfare of the Christian King of Great Britain. Determined to keep open a market where men should be bought and sold, he has prostituted his negative for suppressing every legislative attempt to prohibit or to restrain this execrable commerce. And that his assemblage of horrors might want no fact of distinguished die, he is now exciting those very people to rise in arms among us,

and to purchase that liberty of which he has deprived them, by murdering the people on whom he also obtruded them; thus paying off former crimes committed against the liberties of one people with crimes which he urges them to commit against the lives of another.

Jefferson was not at his most brilliant in this contention, and Congress wisely decided that Americans had better not venture out of their glass houses to throw stones at a monarch whose responsibility for slavery was somewhat less than their own. Another major operation was performed by the delegates with good effect on a long paragraph denouncing the English people, but even in his old age the author resented both excisions: "The pusillanimous idea that we had friends in England worth keeping terms with, still haunted the minds of many. For this reason, those passages which conveyed censures to the people of England were struck out, lest they should give them offence. The clause, too, reprobating the enslaving of the inhabitants of Africa was struck out in complaisance to South Carolina and Georgia. . . ." [20]

Jefferson could be permitted his prejudices, for the Declaration remains one of the most stirring and magnificent messages of all time, a tribute to the good sense of its editors as well as the creative genius of its author. As an essay in political economy, of course, it is not always a model of pure logic. The assault on George III was conducted with more vigor than justice, especially when it is considered that Americans had spared that monarch from any censure until the past six months. Parliament was never mentioned once in the Declaration, though for years the rebels had shrieked to high heaven against such tyrannies as taxation without representation. Now that they were severing themselves from the Empire, however, the Declaration soared above Parliament and other earth-bound institutions by appealing for justification to the rights of man according to natural law.

Jefferson believed that the adoption in Congress on July 4th was speeded by the plague of horseflies which had the delegates slapping at their silk-stockinged legs. At any rate, the amended Declaration came up for a vote late Thursday afternoon and won the approval of twelve colonies, with New York again remaining silent.

Congress also found opportunity on that historic day to pass seven other resolutions ranging from the significant to the trivial. The new nation was named for the first time in the *Journals* when Adams, Franklin and Jefferson were elected to a committee "to bring in a device for a seal of the United States of America." But the legislative mills continued to grind out some of the usual petty business, and a final resolution instructed the Secret Committee "to sell 25 lb. of powder to John Garrison, of North Carolina." [21]

It does not seem to be altogether a coincidence that so few delegates mentioned the Declaration with any show of excitement in their letters. The fact is that Independence Day matured rather gradually as an institution; and of all the participants only John Adams had the reporter's instinct to catch a glimpse of the occasion as posterity would see it. On the morning of July 3rd he snatched time to dash off an exuberant note to his wife: "Yesterday, the greatest question was decided, which ever was decided in America, and a greater, perhaps, never was nor will be decided among men."

Enthusiastic as this appraisal was, Adams must have concluded that he had not gone far enough. That same evening he wrote again to Abigail, and except for the date his letter was prophecy:

"The second day of July, 1776, will be the most memorable epocha in the history of America. I am apt to believe that it will be celebrated by succeeding generations as the great anniversary Festival. It ought to be commemorated, as the day of deliverance, by solemn acts of devotion to God Almighty. It ought to be solemnized with bonfires and illuminations, from one end of this continent to the other, from this time forward, forevermore." [22]

PART THREE

Alliance

It is not easy to be wise for all times, not even for the present — much less for the future; and those who judge of the past, must recollect that, when it was the present, the present was the future.

— GOUVERNEUR MORRIS

Chapter 12

Embarrassment of Riches

THE ghost of Guy Fawkes haunted the State House the Monday after independence was declared. In a letter of July 8th Joseph Hewes informed a friend that "a paper has been privately laid upon Congress Table importing that some dark designs were formed for our destruction, and advising us to take care of ourselves. some were for examining the Cellars under the Room where we set. I was against it and urged that we ought to treat such information with Contempt and not show any marks of fear or Jealousy." [1]

The North Carolina member added that "no notice has been taken of this piece of information which I think is right." But if nothing came of the gunpowder plot, a group of loyalists actually did conspire at a later date to seize delegates wholesale in a raid. The marvel is that no such attempt was ever made. Throughout the war the State House was seldom adequately guarded, and in an age of creeping communication the capture of Congress would have created a political vacuum lasting for months before enough men could be elected to form a new government.

By this time it should have been obvious even to the British and loyalists that the rapid acceleration of the rebellion had been largely due to the Continental Congress. The personal leadership of George Washington had not become a major factor at this date, yet in less than two years the New World parliament of village lawyers, merchants and planters had created a nation. Summing up this achievement, the historian Van Tyne has written that "uncertain as was its authority, lacking any formal grant of jurisdiction or power to govern, Congress was soon carried by the tide of the revolutionary sea on which it was afloat to the utmost bounds of sovereign power. An army, a navy, a treasury arose like magic palaces as Congress rubbed the political lamp." [2]

After the Declaration of Independence crossed the ocean, it is understandable that loyal subjects of George III should have bellowed with rage at the seeming inconsistencies of the American position. But at least one English critic realized that the rebels had been only too consistent and unswerving from the beginning. The pamphleteer John Lind, in *An Answer to the Declaration*, solemnly concluded that "had an angel descended from Heaven with terms of accommodation, which offered less than independence, they would have driven him back with hostile scorn."

This was the work of the upstart revolutionary body, elected in 1774 to petition humbly for redress, which led the colonies all the way to a separate national existence in 1776.

The assembly reached the peak of its power and influence in the summer of the Declaration—a heyday to be recalled with nostalgia by delegates of the next thirteen troubled years. Everywhere the members of the Continental Congress were accorded a degree of voluntary homage that a monarch might have envied. On a journey that autumn John Adams was touched when a poor family refused to accept money for the food that a congressman ate. Almost equally flattering was the fear and hatred expressed by the Tories, who credited the assembly with enough malevolent power to compel an unwilling people to take the plunge into sedition.

This delusion represented a swing in the opposite direction from the wishful thinking of 1775, when so many Tories were still trying to convince themselves of congressional impotence. The truth was that the practical politicians of the State House seldom ventured a pace in advance of the public, though exerting all their talents as propagandists to make sure that public sentiment did not lag or lose step.

No better test could have been had than the reception of the news that independence had been declared. The first celebration took place at Philadelphia on July 8th, after the Declaration was read to an enormous crowd in the State House yard. "Three cheers rended the welkin," John Adams wrote to Chase the next day. "The battalions paraded on the Common and gave us the feu de joie, notwithstanding the scarcity of powder. The bells rang all day and almost all night." [3]

A great "illumination" was held at Princeton, for nothing could give more joy than bonfires and gleaming windows in an age of economized candles. A boisterous crowd at New York toppled over the leaden statue of King George, which was later melted down into bullets to be fired at that monarch's troops. Thirteen volleys were heard in towns which could spare the gunpowder, and there was always enough Madeira to drink thirteen toasts. Only the hackneyed simile of the ripples in the pond could have described the spread of the news, with the last of the celebrations being held as late as September in remote frontier settlements of Georgia.

Congress had not erred in supposing America to be emotionally ripe for independence. The thirteenth colony gave its assent on July 9th, when the New York Convention upheld the Declaration with a resolution that "we approve the same, and will, at the risque of our lives and fortunes, join with the other colonies in supporting it." The express reached Philadelphia six days later, and on the 19th the document was accurately as well as officially entitled "The Unanimous Declaration of the Thirteen United States of America."

There were still dissenters, even in Congress. John Alsop proved not to be entirely a "soft, sweet man" when he wrote to the New York Convention on the 16th that the Declaration was "against my judgment or inclination. As long as a door was left open for a reconciliation with Great Britain upon just and honorable terms, I was willing and ready to render my country all the service in my power . . . but as you have, I presume, by that declaration, closed the door of reconciliation, I must beg leave to resign my seat as a delegate from New York. . . ." [4]

Although Robert Morris signed the Declaration, he insisted months later that it had come prematurely. The defeat meant heartbreak for John Dickinson, who failed of re-election as a delegate. The Pennsylvania patriot took command of a brigade of militia in New Jersey, and on August 7th he wrote to his friend Charles Thomson: "The enemy are moving, and an attack on New York is quickly expected. As for myself, I can form no idea of a more noble fate than . . . to resign my life, if Divine Providence should please so to dispose of me, for the defence and happiness of those unkind countrymen whom I cannot forbear to esteem as fellow-citizens amidst their fury against me." [5]

Gentlemen of that day, most of whom were tough at core, prided themselves on a "sensibility" which made the most of every emotion, including self-pity. John Adams declared that a few months before the Declaration he was shunned "like a man infected with the leprosy. I walked the streets of Philadelphia in solitude, borne down by the weight of care and unpopularity." And now that it was the turn of his opponents in Congress, he could even shed a tear for them when he wrote to Abigail on July 10th:

> Dickinson, Morris, Alsop, all fallen, like grass before the scythe, notwithstanding all their vast advantages in point of fortune, family and abilities. I am inclined to think, however, and to wish, that these gentlemen may be restored at a fresh election, because, although mistaken in some points, they are good characters, and their great wealth and numerous connections will contribute to strengthen America and cement her union.[6]

This mood of poetic melancholy might have been spoiled if he could have guessed that his fallen enemy Dickinson would rise to win new triumphs in Congress. It might even have been disturbing if Adams had foreseen that the conservative of 1776 would live to oppose him as the elderly liberal of 1804, campaigning for the second term of Jefferson as president. Farmer Dickinson was not as fragile as some people supposed.

Not only Robert Morris but also such last-ditch opponents as George Read, Carter Braxton and Ned Rutledge affixed their signatures to the Declaration on August 2nd. The legend that the founding fathers signed on July 4th, often as it has been denied, will probably never be quite vanquished. The *Journals* are somewhat to blame for this fiction. For the text was published under the date of July 4th with the explanation, "The foregoing declaration was, by order of Congress, engrossed, and signed by the following members . . ."

John Trumbull's well-known painting, *The Signing of the Declaration of Independence*, an attraction for generations of tourists visiting the national Capitol, has innocently done its part to fix the error in the American consciousness. But most of the responsibility must be borne by Adams and Jefferson, whose memories betrayed them in their old age.

Both stubbornly insisted nearly half a century later that the document had been signed on that first Independence Day. There is a sufficiency of evidence, however, to prove that no names were attached until August 2nd, after the Declaration had been engrossed on parchment. Several of the immortal fifty-six did not take their seats until after July 4th; and Matthew Thornton of New Hampshire could not have signed before November 4th, his first day in Congress.

In excuse of Adams and Jefferson, it would appear that the signers themselves did not regard the event as a towering landmark at the time. Few of them mentioned the happenings of July 4th or August 2nd in letters that have survived. Apparently they did not dream that posterity would elevate them on a pedestal above the rest of the 342 men who served from first to last in the Continental Congress.

Then, as now, it was plain that some of the worthiest members of the assembly were prevented by circumstances from becoming signers—soldiers in the field, such as Washington and Sullivan; fiery radicals serving their own states, such as Gadsden and Patrick Henry; youthful patriots born a few years too late, such as Madison, Hamilton and Monroe. It was equally obvious, on the other hand, that the men who took their seats after July 4th had become signers of a document to which they contributed little or nothing. In comparison, John Dickinson was more deserving of honor, even though he declined a shrine among the immortals.

The secrecy which attended the signing may also account to some extent for confused recollections. At this historical distance it is hard for citizens of the world's most powerful republic to realize that the founding fathers actually were committing an act of treason when they scrawled their names. Their chances of escaping a British gallows, of course, depended on the fortunes of a war waged against heavy material odds. But in the summer of 1776 it was not prudent for signers to shout from the housetops; and their names were held as a secret record until January 18, 1777, immediately following the news of the stirring victories won by Washington at Trenton and Princeton. On that date Congress ordered an authenticated copy of the Declaration and the names of the signers to be sent to each of the states.

Abraham Clark did not indulge in a mere figure of speech when he speculated as to the possibilities of being "exalted on a high gallows." One of his New Jersey colleagues, John Hart, became the victim of a man hunt a few months after he signed the Declaration at the age of 65. The Hessians looted and burned the home of the Hopewell miller, then pursued him all winter from one hiding place to another. Hart escaped with his health shattered and remained an invalid until his death three years later.

Another New Jersey signer, Richard Stockton of Princeton, was captured by the redcoats late in 1776 and clapped into the infamous Provost Jail at New York after his home had been pillaged and his library burned. A graduate of the first class in the little college, the handsome young lawyer had completed his education in the mother country, gaining the friendship of such Englishmen as Burke, Garrick and Lord Chesterfield. Stockton's captors treated him with a brutality which broke his spirit, so that he signed the British amnesty proclamation. This moment of weakness caused him to be shunned by old friends and neighbors on the rebel side, and he died a lonely and embittered figure before the end of the war.

Eight other signers were fortunate enough to escape an enemy pursuit. Elbridge Gerry got away in his nightshirt, and Thomas Jefferson as governor of Virginia was saved by a margin of five minutes. Even so, the redcoats pillaged one of his plantations and cut the throats of colts too young to be taken away.

Altogether, fifteen of the signers had their homes destroyed. Still others were punished indirectly through their wives or children. The two sons of Richard Henry Lee, unable to return from a school in England, had to endure the mental torture of announcements that their father was to be hanged. Francis Lewis, a wealthy New York merchant when he signed at the age of 63, was ruined within a month by invaders who burned his home and seized his business properties. After capturing his wife, the British subjected the elderly woman to hardships which hastened her death.

Episodes of this sort, violating the codes generally observed in that age of moderate warfare, do not mean that the invaders were monsters. It was simply that many British officers held the rebels to be outlaws without any claim to mercies ordinarily shown to foemen. Congress threatened retaliation on prisoners, and after the early excesses the situation gradually improved. But it was a long and cruel conflict, fought on both sides with the fury of civil strife, and the Americans had the misfortune to be invaded. All but one of the former colonies were overrun at various times, the four principal cities occupied for long periods, and a dozen flourishing towns destroyed entirely or in large part.

Apparently the fifty-six signers were thought to be blacker sheep than other members of Congress by an enemy whose spies reported most of the secrets of the State House. This distinction did not last long, however, and before 1781 more than half the men elected to the assembly suffered wounds, imprisonment, pillage, property destruction or other consequences of the war.

Such penalties were not visioned by many rebels in July, 1776, when it could truly have been said that the cause was threatened by an embarrassment of riches. The American forces, despite their lack of experience and resources, had incurred almost no setbacks save those of the Canadian campaign. Bunker Hill, of course, might technically have been described as a reverse, though the rebels could have wished for other such defeats. Lexington, Ticonderoga, Montreal, Moore's Creek, the siege of Boston—all these were indubitably victories, and they had been won by military novices who captured a large part of their cannon, ammunition and gunpowder from the foe.

The cup was running over when the news reached Philadelphia shortly after July 4th that a great British land and sea force had been repulsed at Charleston. This was the armada commanded by Admiral Parker and General Clinton which had been delayed by storms in its invasion of the Carolinas. Major William Moultrie, defending a fort of palmetto logs named after him, beat off the enemy fleet and troops in a ten-hour action on June 28th, inflicting losses of a ship and 200 killed or wounded soldiers at small cost to himself. Later dispatches told that the British lingered off the coast for a few weeks, then sailed northward toward New York.

Even the failure in Canada was being redeemed by Gates. He had taken command of a force described by Chase and Carroll as "an Army broken and disheartened, half of it under inoculation, or under other diseases; soldiers without pay, without discipline, and altogether reduced to live from hand to mouth." [7] At Crown Point, where the ragged and demoralized remnants had fallen back from the border, the former British officer displayed a genius for reorganization. Using his new powers as "dictator" with firm paternalism, he restored hope and pride and discipline to the northern army before the end of the summer.

Skeptics might have argued that luck had entered into many of the rebel successes. But it was the kind of luck that usually favors audacity, and the letters written by delegates show no lack of faith or courage as Congress prepared to meet the attack on New York. A "flying camp" was created, consisting of militia from the middle states, to be stationed in New Jersey as reserves and reinforcements. On July 16th the assembly ordered that a bounty of $10 be paid soldiers who would re-enlist for a three-year term. And on the 23rd the commander in chief became the subject of a resolution:

> That General Washington be informed that Congress have such an entire confidence in his judgment, that they will give him no particular directions about the disposition of his troops, but desire that he will dispose of those at New York, the flying camp and Ticonderoga, as to him shall seem the most conducive to the public good.[8]

The confidence of Congress was tempered by caution, as Washington learned after writing on the 29th to inquire about the extent of his authority. President Hancock was instructed to reply four days later that Gates had been granted unusual powers only for the limited period of an emergency. "Should Congress ever empower its Generals to fill up vacancies in the Army," the commander in chief was told, "they know of no one in whom they would so soon repose a trust of such importance as in yourself; but future Generals may make bad use of it. The danger of the precedent, not any suspicion of their present Commander-in-Chief, prompts them to retain a power, that, by you, might be exercised with the greatest publick advantage."[9]

No doubt Congress was sometimes guilty of meddling with its generals, though Washington enjoyed a larger measure of trust than the others. But neither hope of victory nor dread of defeat ever tempted the assembly to depart from a policy of keeping the military under civil control. It was a valuable tradition to set for a new nation born painfully in time of war.

Fainter hearts might have been shaken by the enemy's array of armed might. On July 4th, as if in reply to the Declaration, the first sails were sighted off Staten Island. As many as a hundred British ships came up the Narrows in a single day during the next few weeks. After the arrival of the fleet from Charleston, the armada numbered 52 warships and 427 transports.

A total of 34,000 British and Hessian soldiers may not seem impressive in a day of locust tactics based on human tonnage. But the eighteenth century was an age of small establishments made up of highly trained regulars serving long terms. Howe's army was not only the largest ever seen in the New World; it was the largest British expeditionary force of all history up to that date. As a final asset, in addition to an overwhelming artillery train, the invaders brought a military chest amounting to £840,776 in gold. This sum was deemed sufficient for the putting down of the rebellion, either by force or by persuasion. For the Howes were said to be bearing a sword in the left hand and an olive branch in the right, hoping to succeed as peace commissioners rather than conquerors.

Instances of Tories suffering persecution have been cited so often that the other side of the story is often overlooked. Hundreds of loyalists were on hand to greet the British when they landed on Long Island in mid-August. They gave information of American military positions and offered to act as guides. Their zeal also took the form of violence against rebel families, and three Presbyterian churches were burned because they had been patriotic rallying places. At a mass meeting the Tories of Queens County voted to revoke all authority of Congress, and that body passed a resolution which could only be described as a political excommunication of the New York loyalists.

The British and Hessian invaders marveled at the orchards, meadows, fields and well-filled barns of Long Island. As former peasants or slum dwellers, they exclaimed at the opportunities of a country in which a poor man could aspire to own a farm. Even more wonderful to these newcomers, accustomed to the bounties of nature being reserved for the gentry, was the privilege of every American to catch a string of bass, shoot a few canvasback ducks, or pick a bucket of wild berries. These were liberties which could be comprehended even by German mercenaries from a land which had never struck a blow for liberty.

Ambrose Serle, secretary to Lord Howe, related that the British soldiers "seemed as merry as in a Holiday, and regaled themselves with the fine apples, which hung every where from the Trees in great abundance." The Germans did not content themselves with picking fruit. "It is impossible," deplored Serle, "to express the Devastations, which the Hessians have made upon the Houses & Country Seats of some of the Rebels. All their Furniture, Glass, Windows, and the very Hangings of the Rooms are demolished or defaced. This with the Filth deposited in them, makes the Houses so offensive, that it is a Penance to go into them." [10]

The defenders of America's second city could muster fewer than 20,000 men fit for duty. Even so, Washington's force was more deficient in quality than in numbers. Allowing for prejudice, Serle had grounds for describing the rebel host as "the strangest that was ever collected: Old men of 60, Boys of 14, and Blacks of all ages, and ragged for the most part, compose the motley Crew, who are to give the Law to G. Britain and tyrannize over His Majesty's Subjects in America." [11]

With the exception of a few brigades, the militiamen were poorly armed and trained. American victories since Lexington had given them a perilous excess of confidence, based on the New England theory that homespun patriotism could compensate for discipline. Yet any armchair strategist could perceive the vulnerability of Manhattan Island to a combined land-and-sea attack, even though the Americans had stretched a 2,100-foot chain across the Hudson. Washington and the more discerning members of Congress must have realized that they were up against an insoluble dilemma—militarily, New York could not be defended; politically, it could not be abandoned.

At any rate, Congress had other fish to fry these July days. On the 12th a first draft was reported by the committee of thirteen appointed exactly a month earlier "to prepare and digest the form of a confederation." And on the 18th the committee on foreign alliances laid upon the table a model treaty drawn up in detail.

Here it may be recalled that both projects were recommended in the original resolution offered on June 7th by Richard Henry Lee to start the fight for independence. This goes a long way toward explaining the remarkable calm with which so many delegates took the Declaration; they considered it as only one of three gates to be opened before entering the far, green vistas of the promised land.

The day before the Declaration became officially unanimous, John Adams submitted a lengthy report from "the committee appointed to prepare a plan of treaties to be entered into with foreign states or kingdoms." A printed volume of historical treaties supplied by Franklin had given helpful suggestions. In the first draft the contracting parties were designated by Adams as "A" and "B," but the wishful thinking of Congress found expression in a printed version referring candidly to "the most serene and mighty Prince, Lewis the Sixteenth, the most Christian King, his Heirs and Successors, and the United States of America; and the Subjects of the most Christian King, and of the said States." [12]

It is a tribute to the adaptability of Congress that the vocabulary of courtiers could so quickly be adopted by delegates who had just approved another document condemning George III as a tyrant and murderer. But the realists of the State House knew that the new United States would have a hard time weathering the coming storms without foreign aid, if not actually a foreign alliance.

Silas Deane, unable to speak "six consecutive words" in French, had not yet had time to report from his mission. But the delegates were already aware that America had an enthusiastic admirer in the playwright and adventurer Caron de Beaumarchais, author of the recently staged *Le Barbier de Seville*. In 1775 he had met friends of the rebel cause at the London home of John Wilkes and hinted at a conspiracy to send military supplies across the Atlantic on a decisive scale.

The son of a Paris watchmaker, Beaumarchais at the age of 44 had long been accustomed to living by his wits and overcoming the disadvantages of a bougeois birth. He recognized only the nobility of genius, and his insolent attitude toward dull aristocrats was to make him the prototype of the central character in his most famous comedy, *Le Mariage de Figaro*. But even his talents at intrigue would have been unavailing if the ministers of Louis XVI had not long ago converted themselves to the desirability of secret aid for America. Ever since the costly and humiliating defeat of France in the last war, a succession of spies and secret agents had been sent to England's overseas colonies. On the other hand, several Englishmen had scented as early as 1774 the danger of the revolting colonies seeking an alliance with European nations. "You will draw a foreign force upon you," warned Burke in the House of Commons, "if you get in war with the colonies." Lord Chatham was more explicit: "France has her full attention upon you. War is at your doors."

By the summer of 1776 the Comte de Vergennes, foreign minister of Louis XVI, had reached the point where he needed only assurances that his country could have the game without the name. In March and again in May, he proposed to the monarch the possibility of "veiled and hidden aid to appear to come from Commerce." Beaumarchais offered a solution in his scheme of a bogus Spanish mercantile firm, Roderique Hortalez and Company, which would ship munitions across the ocean in exchange for American produce. Vergennes, of course, would piously deny that France had any official knowledge or responsibility in the event of an English protest.

Beaumarchais received a first advance of a million livres from the French treasury, plus the promise of arms from the royal arsenal. But even before the first shipments from Hortalez and Company reached America the following winter, France contrived to give the rebels a great deal of preliminary help. Muskets, gunpowder and other supplies were being smuggled in from French and Dutch ports in the West Indies throughout the summer of 1776.

This assistance was doubtless one of the factors which encouraged Congress to hope that France might eventually consent to sign an outright treaty of alliance. The thirty clauses in the model proposed on July 18th were debated for several days in the committee of the whole. Adams wrote that attempts "were made to insert in it articles of entangling alliance, exclusive privileges, and of warranties of possession," but all these motions failed to pass.

After the adoption, the next obvious step was for Congress to send commissioners to France with a view to promoting a treaty. Deane was already in that country, and on September 27th Franklin and Jefferson were named to join him. When the latter declined, the appointment went to Arthur Lee, a brother of the two Virginia delegates.

There is no evidence that anyone thought it presumptuous for the representatives of thirteen struggling little states to seek an alliance with Europe's most populous kingdom. Nor did the members of Congress show any hesitation about laying the foundation of a future nation on July 12th when the committee of thirteen reported its "Articles of Confederation and Perpetual Union." That same day the committee of the whole ordered eighty copies to be printed with the utmost secrecy, so that the instrument could be "speedily digested and made ready to be laid before the several States for their approbation."

These blithe words would have the taste of crow for delegates forced to eat them in coming months. With parliaments and individuals alike, it can be a kindness that the future is hidden; and on that July day nobody could have anticipated that five years of weary wrangling lay ahead before the Articles of Confederation would at long last be ratified by the states.

It did not seem at all inconsistent to members of Congress that the first draft should have been written by an absent member, John Dickinson, who had led the fight against independence. On the contrary, Robert Morris could still insist two weeks after the Declaration that he opposed independence "because in my poor opinion it was an improper time and will neither promote the interest or redound to the honor of America, for it has caused division when we wanted Union. . . ."[13]

He was not the only delegate to take a gloomy view of the scramble as the states hastened to draw up their own constitutions and elect their own executives. The race had begun in January, when the New Hampshire convention reported. South Carolina came next in March, then Virginia and New Jersey on the very eve of the Declaration. The news of Independence seemed to break down the last barriers, so that the drawing up of constitutions threatened to become the chief American industry of 1776. It was understandable that recent colonies should want to replace the royal charters with instruments of their own creation; but conservatives such as Morris foresaw the danger of the states returning to their former condition of squabbling and disunity.

Another signer, Joseph Hewes, thought that plans for confederation and foreign treaties should have preceded separation. In a letter to a friend on July 28th that hard-working delegate agreed with Morris that "these Capital points ought to have been setled before our declaration of Independence went forth to the world. this was my opinion long ago and every days experiences serves to confirm me in that opinion. I think it probable that we may split on these points, if so our mighty Colossus falls to pieces." [14]

Certainly the Americans of 1776 had a long tradition of constitution making behind them. The historian Fisher has listed eighteen plans for confederation which were suggested before that date, not to mention a total of twenty-nine charters drawn up to govern the various colonies between 1584 and 1732. [15]

The first recorded plan of union came at the early date of 1643, when the New England colonies signed articles of confederation for mutual defense against Indians or any other hostile invasion. In 1696 William Penn proposed a union of the colonies under their own congress and a commissioner appointed by the king as executive officer. Five years later Robert Livingston, of New York, made a concession to sectionalism in his plan for three distinct unions composed of northern, middle and southern colonies.

It is hard for Americans of this age to realize that the year 1776 is but a historical halfway station between the first settlements along the Atlantic seaboard and the present day. At that point the colonies had already experienced a century and a half of political development that is not to be despised. Most of them were accustomed to a degree of local self-government making the subjects of the German princelings seem human cattle in comparison. It was inevitable that such a politically advanced people should envison the advantages of confederation at an early date, and just as inevitable that farseeing Englishmen should anticipate the dangers. Sir William Keith, a capable royal governor of Pennsylvania, had a Machiavellian idea that the mother country should encourage jealousies between colonies. "For while they continue so," he asserted, "it is mortally impossible that any dangerous union can be formed between them."

Yet it was the British authorities themselves, as represented by the Lords of Trade, who called a conference at Albany in 1754 and suggested that the colonies unite to the extent of agreeing on an Indian policy and clearing up the confusion of separate treaties. Benjamin Franklin, then a prosperous, middle-aged burgher of Philadelphia, drew up the best of several plans offered by representatives. It guaranteed local self-government to each colony and provided for a grand council of all under a president-general appointed by the crown with executive powers.

Franklin's "Albany Plan," as it came to be known, is important because it left its mark on so many later schemes for confederation, including the one which he himself suggested in 1775. In 1754, of course, he was a loyal subject of George II; and many of his ideas were adopted in plans for union drawn up by such high Tories as Hutchinson and Galloway to stem the tide of independence. Galloway's proposals were narrowly defeated in the Continental Congress of 1774. The following year conservative sentiment remained so strong that the "violent men" of the assembly deemed it prudent to postpone consideration of Franklin's new plan, entitled the Articles of Confederation and Perpetual Union.

The name and much of the thought of this document went into the draft in John Dickinson's handwriting which the committee of thirteen reported to Congress eight days after the Declaration of Independence. The two plans show a great similarity. Both aimed at a confederation in which an elected assembly should hold such powers as determining war and peace, forming foreign alliances, appointing and recalling ambassadors, regulating the armed forces, deciding general questions of trade, and settling disputes between colonies. Both instruments also specified that expenses were to be met from a common treasury, with the funds to be supplied by states reserving for their own legislatures the right of levying taxes.

In their details the plans often differed. Where Franklin suggested that expenses be apportioned according to the number of male citizens between the ages of 16 and 60. Dickinson's plan broadened the base to include all white inhabitants, regardless of age or sex, as determined by a triennial census. Where Franklin believed that representation should be limited to one delegate in Congress for each 5,000 males between 16 and 60, Dickinson left the number to be decided by each state. Franklin proposed that every delegate in Congress should have one vote, while the Dickinson plan specified "that in determining Questions each Colony shall have one vote." Franklin contented himself with a quorum in Congress consisting of half the members, while Dickinson's plan demanded an affirmative vote of at least seven states to decide most questions, and nine states for issues of grave import. And though Franklin did not limit the number of annual terms that a delegate could serve, Dickinson's draft stipulated that no delegate could be elected for more than three years out of six.

In 1775 Franklin had hoped to welcome into the confederation such British possessions as St. Johns, Nova Scotia, Quebec, the Islands of the West Indies, East and West Florida, and even Ireland. A year later Dickinson mentioned only Canada. Many more differences of the sort could be cited, but in the essentials the two plans show a similar trend of American political thought. Both were the products of a people long accustomed to local self-determination who evinced a marked reluctance to place too much power in the hands of any central government, even their own. Thus the executive authority, if such it could be flatteringly called, was given by Franklin to a council consisting of twelve members of Congress chosen by that body. Dickinson's plan called for a council of state made up of a member from each state. But since neither plan saw fit to allow Congress much power in the first place, there was precious little danger of tyranny from an executive body under the thumb of Congress.

Both instruments made it plain that the Americans of 1776 actually wanted a loose confederation of thirteen states bound together by just enough central authority to transact such affairs of trade, defense, currency and foreign relations as could not conveniently be decided by the states individually.

The wide gap between theory and practice in politics was never more evident than during the summer days in 1776 when the issue was first placed on the threshing floor of Congress. The winnowing began in a hopeful mood. Josiah Bartlett, of New Hampshire, admitting in a letter of July 22nd that the business "goes on but slowly," seemed a little chagrined that nothing had as yet been adopted. A week later he allowed that it still "may possibly take a week or ten days' time"—an estimate that fell short by many months.

Some of the delegates themselves were novices. New Jersey had sent practically a new slate just before July 4th, and just afterwards the revolutionary council in control of Pennsylvania elected George Clymer, Benjamin Rush and George Taylor to replace Dickinson, Willing and Humphreys. "The papers will inform you that I have been thrust into Congress," wrote Dr. Rush on July 21st to General Lee. "I find there is a great deal of difference between sporting a sentiment in a letter, or over a glass of wine upon politicks, and discharging properly the duties of a Senator." [16]

In a letter of the 28th Joseph Hewes grumbled that "much of our time is taken up in forming and debating a Confederation for the united States. what we shall make of it God only knows. I am inclined to think we shall never modell it so as to be agreed upon by all the Colonies."

By the middle of August the controversy had reached a deadlock in which the delegates could agree on nothing except to drop the subject. Ned Rutledge fumed in a letter of the 19th that "it is of little Consequence if we never see it again; for we have made such a Devil of it already that the Colonies can never agree to it."

On August 20th the debates were renewed. It took the balance of the month to finish the preliminary revision; but before any further progress could be made, Congress had new problems thrust upon it with the news of the defeat in the battle of Long Island.

As the first action resembling a formal battle, the clash of August 27th was disillusioning to Americans who had fancied that militiamen could hold their own against European regulars. Washington's generalship, unfortunately, was not any more encouraging than the showing of his troops. The rebel forces, dangerously extended on Long Island, were surprised by redcoats and Hessians closing in on their rear after an all-night turning movement. The best soldiers would have been dismayed by such an attack, and it was to the glory of a few American regiments that they put up a stout fight. But some of the scared militia lads took to their heels, and some of them were spitted on bayonets by green-clad aliens from Hesse and Brunswick. When it was all over, the beaten rebels were fortunate to get away with no more than 1,400 casualties, about two-thirds of them prisoners.

Chapter 13

The Flight to Baltimore

THE tavern at New Brunswick could offer only a small room to Dr. Franklin and John Adams, who became bedfellows in fact as well as politics. Some wakeful moments ensued that September night, and in his *Autobiography* the Massachusetts member recalled the topic of conversation. "The window was open, and I, who was an invalid and afraid of the air in the night, shut it close. 'Oh!' says Franklin, 'don't shut the window, we shall be suffocated.' I answered, I was afraid of the evening air. Dr. Franklin replied, 'The air within this chamber will soon be, and indeed is now, worse than that without doors. Come, open this window and come to bed, and I will convince you.'"

John Adams may sometimes have fallen short as a philosopher, but he was always a good reporter. Although he could not reconcile Franklin's theories with his own experience, he remembered in afteryears that he had "so much curiosity to hear his reasons that I would run the risk of a cold. The Doctor then began a harangue upon air and cold, and respiration and perspiration, with which I was so much amused that I soon fell asleep, and left him and his philosophy altogether, but I believe they were equally sound and insensible within a few minutes after me, for the last words I heard were pronounced as if he was more than half asleep." [1]

Adams was sufficiently convinced to admit in his old age that "there is much truth, I believe in some of the things he advanced, but they warrant not the assertion that a cold is never taken from cold air."

The next morning the three travelers jogged on through New Jersey. For the Continental Congress had elected Ned Rutledge along with Franklin and Adams as peace commissioners on September 7th, thus sending its youngest, oldest and most pugnacious members to meet Lord Howe on Staten Is-

176

land and hear the British terms. The three Americans were courteously greeted by their host at the water's edge, after they crossed from the Jersey shore in a barge sent by Howe. Adams related that they "walked up to the house between lines of grenadiers, looking fierce as ten Furies, and making all the grimaces and gestures, and motions of their muskets, with bayonets fixed, which, I suppose, military etiquette requires, but which we neither understood nor regarded. The house had been the habitation of military guards, and was as dirty as a stable; but his lordship had prepared a large handsome room, by spreading a carpet of moss and green sprigs, from bushes and shrubs in the neighborhood, till he had made it not only wholesome but romantically elegant; and he entertained us with good claret, good bread, cold ham, tongues and mutton." [2]

The cordiality shown by the British admiral was genuine, for he and Franklin had been friends in England. Both of the Howes were such liberal Whigs that Englishmen wondered why George III had chosen them as his peace commissioners. In all the kingdom it would have been hard to find men more friendly to Americans or less inclined to condemn them for their political sins. Blood was thicker than the water of the Atlantic Ocean, and Adams found his host profusely grateful to Americans "for erecting a marble monument in Westminster Abbey, to his elder Brother, Lord Howe, who was killed in the last war, saying, 'he esteemed that honor to his family *above all things in this world.'*"

It had been a sad blow to New York loyalists to find themselves so often snubbed by Howe. Even the diarist Serle was shocked when his employer casually remarked that "almost all the People of Parts & Spirit were in the Rebellion." [3]

At the Staten Island conference, according to Adams, Howe confided "that he felt for America as a brother, and, if America should fall, he should feel and lament it like the loss of a brother. Dr. Franklin, with an easy air, and a collected countenance, a bow, a smile, and all that *naiveté,* which sometimes appeared in his conversations, and is so often remarked in his writings, replied, 'My Lord, we shall do our utmost endeavors to save your lordship that mortification.' His lordship appeared to feel this with more sensibility than I could expect; but he only returned, 'I suppose you will endeavor to give us employment in Europe.'"

The minutes of the conference reveal that Dr. Franklin interpreted the British terms to mean the "unconditional submission" of America. The admiral objected to that phrase, but his guests were not convinced. After taking their leave in a spirit of personal good will, they reported to Congress on September 17th after their return that "it did not appear to your committee that his lordship's commission contained any other authority than that expressed in the act of Parliament, namely, that of granting pardons, with such exceptions as the commissioners shall think proper to make, and of declaring America, or any part of it, to be in the king's peace, upon submission. . . ." [4]

These terms did not tempt delegates who continued to give most of their thought to the depressing military situation. Washington had managed to extricate his battered forces from Brooklyn Heights, where some 9,000 men were threatened with capture, but Manhattan Island offered a precarious refuge. The possibility of further retreats seems to have been frankly recognized by the assembly in a resolution of September 3rd advising Washington "in case he should find it necessary to quit New York, that no damage be done to the said city by his troops, on their leaving it: That Congress having no doubt of being able to recover the same, though the enemy should, for a time, obtain possession of it." [5]

General Howe crossed the East River on the 15th and landed troops above the city. Again Washington barely pulled out in time to escape disaster, and some of his militia brigades did not cover themselves with glory. Representatives of the masochistic school of American historians have commented with severity on the flight of these outnumbered military novices. Evidently some apologies were heard at the time in the State House, for Dr. Witherspoon found it necessary to remind Congress that the instinct of self-preservation was not entirely an American institution: "I wish it were considered, that neither loss nor disgrace worth mentioning has befallen us in the late engagement, not comparable to what the British troops have often suffered. At the battle of Preston, sir, they broke to pieces and ran away like sheep, before a few Highlanders. I myself saw them do the same thing at Falkirk . . . a small part only of the army making a stand, and in a few hours the whole retreating with precipitation."

Grown men had been known to feel like schoolboys when the Scottish divine fixed them with a bleak and righteous gaze. He concluded his brief speech by adding that in the rebellion of 1745 "the Militia of England . . . behaved fifty times worse than that of America has done lately. They generally disbanded and ran off as soon as the rebels came within ten or twenty miles of them." [6]

The president of Princeton might have adduced similar examples from the annals of all nations in all times, since "cowardice" on the battlefield is usually only a harsh name for lack of training. The very day after the American disgrace, another force of green recruits stood like veterans and repulsed British regulars in a hot little action at Harlem Heights.

On the recommendation of the Board of War, Congress voted to offer a bounty of $20 to soldiers "inlisting to serve during the present war, unless sooner discharged." In addition, lands were to be granted to both officers and men—500 acres to a colonel, 450 to a lieutenant colonel, 400 to a major, 300 to a captain, 200 to a lieutenant, 150 to an ensign, and 100 to a noncommissioned officer or soldier.

It was further resolved on September 16th that "eighty-eight battalions be inlisted as soon as possible, to service during the present war." The quotas assigned to the states give an idea of comparative resources as estimated by Congress: Massachusetts and Virginia, 15 battalions each; Pennsylvania, 12; North Carolina, 9; Connecticut, 8; South Carolina, 6; New York, 4; New Jersey, 4; New Hampshire, 3; Rhode Island, 2; Delaware, 1; Georgia, 1.[7]
. As a remedy for the indiscipline contributing to American defeats, Congress adopted new articles of war on September 20th after repealing the old regulations. John Adams had found an opportunity for informal glimpses of militiamen on the trips through New Jersey, and his observations were not reassuring:

> On the road, and at all the public houses, we saw such numbers of officers and soldiers, straggling and loitering, as gave me, at least, but a poor opinion of the discipline of our forces, and excited as much indignation as anxiety. Such thoughtless dissipation, at a time so critical, was not calculated to inspire very sanguine hopes, or give great courage to ambassadors. I was, nevertheless, determined that it should not dishearten me. I saw that we must, and I had no doubt that we should, be chastened into order in time.[8]

As the chairman of the Board of War, Adams did not apologize for modeling the new American articles after the enemy's regulations. "There was extant one system of articles of war," he declared, "which had carried two empires to the head of mankind, the Roman and British; for the British articles of war were only a literal translation of the Roman. It would be in vain for us to seek in our own inventions, or the records of warlike nations, for a more complete system of military discipline. . . . The British articles of war were, accordingly, reported, and defended in Congress by me assisted by some others, and finally carried." [9]

This account was written long afterwards, when Adams could boast that the articles "laid the foundation of a discipline which, in time, brought our troops to a capacity of contending with British veterans, and a rivalry with the best troops of France."

The inducements offered by Congress for long-term enlistments were not so successful. For as wages went up along with other prices, the economic factor began to enter into the equation. The chairman of the Board of War admitted that the number of men who could be enlisted for the duration "would be very small in New England. . . . A regiment might possibly be obtained, of the meanest, idlest, most intemperate and worthless, but no more. We must have tradesmen's sons, and farmers' sons, or we should be without defence." Thomas McKean also testified before Congress as to the situation in his state: "Even in Pennsylvania, the most desperate of imported laborers cannot be obtained in any numbers upon such terms. Farmers and tradesmen give much more encouragement to laborers and journeymen." [10]

Several years later the answer was worked out by a young man with a mind as keen as a surgical instrument. Alexander Hamilton found that the proportion of soldiers to financial resources followed a pattern among the nations of Europe. Applying the same yardstick to his own country, he arrived at the pessimistic conclusion that America simply could not afford an army capable of contending with the forces of the British Empire on equal terms.

One of the backwoods riflemen might have put the same thing more succinctly by saying that the rebels had bitten off more than they could chew. Historians have questioned the patriotism of militiamen who hurried home on the eve of battle when their three-month terms were up; but there is much to be said for the small farmer whose crops represented food for his family the following winter. The British were able not only to pay and equip regiments of American loyalists, but also to provide for wives and children. The result was that during the worst winter of the war the rebels had to face larger forces of their own countrymen, in addition to British regulars and German mercenaries.

The pages of the *Journals* make it plain that military problems took up most of the time of the Continental Congress during the first eight years of its existence. There was no other agency to conduct the war except the assembly and an overburdened commander in chief. And after taking full account of their lapses and mistakes, it remains one of the miracles of history that the new nation won its independence on the battlefield.

Prospects of a final victory could not have seemed bright in the early autumn of 1776. After the Americans abandoned New York, the great fire which destroyed 500 houses was probably the work of looters, though each army blamed the other. News also reached Congress of a second British invasion from the north as Carleton took the historical water route up Lake Champlain, with Ticonderoga as his objective. It was at least a consolation that General Gates defended that fort with a northern army which he had nursed back to good disciplinary health. General Benedict Arnold was meanwhile driving his detachment day and night to build a flotilla in time to fight the British lake squadron.

During the autumn the Articles of Confederation were brought up again from time to time in Congress. Each discussion made it more apparent that Samuel Chase had hit upon the three most controversial points as early as July 30th.

"The Confederacy has engaged our close attention for a week," he wrote to Richard Henry Lee, then in Virginia. "Three great difficulties occur: Representation, the mode of voting, and the claims to the South Sea. The whole might, in my opinion, be settled, if candour, justice, and the real interests of America were attended to. We do not all see the importance, nay, the necessity of a Confederacy." At this point the Maryland member doubtless sighed as he ended his letter with the jeremiad: "We shall remain weak, distracted, and divided in our councils, our strength will decrease; we shall be open to all the arts of the insidious Court of Britain, and no foreign Court will attend to our applications for assistance before we are confederated. What contract will a foreign State make with us when we cannot agree among ourselves?" [11]

Representation and the mode of voting, of course, were merely separate aspects of the same great problem. At the very first meeting of the Continental Congress, this had been the issue which inspired Patrick Henry's oratorical cry, "I am not a Virginian, but an American!" Nevertheless, he had argued as a Virginian that September day in 1774, and the other delegates had argued according to their sectional interests. At the time Congress dodged the question by allowing each colony an equal vote regardless of property or population, though the *Journals* recorded this compromise as a temporary solution. And now the specters laid in 1774 were back to haunt the assembly in 1776, along with all the other issues of confederation.

The "claims to the South Sea" brought up a knotty problem, deeply rooted in colonial history, growing out of the fact that Virginia, North Carolina, Georgia, New York, Massachusetts and Connecticut were avowedly "three-sided" states. On the strength of forgotten Indian treaties or royal charters, all six states insisted on an indefinite right of westward expansion to the Pacific, wherever that fabled sea might be located. The opportunities for squabbles were endless. Virginia's disputed northern boundary cut across territory claimed by four other states. New Hampshire and New York threatened a petty war over a region called Vermont; and Connecticut citizens stood ready to defend their "right" to lands in Pennsylvania. Naturally, the seven "four-sided" states were not content to accept a role as passive bystanders, since their interests were very much involved.

The problems of voting and representation dragged in the related issue of apportioning the costs. But the states which were most strident in demanding a voice on a basis of population or property were usually singing small when it came to incurring a comparable share of the expenses.

Finally, there were honest doubts in the minds of many delegates as to the desirability of all thirteen states uniting under a strong central government. It was not thought unpatriotic in 1776 to suggest the possibility of forming two, three or more American nations on a basis of sectional interests. Nor had anybody been shocked the year before when John Adams predicted to Congress that as he "supposed no man would think of consolidating this vast continent under one national government, we should probably, after the manner of the Greeks, the Dutch and the Swiss, form a confederacy of States, each of which must have a separate government." [12]

After many tribulations America itself was to set the world its greatest example of a federal union on a large and enduring scale. But in 1776 the founding fathers had no models except such loose confederations as the Dutch provinces, the Swiss cantons and the Amphictyonic League of city-states in ancient Greece.

Again, as in the case of independence, it can only be regretted that such an incomplete record has been preserved of the discussions of the Articles of Confederation. Wilson of Pennsylvania, according to John Adams, "moved that the debates should be made public, the doors opened, galleries erected, or an adjournment made to some public building where the people might be accommodated. Mr. John Adams seconded the motion and supported it with zeal. But no! neither party was willing; some were afraid of divisions among the people; but more were afraid to let the people see the insignificant figures they made in that assembly." [13]

The main sources are the reports written from contemporary notes by Adams and Jefferson in their old age. The author of the Declaration has left an account of the arguments on apportionment of expenses, as stipulated in the original draft of Article XI:

> All charges of war and all other expenses that shall be incurred for the common defence, or general welfare, and allowed by the United States assembled, shall be defrayed out of a common treasury, which shall be supplied by the several colonies in proportion to the number of inhabitants of every age, sex, and quality, except Indians not paying taxes, in each colony, a true account of which, distinguishing the white inhabitants, shall be triennially taken and transmitted to the Assembly of the United States.

Samuel Chase brought up the subject of slavery with his motion that the quotas be fixed according to the number of white inhabitants only. The Maryland lawyer "observed that negroes are property, and as such, cannot be distinguished from the lands or personalities held in those States where there are few slaves; that the surplus of profit which a Northern farmer is able to lay by, he invests in cattle, horses, &c., whereas a Southern farmer lays out the same surplus in slaves." [14]

The viewpoint of the northern states was upheld by John Adams, who maintained that "five hundred freemen produce no more profits, no greater surplus for the payment of taxes, than five hundred slaves. Therefore, the state in which the laborers are called freemen, should be taxed no more than that in which are those called slaves."

As a compromise Benjamin Harrison proposed "that two slaves be counted as one freeman." Slaves, he contended, "did not do as much work as freemen . . . that this was proved by the price of labor; the hire of a laborer in the Southern colonies being from £8 to £12 [annually], while in the Northern it was generally £24."

If Chase's amendment should be adopted, said James Wilson, "the Southern colonies would have all the benefit of slaves, whilst the Northern ones would bear the burthen." The Pennsylvania member granted "that freemen work the most; but they consume the most also. They do not produce a greater surplus for taxation. The slave is neither fed nor clothed so expensively as a freeman."

It was the opinion of Dr. Witherspoon "that the value of lands and houses was the best estimate of the wealth of a nation, and that it was practicable to obtain such a valuation. This is the true barometer of wealth."

The amendment was put to the test, Jefferson reported, and defeated by the votes of seven northern and middle colonies. Delaware, Maryland, Virginia and both Carolinas voted in the affirmative, with Georgia being divided.

Article XVII consisted of only a few words: "In determining questions, each colony shall have one vote." But the delegates could at least agree unanimously with Chase that "this article was the most likely to divide us, of any one proposed in the draught then under consideration; that the larger colonies had threatened they would not confederate at all, if their weight in Congress should not be equal to the number of people they added to the confederacy; while the smaller ones declared against such a union, if they did not retain an equal vote for the protection of their rights." [15]

Dr. Franklin was never at a loss for a quip to put over his point. He remarked "that at the time of the Union between England and Scotland, the latter had made the objection which the smaller States now do; but experience had proved that no unfairness had ever been shown them; that their advocates had prognosticated that it would again happen, as in times of old, that the whale would swallow Jonah." But the philosopher "thought the prediction reversed in event, and that Jonah had swallowed the whale;

for the Scotch had in fact got possession of the government, and gave laws to the English people."

As a large-state man, Franklin "reprobated the original agreement of Congress to vote by colonies, and, therefore, was for their voting, in all cases, according to the number of taxables."

The learned Dr. Witherspoon, educated in the subtleties of theology at the University of Edinburgh, made a practice of wearing his cap and gown in the State House. "All men admit that a confederacy is necessary," he answered Franklin. "Should the idea get abroad that there is likely to be no union among us, it will damp the minds of the people, diminish the glory of our struggle, and lessen its importance. . . . If an equal vote be refused, the smaller States will become vassals to the larger; and all experience has shown that the vassals and subjects of free States are the most enslaved." The president of Princeton conceded "that equality of representation was an excellent principle, but then it must be of things which are co-ordinate; that is, of things similar, and of the same nature; that nothing relating to individuals could ever come before Congress; nothing but what would respect colonies."

John Adams, speaking for one of the two largest states, "advocated the voting in proportion to numbers. . . . Reason, justice and equity never had weight enough on the face of the earth, to govern the councils of men. It is interest alone which does it, and it is interest alone which can be trusted. . . . It has been objected that a proportional vote will endanger the smaller States. We answer that an equal vote will endanger the larger."

"The larger colonies," declared Dr. Rush, the dapper Philadelphia physician, "are so providentially divided in situation, as to render every fear of their combining visionary. Their interests are different, and their circumstances dissimilar. It is more probable they will become rivals, and leave it in the power of the smaller States to give preponderance to any scale they please."

The small-state men found an able champion in Stephen Hopkins, former governor of Rhode Island, who asserted that "history affords no instance of such a thing as equal representation. The Germanic body votes by States. The Helvetic body does the same; and so does the Belgic confederacy." After pointing out that the four largest American states outnumbered the others combined, he predicted darkly that they "would govern the others as they should please."

Wilson answered "that taxation should be in proportion to wealth, but that representation should accord with the number of freemen. . . . It has been said that Congress is a representation of States, not of individuals.

I say, that the objects of its care are all the individuals of the State. It is strange that annexing the name of 'State' to ten thousand men, should give them an equal right with forty thousand. This must be the effect of magic, not of reason."

The Pennsylvania lawyer, educated at Glasgow, St. Andrews and Edinburgh universities, had won recognition at the age of 34 as one of the most able men of Congress. In his conclusion he summed up the case for the large-state group:

It is asked, shall nine colonies put it into the power of four to govern them as they please? I invert the question, and ask, shall two millions of people put it into the power of one million to govern them as they please? It is pretended, too, that the smaller colonies will be in danger from the greater. Speak in honest language and say, the minority will be in danger from the majority. And is there an assembly on earth, where this danger may not be equally pretended? The truth is that our proceedings will then be consentaneous with the interests of the majority, and so they ought to be. . . . I defy the wit of man, to invent a possible case, or to suggest any one thing on earth, which shall be for the interests of Virginia, Pennsylvania and Massachusetts, and which will not also be for the interest of the other States.

Neither reason nor eloquence swayed delegates who continued to vote according to large or small states on the most troublesome issue which ever divided the founding fathers. Eleven years later it was to be solved by the famous compromise which appeased the small states by giving them an equal voice in the Senate, while compensating the large states with a House of Representatives based on population.

This provision, as every schoolboy knows, was the work of the Constitutional Convention which met in 1787. It is not so well remembered that every one of the major problems had arisen as early as 1776 in that great laboratory of American political institutions, the Continental Congress. The arguments of the leaders have been recorded in Jefferson's notes. But there were also such plain men as William Williams, the Connecticut merchant and town clerk, whose honest perplexities have come down in a letter of August 12th: "Congress are yet bussie at all Intervals of crouding Business, in Setling a Confederation. it seems to labour hard, and I fear a permanent one will never be settled. . . . What will be the event of Things God only knows."[16]

Even in the discussion of great issues it was seldom that the debates in the State House soared to heights of oratory. As a national patriarch, Thomas McKean wrote: "I do not recollect any *formal* speeches, such as are made in the British Parliament and our late Congresses, to have been made in the revolutionary Congress, though I was a member for eight years. . . . We had no time to hear such speeches; little for deliberation; action was the order of the day." [17]

Williams, who believed that "the Salvation of the Country depends on the Character of Congress," wrote to Joseph Trumbull on October 7th that "the great Affairs generally are well determined, tho sometimes with great Altercation." [18]

Some of the most angry disputes, according to notes taken by John Adams, arose from discussions of Articles XIV and XV, bringing up the explosive question of state boundary claims. [19] Again the delegates were sharply divided according to sectional interests after Chase declared, "No Colony has a right to go to the South Sea; they never had; they can't have. It would not be safe to the rest. It would be destructive to her sisters and to herself."

The Continental Congress never decided an issue which was to have more influence on the future development of the republic. For these disputed lands comprised the vast territory which would be carved into new states after 1789.

Virginia, with her extensive claims to the northwest, had more at stake and a more valid case than the other "three-sided" states. "What are reasonable limits," asked Jefferson. "What security have we, that the Congress will not curtail the present settlement of the States? I have no doubt that the Colonies will limit themselves."

"Every gentleman has heard much of claims to the South Sea," replied Wilson. "They are extravagant. The grants were made upon mistakes. They were ignorant of the Geography. They thought the South Sea within one hundred miles of the Atlantic Ocean. It was not conceived that they extended three thousand miles. . . . Pennsylvania has no right to interfere in those claims, but she has a right to say, that she will not confederate unless those claims are cut off. I wish the Colonies themselves would cut off those claims."

The dispute, like most clashes between the Haves and the Have-Nots, generated more heat than light. The six states with westward claims refused to budge an inch, and each discussion ended with mutterings of a refusal to confederate. Maryland was the most assertive of the seven opposing states, and Chase rose repeatedly to deny "that any Colony has a right to go to the South Sea."

"How came Maryland by its land, but by its charter?" demanded Ben Harrison. "By its charter, Virginia owns to the South Sea. Gentlemen shall not pare away the Colony of Virginia."

Samuel Huntington, the new Connecticut member, supported Harrison.

"Admit there is danger from Virginia, does it follow that Congress has a right to limit her bounds? The consequence is, not to enter into confederation. But as to the question of right, we all unite against mutilating charters. . . . I doubt not the wisdom of Virginia will limit themselves. A man's right does not cease to be a right, because it is large. . . ."

"The smaller Colonies have a right to happiness and security," said Stone of Maryland; "they would have no safety if the great Colonies were not limited. . . . It is said that Virginia is attacked on every side. Is it meant that Virginia shall sell the lands for their own emolument? All the colonies have defended these lands against the King of Britain and at the expense of all."

Jefferson, like Chase, contented himself with reiteration when reason failed; and the day's controversy ended in the usual deadlock as the author of the Declaration protested "against the right of Congress to decide upon the right of Virginia."

Late in August the assembly got as far as ordering a new printing of the Articles, so as to include the revisions authorized up to that time. The delay in resuming the debates—a delay which was to last six months—found an apologist in Edward Rutledge, who explained in a letter of October 2nd: "Our Confederation has been neglected for many weeks because the states have been unrepresented." Only the day before, Congress had taken official notice of such lapses with the resolution "that the president be desired to write letters to the conventions and assemblies of the respective states, requesting that measures be taken, to cause, as speedily as possible, a full representation of the said states in Congress." [20]

The delegates could scarcely have realized that these were the first symptoms of the absenteeism which would become one of the two most persistent ills of the Continental Congress. The other was an almost fatal anemia due to maladjusted finances, and it also might have been diagnosed at this early date. For the ten million dollars issued that spring to carry on the war until the end of the year had lasted only until the end of October. It had become necessary to order another five million, and Congress likewise gave thought to a seemingly painless method of filling the treasury. Although the assembly frowned from time to time on such sins as dancing and profanity, the puritans of 1776 thought nothing of passing a measure which would be denounced as scandalous in the middle of the twentieth century:

Resolved, That a sum of money be raised by way of a lottery, for defraying the expenses of the next campaign, the lottery to be drawn in the city of Philadelphia.[21]

Nearly three weeks later a resolution of November 18th ordered the printing of 100,000 tickets, and it was decided that the first drawing would be held the following March, if not sooner.

The fortunes of Washington's dwindling army went from bad to worse during these autumn weeks. Howe has been criticized for his failure to end the war at a stroke, but experience had taught that rebel marksmen could be dangerous when firing from cover. Another costly lesson was administered at Pell's Point in a decisive little action too often neglected by history. The British general aimed a new surprise blow, sending four brigades by water to disembark in Westchester County and cut off the American retreat. Washington had to depend on 750 Massachusetts troops holding firm on October 18th until the main army could escape. The turning movement planned by Howe as another battle of Long Island became another Bunker Hill on a small scale when the rebels, firing from behind a stone wall, beat off a much larger force of redcoats and Hessians.

A few days later an express reached Philadelphia with news of an American defeat in the north which was even more worthy of being ranked with Bunker Hill. Carleton's invading army of 11,000, greatly outweighing any force that Gates could collect at Ticonderoga, was compelled to halt and fight Benedict Arnold for control of Lake Champlain. Hammers and saws became weapons as both sides waged a race of shipbuilding. In the hard-fought action of Valcour Island on October 11th the 15 leaky rebel vessels suffered so much damage that Arnold completed the destruction of his flotilla. But Carleton's superior squadron took such heavy punishment that he retreated to Canada after deciding to postpone operations until spring.

Washington lost a confused combat on October 28th at White Plains. Instead of pursuing farther, Howe mysteriously fell back to Manhattan Island. His intentions did not become clear until November 16th, when he captured Fort Washington with nearly 3,000 defenders—the largest bag of prisoners the rebels were to lose in the north throughout the war. Both Washington and Greene were guilty of blunders, and their small remaining force was pressed so hard that the last rebels had not left Newark before the enemy entered. It was during this retreat that Thomas Paine, serving as a Pennsylvania militia volunteer, wrote the challenging words of The Crisis:

> These are the times that try men's souls. The summer soldier and the sunshine patriot will, in this crisis, shrink from the service of their country; but he that stands it *now*, deserves the love and thanks of man and woman. Tyranny, like hell, is not easily conquered; yet we have this consolation with us, that the harder the conflict, the more glorious the triumph.

Paine appealed in vain for heaven to inspire a Yankee Joan of Arc—"some Jersey maid to spirit up her countrymen, and save her fair fellow sufferers from ravage and ravishment." Unhappily, a great many inhabitants of the invaded state were selling their produce for British gold and pledging allegiance to the king.

Washington's forlorn army had been reduced to 3,000 effective troops when he reached the Delaware with the foe nipping at his heels. After seizing small boats up and down the river, he crossed to the Pennsylvania side. But this was only a temporary refuge, for the enemy could either build a pontoon bridge or wait for the winter to provide a bridge of ice.

It would be an understatement to say that these were anxious days for Congress. The alarming military situation, crowding out other business, is reflected in a spate of resolutions offering higher bounties for enlistments, appealing to the states to furnish their quotas of troops, and denouncing the profiteers who "with views of avarice and extortion, have monopolized and engrossed shoes, stockings and other necessaries for the army, whilst the soldiers of the Continent, fighting for the liberties of their country, are exposed to the injuries of the weather, at this inclement season." [22]

As the enemy drew nearer, breathing hotly on the backs of the routed rebels, Congress directed the Board of War to prepare for the defense of the American metropolis. After the British reached Trenton the assembly did not need Washington's warning of December 12th "that Philadelphia is their object, and that they will pass the Delaware as soon as possible. Happy should I be, if I could see the means of preventing them; at present I confess I do not." [23]

Congress had already approved on the 10th an "address to the inhabitants of America" which was obviously intended to cushion the blow of Philadelphia's fall. British successes were attributed "not to any capital defeat, or a want of valour in the Army that opposed them, but to a sudden diminution of its numbers from those short inlistments which, to ease the people were at first adopted." The address ended with assurances that "even the loss of Philadelphia would not be the loss of the cause, yet while it can be saved, let us not, in the close of the campaign, afford them such a ground of triumph. . . ."

If George Washington had been cut down by a British bullet at this time, he would doubtless be remembered as a soldier who showed a brief promise at the siege of Boston, only to go the way of Humpty-Dumpty in the New York campaign. His generalship could not have been warmly praised, and it took defeat to bring out his most remarkable qualities of leadership.

On December 11th, as the beaten army stumbled into Trenton, the commander in chief received a message from Secretary Thomson which left no doubt that nerves were becoming strained at the State House. It was the first copy of a resolution, later found among rough drafts of manuscripts, which never attained to the dignity of publication in the *Journals*:

> Whereas a false and malicious report has been spread by the enemies of America, that the Congress was about to disperse:
>
> *Resolved,* That General Washington be desired to contradict the said scandalous report, this Congress having a better opinion of the spirit and vigor of the army, and of the good people of these States, than to suppose it necessary to disperse; nor will they adjourn from the city of Philadelphia in the present state of affairs, unless the last necessity shall direct it.[24]

It might have been supposed that this request, amounting to a polite command, would be accepted with proper humility by a general whose army was wasting away on the thin, bitter gruel of defeat. Instead, Washington returned a gentle rebuke. After "sleeping on" the problem, he wrote a refusal next morning which remains a monument to his integrity and good judgment:

> I last night received the favor of Mr. Thomson's letter, enclosing the proceedings of Congress, of the 11th instant. As the publication of their resolve, in my opinion, will not lead to any good end, but, on the contrary, may be attended by some bad consequences, I shall take the liberty to decline inserting it in this day's orders. I am persuaded, if the subject is taken up and reconsidered, that Congress will concur with me in sentiment. I doubt not, but there are some, who have propagated the report; but what if they have? Their remaining in or leaving Philadelphia must be governed by circumstances and events. If their departure should become necessary, it will be right; on the other hand, if there should not be a necessity for it, they will remain, and their continuance will show the report to be the production of calumny and falsehood. In a word, Sir, I conceive it a matter, that may as well be disregarded; and that the removal or staying of Congress, depending entirely upon events, should not have been the subject of a resolve.[25]

Washington's letter amounted to a courteous veto. Congress took it in good spirit, and the hasty, ill-advised resolution was buried deep in that limbo of things which are better left unsaid.

It would scarcely be a cynicism to add that one of the foremost functions of any parliament is its usefulness as a scapegoat in time of disaster. The Continental Congress of this crisis has been handled roughly not only by historians of the nineteenth century but also some debunkers of the twentieth. The resulting legend resembles the plot of a Grade B motion picture. Congress, as the collective villain, is cast as a group of scared civilians fleeing to Baltimore to save their own skins. In their panic the delegates leave the whole burden to Washington, appointing him dictator of America in a frantic effort to save the cause.

Fortunately for adult tastes, the historical facts tell a more interesting story when they are not strained by the "interpretation" of historians. For weeks Congress met each day in an atmosphere of the wildest rumors. As early as November 16th William Hooper of North Carolina expressed his disgust by using an ancient American epithet in a letter reporting that "the people here have been horribly frightened. The Council of Safety a set of water Gruel Sons of B——s told the people a damned Lie 'that they had certain information that 100 Ships had left Sandyhook for this City'—the people at first believed and trembled, the tories grinned. Rumor trumpeted it for a day." [26]

The question of withdrawing from the imperiled city was of course decided by broader considerations than those of personal safety. But if the courage of the delegates is to be questioned, the statistics of the Continental Congress show a record of military service which has probably never been bettered by any other parliament of history. Of the 342 men elected during the fifteen years, 134 bore arms in either the militia or the Continental army. One was killed in action, twelve seriously wounded, and twenty-three taken prisoners in combat.

When it is recalled that a majority of the delegates had passed the age of 40, the valor of Congress needs no apologies. But it is not the duty of a governmental body to make a futile display of bravado, even though a few members of 1776 felt sheepish about the flight. Robert Morris very sensibly summed up the situation when he wrote to John Jay on January 12th that "meer personal safety I suppose would not have induced many of them to fly, but their security as a body was the object. had any number of them fallen into the Enemies hands so as to break up the Congress, America might have been ruined before another choice of Delegates could be had and in such an event that would have been deemed criminal and rash to the last degree." [27]

On December 11th Congress recommended "to all the United States, as soon as possible, to appoint a day of solemn fasting and humiliation; to implore of Almighty God the forgiveness of the many sins prevailing among all ranks, and to beg the countenance and assistance of his Providence in the prosecution of the present just and necessary war." The following day it was resolved "that this Congress be, for the present, adjourned to the town of Baltimore, in the State of Maryland, to meet on the 20th instant. . . ." [28]

Washington's rebuke seems only to have raised him in the esteem of the assembly. In fact, it could even be said that he won tacit recognition as an executive on that Thursday, December 12th, which dates one of the lowest ebbs of the American cause.

Up to this point Congress had shared the alarms of constituents who showed a pathological distrust of executive power. After using all their political wiles to circumvent royal governors and the king, Americans did not propose to create tyrants of their own. Their new governors were allowed very moderate authority curbed by legislative checks and balances, and several states played safe by setting up executive councils.

Congress, lacking any jurisdiction over territory, any taxmaking or law-giving functions, any constitutional authority whatever, managed to wield more actual power than Parliament while governing entirely by influence. But even at a heavy cost in efficiency, Congress did not trust its own members to carry out administrative duties unless they kept watch over one another in standing committees. The thought of granting executive powers to any individual would have been abhorrent, yet Congress accepted Washington in this capacity down to the end of the war.

The commander in chief had no more constitutional authority, of course, than the revolutionary assembly. He also governed by influence. It would not be too strong a statement, however, to say that he was as much the executive of the United States from 1776 to 1783 as during the eight years of his administration.

Throughout the earlier period the conduct of a war and the regulation of a society in a state of revolution were the great tasks of government. Washington and Congress shared them in a tacit division of powers.

The exchange of December 12th is one of the first examples of this unique relationship. On later occasions Washington again used his "veto," and Congress sometimes overruled as well as accepted his negative. When issues of grave importance arose, he was summoned to confer at the State House; and other questions were mutually decided when a committee of delegates journeyed to meet with him at his headquarters.

Tact, judgment and integrity on both sides had to take the place of the constitutional authority which neither the commander in chief nor the revolutionary assembly had been awarded. There were flashes of resentment, there were doubts and hesitations, there were differences of opinion when co-operation was hardpressed to survive. Even so, it is a demonstrable fact that Washington and the Continental Congress worked together more effectively on the whole than the executive and legislative branches at several periods of the twentieth century.

Chapter 14

Year of the Hangman

THE so-called dictatorial powers conferred on Washington by Congress offer another example of the new relationship developing from the crisis. In a letter of December 20th the commander in chief warned that "ten days more will put an end to the existence of our army." After admitting that little could be done to save Philadelphia, he asked for enough authority to deal with the military emergency.

If, as he reasonably pointed out, "every matter that in its nature is self-evident is to be referred to Congress, at the distance of a hundred and thirty or forty miles, so much time must necessarily elapse, as to defeat the end in view. It may be said, that this is an application for powers that are too dangerous to be entrusted. I can only add that, desperate diseases require desperate remedies; and I with truth declare, that I have no lust after power, but I wish with as much fervency as any man upon this wide-extended continent for an opportunity of turning the sword into the ploughshare." [1]

The very first resolution passed at Baltimore shows a disposition on the part of Congress to grasp the nettle with less caution than usual. Robert Morris, George Clymer and George Walton were honored on the 21st with an unusual degree of trust by being appointed as "a committee of Congress, with powers to execute such continental business as may be proper and necessary to be done at Philadelphia." [2]

The delegates who made this decision realized that they were placing unusual authority in the hands of one man. Not only was Morris the brains of the new committee, but he had long been an outspoken advocate of delegating administrative authority to individuals instead of the usual standing committees. Yet Congress asked only "that the said committee keep up a regular correspondence with Congress, informing them, from time to time, of their proceedings."

After this entering wedge, the assembly did not balk at granting Washington more sweeping powers for six months than had been permitted Gates in a lesser emergency. It would be ridiculous, however, to say that an American "dictator" had been created by the resolution of December 27th:

That General Washington shall be, and he is hereby, vested with full, ample and complete powers to raise and collect together, in the most speedy and effectual manner, from any or all of these United States, 16 battalions of infantry, in addition to those already voted by Congress; to appoint officers for the said battalions, to raise, officer, and equip three thousand light horse, three regiments of artillery, and a corps of engineers, and to establish their pay; to apply to any of the states for such aid of the militia as he shall judge necessary; to form such magazines of provisions, and in such places, as he shall think proper; to displace and appoint all officers under the rank of brigadier general, and to fill up all vacancies in every other department in the American armies; to take, wherever he may be, whatever he may want for the use of the army, if the inhabitants will not sell it, allowing a reasonable price for the same; to arrest and confine persons who refuse to take the continental currency; or are otherwise disaffected to the American cause; and return to the states of which they are citizens, their names, and the nature of their offences, together with the witnesses to prove them.[3]

The last three provisions granted powers that might have been abused by a less worthy recipient; but stern measures seemed justified by the disloyalty and profiteering in New Jersey. Nevertheless, the delegates felt that explanations were in order; and a circular letter of the 30th informed the thirteen states that "Congress would not have Consented to the Vesting of such Powers in the Military Department as those, which the Inclos'd Resolves convey to the Continental Commander in Chief, if the Scituation of Public Affairs did not require at this Crisis a Decision and Vigour, which Distance and Numbers Deny to Assemblies far Remov'd from each other, and from the immediate Seat of War."[4]

On the last day of the year, as if proving the wisdom of the decision, a letter from Washington was read before Congress with the dramatic news of his crossing of the Delaware on Christmas night and capture of the Hessian outpost at Trenton. A bag of a thousand prisoners was not to be despised in this war; and it became an added satisfaction to humiliate the German mercenaries.

Baltimore buzzed with rumors of bold new rebel operations the first week of the year. People were hardened to enduring suspense in that day of tedious communication, but the official confirmation of Washington's victory at Princeton on January 3rd was not read to Congress until ten days later. After the ragged little American army went into winter quarters at Morristown, it appeared that nearly all New Jersey had been won back to the cause. This result was accomplished as much by the depredations of the enemy as the successes of rebel arms. Serle and other intelligent British observers foresaw the consequences of widespread pillage and devastation which spared neither Tory nor patriot. A Committee of Congress, appointed to investigate atrocities, reported on April 18th that "the destruction was very general and often undistinguished; those who submitted and took protection, and some who were known to favor them [the British], having frequently suffered in the common ruin." [5]

The powers given to Washington seem to have sent a ripple of rumors as far as Boston. In a letter to his wife on April 6th, John Adams indignantly denied "that Congress, the last summer, had tied the hands of General Washington, and would not let him fight, particularly on the White Plains. This report was totally groundless. Another was that at last Congress untied the General, and that he instantly fought and conquered at Trenton. This also was without foundation, for as his hands were never tied, so they were not untied. . . . Another report, which has been industriously circulated, is that the General has been made by Congress dictator. But this is as false as the other stories. . . . Congress never thought of making him dictator or of giving him a sovereignty." Adams predicted in his disgust that "such a collection of lies would be a curiosity for posterity." [6]

At any rate, there could be no question that Washington had shown brilliant generalship in the Trenton-Princeton campaign without abusing the powers conferred by Congress. Meanwhile the committee headed by Robert Morris at Philadelphia had gone far toward proving his contention in a letter of December 16th that "if the Congress mean to succeed in this contest, they must pay good executive men to do their business as it ought to be, and not lavish millions away by their own mismanagement. I say mismanagement, because no man living can attend the daily deliberations of Congress and do executive parts of business at the same time." [7]

The response of the delegates to Baltimore, then an overgrown village, fell considerably short of delight. William Hooper, the Wilmington lawyer, wrote to a North Carolina friend on December 28th: "This dirty boggy hole beggars all description. We are obliged, except when the Weather paves the streets, to go to Congress on Horseback, the way so miry that Carriages almost stall on the sides of them. When the Devil proffered our Saviour the Kingdoms of the World, he surely placed his thumb on this delectable spot and reserved it to himself for his own peculiar seat and inheritance." Forceful as this opinion may seem, Hooper had not yet said the worst. Writing to Joseph Hewes after recovering from an illness, he reported that he "had very nearly measured my length under Ground in that worst of all terrestial places, a situation bad as it is yet preferable to being above it long in that wretched place." [8]

A similar note of good-humored hyperbole is found in the complaints of other delegates, for the change of environment seems to have restored a social whirl reminiscent of the early days of Congress in Philadelphia. Baltimore hosts were equally hospitable, and John Adams' diary, silent throughout the busy months of 1776, was filled again with such entries as the following:

> Fri., Feb. 7. Dined about half a mile out of town, at Mr. Lux's, with Dr. Witherspoon, Mr. S. Adams, Mr. Lovel [Lovell], Mr. Hall, Dr. Thornton, a Mr. Harrison. . . . Sat., Feb. 8. Dined at the President's, with Mr. Lux, Messrs. Samuel and Robert Purviance, Captain Nicholson of the Maryland frigate, Colonel Harrison, Wilson, Mr. Hall, upon New England salt fish. The weather was rainy, and the streets the muddiest I ever saw. This is the dirtiest place in the world. [9]

The following week, dining at another Baltimore home in company with Gerry, Sergeant, Samuel Adams, Dr. Rush, Dr. Witherspoon and the Lee brothers, the diarist encountered a curious local custom. Families still possessing a portrait of George III hung it upside down near the floor with this caption in doggerel:

> Behold the man, who had it in his power
> To make a kingdom tremble and adore.
> Intoxicate with folly, see his head
> Placed where the meanest of his subjects tread.

The delegates did not need to be reminded that finances were one of the most urgent problems before Congress. Their own personal expenses gave proof of inflationary prices. John Adams, flying in the face of the copybook maxims, suggested to his wife in a letter of February 17th, "There is a United States lottery abroad. I believe you had better buy a ticket and make a present of it to our four sweet ones. Let us try their luck. I hope they will be more lucky than their papa has ever been, or ever will be." The children did not win, and two months later Abigail spoke for less articulate wives when she reported to her husband "a general cry against the merchants, against the monopolizers, etc., who, 'tis said, have created a partial necessity. That a scarcity prevails of every article, not only of luxury but even the necessaries of life, is a certain fact. Everything bears an exorbitant price." [10]

Intervals between new emissions of Continental money were growing shorter as prices increased, and the dullest delegates could see the connection. Nelson of Virginia wrote to Robert Morris that he "had most as lieve go to a jail as go near the Treasury. The period is not far distant, when the last five millions of Dollars will be exhausted. . . ."

As early as the third day in Baltimore the assembly hit upon the solution which would eventually pull America through the war after every other expedient failed. But little action was taken to support the resolution "that the Commissioners of Congress at the Court of France be authorized to borrow on the faith of the thirteen United States a sum not exceeding two millions sterling, for a term not less than ten years." [11]

At this time some of the members doubted whether a European loan could be negotiated, and others hoped for results from such new schemes as the lottery. Citizens of four New England states, meeting at Providence, demanded in January that Congress pass measures to fix prices. "It must be done," agreed Chase. "The mines of Peru would not support a war at the present high price of the necessaries of life." But that bleak realist Dr. Witherspoon had his doubts. "Remember," he warned, "laws are not almighty."

Few members of Congress had any illusions about paper money. "If we go on emitting money," wrote Thomas Burke, a newcomer from North Carolina, in a letter of February 10th, "the quantity in circulation so enhances the price of things that we shall only make money without being able to get for it more commodities, and it will, of course, destroy its own purpose." [12]

Most of the delegates would have agreed further with Burke that "a Tax seems the only adequate expedient." But they knew that Congress might as well cry for the moon as the tax-levying powers so jealously guarded by the states. After two weeks of intermittent debate the question of price regulation found the assembly divided. "The continent," diagnosed Dr. Rush, "labours under a universal malady. From the crown of her head to the Soal of her feet she is full of disorders. She requires the most powerful tonic medicines. The resolution before you is Nothing but an *Opiate*. It may compose the continent for a night, but She will soon awaken to a fresh sense of her pain and misery." [13]

Congress could only offer such quack prescriptions, already found futile, as its resolution of January 14th that paper money "ought to pass current in payments . . . and be deemed in value equal to the same nominal sum in Spanish milled dollars." As another pink pill to treat an economic plague, it was declared that any American preferring hard money "ought to be deemed an enemy to the liberties of these United States."

The first symptoms of absenteeism, diagnosed the previous autumn, led to a malady as serious as financial ills during the winter in Baltimore. By

February 17th John Adams was commenting on the "melancholy prospect before me of a Congress continually changing, untill very few Faces remain, that I saw in the first Congress. . . . Mr. S. Adams, Mr. Sherman, and Coll. Richard Henry Lee, Mr. Chase and Mr. Paca, are all that remain. The rest are dead, resigned, deserted or cutt up into Governors, etc. at home." [14]

In numbers the assembly had become a rump parliament, averaging from twenty to twenty-five delegates—fewer than half the members who decided the great issues of 1775 and 1776. They met in a large room of a three-story brick home rented from Henry Fite. Baltimore, which had a population of 6,000 in a 1775 census, offered the courthouse after undergoing expense for repairs, but the assembly declined. [15]

Some of the shrinkage of Congress had been inevitable. Franklin sailed for France late in October, and Jefferson set an example for Ned Rutledge and other delegates by serving his own state. This exodus confirmed Robert Morris' stubborn opinion that independence had come too soon. "Mr. Johnson, and indeed all the Maryland delegates, are at home forming a Constitution," he wrote to Gates shortly after Jefferson's departure. "This seems to be the present business of all America, except the Army: it is the fruits of a certain premature declaration which you know I always opposed." [16]

Robert Treat Paine wished that "the inhabitants of the United States were more intent upon providing and manufacturing the Means of defence, than making Governments without providing the Means of their support." William Hooper agreed with Morris in a letter of February 1st: "I lament, my dear Sir, the very small representation which America presents in Congress the members of which will soon be reduced to the number of 22, how unequal to the importance of its councils!" And after four months of a "thin" Congress, the entire New York delegation considered the situation serious enough for a report to the state convention: "Every wise man here wishes that the establishment of new Forms of Government had been deferred; they see that the Union, Vigor and Security derived from Conventions and Committees are not to be found in any State under its new Constitution." [17]

From the viewpoint of getting things done, there was much to be said for the revolutionary conventions and committees of safety created by that first crude instrument of American union, the Association. These local and state councils, bridging the chasm between royal rule and independence, were not curbed by many restraints save of their own hasty improvising. The possibilities for tyranny were endless, and no doubt they were sometimes realized at the expense of Tories or citizens hoping to remain neutral. The effectiveness of the revolutionary conventions and committees, in short, was based upon a directness of approach which made representative government seem cumbersome in contrast. But even in time of war the states could not content themselves indefinitely with a system akin to martial law. Sooner or later the states had to frame their own constitutions; and it is noteworthy that the Marylanders who annoyed Morris were the authors of the most democratic bill of rights yet to be approved in America—a document so enlightened that it eventually became the model for the first eleven amendments to the Constitution of the United States.

New England's two "little republics" were so satisfied with the liberties of their old royal charters that Connecticut kept hers until 1818, and Rhode Island down to the year 1842. Ten of the remaining states drew up new constitutions before the summer of 1777, though some of them had to try again. Altogether, counting the efforts rejected by voters, more than a score of state constitutions were written between 1775 and 1778.

During this period it was inevitable that the Continental Congress, the only substitute for a national government, would lose some of the prestige and influence which had served it instead of authority. Even after the flight to Baltimore it surprised John Adams to find that in a New Jersey loyalist community his party "met with no molestation or insult. We stopped at some of the most noted Tory houses, and were treated everywhere with the utmost respect." [18] Nevertheless, the states were beginning to take such pride in their new constitutions and state governments that less value was attached to a full representation in Congress. Each state was supposed to elect enough delegates so that those in session could be relieved by others, after a specified period, without any interruption in attendance. No fault could be found with the theory; but as it worked out in practice, according to Francis Lightfoot Lee, "the members grow weary, go off, and leave us too thin; which obliges us to call for them." He suspected that there were some "who wish the Congress to be divided and contemptible; as that cant be accomplished, the next thing is, to make the world think it is so." [19]

The greatest menace of absenteeism was that a few delegates so often had it in their power to frustrate the will of a majority of the states. There were complaints of cliques being formed; and nobody found it ironical that the New England states were accused of sectional voting because of being more faithful in attendance than the others.

It was natural that veterans of 1774 should suspect a decline in the quality as well as bulk of Congress when men as able as Patrick Henry, Christopher Gadsden and William Livingston preferred to serve their states. It was obvious that no newcomers could ever fill the shoes of such departed giants as Washington, Dr. Franklin and Thomas Jefferson. Yet some of the delegates who took their seats early in 1777 would also give a good account of themselves—Lovell of Massachusetts, Elmer of New Jersey, Burke of North Carolina.

The number of physicians in the Continental Congress has been remarked by every chronicler. Rush, Elmer, Bartlett, Brownson, Wolcott, Hall, Jones, Thornton and Burke had appeared up to this time, and seventeen more active practitioners were to be elected after 1777. The new North Carolina member, who practiced law as well as medicine, had been born in Ireland thirty years before. No delegate ever took his responsibilities more seriously than Thomas Burke, and his opinion of Congress in a report of February 10th to Governor Richard Caswell may be accepted as an honest and penetrating estimate:

> Of the political principles of the respective States I am not yet able to speak very clearly, for they are kept as much as possible out of view. I conjecture, however, that all are under some apprehensions of combination in the Eastern States to derive to themselves every advantage from the present war, at the expense of the rest. I am not yet satisfied that there is any combination among them. I rather think that they only combine when they have one common interest, which is seldom the case, and I am sure this is not peculiar to them.[20]

March 12th found the assembly meeting again in the State House, after adjourning at Baltimore on February 27th. Philadelphia had come to regard Congress as a civic asset bringing both prosperity and prestige. The delegates themselves were not many, but as the seat of government the little city attracted a stream of visitors with their servants and carriages.

The landladies rejoiced after three months of empty rooms. Spinsters, widows and wives supporting the kind of spouses who are known as "poor providers," the keepers of these Revolutionary boardinghouses deserve their paragraph in history. The Virginia and South Carolina delegates continued to favor the table set by Mrs. Mary House and presided over by her young and attractive daughter, Mrs. Eliza Trist, at the corner of Fifth and Market. Their dining room became Philadelphia's nearest approach to a salon, and both women kept up a correspondence with members of the "family" after they left Congress.

Another place which grew into an institution was Miss Leonard's, under the auspices of Mrs. Yard, where Gerry and Lovell moved on their return from Baltimore. John Adams staked out a little corner of New England at the home of the Duncans, a transplanted Boston couple, between Second and Third on Walnut. Wolcott of Connecticut and Whipple of New Hampshire also were guests.

Sam Adams chose Mrs. Cheeseman's establishment at Fourth and Market. There, according to his distant kinsman, the archrebel had "a curious group of company, consisting of characters as opposite as north and south. Ingersoll, the stamp man and Judge of Admiralty; Sherman, an old Puritan, honest as an angel and as firm in the cause of American independence as Mount Atlas; and Colonel Thornton, as droll and funny as Tristram Shandy. Between the fun of Thornton, the gravity of Sherman, and the former Toryism of Ingersoll, Adams will have a curious life of it. The landlady, too, who has buried four husbands, one tailor, two shoemakers, and Gilbert Tennant, and still is ready for a fifth, will add to the entertainment."

But this boardinghouse seems to have been an oasis in the prim respectability of Philadelphia; for in another letter John Adams sighed to Abigail that the city "is a dull place in comparison of what it was. More than one-half of the inhabitants have removed into the country, as it was their wisdom to do. The remainder are chiefly Quakers, as dull as beetles. From these neither good is to be expected nor evil to be apprehended. They are a kind of neutral tribe, or the race of the insipids." [21]

President Hancock, occupying a furnished house on Chestnut near Fourth, seems to have been the only delegate at this time to have brought his wife. The previous winter John Adams had commented on the "modesty, decency, dignity and discretion" of the recent bride, surrounded as she was by so many unattached men. "Her behavior is easy and genteel. She avoids talking upon politics. In large and mixed companies she is totally silent, as a lady ought to be."

Such descriptions are noteworthy because the era of the Continental Congress, generally speaking, was one of the most exclusively masculine periods of all history. In Paris and other European capitals, women of the day were taking an active part in international politics, often at the expense of conservative moral standards. In London, where codes were more strict, some of the greatest statesmen could be seen in public with their mistresses. But in Philadelphia it would have been an exaggeration to say that women played so much as a secondary part in politics—they played no part at all. The most that could be claimed was that they made a contribution indirectly as Penelopes who kept up the homes and plantations of delegates away for months.

Not only the occupations but the diversions of Congress were masculine— a Sunday canter along the Schuylkill, a hearty dinner of several meat courses, a bowl and pipe at the tavern. One of the most memorable occasions seems to have been the "turtle feast" of the previous August, when the delegates celebrated the signing of the Declaration by devouring sea food, captured on an enemy ship, which was destined for Lord North's table in London.

The letters of such wives as Abigail Adams and Sarah Jay attest that

American women were lacking in neither brains nor charm. That they were both adored and respected is equally evident from letters written by the husbands of an assembly which had few bachelors. Although these messages do not lack for compliments and endearments, there is seldom any "writing down" from a summit of intellectual superiority. Nor did the masculinity of the delegates take the direction of dalliance on lonely nights. Philadelphia had its share of unattached and acquiescent women, and with the exception of several pietists such as Judge Sherman the members of Congress were not puritans. Nevertheless, they set a remarkable standard of marital fidelity as well as temperance over a period of fifteen years. There were few episodes of furtive gallantries; and in an age of universal drinking, there were only one or two delegates who might have been called tosspots.

The most reasonable conclusion is that the men of the Continental Congress had neither time nor taste for dissipation. If they had any weakness at all, it was their chronic state of invalidism—the gout or "hectic humors" enjoyed by so many future octogenarians while working fifteen hours a day. Afterwards their recreation usually took the form of a postman's holiday as they argued politics until midnight in some smoky, candlelit tavern.

The combination of spring weather and the return to Philadelphia increased attendance until every state was represented by the first week of April. The members resolved in a virtuous mood to devote at least two days a week to the neglected Articles of Confederation. Enough progress was made before the month's end so that Burke could report to Governor Caswell on the 29th:

> We have agreed to three articles: one containing the name: the second a declaration of the sovereignty of the States, and an express provision that they be considered as retaining every power not expressly delegated; and the third an agreement mutually to assist each other against every enemy. The first and latter passed without opposition or dissent, the second occasioned two days debate. It stood originally the third article; and expressed only a reservation of the power of regulating the internal police, and consequently resigned every other power.[22]

It had taken a newcomer, later to be famed as the states' rights champion of Congress, to discover that Article III of the Dickinson draft left the states little more power than the regulation of their own internal governments. Such a lapse shocked men believing in state sovereignty, as most of the delegates did. The only surprising result is that there were actually enough dissenters to prolong the debate for two days after Dr. Burke offered an amendment "which held up the principle, that all sovereign power was in the States separately. . . ."

Wilson and Richard Henry Lee led the opposition, but the vote was eleven to one (with Virginia negative and New Hampshire divided) in favor of the amendment. Most of the delegates agreed with Burke that "the Congress should have power enough to call out and apply the common strength for the common defense; but not for the partial purposes of ambition."

Before many years there would be Americans who believed that Congress had cut the infant nation's throat that April day, leaving it to bleed to death in the cradle. But the delegates were in deadly earnest when they feared "the Delusive Intoxication which Power Naturally imposes on the human mind." And though the debates on the Articles proceeded with high hopes that "the whole would soon be passed," Burke had to report on May 23rd: "Since my last we have made no progress in the business of confederation. A difficulty occurs, which, I fear, will be insuperable; that is how to secure in each State its separate independence, and give each its proper weight in the public councils. So unequal as the States are, it will be nearly impossible to effect this: and after all it is far from improbable that the only Confederation will be a defensive Alliance." [23]

The last sentence, probably representing a majority opinion, shows how far Americans were in 1777 from any conception of a compact federal union. A month later, in a letter of June 26th, Sam Adams wrote that "a kind of Fatality still prevents our proceeding a step in the important affair of Confederation." By this time Congress had reached the usual stalemate on the issues of representation and voting. Once more the large and small states exhausted themselves in a hopeless deadlock lasting into July, when the weary delegates dropped the subject of confederation.

Any illusions about soldiers disdaining the mire of politics were shattered by the scheming warriors who made themselves odious to Congress in the spring of 1777. A swarthy and truculent brigadier, aspiring to be a major general, called on the Board of War and convinced John Adams that he had been "basely slandered and libeled." But Benedict Arnold became such a persistent lobbyist for himself as to hurt his own interests. Adams voiced the sentiment of Congress when he exploded, "I am wearied to death with the wrangles between military officers, high and low. They quarrel like cats and dogs. They worry one another like mastiffs, scrambling for rank and pay like apes for nuts." [24]

On February 17th it was decided "that in voting for general officers, a due regard shall be had to the line of succession, the merit of the person proposed, and the quota of troops raised, and to be raised, by each state." [25] This measure, which came to be known as the "Baltimore resolution," appealed to practical politicians because it set three standards for promotion, any one of which could be emphasized for purposes of expediency. But the officers clamored as loudly as ever, and a further complication arose when European soldiers began to turn up in Philadelphia with expectations of a higher rank than native sons who had distinguished themselves on the battlefield.

Although the Continental Congress was made the scapegoat, most of the fault could be traced to Silas Deane and his extravagant promises to foreign volunteers. The original intention had been to accept a few specialists such as engineers, but the American commissioner sent so many adventurers that on March 13th the Committee of Secret Correspondence was directed "to discourage all gentlemen from coming to America with expectation of employment in the service, unless they are masters of our language, and have the best of recommendations." A week later Congress approved a face-saving certificate of rejection stating "that it is wholly and only upon the grounds mentioned in the said resolve, that the bearer is not employed by the United States." [26]

As French interpreter, James Lovell combined a cold perfection in speaking the language with a distaste for the people and customs. An accomplished linguist and mathematician, the former instructor of the Boston Latin School had been imprisoned by the enemy at Halifax in 1775 after differing with his father, one of New England's leading loyalists. At the age of 34 the Massachusetts delegate had the zeal of a fanatic; and in a first interview he dismissed the Marquis de Lafayette and his companions, as one of them complained, "like a set of impostors." Fortunately, the youthful nobleman persevered until he convinced Congress of his integrity, and both he and Baron de Kalb were commissioned major generals. Along with Kosciusko, Steuben and the Chevalier du Plessis, they made a contribution to the cause which more than compensated for any embarrassments suffered at the hands of self-seeking adventures.

A handsome funeral solved the most troublesome of the debacles. After one Du Coudray reached these shores with a contract from Deane giving him command of all artillery and engineer forces, American officers could stand no more. Sullivan, Greene and Knox had written to Congress, threatening to resign, when the newcomer was drowned in the Schuylkill. In their scarcely concealed relief the delegates celebrated this dispensation by resolving "that the corpse of the said Mons. de Coudray be interred at the expence of the United States, and with all the honors of war. . . ."

The relationship between Congress and Washington continued to resemble the functioning of the legislative and executive branches of an established government. When the assembly decided to order retaliations on prisoners for hardships believed to have been inflicted on General Lee after his capture, Washington again used his "veto power" on March 1st: "Here retaliations seem to have been prematurely begun, and are . . . not justified by any General Lee has yet received. In point of policy, under the present situation of our affairs, this doctrine cannot be supported. The balance of prisoners is greatly against us; and a general regard to the happiness of the whole should mark our conduct." [27]

This time the delegates overrode his negative by resolving "that General Washington be informed, that Congress cannot agree to any alteration. . . ." But the commander in chief never hesitated to dissent if he believed himself to be right; and on March 14th, when Congress meddled in strategy, he was even blunt: "Could I accomplish the important objects so eagerly sought by Congress—'confining the enemy within their present quarters, preventing their getting supplies from the country, and totally subduing them before they are reinforced,'—I should be happy indeed. But what prospect or hope can there be of my effecting so desirable a work at this time? The enclosed return, to which I solicit the most respectful attention of Congress, comprehends the whole force I have in Jersey." [28]

The patriotism of Washington shone all the more brightly in contrast to the current feud between Gates and Schuyler, both of whom had their factions in Congress and the army. Although the former was a Virginian, the New Englanders made him their champion; and the New York landed proprietor had the backing of the middle and southern states. Each took care to further his cause in the State House by lobbying methods, and the time came when the delegates wanted to invoke a plague on both their houses. On March 15th, after an insulting letter from Schuyler, they declared it "altogether improper and inconsistent with the dignity of this Congress, to interfere in disputes subsisting among the officers of this army: which ought to be settled . . . in a court martial, agreeably to the rules of the army." The resolution ended by denouncing the language of Schuyler's letter as "ill-advised and highly indecent." [29]

Ever since January 1st there had been superstitious folk who saw in the last three digits of 1777 a portent of the gibbets awaiting American rebels. It was the year of the hangman, and the gallows jokes exchanged in the State House were not so humorous after the imprisonment of Stockton and destruction of other members' homes. It is not likely that many delegates actually feared the noose, but events were to prove that the enemy would go as far as clapping a congressman in the Tower.

Certainly the year 1777 saw the scales removed from the eyes of loyalists who had found comfort in ridiculing the supposed weakness of the Con-

tinental Congress. At first the devout Serle suspected only a misuse of religion when the assembly appointed days of fasting and prayer. Then he
awakened to the fact that these proclamations, by making pastors the agents
of revolt, were being "employed in the Service of Sedition & Rebellion, and
for the Subversion of an Empire . . . an Abuse, the more diabolical as it
pretends to be the more sanctimonious."

Two Tories informed Lord Howe's secretary on January 2nd "that the
Seizure of the Congress had been thought of and even proposed among
some of the first people in Philadelphia." In a diary item of March 17th
Serle noted "a confidential conversation with Mr. Galloway. . . . He told
me of a Plan to seize the Congress, and that 100 men had taken an Oath to
each other to do it." Even the ravages in New Jersey were blamed on "the
diabolical work of a few wicked men, called the Congress, who have opposed Reconciliation and constantly thrown obstacles in its way." [30]

The soldiers of the rebel cause had more hope of pardon, in case of disaster, than the members of the Continental Congress. Nevertheless, that
body added to its political sins on June 14th by creating a minor national
holiday with the resolution "that the flag of the thirteen United States be
thirteen stripes, alternate red and white: that the union be thirteen stars,
white in a blue field, representing a new constellation."

Congress also set the tradition of observing Independence Day on July
4th instead of the 2nd, as John Adams had so reasonably anticipated. Thomas
Burke found it needful to explain the significance of the date when he
reported to Governor Caswell that "the celebration of the fourth of July (the
anniversary of the declaration of Independence) . . . and the 28th of June,
memorable for the defence of Sullivan's Island, were both celebrated here,
and at both a Hessian band of music which were taken at Princeton performed very delightfully, the pleasure being not a little heightened by the
reflection that they were hired by the British Court for purposes very different. . . ." [31]

Any joy the delegates might have taken was soon darkened by news of
military reverses. General John Burgoyne's invading host of 8,500 troops
(counting Hessian, Canadian and Indian auxiliaries) reached Ticonderoga
with the largest train of artillery ever seen in the New World. Only a few
of these guns, dragged to the summit of a near-by mountain, compelled
General Arthur St. Clair to evacuate the fort on July 6th. The reaction of
Congress may be imagined from John Adams' savage comment: "I think we
shall never defend a post until we shoot a general . . . and this event in my
opinion is not far off. . . . We must trifle no more. We have suffered too
many disgraces to pass unexpiated." [32]

Such remarks were hardly calculated to restore good will between Congress and the army at a time of strained relations. As if Burgoyne's invasion were not menace enough, there was also the threat of still larger forces commanded by Howe and Clinton at New York. Howe's intentions remained a mystery even after he loaded his troops in transports and set sail. Not until August 22nd could President Hancock report with certainty to Washington, "This moment an Express is arriv'd from Maryland with an Accott of near Two Hundred Sail of Mr. Howe's Fleet being at Anchor in the Chesapeak Bay."

The commander in chief, then approaching Philadelphia on his march from New Jersey, had been right in supposing the rebel "capital" to be the objective. It could also be assumed that Clinton would move up the Hudson for a junction with Burgoyne.

On the 24th, with the members of Congress watching, the American army passed through the city. There could not have been many light hearts among the onlookers, for inflation was becoming the canker of civilian morale. Current prices in Philadelphia that week, as recorded by John Adams, were double and triple those of 1776: "Four pounds a week for board. . . . Shoes, five dollars a pair. Salt, twenty-seven dollars a bushel. Butter, ten shillings a pound. Punch, twenty shillings a bowl."

The Massachusetts member thought that he had "never lived in my whole life so meanly and poorly as I do now." Yet as he surveyed the situation with all its potentialities of catastrophe, he was not vanquished in spirit. The New Englanders could be petty, they could be provincial, but they were never a faint-hearted race. And it is certain that John Adams meant every word literally when he wrote to Abigail on September 8th:

> But if it should be the will of Heaven that our army should be defeated, our artillery lost, our best generals killed, and Washington fall into Mr. Howe's hands, still America is not conquered. America would yet be possessed of great resources, and capable of great exertions, as mankind would see. It may, for what I know, be the design of Providence that this should be the case. But it would only lay the foundations of American independence deeper, and cement them stronger.[33]

The expression "from the sublime to the ridiculous" had not yet been coined by Napoleon, but nothing else would quite have described the transition of Congress at this time from a mood of courageous realism to one of delirious daydreaming. Henry Laurens, the wealthy, middle-aged South Carolina merchant who had just arrived to represent his state, reported to Governor John Rutledge, "I can hardly forbear concluding that a great Assembly is in its dotage." For while the enemy threatened Philadelphia, Congress was actually planning to capture far-off Pensacola with "an ex-

pedition to West Florida projected by persons out of doors and recommended upon vague and indigested plans and propositions, adopted by a
few within and apparently acquiesed in by a great majority." [34]

The strategists who conceived the plan were confident that a thousand
Americans could (a) proceed by boat down the Ohio and Mississippi, (b)
induce the neutral Spaniards at New Orleans to supply them with cannon,
and (c) march through the forest to combine with several American ships for
a land-and-sea attack on the British fort. The swarthy and thickset South
Carolinian helped to kill this proposal just before Congress had word that
Washington's 11,000 men were defeated on September 11th in the battle
of the Brandywine. And though he extricated them in fairly good order,
there was little to prevent the enemy from taking Philadelphia.

Eliphalet Dyer, representing Connecticut again, dared to hope that "this
plaguy fellow of an How does not disturb us. we are now very Sulky and
determined not to move for him if we can help it." But Howe advanced
the week after his victory, and at three o'clock on the morning of the 19th
the delegates began leaving the city after an urgent warning from Colonel
Alexander Hamilton of Washington's staff.

Even in the hour of peril there were ridiculous moments. Thomas Burke,
not satisfied with the military situation, had been conducting one of the most
vigorous congressional investigations of history. Unarmed but undaunted,
wearing a civilian's garb, he took part in the battle of the Brandywine to the
extent of rallying broken troops of Sullivan's brigade. Returning to Philadelphia, he moved in Congress to have that luckless general discharged as
incompetent. It was a fight between two Orangemen, each as humorless as
he was honest, and Burke wrote directly to Sullivan: "Your personal courage
I meddled not with. . . . My objection to you is, want of sufficient talents,
and I consider it your misfortune, not fault. It is my duty, as far as I can,
to prevent its being the misfortune of my country." [35]

Congress asked for Sullivan's recall, but Washington refused to set a
precedent of punishing defeat. He wrote to President Hancock that he
"must beg leave to defer giving any order about it" and reminded him that
"our situation at this time is critical and delicate, and nothing should be
done to add to its embarrassment."

The delegates straggled out of Philadelphia in their own time and way.
Henry Laurens ate a good breakfast, lit his pipe, and drove in his carriage
to Bristol, where he picked up the wounded Lafayette. James Lovell wrote
to Gates that he "tarried until the 25th, when, the Enemy being within a mile
and without any opposing Troops in the City, I slipt into the Jersies. It
was lucky that I had a young Lady to gallant thither; for 3 or 4 officers who
left Philada. before me were taken. . . ." [36]

Lancaster became the seat of government for a single day, September 27th, when a quorum of Congress held a session in the courthouse. Then the road led across the Susquehanna to York, a farming community of some 1,800 inhabitants. Philadelphia and even Baltimore must have been recalled as metropolitan by the travel-stained delegates who attended their first meeting in the Pennsylvania village on September 30th. But at least they could be sure that there would not be many dull moments ahead—not while Thomas Burke and Henry Laurens were in the assembly.

Chapter 15

Snow on Valley Forge

YORK consisted of but 286 houses nestling in a broad valley between autumn-tinted hills. The members of Congress with their employees, guards and servants were hard put to find accommodations, and the larger residences took in the overflow from the few taverns. Each frosty October morning the ringing of the bell summoned the delegates to the little court-house on the square. President Hancock and Secretary Thomson sat at the judge's desk, and the delegates in their rows of seats were warmed by an enormous wood stove with a pipe extending to the rear wall.[1]

The Board of War, presided over by John Adams, conferred in the law office of James Smith, the 64-year-old delegate from York who had studied at the College of Philadelphia after coming to this country as a penniless Scotch-Irish immigrant. The Board of Treasury, with Elbridge Gerry as chairman, found quarters at the residence of Archibald McClean. Two rooms of this home became the Treasury of the United States for the next nine months as Michael Hillegas supervised the printing of the paper money authorized by Congress. The equipment saw such hard service during the winter that on May 8th the assembly appropriated $56 for repairs described as "sundry contingencies for the money press."

John and Samuel Adams, Gerry, Harrison and Richard Henry Lee shared rooms at a house rented by Daniel Roberdeau, the Pennsylvania member who as a brigadier had recently captured from the foe a sum equal to $22,-000 in silver and turned it over to Treasurer Hillegas. Most of the other delegates, then receiving from $5 to $8 a day as compensation, found lodging in near-by residences, two to a room, and took their meals at taverns. Expenses averaged at least $8 a day for bare necessities, according to an account kept by Dr. Jonathan Elmer which mentions a frugal total of £65 to support himself and horse for seven weeks. Richard Henry Lee, so "land-poor" that he must subsist on his income as delegate, reduced his budget with a monotonous daily fare of roast wild pigeons, bought from the country folk for a few pennies a dozen.

A sober and thoughtful Congress was summoned to the first meetings in York by the courthouse bell which Martin Brenise rang each morning for a daily stipend of two-thirds of a dollar. The easy victory won by Howe and the capture of Philadelphia had demonstrated the material weakness of the states. The need for combining their strength was never more apparent, and on the 3rd the delegates sternly resolved "that the articles of confederation be taken into consideration tomorrow morning." Only twenty-five members, according to the *Journals*, were in attendance: Folsom of New Hampshire; John and Samuel Adams, Gerry, Lovell and Hancock of Massachusetts; Marchant of Rhode Island: Dyer, Williams and Law of Connecticut; Duer and Duane of New York; Roberdeau of Pennsylvania; Chase and Carroll of Maryland; Harrison, Jones and the Lee brothers of Virginia; Penn and Harnett of North Carolina; Brownson of Georgia; and Middleton, Laurens and Thomas Heyward, Jr., of South Carolina.

During the last uneasy weeks in Philadelphia the assembly had passed several war measures which would be remembered with complacency in the future. When Washington discreetly asked "to be excused from making the appointment of an officer to command the northern army," Congress intervened in the Schuyler-Gates feud on August 4th by electing Gates, with eleven states concurring. Ten days later he was granted for a term of four months the "dictatorial" powers which could no longer be called unusual.

Benedict Arnold, soothed with a major general's rank that spring, was sent to Gates as subordinate. And on August 16th the tactics of the war's most important battle were shaped in advance with the resolution: "That General Washington be informed, that, in the opinion of Congress, 500 riflemen, under the command of an active and spirited officer, should immediately be sent into the northern department, to assist in opposing the incursions of the enemy in that quarter." [2]

The pages of the *Journals* since 1775 showed that Congress had taken the lead in recognition of the value of the rifle as a new weapon and of the American frontiersman as a soldier. Washington, though he needed all available strength for the defense of Philadelphia, responded uncomplainingly by sending Colonel Daniel Morgan's crack regiment of riflemen to the northern army.

On August 20th the delegates approved a mild reprimand for that unruly New Hampshire brigadier, John Stark. The very next day they were embarrassed by the news of his victory of the 16th at Bennington over a Hessian detachment from Burgoyne's army. The British general, an unusually humane soldier, had recently been shocked to learn of the killing of an American girl by his Indian auxiliaries. Romanticists of that age liked to shed tears over their heroes or heroines; and they had been weeping the last three years over Goethe's *Werther,* the youth whose burden of unrequited love became too great to bear. But here was a drama from real life with all the elements of grand pathos—Jane McCrea had been slain and scalped by redskins on her way to a forest tryst with her lover, a provincial officer in the British army. Within the next six months the name of this frontier girl became known all over England as well as America, and neither excuses nor apologies could atone for the sorry episode. Not only did the British cause suffer morally, but the affair had the practical effect of arousing the countryside. Militia volunteers flocked by the hundred to reinforce Gates while current doggerel represented Burgoyne as boasting:

> I will let loose the dogs of hell,
> Ten thousand Indians who shall yell,
> And foam and tear, and grin and roar,
> And drench their moccasins in gore. . . .
> They'll scalp your heads, and kick your shins,
> And rip your guts, and flay your skins,
> And of your ears be nimble croppers
> And make your thumbs be tobacco-stoppers.

Congress approved a letter of thanks to Gates on October 4th for the victory he claimed in the first of the two Saratoga engagements—the action of September 19th, known as the battle of Freeman's Farm. But the perfunctory wording of the message reveals that the assembly had no idea of the importance of the events taking place in the wooded country of the upper Hudson. Generals were apt to claim a victory on the slightest excuse, and later dispatches hinted that Burgoyne also boasted a triumph on the grounds of compelling an American retirement.

The next day an express brought the news of another rebel victory at Germantown, where Washington treated Howe to a dawn surprise on October 4th. But subsequent reports indicated that the Americans had been repulsed with severe losses, and four days later the assembly's letter of thanks amounted to a condolence. After observing that "the best designs and boldest efforts may sometimes fail by unforseen incidents," Congress expressed its trust "that, on future occasions, the valour and virtue of the army will, by the blessing of Heaven, be crowned with complete and deserved success."

Grim determination was the mood of the assembly when the Articles of Confederation were debated throughout the second week at York. And it seemed a miracle of progress to settle the most controversial issue in just two days.

Although the doors were still closed, the policy of secrecy had been amended on August 2nd by a resolution "that all proceedings of Congress, and all questions agitated and determined by Congress, be entered on the journal, and that the yeas or nays of each member, if required by any State, be taken on every question as stated and determined by the house." [3]

This reform, now getting its first real test, seemed to have a beneficial effect on members who realized that they might be asked to explain their vote as printed in the *Journals*. The large-state men, opposing an equal vote for each state, tried to put over amendments providing a representative for each fifty or even thirty thousand inhabitants. But on October 10th Henry Laurens could write to his son that Congress had "surmounted one vast point—the Votes are to be by States and not by Voices." The resolution had passed with Virginia dissenting and North Carolina divided.

Next came the equally thorny question of apportionment of public expenses. Laurens wrote that "some sensible things have been said, and as much nonsense as ever I heard in so short a space." After four days of discussion the delegates decided on the 14th in favor of a basis of land values with improvements, "estimated according to such mode as Congress shall, from time to time, direct and appoint." The southern and middle states had defeated the solid New England phalanx by a vote of 5 to 4, with New York and Pennsylvania divided.

It needed no prophet to foresee that both issues—the method of voting as well as the apportionment of expenses—would vex Congress again and again in the future. But the assembly had evidently made up its mind that a patchwork confederation offered more shelter than none, and October 15th saw a decision on the third of the trinity of issues which had split the states hopelessly for the last sixteen months—the claims to the South Sea.

Maryland led the fight against the "three-sided" states, but the influence of Virginia prevailed to defeat three successive amendments giving Congress varying degrees of power to fix the western boundaries. Again it could be foreseen that this settlement, like the other two, had merely banked fires of controversy which would blaze up into flame again and again.

Although each state would have but one vote, the number of delegates was established at not less than two or more than seven. Following is this decision as it was published in the *Journals*:

New Hampshire			Rhode Island		
Mr. Folsom,	no }no		Mr. Marchant,	no }no	
Massachusetts Bay			Connecticut		
Mr. S. Adams,	ay		Mr. Dyer	ay	
J. Adams,	no	ay	Law	ay	ay
Gerry,	ay		Williams	ay	
Lovell,	ay		Virginia		
New York			Mr. Jones	ay	
Mr. Duane	ay	ay	F. L. Lee	ay	ay
Duer	ay		R. H. Lee	ay	
New Jersey			North Carolina		
Mr. Witherspoon	no	no	Mr. Penn	ay	
Elmer	no		Burke	ay	ay
Pennsylvania			Harnett	ay	
Mr. Morris	ay	ay	South Carolina		
Roberdeau	ay		Mr. Middleton	ay	
Maryland			Heyward	ay	ay
Mr. Chase	ay		Laurens	ay	
Smith	ay	ay			
Carroll	ay				

So it was resolved in the affirmative.

As a safeguard against factions entrenching themselves in Congress, the term of service was limited, at the obvious risk of penalizing experience, to three years in any period of six. "By this measure," Edmund Cody Burnett has written, "Congress effectually inoculated itself with the germ of pernicious anemia." [4]

The delegates labored day after day to complete the remaining articles, none of which threatened any serious disagreement. The only concession to executive authority, as represented by the proposed Council of State, was weakened still further by transforming it into the Committee of the States, consisting of a member from each state authorized to carry on during a recess of Congress. But since this committee could hope for no more powers than those which Congress chose to confer, it evolved as a sort of vermiform appendix of government which could only atrophy or burst. As it proved, the outcome would be a bad case of inflammation in the summer of 1784.

By the end of the month a hard-driving Congress had composed its differences so successfully as to complete the Articles of Confederation save for a few last touches. It remained only to await or create a good opportunity for presenting them to the states; and if the delegates could have known, a

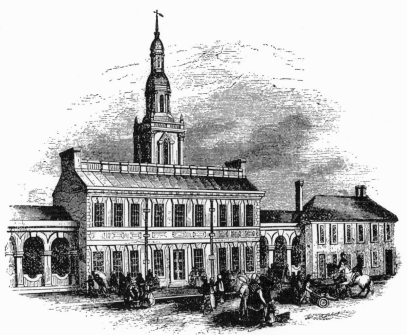

The State House in Philadelphia, later known as Independence Hall, was the home of the Continental Congress from 1775 to 1783, except for two interludes when the enemy threatened.

JOHN ADAMS
portrait by Stuart

THOMAS JEFFERSON
from copper plate by St. Memin

GEORGE WASHINGTON
portrait by Trumbull

JAMES MADISON
portrait by Stuart

JAMES MONROE
portrait by Stuart

The first five presidents of the new Republic were graduates *summa cum laude* of that school of practical politics, the Continental Congress.

JOHN JAY

BENJAMIN FRANKLIN
reprinted from
Harper's Magazine

America's first diplomats and foreign ministers were selected by and from the Continental Congress. Benjamin Franklin was minister to France, and John Jay the minister to Spain. Henry Laurens sailed for Holland as commissioner to negotiate a loan, but was captured and imprisoned in London Tower.

HENRY LAURENS
reprinted from *Harper's Magazine*

EDWARD RUTLEDGE
reprinted from *Harper's Magazine*

THOMAS MCKEAN
reprinted from *Harper's Magazine*

More than a third of the members of the Continental Congress were lawyers or jurists. Many of them, such as the three pictured here, had been educated at the Middle Temple in London.

PEYTON RANDOLPH
portrait by Peale

DR. BENJAMIN RUSH
reprinted from *Harper's Magazine*

DR. DAVID RAMSAY

DR. OLIVER WOLCOTT
reprinted from *Harper's Magazine*

Dr. Wolcott, of Connecticut, Dr. Ramsay, of South Carolina, and Dr. Rush, of Pennsylvania, were three of the physicians who took such a bold part in the decisions of the rebel parliament.

LEWIS MORRIS
courtesy of Independence Hall

CARTER BRAXTON
courtesy of Independence Hall

ARTHUR MIDDLETON
courtesy of Independence Hall

Although the Tories saw themselves as fallen aristocrats, the rebel cause was equally well upheld by old American families such as those represented by the delegates pictured on this page.

CHARLES CARROLL
portrait by Peale, courtesy of Independence Hall

JOHN HANCOCK
portrait by Copley

THOMAS LYNCH, JR.
Brown Brothers

Three of the largest inherited fortunes in the America of that day were risked when these members of the Continental Congress signed the Declaration of Independence on August 2, 1776.

Three members made a specialty of the financial problems of the Continental Congress which baffled their colleagues.

ROBERT MORRIS
reprinted from *Harper's Magazine*

ALEXANDER HAMILTON
miniature by Talleyrand

GOUVERNEUR MORRIS
reprinted from *Harper's Magazine*

FRANCIS LEWIS
courtesy of Independence Hall

PHILIP LIVINGSTON
reprinted from *Harper's Magazine*

Questions of trade and commerce were
in the province of these delegates who
had succeeded as merchants of colonial
America.

WILLIAM WHIPPLE
portrait by St. Memin, courtesy of
Independence Hall

More than a third of the members of the middle-aged Continental Congress volunteered for active war service. Some of them, such as those pictured here, rose to high rank.

THOMAS MIFFLIN

PHILIP SCHUYLER
reprinted from *Harper's Magazine*

JOHN SULLIVAN

THE REV. JACOB DUCHÉ
Brown Brothers

CHARLES THOMSON
Brown Brothers

Three of the salaried employees of Congress were the Rev. Jacob Duché, first chaplain, Charles Thomson, permanent secretary, and Thomas Paine, secretary of foreign affairs.

THOMAS PAINE
portrait by Romney

JAMES DUANE
reprinted from *Harper's Magazine*

JOHN DICKINSON
reprinted from *Harper's Magazine*

John Dickinson, supported by
Wilson, Duane and other conservatives, led the long and bitter
fight in Congress against what he
held to be a premature Declaration
of Independence.

JAMES WILSON
courtesy of Independence Hall

PATRICK HENRY

ELBRIDGE GERRY
reprinted from *Harper's Magazine*

Richard Henry Lee, backed by such ex-members as the Virginia orator and Massachusetts politician, was the fore-most opponent of the proposed new Constitution on the floor of Congress.

RICHARD HENRY LEE
reprinted from *Harper's Magazine*

ABRAHAM CLARK
courtesy of Independence Hall

WILLIAM ELLERY
portrait by Trumbull,
courtesy of Independence Hall

These three members set a record for long and faithful service in the Continental Congress which was never bettered.

ROGER SHERMAN
courtesy of Independence Hall

The revolutionary assembly also had
its chronic troublemakers, such as the
leaders of factions pictured on this page.

SAMUEL ADAMS
reprinted from *Harper's Magazine*

SILAS DEANE

ARTHUR LEE
courtesy of Independence Hall

The City Hall of New York, later known as Federal Hall, became from 1785 to 1789 the eighth and final meeting place of the migratory Continental Congress.

victory had already been won on October 17th which went far beyond their wildest dreams.

First, there had to be one last gloomy moment. On October 8th, just after the reverse at Germantown, the Rev. Jacob Duché turned apostate. Writing from behind the enemy lines at Philadelphia, he implored Washington to abjure the cause and return to the British fold. The commander in chief promptly sent the letter to Congress, which suffered a more painful shock than the one caused by Dr. Church's treason in 1775.

Although the Philadelphia minister had amicably resigned as chaplain, he was still esteemed as the greatest mediator between Jehovah and the Continental Congress. No delegate of 1774 could ever forget his powerful intercession for divine vengeance on that morning when the bells were mourning the supposed destruction of Boston. Such memories only added to the fury of delegates who now denounced Duché as the blackest of traitors. "Poor man!" wrote John Adams. "I pity his weakness and detest his wickedness." Nathaniel Folsom, the self-educated New Hampshire delegate, reported to his own state with indignant spelling, "I inclose you a Coppey of a letter from the Revt. mr. Ducha to general Washington that you may See what a Judas wase a Chaplin to Congress."

The pastor's "treason" might have been judged less harshly if it had not been aggravated by unkind comments on the delegates. "Take an impartial view of the present Congress," he wrote. "What can you expect of them? Your feelings must be greatly hurt by the representation of your native province."

The Lee brothers, who had no small idea of their own worth, probably winced at this point. But in the very next paragraph it was the turn of Pennsylvania: "As to those of my own province, some of them are so obscure that their very names have never met my ears before, and others have only been distinguished for the weakness of their understandings and the violence of their tempers." And if the Yankees, who loved a spicy bit of malice, were inclined to chuckle at the expense of their colleagues, here was a message for them: "From the New England provinces can you find one that, as a gentleman, you could wish to associate with, unless the soft and mild address of Mr. Hancock can atone for the want of every other qualification necessary for the seat he fills?"

Duché had the intimate knowledge to make some pungent comments. But in the end he fell back upon that attitude of social snobbery which so often stultified the loyalist cause. For it was abuse rather than criticism when he described the delegates as "bankrupts, attorneys, and men of desperate fortunes. Are the dregs of a Congress, then, still to influence a mind like yours?" he asked Washington. "Most of them were chosen by a little, low faction, and the few gentlemen that are now among them are well known to be on the balance and looking up to your hand to move the beam."

Never did an actor on the stage of history miss his cue more ineptly than this wretched soul who gave way to discouragement just as the gates of hell were being stormed. It has even been argued that the pastor was a victim of enemy coercion, for he became one of the most miserable of the exiles in England. Long after the war he returned to end his life in America, and Washington received him courteously as president of the new republic.

The first wild reports of a victory over Burgoyne, too fantastic to be credited, reached York on the 16th. Martin Brenise rang the courthouse bell for hours, but no word came from Gates. On the 23rd John Adams wrote to James Warren, "We have had Rumours, which lifted us up to the Stars." That same day he informed Abigail of "news from the committee of Albany through Governor Clinton and General Washington of a capitulation of Burgoyne and his whole army. To this moment we have no express from Gates or any authentic confirmation." [5]

On the 27th, after three more anxious days of "soaking and poaching in the heaviest rain that has been known for several years," Adams was still fretting. In a letter of that date he exploded, "It is impossible to bear this suspense any longer."

It had to be borne, nevertheless, until the very last day of the month, when Colonel James Wilkinson arrived with dispatches from Gates. While the delegates at York were writhing on the rack, the 20-year-old officer had stopped off at Reading to woo the young woman whom he afterwards won in marriage. This romantic interlude did not charm members of Congress, who had to content themselves with a brief verbal report on the 31st, then wait through the whole weekend until Gates' aide could prepare his papers to lay before the assembly on November 3rd.

Considering that the most decisive battle ever fought on American soil remains the most misunderstood, it is not remarkable that the delegates of 1777 got a confused impression. But even the dispatches "sent in a most slovenly manner," as Roberdeau complained, made it gloriously plain that Burgoyne laid down his arms on October 17th after being defeated ten days before in a last desperate attempt to break through the American lines.

During following months it grew equally clear that the military events at Saratoga had often been a sideshow to the personal clash between the two ranking generals. Arnold, rallying about him all of Schuyler's adherents, displayed an insubordination which fully justified Gates in relieving him from command. On October 7th he appeared on the field just in time to lead a final charge which stole the glory of a battle already won, but there is no convincing evidence that he took the slightest part in the hard-fought action of September 19th. The actual battlefield victor of Saratoga was Dan Morgan of the riflemen. Kosciusko, the engineer, deserves great credit for his field fortifications; and as a gifted organizer Gates wrought miracles of order and confidence in an incoherent militia host. Judged on his merits, Arnold was the only one of the four whose absence would not have made any difference in the final result.

At the age of 41 the leader of the riflemen, a rudely educated Virginian who had served as a wagoner in the last war, would not have been thought a gentleman according to the best contemporary standards. Gates seems to have recognized his tactical ability on October 7th, however, by leaving everything to him in the battle of Bemis Heights with the command, "Order on Morgan to begin the game."

Neither friend nor foe could have realized that a new era of tactics was being born on the battlefield where America won her independence. The vicious crack of the rifles at Saratoga emphasized the spectacular futility of redcoats marching shoulder to shoulder in perfect parade step to fire an unaimed volley at forty paces. Morgan's men fought in a deadly silence broken only by the gibbering of the wild turkey calls they used for signaling. Their rifles were instruments of precision as compared to the Brown Bess smoothbores of the foe. Their linen hunting shirts, blending with the autumnal brown of the leaves, were the first modern uniforms of protective coloring. Their tactics, as they scattered to fire from cover, were the methods of woodsmen stalking game, and the handsome British officers were the prey of the man hunt at Saratoga.

Such military considerations, of course, did not interest the members of Congress. They perceived what a heaven-sent political opportunity had been vouchsafed them, and no time was lost in formally adopting the Articles of Confederation on November 15th.

With an eye to public relations, the delegates had already passed a resolution "for getting a printing press erected in this town for the purpose of conveying to the public, the intelligence that Congress may, from time to time, receive." [6] It was further resolved, after the confirmation of the Saratoga news, "to set apart Thursday, the eighteenth day of December next, for solemn thanksgiving and praise" with the earnest recommendation "that servile labour, and such recreation as, though at other times innocent, may be unbecoming the purpose of this appointment, be omitted on so solemn an occasion." [7]

In their hearts the men of the Continental Congress knew that the Articles of Confederation were charged with the gunpowder of future dissension. But as practical politicians they also knew that this opportunity must not be wasted, since a forthcoming exodus of delegates threatened to reduce the membership to barely twenty. Both Chase and Carroll were returning to Maryland for a long stay. Hancock had resigned as president to enter Massachusetts politics, and the two Adamses planned to spend at least a month in Boston. The Articles were frankly rushed through to completion before these members departed; and in a circular letter of November 17th Congress asked the states to ratify them by March 10th:

> Hardly is it to be expected that any plan, in the variety of provisions essential to our union, should exactly correspond with the maxims of political views of every State. Let it be remarked, that, after the most careful inquiry and information, this is proposed as the best which could be adopted to the circumstances of all; and as that alone which affords any tolerable prospect of a general ratification. Permit us, then, earnestly to recommend these articles to the immediate and dispassionate attention of the legislatures of the respective states.[8]

The victory at Saratoga had been won by Morgan, Kosciusko and Gates, but it took all the casuistry of John Witherspoon to save it. For the articles of capitulation had no more than been scanned in Congress when a fatal flaw became apparent. According to the terms of the surrender—the "Convention," to use the euphemism preferred by the vanquished—the prisoners were to be marched to Boston and transported to their homeland in British ships. It was further agreed that they should not be employed again in the war, but the members of Congress found nothing to prevent the recent captives from being used to replace other British soldiers, thus releasing them from guard or garrison duty to fight in America as early as the following spring.

The fruits of victory, in short, were in danger of being snatched from the victors before they could be tasted. Nor could Gates be blamed, since he had been threatened at the time by Clinton's advance on his rear up the Hudson valley. As he explained to Congress, "this delicate situation abridged our conquests and procured Lieutenant General Burgoyne the terms he enjoys."

The delegates were not such innocents as to suppose that the enemy would fail to take full advantage of this weak link in the surrender terms binding them. From the beginning the British had made it plain that they did not consider rebels in a class with other belligerents. This policy had the tacit approval of such royal brothers and sisters of George III as Frederick, Catherine and Maria Theresa, who were just then digesting the territory carved from the living body of Poland. Any one of them would have administered harsher chastisement if dealing with a similar uprising, for the atmosphere in this age of enlightened rulers still held a taint of the divine right of kings. George's brothers and sisters did not wish him any more success than necessary—England was already too successful. But neither did they have any sympathy for the civilians of unfortified towns which had been burned, or for the military prisoners literally rotting away in the dark, unspeakable holds of British prison ships.

It was plainly a case, as Dr. Witherspoon perceived, of God helping those who helped themselves. Anyone with a rudimentary sense of economics could have deduced as early as 1777 that the war would be won by the side which could keep the last brigade in the field. In this strife of attrition each redcoat or Hessian sent across the Atlantic meant another straw added to the tax burden bowing the backs of the English people. The fact that Englishmen themselves did not volunteer in sufficient numbers is not proof of an unpopular war up to this time. Even at the climax of Pitt's magnificent leadership in the last war the American colonies contributed more men and money in proportion to resources than the mother country. Englishmen were not given to volunteering, but neither were they the sort who would consent to the loss of their former colonies until the weight of taxes became too great to bear. Then, and then only, the government upholding the monarch's personal rule would fall.

Dr. Witherspoon realized that such a war of endurance might very well be decided by the factor of a surrendered British army releasing fresh troops for active service in America. Yet it would never do for the rebels to give the appearance of repudiating their general. At this time they were angling not only for a treaty with his Christian Majesty of France but also the crowned heads of Spain, Prussia and Austria.

It was a problem which might have baffled anyone but Dr. Witherspoon, who knew more than one way to skin a cat. A Presbyterian with the artful wiles attributed to Jesuits, he found his first opening when General Burgoyne complained that "the public faith is broke" because his army had not been given the kind of accommodations in Boston which the Convention prescribed.

Congress had meanwhile appointed a committee of investigation, with Witherspoon as chairman, consisting of Dana of Massachusetts, Duer of New York, Francis Lightfoot Lee of Virginia, and Jonathan Bayard Smith of Pennsylvania. On their recommendation the assembly resolved on December 1st that Burgoyne's troops "when they do embark, must be shipped from the port stipulated by the convention of Saratoga and no other." [9]

This meant that the enemy could not gain time by embarking some of the prisoners from Newport and New York, as Howe had requested. The committee answered Burgoyne's charge by accusing him of such minor violations as omitting to return an exact list of troops and failing to surrender all bayonets and cartridge boxes.

On January 2nd Dr. Witherspoon was at last ready to smite the enemy hip and thigh as he stood before Congress in the full dignity of his scholastic gown. He seemed almost to be defending the British troops as he spoke sadly of their violations. Americans, said Dr. Witherspoon, ought "to consider that it was so unexpected, and must have been so humiliating a thing for a whole British army to surrender their arms, and deliver themselves up as prisoners to those whom they had been accustomed to speak with such contempt and disdain—that it is not to be wondered at, if the common soldiers did some things out of spite and ill humor, not to be justified." [10]

The delegates in the little courthouse at York were being treated to a masterly performance. As he continued, the Presbyterian divine appeared to be finding kindly excuses for Burgoyne as well as his men. "But we have here the declared opinion of one of the parties, that the public faith is broken by the other. . . . Therefore we have reason to conclude, that if Mr. Burgoyne is of opinion that the convention is broken on our part, he will not hold to it on his. He would act the part of a fool if he did. It is no consequence to say that his opinion is ill-founded or unjust, as it manifestly is in the present case; for whether it is just or unjust, if it is *really* his opinion (and we should wrong his sincerity to doubt it) the consequences are the same with respect to us."

Dr. Witherspoon was not at a loss when he came to the well-founded British charges that his countrymen had violated Convention terms by not providing the quarters specified for officers and men. "It was very natural," he said, "to suppose that General Burgoyne, accustomed to the splendor of the British court, and possessed with ideas of his own importance, would be but ill pleased with the best accommodations that could be obtained for him and his numerous followers, in one of the frugal states of New England. One would have thought," he continued, twisting the devil's tail harder, "that the recollection of the ruin of Charlestown, the burning of which, if I mistake not, in a letter . . . he calls a glorious light, might have prevented his complaints, even though he had less elbow room than he wished for. But as circumstances stand," concluded Dr. Witherspoon sorrowfully, "by what conduct will we ever be able to satisfy him? When will pretenses ever be wanting to one seeking to prove the convention broken, when it is his inclination or interest to do so?"

While the delegates pondered these sophistries, they may also have recalled Washington's warning in a letter of October 28th to Richard Henry Lee that "unless great delicacy is used in the precautions, a plea will be given them [the British], & they will justify a breach of the Covenant on that part—do they not declare (many of them) that no faith is to be held with Rebels?—did not the English do the very thing I am now suspecting them of, after the Convention of Closter Seven, upon changing their commander? —will they hold better faith with us than they did with the French?"

Washington was referring to the Duke of Cumberland's surrender of a whole army to the French in the last war. His father, George II, repudiated as ruler of Hanover the Convention of Kloster Seven which bound him as monarch of England, and his trickery had the approval if not instigation of the British ministers in 1757.

This historical object lesson influenced Congress to accept the counsel of Dr. Witherspoon and his committee. On January 8th the delegates decided that Burgoyne would not hesitate to take advantage of the "pretended breach of the convention, in order to disengage himself, and the army under him, of the obligation they are under to these United States; and that the security, which these states have had in his personal honor, is hereby destroyed."

> Resolved, therefore, That the embarkation of Lieutenant General Burgoyne, and the troops under his command, be suspended till a distinct and explicit ratification of the convention of Saratoga shall be properly notified by the court of Great Britain to Congress.[11]

At a glance this measure seems guileless enough. On second thought, however, it becomes evident that George III and his ministers would never consent to relations with Congress amounting virtually to a recognition of American independence. Dr. Witherspoon had shown Congress how to eat its cake and have it, and the assembly could afford the generous gesture of allowing Burgoyne to go home on a plea of illness. His troops remained in captivity until the end of the war, when those who had not died or deserted were exchanged.

The decision of the Continental Congress was no trivial factor in a war of attrition. Yet it has shocked the very debunkers and masochists of American history who fashioned a crown of martyrdom for Benedict Arnold. Dr. Witherspoon and the members of his committee must have rested uneasily in their graves until 1932, when Sir Henry Clinton's secret service papers were released to scholars. Then the policy of Congress was fully vindicated by confidential documents proving that the British had schemed to send the Convention troops back into active American service without troubling to use them for releasing other regiments.[12]

The sentimental legend of the neglect and mistreatment of Arnold by the Continental Congress also has been pretty well blasted by these papers. For the historical evidence shows him to have been a cold and avaricious scoundrel who took the initiative in a treason which had no motive except profit.[13]

Cold weather came early that winter and stayed late. The invalids of Congress had more than their usual share of ills, and Eliphalet Dyer confided a medical discovery to a friend in Connecticut. "A deccoction of strong soot with the Yolk of an egg repeated a few mornings will relieve you of your Jaundice," he wrote, "as I have found by repeated experience."

The infirmities of age were also creeping up on Richard Henry Lee. And since a man cannot be too careful about his vision, he wrote to his brother Arthur, a medical graduate of the University of Edinburgh: "My eyes are so extremely injured by their constant application, that without the aid and support of Spectacles I fear I shall soon lose the use of them. I pray you then to procure me a pair of the best Temple Spectacles that can be had. In fitting these perhaps it may be proper to remember that my age is 46, that my eyes are light colored, and have been quick and strong, but are now weakened by constant use. My head thin between the temple." [14]

Even for delegates in good health, the Pennsylvania village offered a dull and cramped life. "Believe me it is the most inhospitable scandalous place I was ever in," complained Cornelius Harnett in a letter. "If I can return once more to my family all the Devils in Hell shall not separate us. The honor of being once a member of Congress is sufficient for me. I acknowledge it is the highest honor a free state can bestow on one of its members. I shall be careful to ask for nothing more," sighed the North Carolina merchant, "but will sit down under my own vine and Fig tree. . . ." [15]

Illness, discontent and the lure of state politics combined to reduce attendance. Henry Laurens, elected president to take Hancock's place, reported to Governor John Rutledge on January 30th that the assembly had "about 21 Members, often 13, sometimes barely 9 States on the floor represented by as many persons." The mornings were occupied until ten o'clock, he explained, with meetings of committees. "If we can then make a house we set till 1 or 2 and never take more than two hours respite, then sit again till 8 or 9." [16]

Oliver Wolcott, returning after an absence, wrote on February 18th that the Connecticut members "hope soon to get into private Lodgings, but We do not know where and find that they are not to be had but with the greatest difficulty and Expence. the latter is so great that I understand that a single Man exclusive of Horsekeeping cannot probably live under at least ten pounds per Week. Everything here bears an enormous price."

Overwork and overcrowding made for short tempers. At the end of a hard winter Thomas Burke waged a one-man war with Congress, which found itself in the painful situation of being too "thin" to discipline him without his own vote. On the evening of April 10th the hot-tempered North Carolina delegate was in his room with a bad cold when President Laurens summoned him to a late session.

"Devil a foot will I go tonight!" he roared, according to the messenger. "It is too late and too unreasonable."

In answer to a second summons Burke asserted "that he will not submit to a tyranny of the majority of this Congress, which would keep him here at unreasonable hours." The following day he declared before the assembly that "he was guilty of no rudeness to Congress; and if he was guilty of an affront, it was to individual members, and required another kind of apology; that he was not convinced he had done any wrong; was not disposed to make any kind of apology; and if he had been guilty of improper conduct, he will answer to his State."

After solemn deliberation Congress decided that Burke had been "disorderly and contemptuous." The resolution of censure added that "the principle upon which he has attempted to justify his withdrawing from the house is dangerous, because it strikes at the very existence of the house, and, as in the present case actually happened, would enable a single member to put an instant stop to the most important proceedings of Congress." [17]

A few days later the states' rights champion returned to North Carolina and appealed to the legislature, which not only upheld his conduct but re-elected him as a delegate.

The mood of Congress is evident from the proclamation in which April 22nd was appointed as a day of fasting and prayer. Americans were exhorted to "confess their iniquities and transgressions, for which the land mourneth; that they may implore the mercy and forgiveness of God; and beseech him that vice, prophaneness, extortion, and every evil, may be done away; and that we may be a reformed and happy people."

The privations suffered by Washington's ragged, half-starved army in the encampment at Valley Forge kept Congress in a mood of anxiety and even guilt. On September 17th and November 14th the commander in chief had twice again been given extraordinary powers of a "dictatorial" nature. Chief among them was the authority "to subsist his army from such parts of the country as are in its vicinity." When he showed great forbearance, Congress scolded him mildly in a resolution of December 10, 1777, for his "delicacy in exerting military authority on the citizens of these states; a delicacy, which though highly laudable in general, may, on critical exigencies, prove destructive to the army and prejudicial to the general liberties of America."

During the next two weeks the relations between Washington and the delegates were strained. Just after Christmas they listened uncomfortably while Secretary Thomson read them a letter written by the general on December 23rd, expressing his candid opinion of gentlemen who seemed to think that soldiers "were made of Stocks or Stones and equally insensible of frost and Snow."

I can assure these Gentlemen that it is a much easier and less distressing thing to draw remonstrances in a comfortable room by a good fire side than to occupy a cold bleak hill and sleep under frost and Snow without Cloaths or Blankets; however, although they seem to have little feeling for the naked, and distressed Soldier, I feel superabundantly for them, and from my soul pity those miseries, wch. it is neither in my power to relieve or prevent . . . and it adds not a little to my other difficulties, and distress, to find that much more is expected of me than is possible to be performed, and that upon the ground of safety and policy, I am obliged to conceal the true State of the Army from Public view and thereby expose myself to detraction and Calumny.

Seldom in history has a president spoken his mind more forcefully to congressmen than this soldier who had been beaten in most of his battles. He might have been dismissed in an hour, but the Continental Congress took its lecture meekly and kept a committee at Valley Forge all winter to make firsthand reports and recommendations. John Adams was no longer a delegate after accepting an appointment as commissioner to France in December. Dana, Folsom, John Harvie and Joseph Reed were appointed to the committee, with Gouverneur Morris and Charles Carroll of Carrollton being added as new members.

In 1777 Congress had made some progress in the direction of administrative reform. Not only had Robert Morris been a blunt critic of the old standing committees; he showed what a competent man could do when he handled the Philadelphia business of Congress during the Baltimore interlude. William Hooper was convinced that "like beginners in every thing else we want Oecomomy, or rather want System. Unless officers are appointed competent to the management of our funds we must be ruined; from a false parsimony in saving hundreds in salaries of proper Officers we are sporting away millions in the want of them." [18]

The assembly elected a committee of five at Baltimore "to prepare a plan for the better conducting the business of Congress by boards composed of persons, not members of Congress." The first result was the reorganization of the office of the secretary of Congress, completed on March 22, 1777. A month later the old Committee of Secret Correspondence became the Committee for Foreign Affairs—a step nearer to our present Department of State—with Thomas Paine being awarded the office of salaried secretary. That same week saw a plan reported for a Board of War composed of men not members of Congress, but it took until October 17th for the measure to be approved. During the winter of Valley Forge a civilian, Richard Peters, served with three soldiers, Gates, Pickering and Mifflin.

It could not be said that the army was neglected. Sometimes, perhaps, there were too many cooks for the watery broth of Valley Forge. Both Gates and Mifflin, the recently resigned quartermaster general, were believed to wish the commander in chief no good; but events would soon prove that he was quite capable of taking care of himself in a political fight.

It was the fop, the cynic and gallant of the Continental Congress who became the moving spirit of the committee at Valley Forge. More than all the rest, Gouverneur Morris made known the hardships of the army and clamored for improvements. Only 25 at the time of his election in 1777, he came from an old and aristocratic New York family of Tory sympathies. Despite his youth, he combined an education at King's College with an extensive experience in state politics. Soon after taking his seat in Congress he joined the committee, and his efforts of the next three months earned him the friendship of Washington.

The young cynic's epigrams were already being quoted. "It is dangerous to be impartial in politics," he wrote to Hamilton. "You who are temperate in drinking have never perhaps noticed the awkward situation of the man who continues to be sober after the company are drunk." There was nothing temperate or impartial about the vigor with which Morris used his pen to awaken the country to conditions at Valley Forge. "The American army, in the heart of America, is on the point of deserting, having nothing to eat," he wrote to Governor Clinton. And in a letter to John Jay he declared, "An army of skeletons appears before our eyes, naked, starved, sick, discouraged."

The new delegate did not spare Congress. "The powerful American Senate is not what we have known it to be. Continental money and Congress have both depreciated," he admitted to Jay. In the very next sentence, however, he expressed his faith that "in the hands of the all powerful Architect of empires the stone which the builders have discarded may easily become the corner stone." [19]

No critics outside the Continental Congress have ever been able to outdo the delegates themselves at making derogatory comments. The winter of York and Valley Forge, as might be expected, found the assembly in a mood for sackcloth and ashes.

"The Love of country and public virtue are annihilated," groaned William Ellery of Rhode Island. "If Diogenes were alive and were to search America with candles, would he find an honest man?" Charles Carroll of Carrollton commented gloomily that "the Congress do worse than ever: We murder time, and chat it away in idle impertinent talk: However, I hope the urgency of affairs will teach even that Body a little discretion." His colleague John Henry, a young Maryland lawyer educated at Princeton and the Temple, believed that "the Avarice of our people and the extravagant prices of all commodities, joined with the imperfect management of Affairs, would expend the mines of Chile and Peru." [20]

Henry did not exaggerate when he summed up in his letter of February 17th some of the difficulties of Congress: "The state of our Army is critical. Four months pay, if not more are due them, and no Money in the Treasury to satisfy their just and reasonable Demands. The press is at work, and attended with all vigilance and care, and has been for some time past; near a million a week is now made; and yet our Demands are greater than we can answer. They come in from all parts of the Continent."

The Maryland member might soon have added a few more troubles to the list. March 10th, the deadline appointed for all thirteen states to have ratified the Articles of Confederation, found only Virginia ready and some of the laggards hostile. And on Friday, March 13th, in keeping with that portentous date, the assembly gave up a long-cherished dream by resolving that "Congress have judged it proper, that the irruption ordered to be made into Canada should be suspended. . . ." [21]

Hopes of Canada's becoming the fourteenth state had never been quite abandoned, in spite of an almost total lack of encouragement. Both the Declaration of Independence and the Articles of Confederation were translated into French; and as late as November 29, 1777, Canada had again been invited into the union. There was something about Our Lady of Snows, as a shivering Briton named the region, which appealed irresistibly to Americans who had grown indifferent to the charms of the Floridas, the West Indies islands or other British possessions. Like a jilted lover whose thoughts turn to rape, Congress ceased wooing only long enough to plan another invasion in the spring of 1778 under the command of Lafayette and de Kalb. But the military resources were found to be deficient, and the army was seething with the feuds which have gone down in history as the Conway Cabal.

It was a time for all men to fall back on such resources of philosophy as they possessed. After three months at Valley Forge, young Gouverneur Morris wrote to Washington: "Had our Savior addressed a chapter to the rulers of Mankind, I am persuaded his good sense would have dictated this text: Be not wise overmuch." [22]

This remark was pondered some days by the father of his country, who was not of a blithe turn of mind. Then he interrupted his weary labors to reply: "Had such a chapter as you speak of been written to the rulers of Mankind, it would, I am persuaded, have been as unavailing as many others upon subjects of equal importance."

Chapter 16

The Treaty with France

AT this point it is mandatory for every writer dealing with the American Revolution to put aside more useful work and devote a solemn chapter to the Conway Cabal. If he chooses to look up the original sources, it will very likely occur to him that there is an astonishing lack of historical proof. The Conway Cabal, in short, consists of little except a name and a legend.

The name refers to a supposed ringleader among the conspirators—General Thomas Conway, an Irish volunteer who had long been in the French service. The legend has it that a clique of officers, plotting with members of Congress to replace Washington with Gates, was detected in the nick of time to save the cause.

There can be no question that members of Congress had criticized Washington. It is sometimes forgotten that this was not only the privilege but the duty of delegates responsible for the conduct of the war. Regardless of personal feelings, they owed it to their country to size up the military abilities of the commander in chief and replace him if he fell short. It was also prudent to keep a watchful eye for the first signs of that greed for political power which so many victorious soldiers have shown. These were considerations which John Adams had in mind when he addressed a warning, quoted in Benjamin Rush's diary, to Congress just after the victories at Trenton and Princeton:

> I have been distressed to see some members of this house disposed to idolise an image which their own hands have molten. I speak here of the superstitious veneration that is sometimes paid to Genl Washington. Altho' I honour him for his good qualities, yet in this house I feel myself his Superior. In private life I shall always acknowledge that he is mine. It becomes us to attend early to the restraining our army.[1]

These were blunt words, gritted out by a fighter, which Washington himself would doubtless have approved. But there were delegates who dealt in innuendo—cryptic and sarcastic little jabs such as those appearing frequently in the letters of James Lovell. Samuel Adams, Richard Henry Lee and Benjamin Rush also have been accused of secret opposition to the commander in chief. There is less question about Dr. Rush than the others, though Adams had to make a special trip back to Boston to square himself in that very Green Dragon Tavern where he had done so much to overthrow Hutchinson and the British colonial authorities.

After examining every scrap of evidence, the researcher can only marvel that a beaten general got off with so little censure. For the most interesting thing about the Conway Cabal is not that a few men criticized the commander in chief—it is the incredible fact that so many men took the attitude as early as 1777 that George Washington was above criticism! There is nothing like it in the entire field of history.

The commander in chief himself showed a remarkable detachment. "But why should I expect to be exempt from censure, the unfailing lot of an elevated station?" he inquired in a letter of January 31, 1778, to Henry Laurens. "Merit and talents, with which I can have no pretensions of rivalship, have ever been subject to it. My heart tells me, that it has been my unremitting aim to do the best that circumstances would permit; yet I may have been very often mistaken in my judgment of the means, and may in many instances deserve the imputation of error." [2]

Conway was the sort of Irishman who cannot open his mouth without putting his foot in it. Originally elected to share the command of the Canadian expedition with Lafayette, he made the mistake of dabbling in the politics of an alien land. The French volunteer, equally guilty in this respect, had the better fortune to be on the winning side. As for Gates, he would doubtless have been willing to accept the supreme command, perhaps even eager. But he took good care not to show his cards.

Soldiers, like college instructors and ministers of the gospel, are wont to display more zeal than skill when playing the politics which they profess to scorn. But Washington was no novice. He had been trained in the hard school of the Continental Congress. When he struck, it was with the silent and deadly swiftness of a hawk scattering a flock of pullets. There was nothing left of the Conway Cabal except a penitent Irishman who had been exposed by the commander in chief as the writer of an inept letter. Next came a hasty scramble for cover on the part of a few congressmen whose devotion to Washington soon became ostentatious. Members of Congress knew when they were beaten in a political free-for-all. Moreover, there had been more smoke than flame in the scheming of all the delegates except Dr. Rush.

Washington, like a giant who does not know his own strength, probably had no idea he was dealing such a crushing blow. Conway resigned and left America after recovering from a desperate wound inflicted by General John Cadwalader in a duel of July 4, 1778. The passive part taken by Gates laid him open to the attacks of the Schuyler and Arnold factions; and it needed only a defeat on the battlefield to make him the victim of more historical injustice than has slandered any other figure of the Revolution.

A scholarly book published in 1940, reviewing every source in detail, presents overwhelming proof that there was no serious and widespread conspiracy to overthrow Washington.[3] Some of his contemporaries were speedily disillusioned after taking alarm at first. Henry Laurens, who usually knew what time it was, calmed the excitable Lafayette in a letter of January 12, 1778: "I think the friends of our brave and virtuous General, may rest assured that he is out of the reach of his Enemies, if he has an Enemy, a fact of which I am in doubt of. I believe I hear most that is said and know the outlines of almost all that has been attempted, and the whole amounts to little more than tittle tattle, which would be too much honored by repeating it." [4]

The breaking up of a hard winter resulted in a springtime influx of delegates, both new and old. "We are now come to the season," commented Lovell in a letter to Sam Adams, one of the absentees, "when certain birds of passage return who seldom appear in our flock during the winter."

It was at this time, about the middle of April, when exciting reports reached America that Lord North planned to send new British commissioners empowered to offer peace on practically any terms. There were even more thrilling rumors of a treaty with France, and optimists could imagine Europe's two most powerful nations running a race across the Atlantic for the favor of America.

"Great Britain means seriously to treat," wrote Gouverneur Morris to Jay on April 28th. "Our affairs are most critical, though not dangerously so. If the minister from France were present as well as him from Britain, I am a blind politician if the thirteen States (with their extended territory) would not be in peaceable possession of their independence, three months from this date. As it is, expect a long war." [5]

An amazing firmness could be shown on any important issue by delegates who had recently been grumbling and bickering. Charles Carroll of Carrollton appears to have voiced the sentiment of the entire assembly in a letter of April 23rd:

> If Lord North's speech is genuine (and I think we have no reason to suspect it to be otherwise) we may fairly conclude that the Administration begin to see the impracticability of reducing these states, or of retaining them, when reduced, in such a state of subordination as to be useful to G. B. . . . In a word, if we guard agt. their insidious offers on the one hand, and can resist their warlike efforts on the other, during the ensuing campaign, I have not the least doubt but that they will acknowledge our Independence next winter, or Spring, particularly if no alliance between these States and some other European power be concluded on the interim.[6]

In a letter written four days later the Maryland delegate emphasized that "no terms, short of Independence, are in my opinion admissible without the utmost danger and disadvantage to these States."

Great Britain, as the rebels suspected, had at last awakened to the imminent peril of finding herself involved in a war against half of Europe. It was the misfortune of the nation which had led the world in political liberalism that the king's supporters were such respectable figures, his opponents such a crew of oddlings, radicals and worse. Lord North, like the monarch himself, was the soul of amiability. Even the opposition found it hard to hate a minister who chuckled until the tears coursed down his fat cheeks upon hearing the latest sarcastic thrust by Chatham.

Burke was so pompous outside the House of Commons that Fox's mistress and gambling debts seemed a welcome contrast. The mind of John Wilkes might have been likened to a garden surrounded by a wall scribbled with indecencies. And anyone could see that Chatham, that terrible old man out of the past, had one foot in the grave and the other in America.

These were the opposition leaders. In contrast, the king's personal rule and American policy were upheld by men whose greatness had to be conceded by the rebels themselves—Edward Gibbon, the historian; Dr. Samuel Johnson, the lexicographer; James McPherson, the author of the Ossian poems; John Wesley, the venerable founder of Methodism. True it was that the first three had been no little influenced by royal rewards, as Gibbon openly boasted. But some of the most exotic butterflies of that age were daintily nourished on corruption, and at least John Wesley had not been bought. He urged his humble followers to render obedience unto the British Caesar.

Dr. Johnson, after the king increased his pension, wrote an abusive pamphlet, *Taxation No Tyranny*, which came out in subsidized editions. McPherson received £500 from the government for his *Right of Great Britain Asserted*, published in ten editions and translated into French. But the most widely read English propagandist was Wesley, whose *Calm Address to the American Colonies* reached a total circulation not far short of 100,000 copies.[7]

These pamphleteers did not escape some censure in England. Dr. Johnson's well-paid efforts were deplored by his admirer Boswell; and A. M. Toplady, the saintlike author of the hymn *Rock of Ages*, called Wesley "a low and puny tadpole of divinity."

Up to the news of Saratoga the war had been a fairly popular cause in England. Commoners as well as the landed gentry had a strong feeling of ownership in regard to colonies, and it seemed to them that George III was fighting for the nation's rights. The only dissenters of any influence were the merchants of a creditor nation who had already lost heavily during the decade of American defiance before 1775. At the outbreak of war the debts and accumulated interest owed by the colonies amounted to the staggering total of five million pounds. London and Glasgow were each involved to the tune of about two millions.

American loyalists asserted that one of the most potent and least publicized causes of the Revolution was this vast debt. On the other hand, Dr. Johnson urged his countrymen to beware of English merchants who placed their profit above the Empire's glory.

After a retirement of two years Lord Chatham returned to the fray on May 30, 1777, with a motion in the House of Lords for a cessation of hostilities. The vote was no closer than might have been expected—28 in favor and 199 opposed.

At the opening of Parliament the following November 18th, Chatham wore the crimson robe of a peer, but it was Mr. Pitt who thundered, "I know that the conquest of English America *is an impossibility*. You cannot, I venture to say it, *you cannot* conquer America. . . . My lords, *you cannot conquer America.*" At the conclusion of his speech he glared at a hostile audience and said, "If I were an American, as I am an Englishman, while a foreign troop was landed in my country, I would never lay down my arms—never—never—never!" [8]

On December 11th, after the news of Burgoyne's surrender, Mr. Pitt pleaded for the conciliation of America in time to prevent an alliance with France. There was still time, if Parliament could be aroused to a sense of the peril, to notify the American commissioners in France and send British peace envoys in a fast ship across the Atlantic. For years the Great Commoner had been in the position of someone shouting alarms to a boatload of deafmutes drifting down the current toward a cataract. Both of the great opposition chiefs, in fact, believed that Englishmen of the era had degenerated. Burke wondered sadly what had become of "the eager, jealous, fiery people" of old;

and Pitt declared that the nation of this decade was "no more like the old England, or England forty years ago" than the decadent Romans of the later Empire were like those of the Republic.[9]

Allowing for the pessimism of minority leaders, this theory has a great deal of support from history. The greatest nations have their periods of sloth and lethargy, and the Englishmen who slept through the personal rule of George III and the loss of America could not even be awakened to the danger of a European war. At this eleventh hour the peers of the realm gazed insolently at the grotesque old man with the raddled face who had been so long the political conscience of Britain.

"Ten thousand brave men have fallen victims to ignorance and rashness," croaked Mr. Pitt. "The only army you have in America may, by this time, be no more. . . . My lords, I contend that we have not, nor can procure, any force sufficient to subdue America. It is monstrous to think of it."

The orator flayed the administration with the lash of his scorn. "Conciliation is at length thought of. Terms are to be offered. Who are the persons that are to treat on the part of this afflicted and deluded country? The very men who have been the authors of our misfortunes! The very men who have endeavored, by the most pernicious policy, the highest injustice and oppression, the most cruel and devastating war, to enslave those people they would now conciliate, to gain the confidence and affection of those who have survived the Indian tomahawk and German bayonet. Can your lordships entertain the most distant prospect of success from such a treaty and such negotiators?" Pitt answered his own question with another of those prophecies which his countrymen had been ignoring and which had such a dismal habit of coming true. "No, my lords, the Americans have virtue, and they must detest the principles of such men. They have understanding, and too much wisdom, to trust to the cunning and narrow politics which must cause such overtures on the part of their merciless persecutors."[10]

Mr. Pitt made one more appearance in Parliament, the most dramatic of all. The date was April 7, 1778, and America had become the ally of the hereditary foe. The bitter old man had to be helped to his feet, for his legs were swathed in flannel bandages. Instead of the crimson robes, this day he wore the old black velvet suit he had made famous in the House of Commons. And in the middle of his final speech, pleading for a stout fight to keep intact the Empire his genius had created, he collapsed with the stroke which caused his death.

But it was not quite the end. Even in death Mr. Pitt had a sure instinct for the theatrical. Two years later, on a May morning in 1780, a British fleet began the bombardment of Charleston. One of the first cannon balls sped across the Ashley River, screamed its way up Meeting Street, past St.

Michael's Church, and took a hand off the statue of William Pitt. It was the right hand—the hand which held a copy of the Magna Carta.

On February 17, 1778, Lord North conceded British defeat in the war by asking Commons to pass a bill for the appointment of commissioners who would be given the broadest powers to offer peace to America on virtually any terms they could obtain.

This was the administration's answer to the news that a treaty with France had been signed on the 6th by the American commissioners in Paris. One of the greatest diplomatic triumphs of world history had been consummated by a benign old gentleman in a blue velvet suit who started life as a Boston printer's devil. No negotiations of a Mazarin or Richelieu ever outshone the tact and subtlety with which Benjamin Franklin represented his struggling young country. Arriving in the autumn of 1776 to ask favors, the elderly philosopher seemed in his kindly way to be conferring them. At least France was grateful, for the manufacture of Franklin medallions and small Franklin busts became a minor industry before the end of 1777. Crowds hailed him at every public appearance, and it was applauded as a historical landmark when Franklin and Voltaire embraced at the Academy of Sciences.

Saratoga proved to be the American trump, but it is a matter of record that Vergennes was convinced of the necessity of open French warfare as early as July, 1777. Even the fall of the American "capital" the following September, exposing Dr. Franklin's own home to pillage, was shrugged off by him with a witticism which his French admirers found truly Gallic in flavor. When Gérard informed him that Howe had taken Philadelphia, the philosopher had a ready and smiling reply, "I beg your pardon, Sir, Philadelphia has taken Howe."

And in his unique way Dr. Franklin had taken Paris.

There was no such thing as a race across the Atlantic between a British peace and a French alliance. The Continental Congress made up its mind in advance and expressed its choice without a dissenting vote. On April 18, 1777, when Washington sent the assembly its first report of Lord North's measure, the delegates presented a solid front. "Whether this insidious proceeding is genuine," wrote Washington, ". . . or contrived in Philadelphia is a point undetermined and immaterial; but it is certainly founded in principles of the most wicked, diabolical baseness, meant to poison the minds of the people and detach the wavering, at least, from the cause." The commander in chief trusted that "it will be attacked in every state, in every part of the Continent."[11]

Congress was just as emphatic. Delegates who had been squabbling all winter were united in dignified firmness on Wednesday, April 22nd, after hearing the report of an exceptionally able committee made up of Gouverneur Morris, Francis Dana and William Henry Drayton. Parliament was accused of trying to weaken and divide America "because the impracticability of subjugating this country being every day more manifest, it is their interest to extricate themselves from the war on any terms." The "wickedness and insincerity" of the enemy were denounced in defiant words:

> The said bill, by holding forth a tender of pardon, implies a criminality in our justifiable resistance; and consequently, to treat with it, would be an implied acknowledgment that the inhabitants of these states were what Britain had declared them to be, rebels. . . . Any man, or body of men, who should presume to make any separate or partial convention or agreement with commissioners under the crown of Great Britain . . . ought to be considered and treated as open and avowed enemies of these United States. . . . The committee beg leave to report it as their opinion, that these United States cannot, with propriety, hold any conference or treaty with any commissioners on the part of Great Britain, unless they shall, as a preliminary thereto, either withdraw their fleets and armies, or else, in positive and express terms, acknowledge the independence of the said states.[12]

In all the history of the United States there has never been a finer hour. For if independence was proclaimed on July 4, 1776, it was surely upheld and sustained on April 22, 1778, in the little courtroom at York. As if to make sure that there could never be any doubt, the decision of the Continental Congress was entered that day in the *Journals*:

> *Resolved, unanimously,* That Congress approve and confirm the said report.

Men of this temper, as William Pitt had long known, could not be conquered. After three years of war the decision of April 22nd was not taken without a realistic idea of the consequences that might await. Earlier in the month Henry Laurens had written to James Duane: "The United States have acted, and 'tis not impossible may be whipped like Children. . . . Let us not be stricken by fear, let us be animated and Wise—there is Wisdom in America, let it be collected—strength and success will be the Issue—but no time is to be lost—I do not hold it impossible, we shall hear of some attempts to accommodation as a prelude to the ensuing campaign . . . but we need not distress our minds by apprehensions that the very first article will be a confirmation of American Independency—and who can dry eyed contemplate submission?"[13]

It is a safe assumption that there were not many dry-eyed members of the Continental Congress on the Saturday evening when the treaties with France reached the Pennsylvania village. After the assembly had adjourned over the Sabbath on May 2nd, the courthouse bell suddenly began pealing with all the brawn of Martin Brenise's arms. The delegates were summoned from taverns and rooming houses to learn that the good news had been brought by Simeon Deane, brother of the commissioner. There were two treaties, one of alliance, and one of amity and commerce, which had been signed in Paris three months before. Congress could not wait to hear them read and held a special meeting that night. There is no record of any celebration over the weekend; but on Monday, the 4th, the assembly gave its approval to each treaty:

Resolved, unanimously, that the same be and is hereby ratified.

Another resolution expressed the sincere wish that "the friendship so happily commenced between France and the United States be perpetual." [14] There was some objection to two minor articles of the commercial treaty; but it was ratified nevertheless, and France later conceded both points.

Wednesday, May 6th, became the official day of rejoicing for both the army and Congress. The Rev. George Neisser, a Moravian minister of York, entered a diary item for that date: "In the evening the entire town, now the capital of the United States, showed its joy at the alliance made with Louis XVI by illuminations." Washington's little army, after the winter of Valley Forge, celebrated with the "grand, noisy, *feu de joy*" for which the boyish Lafayette had been longing. One of the onlookers declared that he had never seen "such unfeigned and perfect joy, as was discovered in every countenance."

Ellery of Rhode Island thought that the treaty of alliance displayed on the part of France "a spirit of magnanimity and a soundness of policy scarcely to be paralleled." But it took a Connecticut Yankee to look at it the other way, and Dr. Oliver Wolcott cautiously allowed that the treaty "seems adapted to secure a lasting Friendship which it is certainly the highest Interest of France to Cultivate." [15]

Most of the delegates, no doubt, were bursting with some share of Samuel Chase's pride. "America," he said, "has now taken her rank among the nations."

On May 6th Congress recommended "to all inhabitants of these states to consider the subjects of his most Christian Majesty as their brethren and allies, and that they behave towards them with all the friendship and attention due to the subjects of a great prince, who . . . hath treated with these United States on terms of perfect equality and mutual advantage, thereby rendering himself the protector of the rights of mankind."

This same day of jubilation saw a committee chosen—Samuel Chase, Richard Henry Lee and Gouverneur Morris—to prepare an address to the inhabitants of the United States. The result, which was largely the product of Morris' pen, achieves the distinction of being probably the most high-flown outburst of rhetoric ever to be approved by the Continental Congress:

> Friends and countrymen: Three years have now passed away, since the commencement of the present war: a war without parallel in the annals of mankind. It hath displayed a spectacle, the most solemn that can possibly be exhibited. On one side, we behold fraud and violence laboring in the service of despotism; on the other, virtue and fortitude supporting and establishing the rights of human nature. . . . The haughty prince, who spurned us from his feet with contumely and disdain, and the parliament which proscribed us, now descend to offer terms of accommodation. While in the full career of victory, they pulled off the mask and avowed their intended despotism; but having lavished in vain the blood and treasure of their subjects, in pursuit of this execrable purpose, they now endeavour to ensnare us with their insidious offers of peace.[16]

Future generations of Fourth of July orators were outdone before they were born by an address which soared upward like a rocket, then burst into a constellation of superlatives and exclamation points. A few weeks later Congress suited the action to the adverb by rejecting all British peace overtures.

On June 4th the three British commissioners reached Philadelphia. Some effort had been made to choose envoys less ignorant than most Britons of conditions in America. George Johnstone had been governor of West Florida and William Eden was a brother of the royal governor so respected in Maryland. The remaining member, the youthful Earl of Carlisle, aspired to become a man of letters and persisted until he wrote two plays.

It would be an understatement to say that the commissioners found the British expeditionary force weakened by disputes. Philadelphia really had taken Howe, for after a winter of idleness and dissipation his army was no longer a keen instrument. Rumors reached the Americans until Gouverneur Morris could write during the darkest days of Valley Forge: "Howe is so afraid that the world will hear of his situation, or that his army will be informed of what is going on in the world, that he examines every letter with severe punishment for those who are caught smuggling. There is mutiny in his army. His officers are resigning."

This was a bit exaggerated, but Serle's diary reveals a growing apprehension. The British had occupied Philadelphia only two months when he wrote that "every thing wears a melancholy aspect; and a Disposition appears very evidently among some principal officers to throw the Blame on others." At the end of the winter Serle deplored the hatreds and jealousies behind the scenes of the famous Meschianza. "Our Enemies," he wrote, "will dwell upon the Folly and Extravagance of it with Pleasure. Every man of Sense, among ourselves, tho' not unwilling to pay a due Respect, was ashamed of this mode of doing it." [17]

The Babylonian spectacle of the Meschianza, or Medley, was intended by the young officers of Sir William Howe's faction as a slap at the Clinton and Cornwallis cliques. The tall, jovial commander at Philadelphia, with his reputation for bravery at Bunker Hill, had long been a hero to every subaltern. Even his vices were those which a soldier could admire—his nights divided impartially between the gaming table and the company of his charming American mistress, Mrs. Loring. When he resigned because his appeals for reinforcements were ignored, the loyalty of his subordinates found expression in the costly extravaganza of May 18, 1778. It is hard to credit the contemporary estimate of £50,000 sterling for silks alone, but undoubtedly the wealthy young officers emptied their pockets for a pageant intended as a protest and rebuke. Present-day tastes are likely to find the Meschianza a little overpowering with its decorated barges, its jousting field, its heralds and trumpeters, its Knights of the Blended Rose, and its gorgeous costumes designed by Captain John André for such Tory belles as Peggy Shippen, Jane Craig, Peggy Chew and Betty Franks.

At a time of war-induced unemployment and misery in the homeland, Serle could only sigh at the prodigality and bad taste of an entertainment advertising the factionalism of the army. It was a painful contrast to find the rebels as firm as a phalanx in their determination to reject any peace which did not offer independence as a preliminary. When General Clinton requested a passport for the commissioners, Washington refused "without being previously instructed by Congress on the subject." Congress in its turn proved to be no more receptive. On Saturday, June 13th, when the commissioners managed by devious means to have their papers delivered, President Laurens held up the packet in full view of the house as if it contained poisonous reptiles. There was some question as to whether the seals ought to be broken at all; and the reading had progressed only to the second page when a slurring reference to the new French allies brought an interruption. Gouverneur Morris leaped to his feet with a motion that the reading be stopped "because of the offensive language against his most Christian majesty." The resolution carried after some debate and the assembly adjourned until Monday.

Not until Tuesday did an indignant Congress finally resolve to hear the balance of the British message. The following day, June 17th, a reply was approved which represented the unanimous vote of all thirty-one delegates as well as all thirteen states. This letter, composed by Gouverneur Morris, declared that Congress are inclined to peace, notwithstanding the unjust claims from which this war originated, and the savage manner in which it had been conducted.

But the concluding paragraph left no doubt as to the only terms that Americans would accept:

> They will, therefore, be ready to enter upon the consideration of a treaty of peace and commerce not inconsistent with treaties already subsisting, when the king of Great Britain shall demonstrate a sincere disposition for that purpose. The only solid proof of this disposition will be, an explicit acknowledgment of the independence of these states, or the withdrawing his fleets and armies.[18]

Again, as on April 22nd, American independence had been confirmed by men who knew that their answer meant the prolonging of the war at the risk of disaster. But there was no faltering. "I have lived to see the day," exulted hard-bitten Thomas McKean, "when, instead of 'Americans licking the dust from the feet of a British minister,' the tables are turned." And James Lovell declared in a letter to Gates: "No peace can take place in Consequence of any Powers we have seen of the King's Commissioners. . . . I can only say, they do not allow *Independence;* therefore they might have tarried at home." [19]

At least there was more reason for confidence in June than in April. Valley Forge had been a severe ordeal, but for the first time the rebels could take pride in a disciplined instrument fit to be compared with enemy regiments. After attempts to impose a Roman sternness had failed, a former Prussian officer succeeded with a policy of sympathy and understanding. The title of "Baron von" Steuben had been his own invention, but there was nothing counterfeit about the veteran's experience and ability as a military preceptor, even though he needed an interpreter to translate his good-humored oaths. One of the few drillmasters of history ever to be loved, Steuben created a spirited army out of the ragged and demoralized mob he found at Valley Forge.

Enemy morale sank to its lowest ebb when the news of General Howe's resignation was followed by the announcement that Philadelphia would be abandoned. This decision struck many Britons as a final admission of defeat, and on May 18th Ambrose Serle wrote despairingly in his diary: "I now look upon the Contest as at an End. No man can be expected to declare for us, when he cannot be assured of a Fortnight's Protection. Every man, on the Contrary, whatever may have been his primary Inclinations, will find it his Interest to oppose & drive us out of the Country." [20]

Before the British commissioners sailed away, Francis Dana, Robert

Morris and Joseph Reed laid before Congress the letters which Johnstone had written them in a futile effort to detach at least a few Americans from the cause. Reed charged that he had refused a bribe of £10,000 with the statement that he "was not worth purchasing, but such as I was, the king of England was not rich enough to do it." Johnstone denied any such attempt, but his letters made good rebel propaganda when published in the *Pennsylvania Packet* of July 21st.

Eden, the most able of the commissioners, attributed the loss of America, which he already took for granted, to the narrowness and insularity of the British governing classes. "It is impossible," he wrote on June 18th, "to see even what I have seen of this magnificent country and not to go nearly mad at the long train of misconducts and mischances by which we have lost it." He regretted "most heartily that our rulers instead of making the tour of Europe did not finish their education by a voyage around the coasts and rivers of the western side of the Atlantic."

Lord Carlisle complained in his letters of mosquitoes as big as sparrows. But he was delighted with a pet raccoon which he took back to London.

Death had already struck down Peyton Randolph, Samuel Ward, Thomas Lynch and half a score of less renowned delegates. The long hours were a strain on the older members; and the next to go was Philip Livingston— "that great, rough, rapid mortal" of 1774—who breathed his last in a York tavern room at the age of 63. At least he did not lack for the constant care of the four physicians then in the assembly.

Congress adopted a policy of honoring each departed member by attending the funeral in a body and proclaiming a month of official mourning. But death must have seemed remote during these vivid June days of 1778 when the delegates could feel the clay of a brave new world between their fingers. Rumors of Philadelphia's evacuation became so persistent that Lovell expressed his disgust in a letter written at York on the 9th: "Here we are still the Sport of Lyars. One day we are told the Enemy are filling their Ditches and preparing to leave Philada. . . . In the next we are informed of new Works and freshly arrived Troops." [21]

Not until the 19th did General Washington notify Congress that the last enemy troops had left the city. It was decided to adjourn from York on the 27th and meet in Philadelphia on July 2nd. The assembly also proclaimed a public celebration on July 4th and resolved that Congress would attend church in a body on Sunday the 5th "to return thanks for the divine mercy in supporting the independence of these states."

After nine months in York there were no ceremonies of leavetaking. Samuel Holten, the newly arrived Massachusetts physician, recorded that on the last evening he "walked out with a number of gentlemen of Congress about a mile to a farmhouse. The people was kind, we eat Cherries and drank whiskey." On July 1st he noted in his diary: "To the City of Philadelphia, 15 miles before breakfast. Dined at a public house, then took Lodging at the Widow Robinson's on Chestnut Street." [22]

Between the dates of these entries had occurred on June 28th the battle of Monmouth—an affair which the Americans might well have called the battle of lost opportunities. The British had left Philadelphia with hundreds of Tory refugees and a baggage train ten miles long. Washington took a parallel route through New Jersey on Clinton's exposed left flank and a confused action occurred at Monmouth. The rebels won a victory and inflicted nearly double their own casualties, but it was the sort of empty triumph that the redcoats had won at Long Island, Brandywine and Germantown. Clinton could congratulate himself on avoiding disaster and keeping his army intact.

The congressmen celebrating independence had reason to be proud of the discipline shown by Steuben's pupils. General Anthony Wayne's Continentals slugged it out with a Guards brigade which was first to break, after losing half its numbers. Such accounts of rebel valor must have heartened the delegates, who dined in a body, according to McKean, "at the new Tavern, where there was an elegant entertainment and a fine band of musick. the firing of a vast number of cannon proved that there was no want of gunpowder."

Richard Henry Lee wrote to his brother Francis that "the Whigs of the City dressed up a Woman of the Town with the Monstrous headdress of the Tory Ladies, and escorted her thro the town with a great concourse of people—Her head was elegantly and expensively dressed. I suppose about three feet high and of proportionable width, with a profusion of curls, &c. &c. &c.—the figure was droll and occasioned much mirth—it has loosened some heads already, and probably will bring the rest within the bounds of reason. . . ." [23]

The joy of home-coming was mixed with anger at the ravages of the enemy. Prominent figures of Congress were the victims of special attention. Franklin's house had been pillaged and his electrical apparatus carried away. Charles Thomson found his summer place a ruin, and John Dickinson's magnificent country estate Fairhill presented a scene of complete and wanton destruction. The home of Congress itself did not escape, and Henry Laurens explained in a letter that the first meeting had to be put off until July 7th because of "the offensiveness of the air in and around the State House, which the Enemy had made a Hospital and left it in a condition disgraceful to the Character of civility. Particularly they had opened a large square pit near the House, a receptable for Filth, into which they had also cast dead horses and the bodies of men who by the mercies of death had escaped from their further cruelties. I cannot proceed to a new subject before I add a curse on their savage practices." [24]

But nothing could take away from the heady feeling of success. On March 10th, the appointed date, only a single state had been ready to subscribe to the Articles of Confederation. Yet on July 14th James Lovell could boast that nine had signed "and there is no doubt but, Georgia, Delaware and Jersey will soon sign. Maryland will take airs and plague us, but upon our determination to confederate with 12 will do what she has always done before—come in without grace." [25]

As early as 1778 the state had a name for perversity. Her delegates had already demanded an amendment to the Articles giving Congress power "to ascertain and restrict the boundaries of the Confederated States which claim to extend to the river Mississippi, or the South Sea." And though the proposal met defeat in June by a vote of six states to five, nobody dreamed that Maryland would hold out against her twelve sisters until 1781.

Not often in this age did something happen before anyone had time to grow impatient. But the Americans who were curious about their new French allies learned the second week in July that they must hasten to prepare a public audience for the minister plenipotentiary of his Most Christian Majesty, the Sieur Conrade Alexandre Gérard de Rayneval.

"Who would have thought," mused the *Pennsylvania Packet,* speaking for thousands of hearts bursting with pride, ". . . that the American colonies imperfectly known in Europe a few years ago, and claimed by every pettyfogging lawyer in the House of Commons, and every cobler in the beer houses of London, as a part of their property, should in the course of three years of a war with Great Britain, receive an Ambassador from the most powerful Monarchy in Europe!"

The cup overflowed when news came that the French fleet commanded by the Comte d'Estaing was sailing from Delaware Bay to New York to co-operate with General Washington. Members of Congress could immediately vision a second Saratoga at the expense of Clinton's army, bottled up on Manhattan Island.

While a crew of workmen renovated the filthy State House, a committee was appointed "to report to Congress on the time and manner of the public reception of Mons. Gérard." The delegates saw no humor in the spectacle of rebels and republicans gravely pondering the fine points of ceremony. The dignity of America was upheld when the committee recommended that "the President shall be seated on a chair raised upon a stage two feet above the ground, and the ambassador on a chair directly opposite to him and raised eighteen inches." The rest of the detailed report was accepted on July 18th, five days after Gérard's arrival.[26]

"Yesterday I had the honor to dine with Le Sieur Gérard," wrote Elias Boudinot to his wife on July 14th. "He is about 50 years of Age, appears to be a Modest, Grave, decent, cheerfull Man—highly pleased with our Country and the Struggles we have made for Liberty. A Committee of Congress were appointed to wait on him at Chester. On their arrival a Barge with 12 Oarsmen dressed in Scarlet trimmed with Silver were ready to receive them. When the Barge was half way to the Ship, she lay on her Oars and fifteen guns were fired."[27]

This was informality as compared to the reception in the State House at high noon on August 6th, after a nervous rehearsal the evening before by the officers of Congress. Admission was by ticket only, and again the New Jersey delegate reported to his wife:

> Our President was seated in a Mahogany armed chair on a platform raised about two feet, with a large table covered with green cloth and the secretary along side of him. The Members were all seated around within the Bar and a large armed chair in the middle opposite the President for the Plenipo. At Twelve Oc. our State Coach and Six waited on the Minister at his Quarters. He was preceded by his own Chariot and two with his Secretaries. The Minister was attended by two Members who introduced him thro' the crowd and seated him in the chair; he then sent to the President (by his Secretary) the Letters from the King of France to Congress, which was opened and read aloud first in French and then in English. It was then announced to the House by the waiting Member, that the stranger introduced was the Minister Plenipotentiary from his Most Christian Majesty, upon which the Minister arose and bowed to the President and then to the House, and the House rising returned the Compliment. The Minister then addressed the Congress and was answered by the President, at which the bowing again took place and the whole concluded. A public dinner succeeded at which was a band of musick and the firing of Cannon.[28]

The New Jersey delegate added with obvious satisfaction that "the whole was plain, grand and decent." Gérard also commented favorably in a private report to his government which noted that twenty-one toasts were drunk while the cannon boomed salutes.

This day would long remain a landmark to delegates whose pilgrimage led through sloughs of despair. Even the Declaration of Independence could not surpass it, and Henry Marchant was moved to the sincere though rhetorical outburst: "The Scene brightens, grows more and more interesting, and calls for new and fresh Exertions of Senatorial Wisdom. We advance into the Circle and Standing of mighty Nations—Adepts in the Policy of Peace and War. May Heaven protect our youth and prove the Friend, Protector and Counsellor of America!" [29]

Nathaniel Scudder, the New Jersey physician who would become the only delegate to give his life on the battlefield, referred to the Articles of Confederation as "the Magna Charta of America." Even Roger Sherman, that shrewd old Yankee veteran of 1774, came as near to enthusiasm as he ever ventured by admitting that "our affairs at present seem to be in a favorable Situation."

Only John Witherspoon was articulate enough to put into words the almost religious spirit of exaltation shared at this moment by members of Congress. In a speech of unknown date in the summer or autumn of 1778 the learned member from New Jersey apologized for gazing hopefully into the future.[30] All ages have their intellectual fashions, and it was the thing at this time to sigh for the vanished glories of the past. Dr. Witherspoon, addressing Congress in his cap and gown, begged leave to make a statement, "though with some risk that it will be thought visionary and romantic. I do expect, Mr. President, a progress, as in every other human art, so in the order and perfection of human society, greater than we have ever seen; and why should we be wanting to ourselves in urging it forward?"

In order not to be thought a sentimentalist, the Presbyterian divine explained, "I am none of those who either deny or conceal the depravity of human nature, till it is purified by the light of truth, and renewed by the spirit of the living God." But Dr. Witherspoon ventured the assertion that the world had improved in the past two centuries. "It is not impossible," he went on, "that in future times all the states on one quarter of the globe, may see it proper by some plan of union, to perpetuate security and peace; and sure I am, a well planned confederacy among the states of America, may hand down the blessings of peace and public order to many generations."

PART FOUR

Victory

*It is not to be expected, from human nature, that the
few should be always attentive to the good of the many.*

— RICHARD HENRY LEE

Chapter 17

The Ailing Physician

AS the years went by, it grew to be a tradition that the quality of the Continental Congress had manifestly declined. Later delegates declared sadly that the halcyon days from 1774 to 1776 would never return. Congressmen of that golden age—even such worthy but limited men as Eliphalet Dyer and Nathaniel Folsom—were conceded to be giants as compared to the brash young fellows who came along a decade later to make up the Congress of Madison and Hamilton and Monroe.

Although John Adams sighed at Baltimore for the vanishing faces of 1774, the *Journals* do not reveal any such twilight of the gods. In an assembly seldom exceeding thirty delegates, no less than eleven members of the first Continental Congress served at one time or another in 1778— Dyer, Sherman, McKean, Chase, Paca, Folsom, Duane, Jay, Hopkins, Samuel Adams and Richard Henry Lee.

Even at this date it had become apparent that nobody would ever fill the shoes of Washington, Franklin, Jefferson or John Adams. Men of that caliber were not common even in an era of political genius. But after giving them their due, it is noteworthy that the revolutionary assembly also developed a high order of secondary talent. From 1774 to 1776 there emerged men of only slightly lower stature than the great leaders—John Jay, James Duane, John Dickinson, Richard Henry Lee, James Wilson, Thomas McKean, Roger Sherman, Stephen Hopkins, Robert Morris. The issues rising immediately after the Declaration were met by an able and opinionated set of newcomers—John Witherspoon, Henry Laurens, Thomas Burke, James Lovell, Charles Carroll of Carrollton. And the bleak winter of Valley Forge brought to the fore still another group which would become known for its works—Gouverneur Morris, John Henry, William Henry Drayton, John Mathews, Nathaniel Scudder, Elias Boudinot, Joseph Reed.

247

Thus did the Continental Congress renew itself.

It would be an injustice in any such summary to overlook the men who contributed faith and courage rather than high abilities. Jesse Root, the Presbyterian parson representing Connecticut, was well endowed with both qualities. When Congress appointed him to write the Thanksgiving proclamation of 1779, he predicted at the climax that American independence would last "as long as the sun and moon shall endure, until time shall be no more." But the minister's colleagues expunged these words as being a bit too fanciful and poetic.

Meriwether Smith, just beginning a long period as a Virginia delegate, had to endure an amount of personal ridicule and dislike that would have crushed a more sensitive soul. This fussy, middle-aged planter was called Fiddlehead by his associates, who wore out all manner of jokes about the doleful tune he played.

William Duer of New York had crammed more than the ordinary amount of adventure into his thirty years. As a young Englishman of good family, he graduated from Eton, served as aide to Clive in India, then emigrated to America in 1767 to become one of the first manufacturers of cotton goods. His closest friend in Congress was a Georgia delegate, Edward Langworthy, who also found life an adventure after starting in an orphan asylum and succeeding as a self-educated journalist and schoolmaster.

It was easier to discover a graduate of a British university in the State House than a man who had toiled at a trade. Although Samuel Huntington had once been an industrious cooper, he learned law and distinguished himself as a Connecticut judge. John Collins, the 60-year-old ex-governor of Rhode Island, came nearest to being an authentic rough diamond. An old sea captain, he visioned Congress as sailing the ship of state "through a Strait among Rocks and Sholes in a thick fog. We may run the ship a Shoar," he wrote dubiously. "She may *poke* through."

There is no need for guesswork as to the bare facts about the 342 men who served from first to last, even though their era did not prefer its truth in the convenient capsule form of statistics. Research has come to the rescue and the lowliest delegate has his sketch in the *Biographical Dictionary of the American Congress, 1774-1927*, published in 1928 by the Sixty-ninth Congress. From this source has been compiled the following table, listing the age groups (at the time of election) of the members whose birth dates are known:

	AGES 20-30	AGES 30-40	AGES 40-50	AGES 50-60	AGES 60-70
Conn.............		6	10	6	1
Del...............	1	6	3	2	
Ga...............		7	6	4	1
Md...............		16	12	6	1
Mass.............		13	6	3	
N. H.............	1	5	9	3	
N. J.............	1	7	12	7	3
N. Y.............	3	13	7	7	1
N. C.............	3	9	9	2	
Penna............		18	14	9	5
R. I.............		4	6	3	2
S. C.............	9	10	5	4	
Va...............	7	16	6	4	1
TOTALS.........	25	130	105	59	15

Thirty-two members were born in the British Isles or West Indies, including such sterling patriots as Hamilton, Robert Morris and Francis Lewis. Third- or fourth-generation Americans, however, were greatly in the majority.

At a time when higher education was a prerogative of aristocracy, the statistics of the Continental Congress do not uphold the loyalists who sneered at the supposed low antecedents of rebel leaders. No less than 123 delegates, according to the biographical sketches, had studied at the six leading American colleges. The following table lists them according to states:

	Conn.	Del.	Ga.	Md.	Mass.	N. H.	N. J.	N. Y.	N. C.	Penna.	R. I.	S. C.	Va.	TOTALS
Princeton.....	3	1	1	3		1	8		2	5	2	2	3	31
Harvard......	2				17	4				1		2		26
Yale.........	14		3		1		1	4		1				24
U. of Penna...		1		4			4		3	6	1	1	1	21
Wm. and Mary				1						1			12	14
King's Col....						1	6							7

That famous London law school, the Inns of Court (usually known as the Temple) led all British institutions with a total of 28 graduates in the Continental Congress, most of them from Maryland, Pennsylvania, Virginia and South Carolina. Eight delegates had studied at Eton as a preparatory school; and the following British or European colleges are mentioned in the biographical sketches:

University of Edinburgh, 8 graduates; Oxford, 3; Cambridge, 3; University of Glasgow, 2; Jesuit College of Saint-Omer (France), 2; University of Dublin, 1; St. Andrews, 1; Halle, 1.

Such famous names as George Washington and Benjamin Franklin, of course, belong among the delegates who studied at no college at all. In this category will also be found Charles Thomson, the Greek and Hebrew scholar. Many of the men in this group had the equivalent of a college education by means of private tutoring. Only about a tenth of the 342 delegates could be classified as "self-educated"—a term usually meaning a few winters in some dame school or a brief period of study under an itinerant schoolmaster.

Glancing at the occupations, it may be noted that there was a great deal of overlapping. Professional men of that day were close to the soil, so that many lawyers could also be called farmers or planters. John Dickinson managed to be both lawyer and landed proprietor, and Thomas Burke was doctor, lawyer, planter and public servant. A few delegates, such as Sam Adams, were officeholders all their lives; and a few others, such as Schuyler and Charles Carroll of Carrollton, were virtually feudal lords. The following table lists the six leading occupations:

	Conn.	Del.	Ga.	Md.	Mass.	N. H.	N. J.	N. Y.	N. C.	Penna.	R. I.	S. C.	Va.	TOTALS
Lawyers, Jurists..	21	6	6	20	10	3	11	15	10	15	4	11	19	151
Planters, Farmers		4	1	5		1	3		10	2	5	10	15	56
Merchants......	1	3	5	1	6	6	3	8	2	12	1	3	2	53
Physicians......	1	1	3		1	3	4	1	2	6	1	2	2	27
Landed Prop....		1		5			2	3				1		12
Ministers.......			2	1		2				2	1			8

There were also a few college instructors, schoolmasters, millers, manufacturers and shipmasters. In a day of handicrafts the trades were very meagerly represented by a sprinkling of printers, carpenters, ironmongers, coopers and surveyors, most of whom had become property owners and local officeholders.

The high percentage of lawyers is not surprising when it is considered that the legal profession offered the surest road to a political career at a time when business ran a poor second to public service. It did not take a long or arduous period of study to pass a bar examination, so that neither wealth nor education was a prerequisite.

If there was any such thing as an "average" member of an assembly made up of assertive individualists, he would have been a lawyer just past the age of 40, a college graduate, a property owner in comfortable financial circumstances, and a recognized political leader in his own state. Nor can his religious preferences be overlooked, for the Congregational and Presbyterian Churches were actively identified with the rebel cause from the beginning. Congregationalism could almost be called the state religion of New England, and the Scotch-Irish patriots of the middle colonies were Presbyterians.

Although the Irish Catholics fought on the loyalist side, no group contributed more to the American victory than the newcomers from northern Ireland, most of them transplanted Scots, who had been pouring into the country since 1750 at the rate of 12,000 a year. Serle described them with distaste as being "disposed absolutely to the present Faction against Government and many of them now principal agitators in these confusions."

The Quakers, the Methodists and the German sects of Pennsylvania tried to remain neutral, but all were regarded as opponents by the more rabid patriots. In the northern states the Anglican Church usually took the side of the king, yet a majority of the Episcopal ministers in Maryland, Virginia and the Carolinas sympathized with the American cause.

One of the most remarkable results of the Revolution was the improvement in the position of the small Roman Catholic minority. In 1774 the rebels had resented it when the Quebec Act guaranteed freedom of worship to their northern neighbors, and the failure of the Canadian campaign of 1775-1776 could in many instances be charged to the bigotry of an undisciplined American soldiery.

Charles Carroll of Carrollton accomplished as much for his church as for his country. Without ever becoming a religious propagandist, he set an example which melted the prejudices of rebel leaders, many of whom had never known anyone of his faith. The wealthiest man in America, educated at Bourges, Paris and London, he had adopted his unusual signature upon inheriting a vast Maryland estate named after his family. His brother John, the priest who cared for the aged Franklin so tenderly on the mission to Canada, became the first Catholic bishop of America after the war and founded the seminary which has grown into Georgetown University.

The necessity for an American policy of tolerance was obvious after the treaty of amity in 1778 with Europe's largest Catholic kingdom. This alliance widened the breach between Americans of opposite political beliefs.

Religious as well as national prejudices were invoked by the loyalists in such verses as the following, sung to the tune of *Yankee Doodle:*

> The French alliance now came forth,
> The Papists flocked in shoals, sir;
> Friseurs, marquis, valets of birth,
> And priests to save our souls, sir.

Rivington's Gazette, the Tory propaganda journal published in New York, declared unblushingly that Gérard had been tendered a handful of soil, upon landing in America, to symbolize French possession. Americans were warned that a new Bastille would be built on these shores by the "frog-eating gentry" who plotted forcible conversions to popery.[1]

It may be, since all men cling to their prejudices, that a great many rebels had moments when they resented a policy of expediency. But bigotry thrives on isolation, and the association of Congregational and Presbyterian patriots with the Carrolls did a great deal to establish freedom of worship as one of the unquestioned liberties of the new nation.

Nothing was too scurrilous in 1778 for the insults exchanged between rebels and loyalists in their newspapers. New York Tories, according to *Rivington's Gazette,* found it a satisfaction to gaze at "an illuminated painting of the Congress whose ambition has almost ruined this unhappy country." The artist had limned the devil at President Laurens' elbow, addressing the delegates "with so significant a grin as seems to indicate his having no doubt of their making his house their home in the infernal regions." The headless statue of Pitt also appeared among the members of Congress "as being one of their kidney and gave a hint of what ought to have been done long ago."[2]

The patriots in their turn were fond of ridiculing the snobbish tendencies of American loyalists. When the British put hundreds of soft-handed refugees to work at fortifying the New York lines, rebel mockery was expressed by the jingle:

> Come, gentlemen Tories, firm, loyal and true
> Here are axes and shovels and something to do!

Words were not the only weapons of the civil war. Massachusetts and North Carolina had already passed laws making it possible to banish Tories. Dr. Zubly, the Georgia loyalist who resigned from Congress, had recently been driven out of that state after the confiscation of his property, though he was allowed to resume his Savannah pastorate before the end of the war. Pennsylvania went so far as to approve legislation which might have resulted in Tories being tried and executed for their beliefs. Washington and other rebel leaders used their influence against such extremes, arguing that reprisals would be invited. But Congress had just returned from York to Philadelphia when the delegates had the melancholy duty of refusing clemency to the families of two condemned Quakers named Roberts and Carlisle. After both had been convicted in a Philadelphia civil court of giving active aid to the enemy, Roberts' wife and children appealed to Congress. A recommendation of mercy would probably have stopped the execution; but the assembly did not intervene, and the two Tories went to the gallows with composure. Roberts, addressing a morbid crowd, declared with his last breath that he did not regret doing his duty for his sovereign.

From the rebel viewpoint, nothing could atone for the hideous guilt of loyalists who led the Indian raids on the New York and Pennsylvania frontiers in 1778, resulting in the massacre of women and children. The indignation of Congress is evident from the wording of the resolution of July 25th, authorizing a punitive expedition against the savages "and tories and other banditti" responsible for the horrors of tomahawk and scalping knife in the Wyoming valley.[3] Lack of military resources made necessary a postponement, but the Six Nations were marked for destruction.

Several resolutions in the *Journals* at various times recommended the recruiting of Indians for strictly military purposes, though little was done about it. As early as Bunker Hill, for that matter, a few Indians volunteered as militiamen. A small number of redskins were used as scouts and woodsmen in the American forces throughout the war; but Congress could stand on its record of trying to keep the frontier tribes neutral by every possible means, including bribery.

Early relations between the patriots and their new allies show an effusive cordiality. Samuel Holten's diary mentions that on August 25th Congress "dined with the French minister at his invitation and about 400 other Gentlemen. The dinner was Grand and Elegant and the band of musick was very agreeable."[4]

Long before the treaty of amity, secret French aid had saved the rebel forces from being defeated by sheer lack of arms. Beaumarchais and his mythical firm of Roderique Hortalez and Company were operating so well by the second month of 1777 that Congress could resolve, like a client placing an order, "that the commissioners at the Court of France, be directed to use their utmost endeavours, to send, without delay, 80,000 blankets, 40,000 compleat suits of cloaths, for soldiers, of green, blue and brown colours, with suitable facings, and cloth of the same colours, with trimmings, sufficient for 40,000 suits more, 100,000 pairs of yarn stockings, fit for soldiers, 1 million flints, and 200 tons of lead. . . ."[5]

Six months later the arms and clothing sent from France had a great deal to do with the victory at Saratoga, which in turn made possible the alliance with England's hereditary enemy. And now that France had declared war, the Americans could hope for naval aid against the overwhelming British superiority on the sea, particularly in American waters.

After a bright beginning, the American navy had run into difficulties, not the least of which were political. Esek Hopkins, the country's first naval commander, fell considerably short of being a Washington in character or ability, though he deserved better than an ignominious dismissal. Captain John Paul Jones also suffered injustices from congressional attempts to satisfy all states in appointing naval officers. During the last six months of 1776 Jones captured or destroyed 5 transports, 2 ships, 6 schooners, 7 brigantines, a sloop and a 16-gun privateer. After these victories he found himself eighteenth on the naval list. And though he paid off the crews of the *Alfred* and *Providence* from his own pocket, the sea fighter was not reimbursed until after the war.

In the summer of 1778, commanding the *Ranger,* Jones conducted the only American operation of the war on English soil when he raided the harbor of Whitehaven, spiked the guns of the two forts, and tried unsuccessfully to burn the shipping. Four days later, after outfighting the superior British sloop-of-war *Drake,* he forced her to strike her colors and accompany him as a prize.

Thrilling to American hearts as these exploits were, they could not alter the fact that the rebels were overwhelmed in their own waters by the enemy's great naval advantage. The treaty with France brought the first prospect of relief. Since her defeat in the last war that kingdom had made tremendous strides toward a goal of a navy strong enough to contend with the victors. The excellence of French ordnance and shipbuilding were acknowledged on the other side of the Channel; but the fleet of Louis XVI continued the old policy of making noble birth a qualification for high command. It would have been heretical in England to create an admiral out of a titled general, yet the gallant Comte d'Estaing and some of his aides were soldiers with no experience of seamanship.

Unhappily for the rebel cause, this was exactly the accomplishment needed for victory in the summer of 1778. While General Washington hemmed in Clinton's army at New York, the French fleet tried to force an entrance into a harbor defended by a much inferior naval force. It is doubtful if the British invasion of America could have survived the blow of another army surrendering nine months after Saratoga, but French seamanship failed in the emergency. Admiral d'Estaing gave up the attempt to get his warships over the harbor shoals, sailing away just before a favorable combination of winds and tides occurred. Washington's army, the best American instrument of the war from a viewpoint of training and equipment, was stranded in Westchester County, unable to attack a strongly fortified British army. The new allies had not yet given up hope of a successful land-and-sea operation. Comte d'Estaing, whose timidity lay in seamanship rather than combat, sailed to Rhode Island to combine with General Sullivan's militia forces in an attempt to capture or destroy the redcoat garrison of 6,000 at Newport. Again the chance of another Saratoga beckoned, and the French admiral boldly assailed a British squadron which came to the rescue. Both fleets were scattered at the outset by a terrific storm which left a record for destruction never equaled until the hurricane of 1938. The French admiral had to put into Boston for heavy repairs, leaving Sullivan and his subordinates to their recriminations after the failure of the land operations.

The alliance which began so amicably was threatened with worse than mutterings when a Boston mob, shouting imprecations on French "monarchy and popery," killed one of d'Estaing's sailors in a street riot. The incident was quickly hushed, and both Lafayette and Hancock did a great deal to restore cordiality. The New England members of Congress helped by lecturing their constituents in letters such as the following, written by Samuel Adams on September 14th to Samuel Savage Phillips:

> I am sorry to hear there is a Disposition in some persons in Boston to cast an odium on the french Admiral for his leaving Rhode Island. In my opinion it is at this Juncture impolitick in the Extreme. Even if his Conduct was thought to be blameworthy Prudence I think would dictate Silence to us. Men of Discretion and Influence will surely by all means check such a Disposition.[6]

John Hancock's weakness for luxury and display served his country well in this crisis. Every day during the autumn of 1778 he entertained as many as forty French officers for dinner in his Boston home. Dolly Hancock sent her servants to milk all the cows pastured on the Common, regardless of ownership, and the former president of Congress wrote to a friend: "I must beg the fav'r of you to Recommend to my man Harry where he can get some Chickens, Ducks, Geese, Hams, Partridges, Mutton, or any thing that will save my Reputation in a Dinner, and by all means some Butter."

Tact on both sides smoothed over differences of opinion before the French warships left Boston for operations in the West Indies. But Americans could not help reflecting at the end of the year that only bitter husks were left of the summer's flourishing hopes. The British, recovering from the jolt of finding themselves involved in a European as well as an American war, were going ahead to fight it out with their usual pluck. They even opened up a new American front in the autumn as warships sailed from New York with troops which captured Savannah.

While Washington's idle army melted away with expiring enlistments, the mood of the State House reflected the change in the fortunes of war. The exaltation of July turned into quarrelsomeness within two months, and a seemingly innocent item of August 15th in the *Journals* became the opening gun of the most savage dispute in the fifteen years of the Continental Congress. Silas Deane, home from abroad, was requested to render "a general account of his whole transactions in France, from the time of his first arrival, as well as a particular state of the funds of Congress, and the commercial transactions in Europe, especially with Mr. Beaumarchais, and to answer such questions as may be asked." [7]

This would appear to be a routine investigation, but the assembly split into two furious factions. Deane's friends, chiefly conservative delegates from the middle and southern states, admitted that his accounts had been carelessly kept but insisted that he was an able and honest public servant. They were opposed by a vociferous group of New Englanders and southern radicals who agreed with Deane's colleague and accuser, Arthur Lee, that he was unworthy of the trust reposed in him.

This dispute was to drag on until Deane ended as a traitor and Lee as a neurotic. The brother of the Virginia delegates, educated as a physician at Eton and the University of Edinburgh, had already shown signs of the unbalanced temperament which caused Franklin to think him insane. Lee suspected most of his associates, including the old philosopher, of crimes ranging from peculation to treason. His charges against Deane started a congressional feud which soon outgrew the original causes, so that Gouverneur Morris commented, "The Storm increases, and I think some one of the tall trees, must be torn up by the roots." Cyrus Griffin of Virginia, writing to Jefferson on October 6th, feared "that Congress will shortly be dissolved. If the large Emissions of Money, and visionary Expeditions do not bring forth our destruction, I greatly fear that *Party* will complete the matter. Congress exhibit not more than two or three Members actuated by Patiotism." [8]

On September 22nd John Mathews of South Carolina wrote to Thomas Bee: "Oh! my worthy friend, never was Child more sick of school, than I am, of this same business I am sent here upon. . . . I am afraid the day will shortly arrive when some men, will be made sensible, that all the future services they can render their Country, can never compensate for the invaluable moments, nay hours, days, and months, they have trifled away, in idle debate." This would seem to be a strong enough opinion, but on October

17th, the anniversary of Saratoga, the London-educated lawyer wrote again to his friend: "A change of Men, or measures, must be speedily effected, or we are lost. It is a melancholy truth, and as I think it is high time it was known, I must tell you, that the American cause never stood so near the pinnacle of destruction as it this day does, and is daily approaching nearer to its downfall." [9]

The frantic note of exaggeration in these jeremiads is another symptom of the malaise of the assembly. It had gone so far by October 22nd that small interest was shown in that congressional panacea for all ills, a projected new invasion of Canada. Instructions were sent to Franklin, holding forth the Newfoundland fisheries as bait, asking him to appeal for French assistance to the extent of 5,000 troops in addition to warships and transports. There was even a spark of the old spirit in the prediction that within a few months "the reduction of Canada might be so far completed that the ships might proceed to the investiture of Halifax." [10]

But the feeble display of enthusiasm soon died out, leaving some of the delegates frankly skeptical. In such gloomy moments the spirit of the Great Jehovah brooded darkly over the Continental Congress, and on October 12th the delegates declared that

> whereas true religion and good morals are the only solid foundations of public liberty and happiness:
> Resolved, That it be, and it is hereby earnestly recommended to the several states, to take the most effectual measures for the encouragement thereof, and for the suppressing of theatrical entertainments, horse racing, gaming, and such other diversions as are productive of idleness, dissipation, and a general depravity of principles and manners. [11]

It may be suspected that Sam Adams inspired this resolution. At any rate, he had written to his wife in similar language only the week before: "I hope the Depravity of Manners is not so great as to exclude all Hopes of Childrens rising up and serving God and their Country in the Room of their Fathers. May Heaven grant us a Time of Reformation!" [12]

The rock-ribbed puritanism of the archrebel might have been more admirable if he had not come into his own as a troublemaker in the Deane-Lee imbroglio. Even the brothers of Dr. Arthur Lee were not such scheming partisans as Sam Adams, who probably did more than any other delegate to keep the feud alive after it would normally have died of inanition.

If the Continental Congress had no other claim to immortality, it should be remembered as doubtless the only parliament of history to consider the question of meeting at the unearthly hour of 5:00 A.M. When this issue came up in the autumn of 1778, there were nine affirmative votes out of thirty, with New York, Pennsylvania and North Carolina concurring.[13] As a somewhat less masochistic measure, it was resolved to meet daily from nine until one and three until six. After a brief experience, Congress found this schedule unsatisfactory and went back to the old hours of ten until three, with committee meetings taking up the balance of a delegate's long day.

Titus Hosmer of Connecticut complained that business went tediously. "When we are assembled several gentlemen have such a knack at starting questions of order, raising debates upon critical, captious or trifling amendments, protracting them by long speeches, by postponing, calling for the previous question, and other arts, that it is almost impossible to get an important question decided at one sitting; and if it is put over to another day, the field is open to be gone over again, previous time is lost, and the public business is left undone."[14]

Up to this time Congress had washed its soiled political linen in private. As early as the autumn of 1775, according to John Adams, insinuations of profiteering were heard behind closed doors. The delegates found it a suspicious coincidence, with Thomas Willing serving in Congress, that the Philadelphia house of Willing and Morris had been awarded a contract for gunpowder "by which the House, without any risk at all, will make a clear profit of twelve thousand pounds at least." Adams added that several delegates had complained. "All think it exorbitant."[15]

Both Willing and his partner Robert Morris were severely criticized for driving a hard bargain at their country's expense, but not a breath of scandal reached the public.

No such constraint prevailed in October, 1778, when Alexander Hamilton, already well known in New York at the age of 22, indulged a fondness for making public accusations which would lead down the years to the most famous duel of American history. Assailing Samuel Chase in a Poughkeepsie newspaper, the young officer wrote: "You have shown that America can already boast one public character as abandoned as any the history of past or present times can produce. It is your lot to have the peculiar privilege of being universally despised."[16]

Hamilton apparently had good grounds for charging the Maryland delegate with forming a monopoly in flour and raising the price more than 100 per cent. The following month Chase failed of re-election to Congress when he remained silent. Never in history has there been a war without profiteering, but the facts scarcely justified William Whipple's reaction to the Chase exposé in a letter of November 24th: "The Spirit of Monopolizing under the name of Speculating rages with great violence through the United States the consequence of which must prove fatal unless the interposition of the Legislatures of the several States can check its fury." [17]

As the year limped toward an end the violence of the Deane-Lee feud could not be contained by the State House walls, and both factions appealed to the public. The bitterness of sentiment is revealed by a letter of December 10th which Francis Lightfoot Lee wrote to his brother Arthur in Paris:

> After having been absent since the beginning of June, I arrived here the 7 of Novr. . . . I was astonished to find out that S. Deane had made so great progress in the Art of intriguing, as to have formed here a very dangerous party who think it necessary to their designs, to remove all the old friends of Liberty and Independence, for which purpose every Lie their invention can furnish, is circulated with the Air of certainty, and the blackest coloring given to actions in themselves indifferent or accidental. This party is composed of the Tories, all those who have rob'd the public . . . with many others, whose design, I fear, is of a much more alarming nature, and a few which wish to succeed to Offices abroad. All these together form a very powerfull body.[18]

The partisans of the other faction were not any more reticent about claiming a monopoly of patriotism and public virtue. Deane appealed to Congress for another hearing several times in the autumn of 1778. Then he went over the heads of the assembly on December 5th. In an address, "To the Free and Virtuous Citizens of America," published in the *Pennsylvania Packet,* he vigorously defended himself and accused his accusers.

The oldest delegates had never seen such a storm as broke on the floor of the State House. Henry Laurens, the short and stocky merchant of Huguenot extraction, was incapable of remaining neutral in anything. Warmhearted, equally impulsive as friend or foe, the 54-year-old president shocked Congress on December 9th by suddenly making a speech of resignation.

In his newspaper letter Deane had not neglected to throw brickbats at Congress as well as Lee. Laurens declared that he felt "my own honor, and much more forcibly the honor of the Public deeply wounded by Mr. Deane's address." But much as he resented it because Deane "arraigns the justice and the wisdom of Congress," the South Carolina member hurled a few stones of his own: "Finally, gentlemen . . . as I cannot consistently with my own honor, or with utility to my country, considering the manner in which Business is transacted here, remain any longer in this chair, I now resign it." [19]

The election of John Jay, regarded as a Deane man, was the answer of Congress. As might have been expected, the Lee faction took Laurens to its bosom after applauding his decision to remain as a delegate.

Once the feud had become public property, the Philadelphia newspapers were filled with articles signed by such pseudonyms as Senex and Plain

Truth and Common Sense. James Duane commented to Governor Clinton in a letter of December 15th, "You will see by the papers a ridiculous squabble between Deane and the Lees." The New York member added that "our late honorable President was exceedingly wounded" but thought that "his zeal transported him a little too far." [20]

Edward Langworth, himself a former newspaperman, denounced the "Phantasticability and absurdity of the President" in a letter to his friend Duer. The Georgia delegate praised Congress for imposing "not the least restraint on the Liberty of the Press. as for my part I shall rejoice to see more publications on the proceedings of Congress. a little gentle Satyr will be useful on many occasions and will restrain the spirit of intrigue and Cabal." [21]

Another heated controversy, second only to the Deane-Lee dispute, found its way into the newspapers. General William Thompson had recently been charged by Congress with using "abusive, disrespectful, and contemptuous expressions" toward a delegate, Thomas McKean. It was not the first situation of the sort. In the summer of 1777 the assembly intervened when a Delaware citizen, Gunning Bedford, challenged Jonathan Dickinson Sergeant to a duel for statements made by the New Jersey member in a debate. Congress declared the offender "guilty of a high breach of the privileges of this house" and ordered him to apologize, which he did. This case set a worthy precedent, but the assembly did not fare so well in the Thompson-McKean dispute. The general won an acquittal which caused Francis Lightfoot Lee to lament that "Congress has no power, and every Villain whome they want to call to account, insults them." This plaint seemed justified when Thompson declared in the *Pennsylvania Packet* that McKean had "behaved like a Lyar, a rascal and a coward." Congress left it to the insulted delegate to answer in his private capacity, though he had incurred Thompson's wrath as a public servant.

More fuel was heaped meanwhile on the flames of the Deane-Lee quarrel by Thomas Paine, who wrote in a Philadelphia newspaper over the pseudonym Common Sense: "If Mr. Deane or any other gentleman will procure an order from Congress to inspect an account in my office, or any of Mr. Deane's friends in Congress will take the trouble of showing themselves, I will give him or them my attendance, and shew them in handwriting which Mr. Deane is well acquainted with, that the supplies he so pompously plumes himself upon were promised and engaged, and that as a present, before he ever arrived in France; and the part that fell to Mr. Deane was only to see it done, and how he has performed that service the public is well acquainted with." [22]

French aid to America in the early part of the war had never been exactly a secret, even in England. Still, Gérard did not care to have it shouted from the housetops that his country had played a two-faced role. On January 5, 1779, the minister protested to Congress about the "indiscreet assertions" of an American public official. He asked the assembly "to take measures suitable to the circumstances" after declaring solemnly for the record "that all supplies furnished by M. Beaumarchais . . . whether merchandise or cannon or military goods, were furnished in the way of commerce."

The Lee partisans called upon heaven to witness that Paine had been persecuted, but they could say little in his defense. After all, he had published articles based on secret papers entrusted to him as paid secretary of the Committee for Foreign Affairs. On the advice of friends, he saved embarrassment by resigning on January 8th. President Jay was instructed to assure Gérard "that Congress do fully, in the clearest and most explicit manner, disavow the publications" which had offended. With tongue in cheek, Congress solemnly expressed its conviction "by indisputable evidence that . . . the great and generous ally of these United States, did not preface his alliance with any supplies whatever sent to America." [23]

Nothing would seem to be lacking to complete the farce, yet only a week after his resignation Thomas Paine had the satisfaction of declining an offer of more lucrative employment at writing propaganda for a foreign nation. The nation was France, and the offer came from Gérard.

Chapter 18

That Froward Hussy, Maryland

E ARLY in 1779 it began to occur to Congress that the Articles of Confederation were no nearer to ratification than ever, though all the
states save one had acceded. John Dickinson returned to the assembly as a
delegate from Delaware, where he owned property, just in time to bring
that state into the fold as the twelfth to sign.

"There now remains Maryland who you know has seldom done anything with a good Grace," grumbled William Whipple, the reformed New
Hampshire slave trader, in a letter of February 7th to Dr. Bartlett. "She has
always been a froward hussey." [1]

Most of the delegates had been certain in July, 1778, that the end of the
year would see the Articles ratified. Six months later Maryland was still
resisting in spite of broad hints that confederation might in a pinch be
managed with fewer than thirteen states. The Virginia delegates were instructed by their assembly on December 19th to submit such a proposition.
But it was not until May 20th that they "laid before Congress an Instrument
from that State impowering them to Confederate with any one or more
States, and they have offered to do so in explicit terms." [2]

These were the words of a report by the North Carolina members, who
recommended that their state take similar action. Maryland had not been
idle meanwhile, and instructions to her delegates were presented to the assembly that very day. Both documents lay side by side on the table of Congress as evidence that eighteen months after adoption the Articles of
Confederation were still a long way from ratification.

There were wheels within wheels, for some of the states had signed only on condition that all the others give their assent. A comparison of the two documents, moreover, was rather to the advantage of Maryland. "Is it possible," asked that froward hussy, "that those states who are ambitiously grasping at territories, to which in our judgment they had not the least shadow of exclusive right, will use with greater moderation the increase of wealth and power derived from those territories, when acquired, than what they have displayed in their efforts to grasp them?" And many members from other states agreed personally with Maryland's succinct answer, "We think not." [3]

Virginia's western land claims were held to be "injurious to more than one half if not the whole of the United States." The Maryland instructions predicted darkly: "Although the pressure of immediate calamities, the dread of their continuance from the appearance of disunion, and some other peculiar circumstances, may have induced some states to accede to the present confederation, contrary to their own interests and judgments, it requires no great share of foresight to predict, that when these causes cease to operate, the states which have thus acceded to the confederation will consider it no longer binding, and will eagerly embrace the first occasion of asserting their just rights and securing their independence."

Maryland made no bones about admitting that jealousy of the prospect of cheap lands and low taxes in a neighboring state had been an influence. One of the delegates, Daniel of St. Thomas Jenifer, who had already shown a keen interest in land speculation, also offered a candid political motive. "Whilst we retain our negative to the present plan of confederation the Door will be open for Justice to be done us," he declared in a letter of June 8th, adding that "the moment it is turned into an affirmative, it will not only be shut, but locked against us." [4]

On May 21st Connecticut appeared to follow the example of Virginia when her delegates presented similar instructions. But there was an important difference, for the New England state specified that Maryland should have the privilege at a later date of entering the confederation on the same terms as other states. Thomas Burke wrote from North Carolina, where he was taking leave of absence, to warn that any "such partial Confederacy may lay the foundation of disunion." The British, he feared, would be encouraged to prolong the war.

On the whole, Maryland got the better of Virginia in this clash of opposing viewpoints. After allowances are made for narrow and parochial interests, the smaller state had spoken eloquently for all America—the America of the future—in the final plea of the instructions to her delegates:

We are convinced policy and justice require that a country unsettled at the commencement of this war, claimed by the British crown, and ceded to it by the treaty of Paris, if wrested from the common enemy by the blood and treasure of the thirteen states, should be considered as a common property, subject to be parcelled out by Congress into free, convenient and independent governments, in such manner and at such times as the wisdom of that assembly shall hereafter direct. . . . We have spoken with freedom, as becomes freemen, and we sincerely wish that these our representations may make such an impression on that assembly as to induce them to make such addition to the articles of confederation as may bring about a permanent union.

Two social events at the beginning of 1779 were mentioned by Samuel Holten's diary. On Tuesday, January 5th, "Genl. Washington invited Congress to dine with him at the city tavern and we dined accordingly." The following Friday "Congress invited Genl. Washington to dine at the city tavern."

It had become a recognized tradition for either the assembly or the commander in chief to suggest the desirability of a conference. This time Washington made the overtures in a letter of December 13th, requesting that he might lay before the delegates "the state of the army, the condition of our supplies, and the requisites for carrying into execution an undertaking that may involve the most serious events."

Duane, Root, Laurens, Meriwether Smith and Gouverneur Morris were appointed as members of a committee to represent Congress. It did not take long to dispose of the last of Washington's three propositions. On January 1, 1779, the committee reported that the proposed invasion of Canada in combination with France "should be deferred till circumstances shall render the co-operation of these states more certain, practicable and effectual." After reviewing the lack of arms and supplies, the committee found it doubtful "that these states will be able to perform their part in the proposed stipulations." [5]

There was another objection which could not be mentioned very tactfully in the report, though it circulated freely "out of doors" and probably reached the sensitive ears of Gérard. It was not altogether provincialism which caused some of the delegates to question the advisability of exposing France to temptation in regard to Canada. After all, France had lost that colony only nineteen years before to American as well as English invaders. France was the mother country in language, religion and customs; and there were members of Congress who feared that blood might prove thicker than the ink with which treaties of alliance are signed.

Washington and the committee frankly recognized that Congress and the states were competing for enlistments. A resolution of January 23rd recommended "that the Commander in Chief be authorized and directed to take the most effectual measures, to reinlist for the continuance of the war, all such of the continental troops as are not expressly engaged for that period, as well as for raising new recruits . . . and for these purposes, besides the bounties of cloathing, and at the expiration of the war, of money and land hitherto provided by Congress . . . to grant to each able bodied soldier now in the service, and who shall voluntarily re-inlist during the war, a bounty according to the circumstances of his present engagement, not to exceed in any case 200 dollars. . . ." [6]

A second resolution asking the states to revoke their bounties met defeat from delegates who knew that it would be wasted effort. As they had anticipated, the states continued to outbid Congress by holding forth the inducement of shorter terms as well as higher rewards. On March 9th the assembly decided on a straight bounty of $200; and legal compulsion was suggested without success to the states in a recommendation that they raise troops "by draughts, or in any other manner they shall think proper."

Ever since the summer of 1776 both British and Americans had attempted to secure the loyalty of doubtful communities by demanding wholesale oaths of allegiance. Both made an even more determined effort to induce opposing soldiers to desert, and the British felt that they had as good a right as Congress to offer American land. It galled the rebels to find it expedient to extend boons to the Hessians accused of the worst looting; but deserters were offered oxen and hogs as well as land in the spring of 1778, even though Congress had no livestock at its disposal.

All available records show that neither side had much success with such attempts. The human cattle from Germany were guarded like prisoners by their own officers, according to the rule laid down by Frederick the Great. A great many captives taken in battle by the Americans remained in this country, but there were few deserters. As for the redcoats, still fewer were tempted by material gains and political liberties surpassing anything they could expect at home after serving a long enlistment. Even the rebels were impressed by British foemen who displayed all the arrogance of Roman legionaries in a barbarian land, making little distinction between American loyalists and patriots.

In the first weeks of 1779 Washington and the committee devoted all their thought to plans for fighting rather than bribing the enemy. One of the commander in chief's most cherished projects had been a request for half pay for officers on a lifetime basis after the war. He proposed it at Valley Forge and Congress passed a measure the following May calling for half pay for seven years if the officer continued in the service until the end of the war without holding any office of profit.

This compromise did not satisfy the general, who again recommended a lifetime basis in January, 1779. Two of Washington's most valuable qualifications for his unique position were his unfailing pessimism and his conviction that practically all human actions sprang from self-interest. The events of the Revolution seldom gave him any reason for changing his mind; and both attitudes colored his arguments in favor of half pay for life. In the first place, looking on the dark side as usual, he thought it very doubtful if many of the comparatively young officers would outlive the seven-year period. And if they did, declared the father of his country, self-interest would cause them to be anxious about their financial security during the limited time on earth remaining to them.

Congress was so little convinced by these lugubrious reasons that only two members supported a motion for Washington's measure. In June the assembly thought better of it after reading an urgent memorial from a group of officers. General John Armstrong, a middle-aged civil engineer just elected as a Pennsylvania member, worked hard for the cause of his former comrades in arms. A committee considering the matter brought in a favorable report, but Congress again defeated half pay for life on August 17th. On December 1st the measure failed for a third time. Washington kept on backing it with his customary persistence; but not until October 21, 1780, did Congress finally agree with him.

Much of the opposition came from New England members who muttered that Washington attended to the interests of officers at the expense of enlisted men. Pension legislation, which would be given so much time by future Congresses, had begun on August 26, 1776, with a resolution providing half pay for life for any soldier as well as officer "so disabled in the service of the United States of America as to render him incapable afterwards of getting a livelihood." On September 23, 1778, the widow and eleven children of the "brave and worthy" Captain Skimmer, killed while commanding the Continental brig *General Gates*, were compensated none too munificently by a resolution providing an annual pension of $400.[7] Other such resolutions appear in the *Journals*, but the recipients were soon to find their pitiful stipends becoming almost worthless as the currency sickened.

Each spring brought dreams of victory to the imagination of delegates who fondly believed that just another campaign would see the war through to a triumphant climax. The fifth summer of the struggle found Washington too weak and Clinton too cautious to attack in force, so that both armies attempted nothing more ambitious than small warfare in the New York area. The improvement in American discipline, however, was demonstrated in the two main military events of the year. General Anthony Wayne's light infantry behaved like veterans when they stormed Stony Point with the bayonet alone, capturing 500 prisoners in the British fort on the Hudson. The other operation, cherished by Congress as its own idea, showed precision in the strategic sphere. During the January conferences Washington had agreed to a large-scale punitive expedition against the New York loyalists and the Indians of the Six Nations. In a summer's efficient campaign General Sullivan's army laid waste the Indian crops and villages before defeating the allies in the battle of Newtown on August 29th.

Neither of these victories had yet been announced when the heat of a Philadelphia summer, combined with the warlike fervor of two delegates, brought forth one of the most incredible proposals ever to be heard on the floor of the State House. John Dickinson moved on July 14th that "Congress immediately adjourn to the place where the Army shall be, and that the members shall respectively join the Militia, and act with them in such important operations as shall be judged most expedient for advancing the welfare of these states." William Henry Drayton, the Oxford-educated South Carolina jurist, promptly seconded a motion which seems to have been made seriously. But Henry Laurens doubtless voiced the ridicule of other delegates when he remarked in a letter of July 17th, "This shews more valour in these Gentlemen than of the wisdom and reflection of grave Senators, but who can restrain the ardor of fighting Men when an opportunity offers?" [8]

The anniversary of the French alliance called for a dinner at the City Tavern, with Congress as host and M. Gérard as the guest of honor. Two days later, on February 8th, he informed the assembly that he had an important secret to communicate. It proved to be a confidential announcement that Spain would probably declare war on Great Britain in the near future.

No prophet foretold that Spain would ally herself with France alone, and on the 15th the French minister asked for a private audience with the committee of the whole. The time had come, he suggested, for Congress to make up its mind as to the major decisions which would inevitably rise from an alliance with Spain and the peace conference. In other words, what did America want from the war? What would she be willing to give up? What were her minimum requirements?

Thomas Burke of North Carolina, Meriwether Smith of Virginia, Samuel Adams of Massachusetts, John Witherspoon of New Jersey and Gouverneur Morris of New York were appointed to a committee for the purpose of making a survey. It took them only a week to conclude that as a preliminary to any negotiation "the liberty, sovereignty, and independence, absolute and unlimited, of these United States, as well in matters of government as of commerce, shall be acknowledged on the part of Great Britain." [9]

Never once, however dark the outlook, was there the slightest wavering on the part of Congress in regard to independence. The committee also drew up twelve other stipulations—six of them positive, and the others intended as bargaining points. The ultimata included certain minimum boundary requirements, the evacuation of American soil, American fishing rights in the waters off Newfoundland, navigation of the Mississippi to the southern boundary of the United States, free trade with a port or ports below that boundary, and the cession of Nova Scotia if France and Spain would lend their support.

From the beginning it could be seen that all but two of these six major stipulations might be settled without too much difficulty. Fisheries and the navigation of the Mississippi were the questions that would split Congress along sectional as well as factional lines. The New Englanders held that Newfoundland fishing privileges were their hereditary right, while the Southerners maintained just as stoutly that the progress of America depended on the navigation of the great river. Neither region could see the other's viewpoint, and the vote on each issue sometimes resulted in all the states north of Maryland going in one direction, and those to the southward pulling away in opposition.

With the sectional lines so firmly drawn, any exceptions could be charged to factionalism. To say that Henry Laurens of South Carolina and the Lee brothers of Virginia voted with the Yankees on the fisheries issue can only be compared to an announcement in this day that senators from the deep South had allied themselves with Republicans on an issue favoring northern urban manufactories. Edmund Cody Burnett, the historian of the Continental Congress, has written that "it would be a fruitful theme to trace the growth of parties during this year 1779, to which the Deane-Lee imbroglio contributed so powerfully. For certain it is that that long-drawn-out controversy not only generated numerous personal antagonisms, but drove such a cleaving wedge between groups in Congress that the cleft remained, views continued to diverge, attitudes refused to harmonize, interests persisted in being irreconcilable, and all this until a time when Deane and Lee had all but been forgotten." [10]

This cleavage explains why three southern delegates voted with a New England group supporting a Virginian against a man from Connecticut. It is also significant that the group had acquired the name of the "Adams-Lee faction" as a tribute to the part played by Sam Adams behind the scenes.

Up to this time it must have given the archrebel some bitter moments to recall the decade before 1774 when he had been the organizer of revolt. In contrast, his five years in the Continental Congress represented a period of obscurity. But the Deane-Lee feud provided just the opening for the tireless cunning of the middle-aged delegate with the benevolent smile and palsied hands. He responded by scheming against his foes in Congress as relentlessly as he had undermined the British authorities ten years before. In fact, he did not trouble to change either the words or the tune; and Sam Adams' opponents of 1779 became the successors of Hutchinson and Gage as enemies of liberty, friends of tyranny and advocates of oppression.

No question before Congress was too great or too small to be fought out along factional lines. Henry Laurens started a new controversy the first week of 1779 by criticizing the accounts of the Secret Committee as kept by Robert Morris two years before. The South Carolina member assured Morris that he did not "insinuate that you have in any respect acted dishonestly." But the close connection between this committee and the firm of Willing and Morris left some doubts as to whether there had been profiteering.

Laurens and Morris exchanged heated letters in the Philadelphia newspapers as other delegates took sides according to their Deane-Lee affiliations. This meant that Laurens was thought a renegade by his colleagues in the South, most of whom were Deane sympathizers. John Penn, the North Carolina lawyer, defended Morris so furiously that his own personal quarrel with Laurens soon became noisier than the main bout. With Congress in this mood, Samuel Sterritt wrote to General Mordecai Gist on January 19th: "The Custom of Duelling is exceedingly prevalent at present in this City. . . . Two Members of Congress, Mr. Lawrence the late President and Mr. John Penn from North Carolina lately decided some nice point of honor by single Combat. Such is the countenance given to that mode of satisfaction by the example of those illustrious heroes in romance, that we have new duels fought every day." [11]

Allowances must be made for exaggeration in this account, for neither Laurens nor Penn missed a day in Congress. But the bitterness of personal feeling cannot be overemphasized in a dispute which sputtered along for eight months. Meanwhile Sam Adams' quill scratched away busily every night as he indoctrinated people with such letters as the following, written to Samuel Cooper on January 19th:

> Mr. Deans Friends are in hopes he will be sent to Holland as a Reward for his good Services, from whence he may probably send or bring another mercantile Letter of Recommendation. Doubtless deep *Commercial* Connections may be formd there. . . . I am sorry to be obliged to think, that a Monopoly of Trade, and not the Liberty of their Country, is the sole Object of some Mens Views. This is the Cake which they hope shortly to slice and share among themselves.[12]

It is understandable that the Lee brothers should have felt deeply on an issue concerning not only family honor but also the best interests of America as they saw them. On May 3rd Richard Henry Lee wrote to Jefferson "that persecuted as I have been by the united voice of toryism, peculation, faction, envy, malice, and all uncharitableness, nothing but the certain prospect of doing essential service to my country can compensate for the injuries I receive." [13]

The debates on the Newfoundland fisheries and navigation of the Mississippi brought up the whole subject of American foreign relations, dragging in Franklin and John Adams along with Deane and Lee. Neither the philosopher's scant gray hairs nor his services in securing a treaty of alliance were enough to spare him from insinuations of misconduct. John Adams, on the other hand, had to endure stings from the Deane faction. For weeks the merits and demerits of the commissioners in Paris were discussed in terms which would have made their ears burn. Finally, after long labor, the mountain of ill feeling gave birth on April 20th to a mouse of a resolution "that suspicions and animosities have arisen among the late and present commissioners . . . highly prejudicial to the honor and interest of these United States." [14]

An attempt to recall Franklin for his testimony met defeat, not without more insinuations against him being heard. Even in 1779 it hardly seems possible that Arthur Lee could have been mentioned in the same breath, but the leaders of factions are not limited by reason. A year later, after tempers had cooled, Richard Henry Lee could still attack Franklin on patriotic grounds in a letter to Sam Adams: "How long my dear friend must the dignity, honor, and interest of these United States be sacrificed to the bad passions of that old man under the idea of his being a philosopher? The philosophy which does not rectify the heart is not the kind of wisdom which it befits republicanism to cherish and to confide in." [15]

When the question of Arthur Lee's fitness to conduct the peace negotiations came up before Congress, not even Gérard and Vergennes could escape being involved. Two Deane men, William Paca of Maryland and William Henry Drayton of South Carolina, persuaded Gérard to give them a formal statement that Lee's ability—his integrity was not in question—did not have the confidence of Versailles and Madrid. The American commissioner had been so indiscreet and quarrelsome, in short, that the two courts did not believe him to be a proper person for such a delicate business. The statement quoted Vergennes as saying, "I confess to you that I fear Mr. Lee and those about him." [16]

On April 30th, when Paca and Drayton laid this statement before Congress, the rage of the Adams-Lee faction knew no bounds. The question of

Lee's recall reached a deadlock on May 3rd. New Hampshire, Massachusetts, Connecticut and New Jersey voted in the negative, New York, Virginia, Maryland and North Carolina in the affirmative, with Pennsylvania, Delaware and South Carolina being divided. Altogether, twenty-two delegates decided against Lee, fourteen upheld him, and one was excused. Elbridge Gerry of Massachusetts broke away from his section by voting with such Deane men as John Dickinson, James Duane, Thomas Burke and Gouverneur Morris.

Resentments were intensified by an epidemic of attacks on Congress in newspaper articles signed by such pseudonyms as Cato, Leonidas, Americanus and O Tempore! O Mores! In some instances it could not be doubted that the authors were the recipients of what would today be known as inside information. Inevitably, members of the assembly suspected one another of divulging secrets or of writing the letters themselves.

"There is as much intrigue in the State House as in the Vatican," John Jay wrote to Washington on April 26th, "but as little Secrecy as in a boarding school." John Armstrong, the ex-general, more the engineer and soldier than the politician, could only groan "that compared to Congress in it's present attitude, I call the Army a bed of ease, a Pillow of Down." [17]

The questions of the fisheries and the navigation of the Mississippi were meanwhile being stormily debated from time to time without making much progress as compared to the other four major stipulations. During one of the interludes Congress spoke the language of courtiers on June 15th when it congratulated Louis XVI on the birth of a daughter and requested him "to oblige us with portraits of yourself and royal consort, that by being placed in our council chamber, the representatives of these states may daily have before their eyes the first royal friends and patrons of their cause." [18] And a few days later, at the Fourth of July banquet for M. Gérard, toasts were drunk to "His Most Catholic Majesty and the other Branches of the Royal House of Bourbon."

Not even the celebration of Independence Day could soothe the animosities of Congress. Henry Laurens and the pontifical William Henry Drayton, differing the more violently because they represented the same state, set some kind of record by quarreling about fireworks. Laurens, whose sense of humor operated at other times, solemnly recorded the arguments. After a French officer asked permission for the exhibition, Drayton remarked "that it had been the practice of all nations ancient and modern to celebrate particular days by festivity, that Greece had instituted the Olympic Games . . . and concluded by hoping the man would be allowed to exhibit his fire works.

"Mr. Laurens rose, expressed his astonishment at the Conduct of his

Honorable Colleague. . . . Does not the gentleman know that his own Country is bleeding at every vein and now probably reduced to the greatest distress?"

The hot-tempered South Carolina merchant added that "the Olympic games and other fooleries brought on the desolation of Greece." He quoted Drayton as replying, "I would have Gentlemen when they talk about history discover that they knew something about it. The Olympic Games were not instituted for the celebration of anniversaries nor did they bring on the ruin of Greece. They were calculated for improving bodily strength, to make men athletic and robust."

Laurens apparently did not think of the proper retort until after his day in Congress, when he ended his notes for July 2nd with the rhetorical query, "Is drinking Madeira Wine from 5 to 9 o'clock, then sallying out to gaze at fire works, and afterwards returning to Wine again, calculated to make men athletic and robust?" [19]

The decision of Congress is shown by an entry for July 5th (the 4th fell on Sunday) in the diary of John Fell, the New Jersey merchant just released from a long British captivity. "Congress adjourned at 12. OClock to hear Mr. Bracenridges [Hugh Henry Brackenridge] Elogium on the Heroes Slain in this Contest. Afterwards there was an Entertainment at the City Tavern. And in the Evening Currious Fire works." [20]

One of the crosses which parliamentarians must bear is the reproaches of constituents for a supposed failure to try brilliant "new" ideas which have long ago been considered. Congressional tempers in 1779 were not sweetened when Leonidas and Americanus and their tribe published newspaper articles to the effect that paper could never take the place of gold. John Dickinson found it hard to conceal the irritation in his reply of July 19th to some financial suggestions from Caesar Rodney, president of Delaware:

We see the wisdom of your proposal to stop the presses—we perceive taxation to be of as much importance as you mention—we are desirous of borrowing on the lowest terms—but, while we have so many thousands to supply with necessaries, and while the demands upon us for the articles we purchase are daily and hourly rising upon us, with such a boundless stretch—to what purpose are loans and taxes? [21]

Throughout 1779 the members of Congress had to submit with as much grace as possible to being constantly reminded that prices were high and profiteers rampant. Delegates whose allowances did not cover expenses were quite able to understand the plight of their constituents. "Speculation here has arrived to such a height, and prices in three weeks encreased 100 per Ct.," raged Daniel of St. Thomas Jenifer in a letter of May 24th. "This has made those Vermins the Speculators become the object of resentment, and a Mob has assembled to regulate prices. what will be the issue God knows. they are now parading."[22]

Before the year ended, the American "capital" was to see several outbreaks of mob violence without any great damage resulting. Edward Langworthy appealed to Congress in July for protection against "outrages I have reason to apprehend." While lodging at the home of Charles Humphreys, a congressman of 1774-1776 accused of profiteering as a Quaker miller, the Georgia member claimed to have been roughly handled by soldiers taking the law in their own hands. He accused Charles Willson Peale of instigating the trouble, but the portrait painter declared the charges to be "groundless, erroneous and unjust."

Congressmen did not need to be reminded of "those Vermins the Speculators" when one of the most distinguished of them was operating under their noses. After requesting the command at Philadelphia on the plea of a Saratoga wound, General Benedict Arnold lost no time at taking advantage of the opportunities awaiting a man of easy conscience in July, 1778. Four days after his arrival, before the shops had time to reopen following the British evacuation, he signed a secret agreement with James Mease, the clothier general, and his deputy William West, in which the three planned to use the public credit instead of their own money to buy goods supposedly for the army and sell them to the public at a huge profit. It was impossible to lose at this game, since anything not wanted at exorbitant prices by the public could simply be turned over to the army for enough to cover expenses. Arnold received his share for protecting the very crimes which as commander he was supposed to detect and punish. The reckless assurance of the conspirators, as well as their distrust of one another, is shown by the contract with their signatures which did not come to light until after Arnold's treason. In the autumn of 1779, however, he scarcely troubled to hide his trail. Arriving in the city without resources except a major general's pay of $332 a month in Continental money—then worth perhaps a third of its face value—the adventurer with the cold gray eyes paraded his contempt for public opinion by giving expensive entertainments for Tories. Soon he moved into the John Penn house on Market Street which had been General Howe's headquarters, and Arnold's coach-and-four and liveried servants became one of the spectacles of Philadelphia.

His unpopularity is understandable. But it was not until the first month of 1779, long after his dealings had been a public scandal, that the Pennsylvania Council indicted him on eight charges. Copies of the resolution, which the newspapers published, were sent to General Washington and the authorities of other states.

The swarthy little general tried later to justify his treason by claiming to have been a victim of congressional persecution at various times. Hence it is interesting to note that the assembly came to his defense on February 16, 1779. Every state but Pennsylvania voted against a motion to suspend the accused man from command, and Congress appointed a committee of investigation.

When four of the charges were thrown out for lack of evidence, the attitude of Congress was openly resented by the Pennsylvania authorities. "By their publications they have directly and positively appealed to the Public and stand as accusers of Congress to their Constituents," declared Gouverneur Morris in the debate of March 26th. "Therefore we cannot consistently with the honor and dignity of this Congress nor consistently with the regard we owe to our Constituents confer with the State of Pennsylvania, before they have made reparation." Meriwether Smith, according to Laurens' notes, expressed himself even more vigorously: "If I had been abused and traduced and held out in print to the Public, shall I as an individual submit to a conference with the Man or any set of Men who have used me in that manner. No Sir!" [23]

This was a sample of the talk heard in the State House. But past events had proved that Congress could not discipline an individual, much less a state, when it came to a showdown. The assembly had little choice but to take a public scolding from the Pennsylvania authorities with as much dignity as it could retain. After incurring this humiliation in an effort to see justice done to Arnold, it would have been disconcerting to know that as usual he blamed Congress. In a letter of May 5th to Washington he wrote: "I little expected to meet the ungrateful returns I have received from my countrymen; but as Congress have stamped ingratitude as a current coin I must take it. I wish your Excellency, for your long and eminent services, may not be paid in the same coin."

The British secret service papers have indicated that a few days before or after writing this letter Arnold began his treason by sending a message to Clinton's headquarters. During his remaining sixteen months in an American uniform he supplied the enemy continually with military information while bargaining for his price of £10,000 for the betrayal of West Point.

The court-martial did not meet until the end of 1779, and Arnold won practically an acquittal in January with a verdict imposing a reprimand for two trivial offenses. Justice has been blind, deaf and dumb in an effort to placate the sulking warrior; for there could be no question of his guilt in using public wagons to transport personal goods for speculation. The mild reprimand from the commander in chief, merely included in the day's orders on April 6, 1780, could scarcely have offended a man who at that time had been a traitor for nearly a year.

Pennsylvania's opposition to Congress in the Arnold affair was only another of the incidents adding to the strain on the twenty-five or thirty men trying to govern a warring country without authority or resources. Sometimes nerves snapped under the tension, and the first physical encounter of the State House occurred on August 31st. It is not surprising that one of the participants should have been Henry Laurens, but the other was the mild-mannered secretary. Both published tedious and humorless justifications in the *Journals* a few days afterwards. "When he . . . seized the bundle [of papers] in my left hand and endeavored to take it by force, I wrenched it from him," wrote Thomson. "But afterward, when he used abusive language and threatened to kick me, I felt my indignation kindled to that degree, that I am glad, I had so far the command of myself as only to put myself in an attitude of defence and say 'you dare not.'" [24]

This ridiculous episode is more excusable when it is realized that both men had been tortured by visits to the bedside of William Henry Drayton, who died of typhus three days later. Only 37 years old, the South Carolina judge had been writing a history of the Revolution to which Thomson and Laurens contributed notes.

Typhus and yellow fever epidemics were to be feared in the Philadelphia of that day. But it was overwork which killed Joseph Hewes of North Carolina, the moving spirit of the marine committee, two months later. He had been first to recognize the ability of John Paul Jones, and the news of the victory of the *Bon Homme Richard* over the *Serapis* reached him on his deathbed.

Delegates looking back over the first five years of the Continental Congress might have been pardoned for reflecting that some of the earlier problems, including independence, were simple as compared to the issues of 1779. President Jay's sincerity cannot be doubted, but there was the air of whistling in the dark when he wrote to Washington on April 21st: "The spending of a few troublesome Years of our Eternity in doing good to this and future Generations is not to be avoided or regretted. Things will come out right, and these States will be great and flourishing." On July 14th, in a letter to Gates, Henry Laurens said pretty much the same thing, but said it with more caution, "I am persuaded all will come right, but not until we shall have waded and plunged through a good deal of wrong. . . ." [25]

Chapter 19

Watchman, What of the Night?

THE nicknames and initials of the delegates of 1779 were so well known to intimates that they could be used as a code of sorts. James Lovell, one of the Adams-Lee strategists, wrote to Arthur Lee on September 21st: "W. H. D. is off the Stage. Jemmy D. and Gov. M. are behind the Scenes; Judge F—l and Wody L—don are on their pillows. But the main Chair is full. The Farmer the Fidler and the Boatswain are active." [1]

This report on the leaders of the Deane faction might be decoded as follows: "William Henry Drayton is dead. James Duane and Gouverneur Morris are absent; John Fell and Woodbury Langdon are ill. John Jay remains in the president's chair. John Dickinson, Meriwether Smith and William Carmichael are up to no good."

Intimacy did not in most cases make for affection, but at least the delegates of 1779 could respect one another for taking a personal loss to serve in Congress. Although many of them were prosperous and even wealthly men "on paper," the consequences of the decline of Continental money were summed up by Richard Henry Lee in a letter of May 3rd to Thomas Jefferson:

> Almost the whole of my landed estate was rented out some years before the war for low cash rents, and under the faith of existing laws which secured me Specie for my rents. The vast sums of paper money that have been issued (& this now being a legal tender for the discharge of rents growing from old contracts) and the consequent depression, has well nigh effected an entire transfer of my estate to my Tenants. This year, Sir, the rent of 4000 acres of fine Land will not buy me 20 barrels of Corn! [2]

Personal financial troubles had a great deal to do with the resignation of the Virginia delegate a few weeks later, despite the need of the outnumbered Adams-Lee faction to be represented. Another Virginia member, the brilliant young Edmund Randolph, an able lawyer at the age of 26, declined an appointment for another year in a letter of October 21st because of the "dependence of my family on the fruits of my profession."

Dr. Nathaniel Scudder of New Jersey wrote on November 21st that "sheer necessity compels me to retire." A month later William Floyd of New York reported to Governor Clinton that "Congress have resolved to Remove from this place the 1st of May next But have not yet Determined on the place where they will Remove to. You will not be surprized at their wish to Quit this City, when you are informed of the amazing Expense of Living here: Beef in the market Current at 3 Doll's pr. lb; pork four . . . and other things in proportion; it Seems as if the Devil was with all his Emmisaries let loose in this State to Ruin our money."[3]

"The expense of living here is intolerable, beyond Conception, and almost insupportable," wrote Nathaniel Peabody of New Hampshire to Dr. Bartlett on Christmas Eve. John Armstrong, the bluff old Pennsylvania engineer, set a precedent worthy of future congressional imitation by admitting that he was bankrupt in ability rather than money. "I am now leaving Congress," he wrote on October 15th, "having exerted the last dregs of any remaining talent I had under various impediments."[4]

The delegates who stuck it out made a grim joke of their service in the assembly. "For God's sake come on to relieve me in Nov., but at the furthest the very beginning of December," implored Cornelius Harnett of his colleague Thomas Burke on October 9th. ". . . I acknowledge it is cruel of me to wish you to return; you have already suffered more in your private concerns than any man who has been in the Delegation for some time past. But you have this Consolation; that, should you fail of receiving your reward in this world, you will no doubt be singing Hallelujas in the next to all Eternity, Tho' I acknowledge your Voice is not very well Calculated for that business."[5]

Neither of the two North Carolina members was destined to outlive the war. Harnett died in 1781 of hardships suffered while a British prisoner. Burke crammed such adventures into his remaining few years as an escape from the British and Tories holding him hostage, but in 1783 he succumbed at the age of 36 to an illness brought on by overwork.

All questions before Congress led sooner or later to the underlying problem of finances. At the beginning of 1779 the Continental currency was heading toward collapse at such a rate that this was obviously the year of crisis.

The financial experts of Congress had long ago concluded that foreign loans offered the only hope of salvation, for it could only be regretted that taxation had been a political impossibility at the outset. On October 22, 1778, detailed instructions were sent to Franklin in regard to the financial debacle.[6] This statement, drawn up by Gouverneur Morris, is worth quoting at length for its diagnosis of American ills:

> At the commencement of the war, it was obvious that the permanent revenues and resources of Great Britain must eventually overbalance the sudden and impetuous sallies of men contending for freedom on the spur of the occasion, without regular discipline, determinate plan, or permanent means of defense. America never having been much taxed . . . and contending against what once was the lawful authority, had no funds to support the war, notwithstanding her richness and fertility. And the contest being upon the very question of taxation, the laying of imposts, unless from the last necessity, would have been madness.
>
> To borrow from individuals, without any visible means of repaying them, and while the loss was certain from ill success, was visionary.
>
> A measure, therefore, which was early adopted, and thence become familiar to the people, was pursued. This was the issuing of paper notes representing specie, for the redemption of which the publick faith was pledged.

Morris explained in a few paragraphs that "this general credit, however, did not last long." His statement continued:

> The monopoly of commodities, the interruption of commerce rendering them more scarce, and the successes of the enemy, produced a depreciation of the paper. And that trace begun, became in itself a source of further depreciation. . . .
>
> This demanded more plentiful emissions, thereby increasing the circulating medium to such a degree as not only to exclude all other, but, from its superabundant quantity, again to increase the depreciation.
>
> The several states, instead of laying taxes to defray their own private expenses, followed the example of Congress, and also issued notes of different denominations and forms. Hence to counterfeit became much easier, and the enemy did not neglect to avail themselves of this great though base advantage. And hence arose a further depreciation.

The multiplicity of emissions, Morris concluded, "not only impairs the value simply in itself, but, as it calls for continued large emissions, so the certainty that everything will be dearer than it is, renders everything dearer than it otherwise would be; and vice versa. Could we possibly absorb a part of the inundation which overwhelms us, everything would be cheaper from the certainty that it would become cheaper."

Congress instructed Franklin: "The above observations . . . you shall lay substantially before the French ministry, and labour for their assistance to remove the difficulties there stated."

Such had been the desperation of Congress that in 1777, nearly six months before the treaty of alliance, the assembly began spending the loans from France not yet received. In other words, Congress went ahead, without any assurance that the lenders would lend, to draw bills of exchange on its commissioners in France, hoping that by some miracle these bills would eventually be accepted.

This quaint financial policy was proposed in June, 1777, by a committee. On the following September 10th Congress took the plunge by resolving that bills of exchange drawn on the Paris commissioners would be used to pay the interest on loan office certificates.

As the next step (December 3rd) the assembly formally instructed the commissioners to seek a loan of two millions sterling at the courts of France and Spain, pledging the faith of the United States, for a term of not less than ten years. There were even designs on the Grand Duchy of Tuscany.

While Congress waited impatiently for results, its representatives in Europe showed their annoyance sometimes. "But Taxation, my dear Sir, Taxation and Oeconomy, are our only effectual Resources," John Adams had written to James Warren in the late summer of 1777. In a letter of February 13, 1779, to the Committee of Foreign Affairs, he seems not to have changed his mind after a year in France: "It would be agreeable to me, indeed, if I were able to throw any light on the subject of finances. As to a loan in Europe, all has been done which was in our power to do, but without the desired effect. Economy and taxation comprehend all the resources that I can think of." [7]

These two words belong in that department of history reserved for such interesting and probably apocryphal remarks as "Let them eat cake!" The fact is that Congress could not and the states would not impose enough taxes to finance a revolution springing from resistance to taxes. As for economy, it is hard to see where reforms could have been introduced into an administration which too often erred on the side of pinchpenny policies.

Nor could it be said that Congress overlooked many means promising to raise money. The lottery had brought in only a trickle, not because Americans of that age were too virtuous to gamble, but because the prizes consisted of the very loan office certificates which had already proved to be a failure. An eager cash market awaited American products in Europe, but there was the British blockade. The Committee of Foreign Affairs, reporting to the commissioners in France on December 2, 1777, bemoaned the issues of

"Continental" which reached a total of thirty-eight million dollars by the end of that year. "Our situation is rendered still worse," the letter continued, "by the impossibility of vending such products as America has largely in store, which are now greatly wanted in Europe, viz: tobacco, naval stores, rice, indigo, etc. The great superiority of the enemy's naval fleet makes it impossible to send those products to sea with a tolerable prospect of safety." [8]

A poll tax on everv inhabitant of America; a duty of 2 per cent on imported commodities; a permanent fund of two millions to be paid in annually by the states over a period of ten years—these were some of the proposals considered by Congress and reluctantly put aside because the states were not ready. The assembly covered the ground so thoroughly that in the autumn of 1778 a committee recommended "that the several States having large uncultivated Territory, beyond what is in their power to govern, be called upon to cede the same to the United States." The committee envisioned not only new independent states but also the sale of millions of acres to provide funds for Congress. This was the very scheme which brought America out of beggary in the end; but like the other ideas for raising money, it had to mature politically.

After making war nourish war by fighting the British with arms captured from them, it was not to be supposed that Congress would neglect any possibility of squeezing the Tories. On November 27, 1777, the struggle entered a new implacable phase with the resolution:

> That it be earnestly recommended to the several states, as soon as may be, to confiscate and make use of all the real and personal estate therein, of such of their inhabitants and other persons who have forfeited the same, and the right to the protection of their respective states, and to invest the money ensuing from the sale in continental loan office certificates, to be appropriated in such manner as the respective states shall hereafter direct. [9]

Harsh as this decision may seem, it is only fair to add that there had been provocations. Loyalists behind the British lines had plundered neighbors adhering to the patriotic side. Even the Tories who contented themselves with selling produce for British gold had aroused the wrath of the rebels. "Long Island has been exceedingly enriched by the war," wrote Serle in the spring of 1777. "Many of the Farmers have been paid £60 or 70 for the Use of their Horses & Waggons alone; and they have acquired great Sums by the Sale of their Cattle. So profitable a time, they own, they never knew before." [10]

Lord Howe, who had little use for Tories, coolly advised Galloway and his friends to negotiate with the rebel authorities after the evacuation of Philadelphia. His brother, Sir William, told a loyalist leader that he had better "make his peace with the states, who, he supposed, would not treat them too harshly."

Conversion rather than persecution had generally been the rebel policy up to the autumn of 1777, but the fall of Philadelphia sharpened antagonisms. Even so, the confiscation resolve did not result in all loyalist property being swallowed at a gulp. Several states actually opposed the measure at first; but as the war went on, adding to expenses as well as resentments, all of them gradually fell in line. Tory owners were given the right of trial by jury in a few states to determine the legality of the seizure, but most of the states simply confiscated by attainder and sold at auction. Needless to add, there were many instances of injustice and shady political dealing. And though the various state laws provided as a rule for the families of Tories deprived of a livelihood as well as property, such humanities were not observed too strictly toward the end of the struggle.

Every long-drawn war results in a financial revolution which destroys old fortunes and creates new. The prizes go to the tough, the cunning and the resourceful, which means that speculators and profiteers are more likely to succeed than men of breeding and culture. The American loyalists who became the impoverished exiles of 1783 saw themselves as fallen aristocrats, yet it is an ironical fact that many had been the profiteers of the last war. Since 1763 they had mellowed enough to be horrified by a newer group of profiteers, especially when the profiteering was done at their own expense. In turn, the *nouveau riche* Americans of 1783 would soon learn to esteem family and position above money, so that two decades later the daughter of a Baltimore speculator named Patterson married the brother of a Corsican *arriviste* named Bonaparte.

This process of social erosion could scarcely have been contemplated in the proper philosophical mood by congressmen who had authorized the printing of sixty-three and a half more millions in "Continental" during 1778 alone, making a total of $101,500,000 by the end of the year. If the acceleration kept on another twelve months at this rate, it could readily be foreseen that the certificates would soon lose all value. There was nothing left except to take some of it out of circulation, and on December 31st Congress voted to destroy two whole emissions amounting to $41,500,000. They could not be redeemed after June 1, 1779, on which date would begin the process of marking them with a circular punch. The bills were "to be afterwards examined and burned, as Congress shall direct."

As an important provision of this same measure, the states were urged to pay their respective quotas of $15,000,000 for 1779 and the next eighteen years, in order to sink the past loans and emissions. A resolution of January

4th appointed a delegate from each state to a committee which set the annual quotas as follows:

New Hampshire	500,000	Pennsylvania	1,900,000
Massachusetts	2,000,000	Delaware	150,000
Rhode Island	300,000	Maryland	1,560,000
Connecticut	1,700,000	Virginia	2,400,000
New York	800,000	North Carolina	1,090,000
New Jersey	800,000	South Carolina	1,800,000 [11]

Georgia's quota was deferred because of the British invasion. An appeal went out to the other twelve states on January 13th in the "Address to the People on the Currency" signed by President Jay, which blamed most of the financial ills on enemy counterfeiting—an accusation which hurt nobody's feelings even if it convinced nobody. Meanwhile the daily expenses of the war had somehow to be met; and on January 14th, just after authorizing the removal of $41,500,000 from circulation, Congress ordered a new emission amounting to $50,000,400.

In less than a month the demands of daily war expenses made necessary an issue of five additional millions on February 3rd, followed by another on February 19th, and still another on April 1st. Thirty-five millions had been added to the grand total when the time came on June 1st to cancel the $41,500,000 designated for withdrawal. Some of these bills were still in circulation, so that the time had to be extended to January 1, 1780.

By May the financial situation had grown so serious that Congress agreed to devote three days a week to those problems alone. On May 22nd the assembly passed a resolution calling upon the states to pay their quotas of forty-five million dollars into the treasury before the end of the year—this burden on top of the quotas of the fifteen millions asked in the resolution of January 2nd.[12]

Large as these sums then seemed, the currency was depreciating at such a frightful rate that if the states paid in full the total would not cover the new emissions necessary in 1779 alone. Nevertheless, the states would have to tax their citizens as Americans had never been taxed before. It remained a question whether the state officials could or would take that political risk, and Congress decided that the crisis called for some powerful rhetoric.

Jefferson has emerged as the most celebrated polemic writer of the era, but nobody ever contributed as many addresses as John Dickinson. It was as a contemporary of James Otis that he composed his *Declaration of Rights* for the Stamp Act Congress, followed by his *Letters of a Farmer in Pennsylvania*. Fifteen years later, in the financial crisis of 1779, the hypercritical editors of Congress again relied upon "the Penman of the Revolution" after rejecting the efforts of two other aspirants.

Dickinson reviewed the failure of emissions, loan office certificates and the lottery. He admitted that there had been speculation, profiteering, monopolizing and incompetence of officials. Then he told the states bluntly "that we are not convinced there has been as much diligence used in detecting and reforming these abuses as there has been in committing or complaining of them."

> In vain will it be for your delegates to form plans of oeconomy, to strive to stop a continuation of these emissions by taxation or loans, if you do not zealously co-operate with them in promoting their designs. . . . We have, on the most mature deliberation, judged it indispensably necessary to call on you for 45,000,000 of dollars, in addition to the 15,000,000 required by a resolution of Congress of the 2nd of January last, in the same proportion, as to the quotas of the several states, with that for the said fifteen million.[13]

The address specialized in plain talk rather than eloquence, but Dickinson put two pointed queries: "Do you imagine that they [your enemies] can now flatter themselves with a hope of conquering you, unless you are false to yourselves? . . . What nation ever engaged in a contest under such a complication of disadvantages, so soon surmounted many of them, and in so short a period of time had so certain a prospect of a speedy and happy conclusion?"

Troubles never came singly to Congress, and a committee appointed to consider the claims of Hortalez and Company estimated on June 1st that the United States was indebted to the extent of "about £200,000 sterling." After admitting that "Mr. Beaumarchais has a just claim on these states for a large sum of money," the committee added vaguely that "it is not in their power, with any degree of exactness, to ascertain the amount." Leave was asked and granted for further investigation into a financial snarl destined never to be satisfactorily unraveled.[14]

Another problem which threatened to become perennial arose from the petty civil war in the Vermont territory claimed by both New York and New Hampshire. Congress appointed a committee on June 1st "to repair to the inhabitants of a certain district known by the name of New Hampshire Grants, and enquire into the reasons why they refuse to continue citizens of the respective states which have heretofore exercised jurisdiction of the said district. . . ."[15]

The cry of "Stop the press!" now reverberated through the land as a popular panacea for financial troubles. Congress was belabored by anonymous newspaper writers until Elbridge Gerry could stand no more. "If such infamous Publications are to pass without proper notice," he grumbled in a speech, "'tis time for Congress to go home and other men come in their stead. . . ."

The member from Massachusetts must have been astonished when delegates from the supposedly autocratic southern states blocked the investigation that he demanded. Although Gerry threatened to resign, Burke and Penn and Meriwether Smith flew to the defense of such gadflies as Leonidas and O Tempore! O Mores! "When the liberty of the Press shall be restrained," said Smith, "take my word for it, the liberties of the People will be at an end."

While Congress struggled against financial collapse, the Chevalier de la Luzerne and his secretary François Marbois were taking a leisured overland trip from Boston to Philadelphia. The new French minister exclaimed at the prosperity of a land in which a farmer thought nothing of owning his acres and a span of oxen. Marbois noted in his journal the variety as well as quantity of foods served at every meal, the sturdy homespun clothing worn by the most humble folk, the absence of anything that a European would call poverty. It was a smiling American countryside which greeted the visitors in the late summer of 1779, and they could only recall with pity the comparative misery of peasants in their own land.

Such inconsistencies are likely to make the entire subject of finance an enigma when it is not a bore. It is hard to remember that currency is only a medium for distributing capital as represented by houses, farms, factories, roads and wharves. Currency is not capital any more than a ship is cargo; but only a few men akin to poets have the gift for seeing rows of digits in terms of the human joys, sorrows, efforts and frustrations which produce a nation's wealth. Alexander Hamilton at the age of 22 was one of these men, and in an undated letter of 1779 to Robert Morris he exploded a good many popular fallacies of the day:

> Most people think that the depreciation might have been avoided by provident arrangements in the beginning, without any aid from abroad; and a great many of our sanguine politicians, till very lately, imagined the money might still be restored by expedients within ourselves. . . .
>
> The idea proceeded from an ignorance of the real extent of our resources. The war, particularly in the first periods, required exertions beyond our strength, to which neither our population nor riches were equal. We have the fullest proof of this, in the constant thinness of our armies; the impossibility, at this time, of recruiting them otherwise than by compulsion; the scarcity of hands in husbandry, and other occupations; the decrease of our staple commodities; and the difficulty of every species of supply. I am aware that the badness of the money has its influence; but it was originally an effect, not a cause, though it now partakes of the nature of both. . . .
>
> It was not in the power of Congress, when their emissions had arrived at the thirty millions of dollars, to put a stop to them. They are obliged, in order

to keep up their supplies, to go on creating artificial revenues; and as these multiplied, their value declined. The progress of the depreciation might have been retarded, but it could not have been prevented. It was, in a great degree, necessary.

The only remedies, declared Hamilton, were a foreign loan and the establishment of "an American bank, instituted by authority of Congress." He pointed out that France and England each had a debt of nearly two hundred million pounds sterling. "The most opulent States of Europe, in a war of any duration, are obliged to have recourse to foreign loans or subsidies. How, then, could we expect to do without them. . . ." [16]

But young Hamilton did not as yet have the ear of Congress. On June 11th, in response to the clamor of "Stop the press!" the assembly declared against any more emissions. Five weeks later the printing press had to be called upon for another five millions. On the first day of September, however, Congress resolved that "on no account whatever" would it go beyond a grand total of two hundred million dollars in "Continental." All but about forty millions had already been issued since 1775, but it was agreed not even to emit this amount unless urgently necessary.

Ten days later, as if to burn its bridges behind it, Congress asked John Jay to write a circular letter announcing the decision to the states. The result was one of the most memorable state papers of the period. In particular, the introductory sentence is worthy of a high place among American quotations:

> In governments raised on the generous principles of equal liberty, where the rulers of the state are the servants of the people, and not the masters of those from whom they derive authority; it is their duty to inform their fellow citizens of the state of their affairs, and by evincing the propriety of public measures, lead them to unite the influence of inclination to the force of legal obligation in rendering them successful. [17]

A legalist as well as a patriot, the 34-year-old president of the assembly offered a convincing proof of the political immutability of America: "On the 4th of July, 1776, your representatives in Congress, perceiving that nothing less than unconditional submission would satisfy our enemies, did, in the name of the people of the thirteen United Colonies, declare them to be free and independent states, and 'for the SUPPORT of that declaration . . . did mutually pledge to each other their LIVES, their FORTUNES, and their SACRED HONOR.' Was ever confederation more formal, more solemn, or more explicit?" demanded John Jay, the patriot. "It has been assented to and ratified by every state in the union." Thus, concluded John Jay, the lawyer, as long as any of the objects were not attained, including the redemption of the Continental currency, the American union "cannot, so far as it may respect such objects, be dissolved, consistent with the laws of God or man."

He admitted that "the time had been when honest men might, without being chargeable with timidity, have doubted the success of the present Revolution . . . but that time is passed. The independence of America is now as fixed as fate. . . ."

The minister of his Christian Majesty, representing a nation soon to be asked for loans, had the moral advantage which a prospective creditor always holds over a prospective borrower. Without going too far beyond his prerogatives, the Sieur de Gérard kept a watchful eye on the debates in Congress. When the questions of the Newfoundland fisheries and the navigation of the Mississippi were still deadlocked after three months, he communicated on May 6, 1779, "the perplexity under which he labors with regard to informing his court of the delays which the negotiation, commenced in the month of February last, meet with. It must be allowed that no affair so important and so pressing has ever experienced so much delay; and the undersigned declares that he can see no reason for warning France and Spain against the sinister interpretations with which attempts are made to inspire them with regard to this conduct." [18]

The French minister, in line with good diplomatic practice, dangled a glittering inducement before the eyes of Congress. Although Louis XVI "has made no engagement to furnish supplies of money to the United States," declared Gérard, the monarch "is desirous to contribute to the re-establishment of the American finances, as far as his own necessities allow him to do so."

Other such hints were thrown out from time to time, but the members of Congress did not respond to either prodding or wheedling. They kept on obstinately debating the two issues at intervals until September, settling them in their own way. The statement supplied by Gérard about Arthur Lee had damaged him with the Adams-Lee delegates, who also resented his messages to Congress. "I am afraid," wrote James Lovell on March 21st, "of the Arts that are used to hurry us into a rash ultimatum. We are told that such is our *first* Business tho' . . . the Observations of a blind man may convince us of the contrary; but forsooth France and Spain are of that opinion fully as say the Lickspittles of the Plenipo." [19]

The New Englanders, who wished to make the fishing rights a rigid ultimatum, were opposed every inch of the way by the Southerners, who did not think the issue important enough, since it did not concern their sectional interests, to endanger a future peace treaty. There was also the question of French and Spanish consent, for the Southerners demanded as a prerequisite that the allies support the ultimatum.

When it came to the navigation of the Mississippi, the shoe pinched the other foot. The New Englanders were interested only in seeing that this issue was not allowed to offend Spain, as a prospective ally with holdings at the mouth of the river.

Three volumes of the *Journals* are largely devoted to contests in which phrases and even words became the subject of fierce debates. The sectional character of the voting is shown by the final decision, as published in the *Diplomatic Correspondence:*

> On motion of Mr. McKean, seconded by Mr. Huntington,
> *Resolved,* That if after a treaty of peace with Great Britain, she shall molest the citizens or inhabitants of any of the United States in taking fish on the banks and places described in the resolution passed on the 22nd day of July instant, such molestation (being in the opinion of Congress a direct violation and breach of the peace) shall be a common cause of the said States, and the force of the Union be exerted to obtain redress for the parties injured.
> On the motion to agree to this, the yeas and nays being required by Mr. Smith,

New Hampshire	Mr. Whipple	Aye
	Mr. Peabody	Aye
Massachusetts Bay	Mr. Gerry	Aye
	Mr. Lovell	Aye
	Mr. Holten	Aye
Rhode Island	Mr. Marchant	Aye
	Mr. Collins	Aye
Connecticut	Mr. Huntington	Aye
	Mr. Spencer	Aye
New York	Mr. Jay	Aye
	Mr. Duane	Aye
	Mr. Lewis	Aye
New Jersey	Mr. Fell	Aye
	Mr. Houston	Aye
Pennsylvania	Mr. Armstrong	Aye
	Mr. Searle	Aye
	Mr. Muhlenberg	Aye
	Mr. McLene	Aye
Delaware	Mr. Dickinson	Aye
	Mr. Van Dyke	Aye
	Mr. McKean	Aye

Maryland	Mr. Carmichael .... No
	Mr. Henry .... No
	Mr. Forbes .... No

Virginia	Mr. Fleming .... No
	Mr. Smith .... No
	Mr. Randolph .... No

North Carolina	Mr. Harnett .... No
	Mr. Penn .... No
	Mr. Burke .... No
	Mr. Hewes .... No
	Mr. Sharpe .... No

South Carolina	Mr. Laurens .... No
	Mr. Mathews .... No
	Mr. Drayton .... No

So it was resolved in the affirmative.[20]

The Southerners were handicapped by the fact that invaded Georgia was not represented. Nevertheless, they managed to keep the fisheries question on the carpet from the middle of February until July 29th, the date of the above resolution. Two weeks later the question of instructions to the minister negotiating the peace came up for discussion. And on August 14th the New Englanders made a further concession by accepting the instruction that "a desire of terminating the war hath induced us not to make the acquisition of these objects an ultimatum on the present occasion."

After a longer though less emotional contest the issue of Mississippi navigation also ended in a compromise. Early in September the French minister hinted strongly that it would not be good policy to alarm a potential ally. On the 17th, therefore, Congress resolved that if Spain should capture Florida after becoming an ally, the United States would guarantee possession "provided always, that the United States shall enjoy the free navigation of the river Mississippi into and from the sea."[21]

This completed Gérard's task in America, and that very day he took his leave of Congress in a private audience. The French minister and President Jay exchanged the full-blown compliments of diplomacy, but a sigh of relief can almost be heard between the lines of John Dickinson's letter to a constituent: "We have dismist him with as honourable Testimonial, respecting his public and private Conduct, as we could give." Undoubtedly the Adams-Lee faction would have slammed the door in Gérard's face if the majority had not insisted on discretion.

Before leaving the subject of foreign relations, Congress took up the accu-

sations hurled at one another by the representatives in Europe. The status
of Franklin had been decided in the early autumn of 1778 when he was
elected sole minister plenipotentiary to the court of France. This appointment had not pleased some of the more rabid Adams-Lee partisans, but
Thomas Burke revealed that a majority of the members "gave little or no
Credit to the charges against him." James Lovell had already written to the
philosopher: "You have escaped all considerable Injuries, tho you have been
comprehended in some propositions not altogether honorary."²²

"Upon the whole," Burke reported to the North Carolina assembly
toward the end of August, "your Delegates could find no sufficient Cause
for degrading any of the foreign Ministers tho they saw plainly that none
Except Doctor Franklin could be any longer useful. . . ." But he added
judiciously "that all of them, not excepting Doctor Lee, had some Merit,
particularly unwearied Attention and Industry."²³

The Adams-Lee group made a perfunctory attempt to have Arthur Lee
chosen for the peace mission, but as experienced politicians they realized
that he lacked support. Next they got behind John Adams and elected him,
after some maneuvering, to negotiate the treaties of peace and commerce
with Great Britain. John Jay had to be content with the appointment as
minister to Spain; and Samuel Huntington was chosen on September 28th
to fill the vacant president's chair.

Luzerne, the new French minister, was described by General Steuben in
a letter to Hamilton as "about thirty-six years of age, though he appears
younger. . . . He appears to be a man of solid sense, and less presumptuous
than the people of quality in that country usually are. His manners are
prepossessing; and they would be more so if he could speak English."²⁴

His secretary Marbois spoke English so well that he soon married a
Philadelphia girl; and in 1803, as the Marquis of Barbé-Marbois, he represented Bonaparte in the Louisiana Purchase. The minister presented his
credentials on November 4th and had his formal audience two weeks later.
This time, however, the ceremonial aroused few comments in the letters of
delegates who were more absorbed by the state of America's finances.

Congress had grimly stuck to its determination not to emit any more
money beyond a grand total of $200,000,000. Necessity led to a resolution
of October 6th, calling upon the states for still more quotas in addition to
those asked in the resolutions of January 2nd and May 21st—this time for
$15,000,000 monthly from February 1 to October 1, 1780. Few delegates
seem to have thought that their states would levy the taxes, and this
pessimistic conclusion proved to be prophecy.

Early in October only three of the sixty millions asked from the states to
defray expenses of 1779 had been received. Congress had no choice except

to keep on ordering emissions until the deadline of the two hundredth million was reached on November 29th.

Facing the certainty of an empty treasury before the end of the year, the delegates snatched desperately at any prospect of foreign loans. Spain loomed as a greater possibility after the appointment of John Jay as minister. In the hope that Holland also might be persuaded, the assembly elected Henry Laurens as commissioner to negotiate a treaty of amity and commerce.

America, of course, was not in a position to wait long months for results— not at a time when funds were lacking to feed and clothe the army from day to day. It could not be forgotten that in 1777 Congress had learned how to annihilate time by drawing bills of exchange on its commissioners across the Atlantic in the faith that they would be accepted. Then the scheme had gone no further than a resolution to pay interest on loan office certificates in such bills. Elbridge Gerry revived the idea in the summer of 1779 by suggesting bonds, payable in eight years, to anticipate European loans not yet consummated. On November 23rd, however, Congress went still further by adopting a plan to draw bills payable at six months' sight on Jay and Laurens. The sale of these bills at the current rate of exchange, it was fondly believed, would tide America over the emergency. For nobody had any doubt that the halting of emissions would soon check the depreciation blamed on the money press.

The desperation of the remedy is apparent from the fact that Jay had not yet reached Spain, let alone negotiating a loan. Laurens, far from being in any position to solicit a Dutch loan, would not depart for ten months on a voyage fated to end in a long captivity in the Tower of London. But the members of Congress could not be choosers. They could only cope with a present crisis by drawing bills of exchange payable in future funds.

Chapter 20

Bricks without Straw

AFTER taking his seat in the early spring of 1780, the new delegate from Virginia needed only a week to perceive that his country was in danger. In a letter to Jefferson of March 27th, James Madison summed up the crisis without exaggeration:

> Our army threatened with an immediate alternative of disbanding or living on free quarter; the public treasury empty; public credit exhausted; . . . Congress complaining of the extortion of the people; the people of the improvidence of Congress, and the army of both; . . . an old system of finance discarded as incompetent to our necessities, an untried and precarious one substituted, and a total stagnation in prospect between the end of the former and the operation of the latter. These are the outlines of the true picture of our public situation.[1]

In this same letter the 29-year-old delegate mentioned "a defect of adequate statesmen" which made the assembly "more likely to fall into wrong measures and of less weight to enforce right ones." But the new member himself brought to the council a political genius such as any nation is fortunate to produce once in a century. Shy and withdrawn, only five and a half feet in height, Madison looked smaller and more solemn because of his habit of dressing entirely in black. It was not at first glance that the force of that personality became apparent, but Dr. Witherspoon had known. Dr. Witherspoon, gathering a preceptor's reward, had induced the young Virginian to return to Princeton for another year of study after his graduation in 1771. Scholarship was all that mattered to an "invalid" haunted by psychosomatic fears of the death which at last overtook him in 1836, the year of Martin Van Buren's nomination for the presidency.

At the time of Madison's arrival as the youngest delegate, nearly four months had passed since December 1st, the date when everyone trusted that some relief might be expected from the stopping of emissions. Instead, the depreciation could and rapidly did grow worse. From a valuation of about twenty for one in December, as compared to Spanish milled dollars, the "Continental" sank to sixty for one on March 14th. "Beef is sold 5, 6, and 8 dollars a pound," added Samuel Livermore in a letter of this date, "and other things in proportion. Expenses are beyond imagination." [2]

The members of Congress, as well as the French visitors, had observed in their travels that the farm lands of America offered a plausible picture of well-being. In rural districts of Virginia and Connecticut it would have been hard to imagine that America was beginning the sixth year of a war against heavy material odds. But Madison knew, as did Hamilton, how difficult a feat of political legerdemain it would be to transfer some of the plenty from the farmer's table to the soldier's mess. Congress had already made the attempt in a resolution of December 14, 1779:

> That all the states shall be called upon to furnish their quotas of such supplies as may, from time to time, be wanted for carrying on the war; and in making the requisitions, due care shall be taken to suit the convenience of the several states; and the articles by them respectively furnished shall be credited towards their quotas of the monies which they are called upon to raise for the United States, at equal prices for articles of the same kind and quality, and for others in due proportion. . . .[3]

In other words, Congress hoped to persuade the states to pay their quotas in bacon and flour and beef instead of the money of a dying currency. It was as good a solution as anything that could have been proposed, but it did not alter the fact that America, as Hamilton had declared, simply lacked the resources to fight the British Empire. Rural prosperity on a small scale could not take the place of commerce and manufactures as the sinews of war, especially at a time when the British naval blockade had America under its thumb.

Congress deserves credit, after all errors are taken into account, for dogged courage in dealing with insoluble financial problems. The new delegate from Virginia had been in the assembly only two months when his mind raced ahead to comprehend the full political implications. "It is to be observed," he wrote to Jefferson on May 6th, "that the situation of Congress has undergone a total change from what it originally was. Whilst they exercised the indefinite power of emitting money on the credit of their constituents they had the whole wealth and resources of the continent within their command, and could go on with their affairs independently and as they pleased. Since the resolution for shutting the press, this power has been entirely given up and they are now as dependent on the states as the King of England is on the parliament." [4]

George Washington, this same month, reached an even more disturbing conclusion. Although the austere legend of the commander in chief has elevated him far above the clamor of politics, nobody had a better understanding. Where Jefferson, Madison and Hamilton had naturally keen intellects whetted to a razor's edge by scholarship, the father of his country had intuition. One of the least educated men of the day in terms of schooling, he was not surpassed even by Lincoln in the political perception which comes from reading the human heart. On May 31st, writing to Joseph Jones, the Virginia physician just returned to Congress for another term, Washington issued a warning which he intended to be considered by other members:

> Certain I am, unless Congress speak in a more decisive tone, unless they are invested with powers by the several States competent to the great purposes of the war, or assume them as a matter of right, and they and the States respectively act with more energy than they hitherto have done, that our cause is lost. We can no longer drudge on in their old way. . . . One State will comply with a requisition of Congress, another neglects to do it; a third executes it by halves; and all differ either in the manner, the matter, or so much in point of time, that we are always working up hill; and, while such a system as the present one or rather want of one prevails, we shall ever be unable to apply our strength or resources to any advantage.
>
> This, my dear sir, is plain language to a member of Congress; but it is the language of truth and friendship. It is the result of long thinking, close application, and strict observation. I see one head gradually changing into thirteen. I see one army branching into thirteen, which, instead of looking up to Congress as the supreme controlling power of the United States, are considering themselves as dependent on their respective States. In a word, I see the powers of Congress declining too fast for the consideration and respect, which are due them as the great representative body of America, and I am fearful of the consequences.[5]

Washington's dependent clauses sometimes gave him trouble. But there was nothing wrong with his deductions. And there was nothing in all American polemic writing up to this time which analyzed more intelligently the factors which would soon bring the country to a choice between chaos and a new constitution.

Late in January the assembly appointed a committee of seven members—Mathews, Ellsworth, Gerry, Burke, McKean, Griffin and Robert R. Livingston—to consult with the new French minister at his request. On the 25th the committee reported that Luzerne "had it in command from his king to impress upon the minds of Congress, That the British cabinet have an almost insuperable reluctance to admit the idea of the independence of these

United States and will use every possible endeavor to prevent it. . . ." There was a further warning "that should the enemy be in possession of any part of these United States at the close of the next campaign, it will be extremely difficult to bring Great Britain to acknowledge their independence."[6]

The messages of Luzerne as well as Gérard followed a pattern which should have become familiar to Congress. From the viewpoint of ministers representing an old European kingdom, the Americans were rebelling British colonists who could be urged to do the mother country a great deal of harm. All the better if they could be helped to the point of winning their independence, though the French monarch abhorred republican institutions as much as did his brother across the Channel. It was worth a considerable investment for France to rob the hereditary foe of her fairest colonies and establish a hostile nation, and French policy spoke with firm but benevolent paternalism. After the usual warning of the consequences awaiting a half-hearted effort in the next campaign, Luzerne promised naval aid if possible.

Naturally, the French minister wished to know "what force the United States can bring into the field next campaign." Congress informed him on January 31st "that the United States have expectations, on which they can rely with confidence, of bringing into the field an army of twenty-five thousand effective men, exclusive of commissioned officers." It was asserted that supplies "can certainly be obtained within the United States" for this force and any troops that his most Christian Majesty might send. As for money, the penniless assembly declared with proud assurance "that Congress rely on the contributions of the States by taxes and on moneys to be raised by internal loans for the pay of the army."[7]

This statement has been cited as an example of the foolish optimism that Congress could display in the hour of peril. It is rather an evidence of a determination which did not hesitate at beguiling an ally—the same determination with which the Continental Congress drove relentlessly toward independence while protesting loyalty to George III. The aid of France was essential to American victory if not to survival in the next campaign, and Congress would doubtless have promised to raise, pay and supply an army of a million men.

It is not likely that Luzerne was much deceived. Only once before had the rebels been able to raise an army as large as 20,000 men, and both moral and material resources were at their height in 1776. Even so, this host of untrained militiamen had melted away after a few defeats in the New York campaign.

In the winter of 1779-1780 Washington's unpaid and half-starved army at Morristown had become so weak that the Tories could boast with absolute truth that more Americans were fighting for the king than for independence. New York, the center of loyalists from all the colonies, could show in 1779 two brigades ready to take the field and thirteen regiments in process of recruiting—the New York Volunteers, Queen's Rangers, Loyal Americans, Orange Rangers, Pennsylvania Loyalists, Maryland Loyalists, Roman Catholic Volunteers, West Jersey Volunteers, Chasseurs, Royal American Reformers, Volunteers of Ireland, British Legion, Guides and Pioneers. "The real service rendered the British by the Tories was not through these associated bands," a historian of the loyalists has asserted, "but by the thousands of individuals who enlisted in the regular army. New York alone furnished about 15,000 men to the British army and navy, and over 8,000 loyalist militia. All the other colonies furnished about as many more, so that we may safely state that 50,000 soldiers, either regular or militia, were drawn into the service of Great Britain from her American sympathizers." [8]

About 30,000 German mercenaries fought in America. The forces of British regulars are harder to estimate, since they shuttled between America and Canada or the West Indies. But it is a moderate estimate that at least 40,000 redcoats served for long periods in the Revolution. The total of the king's troops, plus a superiority in naval power which doubled their military value, amounted to some of the heaviest odds ever overcome in history. For while the rebel forces fluctuated even more than those of the enemy, Washington could seldom count on a main army of more than 10,000 poorly provided men after the peak of 1776. During the entire eight years, it is true, American enlistments added up to a total of more than 300,000; but nine-tenths may be considered militia recruits who volunteered for a term of one to three months and usually saw no action. Thus in the critical winter of 1779-1780 Washington had as few as 5,000 effectives at Morristown. Their fitness may be judged from a report of the Board of War to Congress on March 10th "that by the return of the Commissary General of Issues it appears that there is not now Bread on hand for ten days." [9]

In spite of such shortages, the Board of War assured Congress on February 1st that America could raise an army of 35,211 men. This figure provided a margin of safety over the total promised Luzerne, and Congress omitted the customary verb "recommended" from its resolution of the 10th. This time the states were "required to furnish, by draughts or otherwise, on or before the first day of April next, their respective deficiencies" of the quotas assigned to them.[10]

A resolution of the 25th fixed the quotas of supplies for each state. Massachusetts, for instance, was asked for 56,000 hundredweight of beef, 12,126 bushels of salt, and 195,638 gallons of rum.

It is noteworthy that no dependence was placed in the undermanned little American fleet, bottled up by the British blockade. In a letter of April 26, 1779, Washington had begged leave to ask John Jay "what are the reasons for keeping the Continental frigates in port? If it is because hands cannot be obtained to man them on the present encouragement, some other plan ought to be adopted to make them useful." President Jay replied that "while the maritime affairs of the continent continue under the direction of a committee they will be exposed to all the consequences of want of system, attention and knowledge. The marine committee consists of a delegate from each state. It fluctuates, new members constantly coming in and old ones going out. Three or four, indeed, have remained in it from the beginning, and few members understand even the state of our naval affairs, or have time or inclination to attend to them." [11]

This does not mean that the rebels failed to give a good account of themselves on the sea, considering the hopeless odds against them. During the eight years the 46 American war vessels, with their 1,242 guns and swivels, captured or destroyed 196 enemy craft. The 792 privateers, carrying more than 13,000 guns and swivels, captured or destroyed at least 600 British merchant ships worth eighteen million specie dollars with their cargoes. [12]

Although privateering accomplished greater results, it crippled the infant navy by attracting seamen with its lure of prize money. Speculation reached the point where some of the greatest patriots owned a share in a marauder which stood to pay for itself or lose all in a single voyage. But it must be remembered that, if the British losses in merchant ships were heavy, the royal navy wiped out American seaborne commerce and bottled up the fleet.

On January 31st Congress practically made French naval aid a stipulation by informing Luzerne "that the United States, with the assistance of a competent naval force, would willingly, during the next campaign, carry on the most vigorous offensive operations. . . . That without such naval force, little more can be attempted by them than straitening the quarters of the enemy."

When no improvement in the financial situation resulted from stopping the money press, Congress resolved on March 18th to establish a basis of one-fortieth of face value for the redemption of "Continental." Thus the two hundred million dollars of the debt were reduced to five millions, though not without some damage to the good name of an assembly which only six months before had promised that the bills would be redeemed at par.

Once again, however, Congress felt that dire necessity justified a not too scrupulous decision. Funds must be had to carry on the war—funds which the states were not sending according to their quotas. As the old bills came in for destruction, new ones were to be issued at a rate not to exceed one-twentieth of the nominal sum. Redemption was to be in specie at the end of six years, plus interest at 5 per cent payable in bills of exchange drawn on the commissioners and ministers in Europe.

Americans in general accepted the decision as a confession of a financial debacle if not actual bankruptcy. Vergennes protested months later that an exception should be made in favor of French allies who had accepted the money in good faith. Worse yet, from the viewpoint of the harassed delegates, the measure did not have the anticipated effect of breathing new life into the dying currency. The rate of depreciation during the next two months is indicated by a petition of the New York delegation to Governor George Clinton on June 2nd: "We must entreat your Excellency to recommend a suitable Provision for us without Loss of time. They demand from us £270 Cont. money a week for a gentleman and Servant exclusive even of Table beer, everything else is in proportion, and exchange 60 to one." [13]

Perhaps the greatest benefit came from the growing realization that Congress must have a more respectable measure of authority, not to mention a more dependable source of income. Just as the assembly had learned to accept Washington with the trust usually paid to a constitutional executive, so the great leader used his influence in the spring of 1780 to persuade his countrymen that more powers should be given to Congress. "It were devoutly to be wished," he wrote on April 3rd, "that a plan could be adopted by which everything relating to the Army could be conducted on a general principle under the direction of Congress."

For purposes of efficiency he suggested that Congress place such powers as it possessed in the hands of a special executive committee small enough to act with energy and decision. Many delegates regarded it as a dangerous step, but a resolution of April 6th set up a committee of three to reside at Washington's headquarters. The members chosen ten days later were Philip Schuyler of New York, Nathaniel Peabody of New Hampshire and John Mathews of South Carolina.

It had already been manifested that the states were not likely to furnish either money or supplies without persuasion. On March 28th, after attending the funeral of James Forbes, a Maryland member who died after a brief illness, Congress appointed a committee to compose a letter to the executives of the thirteen states. The first draft, submitted six days later, did not err on the side of evasion: "There is no money in the treasury, and scarce any provisions in the public magazines. The states are greatly deficient in the quotas of money, they have been called on for. More than fifty millions of dollars, of the quotas that have come due to this time, remain unpaid." [14]

It took nearly a month and many rejected efforts before Congress approved on April 24th a letter written by John Churchill Houston, the scholarly

Princeton instructor representing New Jersey. Only six paragraphs in length, it was deemed to be the right compromise between prodding in the ribs and patting on the back:

> The resources of our country, even after a five years' obstinate and lasting war, are still abundant; and in articles, the most essential, scarcely impaired. The spirit of the people is free to produce them. All that is wanting is an established medium of negotiation to be applied in effecting it. . . . The crisis calls for exertion. Much is to be done in a little time.[15]

The committee at headquarters, as it came to be known, was meanwhile unlimbering some of its heaviest rhetorical guns and taking aim at recalcitrant states. It could never be said that Congress had chosen men unsympathetic to the army. As a recent general, Schuyler partook of the military viewpoint; and John Mathews embarrassed Washington with the vehemence of his partisanship.

When informed that British invaders might pillage his plantation, the fiery South Carolinian wrote to a friend: "Let them keep it, and the Devil help them with it." Displaying a like scorn of consequences, he spoke his mind in the most emphatic terms to Congress as well as the state executives. In a circular letter of May 25th Mathews and his colleagues informed the states "that the Army was five months pay in arrears, that it has Seldom or ever, since it took this cantonement, had more than Six days provision in advance." This same week the committee at Morristown fired a blast at Congress: "Persuaded, sir, that to be silent on such occasions would be criminal, We will address our Compeers with decency, but with Freedom. We will advise them, that something more is necessary than mere recommendations, or they will lose an army, and thereby risk the loss of an Empire. Times and exigencies render it sometimes necessary for the Governing powers to deviate from the strict lines of conduct which Regular Constitutions prescribe. We entreat Congress seriously to consider Whether such times and exigencies do not now exist."[16]

This was an outspoken invitation for Congress to seize some of the powers held by the states, but there were no incipient Cromwells in the State House to lend an ear. The assembly continued to jog along at the same old sober pace when Luzerne communicated to President Huntington "that the king, in consequence of his affection and friendship for the United States . . . has resolved to send to this continent a re-enforcements of troops, intended to act against the common enemy, and of vessels, which will be employed in assisting the operations of the land troops."[17] And though such a suggestion was not in his province, the French minister requested Congress "to consider whether the course most proper to be adopted under these circumstances be not to appoint, without the least delay, a small committee, who shall repair to the army, furnished with instructions, and there fix upon measures, which shall be carried into execution immediately upon the arrival of the land forces, under the command of the Count de Rochambeau. . . ."

Another broad hint that Congress should wield more authority! The assembly gave its answer three days later in President Huntington's announcement of the good news. All states save the three southernmost, then resisting the foe, were solicited for an extra contribution of ten million dollars before July 15th. But the scowl and outthrust jaw of dictatorship were quite lacking from the appeal: "Congress have no resources but in your Spirit and Virtue, upon these they confidently rely." [18]

By the middle of June the committee at Morristown, sending circular letters directly to the states, rivaled in importance the parent council. The idea of more authority for Congress began to sprout within Congress itself; and on the 15th a committee headed by the forthright Robert R. Livingston made a direct request in a first draft of an address to the states. After referring to the "supineness and false security" of states which had not given aid, the address asked:

> What, then, can justify any in withholding it? is the present ease or convenience of the subjects to be put in competition with the lasting happiness of millions? Do the rulers fear at this critical period to exert their utmost authority? . . . A Common Council involves the power of direction. Let not our measures be checked or controuled by the negligence or partial views and interests of separate communities, while they profess to be members of one body. . . . Let us awake before the season of successful exertion has passed. [19]

A majority of Congress did not agree that more "power of direction" should be given to the "Common Council." These passages were deleted and the space filled as usual with appeals to the patriotism of the states. And as usual the states responded with a woeful fraction of their quotas of money and supplies.

The states seemed to have decided that Congress would find a way, as it had always done in the past. Their faith was justified when more bills of exchange were ordered to be drawn on Franklin and Jay, at sixty days' sight, and offered for sale. On July 11th the Committee of Foreign Affairs wrote to Franklin with the humility of an old drunkard who has fallen from grace:

> After the repeated remonstrances you have made to Congress on the Subject of Bills of Exchange the inclosed Resolution, we are well aware, will need an apology. . . . Congress attending to your letters and Representations have only taken this Step with Reluctance. But the present crisis . . . has induced Them to risque the Sum mentioned. The Bills will not be drawn faster than

indispensible Exigencies may require, and it is to be hoped that this mode of commanding Cash will not be again resorted to.[20]

Only a few traces are left in the *Journals* of a "Committee for encreasing the powers of Congress" headed by Robert R. Livingston, which apparently got as far as drawing up an "Application to the State Legislatures." There was also a copy of a resolution asserting the authority of Congress to act in procuring supplies. But neither the application nor the resolution ever got beyond the committee, which in its turn soon died a natural death. A few weeks later Ezekiel Cornell of Rhode Island wrote to a friend: "Congress in general appear exceedingly easy in the present situation of affairs. There doth not appear the most distant wish for more powers, but rather on the contrary, a wish to see their States without control (as the term is), free, sovereign, and independent." [21]

This Independence Day was celebrated in a sedate manner when Congress and the French minister attended the graduation exercises of the University of Pennsylvania. The students had composed a dialogue filled with such passages as the following:

> How like a tree just planted in the soil,
> And striking root, did independence bear
> The black and bellowing blasts of seventy-six.
> The shaking did her good,
> And fixt her but the faster in her place.[22]

It might have been hoped that these lines contained more truth than poetry, but the gentlemen of the State House were not too exacting. Still, it must have occurred to them that the political winds of 1780 were not exactly zephyrs. In the middle of July the Comte de Rochambeau landed at Newport with 6,000 men; and despite the assurances given Luzerne six months before, the states had fallen far behind in their quotas of troops as well as supplies.

But if America was in no position to conduct a vigorous campaign, neither was France. A British fleet under Admiral Graves promptly bottled up the French land-and-sea forces in Rhode Island, and a second contingent could not even get away from Brest.

Americans had reason to be worried when they recalled Luzerne's warnings that Britain might insist on a title to the American soil left in her possession at the end of hostilities. There could be no doubt that the invasion of the South had been planned with this end in view. Following the capture of Savannah late in 1778, the British soon controlled all Georgia. The seaport successfully withstood a siege by French and American forces the next autumn, repulsing an assault in which Count Pulaski fell mortally wounded.

The northward sweep into the Carolinas was methodical, with forts being established at strategic points. The climax came on May 12, 1780, when Charleston and 5,000 defenders under General Benjamin Lincoln surrendered to a much larger British land-and-sea force. In point of numbers the capitulation ranked as the foremost American disaster of the war, though two-thirds of the men consisted of militia and even armed slaves.

Congress responded with energy. A decision of June 13th placed General Gates in command of the southern army and gave him authority to call on Virginia and the Carolinas for troops and supplies. The resolution went so far as to empower him "to take other such measures, from time to time, for the defence of the southern states as he shall think most proper."

A rumor had spread that the enemy would offer the eleven northern states their independence on condition that Great Britain retain Georgia and South Carolina. Congress had in mind its French allies as well as credulous Americans when it reiterated a principle on June 23rd with the unanimous resolution:

> That the said report is insidious and utterly void of foundation.
>
> That this Confederacy is most sacredly pledged to support the liberty and independence of every one of its members; and, in a firm reliance on the divine blessing, will unremittingly persevere in their exertions for the establishment of the same, and also for the recovery and preservation of any and every part of these United States that has been or may hereafter be invaded or possessed by the common enemy.[23]

The faith of this declaration was scarcely justified by works. A squabble between Congress and General Nathanael Greene, discreditable to both, ended in the resignation of the only quartermaster general who had been able to cope with that thankless job. The committee at headquarters, far from easing military burdens, only added to them. John Mathews, the guiding spirit, had courage, energy, integrity—everything except the blessed qualities of patience and common sense. Relations between him and Congress were already strained when a group of officers presented a memorial asking for more pay on the grounds of currency depreciation. Their arguments were reasonable and Ezekiel Cornell wrote to his friend General Greene on August 15th, "Congress was not so angry at the Memorial of the General Officers as you imagined." Cornell may have been thinking of parliaments in general when he added sagely, "We are not apt to be angry at any thing we can evade." [24]

At this time Mathews took it upon himself to put out a circular letter to the states during the temporary absence of Peabody and Schuyler. His intentions were better than his tact, and he did not help the cause with curt references to the "extraordinary backwardness of some States." Next it occurred to the excitable South Carolinian that it would be a good idea to lecture Congress on its attitude toward the army. "It may be asked whether Congress are to be dictated to, by their Officers?" he wrote to President Huntington on August 6th. Although nobody had asked, Mathews answered "that on the present occasion they must; necessity compels them to it, and it is a duty they owe their constituents, not to suffer punctilio to militate against their essential interests." This unsolicited criticism might have been forgiven him, but next he exploded with more emotion than prudence, "Remember the Gentleman at the head of your Army. . . . For God's sake! have some regard for his feelings." [25]

On August 12th Congress passed a resolution recommending that soldiers as well as officers be paid more money to compensate for depreciation. And this same day Mathews and his colleagues were summarily recalled from headquarters. The delegates were particularly annoyed by the assumption of Mathews that Washington had no other friend in Congress. The reception given the South Carolina member on his return to the State House may be pictured from his letter of September 15th to the commander in chief: "Although I had heard a good deal, and seen something, of the rancour of these demagogues yet I never imagined it had risen to that height, I was made to *feel* it had done, upon my resuming my seat in Congress." [26]

All hopes of an active campaign with the French vanished before autumn. America's financial plight could be shown by columns of figures, but it is better illustrated by a letter to President Huntington from Jacob Hiltzheimer, keeper of the stables:

> I take the Liberty to Inform your Excellency that the Horses in my care belonging to Members of the Hon'ble the Continen'l Congress have been without grain some time and now with out hay too. Some time ago I Bought Hay on Credit to the amount of about 20000 Dollars with a promise to pay in a short time but could Not comply for want of Money wherefore it is out of my Power to Purchase any more without paying for it at the time.[27]

It might have been supposed by members of Congress trusting in the law of averages that American fortunes at this time could only take a turn for the better. But there were deeper sub-basements of gloom to be explored, for within the next few weeks the assembly would have the news of Arnold's treason and the worst American battlefield defeat of the war.

Never did the course of the American Revolution bear more resemblance to the plot of a stock melodrama, at least from the viewpoint of observers blessed with the privilege of hindsight. The rule of technique prescribing that the happy ending must be preceded by an agony of suspense was faithfully followed in news reaching Congress on August 31st. "I have this day," wrote President Huntington to Washington, "received from General Gates dispatches, containing the disagreeable Intelligence of the total Defeat of the Army under his Command. . . ." [28]

The American force of 3,000 men had not merely been defeated by the 2,200 redcoats and loyalists under Cornwallis. It had been outgeneraled, outfought, routed, and virtually destroyed. For this was no empty tactical triumph such as Long Island and Brandywine. Camden compared favorably with the most decisive American victories, and it had been largely won by Americans over Americans. Although the loyalists had been a long time in arming, the decisive blows on August 16th were struck by Tarleton's dragoons, recruited from among southern Tories, and Lord Rawdon's Volunteers of Ireland, raised in Pennsylvania.

De Kalb, the American second in command, died of wounds and the defeated general paid with his reputation. His old enemies of the Gates-Schuyler feud did not neglect their opportunity, though Greene testified later that neither Gates' courage nor judgment had been at fault. Nevertheless, such a competent job of character assassination was done by Hamilton, Schuyler's son-in-law, that his victim remains to this day the only prominent Revolutionary soldier without a full-dress biography.

It may even be that the fallen idol's enemies overdid their clamor, for General James Mitchell Varnum wrote to Gates on February 15th: "Misfortune is construed into Wickedness or Weekness, and the shining Merits of Years are enveloped in the illfated Events of an Hour. How ungenerous is the human Heart when under the Controul of tumultuous Passions!" [29] Congress did not press the inquiry into Gates' conduct ordered on October 5th, and a resolution of the following May directed "that Major General Gates be informed, that he is at liberty to repair to headquarters, and take such command as the Commander in Chief shall direct." Washington showed no lack of confidence and Gates ended the war as America's second soldier in rank.

The news of Benedict Arnold's frustrated attempt to betray West Point came as an anticlimax after Camden, though the members of Congress must have shuddered at the narrowness of the escape. That the traitor's financial affairs had already aroused suspicion is hinted by a letter from James Lovell to Nathaniel Peabody on October 3rd: "Many are *mightily shocked* by the West Point plot: I presume you escaped *that* degree of surprise respecting Arnold's *baseness*, as you had been *prepared* here on 'the Com'tee for his accounts.'" [30]

For the moment the rebels had no army worthy of the name to oppose the British in the South, though it appeared that Virginia might be invaded next. Secretary Charles Thomson was not a strategist, but he did not make the mistake of blaming Gates. "To our want of money may be ascribed the Enemy's success in Carolina," he wrote to Jay on October 12th. "For although Congress had timely notice of Sir Henry Clinton's intentions last fall and notwithstanding his tedious passage and the slowness of his proceedings after his arrival . . . yet for want of money Congress could not forward with sufficient dispatch the succor intended. . . ."[31]

The fact that Congress and Greene were not on the best of terms did not prejudice that body against electing him to command in the South. Vigorous measures were taken to create a new army in spite of the financial difficulties. John Sullivan, returned to Congress as a New Hampshire delegate, headed a committee appointed on November 7th to raise money. There was a note of touching candor in the confession that during the past "most of our difficulties have arisen from an Ignorance of Finance." In a studious spirit the committee took up the study of David Hume's *Essays*, but this adventure in education did not lead to financial reforms. The extent of the depreciation is revealed by Dr. Jones' expense account, listing a total of £7,162, Continental money, for board, lodging and washing for himself and a servant from April 3rd to September 7th. "As to the condition of the money here," wrote Oliver Wolcott on January 3rd, "the apparent discount is seventy-five for one. . . . The practical discount is 100 for 1." [32]

Just at this time, when it must have seemed that the American cause could not bear the weight of another disaster, an express reached Philadelphia on the afternoon of January 3rd with the first account of the dispute over enlistment terms which caused a mutiny of the Pennsylvania regiments stationed in New Jersey. Wild rumors spread through the city that the entire army had gone over to the enemy and would soon march on Philadelphia. Congress appointed a committee consisting of John Sullivan, John Mathews and Dr. Witherspoon to co-operate with the Pennsylvania Council in an effort to quell the insurrection. There ensued a week of suspense, then Sullivan's report from Trenton on January 10th came as good news:

> As an earnest of their Sincerity they [the mutineers] have this night sent to us under a strong guard, the two spies sent out by S'r Henry Clinton with offers of terms to them. . . . In short the whole progress of this affair except the first Tumult has been conducted on their part with a consistency, firmness and a degree of Policy mixed with candor that must astonish every theorist on the nature of the American soldiery; and cover S'r Harry with Shame and Confusion, if not stigmatize him with the appelation of the Prince of Blunderers. . . .[33]

The long-dreaded uprising of unpaid and half-starved soldiers had occurred, and they had shown themselves to be such patriots as to put some of
their social betters to shame. Nor could it have been said that the congressional committee was niggardly in recommending on January 24th that
"not only every thing justly due to the Soldiers of the Pennsylvania Line
should be granted, but that a construction favorable to them should be
put upon the form of enlistment. . . ." The committee urged that Congress
confirm General Wayne's amnesty to the mutineers and declared that
"this disturbance however unhappy and threatening at first, has now afforded an undeniable and pleasing proof of the firm attachment of the Soldiery as well as of the Country in general to the American cause." [34]

After this heartening outcome, anyone familiar with the technique of
melodrama might have suspected that the turning point had been reached.
All doubts should have been dispelled the first week of February, when the
assembly of Maryland passed an act which the older members of Congress
doubtless hailed as a miracle. At last that froward hussy had joined her
twelve respectable sisters, and it could be proclaimed throughout the land
that after three and a half years of waiting the Articles of Confederation
would be ratified on March 1, 1781.

Chapter 21

The News from Yorktown

WHEN American fortunes were at their lowest in 1780, the rebels had the satisfaction of knowing that their enemy was in no position to gloat. British agents sought new loans in Europe at high interest rates to add to a national debt of two hundred million pounds sterling. Unemployment and the decay of trade were acknowledged after France and Spain became enemies. John Wesley, whose mission took him all over England each year, lamented that thousands of idle workmen were walking shadows for want of bread, and some had actually perished of starvation. Although the founder of Methodism still upheld the royal cause, he warned Lord Dartmouth that the masses were ripe for rebellion.

John Adams kept Congress informed from Paris as to British unrest and misery. From the last month of 1779 to the third month of the following year, according to his reports, no less than twenty-five English counties passed resolutions denouncing the waste of public funds, the undue influence of the crown, and the corruption of Parliament. On March 28th the county of York came out boldly with a declaration blaming the American war as the cause of England's troubles. The freeholders of Surrey followed suit two weeks later by resolving without a dissenting vote "that the American war, originating from the corrupt influence of the crown and the ill-founded assertions of the king's ministers in Parliament is the cause of the present calamitous situation of the country." [1]

These were not the vaporings of London radicals; they were the protests of solid, middle-class Englishmen with both feet on the ground. What might have been the result of this movement in the spring of 1780 will never be known, for the whole nation was suddenly shocked into conservatism by the terrible Gordon riots. Once John Wilkes could undoubtedly have led the English masses to political reforms. But the radical of 1770 had become a weary and jaded politician in 1780, holding the lucrative office of chamberlain of the City. Meanwhile a more dangerous agitator had appeared in the person of Lord George Gordon.

Rabble-rousers throughout history have found it expedient to direct popular hatred against a racial or religious minority. But this half-mad Scottish peer happened to be a fanatic in deadly earnest. He drew attention away from George III and the American war by transforming political grievances into blind religious prejudice. London was at the mercy of the mob for three June days. The House of Commons was threatened and the Bank of England actually attacked by rioters who set fire to Newgate, destroyed Catholic chapels and pillaged like an army of invading barbarians.

George III and John Wilkes, the opponents of 1770, stood shoulder to shoulder in this crisis as the two men whose firmness saved London. Wilkes sacrificed the remnants of his influence by calling in troops who put down the uprising after 450 people had been killed or wounded and property worth millions ruined. Gordon was tried for high treason but acquitted, and the chief result of his Protestant crusade was the postponement of English political reforms.

The British turned their victories at Charleston and Camden to good account as an antidote for dissatisfaction with the war. Then fortune frowned on the invaders, who had two small armies destroyed within a few months.

The clash at King's Mountain on October 7, 1780, was entirely a civil war battle. Colonel Patrick Ferguson, the most able of the British partisan leaders, was slain and his whole force of 1,100 loyalist troops reduced to killed, wounded or prisoners by a hastily improvised army of Carolina frontiersmen armed with rifles.

On January 17th, in another Carolina border action, General Daniel Morgan created the tactical masterpiece of the war at the expense of Colonel Banastre Tarleton. At a cost of 60 casualties the Americans killed, wounded or captured 900 foemen of an army numbering a thousand. The tactics of Cowpens impressed General Greene so much, moreover, that he adapted them with good effect in the three battles of his southern campaign.

Congress had to bear the guilt of a good many military errors, both of commission and of omission. But the assembly could claim the credit not only for the development of rifle tactics but also for the long overdue promotion of Morgan to a brigadier's rank in a resolution of October 13, 1780. In an age of frank class distinctions the burly "Old Wagoner" had the speech and mannerisms of the ranks, even to the extent of administering discipline with his fists. His acceptance as a gentleman had not been impulsive, and Congress tacitly rebuked the officers on March 9th by voting a gold medal for the victor of Cowpens. Before the end of the war, it is only fair to add, Washington and such generals as Greene, Wayne and Lafayette were corresponding with Morgan on the most friendly terms.

The slight coolness of earlier years was a symptom of something more than social snobbery. For the struggle against Great Britain released another revolution—the uprising of frontier Americans against the village politicians of New England and the tidewater aristocrats of the South. Lean and hard men, bitter Calvinists, aggressive democrats, these new Americans had already developed a future leader in a lanky Carolina boy who took a saber slash in the arm rather than polish a British officer's boots. The boy's name was Andrew Jackson and he was thirteen years old when the redcoats made him a prisoner in the spring of 1781.

From time to time during the past year Congress had done what it could to hasten the ratification of the Articles of Confederation. As individuals a few delegates might denounce Maryland's obstinate stand, but men of foresight recognized that all states were concerned with the disposal of the western lands.

On September 6, 1780, Congress "recommended to those states, who have claims to the western country, to pass such laws, and give their delegates in Congress such powers as may effectually remove the only obstacle to a final ratification of the articles of confederation; and that the legislature of Maryland be earnestly required to authorize their delegates in Congress to subscribe to the said articles." [2]

Only a month later Congress caught a more dazzling glimpse of the power and the glory. But the canny politicans of the small states, holding a majority, inserted a provision for keeping all future states small in a resolution of October 10th:

> That the unappropriated lands that may be ceded or relinquished to the United States, by any particular states, pursuant to the recommendation of Congress on the 6th day of September last, shall be disposed of for the common benefit of the United States and be settled and formed into distinct republican states, which shall become members of the federal union, and have the same rights of sovereignty, freedom and independence, as the other states; that each state which shall be so formed shall contain a suitable extent of territory, not less than one hundred nor more than one hundred and fifty miles square, or as near thereto as circumstances will admit. [3]

This vision of dozens of square, sturdy little Connecticuts fitting neatly into the political vacuum on the other side of the Alleghenies did not arouse any enthusiasm in Virginia. Not only did that state have the best claim to the most western territory, but she had defended it with her own blood and money. For the whole war held no brighter adventure than the expeditions of 1778 and 1779 in which George Rogers Clark's little band captured the British outposts on the Mississippi and brought the "hair-buyer" Hamilton home as a prisoner.

All along it had been obvious that some of the "three-sided" states valued their western claims chiefly as bargaining points to gain political concessions. Gradually it occurred to them that it would be more profitable to make a gesture of renunciation and share in the vast area west of the mountains. By the end of 1779 this sentiment had spread until Robert R. Livingston could report "a violent inclination in most of the States to appropriate all the western lands to the use of the United States."

General Schuyler made a special trip from Albany in the spring of 1780 to propose a recommendation of Congress that at least part of the western lands be immediately relinquished for the benefit of the United States. Congress appointed a committee of investigation consisting of James Duane of New York, Joseph Jones of Virginia, Willie Jones of North Carolina, John Henry of Maryland and Roger Sherman of Connecticut. Their report lay on the table until autumn, then inspired the resolutions of September and October.

The America of the future was indebted to Maryland for courage as well as less exalted motives such as jealousy of a neighbor. But it is to the credit of Virginia that the state had congressmen as farsighted as Madison and Dr. Jones, both of them keeping in close touch with Thomas Jefferson. They were willing even to scale down the actual expenses incurred by Virginia alone for establishing garrisons in the huge domain wrested by Clark from the foe. The movement had another impetus in October, 1780, when the Connecticut assembly agreed to cede that state's lands. Then on January 2, 1781, the Virginia assembly passed an act of cession which put the issue of ratification squarely up to Maryland.

The conventions which usually keep a diplomat from interfering in the affairs of a foreign state were observed by Luzerne even less scrupulously than by Gérard. Weak as the French minister might be on English verb forms, he knew exactly what went on behind the closed doors of the State House. He had his own pet projects in Congress and did not hesitate to use his influence as the envoy of a nation able to grant favors.

Luzerne had long been an advocate of confederation when the Maryland delegates, early in January, earnestly solicited French naval aid to defend that state from British naval raids in Chesapeake Bay. The French minister intimated very courteously that it would be a good time for Maryland to strengthen the American cause by changing her mind about ratification. Maryland saw the point and the state assembly passed an act of approval at the end of the month. Congress appointed March 1st for a ceremony thus described in the diary of Thomas Rodney:

> By a Signal given at the State House the Completion of this grand Union and Confederation was announced by Firing thirteen cannon on the Hill and the same number on board Captn. Paul Jones Frigate in the Harbour. At Two OClock the Members of Congress and a great number of Gentlemen waited on the President of Congress to Congratulate him on this occasion; and partook of a Collation prepaired at his House for that purpose. In the evening there was a grand exhibition of fireworks at the State House, and also on board Paul Jones Frigate in the Harbour, and all the vessels in the Harbour were Decorated and illuminated on this occasion and great joy appeared in every Countenance but those of the Disaffected.[4]

In the hour of rejoicing the *Pennsylvania Packet* paused to pity a toppling foe. Despite the grumbling which went on continually, such was the confidence of Americans in their cause that references may also be found in the letters of Washington, Franklin and John Adams to the approaching collapse of the British Empire. Thus the following passage probably represented at the time the opinion of most of the members of the Continental Congress:

> But Britain's boasted wealth and grandeur are crumbling to pieces, never again to be united . . . and, if she persists in her present self-destroying systems, there will be a time when scarcely a monument of her former glory will remain. The fragments of her empire, and its history, will then be of little other use to mankind, but, like a ruined tower on a dreary coast, to serve as a landmark to warn against the shoals on which her political navigators had ship-wrecked that infatuated nation.[5]

The celebration on March 1st was heartfelt, but the more able members of Congress knew perfectly well that the Articles of Confederation had been outgrown before they were ratified. Events of the past three and a half years had proved again and again the need of a constitution giving more powers to Congress as well as its own source of income for "continental" purposes.

For months the leaders had agreed among themselves that the Articles were inadequate. "The fundamental defect is a want of power in Congress," wrote Hamilton to Duane on September 3, 1780. "It is hardly worthwhile to show in what this consists, as it seems to be universally acknowledged."[6]

Legalists could and did point out that the Continental Congress had never since 1774 been wholly lacking in authority. But its powers had been so vaguely defined, so confused and contradictory, that the total effect was much the same. In this same letter Hamilton admitted that "Congress have done many of the highest acts of sovereignty, which were always submitted to. . . . But the Confederation itself is defective," he insisted, "and requires to be altered. It is neither fit for war or peace."

The states themselves had on occasion recognized that Congress must have more authority. On October 10, 1780, the New York legislature went so far as to resolve (at a time when many states were deficient in furnishing their quotas of money and supplies) that Congress be given the power "to march the Army, or such part of it as may be requisite, into such State; and by a Military Force, compel it to furnish its deficiency."

Washington, upon learning of this act, declared, "I am convinced it is essential to our safety that Congress should have an efficient power. The want of it must ruin us."

Next, the representatives of the four New England states, meeting at the so-called Hartford Convention on November 8th, not only endorsed the New York resolution but laid it before Congress for consideration the following month. There the opposition of a small radical group, chiefly New Englanders led by Sam Adams, was strong enough so that the proposition did not come up for a vote. It could readily be seen, moreover, that any future attempt of Congress to vote itself more authority would be opposed as "tyranny" by the Yankee phalanx.

As long ago as 1776, in a burst of introspection, that great reporter John Adams had analyzed the New England character. "My countrymen want art and address," he confessed. "They want knowledge of the world. They want the exterior and superficial accomplishment of gentlemen, upon which the world has set so high a value. In solid abilities and real virtues they vastly excel, in general, any people upon this continent. Our New England people are awkward and bashful, yet they are pert, ostentatious, and vain; a mixture which excites ridicule and gives disgust. They have not the faculty of showing themselves to the best advantage, nor art of concealing this faculty." But Adams proved himself to be a New Englander in good standing when he added that "New England must produce the heroes, the statesmen, the philosophers, or America will make no great figure for some time." [7]

Sam Adams and his faction, of course, were not the only obstructionists of Congress in 1781. The Civil War and Reconstruction were still far in the future, but it could already be seen that these traditions would be created at the earliest opportunity. For the Southerners in Congress could be quite as provincial as any Yankee with their attitudes, their sentimentalities, their outbursts of petulance varied with periods of indolence. "Were an angel from heaven," declared John Mathews of South Carolina, "to perch on the back of the Presidents Chair and proclaim the immediate annihilation of the southern States, unless something vigorous and effectual was done, and even point out the mode, I sincerely believe, as soon as he had taken his flight, and the surprise had subsided, they would just sink again into the same torpid State in which he found them." [8]

It was the fate of the issue of congressional powers to be ground to dust rather than grist between the upper and nether millstones of sectional politics. In this instance the New Englanders, with their fear of political power, were most to blame.

Delegates not so fortunate as to have been born in this region must sometimes have reflected that the Revolution could never be won without the New Englanders—or with them. Alexander Hamilton, in a letter to Isaac Sears of October 12, 1780, spoke for a large group which believed that all the gains since 1775 were endangered by the lack of an efficient administration:

> It is impossible that the contest can be much longer supported on the present footing. We must have a Government with more power. We must have a foreign loan. We must have a Bank, on the true principles of a Bank. We must have an Administration distinct from Congress, and in the hands of single men under their orders. [9]

The Articles of Confederation, it was generally admitted, had been put together in desperation before America had the assurance of Saratoga and the French alliance. Long before March 1, 1781, the only question among most American leaders had been whether to patch up a faulty constitution or start all over again with a constitutional convention. As early as September, 1780, Hamilton had urged that such a convention "should assemble the first of November next. The sooner the better." He declared that "the first step must be, to give Congress powers competent to the public exigencies. . . . The Confederation, in my opinion, should give Congress complete sovereignty; except to that part of internal police which relate to the rights of property and life among individuals, and to raising money by internal taxes." [9]

Beginning with Paine's *Common Sense* in 1776, there are many instances of a constitutional convention being proposed before 1786. But the time was not ripe five years earlier, and Congress went ahead in the spring of 1781 to make the best of the Articles. Before starting the new regime, the assembly decided on March 20th to proclaim another day of fasting, humiliation and prayer—always a sign of tribulation. The members of the Continental Congress were very consciously the agents of Jehovah when they summoned all Americans to "prostrate themselves before our Creator

... that we may, with united hearts, confess and bewail our manifold sins and transgressions, and by sincere repentance and amendment of life, appease his righteous displeasure." [10]

First of all, the question arose as to how many states constituted a quorum, since the Articles were vague about it. Congress decided on nine the first week in March, though a quorum of seven for ordinary business was allowed two months later. The Articles were interpreted to mean that no measure could be adopted without the assent of seven states; and important measures must have the approval of nine states, or two-thirds.

Although no member could serve more than three years in any period of six under the new regime, it remained a question as to whether the term started on March 1st or included previous service. The first interpretation prevailed by tacit consent, for some of the most respected members had already served more than three years.

There could be no doubt, according to the Articles, that each state must be represented by at least two delegates. This meant that New Hampshire and Rhode Island, with but a single delegate each on March 1st, would be without a vote until reinforcements arrived. Congress set a precedent, however, by permitting the lone members to join in debates and sit on committees.

Where the assembly had simply been known as "the Congress," it became "the United States in Congress Assembled" under the Articles. On the whole, however, business went on pretty much as it had before March 1st. President Huntington continued to sit in the chair until his resignation because of ill-health on July 6th, whereupon he was replaced by Thomas McKean of Delaware.

The proponents of more power for Congress did not let the transition period go by without a determined effort. A committee consisting of three warm advocates, Madison of Virginia, Duane of New York, and Varnum of Rhode Island, was appointed to search the Articles for interpretations. All three members being lawyers, they reported in six days that Article XIII "implied" the power of Congress to enforce all provisions of the Confederation in these words: "Every state shall abide by the determinations of the united states in congress assembled, on all questions which by this confederation are submitted to them."

The committee recommended an amendment to the Articles of Confederation authorizing Congress, in case any state should refuse to abide by one of the determinations, "to employ the force of the United States by sea as by land to compel such state or States to fulfil their federal engagements." After a long delay and a brief debate the proposal was turned over to a grand committee consisting of a member from each state on May 2nd. But the probable fate of any attempt to provide Congress with coercive powers could have been predicted by John Sullivan as early as March 6th. "The choice of a Minister of War," he wrote to Washington on that date, "is postponed to the first of October. This was a manoeuvre of Saml. Adams and others from the North, fearing that as I was in nomination the Choice would fall on me who having apostacized from the true New England faith, by sometimes voting with the Southern States am not eligible." [11]

The New Hampshire soldier referred to the campaign for administrative reform aiming at the appointment of a single responsible head for departments such as war, marine, finance and foreign affairs, hitherto administered by boards or committees. This plan had long been hanging fire, but until the spring of 1781 it could make no progress against the faction which preferred inefficiency to any risk of despotism. The once vital Committee of Foreign Affairs had declined meanwhile until James Lovell could inform Arthur Lee in the summer of 1779 that "there really is no such Thing as a Com'tee of foreign affairs existing—no Secretary or Clerk—further than that I persevere to be the one and the other." The hard-working Boston schoolmaster seldom finished his correspondence before midnight, since Franklin, Jay and John Adams had to depend on him for information about America. No delegate could bear such a burden in his "spare time," and Jay complained on October 27, 1780:

"One good private correspondent would be worth twenty standing committees, made up of the wisest heads in America, for the purpose of intelligence. What with clever wives, or pretty girls, or pleasant walks, or too tired, or you do it, very little is done, much postponed, and much more neglected." [12]

James Duane, an old campaigner for reforms in foreign affairs, was named with James Lovell and William Churchill Houston on a committee of investigation. They brought in a report during the summer of 1780 which came up for consideration in December. Other delegates had been urging the necessity for changes in the administration of war, marine and finance. "All Publick Departments," commented John Sullivan in a letter of November 15th, "are now arranging upon oeconomical Principles."

This proved to be a bit premature. Not until January 6th did Congress agree to replace the Committee of Foreign Affairs with an executive secretary. And it took the news of Maryland's intended ratification before Congress decided on February 7th "that there be a Superintendent of Finance, a Secretary at War, and a Secretary of Marine." [13]

After eighteen months in Philadelphia the Chevalier de la Luzerne wielded so much influence that he may almost be considered one of the heads of the American government. A county in Pennsylvania was named after him, just as a frontier Vermont village paid a like compliment to Vergennes. Friendly, tolerant and worldly-wise, the Bourbon diplomat found Congress a constant spectacle. On March 16, 1780, when tempers were frayed by financial troubles, Luzerne reported to Vergennes with amused interest an encounter on the floor of the State House: "We saw, some weeks ago, a delegate James Searle of Pennsylvania and the Secretary of Congress attack each other with canes in the open Senate, wound each other in the face, and on the morrow peaceably retake their seats." A year later Luzerne knew why the advocates of executives for departments were making tedious progress. "Divisions prevail in Congress," he wrote to Vergennes on March 25, 1781, "about the new mode of transacting business by secretaries of different departments. Samuel Adams, whose obstinate and resolute character was so useful to the revolution in its origin, but who shows himself very ill suited to the conduct of affairs in an organized government, has placed himself at the head of the advocates of the old system of committees of Congress, instead of relying on ministers, or secretaries. . . ." [14]

Despite the hostility of this group, executives were named in 1781 for three new departments. Factional jealousies delayed the appointment of a secretary for foreign affairs until August 10th, when Robert R. Livingston accepted. February 20th saw the election of Robert Morris as superintendent of finance, but it took until October 30th to appoint Benjamin Lincoln as secretary of war. No secretary of marine was elected after Alexander McDougall declined, and the superintendent of finance took over the duties temporarily.

While slow advances were being made in this direction, the grand committee had been considering since May 2nd the recommendation of Madison, Duane and Varnum that Congress be allowed the coercive powers held to be "implied" in Article XIII. Thomas Burke warned from the beginning that any such attempt "would give a dreadfull alarm to their Constituents who are so jealous of their Liberty." And General Varnum had written a month earlier to Governor William Greene of Rhode Island:

My Duty, or a mistaken Idea of it, obliges me to hazard a Conjecture, That the Time is not far distant when the present American Congress will be dissolved, or laid aside as useless, unless a Change of Measures shall render their Authority more respectable. . . . If the kind of Government sufficiently energetic to obtain the Objects of Peace when free from invasion, is too feeble to raise and support Armies, fight Battles, and obtain compleat Victory, I know of but one eligible Resort in the Power of the United States. That is to form a Convention, not composed of Members of Congress . . . to revise and refraim the Articles of Confederation. [15]

On July 20th the grand committee brought in a report ignoring the proposal of more powers for Congress. Sam Adams and his faction had scored to this extent, but the proponents managed to gain the appointment of a third committee—General Varnum, Oliver Ellsworth, Edmund Randolph— "to prepare an exposition of the Confederation."

A month later, in a report worthy of a rank among American documents, this committee offered twenty-one provisions for the strengthening of the Articles, including seven new powers which the states were urged to relinquish to Congress. Coercive authority was provided in a clause proposing that Congress be empowered "to distrain upon the property of a State delinquent in its assigned proportion of Men and Money."

The value of the report does not lie in any immediate results, for it was set aside to be debated on a "to Morrow" which never dawned. But the thought of the committee had not been lost, since nearly all of the twenty-one provisions anticipated to some extent the particulars of the Constitution of 1787. The nature of the opposition which barred them from further consideration at this time is revealed by an entry of April 13th in Thomas Rodney's diary: "A resolution was moved by Genl. Varnum, introduced by words like the man himself, arora borialis fine indeed but not well adapted to the occasion for Conferring on John Paul Jones what he well deserved— The Thanks of Congress and a gold Meddal. . . . These favours were opposed in some measure as untimely by that Cautious Senator S. Adams, who only urged that such favours being the highest in the power of the States (and next to those of Heaven) aught to be granted with cautious delibration." [16]

While watchdogs such as Sam Adams were guarding the liberties of America, there was not much prospect that the powers of Congress would be increased. Yet no study of the Constitution of the United States can afford to neglect the foundation built in 1781.

There were never more outspoken critics of Congress than the members themselves, but among the brickbats may sometimes be found a modest bouquet. "Congress may err," wrote James Duane to Washington on December 9, 1780; "they are not exempt from State and national prejudices; they are likely to be deceived: But nothing is more certain than that in the common Cause their Intentions are pure, their Zeal, their Cares, their pains unbounded; and the time will come, when if their measures are not admired they will be approved." [17]

Such was the New York delegate's own zeal that a few months later, at a time when living expenses came out of his own pocket, he had the task of placating Mrs. Duane. It was as a harassed husband rather than a statesman that he wrote on March 6, 1781: "But remember my dearest polly that I did not engage in the delegation of the present critical year but with your own free approbation. . . . I feel my dearest Polly the force of your observation that 'altho the State requires my assistance, I have a tender and affectionate Wife and a young Family who require my Care.' But what can I do? . . . When called upon by the Voice of my Country cou'd I refuse in a cause which my Conscience approved?" At this climax Duane set an example for future husbands by ending on a firm note: "No—an Active part I must take either in *Council* or in *Field.*" [18]

It hardly seems possible that this was the delegate who allied himself with Galloway against several patriotic measures in 1774. If the opponents of independence in the spring of 1776 had been liquidated according to modern Fascist and Communist technique, not only Duane but also John Dickinson, Robert Morris and James Wilson would have been occupying unmarked graves in some concentration camp instead of developing into patriotic leaders of 1781.

Never in the whole fifteen years did attendance in Congress demand more personal sacrifices. The final collapse of "Continental," so long dreaded, took place that spring in an atmosphere of frantic speculation. "We are in an uproar here about the money," James Lovell wrote to Samuel Holten on May 8th. "Sailors with clubs parade the streets instead of working for Paper." After mentioning that paper was 180 and 200 for one, Lovell declared that "the old continental is dying by Yards not Inches." Just five days later, so rapid was the depreciation, Samuel Livermore reported in a letter of May 13th, "The old continental is as low as 500 for one." [19]

Not only the new departments but some of the state delegations found it hard to continue in operation. "What the Maryland Delegates will do for want of Money, I do not know," wrote Jenifer, "but there is one mode by which they can be supplied *i. e.* to order a quantity of Superfine flour, to be manufactured at the Head of the Bay. Superfine flour will command hard money." [20]

Speculators bought bills at a cheap rate of exchange, then rode day and night to reap a profit in another state. There were also cruel losses. John Witherspoon related that his son-in-law sold Virginia property worth several thousand pounds, but on the way back to New Jersey the continental money "perished in his hand in one Week."

Some of these tragedies had been prevented on March 16th, when Congress strongly recommended to the states the repeal of all tender laws. Otherwise a debtor would have been within his legal rights in compelling a creditor to accept worthless paper for a long-standing obligation. Even so, hundreds of creditors had already been ruined, and hundreds of debtors were on their way to establishing a crude new postwar plutocracy.

Desperate as the situation was, Americans seemed more hopeful than they had been the preceding year. At least something was being done about it in 1781. Robert Morris, taking office on May 14th, presented a plan three days later for the establishment of a national bank. Only three days after it came before Congress, that body gave its approval; but it took until the first month of 1782 for the bank to be incorporated and opened for business.

The requisition system, introduced and retained for lack of anything better after the printing press era, had proved to be a failure from the beginning. Some of the states made praiseworthy efforts to raise their quotas of men, money and supplies on time. But there were too many inducements for delay, evasion and selfish local politics. John Mathews, for once being moderate in a judgment, declared that "whilst the states were left *ad libitum,* some of them would do a great deal, some a little, some scarcely anything." In a letter to a Massachusetts friend, James Lovell inquired, "If you know of a Compliance with one Requisition of Congress, *in Time and Quantity,* do let me have it that I may show it to the Delegates of the 12 States who cannot produce a single Instance." [21]

A committee consisting of James Duane, Oliver Wolcott and William Sharpe submitted a frank report on April 18th which declared that as the only means of survival "Congress were obliged to raise money by drawing bills on their ministers abroad; although they had not sufficient assurances that these bills would be honored." [22] On May 22nd, following a suggestion of this committee, the assembly adopted the forthright measure of collecting the next month's quotas by drawing drafts on the states at one month's sight.

The pursuit of a foreign loan had led in December, 1780, to the election of Colonel John Laurens, son of the former president, as an "envoy extraordinary . . . to go to the Court of Versailles, to make, in concert with Mr. Franklin, the public representations of the United States." In a vain hope that Catherine the Great might be persuaded to aid the cause of rebellion, Francis Dana of Massachusetts was appointed minister and sent on a wild-goose chase to Russia. Word had not yet reached Philadelphia that the mission of Henry Laurens to Holland was nipped in the bud by his capture at the start of the voyage.

The financiers of Congress had long recognized that the assembly must have some source of income independent of the states. As early as the autumn of 1778 a committee headed by Gouverneur Morris suggested a duty of 2 per cent on imported commodities. Variations of this plan were heard from time to time until February 3, 1781, when Congress resolved:

That it be recommended to the several states, as indispensably necessary, that they vest a power in Congress, to levy for the use of the United States, a duty of five per cent., *ad valorum,* at the time and place of importation, upon all goods, wares and merchandises of foreign growth and manufactures, which may be imported into any of the said states from any foreign port, island or plantation. . . .[23]

Nobody expected that the impost, as it came to be known, would pass immediately. The anticipated annual income of 600,000 to 700,000 specie dollars, as Mathews estimated, was "but a trifle as compared to our wants." Still, the impost could be considered a step toward financial independence as well as added powers for Congress.

Hopes of French aid in the early spring of 1781 were shattered when Congress received a scolding instead. Never was the paternalism of the French minister more stern than in the memorial read before the assembly on Saturday, March 24th:

The Chevalier de la Luzerne will not dissemble that his court was exceedingly surprised on being informed of the step which Congress had taken in disposing of bills drawn on their ministers, although they could not be ignorant that they had no funds for disposing them. This is a conduct totally inconsistent with that order which his majesty is forced to observe in his finances, and he has no doubt but, in future, Congress will most studiously avoid a repetition of it. He has nevertheless resolved to discharge the bills which became due last year, to the amount of one million of livres; and it is probable that his majesty will be able to provide funds to the amount of three millions for the discharge of those which will become due in the course of the present year.[24]

The acceptance of the bills of exchange doubtless compensated to a great extent for the reproof.* And only two months later another memorial from Luzerne on May 25th brought the tremendous news that "the king has . . . resolved to give a new proof of his affection. . . . The subsidy which the king has resolved to grant to the thirteen United States amounts to six millions of livres turnois, independent of the four millions which the ministry have enabled Dr. Franklin to borrow for the service of the current year."[25]

Again the old philosopher had saved his country, though the feat had been a little more difficult this time because of the blunders of the special envoy sent by Congress.

Never since 1778 had the American forces been able to count on the juxtaposition of the men, the money, the supplies and the naval power— a combination enjoyed consistently by the enemy. In the early summer of

* Five livres had about the value of a Spanish milled dollar.

1781, however, Morris had the money and Washington the assurance that Rochambeau's troops and all possible naval aid would be placed at his disposal. As a final gracious gesture, the proud old French regiments were acknowledging the position of the American commander as allied generalissimo.

The members of Congress played the part of evangelists by exhorting their constituents to strain every nerve. The states responded energetically with money and supplies for an army which only recently had been compelled to choose between "living on the country" and literally starving. Such was the change in public spirit that Washington dropped his habitual pessimism long enough to predict in a letter of June 7th "that it is in our power to bring the War to a happy conclusion." The very American earth and skies seemed to be doing their part; and a letter from President McKean to Washington on July 14th rejoiced at the crops:

> We are blessed with a most plentiful harvest; in this State the corn is greater in Quantity and better in quality than any year of the last twenty, and the country teems with fruit. The Legislatures in most of the States have imposed very considerable Taxes, tho' perhaps not equal to the exigencies of our affairs, yet they appear to be as heavy as the People can bear. . . . Public and private credit and confidence are restoring fast, and the trade and commerce of this city really flourish.[26]

Military operations in the South took on an added importance after Luzerne's new warning of May 26th that the expected mediation by the Russian and Austrian courts would probably be on a *uti possidetis* basis, which meant that Great Britain would claim the American territory in her possession. With the invaders overrunning three southern states at this date and threatening Virginia, the outlook was dark until the reports of Greene's masterly campaign reached Philadelphia. Even military amateurs could perceive that American tactical defeats in the Carolinas were leading to strategic gains. After the "victory" won by Cornwallis at Guilford, costing him nearly 40 per cent of his army, the British general abandoned North Carolina to the rebels and marched into Virginia for recuperation. Nicholas Van Dyke of Delaware believed that Greene had only "to keep up the ball awhile, and he must effectually ruin his Lordship. Two more such victories would probably Burgoyne him and his veterans."[27]

Stories of British outrages were brought to Philadelphia by the homeless prisoners just exchanged by the enemy as captives of Charleston and Savannah. They included such alumni of Congress as Thomas Heyward, Edward Rutledge, Richard Hutson, George Walton, Arthur Middleton and Noble Wymberly Jones. The assembly arranged a loan of $30,000 for the refugees and remembered another old friend by empowering Franklin "to offer Lieutenant General Burgoyne in exchange for the Hon. H. Laurens."

Until the last days of August the delegates appeared to have shared with the foe the delusion that Washington and Rochambeau were joining forces for an attack on New York. This had been the original idea, but the prospect of French naval support in the South induced the allied generalissimo to plan a combined land-and-sea campaign to isolate Cornwallis, then fortifying Yorktown. On August 23rd, as the American troops pelted southward in forced marches, closely followed by the French, John Mathews wrote to General Greene:

> The prospect brightens my friend! and opens to us the most flattering view of the end of all our toils, that I have yet seen, since the commencement of this revolution. Whether the year 1781 will be the oera of America's substantial independence I will not venture to pronounce, but a secret impulse informs me, that it will be the grand Epocha of her glory . . . and raise her into consequence among the nations of the earth. . . .[28]

On September 2nd the vanguard of the American army hurried through Philadelphia without ceremony, for Washington did not care to expose his unpaid troops to city temptations. Monday, the 3rd, was perhaps the greatest day in the lives of the little group of delegates standing outside the State House. Four of them had attended the very first meetings of the Continental Congress in 1774—Roger Sherman, Samuel Adams, James Duane and President Thomas McKean. All of them must have been a little shabby and threadbare, these middle-aged men in cocked hats who waited in the September sunshine. Few patriots had any hard money to spare for clothes these days, and it had been seven years since America imported many velvets and linens fit for a gentleman.

The crash of marching feet grew louder, keeping time to the drums and music. Up Front and Chestnut Streets came the white-clad ranks, for Rochambeau had ordered the French officers "to salute Congress as a crowned head and the President as a first prince of the blood."

The assembly never had a president of more aggressively republican ideals than tough, grizzled Thomas McKean. But a letter written next day by Samuel Livermore of New Hampshire hints that the delegates relished their new honors:

> The members of Congress were at the door of the state house and recd. from the officers of the army as they passed a royal salute. The ceremony on their part was to let fall the point of the sword, likewise the colours, and the members of Congress took off their hats. The engaging figure and behaviour of the officers of all ranks, their dress, the cavalry, musick, arms, artillery, the

figure and behaviour of the privates, and the uniform motion of the whole, afforded the most pleasing prospect of the kind I ever saw.[29]

On Wednesday afternoon, after the second French contingent encamped on the Common, the Soissonois regiment entertained the public with maneuvers while Luzerne gave a dinner for Congress and the officers. Robert Morris could not be present, for he had promised Washington to scrape together $20,000 in hard money, so that the American troops could have a month's pay.

The suspense must have been uncommonly hard to bear during the next six weeks. It did not take any great military knowledge to realize that an allied victory depended on many undependable factors. Admiral de Grasse's supporting fleet might not arrive in time, or it might be defeated by Admiral Graves. Cornwallis might escape from the Virginia peninsula with his 7,000 men, or he might be reinforced from New York. After it was all over, Franklin marveled that the French and American forces "should with such perfect concord be assembled from different places by land and water, form their junction punctually without the least regard for cross accidents of wind or weather or interruption from the enemy; and that the army which was their object should in the meantime have had the goodness to quit a situation from whence it might have escaped, and place itself in another from whence an escape was impossible." [30]

On September 8th (though the news did not reach Congress for five weeks) General Greene fought the last battle of the war at Eutaw Springs in South Carolina. Again he could claim no better than a draw in tactical respects, but after losing nearly half their army the British had to retreat to the seacoast. In ten months the American general had cleared the south of invaders except for a last garrison at Charleston. It was by far the most brilliant campaign of the Revolution.

Congress had the satisfaction of dabbling in the strategy of Yorktown. At eight o'clock on the evening of October 14th President McKean sent Washington a hurried express with "copies of two original letters from Sir Henry Clinton to Lord Cornwallis, which I have in cyphers, and which have been faithfully decyphered by Mr. Lovell." [31]

Although the information did not reach Yorktown in time to be of any help, the State House had taken on for forty-eight hours the atmosphere of a spy novel. Clinton's letters had been captured from the crew of a small vessel off the New Jersey coast and rushed to Philadelphia. After two days and nights of concentrated effort, James Lovell "cracked" the British code. "I found, as I had before supposed," he explained in a letter to Washington, "that they sometimes use Entick's Dictionary marking the Page Column and

Word as 115.1.4. . . . . The use of the same Cypher by all the British Commanders is now pretty fairly well concluded."[32]

Owing to British excesses in the Carolinas, feeling against the enemy ran higher than at any time of the war. Congress had to resist the importunities of southern delegates clamoring for reprisals. Even a philosopher as benign as Dr. Franklin could not help recalling in 1781 one of his last evenings in England when "General Clarke had the folly to say in my hearing at Sir John Pringle's that with a thousand British grenadiers he would undertake to go from one end of America to the other, and geld all the males, partly by force and partly by a little coaxing."[33]

A great many other British boasts were coming home to roost on the drooping standards of Cornwallis' army. Under the gray October skies the beleaguered troops were helpless against the pounding of the allied guns, for the end was never in doubt after Admiral de Grasse won a brief mastery of the sea. On the 17th, four years to the day after the surrender at Saratoga, Cornwallis agreed to capitulate. The redcoats marched out two days later to the music of *The World Turned Upside Down* and laid down their arms. Some weeks would pass before Lord North heard the news, but his anguished cry must have been anticipated by the thoughts of the British officers at Yorktown:

"It is all over! It is all over!"

The first authentic information reached Philadelphia when Colonel Tench Tilghman, one of Washington's aides, clattered into the sleeping streets at three o'clock on the morning of the 22nd. Elias Boudinot tore open a letter already written to his wife to scrawl a hasty message ending with a fervent "God be praised!" Then he dashed off a letter to a friend with an account of the French and American troops "giving quarters to the *abject Brittons* on their Knees begging for mercy."[34]

The salutes, the ceremonies, the fire works and the illuminations would take place on Wednesday, the 24th, after the official dispatch came from General Washington. But on the Monday morning of this first exciting report, Congress as usual had to deal with an urgent financial problem. "When the messenger brought the news . . . it was necessary to furnish him with hard Money for his Expenses," Elias Boudinot recalled afterwards. "There was not a sufficiency in the Treasury to do it, and the Members of Congress . . . each paid a dollar to accomplish it."[35]

Chapter 22

The Shadow and the Substance

DURING the first months of 1782 Congress found itself in a peculiar and painful situation. It could hardly be doubted that Yorktown had brought the war to a finish, yet an American army had to be kept in the field against the possibility of the enemy making a final effort. And while it had been hard enough to maintain an army without funds, Congress could foresee what a difficult and dangerous undertaking it might be to disband an army without funds. The unpaid soldiers had been long-suffering, but it could not be hoped that the next mutiny would end happily.

Postwar adjustments are troublesome enough for an established government with money in the treasury. But in 1782 the postwar adjustments had begun before anyone could be sure that the conflict had ended. As a consequence, Congress had to tackle the problems of peace with one hand and those of defense with the other.

Although it had taken the last of the French subsidy to finance the Yorktown campaign, Luzerne informed Congress on September 24, 1781, that "the king for the next year cannot continue any supplies to the United States. . . . That it is time for them to relieve his majesty from the heavy burdens of a war which he had undertaken and carries on for their sakes." [1]

The French minister appended a list of sums furnished by his country in 1781 alone to the total of 15,699,501 livres, including the six millions of the royal subsidy and the 3,416,000 representing advances drawn on Franklin. The members of Congress could only admit with gratitude that America owed her independence to French aid. On the other hand, France could congratulate herself on a military bargain. At a total cost amounting

324

to less than England's expense for hiring 30,000 German mercenaries, France had nourished a revolution which robbed her hereditary foe of the world's richest colonies. It was a noble and economical revenge for the loss of Canada in the last war.

Nor was there anything niggardly about an ally who might have left the Americans abruptly to their own devices after Yorktown. In the autumn of 1781 Luzerne began a gradual weaning process with the announcement that his Most Christian Majesty had offered "his guarantee for ten millions of livres tournois, to be borrowed in Holland, for account of the United States." [2]

While John Adams attempted to negotiate a loan in the Netherlands, the requisition system functioned more lamely in his homeland than it ever had before Yorktown. The superintendent of finance drew up a plan for the states to pay their quotas of eight million dollars in quarterly installments, beginning on April 1, 1782. But their indifference and neglect caused him to present a complaint to Congress on February 11th. The Confederation, declared Robert Morris bitterly, had given Congress "the privilege of asking everything" but had secured for the states "the prerogative of granting nothing."

The Philadelphia merchant did not pretend to a gift for words, but no "penman" of Congress could have stated the case more forcefully. If there was any complacency left, he shattered it by declaring that the states had defaulted "while all Europe gazed in astonishment at the unparalleled boldness and vastness of claims mingled with an unparalleled indolence and imbecility of conduct." [3]

Congress thought at once of its two favorite remedies—appointing a committee and drafting an address. But after rejecting the best efforts of Daniel Carroll and several other aspiring writers, the assembly decided that this case called for a more powerful prescription. John Rutledge of South Carolina and George Clymer of Pennsylvania, two veterans of the early years who had returned, were selected to visit the states to the southward in person and make an appeal in the strongest terms. Two ordained ministers, Joseph Montgomery of Pennsylvania and Jesse Root of Connecticut, left on a similar mission among the eastern states.

Parson Root, writing to his colleague Williams in 1781, had inquired, "Is not this a wonderful paradox—that there is in the States such a plenty of money that it is worth nothing—at the same time such a vast plenty of provisions and goods and yet no money to purchase them—and the people Complaining they Cant pay their rates." [4] Such phenomena, which have puzzled people of other ages, must have troubled the Connecticut member even more deeply after his persuasions failed to arouse the eastern states. On

June 1st, when the four delegates left on their tours, the payments from the states for 1782 had reached a total of $20,000—scarcely enough for a single day's expenses. Of the four millions due on July 1st, only $50,000 materialized. And the effect of personal appeals may be judged by the fact that on September 1st a total of $125,000 had been received of the six millions hoped for on this date.

The four financial evangelists could report promises and the "strongest assurances" from the states they visited—every encouragement except the actual cash. Worse yet, Montgomery made the belated discovery that some of the states were levying taxes for their quotas and devoting the receipts to their own purposes.

The harassed financiers of 1782 could at least take pride in the new bank established by Robert Morris with a capital of $400,000 from stock subscriptions. In midsummer, after it had been in operation for six months, the Connecticut delegates reported to Governor Trumbull that "the Financier's notes and bank bills are in full credit and paid on sight and are rather preferred to money by the merch'ts here."

Until the British surrender it could usually be said that the states were making an effort which reached quite respectable proportions in the spring and summer of 1781. But after Yorktown the centrifugal tendencies of the Confederation became every day more apparent. Absenteeism had not troubled a great deal since 1777 and 1778, when it could often be blamed on the isolation of Baltimore and York. But the news of the victory had barely been announced when the newly elected president, John Hanson of Maryland, found it necessary to send a circular letter to six state executives on November 15, 1781:

> Congress feel themselves reduced to the disagreeable necessity of directing me to write to your Excellency respecting the deficiency of a Representation from your State. . . . The most important powers Vested in Congress by the Confederation lie dormant at this time by reason of the unpunctuality of the Delegates of six States, in point of attendance: and some of these powers too indispensably necessary to be exercised at this great and important Crisis.[5]

Both Washington and Franklin warned repeatedly that America dared not let her sword rust in 1782. Elias Boudinot, voicing the anxiety of Congress, wrote to his brother on February 20th: "There is not the least prospect of Peace or scarcely the probability of it—on the contrary every measure is adopting in England to send over a large body of Hanoverians and some British regulars early in the Spring. The Com'r in chief expects the next campaign to be the most important of any that has been or will be in America this war." Here the New Jersey member probably shook his head sadly as he continued: "Alas! we are distressed with the languor and Inactivity of the States. All that can be done by Congress, has been, to rouse them from their Lethargy, but all is treated as a matter of course." [6]

The assembly of 1782 shows a curious blend of unknown names and delegates who made their mark in the early years. Eight of the states were represented by hardy perennials—Eliphalet Dyer and Oliver Wolcott of Connecticut; Thomas McKean of Delaware; George Walton of Georgia; Abraham Clark, Jonathan Elmer and John Witherspoon of New Jersey; James Duane and William Floyd of New York; Thomas Mifflin and George Clymer of Pennsylvania; William Ellery of Rhode Island; Arthur Middleton and John Rutledge of South Carolina.

Altogether, five delegates of the first Continental Congress and nine signers of the Declaration of Independence served at various times in 1782, though the assembly could seldom produce a total of more than twenty-five members.

Several other well-remembered figures were elected but did not attend—Caesar Rodney of Delaware; John Hancock of Massachusetts; Samuel Chase of Maryland; and James Wilson of Pennsylvania. Nathaniel Scudder of New Jersey had been killed two days before Yorktown while leading his militamen against the enemy in New Jersey. John Dickinson, Thomas Burke, William Paca, John Penn, Nathaniel Folsom, Stephen Hopkins, John Sullivan, James Lovell and John Mathews retired permanently, either for personal reasons or to serve their own states. Some of the sacrifices made by delegates of these years can be imagined from a letter written to a friend in Scotland by John Witherspoon, explaining why he dropped out for a few months: "I have now left Congress, not being able to support the expense of attending it. . . . Professor Houston, however, our professor of mathematics, is a delegate this year; but he tells me that he will certainly leave it next November. I mention this circumstance to confirm what I wrote you formerly, that the members of Congress in general, not only receive no profit from that office, but I believe five out of six of them, if not more, are great losers in their private affairs." [7]

John Jay, Henry Laurens, Robert Morris and Robert R. Livingston would continue to serve in other fields. But perhaps the most noticeable gap of all, as if a cornerstone had vanished from the State House, resulted from the retirement of Samuel Adams. The spectacle of his old political pupil John Hancock being elected governor of Massachusetts year after year was more than the archrebel could bear, especially when the successful candidate set a tradition of giving balls or banquets of celebration. "Our Bradfords, Winslows & Winthrops would have revolted at the idea of opening scenes of Dissipation & Folly," he wrote to John Scollay after one of these orgies. "I love the People of Boston. I once thought, that City would be the *Christian* Sparta. But Alas! Will men never be free! They will be free no longer than while they remain virtuous." [8]

Sam Adams returned in 1781 to liberate Boston according to his own lights. But the voters preferred overwhelmingly to be enslaved to the voluptuous pleasures introduced by Hancock, and Adams soon became a lieutenant in the political machine he had created.

He would have found the Philadelphia of 1782 quite as sinful as Boston. The Chevalier de la Luzerne, who disliked music and could not dance a step, gave a concert and ball every other week at the large town house he had rented from John Dickinson. More of the delegates were bringing their wives and daughters these days, so that the French minister's affairs were well attended. The iron, vermin-proof bed he had imported—the first of its kind in the New World—was the talk of the town, especially after a bolt of lightning struck one night and reduced it to molten metal. Luzerne, fortunately, was away on a trip to Virginia.

Among the newcomers to Congress this year were several men who had already made a name for themselves as public servants—Alexander Hamilton of New York; Richard Peters of Pennsylvania; Ralph Izard of South Carolina; Arthur Lee of Virginia. Although the Deane-Lee feud had become only a memory, it was still the greatest issue of the day to the neurotic Virginia delegate, who saw himself making "vain efforts to redeem an infatuated Majority from the bondage of folly and private interest." His suspicions seemed to be justified in the last days of 1781 when letters were laid before Congress which left little doubt of Silas Deane's disloyalty if not actual treason.

"On whichever side Mr. Deane's letters are viewed they present mysteries," James Madison wrote to his friend Edmund Randolph. "But it is unnecessary to rely on these publications for the real character of the man. There is evidence of his obliquity which has for a considerable time been conclusive." [9]

Time would prove that Silas Deane had been sinned against as well as sinning. After returning to France in 1780, disgruntled because Congress had not settled his accounts, he drifted to Antwerp and took pay from the British secret service. The rewards were so meager that he lived in poverty-blighted European exile after the war, dying on shipboard in 1789 while sailing to Canada. The sequel had to wait until 1842, when a later Congress recognized the justice of his grievances by paying his heirs $37,000.

As a delegate in 1782, Arthur Lee became a nuisance with his suspicions of everyone who did not agree with him. "The detection of Mr. Deane," he wrote to James Warren on April 8th, "seems not to have drawn any punishment nor even odium on those who countenanced and profited by his wickedness. Among these Dr. Franklin and Mr. R. Morris are the most conspicuous." [10]

Hatred of the enemy, far from subsiding after Yorktown, reached new heights of fury. Reprisals had been monotonously threatened by Congress for seven years, but not until the late date of 1782 did the assembly go so far as to direct that a British officer be selected by lot and hanged as an innocent victim for the crimes of his countrymen. From May until November the life of the youthful Captain Charles Asgill hung in the balance, and the case took on international importance when Vergennes intervened.

There would have been no problem at all if other British officers had shown as much humanity and good sense as Sir Guy Carleton, the new commander in chief at New York, who had been his country's most able soldier as well as administrator. But it was his misfortune to inherit an awkward situation caused by the excesses of Britons who did not believe that rebels were entitled to the customary mercies and courtesies. The consequences of this policy, from the American viewpoint, were summed up in the report of September 27, 1781, by a committee appointed to investigate the "barbarities" of the foe:

> The flourishing villages of Charlestown and Falmouth in Massachusetts, in the year 1775, Norfolk in Virginia in 1776, Kingston in New York in 1777, Bristol in Rhode Island and Bedford in Massachusetts in 1778, Fairfield and Norwalk in Connecticut in 1779, Springfield and Connecticut Farms in New Jersey 1780, and Georgetown in South Carolina and New London and Groton in Connecticut in 1781, have been consigned by these enemies of Mankind to wanton conflagrations! [11]

After reviewing the massacre of American prisoners of war at Fort Grinnell by Benedict Arnold's redcoats, the committee suggested a resolution "if the British Army and Navy continue their present system of inhumanity in burning defenceless villages, or houses, or in murdering inoffensive citizens or prisoners of war, that the War and Marine Departments cause all persons taken in such acts of burning to be immediately consigned to the flames, or afterwards if captivated to be put to death."

Such extremes were not considered seriously, but all delegates resented the continual violations of accepted military or diplomatic immunities at the expense of Americans. As an American envoy Henry Laurens had been imprisoned in the Tower for a year on "suspicion of treason," suffering hardships which broke the health and spirit of the middle-aged South Carolinian. And as an American soldier Colonel Isaac Haynes went to his death in Charleston, condemned to hang for no other offense than resisting in the field. The injustice of this case had been so obvious that some of the British officers protested the decision of the court-martial.

There were of course many generous foemen who earned American respect and admiration, but a long train of grievances had accumulated when Congress learned on April 29, 1782, that Captain Josiah Huddy had been hanged on the 12th for doing his duty as a New Jersey militia officer. This was the last straw, and the assembly decided on a reprisal when the enemy refused to give up the guilty British officer, Captain Richard Lippincott. It was the misfortune of Captain Charles Asgill to be the prisoner whose name was drawn. Sir Guy Carleton, who denounced the execution of Huddy, did his best to save the innocent British officer, but Congress determined anew that Asgill must pay on the gallows. When the enemy commander reminded the assembly of the proposed victim's youth and innocence, he was in turn reminded that the late Captain Huddy also had been young and innocent.

The new crisis in Vermont this year added to the feeling against the British, who were accused of plotting to detach the rebellious district from the Confederation. From a territorial dispute involving New York and New Hampshire, the issue had developed into the embarrassing problem of whether Congress dared heed the aspirations of this frontier area to become an independent state. Any such encouragement would naturally be resented by the two claimants to the territory. The Vermonters did not hesitate to hint that they might throw in their lot with Great Britain if the United States would not listen. British deviltries were suspected by delegates such as William Few of Georgia, who saw "no reason to believe that it is their intention to yield us our Independence or cease to exercise every means in their power to injure and destroy us. Finding they cannot by force accomplish their diabolical designs they are now trying the effect of artifice and Intrigue." [12]

Other members of Congress viewed the recurring issue less as a menace than a crashing bore. "I shall proceed to the old story of Vermont, and that is worn a little threadbare," reported Samuel Livermore of New Hampshire to his state on March 2nd. "The debate will be taken up again in a few days; but what will be done I know not. I fear some would sacrifice the peace of N.H and N.Y. both to gratify their darling Vermont; others will never agree to any terms that suppose the existence of their independence. Between these two partys no one proposition respecting them can be agreed on." [13]

Gradually the Vermont question had come to be closely associated with the problem of western land claims. James Madison, in his notes of May 1st, declared that the independence of Vermont and its admission into the Confederation were advocated by the New England states, with the exception of New Hampshire, "from antient prejudice agst. N. York" and "from the accession of weight they might derive from it in Congress." He added that Pennsylvania, Maryland and New Jersey favored the Vermont cause as part of their opposition to western land claims, particularly those of Virginia. New York and New Hampshire had grounds of self-interest; and Madison explained that Virginia, Georgia and the Carolinas also were against Vermont for these reasons: "1. an habitual jealousy of a predominance of Eastern Interests. 2. the opposition expected from Vermont to Western claims. 3. the inexpediency of admitting so unimportant a state to an equal voice in deciding the peace. . . ."[14]

Practically the same division of states, according to Madison, prevailed in the issue of the western land claims "opposed by Rhode Island, N. Jersey, Pennsylvania, Delaware and Maryland. . . . The western claims, or rather a final settlement of them, are also thwarted by Massachusetts and Connecticut." He listed the proponents as "Virga., N. and S. Carolina, Georgia and N. York, all of those states being interested therein. . . . The claim of N. York is very extensive, but her title very flimsy. She urges it more in the hope of obtaining some advantage, or credit, by its session, than of ever maintaining it."

While Virginia's proposed cession of western lands impended, Vermont's cause lost rather than gained ground because her politicians threatened to go over to the enemy. Any prospect of the district becoming a British wedge driven into the Confederation was alarming, and some of the resulting indignation doubtless influenced the decision to hang Captain Asgill for the crimes of his countrymen. The young officer's fate depended on final hearings held the first week of November, and Elias Boudinot reported that he and Duane led the opposition against a large majority determined on the execution. The dramatic outcome was related in the matter-of-fact style of a letter written by Madison to Edmund Randolph on November 5th:

> In the midst of our perplexities a letter arrived from Genl. Washington inclosing an intercession from the Count de Vergennes in favor of the life of young Asgill, founded on a most pathetic and importunate memorial from his mother. The Ct. writes to Genl. Washington, as he says not in the quality of a public minister, but of a man who feels the force of Mrs. Asgill's supplications. He backs his intercessions, however, with the desire of the King and Queen who were much affected by the memorial. . . .[15]

In spite of the slow voyages of sailing ships, there had been barely enough time for the English mother to make an effective plea. A request from Vergennes could not be ignored, and Congress resolved immediately to spare Asgill and set him free. But there were still recalcitrant members who resented the enemy's tacit assumptions that the neck of a British officer was more precious than the life of Captain Huddy, who also had a mother. These dissenters managed the following day to pass a resolution authorizing Washington to take summary reprisals if the enemy should commit further acts contrary to the laws or usage of war.

Every month brought some new crisis in the maintenance of an army living from hand to mouth. Madison wrote on October 29th that "the state of the public finances has already compelled the Superintendent to give a discharge to the former contractors, and to accept of a new contract, by which thirty per cent. is added to the price of a ration in consideration of credit for three months." [16]

In June, after repeated rumors of peace negotiations, Congress thought of reducing army expenses by reducing the army itself. But with New York and Charleston still occupied, it would never do to sacrifice safety to economy. The assembly contented itself on August 7th by recommending a plan of voluntary retirement for officers, beginning on the first day of the new year.

Although Washington gave his approval, he also called attention on October 2nd to the grievances of officers and soldiers due to "the total want of Money, or the means of existing from one day to another . . . the distress of their Families (i e such as are Maried), at home, and the prospect of poverty and misery before them."

Army officers, state officials, members of Congress—each group felt that its burdens were heaviest of all. John Ambler, treasurer of Virginia, wrote to James Madison on May 11, 1782: "I sincerely wish our Treasury would enable us to make you a remittance. We have not had ten pounds Specie in it since my coming into office, and it is to be feared there will not any come in for a long time. . . . The officers of Civil Government here have not been paid for the last ten months." [17]

Madison in turn explained to his friend Randolph how it was possible for a member of Congress to live from month to month without any income. In a letter of August 27th he confided that he had "for some time past been a pensioner on the favor of Haym Salomon, a Jew broker." And he added on September 30th, "The kindness of our little friend in Front street, near the coffee-house, is a fund which will preserve me from extremities, but I never resort to it without great mortification, as he obstinately rejects all recompense. The price of money is so usorious, that he thinks it ought to be extorted from none but those who aim at profitable speculations. To a necessitous Delegate he gratuitously spares a supply out of his private stock." [18]

This patriot of the money marts landed in New York just before the war as a Polish Jew who had worked for the liberation of that country. For several years he aided the rebel cause with undercover activities, being twice captured by the British. Arriving in Philadelphia in 1778 with his health shattered by imprisonment, he rapidly made and spent a fortune as a broker in bills of exchange. Within a few years he advanced in specie a total of $211,678 to the United States, not to mention the countless gifts or loans without interest to individuals such as Madison. When Haym Salomon died in 1785 at the age of 45, leaving a penniless family, his patriotic benefactions reached an estimated total of more than half a million dollars. Several years later Congress recognized the validity of many of these claims, but no payments were ever made to the heirs.

Western lands and the impost continued to offer the only hope of a "continental" source of income. Although the cessions passed by the New York, Connecticut and Virginia legislatures had been the means of bringing Maryland into the Confederation, they were so riddled with conditions as to raise many new doubts. Thus after briefly looking the gift horse in the mouth, the other states began to clamor for modifications.

The validity of conflicting and overlapping claims had not been settled by offers of cession. Not only the states but several private land companies had claims, and it would have taken a Solomon to make head or tail of the confusion.

The issue took on added importance after personal appeals fared no better than written addresses when it came to persuading the states to pay their quotas fully and promptly. On May 24th the superintendent submitted a list of current expenses with the comment, "Congress will perceive that every sous we can command during the year 1782 is already anticipated." [19]

A grand committee consisting of a member from each state reported on September 4th "that it is their opinion that the western lands if ceded to the U. S. might contribute towards a fund for paying the debts of these States." After weighing this report Congress resolved with more desperation than hope "that one million two hundred thousand dollars be quotaed on the states, as absolutely and immediately necessary for payment of the interest on the public debt." [20]

Considering that the states had paid only a woeful fraction of former quotas, it could hardly have been seriously anticipated that they would do any better this time. In the matter of western lands some progress seemed to be made on October 28th when Congress voted to accept the cession of New York. But James Madison wrote to Randolph on November 5th that "the acceptance of this cession *singly* met with a negative from Virginia for obvious reasons. . . . Upon the whole New York has . . . succeeded in a very important object by ceding a claim which was tenable neither by force nor by right; she has acquired with Congress the merit of liberality, rendered the title to her reservation more respectable, and at least dampt the zeal with which Vermont has been abetted." [21]

Virginia, having good reason to suspect a political combination, cooled on the subject of cession. The whole issue of western lands had reached a stalemate in December when Congress risked its prestige in a resolution of the 5th denouncing Vermont's bid for independence as "dangerous to the Confederacy" and threatening "effectual measures to enforce a compliance" with its decisions.

Recalling past occasions when some state had defied Congress, it should have been no surprise to that body on February 4, 1783, to be opposed by Vermont. Governor Thomas T. Chittenden sent an "indecent and tart remonstrance" declaring in effect that his Green Mountain Boys were perfectly able to whip not only their old foes in New York but all the other twelve states if necessary.

Congress was becoming accustomed to a diet of crow these days. Only recently the Rhode Island delegates had pointed an accusing finger at the assembly and called on their state legislature to "preserve the Liberties of the United States and transmit them to posterity" by rejecting the proposed impost measure. This piece of impertinence could not be dismissed lightly, for it represented a brazen attempt on the part of one state to profit at the expense of the others. Insult had been piled on injury, moreover, by such crude appeals to local prejudice as to disgust a self-respecting politician.

There had been in the past any number of stubborn and opinionated delegates. But it might truthfully have been said that Congress had never been afflicted with a calculating demagogue until David Howell of Rhode Island took his seat in the summer of 1782. A graduate of Princeton, the 35-year-old instructor at the College of Rhode Island (Brown) declared on August 3rd for the benefit of his constituents that "as you go southward, Government verges toward Aristocracy. In New England alone have we pure and unmixed democracy and in Rhode Island . . . it is in its perfection. I hope it may be long preserved. Should our little State have the credit of preventing the 5 per Cent. from taking effect it would be to us an additional gain." [22]

Since the original resolution of February 3, 1781, eleven states had given their consent to the measure aiming to provide Congress with the income from an *ad valorem* duty. With the accession of Maryland on July 15, 1782, only Georgia and Rhode Island were left. The grand committee recommended in October that a special appeal be made to these states. Immediately the two new Rhode Island delegates, Howell and his echo Jonathan Arnold, sent a message of their own to the state legislature, violently denouncing the measure as the "Yoke of Tyranny."

Up to this point they were of course within their rights. A brief truce ensued, for the Articles of Confederation provided that the new federal year begin on the first Monday in November. Elias Boudinot was elected president on the 4th, and Congress had word a few days later that the legislature of Rhode Island had defeated the impost.

On December 6th the assembly decided to send a deputation to harangue the Rhode Island legislators. That very same day it became unofficially known that David Howell was the author of a letter published in the Boston *Gazette*, commenting on John Adams' progress in Holland: "The loan he is negotiating fills as fast as could be expected. The national importance of the United States is constantly rising in the estimation of European powers and the civilized world. Such is their credit, that they have of late failed in no application for foreign loans, and the only danger on that score is that of contracting too large a debt." [23]

So far there was little truth in a statement which could only be considered as an indirect and unprincipled attack on the impost. But the letter ended with the quite accurate revelation, violating the congressional pledge of secrecy, that Sweden had proposed a treaty with the United States.

Howell had to acknowledge that he had written the letter and others of a similar tone. He and his colleague Arnold defended themselves on the grounds of the "freedom of speech and debate in Congress" guaranteed by the Articles of Confederation. The assembly not only administered a stern rebuke but asked Robert R. Livingston, the secretary of foreign affairs, to communicate to the governor of Rhode Island the official truth about the slow progress of the loan in Holland. This amounted to branding Howell publicly as a liar, but his popularity at home did not suffer.

Congress had to bear up under a worse shock when the news came in December that Virginia, of all states, had suddenly and inexplicably repudiated her approval of the impost measure. The deputation had to be recalled after leaving Philadelphia with high hopes of converting the Rhode Islanders. Even Madison had no explanation of his state's behavior except to say that "many have surmised that the emnity of Doctor Lee against Morris is at the bottom of it."

At any rate Congress had not given up hope. Both issues, the impost as well as western lands, would be brought up again. And if the Vermont and

Rhode Island incidents had been humiliating, the assembly had shown this very summer that it could act with firmness and dignity to settle a dispute between states. The Wyoming land controversy between Connecticut and Pennsylvania—older than Congress itself—was submitted to that body according to a provision of Article IX of the Confederation. On August 12th five commissioners were appointed as a court of inquiry—William Whipple, Welcome Arnold, William Churchill Houston, Cyrus Griffin and David Brearley. They reported a unanimous decision on December 30th "that the jurisdiction . . . of all the territory lying within the charter boundary of Pennsylvania and now claimed by the State of Connecticut, do of right belong to the State of Pennsylvania."

But this was another of the specters which would rest uneasily and return again to disturb Congress.

Rumors of approaching peace negotiations were heard often in the spring of 1782, though all the American leaders warned against any relaxation of warlike vigilance. Great Britain was suspected of making a final effort to create dissension between allies, but on May 13th Congress found an opportunity to proclaim in the language of diplomacy its affection for France. Since Gérard's reception in 1778 there had been no more ceremonious occasion than this public audience for Luzerne, "in order that he might deliver to the United States in Congress assembled a letter which he had rec'd from his most Christian Majesty to them announcing the birth of a Dauphin." The report of Secretary Thomson continued:

> The Minister came in his own coach to the State house, being escorted by the city troop of light horse. At the State house he was rec'd with military honors, and being met at the foot of the steps by two members deputed for the purpose he was by them introduced to his seat. The house was arranged in the following order—the President in a chair on a platform raised two steps from the floor with a large table before him. The members of Congress in chairs on the floor to his right and left with small tables before them. The tables were all covered with green cloth. . . . Next to the Members of Congress on the left of the chair stood the principals of the three executive departments namely the superintendant of finance the Sec'ry at War and the Sec'ry for foreign affairs.

The president and council of Pennsylvania also were present, as well as two hundred prominent citizens admitted by ticket. Every detail of the ceremony had been prescribed in advance:

> The Minister was conducted into the Congress Hall by the two members who had received him at the foot of the steps of the outward door. As he entered the bar the president and the house rose, the president being covered.

The Minister as he advanced to his chair bowed to the president who took off his hat and returned the bow. The Minister being uncovered. The Minister then bowed to the members, on each side of the chair, who were standing uncovered but did not return the bow. The Minister then sat down and put on his hat. . . . After a pause of about a minute the Minister arose and taking off his hat addressed the United States in Congress assembled in a short speech delivered in French.

Secretary Marbois presented the letter from his Most Christian Majesty to President Boudinot, and an interpreter read it in English.

Whereupon the president, the Members and the Minister rose the President being covered, but the Members and the Minister uncovered; and the president on behalf of the United State addressed the Minister in a short speech after which they all sat down and after a short pause the Minister rose, whereupon the president and the members rose. The Minister then bowed to the president and members and withdrew, the members who introduced him reconducting him to the foot of the steps at the outward door.[24]

In spite of such public protestations of amity, it was no secret to Luzerne that Congress had a small anti-Gallican party led by Arthur Lee. This veteran troublemaker, who believed Philadelphia to be the "bosom of Toryism," tried without success to have Franklin and Jay excluded from the peace negotiations in Europe.

Lee's opponents, on the other hand, seized every opportunity to show the good will of Congress. Thus on June 13th the assembly sent its condolences to Louis XVI on "an event which has disturbed your majesty's felicity; and unite with you in offering that tribute of sorrow to the memory of your most dear and beloved aunt, the Princess Sophia Elizabeth Justina of France. . . ."

September brought word that John Adams had been able to arrange a loan of five million guilders in Holland—a sum equal to twice as many French livres, or about £400,000 sterling. The partial subscription of a million and half guilders "is a most seasonable relief to the Department of Finance, which was struggling under the most critical difficulties," commented Madison on the 17th. A week later he informed Randolph that "our Ally has added another important link to the chain of benefits by which this country is bound to France. He had remitted to us all the interest which he has paid for us, or was due to him on loans to us, together with all the charges attending the Holland loan; and has, moreover, postponed the demand of the principal till one year after the war, and agreed to receive it then in twelve successive annual payments. These concessions amount to a very considerable reduction of the liquidated debt." [25]

Before this news crossed the ocean, Congress found an opportunity to offer a handsome testimonial of its gratitude to France. A French warship of 74 guns having sunk in an accident, the delegates recalled that America's largest warship had not been launched for lack of funds. On September 3rd the assembly resolved "to present the *America*, a 74 gun ship, in the name of the United States, to the Chevalier de la Luzerne, for the service of his most Christian Majesty." [26] Any lingering doubts as to the amity between the allies should have been dispelled, in spite of the muttering of Arthur Lee's faction, by the statement of policy on October 4th:

> *Resolved, unanimously,* That Congress are sincerely desirous of an honorable and permanent peace; that as the only means of obtaining it, they will inviolably adhere to the treaty of alliance with his Most Christian Majesty, and conclude neither a separate peace or truce with Great Britain; that they will prosecute the war with vigor, until, by the blessing of God on the united arms, a peace shall be happily accomplished, by which the full and absolute sovereignty of these United States having been duly assured, their rights and interests, as well as those of their allies shall be effectually provided for and secured. [27]

Even the financial situation, bad as it was, showed some improvement after the news of the progress made with the loan in the United Provinces. Congress rebounded so far as to resolve on September 13th "that a sum not exceeding four millions of dollars, exclusive of the money which Mr. Adams may obtain by the loan now negotiating in Holland, he borrowed in Europe on the faith of the United States of America. . . ." [28]

As usual, every attempt was made to draw in advance on these prospects before the loans ever materialized into cash.

Luzerne had good news for Congress on September 24th with the report, based on verbal assurances of the English agent at the court of France, "that the king of England, in order to facilitate peace, was disposed to treat of the independence of the United States." This statement seemed to be nullified by the news in October that the English monarch could bring himself only to refer to his former colonies in such vague terms as "any other Princes or States concerned."

Americans would never have believed that their stiff-necked adversary had seriously contemplated abdication this very year when he was compelled to accept a Rockingham ministry after Lord North's fall. The personal rule of the "Patriot King" had come to an abrupt end of disillusionment. George III went so far with his decision in 1782 as to compose a message for Parliament; and again the following year he drew up a tentative instrument of abdication when the defeat of Shelburne seemed to leave no alterative to the Fox-North coalition. In both drafts the monarch admitted with the dignity of complete candor that he had failed.

Americans had denounced him as a tyrant so long that they had forgotten how honest George III could be on occasion. After the disturbing news of October they had to endure long weeks of suspense and anxiety. Then on December 23rd official dispatches confirmed the report that a British commission had authorized Richard Oswald to treat with the commissioners of "the Thirteen United States of America."

No Christmas gift could have been received more thankfully than these five words. For the first time Americans dared to allow themselves the hope that there could be no further doubt about the winning of their independence.

So slow were the communications that another long period of waiting ensued. February 13th brought the news, as one delegate phrased it, of "the humble language in which the once haughty monarch of Great Britain has addressed his Parliament." But not until the morning of March 12, 1783—eight years, lacking a month, after the shot heard round the world —did Captain Josiah Barney reach these shores with official dispatches confirming that the provisional treaty between the United States and Great Britain had been signed on the 30th of November.

Some lofty sentiments were expressed in toasts and orations. But John Montgomery probably came nearest to speaking for the common man who had weathered the trials and transitions of the past eight years. The Pennsylvania delegate, who held the distinction of being the worst speller of Congress, declared proudly that "amirrica will be free and I have reason to belive that the terms of peace for us will be favourable. poor torris must now hang thire heads. the day is now Come when the sun will Raise on amirrica never to set. I look forward with Pleasure to the happey days that our Children will see." [29]

PART FIVE

Union

Democratical States must always feel *before they can*
see: — *it is this which makes their governments slow*
— *but the people will be right at last.*

— GEORGE WASHINGTON

Chapter 23

Congress Takes to the Road

THE terms of the provisional treaty between Great Britain and the United States were more favorable than anybody had dared to expect. Richard Peters of Pennsylvania undoubtedly spoke for Congress as a whole when he wrote to General Gates on March 13, 1783:

> These preliminaries contain everything we ought to wish. The Boundaries are eligible as we have the complete Navigation of the Lakes and that of the Mississippi, our Lines running thro' those Waters. Our Fisheries were secured in the most ample manner. There were some Articles which were inserted to save british Pride wherein it is agreed that Congress shall *earnestly recommend* to the States a Restoration of Property to those Loyalists who have not taken up Arms. But the States will be left of course to their own Way of thinking as to Compliance with this recommendation. . . .[1]

James Madison, always reserved in his judgments, thought that the treaty "appeared to Congress on the whole extremely liberal." President Elias Boudinot allowed himself a moment of exultation in a letter to James Searle: "The Contemplation of this Epoche, almost overcomes me at times. It opens a new scene to Mankind, and I believe is big with inconceivable Effects in the political and I hope in the moral world."[2]

Even the New Englanders, notoriously hard as they were to please, had no complaints about the securing of their local interests by way of Newfoundland fishing rights. All members of Congress seem to have understood that the American commissioners had to make a concession in the article recommending the revision of state confiscation laws. As William Floyd of New York saw it, the British ministers wished to be able to assure the Tories "that they had attended to their Interest as far as Lay in their power." For every delegate realized that any serious attempt to restore this property would be out of the question.

343

Far from thinking that the United States had received a poor bargain, the members of Congress felt on the contrary that the country had taken an unfair advantage of its French allies. After all, Congress had affirmed again and again that it would "undertake nothing in the negotiations for peace or truce without their consent or concurrence." Congress had put itself on record against any efforts to drive a wedge between France and America. Yet in spite of such protestations the American commissioners had signed a treaty with the common enemy after entering into separate and secret negotiations. One of the articles, in fact, consisted of a secret provision concerning West Florida which neither France nor Spain could be expected to endorse.

John Jay and John Adams, as it proved, had suspected France of a disposition to favor her Spanish allies at American expense. Dr. Franklin, though he differed with them, had little choice but to concur. The old philosopher had been so bold in his preliminary talks with Oswald as to suggest that Canada ought to be ceded to the United States in reparation for British war crimes, as represented by the employment of Indians and the burning of American towns. This proposal was too audacious for Jay and Adams, and the latter wrote that "Franklin's cunning will be used to divide us; to this end he will provoke, he will insinuate, he will intrigue, he will manoeuvre."

Franklin signed along with his younger colleagues on November 30th, and afterwards he had the delicate task not only of explaining to Vergennes but also of asking for more money. Needless to add, the greatest diplomat of American history succeeded in both assignments. Vergennes administered a courteous rebuke for the record. Franklin countered with his most exquisite subtlety; and an additional six million livres were made available to the United States. The first six hundred thousand left on the ship which brought the provisional treaty, and the balance was to be paid quarterly in 1783.

The commissioners had of course violated the instructions of Congress. And even though allowances had to be made for time and distance, Madison expressed the misgivings which occurred to other members. He and his friend Randolph corresponded in a cipher (which both fondly imagined to be impenetrable, perhaps because it gave them so much trouble to transcribe) as represented by the italicized words in this letter of March 18th:

> The *dilemma to which Congress are* reduced is *infinitely perplexing. If they abet the proceedings of their Ministers, all* confidence *with France is at an end* which in the event of *a renewal of the war, must be dreadful* as in that *of peace it may* be *dishonorable. If they* [dis]*avow the conduct of their Ministers,* by *their* usual *frankness of communication,* the most serious *inconveniences* also *present* themselves. The torment of this *dilemma cannot be*

justly conveyed without a fuller recital of facts than is permitted. I wish you not to hazard even an interlined decypherment of those which I have deposited in your confidence.[3]

Madison shrewdly conjectured that

in this business Jay has taken the lead & proceeded to a length of which you can form little idea. Adams has followed with cordiality. Franklin has been dragged into it.

There is little evidence of alarm in Congress over the provision which validated American debts with British merchants incurred before 1775. But Madison's notes of debates make it plain that the peace commissioners came in for some harsh words on the floor of Congress. John Francis Mercer of Virginia "gave it as his clear & decided opinion that the Ministers have insulted Congress. . . . He felt inexpressible indignation at their meanly stooping, as it were to lick the dust from the feet of a nation whose hands were still dyed with the blood of their fellow citizens." Alexander Hamilton of New York "urged the propriety of proceeding with coolness and circumspection. He thought it proper in order to form a right judgment of the conduct of our Ministers, that the views of the French & British Courts should be examined." [4]

The delegates knew that in the end they would have to uphold their commissioners with every outward show of approval. Even so, nearly a month passed after the receipt of the provisional treaty before Congress proclaimed a cessation of arms on April 11th. And on Tuesday, the 15th, it was unanimously resolved "that the said articles be ratified and that a ratification in due form be sent to our Ministers Plenipotentiary at the Court of Versailles. . . ." [5]

Some humble pie had to be eaten by Congress before that body could congratulate itself on the new financial sustenance from France. "Our people certainly ought to do more for themselves," declared Dr. Franklin in a letter accompanying the first installment of the six million livres. "It is absurd the pretending to be lovers of liberty while they grudge paying for the defence of it." He added that Europeans were surprised because the states did not meet their quotas and would not consent to such a reasonable duty as the 5 per cent impost. "The knowledge of these things has hurt our credit and the loan in Holland. . . . The foundation for credit abroad should be laid at home. . . ." [6]

Luzerne did not let the occasion pass without getting in a dig. On March 15th he gave it as his opinion to Robert Morris that "the affairs of your finances, far from being bettered since the month of September . . . have on the contrary gone backward; so that I perceive no certainty of the reimbursement of the sums formerly lent, or of those which are now so. . . . I am commanded to inform you, in the most positive terms, that it will be impossible for the king, in any case whatever, to obtain new advances for Congress for the next year." [7]

It had not been long since a committee appointed to confer with the superintendent of finance reported (January 10th) that "he has been under the necessity of drawing bills to an amount beyond the known funds procured in Europe. . . . That the loans come in so slow that he cannot comply with his contracts and obligations nor provide for the maintenance of the army without continuing to draw." [8] Congress decided unanimously to keep this information a secret. With the same secrecy and unanimity it was resolved "that the superintendent of finance be and he hereby is authorized to draw bills of exchange from time to time, according to his discretion upon the credit of the loans which the ministers of the United States have been instructed to procure in Europe, for such sums, not exceeding the amount of the money directed to be borrowed, as the publick service may require."

Two weeks later Congress agreed to a contract between France and the United States which put the amount of the debt at eighteen million livres. Beginning the third year after peace, twelve annual installments of one and a half millions were to be paid; and his Most Christian Majesty made a gift of all arrears of interest at 5 per cent to the date of the treaty.

On January 29th the assembly resolved itself into a committee of the whole "to consider of the most effectual means of restoring and supporting public credit." It had recently occurred to Pennsylvania to pay United States creditors out of state funds collected for the quotas. Such a scheme, if adopted by other states, threatened to dry up the trickle of funds received from the quotas. Congress sent a plain-spoken remonstrance with the advice that Pennsylvania would do better to pay her quotas in full and on time.

After wrestling a few more days with financial problems, the committee of the whole turned them over to a smaller committee made up of Alexander Hamilton of New York, James Madison of Virginia, Nathaniel Gorham of Massachusetts, John Rutledge of South Carolina, and Thomas FitzSimons of Pennsylvania. News from the prolonged discussions must have leaked out occasionally, for Stephen Higginson of Massachusetts wrote in a letter of April 7th:

> We are still hammering on a strange, though artful, plan of finance, in which are combined a heterogeneous mixture of imperceptible and visible, constitutional and unconstitutional taxes. It contains the impost, quotas, and cessions of Western lands, and no part of it is to be binding unless the whole is adopted by all the States. The connection and dependence of one part on

another is designed to produce the adoption of the whole. The cessions are to serve as sweeteners to those who oppose the impost; the impost is intended to make the quotas more palatable to some States; and the receiving it in whole is made necessary to secure the adoption of the whole, by working on the fears of those States who wish to reject a part of it only. . . .[9]

The four best financial minds of the country had been at work more than a month on this scheme—Hamilton and Madison conferring with Robert Morris and his assistant Gouverneur Morris. The cynic and gallant of 1779 had lost a leg the following year from an infection which set in after a carriage accident. But the handicap of a stout oaken peg did not crush the spirit of a man who could say, "The art of living consists, I think, in some degree in knowing how to be cheated." While first learning to hobble around, after months in bed, Gouverneur Morris put out an elaborate report on American finances, suggesting for the first time the decimal system and the terms "dollar" and "cent."

The plan which Higginson thought so wonderful was adopted by Congress on April 18th, but with a weakening of the clause providing that all or none of the provisions must be accepted. "As it stands, it will answer the purposes intended," commented Dr. Jones in faint praise, "if the States will grant their concurrence."

Every requisition had found several states complaining that they were being asked for more than their share. To meet this situation, Congress had already (February 17th) urged the states to make a survey of lands, buildings, and number of inhabitants before March 1, 1784. Again in the plan of April 18th the states were requested to take a census, so that their contributions should be "in proportion to the whole number of white and other free citizens and inhabitants, of every age, sex and condition, including those bound to servitude for a term of years, and three fifths of all other persons comprehended in the foregoing description, except Indians, not paying taxes."

Of late the assembly had not been placing as much reliance on addresses and circular letters, since the states had demonstrated that they could ignore the most stirring appeals. But with no funds for discharging an unpaid army, Congress asked Madison, Hamilton and Ellsworth to prepare an address, approved on April 26th. The first two pages, as published in the *Journals*, give a clear and straightforward summary of American finances at the end of the war. The total debt of the United States amounted to $43,000,000, and the annual interest to $2,415,956. The impost would bring in an estimated annual income of $916,000, if passed by the states, and they were asked to tax themselves to pay the balance of the interest. "For the discharge of the principal . . . we rely on the natural increase of the revenues from commerce, from requisitions to be made . . . and on the prospect of vacant territory." Madison, who wrote most of the address, was not given to rhetorical flights; but he ended with an earnestness more convincing than the most glittering phrases:

> The plan thus communicated and explained by Congress, must now receive its fate from their constituents. . . . No instance has heretofore occurred, nor can any instance be expected hereafter to occur, in which the unadulterated forms of republican government can pretend to so fair an opportunity of justifying themselves by their fruits. In this view the citizens of the United States are responsible for the greatest trust ever confided to a political society.[10]

On May 9th, at the request of the assembly, President Boudinot informed the states "that it is the earnest desire of Congress that such of the legislatures as are neither sitting, nor about to sit in a short time, may be convened with all possible expedition."

Three months' pay for the army, urged by Washington as a necessary minimum, amounted to about $750,000; but the superintendent of finance told Congress bluntly that he saw no prospects for raising such a sum. In January he had given notice of his resignation unless some means of raising revenues could be put into effect before the end of May. Robert Morris was never in his life able to resist a speculation, and there were occasions when he did not stop short of profiteering. But whatever the Philadelphia merchant took with his left hand, he gave back tenfold with his right; and in the spring of 1783 he was personally answerable for about half a million dollars.

Bitter as the outlook might be, James Madison had not lost hope. "The sweets of peace begin to be amply enjoyed notwithstanding its delay," he wrote to Edmund Randolph on May 13th. "All foreign commodities have fallen to a price, almost below example, whilst the produce of the Country has proportionally risen beyond former prices. Salt is already down at 1/4 D'r per bushel and wheat up at 8/ per do."[11]

There could be no question that the average American citizen was better off than he had been at any time in the past few years. This state of affairs only added to the discontent of the unpaid soldiers, and Richard Peters wrote to General Steuben on April 13th: "The difficulty which heretofore oppressed us was how to raise an army. The one which now embarrasses us is how to dissolve it. Everything Congress can do for the Satisfaction of our deserving Soldiers will be done. But an empty Purse is a Bar to the Execution of the best Intentions." Here the Pennsylvania lawyer must have indulged in a wry chuckle as he added, "We have just under Consideration a Plan for establishing a Mint. All we want to put it into Execution is the *necessary Metal.*"[12]

The officers, with General Alexander McDougall as spokesman, had presented an urgent memorial to Congress. Their grievances, it was declared, "were verging to that state which we are told will make a wise man mad." There were indications, however, that observant Americans had ceased to blame Congress blindly. McDougall, who had just been elected as a delegate himself but declined, asserted that "the most intelligent and considerate part of the army were deeply affected by the debility and defects in the federal Government, and the unwillingness of the States to cement and invigorate it."

Although Dr. Burke died this year, his state had a worthy successor in Hugh Williamson, educated at Edinburgh and Utrecht, who had practiced medicine in Philadelphia before settling in North Carolina to become surgeon general of the militia. In a letter of February 17th he wrote from the viewpoint of a congressman unable to offer the soldiers anything except sympathy:

> The framers of our Confederation, with reverence be it said, were not infallible. . . . We borrow money, and have not the means of paying sixpence. There is no measure, however wise and necessary, that may not be defeated by any single State, however small or wrong-headed. The cloud of public creditors, including the army, are gathering about us; the prospect thickens. Believe me, that I would rather take the field in the hardest military service I ever saw, than face the difficulties which await us in Congress within a few months.[13]

Only General Washington's great personal influence brought the army through the crisis of the so-called Newburgh Addresses. An anonymous agitator twice urged the officers, then stationed at Newburgh on the Hudson, to revolt against "a country that tramples on your rights, disdains your cries, and insults your distresses." Both Washington and Congress came under the lash of a writer (supposed to have been Major John Armstrong, Jr.) with a gift for sarcasm and invective. "Can you then consent to be the only sufferers by this revolution," the officers were asked, "and retiring from the field, grow old in poverty, wretchedness and contempt?. . . Attend to your situation and redress yourselves. If the present moment be lost, every future effort is in vain; and your threats then, will be as empty as your entreaties now."[14]

After hearing the address of Washington on March 15th, the officers called a meeting, presided over by General Gates. By a unanimous resolution they rejected "with disdain, the infamous propositions contained in a late anonymous address."

The news of the provisional treaty with Great Britain, a few days later, offered at least the hope of resuming civil life. The old controversial issue of half pay for officers came up again, and after several false starts Congress resolved on March 22nd to commute half pay for life into full pay for five years—a change more to the satisfaction of the officers. But as the time approached for disbanding the army, President Boudinot could only call upon the states "in the most earnest manner to make every effort in their power to forward the collection of taxes." There was as usual no response worth mentioning; and on May 2nd, despite the admonitions of Luzerne, it was resolved to beseech his Most Christian Majesty to add three million livres to the amount granted for 1783.

It occurred to several cautious members meanwhile that perfidious Albion might attack a defenseless America in spite of the provisional treaty. Instead of discharging the soldiers, Congress decided to furlough them with notes for three months' pay and the promise of their discharge as soon as the definitive treaty of peace should be signed. But owing to the delay in forwarding the notes, Washington reported on June 24th that most of the men had left camp "with perfect good humor but without the settlement of their Accounts or a farthing of money in their pockets."

Never in history has an army deserved more or received less. For events had already justified the plaint of the officers in their memorial that "shadows have been offered to us while the substance has been gleaned by others."

Unkind things were so often said about Congress that it must have been flattering when several towns suddenly aspired to play host. Maryland showed a modern spirit by offering the State House at Annapolis, plus a "mansion house" as the president's residence, and a subsidy of £30,000 for the building of new inns and public offices. Another offer, according to a letter of June 4th by Oliver Ellsworth, "had before been made by the State of New York of the town of Kingston. Which, or whether either of them, will be accepted is uncertain; tho' it is generally agreed that Congress should remove to a place of less expense, less avocation and less influence than are to be expected in a commercial and opulent city." [15]

The Virginia delegates reported to Governor Benjamin Harrison "that a more Central Situation for Congress, accompanied with other equal or Superior advantages might possibly be more agreeable" than the New York proposition. They suggested "that an Offer of a Small tract of Territory by Virginia and Maryland in the Neighborhood of Georgetown or Potowmack might meet with the Acceptance of Congress in Preference to that offered by New York. . . ." [16]

This is the first mention of the site which became known as the District of Columbia, though a great many political deals would have to be made before the idea burgeoned into a fact. The possibility of leaving Philadelphia had been suggested in Congress from time to time for several years; but on a June afternoon in 1783 the delegates were shocked into an indignant departure. This experience was described by Benjamin Hawkins of North Carolina in a letter of June 24th, written three days after the event:

> On Saturday about 12 O'clock two hundred and eighty armed Soldiers led by Serjeants marched to and surrounded the State house. . . . They sent in a very indecent letter . . . demanding an answer in fifteen minutes, or they would let in an enraged Soldiery on them. About three o'clock the members of Congress returned to their respective Houses without meeting any personal insult, and in a short time the Soldiers returned to the Barracks. Congress have expressed their sense of this mutiny and insult, to the Executive [Council of Pennsylvania] who are either too timid or indecisive to quell the mutiny and bring the heads of the mutineers to punishment. . . .[17]

The soldiers who bore the brunt of the war had already gone home in an orderly manner. Washington declared that the Pennsylvania mutineers were "Recruits and Soldiers of a day" who had "very few hardships to complain of." John Montgomery, a Pennsylvania delegate, described them as "the off-scourings and filth of the earth," adding that few had been in the service longer than five months.

The trouble began on June 19th. Word came to John Dickinson, president of the Pennsylvania Executive Council, that eighty soldiers from a Lancaster regiment had set out for Philadelphia "to obtain justice," though their accounts were being settled. Congress appointed a committee consisting of Alexander Hamilton, Oliver Ellsworth and Richard Peters to confer with the state authorities. Little anxiety was felt, however, even when the troops reached the city on Saturday morning, the 21st, and took possession of barracks occupied by several hundred other discontented soldiers.

Congress had adjourned as usual until Monday when the situation grew so alarming that President Boudinot called the members together at noon. Dickinson decided that he could not rely on the temper of the militia to put down the disturbance. Another Pennsylvanian, General Arthur St. Clair, tried without success to persuade the soldiers to disperse after several hundred gathered outside the State House with muskets and fixed bayonets. A message to Congress from the mutineers demanded authority to appoint their own officers "or otherwise we shall instantly let in those injured soldiers upon you, and abide by the consequences. You have only twenty minutes to deliberate on this important matter."

James Madison recorded in his notes the agreement of the delegates that "Congs. shd. remain till the usual hour of adjournment, but without taking any step in relation to the alleged grievances of the Soldiers, or any other business whatever. In the meantime the Soldiers remained in this position, without offering any violence, individuals only occasionally uttering offensive words and wantonly pointing their Muskets to the Windows of the Hall of Congress. No danger from premeditated violence was apprehended. But it was observed that spiritous drink from the tippling houses adjoining began to be liberally served out to the Soldiers, and might lead to hasty excesses. None were committed however, and about 3 O'C., the usual hour Cong. adjourned; the Soldiers, tho in some instances offering a mock obstruction, permitting the members to pass thro their ranks. They soon afterwards retired themselves to the Barracks." [18]

Dickinson found himself in a most unhappy position. He appears to have had good reasons for not relying on the militia, but his old associates in Congress charged his hesitation to a politician's fear of offending constituents. "The conduct of this state was to the last degree weak and disgusting," Hamilton reported to Governor Clinton. "In short they pretended it was out of their power to bring out the militia, without making the experiment." [19]

President Boudinot sent an express, written an hour after the adjournment, to General Washington. The mutineers, he declared, "have secured the public Magazine, and I am [of] opinion that the worst is not yet come. . . . It is therefore the wish of the Members who were assembled, that your Excellency would direct a movement of some of your best troops . . . towards this City; as it will be of the most dangerous consequence, if a measure of this kind is to be put up with, and no one can tell where it will end." [20]

Congress met again in the State House that Saturday evening at the risk of becoming involved in a riot. The committee was directed, according to Madison's notes, "to confer anew with the Executive of the State and in case no satisfactory grounds shd. appear for expecting prompt and adequate exertions for suppressing the mutiny & supporting the public authority, authorizing the President . . . to summon the members to meet at Trenton or Princeton in New Jersey."

Again Dickinson had little choice but to express his doubts of the Pennsylvania militia's dependability. The tense situation, Madison related lasted two more days:

> Reports from the Barracks were in constant vibration. At one moment the Mutineers were penitent & preparing submission; the next they were meditating more violent measures. Sometimes the bank was their object; then the seizure of the members of Congress with whom they imagined an indemnity for their offence might be stipulated. On Tuesday after 2 O'Clock, the efforts of the State authority being despaired of, & the reports from the Barracks

being unfavorable, the Committee advised the President to summon Congress to meet at Princeton, which he did verbally as to the members present, leaving behind him a general Proclamation for the Press.

The trouble was settled a week before the troops reached Philadelphia. Most of the mutineers laid down their arms on Wednesday, the 25th, after naming a captain and lieutenant as ringleaders. These officers cheated the hangman by hiding away in a ship crossing the Atlantic, and Congress pardoned several sergeants.

After the departure of Congress the burghers of the city sighed whenever they thought of the thousands of dollars which would no longer be spent every month. Overtures were made to the assembly by such Philadelphians as Benjamin Rush, but a majority of the delegates agreed with Theodorick Bland. It infuriated the Virginia member when he "considered what pernicious Instruments Congress might have been made in the hands of a Lawless band of Armed Desperado's, and what fatal consequences might have ensued to the Union in General, had they remained Impotent and Passive Spectators of the most outrageous Insult to the Government. . . ." [21]

The college buildings were offered to Congress, but Eleazer McComb of Delaware held that "this town is too small for our accomodation." Madison and his Virginia colleague Dr. Jones grumbled about the necessity of sharing a bed in a room just ten feet square. And though John Montgomery could look on the bright side as usual, it may be suspected that his vision was not too penetrating. "Congrass has been well Received at this Pleace," he wrote to Benjamin Rush on June 27th, "and Evry Exertion made by the good Pepole for thire Comfortable accomodation the Inhabitants presented a Polite address to Congrass and Evry mark of respect has been paid to us." But even the gladsome Pennsylvania farmer had to admit a month later in a letter to William Irvine that "we have Done Little Bussiness since we Came to this place haveing Offen but Six states represented and indeed we Can do but little at such a Distance from the Publick offices they being all at Philad'a and will Continue thire." [22]

Not until July 29th were nine states represented so that Congress could ratify the treaty with Sweden which had come up for discussion before the departure from Philadelphia. That same week the assembly invited General Washington to visit Princeton for conferences toward "the formation of a peace establishment." This term, according to Madison, referred to "a system for foreign affairs, for Indian affairs, for military and naval peace establishments; and also to carry into execution the regulation of weights and measures and other Articles of the Confederation not attended to during the war." With more sincerity than is customary, Congress had just "ordered that an equestrian Statue of George Washington be made by the best artist in Europe . . . and erected at the Place where the Residence of Congress shall be established. . . . Pennsylvania and especially Philadelphia are now exceedingly anxious for the Return of Congress to that city," continued Ezra L'Hommedieu of New York in a letter of August 15th. "'Tis no wonder; they now see that it makes an Add'n of 100,000 Dollars at least to the State P. Annum." [23]

A petition with the signatures of 873 Philadelphians failed to melt the hearts of delegates from other states, for on August 14th Congress decided by a vote of 8 to 2 not to return to its old residence. Benjamin Rush, convinced that the grapes were sour, asserted that "the Congress is abused, laughed at and cursed in every company." Richard Peters, another loyal Pennsylvanian, expressed his opinion by resigning from the assembly. "I am much the happiest," he wrote, "when I hear or think nothing of that erratic meteor which arose with so much splendor and I fear will set with no small disgrace." [24]

Congress returned again and again to the subject during its four months in Princeton. For the angry departure from Philadelphia had matured into a conviction that the United States ought to have a seat of government with its own domain and jurisdiction. Barring the disgruntled Pennsylvanians, there were few delegates with souls so dead that they could not picture an empty tract filling with noble buildings and stately avenues. It was even suggested that Congress should move as far west at Fort Pitt (Pittsburgh) to show its faith in the future of the vast region across the mountains. Most of the members found this suggestion too drastic; but on October 7th, after much discussion, it was resolved "that Buildings for the use of Congress be erected on or near the banks of the Delaware, provided a suitable district can be found . . . for a federal town." [25]

Lest the southern states should feel neglected, Congress further resolved ten days later

> that the providing buildings for the alternate residence of Congress in two places, will be productive of the most salutary effects, by securing the mutual confidence and affections of the States, and preserving the federal balance of power:
>
> It is therefore, Resolved, That buildings be likewise erected for the use of Congress, at or near the lower falls of Potomac or Georgetown; provided a suitable district on the banks of the river can be procured for a federal town. . . . [26]

Even the most enthusiastic dreamers had to admit that some time must elapse before Congress could move into its splendid new marble halls. As a provision for the immediate future, however, the assembly showed the same large and impartial spirit by deciding on October 21st "that until the buildings to be erected on the banks of the Delaware and Potomac shall be prepared for the reception of Congress, their residence shall be alternately at equal periods, of not more than one year, and not less than six months, in Trenton and Annapolis; and the President is hereby authorized and directed to adjourn Congress on the 12th day of November next, to meet at Annapolis on the twenty-sixth day of the same month. . . ." [27]

The Massachusetts delegates, reporting to their state assembly, explained that a single federal town would "soon subject us to an oligarchy or aristocracy; but an alternate residence, in two places, has an evident tendency to prevent such Influence." President Boudinot, on the other hand, found it deplorable that "we are in future wandering Stars and to have our Aphelion and Perihelion. I augur great evil from the measure and cannot help thinking of Rome and Constantinople." [27]

The resolutions envisioning new seats of government were passed while Congress struggled with the problems of arranging a formal reception for the new Dutch minister at Princeton. The fact that the United States had no minister of foreign affairs added to the difficulties; for Robert R. Livingston had resigned at the end of 1782, largely because of the inadequacy of the salary. At the request of Congress he continued in office until June, whereupon Secretary Thomson took over the duties as best he could. Politics delayed the choice of a successor until 1784, when John Jay was elected to begin his service early the following year.

In January the assembly had ratified the treaty of amity and commerce which John Adams negotiated with the States-General of the Netherlands. The first week of October brought word that the new minister, Peter John van Berckel, had arrived in Philadelphia. "Congress," complained Madison, "are in a charming situation to receive him in an obscure village . . . and without even a Minister of F[oreign] A[ffairs]." The superintendent of finance was hastily summoned from Philadelphia to fill this gap, but there remained the problem of translating the Low Dutch of the credentials. Someone recalled that the recently elected New Jersey member, Frederick Frelinghuysen, could read the language; and Mynheer van Berckel finally had a reception which pleased neither him nor his hosts.

Thomas FitzSimons of Pennsylvania, in a letter of November 6th to Richard Peters, disclosed that the visitor had been "not a little disappointed at his Reception. he told me very politely that the States of Holland, to do honor to their 1st Embassy to the United States had sent their Minister with a Respectable fleet, that when Mr. Adams arrived in Holland the states sent a person to receive him and provide a proper place for his reception.

. . . he appears to be a very Genteel Sensible man Speaks English well, and to have felt Exceedingly What I Imagine he thinks the Neglect that he had been treated with." [28]

Long after this embarrassment had been forgotten, the delegates would remember their two receptions in 1783 for the leader whose statue had already been ordered. George Washington somehow had the quality of endowing even an informal affair with the dignity of a state occasion. On August 26th Congress gave him an audience and congratulatory address at Princeton, and in a letter of September 9th David Howell described a dinner attended by the delegates: "The tables were spread under a marquis, or tent taken from the British. The repast was elegant but the General's company crowned the whole. . . . I observed with much pleasure that the General's front was uncommonly open and pleasant, the contracted, pensive phiz betokening deep thought and much care . . . is done away, and a pleasant smile and a sparkling vivacity of wit and humor, succeeds." [29]

The Rhode Island delegate, who remains unique in finding Washington sparkling, recorded that President Boudinot and the French minister were seated on either side of him. He did not mention the shabby figure invited by the commander in chief as his personal guest—Thomas Paine, who had published twelve *Crisis* papers during the war. This was Washington's way of showing his approval of a needy patriot; for Paine had written President Boudinot that summer, asking for employment. Many of the members of Congress privately considered the pamphleteer on a social level with hostlers, and it is not likely that the Virginia aristocrat had a much better opinion. But he had an unyielding sense of justice; and it was due to his championing that bequests from New York, Pennsylvania and Congress freed Tom Paine from financial worries.

Since 1781 Washington had been the foremost advocate of more authority for Congress. "No man in the United States is, or can be, more deeply impressed with the necessity of a reform in our present Confederation, than myself," he wrote to Hamilton on March 31, 1783; "no man, perhaps, has felt the bad effects of it more sensibly; for, to the defects thereof, and the want of powers in Congress, may justly be ascribed the prolongation of the war, and consequently, the expenses occasioned by it." [30]

In a generation of great political minds, Washington stands out because of a practical intellect which gained rather than suffered from his lack of scholarship. His thoughts were original and intuitive, uncomplicated by the tenets of other minds and other ages. Thus at a time when most American leaders blamed the failure of the requisition system on the sacrifices it demanded, Washington could hold a contrary opinion in a letter to Joseph Reed of July 4, 1780:

> When any great object is in view, the popular mind is roused into expectation, and prepared to make sacrifices both of ease and property. If those, to whom they confide the management of their affairs, do not call them to make these sacrifices, and the object is not attained, or they are involved in the reproach of not having contributed as much as they ought to have done towards it, they will be mortified at the disappointment, they will feel the censure, and their resentment will rise against those, who, with sufficient authority, have omitted to do what their interest and their honor required. Extensive powers not exercised as far as was necessary have, I believe, scarcely ever failed to ruin the possessor.[31]

The difficulty which popular opinion has always felt in understanding and "humanizing" Washington may be due to the fact that he occupies a lonely position as one of the world's greatest political thinkers. Although the rule of the majority could not always have been to his personal taste, neither Jefferson nor Jackson nor Lincoln ever got closer to the heartbeat of popular government than Washington in the words already quoted on the title page of this section:

"Democratical States must always *feel* before they can *see:*—it is this which makes their governments slow—but the people will be right at last."[32]

It is one of the wonders of history that such a man, so little endowed with the traits which win popularity, should have been idolized in his own generation. The *Journals* do not record any important resolutions being passed as a result of the Princeton conferences, but policies were shaped for the future. A few months later, after word had been received of the signing of the definitive treaty of peace on September 3rd, the last meeting between Washington and the Continental Congress took place at Annapolis.

After electing Thomas Mifflin, the belligerent Quaker, as its new president the first week of November, the assembly adjourned at Princeton to meet at the Maryland capital on the 26th. As usual, the members straggled in belatedly, and on December 23rd there were still not nine states to ratify the peace with Britain when Washington had his final audience. The senate chamber of the Maryland State House had a fireplace on one side and a gallery in the rear. President Mifflin presided from the dais in front, and Washington stood beside the desk of Secretary Thomson to read his farewell address. Of all the delegates listening, only Mifflin and possibly Thomas Jefferson had been present on that June day in 1775 when the Continental Congress elected Washington to the command he was resigning eight and a half years later. They must have recalled that although the Virginian had not solicited the honor, he had used the power of suggestion by wearing his uniform while attending as a delegate. It might also have been recollected that the Congress of 1775 deserved more credit for politics than for prophecy.

James McHenry, a young Maryland delegate, wrote that evening to his sweetheart, Margaret Caldwell: "Today my love the General at a public audience made a deposit of his commission and in a very pathetic manner took leave of Congress. It was a solemn and affecting spectacle; such an one as history does not present. The spectators all wept, and there was hardly a member of Congress who did not shed tears. The General's hand which held the address shook as he read it." [33]

Congress, of course, could not let such an occasion pass without an "elegant public dinner" at which were heard the customary thirteen toasts and thirteen salutes from the cannon. New England and Sam Adams must have seemed far away that evening when the delegates enjoyed themselves at a grand ball given by Governor William Paca in the State House. The following April, when the bill was presented for the dinner, the assembly voted a payment of $654 75/90 to George Mann, tavernkeeper of Annapolis. A committee explained "that the entertainment was given to a numerous assemblage of guests, was exceedingly plentiful, and the provisions and liquors good in their kind." But Congress had these words stricken from the record, since it is just as well for the constituents not to know too much.

Chapter 24

The Winning of the West

NOT much more than a village in size, Annapolis had the atmosphere of a capital. Here for the first time the Continental Congress did not consider it needful to frown upon such worldly diversions as horse racing, dancing and the theater.

The war having ended, delegates no longer had to set an example of the sterner virtues. "Eight of us lodge in one house," wrote Samuel Dick of New Jersey to a friend on March 18, 1784, "and our Time at home is Spent agreeably enough whilst the polite Attention of the Gentlemen of the Town engages all our leisure hours in Visits and Amusements. The Players Exhibit twice a week and there is a Brilliant Assembly or Ball once a fortnight to which we have Standing Cards of Invitation." [1]

Already a mellow old town in 1784, Annapolis had long observed city planning and zoning ordinances. The government buildings were located in State Circle, 538 feet in diameter, while the smaller Church Circle provided a setting for St. Anne's. From these hubs the narrow streets went out like crooked spokes—Prince George Street, Duke of Gloucester Street and West Street, which became the mile straightaway racetrack at the edge of town. The various sections were zoned according to residences for the gentry, shops, warehouses, and small industries such as brewing, tanning and weaving.

Although there were fewer than four hundred buildings on the peninsula between the Severn and Spa Creek, the little capital was the social center for the families of near-by country estates. No town in America could put on a more luxurious display of silks, satins, silverware, coaches, sedan chairs and liveried servants.

Roger Sherman, returning to Congress after an absence of two years, kept his puritanical ideals intact. But David Howell went so far as the confession

359

in a letter of February 21st: "Had my education in youth, or did my present taste admit of my participating in the amusements of this place such as plays, Balls, Concerts, routs, hops, Fandangoes and fox hunting, or I may add did my finances admit of mixing with the *bon-ton,* time might pass more agreeably. . . ." [2]

Elbridge Gerry, the wily Massachusetts politician, saw advantages in the fact that some of his colleagues as well as the Annapolis folk were intent on amusement. In a letter of April 21st to Samuel Holten he paid a left-handed compliment:

> You want to know how I like Annapolis. It is of all places the best for transacting publick Business, there is very little private Business in the place, and the Inhabitants are almost universally disposed to enjoy themselves. Balls, Plays, dining and Tea parties, engross the Time of the Ladies, Hunting, Fishing, Gaming, Horseracing, etc. that of the Gentlemen. those of Congress who are wholly devoted to Pleasure . . . may indulge their Inclination by being courteous and attentive to the inhabitants; those who are for dispatching the publick Business, will never be interrupted by the Citizens of Annapolis, for the Idea of Business to them is neither agreeable nor reputable. . . . [3]

More delegates of the early years were back in the assembly during the second half of 1783 or the early months of 1784: Oliver Ellsworth and Roger Sherman of Connecticut; Thomas Stone of Maryland; Francis Dana and Elbridge Gerry of Massachusetts; James Wilson and Thomas Mifflin of Pennsylvania; William Ellery of Rhode Island; Thomas Jefferson of Virginia.

A tall, serious young Virginia member named James Monroe had been but a 16-year-old student at William and Mary when the Continental Congress first met in 1774. "I am called to a theatre to which I am a perfect stranger," he wrote to Richard Henry Lee on December 16, 1783. "There are before us some questions of the utmost consequence that can arise in the councils of any nation." After listing these issues at formidable length, the newcomer ended in a respectful tone: "It is my desire to hear from you as frequently as possible, and upon these subjects before us. . . ." [4]

The new Maryland delegate, Dr. James McHenry, who had studied under Benjamin Rush and served as a surgeon in the war, upheld the assembly's tradition of spunky physicians. Madison and Hamilton had done a great deal to increase the prestige of Congress among the young men of the country. Either could be a sharp critic on occasion, but both were quick to defend Congress against the senseless and unthinking abuse which must be endured by every parliament. Madison, writing to Governor Benjamin Harrison, declared at a gloomy moment of 1783: "Your Excellency will readily conceive the dilemma in which Congress are placed, pressed on one side by justice, humanity and the public good to fulfill engagements to which their funds are incompetent, and on the other left without even the resource of answering that everything which could have been done has been done." [5]

This same year Alexander Hamilton wrote his *Vindication of Congress*. The following paragraphs are part of the fragment preserved of one of the first pamphlets to urge the necessity for a new constitution:

It is therefore painful to hear, as is too fashionable a practice, indiscriminate censure heaped upon Congress for every public failure and misfortune, without considering the entire disproportion between the means which that body have it in their power to employ, and their responsibility. . . . The good deeds of Congress die, or go off the stage with the individuals who are the authors of them, but their mistakes are the inheritance of those who succeed. . . .
Congress stand in a very delicate and embarrassing situation. On the one hand, they are blamed for not doing what they have no means of doing; on the other their attempts are branded with the imputations of a spirit of encroachment, and a lust of power. In these circumstances, it is the duty of all those who have the welfare of the community at heart, to unite their efforts to direct the attention of the people to the true source of the public disorders— the want of an EFFICIENT GENERAL GOVERNMENT—and to impress upon them this conviction, that these States, to be happy, must have a stronger bond of UNION, and a CONFEDERATION capable of drawing forth the resources of the country. [6]

Youth was not held against a man in the prevailingly middle-aged Continental Congress. James Monroe, Alexander Hamilton, Edward Rutledge, Gouverneur Morris and Francis Kinloch all took their seats before celebrating their twenty-sixth birthdays. James Madison, Edmund Randolph, James McHenry, Charles Pinckney and Rufus King were not yet thirty.

There is no evidence that any of the newcomers were patronized on the grounds of immaturity. At the other extreme, the founding fathers did not believe that a man was ready for the scrapheap when he passed his physical prime. Benjamin Franklin and Stephen Hopkins, the patriarchs of the assembly, demonstrated what could be accomplished by members elected when they were nearly seventy.

Young Monroe knew a rising star when he saw one. He hitched his wagon to the political genius of his colleague Thomas Jefferson, back in Congress after an interlude of seven years as a leader in his own state. The two took their meals together and served on some of the year's most important committees.

After eight months of rebuffs or neglect, it could no longer be hoped that the states would accept as a whole the "artful" financial plan of April 18, 1783, drawn up by Hamilton and Madison with a view to gaining a wholesale approval of the impost, western land cessions and a revised quota system. Neither of the authors served in Congress during 1784; and Jefferson recognized that the components of the plan must be salvaged piecemeal, if at all.

It goes without saying that the new year found Congress in a desperate financial situation. This had long been the normal state of affairs, for the end of the war had taken away the last great incentive for meeting quotas. Robert Morris presented a statement for January 1, 1784, showing the payments to that date on the requisition of October 30, 1781, for eight million dollars:

	Paid	Due
New Hampshire	$ 3,000	$ 370,598
Massachusetts	247,676	1,059,919
Rhode Island	67,878	148,836
Connecticut	131,577	615,618
New York	39,064	334,533
New Jersey	102,044	383,674
Pennsylvania	346,632	774,161
Delaware	Nothing	112,085
Maryland	89,302	844,693
Virginia	115,103	1,192,490
North Carolina	Nothing	622,677
South Carolina	344,301	29,296
Georgia	Nothing	24,905
	$1,486,512	$6,513,488

These figures picture the endless crisis of Congress more forcefully than the most eloquent address to the states. Jefferson saw in the western lands the best hope of revenue, though he was vastly more interested in the political aspects of carving new states out of the wilderness. Before that issue could be tackled, however, there was the immediate problem of ratifying the definitive peace treaty. "The departure of a member two days hence leaves us with only six states and of course stops all business," Jefferson reported to Governor Benjamin Harrison on December 24, 1783. "We have no certain prospect of nine within a given time; chance may bring them in, and chance may keep them back; in the meantime only a little over two months remain for their assembling, ratifying and getting the ratification across the Atlantic to Paris. All that can be said is that it is yet possible." [7]

A group of delegates urged that seven states were sufficient, but the majority doubted the validity of such a ratification. The urgency was intensified by news from across the Atlantic that the treaty had not been well received in England. America's old friend Burke became its most bitter opponent in Commons, with the younger Pitt remaining the sole defender of ability.

The time would come when the ruling classes of England could agree with Jefferson that "the mass of mankind has not been born with saddles on their backs, nor a favored few booted and spurred, ready to ride them legitimately, by the grace of God." The American Revolution had prevailed chiefly because it represented the victory of a dynamic new social order over a dying society entrenched in the ruins of a crumbling economic system. Englishmen themselves would adopt most of the political gains of the American Revolution in the Reform Bill of 1832; but early in 1784 there were good reasons for fearing that Great Britain might disavow an unpopular treaty if the United States did not act within the period of six months specified for the exchange of ratifications.

Richard Beresford, the 28-year-old, Temple-educated lawyer representing South Carolina, became at this anxious moment the most important delegate of the Continental Congress. Lying ill in Philadelphia, he appeared to personify the difference between ratification and failure. Jefferson declared that "if Beresford will not come to Congress, Congress must go to him for this one act." But it did not prove necessary to hold a special session in the Charleston delegate's sick room. He crept wanly into Annapolis on January 14th, partially recovered, and that same day it was

> Resolved, unanimously, nine states being present, that the said definitive treaty be, and the same is hereby ratified by the United States in Congress assembled.[8]

In accordance with the terms of the treaty, Congress also "earnestly recommended" by a unanimous vote that the state legislatures restore confiscated estates to British subjects and American loyalists who had not borne arms against the United States. There were no delegates so credulous, of course, as to believe for a minute that this resolution would ever be heeded by the states.

It remained doubtful whether the American ratification could be delivered to Paris before the deadline of March 3rd. Although Congress sent three copies in the hope that one would arrive in time, the first ship ran aground and had to return to port. Several weeks went by before another sailed, but the British ministers did not object to a date of May 12th for the exchange.

From the adjournment at Princeton until March 1st there were only three January days in the entire four months when Congress had enough states on the floor to transact important business. Several disgusted delegates proposed a warning to the delinquent states that the assembly would adjourn if the plague of absenteeism continued. "Admonition after admonition has been sent to the states, to no effect," Jefferson wrote to Madison on February 20th. "We have sent one today. if it fails, it seems as well we should all retire."

On the first day of March, with nine states on the floor at last, Virginia laid her deed of cession before Congress. The cession of January, 1781, which had brought Maryland into the Confederation, met with a refusal from Congress in October because of its unsatisfactory conditions. In the autumn of 1783 the assembly specified new terms which would be acceptable, and Virginia immediately drew up a deed ceding her territory north and west of the Ohio. Thus the United States came into a wilderness empire which eventually made five new states.

Jefferson visioned ten in the year 1784 and designated their boundaries in his report. He even went so far as to name them, and the Continental Congress deserves the everlasting gratitude of posterity for rejecting such frightful fancies as Sylvania, Cherronesus, Michigania, Assenisipia, Metropotamia, Illinoia, Polypotamia and Pelisipia. Saratoga would have been endurable; but only the tenth name, Washington, found lodgment 105 years later on the other side of the continent.

A revised plan, with the boundaries and names left out, was debated on March 22nd. Jefferson led a valiant fight to have slavery prohibited after 1800 in the new states, but the proposition could not gain enough support. New York, Pennsylvania and the four New England states were in favor, with Maryland, Virginia and South Carolina opposed, North Carolina divided, and New Jersey unable to vote.

April 23rd saw the adoption of an amended act providing for temporary government in any district of the ceded territory upon the petition of the inhabitants. The district could send a delegate to Congress with the right of debating but not of voting. After a minimum of 20,000 free inhabitants had been acquired, Congress could authorize the calling of a convention to draw up a permanent constitution and government under specified conditions. And after the number of inhabitants equaled the population of the smallest of the original thirteen states, the territory could be admitted into the Confederation on equal terms.

Jefferson acted as chairman of the committee which drew up an "Ordinance for ascertaining the mode of locating and disposing of lands in the western territory." Following a first reading on May 7th, the plan met with an overwhelming defeat on the 28th, with only North Carolina voting in favor. The other states were not so much opposed as undecided, and the question of disposing of the lands had to wait nearly a year for an agreement of minds.

Negotiations with the Indians were being completed this spring, and it remained for Connecticut, Massachusetts and North Carolina to submit acceptable cessions of the lands they claimed. But the West had actually been won with the act of April 23rd; and most of the credit belonged to three Virginians who would live to become presidents of a republic which included the new states created out of the territory ceded by Virginia.

Writing in cipher, Jefferson gossiped to Madison in a letter of February 20th about a quarrelsome colleague. "Lee finding no faction among the men here," he commented with distaste, "entered into that among the women which rages to a very high degree. A ball being appointed by the one party on a certain night, he undertook to give one and fixed it precisely on the same night. This of course has placed him in the midst of the mud. He is courting Miss Sprig a young girl of seventeen and of thirty thousand pounds expectation." [9]

It may be that Jefferson did not notice the factions scheming under his nose, but even the allurements of romance and fortune could not prevent the middle-aged Arthur Lee from plotting against Robert Morris. The Virginia delegate managed to convince a small group of New Englanders, after working on their pathological fear of tyranny, that the country was in peril from an incipient oligarchy headed by the superintendent of finance.

Samuel Osgood of Massachusetts sounded the alarm in a letter of January 14th to John Adams: "Our Danger lies in this—That if permanent funds are given to Congress, the aristocratical Influence which predominates in more than a major Part of the United States, will finally establish an arbitrary government in the United States." [10]

Even a few members could wield an inordinate influence in the "thin" Congress of 1784. Concrete examples were offered by Elbridge Gerry in April, when he made a motion:

That the legislatures of the several states be informed, that whilst they are respectively represented in Congress by two delegates only, such a unanimity for conducting the most important public concerns is necessary as can rarely be expected. That if each of the thirteen states should be represented by two members, five out of the twenty-six, being only a fifth of the whole, may negative any measure requiring the voice of nine states; that of the eleven states now on the floor of Congress, nine being represented by two members from each, it is in the power of three out of twenty-five, making only one-eighth of the whole, to negative such a measure. . . . [11]

Lee and half a dozen New England members had an influence out of all proportion to their numbers. Osgood, as their spokesman, went so far as to assert that Morris was "Ambitious of becoming the first Man in the United States" but that his principles "do not comport so well with Republicanism, as Monarchy."

Whenever a faction volunteers to save the country at all costs, the perils of the country are likely to be increased. The superintendent of finance had been trying to retire for months, so that he could not have been much offended in March at plans to abolish his office and replace it with a board consisting of three commissioners of finance. Daniel of St. Thomas Jenifer, Oliver Ellsworth and William Denning were elected on June 3rd, just before Congress adjourned. All three declined the thankless position, and it took many more months to get the new board on a functioning basis.

One of the last recommendations of the outgoing superintendent of finance was a proposal of currency reforms based on the adoption of the decimal system. This measure came up before a committee headed by Jefferson, who added improvements of his own while crediting Gouverneur Morris with the original idea. Some of the difficulties which had bedeviled Americans under the old system are evident from the paper which Jefferson laid before Congress:

> The most *easy ratio* of multiplication and division, is that by ten. . . . Everyone remembers that, when learning Money-Arithmetic, he used to be puzzled with adding the farthings, taking out the fours and carrying them on; adding the pence, taking out the twelves and carrying them on; adding the shillings, taking out the twenties and carrying them on; but when he came to the pounds, where he had only tens to carry forward, it was easy and free from error. The bulk of mankind are school-boys through life. These little perplexities are always great to them. . . . If we adopt the Dollar for our unit, we should strike four coins, one of gold, two of silver, and one of copper, *viz.*:
>
> 1. A golden piece, equal to ten dollars:
> 2. The Unit or Dollar itself, of silver:
> 3. The tenth of a Dollar, of silver also:
> 4. The hundredth of a Dollar, of copper.[12]

In his old age Thomas Jefferson had every reason to congratulate himself on taking the principal part in the introduction of the decimal system. He even proposed in 1784 the ancestors of the present-day nickel, quarter, and half dollar: "Perhaps it would not be amiss to coin three more pieces of silver, one of the value of five-tenths, or half a dollar, one of the value of two-tenths, which would be equal to the Spanish pistereen, and one of the value of five coppers, which would be equal to the Spanish half-bit."

Again as in 1776, Jefferson regarded oratory as a low and time-destroying art. "Our body was little numerous," he wrote of the assembly of 1784 in his *Autobiography*, "but very contentious. Day after day was wasted on the most unimportant questions." While listening to delegates "afflicted with the morbid rage of debate," it struck the author of the Declaration "that to refute indeed was easy, but to silence was impossible." Jefferson pointed to Franklin and Washington as worthy examples: "I never heard either of them speak ten minutes at a time, nor to any but the main point, which was to decide the issue. They laid their shoulders to the great points, knowing that the little ones would follow of themselves." [13]

The harassed men who framed the Articles of Confederation had thought it a good idea to break up factions by allowing no delegate to serve more than three years out of six. In the spring of 1784 this provision was used as a weapon by every faction in Congress to get rid of troublesome opponents. David Howell, one of the last to be selected as a victim by the committee of investigation, reported on May 22nd to Governor Jabez Brown of Rhode Island: "I have been in hot water for six or seven weeks, ever since business has been taken up in earnest. Thank God, we have hitherto carried every point. I have received two written challenges to fight duels; one from Col. Mercer, of Virginia, the other from Col. Spaight, of No. Carolina. . . . I answered them that I meant to chastise any insults I might receive and laid their letters before Congress." [14]

Ephraim Paine of New York wrote to Robert R. Livingston on May 24th that he had "expected in congress to find justice sit enthroned, supported by all the virtues. Judge, then, how great was my disappointment when I found caballing, selfishness and injustice reign almost perpetually; and in place of that good order and decency which ought to preside in all public bodies, especially in that august one, tumult and disorder prevail, even to the degree of challenging, in the house." The familiar geographical lines drawn in this dispute were revealed in one of his concluding sentences: "The Southern nabobs behave as though they viewed themselves a superior order of animals when compared to those of the other end of the confederacy; this, sir, you know, does not agree with the great spirits of the Northern gentry. . . ." [15]

In a day of dueling it is remarkable that no delegate ever was killed or seriously wounded as the result of a dispute arising on the floor of Congress. Lachlan McIntosh, elected by Georgia for 1784 (he did not attend), was remembered as the slayer of Button Gwinnett, a signer of the Declaration, though their duel had nothing to do with Congress. But even at this date the northern delegates felt no shame in disdaining a challenge after making it plain that they would not hesitate to defend themselves.

Samuel Osgood had stirred up such enmity in his efforts to save the country that he became the first delegate to be actually ousted on the grounds of having served three years since March 1, 1781. The members of his faction contested the decision to no avail, and on his way home the ex-member wrote to Gerry: "Farewell all Connection with public Life. I am inexpressibly disgusted with it."

The ax fell next on the two Delaware delegates, James Tilton and Gunning Bedford, Jr. But when it came the turn of Howell and Ellery of Rhode Island, both fought back so furiously that the motion to unseat them lacked seven votes of carrying. Secretary Thomson mentioned that the debates "were conducted with a good deal of warmth." And James Monroe wrote on May 25th: "I never saw more indecent conduct in any Assembly before." [16]

Everyone soon realized that if this method of settling grudges continued, there would be too few delegates left to conclude the business of an already thin assembly. For some time it had been urged "out of doors" that both Congress and the country would gain if that body took a vacation after sitting almost continuously since Lexington. The Confederation appeared to offer a solution in Article IX, providing for a Committee of the States, limited to one delegate from each, empowered to sit during a recess of the parent body. Jefferson pleaded the necessity of preserving a "visible head" of the federal government; and late in April the delegates resolved to adjourn on June 3rd, leaving behind a Committee of the States.

During the few intervening weeks the assembly hastened to settle unfinished business. The question of a peacetime military establishment for a population of three millions was decided by the resolution of June 2nd "that the commanding officer be, and he is hereby directed to discharge the troops now in the service of the United States, except 25 privates, to guard the stores at Fort Pitt, and 55 to guard the stores of West Point and other magazines, with a proportionate number of officers; no officer to remain in service above the rank of captain, and those privates to be retained who were enlisted on the best terms." [17]

Certainly the United States of 1784 could never have been accused of harboring warlike ideas.

At least one other issue had found the delegates in harmony: they all believed that treaties of amity and commerce should be concluded with the remaining states of Europe. Terms were decided in April for such future pacts, though a year had gone by without Congress being able to agree on Robert R. Livingston's successor. The news that John Jay planned to return to America suggested an acceptable candidate, and he became the new minister of foreign affairs.

Congress passed a resolution asking that it be vested by the states with extensive powers over foreign commerce for a period of fifteen years. Franklin and John Adams obviously could not handle all the new projects in this sphere, and Thomas Jefferson was chosen on May 7th as a third minister. Thus his career in the Continental Congress ended that month, for he left immediately to take passage on one of the first ships to Europe.

Arthur Lee, Osgood and their little group had long insisted that the Chevalier de la Luzerne was implicated with Robert Morris in the suspected monarchal plot. But when the French minister announced his leave-taking in an audience of April 6th, the most effusive compliments and good wishes were exchanged on the floor of Congress. Luzerne took great pleasure in informing Congress of the arrival of the portraits of their good friends Louis XVI and Marie Antoinette, which had been requested in June, 1779. But there were no walls appropriate for the display until those splendid new marble buildings should arise from the banks of the Delaware and Potomac. Hence the canvases went into safekeeping for a year before they adorned the Council Chamber in New York. They followed the new national government to Philadelphia and Washington, then vanished without explanation to provide one of the minor mysteries of American history.

At the last moment Congress deftly dodged when New York tried to bring up that everlasting Vermont problem. This evasion caused Charles DeWitt to complain to Governor Clinton of a plot being "formed and perhaps wrought into System to take that Country from us." But Congress continued to turn its back until the adjournment of June 3rd, when it resolved to meet again at Trenton on October 30th.

The Committee of the States started bravely by holding a first meeting the very day after the parent body ceased to deliberate. Samuel Hardy of Virginia was elected chairman, then the committee itself adjourned until June 26th. "There seems to be an apprehension generally prevail'g here," wrote Francis Dana, the Massachusetts member, in a letter of the 17th, "that we shall not make up a Committee of the States. I am very indifferent about it, because I am satisfied the public Interests will receive no prejudice from the circumstance of their *not* meeting." [18]

Not until July 8th was there finally a quorum of nine members representing as many states: Chairman Hardy of Virginia; Francis Dana of Massachusetts; Jonathan Blanchard of New Hampshire; Edward Hand of Pennsylvania; Jeremiah Townley Chase of Maryland; Samuel Dick of New Jersey; Richard Dobbs Spaight of North Carolina; Jacob Read of South Carolina; William Houstoun of Georgia.

Relations were friendly enough at the outset, judging by a letter written to his wife on July 7th by Samuel Dick, the hearty New Jersey physician: "Tho' here but two days I have been Invited to three Dinners, have Eat four, and din'd with two hundred Gentlemen—On Monday with the Society of the Cincinati and the Governer of this State, and Yesterday with the Citizens of Annapolis. . . . The Committee are Quartered in two houses Except Mr. Chace who lives in town. Mr. Dana . . . from Boston, Mr. Blanchard (my former Housemate) from New Hampshire, General Hand from Pennsylvania and Myself (all in the Married Row) Lodge at Mrs. Brices—four other Gentlemen of the Com'ee being Batchelors dine together in their own Stile." [19]

The powers of the committee had been limited by Congress to routine decisions. But at the end of July the nine delegates at Annapolis had good news which cleared up a nagging anxiety of months. Francis Dana rejoiced in a letter of the 30th:

> The Committee of the States have this day received his British Majesty's Ratification of the Definitive Treaty of Peace between the United States of America, and himself, bearing date the 9th of last April; and which was exchanged for that of the United States on the 12th of May following at Passy. Thus the last hand is now put to that great and glorious Work. The Ratification will soon be published by order of the Committee of the States. [20]

This same week also brought word that the Rhode Island assembly had again rejected the impost, as proposed in the financial plan of April 18, 1783. John Montgomery, writing to Edward Hand, swore that "the Cursed State ought to be erased out of the Confederation, and I was going to say out of the earth, if any worse place could be found for them." Jacob Read's letter of July 30th to Nathanael Greene crackled with indignation: "Your State has once more damped our hopes and thrown things into Confusion, the Consequences will I fear be fatal in Europe. . . . God send some change of Sentiment may take place in your Councils! Without it were are lost." [21]

No good excuse could be found for Rhode Island in 1784. Throughout the history of the United States there has been no more troublesome question than states' rights when it serves as a Trojan horse for the forces of greed and selfish interests. Rhode Island was rebuked most convincingly by the representative of a state which would become the champion of secession three generations later. On August 13th Jacob Read of South Carolina wrote to Washington:

> Let the Blame fall where it ought, on those whose attachment to State Views, State Interests and State Prejudices is so great as to render them eternally opposed to every Measure that can be devised for the public good. The evil is not however as yet intirely incurable. I hope and trust the Next

Congress will be more wise and able to avert the Mischiefs that appear to me to threaten the Union. If that cannot be done, we must look about and see if some more efficient form of Government cannot be devised. I have long entertained my doubts of the Present form even if the States were all disposed to be honest, and I am sorry to say such a conclusion would however be against premises.[22]

Both Rhode Island and Connecticut were reproached for their failure to be represented on the Committee of the States. On August 11th Francis Dana and Jonathan Blanchard added to the guilt of New England by taking French leave after the other members refused to vote an adjournment. Dr. Dick started home soon afterwards, leaving only six members unable to do business. They stuck it out for ten more days, trying vainly to summon enough substitutes for a quorum; and then the Committee of the States disintegrated beyond repair.

Charles Thomson led the list of mourners. As early as July 23rd he masked his anxiety with a genial tone in a letter to Read, who had a reputation as a gay bachelor: "I acknowledge, my dear sir, the beauties and agreeable situation of Annapolis, and will admit that the graces and charms of its nymphs are not excelled by those of the inhabitants of Calypso's isle. . . . But these are not the objects of the patriot's pursuit. The dance, the ball, and continued round of pleasure are not the means of promoting the interests of his country. . . . I confess, therefore, I should not be sorry if some kind mentor, I care not whether in the form of a mosquito or a fever and ague were to drive you from that enchanting place into the walks of politics, and force you to turn your attention to the concerns of this young and rising empire which demands your care." By August 13th Thomson had become so worried that he sent a hasty note from his Philadelphia home to Chairman Hardy: "Can it be possible that gentlemen will take such a rash step as to dissolve the Committee and leave the United States without any head or visible Authority?"[23]

The thin, scholarly secretary must have found it painful that a dissolution instead of a celebration should mark the tenth anniversary of the Continental Congress. On September 5th a decade would have passed since half a hundred Americans from twelve colonies first met in Philadelphia with only the authority to remonstrate and petition for redress. The most fiery patriots of 1774 had not dreamed of separation and a long war aiming at a new national existence. And now that these objects had been attained, Americans were finding their responsibilities no bed of roses.

Nobody took a more protective interest in the Continental Congress than Charles Thomson, the one man who had attended practically every day's meeting of the ten years. All the records were preserved in the foolscap folio volumes of his "rough *Journals*" and afterwards rewritten in his meticulous script. It is not likely that any American of the age knew more about the delegates, and posterity is the poorer because Thomson did not write the history of the Continental Congress which he planned to the extent of hoarding material. Legend has it that after finishing his translation of the Bible he destroyed most of these papers in his declining years, leaving only his correspondence with Franklin and Jefferson plus a few other fragments.

Jacob Read poked fun at the departed New Englanders with a mock advertisement offering a reward for the two runaways, "Jonathan and Squinting Frank"—Blanchard and the recent minister to Russia, Francis Dana. But Thomson was deadly serious when he wrote to the London-educated South Carolina lawyer on September 27th, after all hope had vanished for reviving the Committee of the States: "Whatever little politicians may think, time will evince that it is of no small consequence to save appearances with foreign nations, and not to suffer the federal government to become invisible. A government without a visible head must appear a strange phenomenon to European politicians and will I fear lead them to form no very favorable opinion of our stability, wisdom or Union." [24]

The prestige of Congress itself, due to meet at Trenton on October 30th, suffered from the collapse of the Committee of the States. John Francis Mercer, the Virginia hothead, blew up with a terrific explosion: "If I do not find the ensuing Congress of a very different complexion than the last and disposed to be very decisive, I will no longer degrade the character of a human being by continuing an useless Cypher among others, who are become as contemptible to the world as they have long been to themselves." He avowed that he had left his home only because of "a desire that the State of Virginia might show her respect for the Confoederal Government, if it is not a prostitution of the name of Government to apply it to such a vagabond, strolling, contemptible Crew as Congress. . . ." [25]

As usual, that body was saved from futility by a few patient, hard-working men serving at a sacrifice. James Monroe wrote to his friend Madison from Trenton on November 7th: "We have yet only 5 States, & not a man from the Eastward except Mr. Holten, there is nothing new without doors which I have not communicated to the Governor." Again the New England states were the chief offenders, and Monroe could only inform Madison a week later that "we have no Congress nor is the prospect better than when I wrote you last." [26]

Richard Henry Lee, again representing Virginia, wrote to a friend on the 19th: "We have but Six States and a half represented. But one delegate as yet from the eastward, whence formerly proceeded the most industrious attention to public business. I do not like this lentor, this strange lassitude in those who are appointed to transact public affairs. I am here placed in the house of a Mr. Howe, where I have a good warm bedchamber, and other conveniences to my satisfaction. The Streets of the Village in this rainy season, are most disagreeably wet and muddy." [27]

At last, on the afternoon of November 29th, seven states were represented at Trenton. Only minor business could be transacted by this number, but the following day saw Richard Henry Lee elected president after a dozen ballots. The successful candidate gave attention to his wardrobe in a letter to his nephew, Thomas Shippen:

> The question for consideration is shortly this—Will the fashion permit an old grave Member of Congress to wear black breeches; it being remembered that he means to accompany the black breeches with black Silk Stockings & white Shoe and Knee buckles—if this should be answered in the affirmative (which I very much hope) the next question is, what sort of black—for black Silk Net it cannot, must not be—Remember again, that except black cloth, black plush, or too thick black Silk—any black Material that is Neat, genteel and warm, and durable will suit me here. . . .[28]

It took most of December to decide the question of a meeting place "until proper accomodations in a foederal town shall be erected." A motion to repeal the measures establishing alternate temporary residence in Annapolis and Trenton met defeat, though only the New Jersey and Rhode Island delegations voted in favor of Trenton for the coming year. Philadelphia lost by the margin of two states and would have carried the day if Maryland and Delaware had been represented. Newport received only the vote of its own state, which left New York leading the field by a process of elimination.

John Jay, serving as a New York delegate before taking up his duties as the new secretary of foreign affairs, cannily insisted that his acceptance of the office depended on Congress doing less wandering. He submitted New York City as a suitable haven for a long stay; and on December 24th all the states save Pennsylvania and Georgia agreed with him. Thus it was that Christmas Day found the delegates once more packing their saddlebags for a journey to the eighth and last dwelling place of the gadding Continental Congress.

Chapter 25

Through a Glass, Darkly

NO city of the country had suffered or gained as much from the war as New York. Partially destroyed by two fires and occupied by the enemy for seven years, it had supported several times its normal population, counting British troops and Tory refugees. Thousands of pounds in gold had been spent by the invaders, and afterwards the patriots had a revenge of wholesale confiscations. They had endured too much themselves to sense the tragedy of thousands of fellow Americans of loyalist convictions—the exiles who sailed away in 1783 to find new homes in an alien land.

America never knew a boom town which grew more lustily than this overcrowded New York of the postwar era. Several new fortunes were in process of being created for every one that had been lost. Congress had its Council Chamber in the most impressive structure of the island—the City Hall at the corner of Wall and Nassau Streets. Broadway, the busiest thoroughfare, started at the Battery and lost itself in fields and meadows about a mile northward. King's College, a three-story stone building at Church, Murray and Barclay Streets, represented culture. But the social centers of the town were the Merchants' Coffee-House at Pearl and Water Streets, and Fraunces' Tavern at the corner of Broad and Pearl.

With the exception of the Pennsylvanians, most of the delegates liked New York. William Ellery wrote to his brother on January 28th: "The gentlemen of this city take great notice of members of Congress. Their cards are as frequent as leaves, and their tables are sumptuous." David Howell, in a letter of February 9th, noted that "the expenses of living here are greater than at any other place where I have attended Congress." But he added "that eleven states are now on the floor and a great deal of harmony prevails." [1]

374

New York's new mayor was that well-known ex-member of Congress, James Duane. He formally tendered the City Hall, and in its acceptance the assembly specified that "the whole of which (except the court and jury rooms) will be necessary for the sessions of Congress." [2]

The new year began with the usual financial troubles caused by the deficiencies of the states in meeting their quotas. "The public creditors press so hard," wrote Samuel Holten plaintively on April 11th, "there is not much pleasure in being a member of Congress, unless a man can bear duning very well." The states could bear it only too well when it came to requisitions; and a new anxiety arose as the ministers reminded Congress of the interest coming due on foreign loans.

It was not a propitious moment for the presenting of war claims, but New York made a valiant attempt, considering that lobbying was then in its infancy. On February 18th, so warm were the city's protestations of affection, Congress felt constrained to thank the Corporation of the Chamber of Commerce. The merchants were assured "that the extension and prosperity of trade shall not cease to be considered as intimately connected with the happiness and prosperity of the United States of America." The artificers, tradesmen and mechanics of the city, who also loved Congress, were thanked in an accompanying resolution for "their cordial welcome and expressions of Confidence." [3]

James Monroe, Rufus King, William Samuel Johnson, James McHenry and Samuel Hardy served on a committee appointed to consider the "memorial from the merchants of New York, setting forth the peculiar losses they have sustained during the late war, by their exertions to support the credit of the paper currency. . . ." After deliberating several weeks the committee set a precedent with its report of March 28th:

> That they are impressed with a thorough conviction of the heavy losses they [the New York merchants] have sustained during the late war from the depreciation of the paper currency, loan-office certificates and other public securities. That when the Committee, in addition to such losses, contemplate the merit of those who suffered them, it cannot but increase their concern, that the power of relief is not within the compass of the federal resources, without making a discrimination between them and other citizens in different parts of the Union, who have sustained losses of the same nature and in a similar extent. [4]

This was a polite way of intimating that dinners at the Coffee-House could be accepted only as social obligations. The New Yorkers were advised to refer such claims to their own state legislature. Rhode Island fared no better a few months later after asking compensation for damage to buildings of the College of Rhode Island by American and French troops occupying them as barracks. A committee headed by Rufus King brought in a favorable report, but Congress put its negative on such a dangerous precedent.

The delegates were unanimous, however, in granting a pension to "Elizabeth Thompson, late a domestic in the family [staff of officers] of the Commander in Chief during the war . . . reduced at the advanced age of 81 years to poverty and distress." In a like spirit, responding to the plea of an Indian who rose to a high rank as officer, Congress voted six hundred dollars "to relieve lieut. colonel Lewis Atayataghrongthta, from the distresses in which his zeal for the service of the United States has involved him. . . ." [5]

On the other side of the ocean Parliament was voting millions of pounds to compensate American loyalists for their losses. It is not so well known that the United States also had a minor problem of the sort, as represented by the Canadians who upheld the rebel cause and emigrated to this country after the war. These newcomers were remembered by Congress in a resolution of April 13, 1785:

> That Jonathan Eddy, and other refugees from Nova Scotia, on account of their attachment to the interest of the United States, be recommended to the humanity and particular attention of the several states in which they respectively reside; and that they be informed, that whenever Congress can consistently make grants of land, they will reward in this way, as far as may be consistent, such refugees, as may be disposed to live in the Western Country. [6]

At a time of so many requests for money, Congress must have found it a welcome change when John Dickinson actually offered to pay an annual rental for a ten-year lease of empty army warehouses at Carlisle, Pennsylvania. The former delegate, in the new role of educator, proposed to turn these public buildings into classrooms. Congress accepted with alacrity on February 7th, and Dickinson College has had a continuous existence ever since.

There may have been some reason for Rhode Island and New York to suspect that their claims suffered from the hostility which they had shown toward the 5 per cent impost. For Congress was no longer turning the other cheek. On April 2nd, after Georgia too decided against the impost, William Houstoun reported to Governor Samuel Elbert "that the whole body of Congress are become so clamorous against our State, that I Shudder for the consequences . . . that it is very seriously talked of, either to make a tryal of voting Georgia out of the Union or to fall upon some means of taking coercive measures against her." [7]

Chief Justice George Walton, a former delegate, stumped the state as the champion of Congress. As a result the grand jury of Chatham County solemnly indicted the Georgia legislature on March 5, 1785:

We present, as a very great grievance, the inattention of the Honourable the Legislature to the requisition made by the Honourable the Congress of the United States for laying an impost of five per cent on goods, wares, and merchandise, imported into this state. . . . The requisition of Congress is founded in equity and justice, nor can we reasonably expect to enjoy the advantages of the Union, unless we contribute to its support.[8]

After the grand juries of Richmond and Liberty Counties returned similar indictments, the chastened legislature repealed its decision against the impost early in 1786.

Connecticut had taken a slap at Rhode Island by passing an act authorizing Congress to put the impost into effect after it gained the assent of twelve states. It seemed a neat bit of poetic justice for Rhode Island to be threatened with the possibility of a neighboring state collecting a duty on her products. But the joke lost its savor when several of the states passed laws discriminating against the commerce of their neighbors as if they were alien nations.

Here was a situation which might conceivably lead to disorder and even anarchy as reprisals multiplied. The problems arose just at a time when Congress had been hoping that the states would soon invest it with the power of regulating both interstate and foreign commerce. James Monroe, William Houstoun, Richard Dobbs Spaight, Elbridge Gerry and William Samuel Johnson were elected before leaving Trenton as a committee to report on this issue.

In the lack of any restrictions on the importation of British goods, the merchants of Great Britain were reaping a harvest in American ports. It was especially galling to American merchants, moreover, to watch their competitors from across the Atlantic pocketing so much of the hard money. Pierse Long of New Hampshire, a merchant himself, wrote on January 31, 1785: "It is amazing to see the quantity of Vessels in this City from all parts of England now in this Harbour carrying our goods to market, and a delay has so long been made to draw an equitable line of proceeding. I hope very soon there will be an end put to so diabolical a trade."[9]

The potentialities of American seaborne commerce, on the other hand, were shown dramatically when the *Empress of China*, which had been granted sea letters by Congress in 1784, docked at New York the following spring with an exotic cargo of teas, silks and spices. The delegates visiting the ship received presents sent from China by the Fuen (chief magistrate) of Canton "as a mark of his good disposition towards the American nation."

Massachusetts did not propose to wait until the other states got around to amending Article IX of the Confederation so as to authorize Congress to regulate trade. On June 23, 1785, Massachusetts passed an act of her own for this purpose and urged the other states to take similar steps. The legislature made it plain, however, that it intended this measure to be only temporary, serving until Congress might be vested "with a *well guarded* power to regulate the trade of the United States."

As the suggestion of Governor Bowdoin, the legislature passed resolutions on July 11th declaring the powers of Congress inadequate and asking that body to call a convention of delegates from all the states "to revise the Confederation and report to Congress how far it may be necessary in their opinion to alter or enlarge the same in order to secure the primary objects of the Union."

The three delegates, Gerry, King and Holten, were requested to present these resolutions to Congress. Massachusetts had shown public-spirited leadership, but her representatives at New York took the bit in their teeth by withholding the resolutions. In a message of September 3rd, signed by Gerry, they justified their refusal:

> We are apprehensive and it is our Duty to declare it, that such a Measure would produce thro'out the Union, an exertion of the Friends of an Aristocracy, to send Members who would promote a Change of Government. . . . 'More power in Congress' has been the Cry from all quarters; but especially of those whose Views, not being confined to a Government that will best promote the Happiness of the people, are extended to one that will afford lucrative Employments, civil and military. such a government is an Aristocracy, which would require a standing Army, and a numerous Train of pensioners and placemen to prop and support its exalted Administration. . . . We are for increasing the power of Congress, as far as it will promote the Happiness of the people; but at the same Time are clearly of Opinion that every Measure should be avoided which would strengthen the Hands of the Enemies to a free Government.[10]

This strange outburst had been inspired chiefly by the suspicions of the Massachusetts delegates as they viewed the first of those veterans' organizations which have cut such a figure in American politics—the Society of the Cincinnati, made up of Revolutionary army officers. The provision for hereditary membership alarmed the Yankees, who immediately scented the beginnings of an American peerage. As early as May, 1784, Gerry had written from Annapolis that "the total Abolition of this Institution must in all Events be affected, or we may bid a final adieu to every pretension of Freemen."

Glancing back from this historical distance, it seems absurd that anyone should have suspected recent Continental majors of plotting to become earls. Yet it could not be denied that in 1785 many good Americans did not consider it treasonable to discuss the possibility of a New World monarchy if no other form of adequate central government could be established. "Shall we have a king?" John Jay wrote to Washington some months later. "Not in my opinion while other experiments remain untried." [11] Gouverneur Morris spoke for an influential group which "believed a monarchical form to be neither solid nor durable. They conceived it to be vigorous or feeble, active or slothful, wise or foolish, mild or cruel, just or unjust, according to the personal character of the prince." But it was his opinion "that the duration of our government must, humanly speaking, depend on the influences which property shall acquire; for it is not to be expected that men who have nothing to lose will feel so well disposed to support existing establishments as those who had a great interest at stake." [12]

The New Englanders were not the only ones to be alarmed at the possibility of the Society of the Cincinnati spawning an American nobility. Aedanus Burke of South Carolina sounded the tocsin in a pamphlet of wide circulation. And one of the most deplorable results was the agreement of the Massachusetts legislature with Elbridge Gerry that "plans have been artfully laid, and vigorously pursued, which had they been successful, We think would inevitably have changed our republican Governments, into baleful Aristocracies."

Instead of rebuking her delegates for not carrying out instructions, Massachusetts rescinded the resolution suggesting that Congress call a convention to revise the Articles of Confederation. This was the deathblow to a proposal which might conceivably have saved the country at least a year of travail before the adoption of a new constitution.

The wrath of the merchants increased meanwhile because Congress lacked the authority to protect them from British competition. "What can be done?" wrote Rufus King on May 19th. "Eight states only have complied with the recommendation of last year for granting to Congress power to prohibit certain importations and exportations." [13]

James Monroe, chairman of the committee working for this amendment, wrote to Jefferson on July 15th: "Some gentn. have inveterate prejudices against all attempts to increase the powers of Congress, others see the necessity but fear the consequences. . . . What will or will not be done ultimately in this business is uncertain." Exactly a month later, writing to Jefferson again, the young Virginian added that "the report proposing to invest congress with the power to regulate commerce hath twice been before congress in committee of the whole. It met with no opponent except the president [Samuel Holten, chairman], by this I do not mean that there were no others oppos'd to it, for the contrary is the case. They however said but little or rather committed their side of the question to his care. In favor of it there were but few speakers also." [14]

While this reform and the impost went begging in 1785, Congress made exhilarating progress toward its goal of deriving income from western lands. For the ordinance which came up for attention in March was debated in April and actually passed in May.

The original ordinance, it will be recalled, had met defeat by a vote of eight states to one in May, 1784. Not only had the delegates smoothed over many differences during the ensuing year, but the leadership of George Washington became a factor after his westward journey in the autumn of 1784. The father of his country was frankly interested in the speculative as well as political aspects of western lands, and his own personal holdings eventually totaled many thousands of acres. In his wonted fashion, he quietly asserted his influence by writing letters to two members of Congress, Jacob Read and Richard Henry Lee, who promptly disseminated his views throughout the assembly.

All the delegates realized that this issue could not safely wait much longer. The great western migration had begun even before the war ended. Some of the choicest lands had already been claimed on the frontier legal principle of squatter's rights; for possession usually constituted nine points of the law when enforced with a long rifle. The pioneering of a later day won a greater fame, but there never was a more rough-and-ready west than the one opened up just after the American Revolution. A young man and woman could start life on the other side of the mountains with only a few possessions and wrest a homestead from the forest. Thousands of them had already done so before 1785, and there would soon be the problem of these districts clamoring in no mild terms to be admitted as states.

A grand committee, consisting of a member from each state, reported a new ordinance on April 12th. Congress split sectionally on the issue, with Rufus King of Massachusetts championing the northern interests and William Grayson of Virginia leading the southern delegates. The middle-aged Virginia lawyer, a graduate of Oxford and the Temple, summed up the arguments in a letter of April 15th to George Washington:

> Some gentlemen looked upon it as a matter of revenue only and that it was true policy to get the money with't parting with the inhabitants to populate the Country, and thereby prevent the lands in the original states from depreciating. Others (I think) were afraid of an interference with the lands now at market in the individual States. part of the Eastern Gentlemen wish to have the lands sold in such a manner as to suit their own people who may

chuse to emigrate. . . . But others are apprehensive of the consequences which may result from the new States taking their position in the Confederacy.[15]

Popular education, then in its infancy, received one of the greatest boosts of history from the regulation that one section of every township should be reserved for the maintenance of public schools. This provision met with general approval, but a storm of opposition swamped the proposal that another section be set aside "for the support of religion, the profits arising therefrom . . . to be applied for ever according to the will of the majority of male residents of full age within the same." As individuals several members lent their support, though Madison wondered how anyone could uphold a regulation "so hurtful to the sale of the public land, and smelling so strongly of an antiquated Bigotry." Other delegates foresaw the endless religious disputes which would result, and a majority of the states voted for expunging the clause.

On May 8th Grayson could report to Washington: "The price is fix'd at a dollar the acre liquidated certificates. The reason for establishing this sum was that a part of the house were for half a dollar, and another part for two dollars and others for intermediate sums between the two extremes, so that ultimately this was agreed upon as a central ground. If it is too high (which I am afraid is the case) it may hereafter be corrected by a resolution."[16]

Twice in May the attendance fell below nine states, but the debates continued as various amendments were introduced. May 23rd saw the adoption of the ordinance. "And if it is not the best in the world," Grayson wrote to Madison five days later, "it is I am confident the best that could be procured for the present. There was such a variety of interests, most of them imaginary, that I am only surprised that it is not more defective. The Eastern people who before the revolution never had any idea of any quantity of Earth above a hundred acres, were for selling in large tracts of 30,000 acres while the Southern people who formerly could scarce bring their imaginations down so low as to comprehend the meaning of a hundred acres of ground were for selling the whole territory in lots of a mile square." And the Virginia member ended with a line which might be applied to most of the decisions of democracy, "In this situation we remained . . . with great obstinacy on both sides, until a kind of compromise took effect."[17]

In a letter of June 13, 1785, Richard Henry Lee estimated the financial results which could be expected from the ordinance:

> This will present about 10 Millions of Acres for sale at one dollar an Acre of Liquidated Certificate value. Subsequent treaties to be held with the Indians will extinguish their claims to about 20 millions more which it is intended to devote to the same purpose and which will very nearly pay off our whole domestic debt. The foreign then will not be found oppressive.[18]

Congress soon had a reminder that it would be wise not to delay the surveying and selling of the western lands. North, south and west, all along the frontier, Americans were breaking away from the old traditions. "A very considerable part of No. Carolina has revolted," Grayson wrote to William Short on June 15th. "They have assumed the powers of Governm't and a Capt. Cocke was here the other day with authority from them to solicit admission. Georgia has laid off a county on the Mississippi called Bourbon and settlers are gathering fast about the Nachez. There is a report that the province of Maine begins to make speeches respecting independence; Vermont remains as it did when you left us." [19]

This account, highly colored as it was, gave an idea of the problems awaiting in the near future. North Carolina had ceded her western territory on June 2, 1784, with a number of conditions and reservations, one of them being that Congress accept within a year. The following November the state repented of its generosity, and the repeal gave the "over-mountain men" an excuse for setting up a government of their own.

Congress turned a deaf ear to the plea of the frontier district calling itself Franklin, which subsequently became the state of Tennessee. Instead, the assembly appealed to North Carolina's "principles of magnanimity and justice," and eventually that state passed a satisfactory act of cession.

Again in the early spring of 1785 it came to the attention of Congress that the United States had acquired some recent inhabitants who did not speak the language. A second memorial from the old French settlements on the Mississippi pointed out that they had been political orphans since their conquest by George Rogers Clark. The assembly decided "that one or more commissioners be appointed to repair to the Kaskaskies and Illinois settlements," but as usual nothing was done about it.

These days found Congress no longer in a mood to apologize for such shortcomings. The blame was being placed where it belonged—on the states which were not doing their part. As a record of the absenteeism which so often halted business, Secretary Thomson presented an abstract of attendance from the first Monday in November, 1784, to July 29, 1785. There were 169 days when Congress met, and the following table lists the total number of days that each state was represented on the floor:

New Hampshire	120	Pennsylvania	130
Massachusetts	152	Delaware	30
Rhode Island	136	Maryland	115
Connecticut	106	Virginia	162
New York	146	North Carolina	96
New Jersey	126	South Carolina	142
		Georgia	66

There had been 14 days when fewer than seven states were represented, and 28 other days when Congress lacked a quorum of nine states. Barely a quorum had been mustered on 49 days; ten states were on the floor 40 times, eleven states 32 times, and twelve states only 6 times. After surveying this record, Congress decided on August 17th that Secretary Thomson should transmit to the legislatures a monthly record of attendance. Blanks were ordered to be printed for the purpose. The preamble to the resolution stated bluntly that the neglect of "the great Interests of the Union" could generally be traced to the "evils which solely result from an incompleat representation." [20]

A test of a few months demonstrated that the backward states could not be shamed into better attendance. On the last day of January, 1786, Chairman David Ramsay sent them a memorial:

> Three months of the federal year are now compleated and in that whole period no more than seven states have at any one time been represented. No question except that of adjourning from day to day can be carried without perfect Unanimity. The extreme difficulty of framing Resolutions against which no exception can be taken by any one State, can scarcely be conceived but by those whose unfortunate situation has led them to experience the perplexing embarrassment.[21]

Congress may have hoped to recapture its past glories in November, 1785, by electing John Hancock president for a second time, though he had not yet appeared as a Massachusetts delegate. The Boston sybarite accepted, but on December 4th Rufus King found it necessary to apologize because the president's house and carriage in New York were not up to Beacon Hill standards. During the interim the assembly filled the gap by creating a new title, "Chairman of Congress," and electing David Ramsay. The South Carolina physician had a brother, Nathaniel Ramsey, representing Maryland at this time. Both were Princeton graduates, both had been wounded and captured during the war; but each had his own way of spelling the family name.

Hancock kept Congress waiting until the following June before resigning on grounds of ill-health. Nathaniel Gorham, the Massachusetts judge, was elected in his place.

The states were remiss not only in paying quotas but also in compensating their own delegates for the high cost of living in postwar New York. "I am in arrears for my board," William Ellery of Rhode Island reminded Governor Greene on October 24, 1785, "and unless I am supplied with about 100 doll's, I shall be under the painful and disagreeable necessity of leaving New York indebted to the person with whom I have boarded." [22] He explained that only personal loans had enabled him to meet his other expenses.

William Samuel Johnson of Connecticut informed Governor Matthew Griswold on November 11th "that I have not by me, nor in my Power, cash sufficient to support me even for a single week at N York, and must therefore beg yr. Excellency to give such directions where it may be proper as will tend to furnish what may be necessary. . . ." [23]

Some of the best-known delegates of the early years dropped out of Congress before it moved to New York—Roger Sherman, Eliphalet Dyer, Thomas McKean, John Witherspoon, Robert Morris, James Duane and Elias Boudinot. But there were as usual some hardy perennials springing up after a long absence—Samuel Holten of Massachusetts, John Langdon of New Hampshire, Robert R. Livingston of New York, William Ellery of Rhode Island, John Henry of Maryland, Richard Henry Lee of Virginia, William Churchill Houston of New Jersey. In a letter to James Madison of November 28, 1785, William Grayson gave a picture of the living conditions of delegates in New York:

> The inconvenience which Members of Congress have experienced here this last year from living at common boarding houses, and mixing with the landlady her Aunts cousins and acquaintances and with all other sorts of company has been complained of loudly; We have not, I confess suffered in this way, though we have purchased the exemption at a dear rate to our purses; we have a house though a small one, and yet that same house has went deep into our allowances; so that our dignity has almost eat up our finances. I understand some of the States mean to relieve their delegates from the weight of this inconvenience by establishing a kind of State house at the expense of each State: Although I cannot help admiring the idea of doing something yet I think the plan of jumbling all together whether grave or gay married or single like Falstaff in the buck basket, heel to point, altogether improper; I should rather suppose (if the legislature gets into a merry mood,) that it would be better to allow each delegate a certain sum of money, provided he disburses the same in House rent. . . .[24]

At no period of the fifteen years were there more romances in Congress. Charles Thomson wrote to Jefferson on April 6, 1786, that "Messrs. Read, Gerry and Monroe are married and Osgood on the brink of matrimony." The Virginia delegate had won the lovely and accomplished daughter of a British army officer who remained in this country. Stephen Mix Mitchell wrote to an absent delegate on February 21st that "our friend Monro was married and next morning decamp'd for Long Island with the little smiling Venus in his arms, where they had taken house, to avoid fulsome Compliments during the first Transports and we have not yet seen him in Town." [25]

When Spain announced the appointment of a new minister, Don Diego de Gardoqui, the smokers of Congress were worried. "It will be unfortunate for us," Richard Henry Lee wrote in a letter of June 4, 1785, "if Mr. Gardoque should not be a Smoker and so not be provided with Havanna Segars. The most worthy Don Juan Miralles used to supply us so copiously that he has occasioned us to loose all appetite for other smoking." [26]

Miralles had been sent to report to his country on American ambitions in the West. Apparently he confided that Spanish interests were endangered, for his successor had instructions not to concede the right of the United States to navigation of the Mississippi.

Gardoqui had his formal audience on July 2, 1785. Congress addressed him by his self-styled title of "Encargado de Negocios," not being quite sure what degree of authority those high-sounding words implied. The newcomer was not so generous as Miralles with his cigars, and his stand on the question of the Mississippi threatened at times to precipitate hostile relations.

Congress itself was divided into two camps. The delegates of the northern and eastern states were quite willing to sacrifice navigation of the river in order to gain trade concessions. Secretary Jay leaned toward their viewpoint, though he had instructions to the contrary. The attitude of the southern states may be guessed from the report of Monroe to Governor Patrick Henry on August 12, 1786: "I soon found in short that Mr. Jay was desirous of occluding the Mississippi and making what he term'd advantageous terms in the treaty of commerce the means of effecting it." His object, according to Monroe, was "to extricate himself from the instructions respecting the Mississippi. . . . We found he had engaged the eastern states in the intrigue, especially Mass. . . ." [27]

Thus began a tug of war between two schools of Americans—those who faced the Mississippi and those who gazed out over the Atlantic; those who believed that the new nation's destiny lay in opening up the West and those who envisioned a future built upon a foundation of seaborne commerce with Europe.

These same differences of opinion prevailed to a lesser extent in relations with Great Britain. It galled the Southerners that British garrisons were still occupying Detroit, Niagara, Sandusky, Oswego and other posts on American soil in defiance of the peace terms. But the trade-minded Americans of the seaport cities, with John Jay again concurring, were ready to concede that the United States had given provocation. Lord Carmarthen, the British secretary of state, coolly admitted that his country had been violating the seventh article of the treaty. But he submitted more than a hundred pages of evidence to support his contention that the United States had not carried out her agreement to pay debts owed to British creditors before the war. The report ended with the promise "that whenever America shall manifest a real determination to fulfill her part of the treaty, Great Britain will not hesitate to prove her sincerity to co-operate in whatever points depend upon her for carrying every Article of it into real and complete effect." [28]

John Adams, recently elected minister to Great Britain, argued that the United States had been paying these prewar debts as rapidly as could be expected from a new nation impoverished by war. Thomas Jefferson, who visited England for two months in 1786, wrote to John Page on May 4th: "That nation hate us, their ministers hate us, and their king, more than all other men. They have the impudence to avow this, though they acknowledge our trade important to them." [29]

The Southerners and Westerners had good grounds to suspect British agents of inciting Indian hostilities while occupying outposts on American soil. But John Jay took every opportunity to promote better commercial relations between the recent enemies. He had the interests of the eastern seaports primarily in mind when reporting to Congress on March 29, 1787:

> Your Secretary has (he thinks with Candor and Impartiality) investigated the cause of the Complaints subsisting between the two Countries, and he would not be candid were he not to confess that in his Opinion Britain has more Reason to complain of the United States than the United States of Britain since the Peace. [30]

James Monroe was not an excitable young man, but he believed that leaders of the northern and eastern states were actually contemplating a withdrawal from the Confederation. "Certain it is," he warned Governor Patrick Henry on August 12, 1786, "that committees are held in this town of Eastern men and others of this State upon the subject of a dismemberment of the States east of the Hudson from the Union & the erection of them into a separate govt." [31]

Evidence that the Virginia delegate was not unduly suspicious may be found in the letters of some of the New England members. Theodore Sedgwick of Massachusetts wrote to Caleb Strong on August 6, 1786:

> It well becomes the eastern and middle States, who are in interest one, seriously to consider what advantages result to them from their connection with the Southern States. They can give us nothing, as an equivalent for the protection they derive from us but a participation in their commerce. . . . Even the appearance of a union cannot in the way we now are long be preserved. It becomes us seriously to contemplate a substitute; for if we do not controul events we shall be miserably controuled by them. No other substitute can be devised but that of contracting the limits of the confederacy to such as

are natural and reasonable, and within those limits instead of a nominal to institute a real, and an efficient government.[32]

Another threat to the rapidly crumbling Confederation could be seen in a financial situation which had gone from bad to worse to intolerable. On June 27, 1786, the new Board of Treasury (Samuel Osgood, Arthur Lee and Walter Livingston) predicted that "we do not conceive it probable that even the sum of Three hundred thousand Dollars in Specie, will be paid into the General Treasury in the present Year. . . ."

The income of the past two years had not been enough for the bare expenses of government, so that nothing remained for the payment of interest on loans. In a resolution of July 6, 1785, Congress had adopted the dollar as the money unit of a decimal system. But the Board of Treasury warned a year later that several states were experimenting again with paper currency. The report concluded: "Nothing occurs as a probable mode of relief, but a Sale in Europe of the Western Territory, which has been ceded to the United States. To attempt new Loans, whilst no Funds are established for paying the Interest and principal of former ones, would in all probability be fruitless; even if it could be done consistently with those Maxims of prudence and Public Integrity, which ought to Characterize the Proceedings of every Nation." [33]

Another determined effort to push the impost met with failure in the spring of 1786. Rhode Island had given a partial assent, and the Georgia legislature concurred after being indicted by several grand juries. This left only New York, and that state defied Congress by levying an impost of her own on the products of Connecticut and New Jersey. Nathaniel Gorham wrote that only the influence of Congress prevented the two states "from entering the lists with N. York and bloodshed would very quickly be the consequence."

New Jersey decided on a retaliation that was more calculated to injure Congress than New York. "Our foederal distresses gather fast to a point," wrote Henry (Light-Horse Harry) Lee of Virginia to Washington on March 2nd. "New Jersey has refused the requisition and will not grant a shilling, until New York accedes to the impost." [34]

Congress had grown accustomed to states falling behind in their payments, but a flat refusal set an example too dangerous to be tolerated. It was resolved on March 7th to send a committee to plead with the New Jersey legislators, and the choice fell on three of the most able delegates—William Grayson of Virginia, Nathaniel Gorham of Massachusetts, and Charles Pinckney of South Carolina. All three made speeches at Trenton and persuaded the legislature to rescind its decision. Two months later New York announced that it had at last granted the impost, but Congress found the act so riddled with conditions that it had to be refused. Stephen Mix Mitchell concluded that the legislature had "step'd as twere out of their way to give Congress a Slap in the face."

In August it became necessary once more to appoint delegates as evangelists to a recalcitrant state. "Monroe and I were sent to the legislature at Phila.," Rufus King recorded in his notes. "Pennsylvania, which had paid her quota more freely than many others, adopted certain regulations, according to wh. instead of paying her quota into the general Treasury, she assumed to distribute it among her own citizens, holding claims on the general Treasury. This assumption increased the financial embarrassment of Congress, and, if followed, would have put an end to the contributions of other states." [35]

The Massachusetts member confessed that stage fright ruined his first attempt at a speech in Philadelphia, but the second time he succeeded "without trepidation and to my own satisfaction." Again a wayward state had been made to see the light, but the proposed address of Congress on October 9th set a new standard for both gloom and candor. The federal finances, so the states were told, had been "deranged from a non performance on your part of that duty which your Constitution and the Confederation imposes upon you." [36] A total of only $971,475 had been paid into the treasury during the two years up to January 1, 1786. The address reached a climax in the most authoritative tone ever assumed by Congress:

> We, the United States in Congress Assembled by Virtue of the powers Vested in us by the Confederation do call on you as members of the Confederacy to pay into the general Treasury at the time stipulated your respective Quotas of the present requisition for the support of the general Government.

A week later Congress backed down by deciding not to send such a brusque message. The delegates settled for a unanimous resolution that the states be "required" to pay their quotas of $530,000 in specie before June 1, 1787. But it is not likely that anyone had the faintest hope of any such sum ever being received. For the prediction made by George Washington in a letter of July 6, 1780, had become an acknowledged fact:

> . . . I give it decisively as my opinion—that unless the States will content themselves with a full and well-chosen representation in Congress and vest that body with absolute powers in all matters relative to the great purposes of the war, and of general concern . . . we are attempting an impossibility, and very soon shall become (if it is not already the case) a many-headed monster— a heterogenious mass—that never will or can steer to the same point. The contest between the different States now is not which shall do the most for the common cause—but which shall do least. . . .[37]

The marvel is only that the United States managed to stagger along on such a basis for six more years. But in the early weeks of February, 1787, when James Madison returned as a delegate, the end was in sight. It was as a realist, not a pessimist, that this genius of practical politics wrote to Edmund Pendleton on February 24th:

> Indeed the Present System neither has nor deserves advocates; and if some very strong props are not applied will quickly tumble to the ground. No money is paid into the public Treasury; no respect is paid to the federal authority. Not a single State complies with the requisitions, several pass them over in silence, and some positively reject them. The payments ever since the peace have been decreasing, and of late fall short even of the pittance necessary for the Civil List of the Confederacy. It is not possible that a Government can last long under these circumstances.[38]

The only symptoms of collapse that had been spared the federal authority up to this point had been armed revolt and civil warfare. But the last months of 1786 brought even these calamities. Henry Knox returned with an alarming report on October 16th after Congress had sent him to investigate the disturbances in western Massachusetts known to history as Shays' Rebellion. The portly secretary of war asserted that "great numbers of people in Massachusetts and the neighboring states avow the principle of annihilating all debts public and private." Knox foresaw "dreadful consequences which may be expected from wicked and ambitious men, possessing the command of a force to overturn, not only the forms, but the principles of the present constitution. . . . I conceive my Official duty obliges me to inform Congress . . . that unless the present commotions are checked with a strong hand, that an armed tyranny may be established on the ruins of the present constitutions." [39]

Chapter 26

The Law of the Land

FOUR days after hearing Secretary Knox's report, Congress resolved unanimously to triple the size of the army by enlisting 1,340 new troops on a wartime basis of three years. Even more significant was the provision that they be raised from the following states in these numbers: Massachusetts, 660; New Hampshire, 260; Rhode Island, 120; Connecticut, 180; and 60 each of calvary from Maryland and Virginia.

This specification should have left no doubt where the new soldiers were to be employed. But the committee consisting of Charles Pettit, Henry Lee, John Henry, Charles Pinckney and Melancton Smith explained that "as it is not expedient that the causes should be publickly assigned for the raising of such troops . . . they have thought it proper, in a separate report on the intelligence received from the Western Country, to recommend the Augmentation of the troops in the service of the United States." [1]

In other words, the public was to be given the impression that the soldiers were being enlisted for the purpose of fighting redskins in the West, not fellow Americans in Massachusetts. Congress approved by adopting the report without a dissenting vote. Another unanimous resolution asserted that "Congress would not hazard the perilous step of putting arms into the hands of men whose fidelity must in some degree depend on the faithful payment of their wages had they not the fullest confidence . . . of the most liberal exertions of the money holders in the State of Massachusetts and other states." This was a none too subtle hint that states calling for federal aid in putting down insurrections would do well to pay their quotas fully and promptly.

The members of Congress deserve no reproach for believing that the Massachusetts rebels were indeed "wicked and ambitious men" bent on the overthrow of the government. These unfortunates were not in a position to tell their side of the story—taxes exceeding the entire cash income of many farm families; farm interest rates ranging from 20 to 40 per cent; corrupt courts serving the interests of moneylenders and profiteers. The debtors of western Massachusetts, in short, were being almost literally devoured by as rapacious and shortsighted a group of creditors as ever committed usury. In Worcester County alone a single year's lawsuits, most of them to collect debts, involved as many litigants as there were inhabitants. Twenty times as many men had been jailed for debt as for all other offenses combined; and the courts authorized creditors to collect by selling every last scrap of a debtor's property—his house and tools, his cow and oxen, even his bed and table.

There were, it is true, a good many malcontents who joined the uprising in the hope of evading just obligations. But Captain Daniel Shays himself had made a distinguished record as an officer at Bunker Hill, Ticonderoga, Saratoga and Stony Point. Most of his followers were decent, hard-working farmers driven to desperation. In the autumn of 1786 they took up arms and forcibly closed the courts which had become the instruments of their creditors. It is one of the ironies of American history that Sam Adams led the chorus of bloodthirsty denunciations of Shays and his men. The hangman would have been kept busy if the archrebel had had his way, but Governor John Hancock intervened on the side of mercy after General Lincoln restored order in 1787 with little trouble or bloodshed. Shays escaped to Vermont and was pardoned the following year. Instead of mounting a gallows, he lived until 1825 to see the development of a nation in which even a debtor had his rights.

The uprising had the immediate effect of throwing such a fright into the moneyed classes of New England as to overcome the prejudices against a strong central government which thrived in this section. Thus it might even be conjectured that Shays' Rebellion tipped the balance in favor of the United States Constitution that won ratification in 1788 with so much difficulty.

As a sign of the times, Charles Pinckney's speech before the New Jersey legislature on March 13, 1786, is evidence that the members of Congress had reached the point of publicly advocating a constitutional convention. "Though our present disorders must be attributed in the first instance to the weakness and inefficiency of the general government," said Pinckney, "it must still be confessed that they have been precipitated by the refractory and inattentive conduct of the states; most of whom have neglected altogether the performance of their federal duties. . . ." As a remedy, he advised that New Jersey "ought immediately to instruct her delegates in Congress, to urge the calling of a general convention of the states, for the purpose of revising and amending the federal system. In this constitutional application, she will meet with all the attention and support she can wish." [2]

The brilliant young Charleston lawyer left a message at Trenton which is of timeless application: "Be assured, sir, the united states can have no danger so much to dread as that of disunion; nor has the federal government, when properly formed, any thing to fear, but from the licentiousness of its members."

American political consciences could no longer gain ease in 1786 by blaming Congress. Charles Pettit of Pennsylvania, in a doleful letter to Jeremiah Wadsworth on May 27th, presented a panorama of America as seen from the viewpoint of that assembly:

> . . . Our Funds exhausted, our Credit lost, our Confidence in each other and in the federal Government destroyed. Resolutions unexecuted; Requisitions but partially complied with in the best of the States, in others not at all; Recommendations as little regarded as the cries of an Oysterman. The States separately pursuing their own whimsical Schemes of dangerous Experiment, regardless of federal System, and destroying their own Strength by intoxicating Draughts of Liberty run mad.[3]

Rhode Island's very name became a byword after the legislature tried to pay its obligations with a depreciated paper currency. The Rev. James Manning, first president of Brown College, wrote to his colleague Nathan Miller on June 7, 1786, after arriving in New York as a delegate: "Alone here for more than a Month; reduced to the very last guinea and a trifle of Change . . . my Lodging, washing, Barber's, Hatters, Taylors Bills, etc. not paid." [4] More neglect of this sort put the two Rhode Island members in a mood to rebuke their own state when reporting to Governor John Collins on September 28, 1786:

> Your Excellency will be made acquainted, by Congress, that no paper, emitted by the States, will answer federal purposes. . . . We need not, Sir, inform you how it wounds our feelings, in every company, as well as in the Gazettes, to hear and see the proceedings of our Legislature burlesqued and ridiculed; and to find that Congress and all men of sober reflection reprobate, in the strongest terms, the principles which actuate our administration of governm't. We are Citizens of Rhode Island and are most sensibly affected with everything which militates to the dishonour of the State. Your Delegates further beg to observe, that if those measures are continued . . . they will infalliably terminate in the ruin of the state; and have no inconsiderable share in the subversion of the Union.[5]

It must have seemed incredible in 1786 that there ever had been a day when the assembly was strong enough to be called King Congress. Henry Lee had a reputation for courage in combat, yet his letters show the effects of the alarms sweeping the country. On October 17th he wrote to Washington that "we are all in dire apprehension that a beginning of anarchy with all its calamitys has approached and we have no means to stop the dreadful work." The very next day Charles Pettit of Pennsylvania reported more rumors to Benjamin Franklin, who had recently returned from Europe: "A total abolition of all Debts both public and Private, and even a general distribution of Property, are not without Advocates." The Massachusetts rebels, said Pettit, were gaining strength. "It is conjectured . . . that foreign Influence has no little weight in their Councils—that they had a great Degree of Systematic Order in their Measures, and are ready on an Alarm to come forth with an organized Army of not less than 10,000 Men armed and officered." [6]

William Grayson wrote to Madison a few weeks later that "it is supposed that Vermont is leagued with them [Shays' followers], and that they are secretly supported by emissaries of a certain nation." And Edward Carrington reported to Governor Randolph: "It is said that a british influence is operating in this mischievous affair. . . ." [7]

Few members of Congress could have supposed that within a year the United States would be given the opportunity to adopt an entirely new constitution providing for a decently strong central government. The first impulse in this direction had come from a trade conference, later known as the Annapolis Convention, which in turn sprang from the effort of Maryland and Virginia to settle problems of commerce on the Potomac. Their commissioners met at Alexandria and Mount Vernon in the spring of 1785 and adjusted differences so satisfactorily that they agreed to invite Delaware and Pennsylvania to a new conference.

When James Madison learned of this proposal, he urged that commissioners be invited to Annapolis from all thirteen states for "the purpose of digesting and reporting the requisite augmentation of the power of Congress over trade." But even Madison had no idea in the spring of 1786 that the meeting would go so far as to call a constitutional convention. "If it should come to nothing, it will, I fear confirm G. B. [Great Britain] and all the world in the belief that we are not to be respected, nor apprehended as a nation in matters of commerce. The States are every day giving proofs that separate regulations are more likely to set them by the ears, than to attain the common object." [8]

Madison's skepticism seemed to be justified on the first Monday in

September when only five states sent delegates—New York, New Jersey, Pennsylvania, Delaware and Virginia. "Many Gentlemen both within & without Congs. wish to make this Meeting subservient to a plenipotentiary Convention for amending the Confederation," he informed Jefferson on August 12th. "Tho' my wishes are in favor of such an event, yet I despair so much of its accomplishment at the present crisis that I do not extend my views beyond a commercial Reform. To speak the truth I almost despair even of this." [9]

At this time it seemed more likely that Congress itself would revise the Confederation. An effort had been made this very summer when seven amendments were proposed on August 7th by a grand committee appointed for that purpose. These reforms were designed to enforce full and regular attendance, to give Congress the authority to collect requisitions, and to vest Congress with exclusive powers of regulating interstate as well as foreign commerce.

It is conceivable that the Confederation might have had a longer life if the amendments had passed. Intelligent and realistic attempts to cope with the foremost handicaps, they were provided with "teeth" for enforcement. August 14th had been the date set for debate, but before that time Congress became embroiled in another sectional struggle arising from Gardoqui's refusal to yield the navigation of the Mississippi. Such an attitude was understandable on the part of a Spanish diplomat, but the southern delegates were infuriated by John Jay's seeming acquiescence. In a report to Congress of August 3, 1786, the secretary of foreign affairs recommended that the present generation "forbear to use the Navigation of that River below their territories to the Ocean." Jay reasoned that "as the Navigation is not at present important, nor will probably become much more so in less than twenty five or thirty years, a forbearance to use it while we do not *want it,* is not great sacrifice." [10]

Such arguments struck many of the members as sophistries intended to beguile the states looking westward, so that the eastern seaports could profit by wresting commercial concessions from Spain. For the eastern delegates made no secret of their prejudice against any policy encouraging the settling of the new lands. Rufus King declared that he regarded "every immigrant to that country from the Atlantic States, as forever lost to the Confederacy."

No issue had more dangerous potentialities of splitting the Confederation into two or three American nations of irreconcilable interests—a prospect frankly and even approvingly discussed in letters of the New Englanders. This question, along with the impost and requisitions for the coming federal year, was still uppermost on September 17th when Rufus King reported to Governor Bowdoin:

The Delegates from New York to the annapolis convention passed through this place this morning on their way home. from them I learn that the Delegates from only Five States assembled at annapolis, that the powers of even these Five were materially different; and that from a consideration of the small number of States which had sent Delegates . . . they had agreed in a recommendation to the States that a convention of Delegates should be held at Philadelphia in May next for the purpose of a *general revision* of the confederation, and a Report to Congress, and also to the several Legislatures.[11]

Most of the other members of Congress were not even interested enough to mention the event in their letters. Two weeks later King wrote to John Adams that the Annapolis Convention had "terminated without credit or prospect of having done much good. . . . Whether the states will accede to the proposition of a convention at Philadelphia in May, is yet uncertain." [12]

Only five states, it is true, had sent delegates to Annapolis. But among them had been two first-rate political minds—Alexander Hamilton of New York and John Dickinson of Delaware. (Nobody seemed to think it unusual for Dickinson and McKean to serve both Delaware and Pennsylvania in turn.) As chairman, Dickinson signed the report, though Hamilton drafted most of it. The commissioners, it was explained, had not considered it "advisable to proceed on the business of their mission under the Circumstances of so partial and defective a representation." The report pointed out "that the power of regulating Trade . . . may require a corresponding adjustment of other parts of the Federal system." These questions were declared to be "of a nature so serious as in the view of your Commissioners, to render the situation of the United States delicate and critical, calling for an exertion of the United virtue and wisdom of all the Members of the Confederacy." Hence it was recommended that all thirteen states appoint delegates "to meet at Philadelphia on the second Monday in May next, to take into consideration the situation of the United States, to devise such further provisions as shall appear to them necessary to render the constitution of the Federal Government adequate to the Exigencies of the Union." [13]

Three months passed that winter without any Congress at all. From November 3, 1786, to the following February 2nd, only a single day found as many as seven states on the floor. The ravages of absenteeism were shown by a table which Secretary Thomson later prepared as a record of attendance during the whole federal year of 1786-1787.

Eleven states had been fully represented on 4 days; ten states on 6 days; nine states on 39 days; eight states on 35 days; seven states on 28 days; and six or fewer states on 102 days.[14] Following are the statistics of absenteeism at its worst:

	2 or More Delegates	One Delegate	No Delegates
New Hampshire	Days 4	Days 23	Days 85
Massachusetts	104	8	0
Rhode Island	13	50	49
Connecticut	53	13	46
New York	112	0	0
New Jersey	103	4	5
Pennsylvania	101	6	5
Delaware	74	26	12
Maryland	7	30	75
Virginia	106	2	4
North Carolina	104	2	6
South Carolina	62	23	27
Georgia	84	23	5

Congress elected Arthur St. Clair of Pennsylvania as its new president on February 2nd. Next, the delegates argued the question of the forthcoming constitutional convention, for Virginia had already taken the lead by electing a slate of representatives which included George Washington. Rheumatism and other ills of the flesh were troubling him at the age of 55, but he threw the great weight of his influence into the scale. It could also be anticipated that Benjamin Franklin, just past 81, would as usual place his country's welfare above personal considerations.

Shays' Rebellion had been an object lesson to New Englanders who might otherwise have hung back. After several days of debate, Madison wrote to Washington that "Congs. have been much divided and embarrassed on the question whether their taking an interest in the measure would impede or promote it." [15] New York helped to make up doubtful minds by instructing her delegates to enter a motion recommending the convention, and a grand committee of Congress brought in a favorable report. The concurrence of the Massachusetts members settled it, and on February 21st the assembly resolved:

> That in the opinion of Congress it is expedient that on the second Monday in May next a Convention of delegates who shall have been appointed by the several States be held at Philadelphia for the sole and express purpose of revising the Articles of Confederation and reporting to Congress and the several legislatures such alterations and provisions therein as shall when agreed to in Congress and confirmed by the States render the federal Constitution adequate to the exigencies of Government and the preservation of the Union. [16]

At least there was no disagreement as to the need for powerful remedies to cure America's political ills. Madison, though little given to exaggeration, wrote to Edmund Pendleton on February 24th: "The late turbulent scenes in Massts. & infamous ones in Rhode Island, have done inexpressible injury to the republican character in that part of the U. States; and a propensity towards Monarchy is said to have been produced by it in some leading minds. The bulk of the people will probably prefer the lesser evil of a partition of the Union into three more practicable and energetic Governments." [17]

Madison dreaded even this lesser evil so much that he urged the "real friends of the Revolution to exert themselves in favor of such an organization of the confederacy as will perpetuate the Union, and redeem the honor of the Republican name."

The issue of Mississippi navigation came up again in March, aggravated by wild tales of Spanish seizures and confiscations at the expense of Americans in the West. The members of Congress must have had a shock when Secretary Jay laid before them on April 13th a letter from one Thomas Green of Louisville: "The Commercial Treaty with Spain is considered to be cruel, oppressive and unjust. The prohibition of the navigation of the Mississippi has astonished the whole Western Country. To sell us and make us vassals to the merciless Spaniards is a grievance not to be borne. . . . The minds of the people here are very much exasperated against both the Spaniards and Congress." Another letter "to a New Englander from a resident of the Falls of Ohio" struck an even more defiant note:

> Do you think to prevent the emigration from a barren Country loaded with Taxes and impoverished with debts to the most luxurious and fertile Soil in the world? Vain is the thought and presumptuous the supposition! . . . Preparations are now making here (if necessary) to drive the Spaniards from their settlements, at the mouth of the Mississippi. . . . You are as ignorant of this Country as Great Britain was of America. These hints if rightly improved, may be of some service, if not blame yourselves for the neglect.[18]

The bewildered members of the Continental Congress, if they had but realized, were dealing with the phenomenon of migration—a cosmic force which had been powerful enough to inundate the Roman Empire. In 1787 could be felt the first impulse of that human tidal wave which swept irresistibly across a continent in a few generations. Half a century later the term "manifest destiny" would be coined, but the Continental Congress could only wonder at the political ferment all along the frontier, in Maine and Vermont as well as in Kentucky and the district calling itself Franklin. The reproach that Americans of the seaboard could not understand the West is borne out by their comments. Even James Monroe, sympathetic as he was to western aspirations, returned from a long trip of inspection to offer, these opinions in a letter to Jefferson of January 19, 1786:

A great part of the territory is miserably poor, especially that near lakes Michigan & Erie & that upon the Mississippi & the Illinois consists of extensive plains wh. have not had from appearances & will not have a single bush on them, for ages. The districts therefore within wh. these fall will perhaps never contain a sufficient number of Inhabitants to entitle them to membership in the confederacy. . . .[19]

The area described by Monroe included some of the most populous sections of present-day Ohio, Indiana and Illinois. But if he and his fellow delegates fell short as prophets, they knew that the western situation might explode at any minute. "From the Temper visible in some of the Papers sent us from the Western Country," Jay reported to Congress, "as well as from the intelligence they convey, your Secretary apprehends that the period is not far distant when the United States must decide either to wage War with Spain, or settle all differences with her by Treaty, on the best Terms in their power." [20]

When Jay informed Congress that he had adjusted a treaty with Gardoqui which relinquished American rights to navigation of the lower Mississippi, the southern delegates reached their boiling point. Led by Madison, they fought to have Jefferson sent to Madrid for negotiations. Jay managed to rally a majority in Congress to his defense, and Gardoqui himself became so alarmed that he made every effort to tread lightly. But the factor which did most to ease the tension was the Convention at Philadelphia. It provided such brisk competition that from May 11th until after July 4th there were not enough states on the floor for a quorum in Congress.

Some of the most prominent figures at Philadelphia were delegates both to Congress and to the Convention—John Langdon and Nicholas Gilman of New Hampshire; Nathaniel Gorham and Rufus King of Massachusetts; William Samuel Johnson of Connecticut; Jonathan Dayton of New Jersey; James Madison of Virginia; William Blount of North Carolina; Charles Pinckney and Pierce Butler of South Carolina; William Few and Abraham Baldwin of Georgia.

Congress could not do business while these men were in Philadelphia, though Secretary Thomson managed to lure enough of them back to New York for a quorum in July. Several of the mutual delegates tried to shuttle back and forth between the two cities, but the transportation of 1787 was not equal to such demands.

Only a few of the men at Philadelphia had never served at any time in the Continental Congress. On the other hand, a dozen veterans of the first few critical years of that assembly were sitting again in the State House— Benjamin Franklin, George Washington, John Dickinson, Roger Sherman,

John Rutledge, Thomas Mifflin, John Langdon, Oliver Ellsworth, George Read, William Livingston, Robert Morris, Gouverneur Morris, James Wilson and George Wythe.

Although Congress had left Philadelphia in wrath, there had never been such a spiritual home as the State House with its high windows and white-paneled walls. Never had there been such shelter from the summer sun and winter blasts as was provided by the seven-foot walls enclosing the bare yard with its few elms. These walls had also provided privacy for some of the decisions shaping the American future; for the term "out of doors" could often be taken literally in connection with informal political deals.

Nostalgia as well as curiosity inspired a motion on April 11th that Congress adjourn at New York on the last Friday of the month and move to Philadelphia to meet on the first Monday in June. This measure failed by a narrow margin, but a letter from William Grayson to James Monroe on May 29th records the discontent of the rump parliament left behind in the City Hall:

> The draught made from Congress of members for the Convention has made them very thin and no business of course is going on here: I do not believe that this will be the case untill that body shall be dissolved, which I hardly think will be the case these three months. What will be the result of their meeting I cannot with any certainty determine, but I hardly think much good can come of it: the people of America don't appear to me to be ripe for any great innovations.[21]

The delegates of twelve states meeting at Philadelphia succeeded fairly well at first in keeping their proceedings secret, judging by the letters of members of Congress. Nathan Dane wrote to Rufus King on June 19th: "I fully agree to the propriety of the Convention order restraining its members from communicating its doings, tho' I feel a strong desire and curiosity to know how it proceeds. I think the public never ought to see anything but the final report of the Convention—the digested result only. . . ."[22]

Most of the delegates had not anticipated anything more drastic than revising the Articles of Confederation; nor did the credentials from a single state authorize the framing of a new constitution. Charles Pinckney brought to Philadelphia the amendments proposed the summer before in Congress, but again there was the fatal clause that a change in the Articles must be "confirmed by the legislatures of every state." This was a serious handicap at a time when one of the states had seceded for all practical purposes. "Rhode Island has negatived a motion for appointing delegates to the Convention, by a majority of twenty two votes," Madison wrote to Edmund Randolph on April 2nd. "Nothing can exceed the wickedness and folly which continue to reign there. All sense of character as well as right is obliterated." [23]

The men conferring in the State House had the good sense to realize that they might better go home than limit themselves to revision. Still, it is almost impossible for a present-day American to realize what a mental struggle it took for most of them to accept those three words, "We, the people." All past conceptions of American government had been built on the familiar foundation of states exercising semi-independent powers. Not only did several of them have their own currency and customs duties in 1787, but also their own "navies" and separate little "armies" of militia. Even the advocates of more authority for Congress had in effect recognized the sovereignty of the states by suggesting various schemes of coercion. Early in June the members of Congress seem to have had more than an inkling that unusual measures were brewing at Philadelphia. For there is an air of suppressed excitement in Edward Carrington's letter of June 9th to Thomas Jefferson:

> . . . the Convention, as a Beacon, is rousing the attention of the Empire. The prevailing impression as well in, as out of, Convention, is, that a foederal Government adapted to the permanent circumstances of the Country, without respect to the habits of the day, be formed, whose efficiency shall pervade the whole Empire: it may, and probably will, at first, be viewed with hesitation, but . . . its influence must extend into a general adoption as present fabric gives way. That the people are disposed to be governed is evinced by their turning out to support the shadows under which they now live, and if a work of wisdom is prepared for them, they will not reject it to commit themselves to the dubious issue of Anarchy. [24]

Despite the pledge of secrecy, the major decisions could not be kept long from members of Congress. Richard Henry Lee had declined on grounds of propriety to serve as a delegate to both councils. But on his way to New York the first week in July he "found the Convention at Philadelphia very busy and very secret. it would seem however, from variety of circumstances," he wrote to his brother Francis Lightfoot on the 14th, "we shall hear of a Government not unlike the B. Constitution, that is, an Executive with 2 Branches composing a federal Legislature and possessing adequate Tone." [25]

A letter written five days later also indicates that members of Congress now had a pretty good idea of what was going on in the State House. William Blount of North Carolina, who returned to Congress on July 3rd, confided in a letter to his brother the news from the Convention:

> The general outlines were to have a National Assembly composed of three Branches the first to be elected by the People at large and to consist of about 70 Members, the second Branch of a less Number to be chosen by the respective

Legislatures for a longer Duration and the third an Executive of a single Man for a still longer Time. I must confess not withstanding all I heard in favour of this System I am not in sentiment with my Colleagues for . . . I still think we shall ultimately and not many Years just be separate and distinct Governments perfectly independent of each other.[26]

The misgivings of the North Carolina farmer, who became a congressman under the new government a few years later, were shared by a great many other Americans. All that sweltering summer—the hottest that oldsters could recall since the middle of the century—men discussing the great topic of interest grew worried at the thought of an individual becoming chief executive. The events of 1776 were still so recent that such an idea smelled of monarchy if not actually tyranny. Scarcely less radical was the "Great Compromise" which gave the small states equal representation in the Senate, and the large states proportional representation in the lower branch of the national legislature. But most dubious of all, perhaps, was the provision for members of the House of Representatives to be elected by popular vote. Even such a sturdy Yankee as Roger Sherman, himself a countrified man of the people, had declared on the floor of the Convention his opinion that the people should have "as little to do as may be about the Government."

These were some of the doubts and fears felt by Americans of 1787 in reaction to rumors of the decisions being made behind the closed doors of the State House. On August 18th the Convention even deemed it necessary to publish in the *Pennsylvania Herald* an unofficial denial of a wild tale that plans were afoot to import Frederick Augustus, Duke of York and second son of George III, as king of the United States.

The members of Congress found their long term of idleness hard to endure. Nathan Dane, in a letter of May 31st to Rufus King, mentioned "how disagreeable this apathetic mode of doing business in Congress is. it appears to me to make the government appear more feeble than it even is, and to have a pernicious effect on the public mind and feelings." A few weeks later Charles Thomson wrote to William Bingham about the "alarm the secession of the Members from Congress at this crisis has spread through the eastern states. Were I to hazard an opinion it would be that the peace of the union and the happy termination of the Measures of the Convention depend on the Meeting and Continuance of Congress and keeping up a form of Government until the New plan is ready for adoption."[27]

It could scarcely have been imagined in this twilight of the Continental Congress that the assembly would suddenly spring to life in July and pass one of the five greatest documents of the entire Revolutionary era.

The secretary of Congress rounded up the members of enough states for a quorum by "stealing" men away from the Convention. William Blount reported to Governor Caswell on July 10th that while he and Benjamin Hawkins were at Philadelphia they "received a letter from Charles Thomson informing us that our presence would complete seven states in Congress and that a Congress was necessary for the great purposes of the Union; whereupon we returned here on the 4th Instant and formed a Congress and we consider ourselves bound to continue until some other State comes up of which we are in hourly Expectation and then I shall proceed to the convention. . . ." [28]

It became the fate of the Continental Congress that after thirteen years of striving in vain for an adequate source of income, funds promised to pour into its lap just as it was being superseded by a new government. Even such a reasonable request as the impost had been refused, and yet this summer found a persuasive lobbyist visiting New York with glib talk of millions. The Rev. Manasseh Cutler of Massachusetts, representing the Ohio Land Company newly formed of New England investors, placed before the delegates some cogent arguments which indicated that western lands would soon provide the solution for financial troubles. But first it seemed expedient to pass the long-postponed "Northwest Ordinance" for the government of the people who would occupy the lands.

Discussions of the provisions, it will be recalled, had made a good deal of progress in the early spring of 1784, when Thomas Jefferson was in Congress. Then the foundation had been laid, and the original blueprint remained as a guide. Hence it did not take long for a committee consisting of Richard Henry Lee, John Kean, Nathan Dane, Edward Carrington and Melancton Smith to report on July 11th "An Ordinance for the Government of the territory of the United States North West of the river Ohio." Never did a measure go more swiftly through the legislative mill; for it had a second reading on July 12th and was passed on Friday, the 13th, with but a single negative. The vote, as published in the *Journals*, was as follows:

Massachusetts		*Virginia*	
Mr. Holten	ay ⎱ ay	Mr. Grayson	ay ⎱
Mr. Dane	ay ⎰	Mr. R. H. Lee	ay ⎬ ay
New York		Mr. Carrington	ay ⎰
Mr. Smith	ay ⎱	*North Carolina*	
Mr. Haring	ay ⎬ ay	Mr. Blount	ay ⎱ ay
Mr. Yates	no ⎰	Mr. Hawkins	ay ⎰
New Jersey		*South Carolina*	
Mr. Clark	ay ⎱ ay	Mr. Kean	ay ⎱ ay
Mr. Schureman	ay ⎰	Mr. Huger	ay ⎰

Delaware		*Georgia*	
Mr. Kearny	ay ⎫ ay	Mr. Few	ay ⎫ ay [29]
Mr. Mitchell	ay ⎭	Mr. Pierce	ay ⎭

Posterity is indebted to Abraham Yates, the Albany ex-sheriff, for this record. In order that his lone negative might long be remembered, he demanded that the yeas and nays be published. This difference of opinion did not win him any praise from following generations, for the Northwest Ordinance remains to this day one of the greatest achievements of the Continental Congress. Like its great predecessors, the Association, the Declaration, and the Confederation, it has the merit of a brevity which has become a lost art in the papers of subsequent Congresses. Only six articles and eight pages, as published in the *Journals*, were needed to present a system of government which proved to be more advanced and liberal in some respects than the Constitution then being debated at Philadelphia.

Important as the measure was, Congress did not seem to think that it called for the assent of nine states. Or it may be that Secretary Thomson had no hope of gathering more than eight. At any rate, the decision of eighteen delegates, one of whom differed emphatically, gave the United States its measure for the government of the vast empire on the other side of the mountains.

If the Northwest Ordinance needed only three days for passage, it must be remembered that it had been debated at various times for three years. The act of April 23, 1784, had placed the number of inhabitants necessary for statehood as equal to the smallest of the thirteen states. But the definitive ordinance of 1787 specified 60,000 free inhabitants and limited the number of states to be created from the area at not less than three or more than five. As soon as a district had 5,000 free male inhabitants, representatives could be elected to an assembly. Congress was to appoint for the entire area a governor and three judges whose duties were described as follows:

> The governor, and judges or a majority of them shall adopt and publish in the district such laws of the original states criminal and civil as may be necessary and best suited to the circumstances of the district and report them to Congress from time to time, which laws shall be in force in the district until the organization of a general assembly therein, unless disapproved by Congress; but afterwards the legislature shall have authority to alter them as they shall think fit.

The legislature and council of a district were also empowered "to elect a Delegate to Congress, who shall have a seat in Congress, with a right of debating, but not of voting, during this temporary Government."

Richard Henry Lee, in letters written that month, described the Northwest Ordinance as "much more tonic than our democratic forms on the Atlantic are." He mentioned the need for a "strong toned government" over "the rude people who will probably be the first settlers there." [30] It is strange that this great champion of popular rights should not have paid more tribute to such provisions in the Ordinance. For the measure guaranteed not only the rights of habeas corpus and trial by jury but also a number of safeguards for the protection of individual liberties which were later incorporated in the so-called Bill of Rights of the permanent Constitution.

The United States has justly been branded with the reproach of legalizing slavery within its own borders after proclaiming liberty to all the world. Hence it is worth noting that the act of 1787 represents one of the first great blows of modern history to be struck at that ancient evil. William Wilber-force, the famous English reformer, had to wait until 1807 before he accomplished much in the House of Commons; but two decades earlier the Continental Congress proclaimed in Jefferson's words:

> There shall be neither Slavery nor involuntary Servitude in said territory otherwise than in the punishment of crimes, whereof the party shall have been duly convicted. . . .

At a time when popular education remained a dream in most parts of the Old World, the Northwest Ordinance provided that "Schools and the means of education shall always be encouraged." These were not empty words, since the income from a section of land in every township was to go for public schools. The Ordinance also set a standard for Indian dealings which might have saved a good many blots on the national honor if it had been more often honored in practice:

> The utmost good faith shall always be observed towards the Indians, their lands and property shall never be taken away from them without their consent; and in their property, rights and liberty, they shall never be invaded or disturbed, unless in just and lawful wars authorized by Congress; but laws founded in justice and humanity shall from time to time be made, for preventing wrongs being done to them, and for preserving peace and friendship with them.

Congress did not forget "the french and canadian inhabitants and other settlers of the Kaskaskies, Saint Vincents and the neighbouring villages." These wards by conquest were very sensibly guaranteed "their laws and customs now in force among them relative to the descent and conveyance of property."

Because rather than in spite of its brevity and simplicity, the Northwest Ordinance is worthy of a place among the great instruments of history which men have devised for their own government. Before the end of the year

Congress added the finishing touches by appointing Arthur St. Clair of Pennsylvania as the first governor. James M. Varnum of Rhode Island, Samuel Holden Parsons of Massachusetts and John Cleaves Symmes of New Jersey were chosen as the three judges.

Soon after the passage of the Ordinance several delegates returned to Philadelphia. On August 3rd Congress found itself again lacking a quorum until September 20th, the day which brought the long-awaited report from the Convention. The response to this exciting event boosted the attendance up to nine states immediately and eleven states within a week.

The *Journals* are significantly silent as to the proceedings on September 26th, when the new Constitution came up for debate. But the next day Richard Henry Lee offered a motion, seconded by Melancton Smith of New York, that the document be passed on without comment "to the executive of every state in this Union to be laid before their respective legislatures." As justification for this decent burial, the Virginia delegate cited the thirteenth article of the Confederation, which "limits the power of Congress to the amendment of the present confederacy of thirteen states, but does not extend it to the creation of a new confederacy of nine states."

The other delegates knew very well that Lee was not merely quibbling about a point of law. As the foremost opponent of the Constitution in Congress, along with Nathan Dane, he hoped to send it hastily to the states without a recommendation by that body. When this proposal was voted down, he introduced new tactics which were described by Madison in a letter of October 16th to Jefferson:

> When the plan came up before Cong. for their sanction, a very serious effort was made by R. H. Lee and Mr. Dane from Mass'ts to embarrass it. It was first contended that Congress could not properly give its positive countenance to a measure which had for its object the subversion of the constitution under which they acted. The ground of attack failing, the former gentleman urged the expediency of sending out the plan with amendments, and proposed a number of them corresponding with the objections of Col. Mason. This experiment had still less effect. In order however to obtain unanimity it was necessary to couch the resolution in very moderate terms.[31]

Of course, it was known in Congress by this time that Elbridge Gerry, George Mason and Edmund Randolph, along with a few other delegates at Philadelphia, had shown their disapproval of certain provisions by refusing to sign the Constitution. In a letter to Randolph of October 16th, Lee complained that he had been overwhelmed on the floor of Congress by delegates prejudiced in favor:

With the Constitution came, from the Convention, so many members of that body to Congress, and of those, too, who were among the most fiery zealots for their system, that the votes of three states being of them, two states divided by them and many others mixed with them, it is easy to see that Congress could have little opinion on the subject. Some denied our right to make amendments; whilst others, more moderate, agreed to the right, but denied the expediency of amending; but it was plain that a majority was ready to send it on, in terms of approbation.[32]

Congress needed but two days to make up its mind. For the *Journals* of September 28th record the only recommendation that could have been passed without a dissenting vote:

Congress having received the report of the Convention lately assembled in Philadelphia

Resolved Unanimously that the said Report with the resolutions and letters accompanying the same be transmitted to the several legislatures in Order to be submitted to a convention of Delegates chosen in each state by the people thereof in conformity to the resolves of the Convention made and provided in that case.[33]

This was not, to be sure, much of a tribute. But it was at least better than a funeral without flowers. And it was the signal for a furious battle of words such as America had not known since the days of 1776.

Chapter 27

And On with the New

AFTER a century had passed, nobody challenged Gladstone when he
lauded the Constitution of the United States as "the most wonderful
work ever struck off at a given time by the brain and purpose of man."
But in 1787 it is not likely that this appraisal would have been accepted
even by the makers of that document. Not a single one of them, judging by
surviving writings, appears to have felt that the instrument was perfect.

Gouverneur Morris, the "penman" who had most to do with the style
of the definitive Constitution, declared that "while some have boasted of it
as a work from Heaven, others have given it a less righteous origin. I have
many reasons to believe that it is the work of plain honest men, and such,
I think, it will appear."

Above all, the Americans of 1787 could never have agreed with Gladstone
that the work had been struck off at a given time. They knew that it had
evolved from a vast fund of experience, much of it painful, accumulated
in that great laboratory of political science, the Continental Congress. Not
only had the brain and purpose of the makers contributed to the instrument,
but the very bones and sinews of men who had been patiently jogging along
country roads for thirteen years to attend sessions of the Continental
Congress.

The other four great documents of the American Revolution had been
reported, debated, revised, and approved on the floor of the assembly. But
the Constitution is even more truly the product of the Continental Congress
because it was hammered out of the hard metal of theory tempered by
practice. All the makers, with but a few minor exceptions, had had from
two to ten years' experience in the Continental Congress. They did not
have to guess as to the probable workings of the provisions they wrote into

407

the Constitution. They knew the answers as nearly as men could learn from the hopes, dreams, successes and failures of an assembly trying to function as a central government without adequate powers.

Knowledge of revolutions was meager in 1787 as compared to the middle of the twentieth century. The men of the Convention had not been given such an opportunity to observe the cycle taken by most political upheavals— from liberty to anarchy, then back to tyranny. Yet the writings of the day show a grave and realistic outlook. That great federalist Benjamin Rush warned his countrymen in the opening sentences of his *Address to the People of the United States,* published a few months before the Convention:

> There is nothing more common than to confuse the terms of the American revolution with those of the late American war. The American war is over; but this is far from being the case with the American revolution. On the contrary, nothing but the first act of that great drama is closed. It remains yet to establish and perfect our new forms of government; and to prepare the principles, morals and manners of our citizens, for those forms of government, after they are established and brought to perfection.

George Washington, as president of the Convention, signed the letter which went out to the states. Only five paragraphs in length, it answered in advance the objections which were sure to be brought up by the states' rights men:

> It is obviously impracticable in the foederal government of these States, to secure all rights of independent sovereignty to each, and yet provide for the interest and safety of all. Individuals entering into society, must give up a share of liberty to preserve the rest. . . . It is at all times difficult to draw with precision the line between those rights which must be surrendered, and those which may be reserved; and on the present occasion this difficulty was increased by a difference among the several States as to their situation, extent, habits, and particular interests. . . . In all our deliberations on this subject we kept steadily in our view that which appears to us the greatest interest of every true American, the consolidation of our Union. . . .[1]

Now that the Constitution has been functioning for a century and a half, its opponents of 1787 are too likely to be dismissed as selfish obstructionists or reactionaries. It is too easy to forget that George Mason and Edmund Randolph led a losing fight on the floor of the Convention to abolish slavery, which the former condemned as "diabolical in itself, and disgraceful to mankind."

Richard Henry Lee took the equally unpopular course of opposing the Constitution in Congress because he believed that it did not provide for essential individual liberties. After losing the first skirmishes, he kept on stubbornly battling for amendments. "The necessary alterations," he declared in a letter of October 2, 1787, to William Shippen, "will by no means interfere with the general nature of the plan, or limit the power of doing good; but they will restrain from oppression the wicked & tyrannic. If all men were wise and good there would be no necessity for government or law— But the folly & the vice of human nature renders government & laws necessary for the Many, and restraints indispensable to prevent oppression from those who are entrusted with the administration of one & the dispensation of the other." [2]

Lee and his colleague William Grayson damned the Constitution for quite opposite reasons—the one because he thought it too strong, the other because it seemed too weak. "Upon the whole," commented Grayson in a letter of November 10th to William Short, "I look upon the new system as a most ridiculous piece of business—something (*entre nous*) like the legs of Nebuchadnezar's image: It seems to have been formed by jumbling or compressing a number of ideas together, something like the manner in which poems were made in Swift's flying island. However bad as it is, I believe it will be crammed down our throats rough and smooth with all it's imperfections. . . ." [3]

Hamilton, Gouverneur Morris and many other Americans of undoubted patriotism agreed with Grayson that a consolidated government was preferable to a federal union. No better argument could have been advanced than to cite the new plague of absenteeism which prostrated the Continental Congress as soon as that body recovered from its first excitement. By the middle of October the attendance had dropped to seven states, and early in November only five were on hand to greet the new federal year. Their salutations were in vain, for the balance of the calendar year passed without a single day's quorum. Necessary as it was to preserve a visible head of the government until the new constitution should be ratified or rejected, Secretary Thomson could not persuade the governors that "the honor and interest of the Confederacy require a speedy and constant representation in Congress. . . ."

The financial situation in the autumn of 1787 was worse than ever, though the western lands held out hope of relief. On September 29th the Board of Treasury reported that "it appears altogether impracticable, in the present state of the Federal Government to make the Interest or Honor of the Union coincide with what the several States appear to judge for their convenience in this respect." Madison confirmed this gloomy view in a letter of December 20th to Thomas Jefferson:

> The States seem to be either wholly omitting to provide for the federal Treasury, or to be withdrawing the scanty appropriations made to it. The latter

course has been taken up by Massachusetts, Virginia and Delaware. The Treasury Board seems to be in despair of maintaining the shadow of government much longer. Without money, the offices must be shut up, and the handful of troops on the frontier disbanded, which will probably bring on an Indian War, and make an impression to our disadvantage on the British Garrisons within our limits.[4]

The North Carolina delegates, cooling their heels in New York, were asked by the legislature of their state to report on federal affairs. The answer should have been more persuasive than the most eloquent rhetoric as an argument for a new constitution:

> To describe the present state and circumstances of the Union, we may declare in one word that we are at the Eave of a Bankruptcy and of a total dissolution of Government. Since the close of the War there has not been paid into the General Treasury as much money as was necessary for one year's interest of the domestic and foreign debt, and Congress have been reduced to the dreadful alternative of borrowing principal to pay interest. Our efforts at home to this end were ineffectual; abroad where we were not known and where enthusiasm for liberty enrolled us among the most deserving of mankind, we were more Successful. The deception cannot be much longer kept up and unless something can be done before the close of the ensuing year we must cease to be a United Government. Our friends must give us up, and we shall become a laughing stock to our enemies.[5]

Congress had not been snubbed so much as forgotten during these exciting months while men all over the country were arguing the great question. The failure of the impost having taught how difficult it was to induce all thirteen states to agree, it had been wisely provided that the Constitution could be ratified with the assent of nine. Pennsylvania, Delaware and New Jersey led the way before the end of the year, and Georgia, Connecticut and Massachusetts followed during the first two months of 1788. Maryland and South Carolina ratified in April and May, leaving it to New Hampshire to become the ninth state on June 21st.

This gave the Constitution its vital minimum, but the advocates did not feel that their victory would be complete without the approval of such large and influential states as Virginia and New York. By the spring of 1788 every American had become either a Federalist or an Antifederalist, and was telling his neighbor so in a loud voice. Ammunition for these tavern and street-corner debates was supplied to the friends of the Constitution by the brilliant *Federalist* essays of Hamilton and Madison. Not so well known, since they upheld the losing side, were Richard Henry Lee's *Letters of the Federal Farmer*, urging the need for a less consolidated government paying more attention to individual rights.

Twelve years had passed since the 55-year-old Virginia planter offered the original motion for American independence. In 1776 his chief opponent had been a man of his own physical and intellectual type—a thin, nervous and sensitive fighter with the courage to champion an unpopular cause. Now the situation was reversed, and John Dickinson took a leading part in advancing the Constitution while Richard Henry Lee warned that a hasty ratification would be repented. John Dickinson did much to gain the immediate assent of Pennsylvania and Delaware, while Richard Henry Lee was quite as influential in causing Virginia to hesitate.

Neither in 1788 nor in 1776 did the voice of the minority go unheard. John Dickinson served his country well in preventing a premature Declaration of Independence; and Richard Henry Lee deserved more credit than any other individual for the amendments included in the Bill of Rights.

Abraham Clark in the summer of 1776 had personified the plain, everyday American with his acceptance of independence. In the summer of 1788, his tenth in the Continental Congress, the 62-year-old New Jersey surveyor was still plodding down the middle of the road, slightly left of center. Twelve years before, he had speculated as to whether he might not be "exalted on a high gallows" for his part in approving and signing the Declaration of Independence. And in a letter to a friend of July 23, 1788, he described his travail in accepting the Constitution:

> I never liked the System in all its parts. I considered it from the first, more a Consolidated government than a federal, a government too expensive, and unnecessarily oppressive in its Operation: Creating a Judiciary undefined and unbounded. With all these imperfections about it, I nevertheless wished it to go to the States from Congress just as it did, without Censure or Commendation, hoping that in Case of a general Adoption, the Wisdom of the States would soon amend it in the exceptionable parts. Strong fears however remained in my mind untill I found the Custom of Recommending amendments with the Adoptions began to prevail. This set my mind at ease.[6]

The New Jersey surveyor was not the only patriot to fear the plunge into the unknown as represented by a strong federal judiciary and a single executive with veto powers. Yet it was the implication of those three words "We, the people" which most disturbed men long accustomed to the sovereignty of the states. Patrick Henry, George Mason and William Grayson were the leading opponents of the Constitution in Virginia. Madison, John Marshall and Henry Lee fought for ratification, supported by Edmund Randolph after his "apostasy" from the Antifederalists. Weeks of furious debate led up to the decision of June 25th, when the state convention decided by a vote of 89 to 79 in favor of ratification.

The fight in New York was almost as bitter, with Hamilton, Jay and

Robert R. Livingston opposing George Clinton, Melancton Smith and the other Antifederalists. The state voted for ratification on July 26th, but North Carolina did not come into the fold as the twelfth state until the late date of November 19th after finding it necessary to call a second convention.

Acceptance of the Constitution could never be unanimous, but it must have been a satisfaction to contemplate the spectacle of stubborn little Rhode Island in outer darkness. The whole history of the Confederation, beginning with its own ratification, had been filled with dreary interludes in which a single state had the power to block the will of the other twelve. This time the majority went their way without interference, and the wayward sister crept sheepishly back into the Union on May 29, 1790. Even so, the state convention did not reach its decision until after the federal Senate passed a bill severing commercial relations between the United States and Rhode Island.

Congress was relegated to the unwonted role of bystander during the months when most of the state conventions were meeting. Not until January 21, 1788, did enough delegates reach New York so that seven states could elect Cyrus Griffin of Virginia as president two days later. Even this step, according to Samuel Alleyne Otis, was taken in a dutiful spirit to "preserve the forms." He added in a letter of February 6th to James Warren, "I need not enlarge upon the weak state of the Federal government; Many circumstances contribute to debase its dignity." [7]

Although Otis mentioned that "Congress have it in contemplation to adjourn in the Spring," the assembly continued in session. On February 19th Madison informed Jefferson that "the Public here [New York] continues to be much agitated by the proposed federal Constitution and to be attentive to little else. . . . Congress have done no business of consequence yet, nor is it probable that much more of any sort will precede the event of the great question before the public." [8]

Day after day went by with nothing accomplished, so that Nathan Dane could only report to Samuel Holten in a letter of March 15th: "There has been a Congress most of the time for two months past and part of the time nine States assembled but we do very little business. Indeed we have but very little to do. It does not appear to be the intention of Congress to engage in any important business, an adjournment has been mentioned for a few months." [9]

Under these circumstances it is not remarkable that a number of delegates should have found something better to occupy their time. Throughout March and April the attendance varied between three and six states. "Here we remain in an idle situation," grumbled Dane on April 18th; and as late as May 3rd the Rev. Paine Wingate of New Hampshire wrote that "we have not had a Congress until yesterday for some time past, owing to two or three members going out of town." [10]

During the idle months a great deal of unfinished business had accumulated. As early as January 24th the *Journals* mentioned the receipt of a letter "from John Fitch praying Congress to grant him a premium for his invention of a *steam boat* for applying steam to work a boat against wind and tide without sails or men to labour." [11] The inventor did not receive much encouragement from Congress, but he persevered with several state legislatures until he was conveying passengers for hire on the Delaware in the summer of 1790.

Congress could not make up its mind whether a government in suspense should go on functioning or merely keep adding to the heap of unfinished business. Even some of the military accounts had not been adjusted at this late date, five years after the conclusion of peace. And though the Ordinance had been passed for the government of the western lands, the cessions of Georgia and North Carolina remained to be accepted. Worse yet, some of the issues already settled, such as the Wyoming valley dispute between Pennsylvania and Connecticut citizens, had broken out into a rash of new problems.

There had been no doubt for a long time that Vermont would achieve statehood by hook or by crook. On June 2nd, with nine states in attendance again, the committee of the whole reported "that in their opinion it is expedient that the district of Kentucky be erected into a separate state. . . ." [12] The politicians of Congress could see how neatly Vermont would pair with Kentucky, just as Maine would offset Tennessee at a later date, thus preserving the balance of power between northern and southern interests. But before the Kentucky question could be settled, Congress learned on July 2nd that New Hampshire had become the ninth state to ratify the new Constitution. This news offered an excellent excuse to drop the discussion while a committee deliberated on the problems of "putting the said constitution into operation."

As if this were not excitement enough for one week, a miracle occurred in the City Hall a few days later. Peleg Arnold's quill must have sputtered in agitation when he communicated the dramatic, the incredible news to Welcome Arnold in a letter of July 11th: "We have this Day Thirteen States on the Floor of Congress which has not been until the present case Since the year 1776.* Ten States having Ratified the New Constitution, Congress are now Deliberating on the time for the States to appoint Ellectors, to Choose a President, and when Proceedings Shall commince under said Constitution." [13]

* More accurately, since the Confederation of 1781.

After the countless letters Secretary Thomson had written to governors, pleading for a quorum in Congress, he must have beamed as he recorded the thirty-eight names under the thirteen states:

NEW HAMPSHIRE—Paine Wingate, Nicholas Gilman;
MASSACHUSETTS—Nathan Dane, Theodore Sedgwick, Samuel Alleyne Otis;
RHODE ISLAND—Peleg Arnold, Jonathan J. Hazard;
CONNECTICUT—Benjamin Huntington, Jeremiah Wadsworth, Pierrepont Edwards;
NEW YORK—Ezra L'Hommedieu, Egbert Benson, Alexander Hamilton, Abraham Yates;
NEW JERSEY—Abraham Clark, Jonathan Dayton;
PENNSYLVANIA—William Irvine, Samuel Meredith, John Armstrong, William Bingham, James R. Reid;
DELAWARE—Dyre Kearny, Nathaniel Mitchell;
MARYLAND—Joshua Seney, David Ross, Benjamin Contee;
VIRGINIA—Cyrus Griffin, James Madison, Edward Carrington, Richard Henry Lee, John Brown;
NORTH CAROLINA—Hugh Williamson, John Swann;
SOUTH CAROLINA—Daniel Huger, John Parker, Thomas Tudor Tucker;
GEORGIA—William Few, Abraham Baldwin.

It was no mystery to the politicians of Congress why absenteeism had ceased so abruptly. No state cared to be without a voice at a time when the outlines of the future government were being shaped. Even Rhode Island, after refusing to send delegates to the Convention, did not propose to be left out in the cold.

Before many decisions could be made, the delegates were drawn into America's most strident celebration of the ratification of the Constitution. The fact that New York herself had not yet ratified did not dampen the enthusiasm of the city on July 23rd. New York meant to outdo the festivities at Philadelphia in December and Boston in February. These occasions had featured allegorical ships of state, paraded through the streets on wheels; but New York created the masterpiece of them all in the *Hamilton*—"a Frigate of thirty-two guns, twenty-seven feet keel, and ten feet beam, with galleries and everything complete and in proportion, both in hull and rigging; manned with upwards of thirty seamen and marines, in their different uniforms."

Thirteen guns gave the signal for the "grand procession." Abreast of old Fort George on Bowling Green, where President Griffin and the members of Congress awaited, the *Hamilton* fired another salute of thirteen guns, followed by three cheers from the crowd. The delegates "politely acknowledged" this ovation, and Hugh Williamson mentioned in a letter of the 26th that "Congress were invited to dine with the company, some thousands under a particular pavilion in the fields. The other states attended," he added sadly, "but the North Carolina delegates stayed at home." The delay in his state's ratification was still troubling the Edenton physician when he wrote to a friend on August 23rd that "North Carolina has at length thrown herself out of the Union, but she happily is not alone; the large, upright, and respectable state of Rhode Island is her associate." [14]

After recovering from its holiday, Congress found no lack of problems clamoring for immediate attention. Georgia had presented a cession of her western lands which had to be refused because of unsatisfactory provisions. Reports of violence had come from the Wyoming valley, and on July 25th Congress resolved "that the Secretary of War direct the detachment of troops marching to the westward to rendezvous in Easton in Pennsylvania and from thence march into the county of Luzerne for quelling the disturbances in that county. . . ." [15]

Foreign affairs were unsettled. Jefferson and Adams had been able to borrow another million guilders in Holland on the strength of a new Constitution being established, but Congress had not as yet been given the contract to ratify. British troops continued to occupy half a dozen forts on American soil, and relations between the recent enemies were not cordial. Jay still insisted, according to Madison's notes of debates, that "the U. S. were more in the wrong in the violation of the Treaty of Peace than G. B. But still the latter were not blameless." Madison, however, resented "the indignity of G. B. in neglecting to send a public minister to the U. S. notwithstanding the lapse of time since Mr. Adams' arrival there" and believed "that self-respect seemed to require that the U. S. should at least proceed with distrust & reserve." [16]

London newspapers filled with sensational accounts of anarchy in America had reached these shores. "The british Courtiers are ridiculing our situation very much," Cyrus Griffin wrote to Thomas FitzSimons on May 27th, "and tell Mr. Adams in a sneering manner when America shall assume some kind of Government then England will speak to her." [17] At least, such evidences of an unfriendly British attitude had been put to use by the Federalists urging ratification of the Constitution.

Even the relations with America's recent ally had become much less cordial since the great days of Gérard and Luzerne. The Comte du Moustier, the new French chargé d'affaires, had his public audience on February 26, 1788. Then a scandal developed when the ladies of Congress learned that he had brought his mistress, Madame de Brehan, who happened to be neither young nor alluring. John Armstrong, Jr., wrote to Horatio Gates on May 30th that "if France had wish'd to destroy the little remembrance that is left to her and her exertions—she would have sent just such a Minister —distant, haughty and penurious—and entirely govern'd by the caprice of a little, singular, whimsical, hysterical old woman whose delight is in playing with a negro child and caressing a monkey." [18]

Madison felt concern over a situation threatening political as well as social consequences. "Moustier proves a most unlucky appointment," he wrote to Jefferson on December 8, 1788. "He is unsocial proud and niggardly and betrays a sort of fastidiousness toward this country. He suffers also from his illicit connection with Madame de Brehan, which is universally known and offensive to American manners. She is perfectly soured toward this country. The ladies of New York . . . have for some time withdrawn their attention from her. She knows the cause, is deeply stung by it, views everything thro' the medium of rancor and conveys her impressions to her paramour over whom she exercises despotic sway." [19]

This imbroglio and more important business had to wait until decisions were made as to the establishment of the new government. There was nothing that the migratory assembly could debate with more gusto than the prospect of a new meeting place. Seldom in its history had the Continental Congress been flattered, and most of these occasions were connected with lobbying efforts to transfer the seat of government. Even little Wilmington entered her bid in the summer of 1788 with disastrous results to the leading candidate. On August 11th Madison wrote to Edmund Randolph that "Philadelphia was first named . . . and was negatived by the voice of one from Delaware, who wished to make an experiment for Wilmington. New York came next into view. Lancaster was opposed to it and failed. Baltimore was tried next and to the surprize of every one had seven votes." [20]

Philadelphia's narrow defeat became the more bitter when New York finally won by virtue of the vote of the despised Rhode Island delegation. Next came the question whether that state and North Carolina were qualified to decide questions of a new government which they had not yet accepted. Such comparisons hurt the feelings of the North Carolina members, who declared indignantly that they did not care "to have North Carolina associated in any vote with Rhode Island."

New York's majority remained under a cloud until September 13th, when the opponents yielded, according to Madison, for fear of "strangling the Government in its birth." This same Saturday morning the Continental Congress passed the last important resolution of its history—a resolution which was that assembly's own death warrant:

> That the first Wednesday in Jany. next be the day for appointing Electors in the several states, which before the said day shall have ratified the said constitution; that the first Wednesday in feby. next be the day for the electors

to assemble in their respective states and vote for a president; and that the first Wednesday in March next be the time and the present seat of Congress the place for commencing proceedings under the new constitution.[21]

If the delegates felt any sentimentality about the occasion, their letters do not reveal it. Most of them appeared to be in a hurry to start home before the members of the new Congress were selected. Neither the word nor the practice of electioneering found much favor in that day; for eighteenth-century gentlemen preferred to believe that a public servant should neither seek nor refuse office. But there are exceptions to the best of precepts, and any politician knows how fatal it is to blush unseen. Thus it was probably not pure coincidence that thirteen of the thirty-eight delegates returned to New York the following year as senators or representatives. In addition, so many former members of the Continental Congress were elected to the first United States Congress that they controlled both Houses.

Among the new senators were such old friends as William Samuel Johnson, Oliver Ellsworth, George Read, William Few, John Henry, Charles Carroll of Carrollton, John Langdon, Jonathan Elmer, Rufus King, Philip Schuyler, Benjamin Hawkins, Pierce Butler, Ralph Izard, William Grayson and Richard Henry Lee.

The House of Representatives listed other familiar names—Roger Sherman, Abraham Baldwin, Daniel Carroll, Elbridge Gerry, Abiel Foster, Samuel Livermore, Elias Boudinot, Hugh Williamson, William Floyd, George Clymer, Thomas FitzSimons, Daniel Huger, James Madison and Theodorick Bland.

It could never have been said that the republic had shown ingratitude toward the men who guided American destinies through the era of the Revolution.

Again on September 18th the attendance shrank to fewer than seven states. It remained at this level until the 25th, when the return of several wandering delegates restored a quorum. With so many pieces of unfinished business left to choose from, it seems odd that Congress should first have considered a problem going all the way back to the year 1776. The Board of Treasury reported that the claim of Caron de Beaumarchais "has no other Voucher to support it, than a copy of a certificate, said to have been signed by Silas Deane." Further evidence indicated "that the supplies sent out from Mr. Beaumarchais, were only made through him, as a private Agent of the Court." Congress put off decision until October 1st, when it was resolved "that the settlement of the accounts of Mr. Caron de Beaumarchais . . . cannot be deemed binding on the United States the said Mr. Deane not being vested with any authority to make such settlement." [22]

The next day Congress lost its home. New York had undertaken to re-model the City Hall before the new government moved in; and the old assembly adjourned for four days, according to George Thatcher in a letter of October 2nd, "to meet in the Rooms where Mr. Jay kept his office. This has become necessary, as the Old Hall and Court Room are to be new-modeled; and the workmen made such a continual noise that it was impossible to hear one another speak. I should not wonder if by the middle of next week Congress were to adjourn without delay. Many are uneasy and are for going home." [23]

On October 6th, following the interlude, six states were represented in the new quarters, but only three the next day. Then the attendance came back to seven again; and if the delegates had but suspected, they transacted the last official business of the Continental Congress on Friday, October 10, 1788.

It was fitting that the final motion should have been put by Abraham Clark. The New Jersey delegate, after recording his first vote for the Declaration of Independence, had been a member since the summer of 1776, barring one or possibly two years when he could not afford to attend. On this October day Clark moved, and Hugh Williamson seconded, that the secretary of war be directed to hand out no more bounties of land to ex-officers who had neglected to account for funds received by them as pay-masters during the war.

It was further appropriate that this last motion should have lost—the entire history of the Continental Congress had been a record of stubborn men inching ahead, making an occasional gain after a succession of losses. The following Monday only two states were on hand, plus a sprinkling of additional delegates. And from October 21st to the end of the month, Secretary Thomson could list a total of only thirteen individuals.

At least, Peleg Arnold of Rhode Island had not lost hope. He had heard many unkind things said about his state, and he had nearly run out of personal funds. But he could still write to Governor John Collins on October 20th "that my Situation renders it Expedient for the State to make further Provision for my support. Such Matters as are unfinish'd at the end of this Year, and others that concern the Union will be taken into Consideration by the Congress which are to assembly the first monday in Novr. next." [24]

Samuel Alleyne Otis stuck it out until that very day. "Brother Thatcher has left me several days since," he wrote to Nathan Dane on October 29th, "and not being . . . more than 4 or 5 members here, and no prospect of new Congress until Decem'r, I determine on Monday . . . to sett off for Massachusetts." [25]

James Madison suspected that the Continental Congress had already come to the end of the road. "It is pretty certain," he wrote to Jefferson on October 17th, "that there will not be a quorum . . . again within the present year, and by no means certain that there will be one at all under the old Confederation. . . . The States which have adopted the New Constitution are all proceeding to the arrangements for putting it in action in March next." [26]

Instructions from the states left no doubt that a Bill of Rights would be appended to the new Constitution. But Madison worried about the outlook for the vice-presidency. "As the president will be from a Southern State," he continued in cipher, "it falls almost of course for the other part of the Continent to supply the next in rank. . . . The only candidates in the Northern States brought forward with their known consent are Handcock and [John] Adams, and between these it seems probable the question will lie. Both of them are objectionable. . . . Handcock is weak ambitious a courtier of popularity, given to low intrigue, and lately reunited by a factious friendship with S. Adams. J. Adams has made himself obnoxious to many, particularly in the Southern States."

While such questions of the future were being discussed throughout America, the Continental Congress seemed all the more a relic of the past. Yet so firmly established were American habits of representative government, it appeared for a few weeks early in 1789 that there might still be a spark of life left in the dying Confederation. On January 13th the new Pennsylvania delegate, Tench Coxe, wrote to Benjamin Rush from New York that "four states are represented and three in part." He added confidently, "A Quorum from seven will be here by the 20th, when a president will be chosen. Mr. Wadsworth has been mentioned to me." But this date passed, and a week later the Philadelphia merchant had lost much of his assurance when writing to James Madison:

> I have been here about a Fortnight during which time we have not made a Congress. So. Carolina, Virga. Pennsa., N. Jersey, and Massachusetts are represented. There is one member from each of the states of Rhode Island, N. Carolina and Georgia. . . . I very much wish we may make a house in a week or ten days, as I think the Appearance in Europe, and perhaps even here, of the old Congress being in full operation and tranquilly yielding the seats to the new would have a good effect. The representations in Europe have been extremely gross, and must have an unfavorable effect upon Emigration in the poorer ranks of life. [27]

Within two days the attendance took such a spurt that Congress came within a single member of having a quorum. John Dawson, a new Virginia delegate who had been eleven years old when the first Continental Congress met, wrote to Madison on January 29th: "We have six states on the floor *viz*. Massachusetts-bay, New York New Jersey Pennsylvania S. Carolina and Virginia; and a member from Rhode Island, North Carolina and Georgia. . . . Connecticut you know can come in any time; we therefore expect in three or four days to have nine states represented. . . ."[28]

It is unfortunate that such hopefulness had to be dashed, but Samuel Alleyne Otis admitted to Madison in a letter of February 4th that "it appears doubtful whether nine States will ever again assemble."

The rest of the story is told in the brief entries of the *Journals*. Day by day, Secretary Thomson recorded the new arrivals, and those of January make a brave showing—James R. Reid of Pennsylvania and Robert Barnwell of South Carolina in a single morning. Then Abraham Clark on the 8th and Tench Coxe on the 10th until the high point was reached at the end of the month.

In February the names are far apart—David Ross of Maryland on the 6th, John Gardiner of Rhode Island on the 12th, David Gelston of New York on the 18th. From that date until the end of the month appears a gap representing the days when Secretary Thomson showed up in solitary grandeur at the City Hall soon to be known as Federal Hall. Then, only two days before the date set for the new Congress to meet, the last entry of all is found in the *Journals*:

Monday, March 2, 1789. Mr. Philip Pell from New York.

The office remained open for several more weeks, but nobody called to relieve Secretary Thomson's loneliness. And on March 18th he sent his last official communication to the governors of the several states:

I have now the honor to transmit to your Excellency herewith enclosed two Copies of the Thirteenth Volume which closes the Journal of the United States in Congress assembled. That the change which has been made with so much order and tranquillity may answer the end proposed and promote and secure the happiness prosperity and glory of the Union is my most fervent prayer.[29]

There were still a number of delegates in New York, even if they did not think to call on Secretary Thomson. Dr. Hugh Williamson of North Carolina and a few others remained to take their seats in the new Congress. And it was as a spectator that Samuel Alleyne Otis lingered until enough senators and representatives arrived in April to elect George Washington president and John Adams vice-president.

Loyalty to the Continental Congress had never been conspicuous, but Otis could not help twitting the members of the new assembly. "Is it not a little wonderful," he wrote to Nathan Dane on March 28th, "that with all the zeal in favor of the New Government the members cannot be collected to administer it? The business was to have commenced 4th March and 24 days have elapsed without making a quorum, nor do I think it will be effected before Tuesday or Wednesday of the next week." [30]

Nobody took the transition more calmly than Charles Thomson, the one man who had been a witness to the entire pageant of the Continental Congress. With the exception of a vacation while the Committee of the States met, he had been present nearly every day since the first session began in the late summer of 1774.

During these lonely hours in the spring of 1789, waiting for delegates to show up at the City Hall, he had no lack of leisure for glancing back over the past fifteen years. From his desk beside the president's chair, he had become familiar with the faces, foibles and abilities of all the 342 delegates. In an assembly made up so largely of middle-aged men like himself, the law of averages prescribed that a number of them—fifty-seven, to be exact— would never live to see the new nation come into being. Thomson himself remained among the few who were privileged to witness the future as well as past of the members of the Continental Congress. Although he celebrated his sixtieth birthday in 1789, he remained on the scene until the third decade of the next century, long after cocked hats and knee breeches had become a curiosity.

As a scholar of history, Charles Thomson must have noted that most revolutions fail because they are unable to set up an adequate new structure of government in place of the one they have torn down. For the experience of time proves that it is easier to build a new gallows than to frame a new constitution, and political opponents can be condemned to death with less effort than it takes for training men to fill their shoes.

Peoples of all ages have found the establishment and maintenance of good government the most difficult of human undertakings. In 1789 the fingers of two hands would have sufficed to number the systems since the dawn of history which had administered wisely and beneficently for any length of time. And even though the new American republic started with the advantages of a Constitution allowing a decent degree of authority as well as liberty, that great realist George Washington frankly used the word "experiment" in his inaugural address to the members of the first Congress:

> The preservation of the sacred fire of liberty and the destiny of the republican model of government are justly considered as deeply, perhaps as finally, staked on the experiment intrusted in the hands of the American People.

As a scholar of ancient languages, Charles Thomson must have traced the streams of Greek and Hebraic thought flowing down the centuries into the five great documents of the American Revolution. But theory is not enough. Good government depends as much on the day-by-day working of practical politics; and in 1789 the American experiment could avoid some of the errors demonstrated during the past fifteen years in a laboratory of administration.

Before his death at the age of 95, Charles Thomson saw the new nation governed as well as conceived by men trained in the Continental Congress. The first five presidents of the United States were graduates of that school for statesmen, as well as four of the first five vice-presidents. The following state and federal offices were also filled by former members of the revolutionary assembly:

United States senators or representatives, 76; cabinet members, 8; ministers to foreign nations, 8; federal judges, 29; governors, 46; state judges, 64; state legislators, 159.[31]

Thomson retired from public life in 1789 to work patiently at his Pennsylvania home on his translation of the Bible. As spectator rather than participant during the next thirty-five years, he must have conceded before his death in 1824 that the American experiment had at least passed safely through the first precarious stages. But even at this date he was not the last of the grand old men of the Continental Congress. John Adams and Thomas Jefferson lived until the fiftieth anniversary of the Declaration of Independence, dying a few hours apart on July 4, 1826. And the survivor of all the signers was a former Maryland member who had accompanied Benjamin Franklin in the spring of 1776 on a trip of thirty-six days from Philadelphia through the wilderness by sled, wagon and flatboat to Montreal. Charles Carroll of Carrollton, aged 95, was still living in the autumn of 1832, and during the past four years he had been a director of the new Baltimore and Ohio Railroad Company.

Appendix

Appendix

SEATS OF THE CONTINENTAL CONGRESS

Philadelphia	September 5, 1774, to October 26, 1774
Philadelphia	May 10, 1775, to December 12, 1776
Baltimore	December 20, 1776, to March 4, 1777
Philadelphia	March 5, 1777, to September 18, 1777
Lancaster	September 27, 1777 (one day only)
York	September 30, 1777, to June 27, 1778
Philadelphia	July 2, 1778, to June 21, 1783
Princeton	June 30, 1783, to November 4, 1783
Annapolis	November 26, 1783, to June 3, 1784
Trenton	November 1, 1784, to December 24, 1784
New York	January 11, 1785, to March 2, 1789

PRESIDENTS OF THE CONTINENTAL CONGRESS

Peyton Randolph, Virginia	*Elected*	September 5, 1774
Henry Middleton, South Carolina		October 22, 1774
Peyton Randolph, Virginia		May 10, 1775
John Hancock, Massachusetts		May 24, 1775
Henry Laurens, South Carolina		November 1, 1777
John Jay, New York		December 10, 1778
Samuel Huntington, Connecticut		September 28, 1779
Thomas McKean, Delaware		July 10, 1781
John Hanson, Maryland		November 5, 1781
Elias Boudinot, New Jersey		November 4, 1782
Thomas Mifflin, Pennsylvania		November 3, 1783
Richard Henry Lee, Virginia		November 30, 1784
John Hancock, Massachusetts *		November 23, 1785
Nathaniel Gorham, Massachusetts		June 6, 1786
Arthur St. Clair, Pennsylvania		February 2, 1787
Cyrus Griffin, Virginia		January 22, 1788

* John Hancock did not serve a day of this term. The following May he resigned on grounds of ill-health.

MEMBERS OF THE CONTINENTAL CONGRESS

CONNECTICUT

Andrew Adams, 1778-1782
Josiah P. Cooke, 1784-1785, 1787-1788
Silas Deane, 1774-1776
Eliphalet Dyer, 1774-1779, 1782-1783
Pierrepont Edwards, 1788
Oliver Ellsworth, 1778-1783
Titus Hosmer, 1778
Benjamin Huntington, 1780, 1782-1783, 1788
Samuel Huntington, 1776, 1778-1781, 1783

William S. Johnson, 1785-1787
Richard Law, 1781-1782
Stephen M. Mitchell, 1785-1788
Jesse Root, 1778-1782
Roger Sherman, 1774-1782, 1784
Joseph Spencer, 1779
Jonathan Sturges, 1786
James Wadsworth, 1784
Jeremiah Wadsworth, 1788
William Williams, 1776-1777
Oliver Wolcott, 1776-1778, 1781-1783

Elected but did not serve—Joseph Trumbull, Erastus Wolcott, Jedidiah Strong, John Treadwell, William Pitkin, William Hillhouse, John Canfield, Charles Church Chandler, John Chester

DELAWARE

Gunning Bedford, Jr., 1783-1785
John Dickinson, 1779
Philemon Dickinson, 1782-1783
Dyre Kearny, 1787-1788
Eleazer McComb, 1783-1784
Thomas McKean, 1774-1776, 1778-1782
Nathaniel Mitchell, 1787-1788
John Patten, 1786

William Peery, 1786
George Read, 1774-1777
Caesar Rodney, 1774-1776
Thomas Rodney, 1781-1782, 1786
James Tilton, 1783-1784
Nicholas Van Dyke, 1777-1781
John Vining, 1784-1785
Samuel Wharton, 1782-1783

Elected but did not serve—John Evans, James Sykes, Henry Latimer, John McKinly, Samuel Patterson, Isaac Grantham

GEORGIA

Abraham Baldwin, 1785, 1787-1788
Nathan Brownson, 1777
Archibald Bulloch, 1775
William Few, 1780-1782, 1786-1787
William Gibbons, 1784
Button Gwinnett, 1776
John Habersham, 1785

Lyman Hall, 1775-1777
John Houstoun, 1775
William Houstoun, 1784-1786
Richard Howley, 1781
Noble Wymberly Jones, 1781-1782
Edward Langworthy, 1777-1779
William Pierce, 1787

GEORGIA—(continued)

Edward Telfair, 1778, 1780-1782
George Walton, 1776-1777, 1780-1781

John Walton, 1777
Joseph Wood, 1777-1778
John J. Zubly, 1775

Elected but did not serve—Joseph Clay, Benjamin Andrew, Samuel Stirk, Lachlan McIntosh

MARYLAND

Robert Alexander, 1776
William Carmichael, 1778-1779
Charles Carroll of Carrollton, 1776-1778
Daniel Carroll, 1781-1783
Jeremiah T. Chase, 1783-1784
Samuel Chase, 1774-1778
Benjamin Contee, 1788
James Forbes, 1778-1780
Uriah Forrest, 1787
Robert Goldsborough, 1774-1776
John Hall, 1775
John Hanson, 1780-1782
William Harrison, 1786
William Hemsley, 1782-1783
John Henry, 1778-1780, 1785-1786
William Hindman, 1785-1786
John E. Howard, 1788

Daniel of St. Thomas Jenifer, 1779-1781
Thomas Johnson, 1774-1776
Thomas Sim Lee, 1783
Edward Lloyd, 1783-1784
James McHenry, 1783-1785
Luther Martin, 1785
William Paca, 1774-1779
George Plater, 1778-1780
Richard Potts, 1781
Nathaniel Ramsey, 1786-1787
John Rogers, 1775-1776
David Ross, 1787-1789
Benjamin Rumsey, 1777
Joshua Seney, 1788
William Smith, 1777
Thomas Stone, 1775-1778, 1784
Matthew Tilghman, 1774-1776
Turbutt Wright, 1782

Elected but did not serve—Richard Ridgely, Gustavus Scott, Edward Giles

MASSACHUSETTS

John Adams, 1774-1778
Samuel Adams, 1774-1782
Thomas Cushing, 1774-1776
Francis Dana, 1777-1778, 1783-1784
Nathan Dane, 1785-1788
Elbridge Gerry, 1776-1780, 1783-1785
Nathaniel Gorham, 1783, 1786-1788
John Hancock, 1775-1778
Stephen Higginson, 1783

Samuel Holten, 1778-1780, 1783-1785, 1787
Jonathan Jackson, 1781-1782
Rufus King, 1784-1787
James Lovell, 1777-1782
John Lowell, 1782
Samuel Osgood, 1781-1784
Samuel A. Otis, 1787-1789
Robert Treat Paine, 1774-1776

MASSACHUSETTS—(continued)

George Partridge, 1779-1782, 1787   George Thatcher, 1788-1789
Theodore Sedgwick, 1785-1786, 1788   Artemas Ward, 1781

Elected but did not serve—James Sullivan, James Bowdoin, Timothy Edwards, Caleb Strong, Timothy Danielson, Tristram Dalton

NEW HAMPSHIRE

Josiah Bartlett, 1775-1778
Jonathan Blanchard, 1783-1784
Nathaniel Folsom, 1774, 1777-1780
Abiel Foster, 1783-1785
George Frost, 1777-1779
John Taylor Gilman, 1782-1783
Nicholas Gilman, 1787-1789
John Langdon, 1775-1776, 1786-1787
Woodbury Langdon, 1779-1780

Samuel Livermore, 1780-1783, 1785-1786
Pierse Long, 1784-1786
Nathaniel Peabody, 1779-1780
John Sullivan, 1774-1775, 1780-1781
Matthew Thornton, 1776-1777
John Wentworth, Jr., 1777
William Whipple, 1776-1779
Phillips White, 1782-1783
Paine Wingate, 1788-1789

Elected but did not serve—Ebenezer Thompson, Timothy Walker, Jr., Joshua Wentworth, George Adkinson, Benjamin Bellows, Moses Dow, Elisha Payne

NEW JERSEY

John Beatty, 1783-1785
Elias Boudinot, 1778, 1781-1783
William Burnet, 1780-1781
Lambert Cadwalader, 1784-1787
Abraham Clark, 1776-1778, 1780-1783, 1786-1788
Silas Condict, 1781-1783
Stephen Crane, 1774-1776
Jonathan Dayton, 1787-1788
John De Hart, 1774-1776
Samuel Dick, 1783-1785
Jonathan Elmer, 1777-1778, 1781-1783, 1787-1788
John Fell, 1777-1780
Frederick Frelinghuysen, 1779, 1783
John Hart, 1776

Francis Hopkinson, 1776
Josiah Hornblower, 1785-1786
William C. Houston, 1779-1781, 1784-1785
James Kinsey, 1774-1775
William Livingston, 1774-1776
James Schureman, 1786-1787
Nathaniel Scudder, 1778-1779, 1781
Jonathan D. Sergeant, 1776-1777
Richard Smith, 1774-1776
John Stevens, 1784
Charles Stewart, 1784-1785
Richard Stockton, 1776
John C. Symmes, 1785-1786
John Witherspoon, 1776-1782

Elected but did not serve—John Cooper, John Neilson, William Paterson

NEW YORK

John Alsop, 1774-1776
Egbert Benson, 1784, 1787-1788
Simon Boerum, 1774-1775
George Clinton, 1775-1776
Charles De Witt, 1784
James Duane, 1774-1779, 1781-1783
William Duer, 1777-1778
William Floyd, 1774-1776, 1779-1783
Leonard Gansevoort, 1788
David Gelston, 1789
Alexander Hamilton, 1782-1783, 1788
John Haring, 1774, 1785-1787
John Jay, 1774-1779, 1784
John Lansing, Jr., 1785
John Lawrance, 1785-1787
Francis Lewis, 1775-1779, 1781-1783
Ezra L'Hommedieu, 1779-1783, 1788

Philip Livingston, 1775-1778
Robert R. Livingston, 1775-1776, 1779-1781, 1785
Walter Livingston, 1784-1785
Isaac Low, 1774
Gouverneur Morris, 1778-1779
Lewis Morris, 1775-1777
Alexander McDougall, 1781
Ephraim Paine, 1784
Philip Pell, 1789
Zephaniah Platt, 1785-1786
Philip Schuyler, 1775, 1777, 1779-1780
John Morin Scott, 1780-1782
Melancton Smith, 1785-1787
Henry Wisner, 1775-1776
Abraham Yates, 1787-1788
Peter W. Yates, 1786

NORTH CAROLINA

John B. Ashe, 1787
Timothy Bloodworth, 1786
William Blount, 1783, 1786-1787
Thomas Burke, 1777-1781
Robert Burton, 1787
Richard Caswell, 1774-1775
William Cumming, 1785
Cornelius Harnett, 1777-1779
Benjamin Hawkins, 1782-1783, 1787
Joseph Hewes, 1774-1777, 1779
Whitmill Hill, 1778-1780
William Hooper, 1774-1777
Samuel Johnston, 1780-1782

Allen Jones, 1779-1780
Willie Jones, 1780-1781
Abner Nash, 1782-1783
John Penn, 1775-1780
William Sharpe, 1779-1781
John Sitgreaves, 1784-1785
Richard D. Spaight, 1783-1785
John Swann, 1787-1788
James White, 1786-1788
John Williams, 1777-1779
Hugh Williamson, 1782-1785, 1787-1788

Elected but did not serve—Ephraim Brevard, Adlai Osborn, Thomas Person, Charles Johnson, Joseph McDowell, Nathaniel Macon, Alexander Martin, Thomas Polk, Benjamin Smith, John Stokes

PENNSYLVANIA

Andrew Allen, 1775-1776
John Armstrong, 1779-1780, 1787-1788

Samuel J. Atlee, 1778-1782
John B. Bayard, 1785-1786
Edward Biddle, 1775

Pennsylvania—(continued)

William Bingham, 1786-1788
William Clingan, 1777-1779
George Clymer, 1776-1778, 1780
Tench Coxe, 1788-1789
John Dickinson, 1774-1776
Thomas FitzSimons, 1782-1783
Benjamin Franklin, 1775-1776
Joseph Galloway, 1774
Joseph Gardner, 1784-1785
Edward Hand, 1784-1785
William Henry, 1784-1785
Charles Humphreys, 1774-1776
Jared Ingersoll, 1780
William Irvine, 1787-1788
David Jackson, 1785
James McClene, 1779-1780
Timothy Matlack, 1781
Samuel Meredith, 1786-1788
Thomas Mifflin, 1774-1775, 1783-1784
John Montgomery, 1782-1784
Joseph Montgomery, 1781-1782
Cadwalader Morris, 1783-1784

Robert Morris, 1776-1778
John Morton, 1774-1776
Frederick Muhlenberg, 1778-1780
Richard Peters, 1782-1783
Charles Pettit, 1785-1787
Joseph Reed, 1778
James R. Reid, 1787-1789
Samuel Rhoads, 1774
Daniel Roberdeau, 1777-1779
George Ross, 1774-1777
Benjamin Rush, 1776-1777
Arthur St. Clair, 1786-1787
James Searle, 1778-1780
William Shippen, 1779-1780
James Smith, 1776-1778
Jonathan B. Smith, 1777-1778
Thomas Smith, 1781-1782
George Taylor, 1776
Thomas Willing, 1775-1776
James Wilson, 1775-1777, 1783, 1785-1787
Henry Wynkoop, 1779-1782

Elected but did not serve—Matthew Clarkson, William Montgomery

Rhode Island

Jonathan Arnold, 1782-1784
Peleg Arnold, 1787-1789
John Collins, 1778-1783
Ezekiel Cornell, 1780-1782
William Ellery, 1776-1785
John Gardiner, 1788-1789
Jonathan J. Hazard, 1788
Stephen Hopkins, 1774-1777

David Howell, 1782-1785
James Manning, 1785-1786
Henry Marchant, 1777-1779
Nathan Miller, 1785-1786
Daniel Mowry, Jr., 1781
James M. Varnum, 1781, 1787
Samuel Ward, 1774-1776

South Carolina

Robert Barnwell, 1788-1789
Thomas Bee, 1780-1782
Richard Beresford, 1783-1784
John Bull, 1784-1787
Pierce Butler, 1787-1788

William H. Drayton, 1778-1779
Nicholas Eveleigh, 1781-1782
Christopher Gadsden, 1774-1776
John L. Gervais, 1782-1783
Thomas Heyward, Jr., 1776-1778

South Carolina—(continued)

Daniel Huger, 1786-1788
Richard Hutson, 1778-1779
Ralph Izard, 1782-1783
John Kean, 1785-1787
Francis Kinloch, 1780
Henry Laurens, 1777-1780
Thomas Lynch, Sr., 1774-1776
Thomas Lynch, Jr., 1776
John Mathews, 1778-1782
Arthur Middleton, 1776-1777, 1781-1782

Henry Middleton, 1774-1776
Isaac Motte, 1780-1782
John Parker, 1786-1788
Charles Pinckney, 1784-1787
David Ramsay, 1782-1783, 1785-1786
Jacob Read, 1783-1785
Edward Rutledge, 1774-1776
John Rutledge, 1774-1775, 1782-1783
Thomas T. Tucker, 1787-1788

Elected but did not serve—Paul Trapier, Rawlins Lowndes, Alexander Gillon, William Moultrie, Thomas Sumter

Virginia

Thomas Adams, 1778-1779
John Banister, 1778
Richard Bland, 1774-1775
Theodorick Bland, 1781-1783
Carter Braxton, 1776
John Brown, 1787-1788
Edward Carrington, 1785-1787
John Dawson, 1788
William Fitzhugh, 1779
William Fleming, 1779-1780
William Grayson, 1785-1787
Cyrus Griffin, 1778-1780, 1787-1788
Samuel Hardy, 1783-1785
Benjamin Harrison, 1774-1777
John Harvie, 1777-1779
James Henry, 1780-1781
Patrick Henry, 1774-1775
Thomas Jefferson, 1775-1776, 1783-1784
Joseph Jones, 1780-1783

Arthur Lee, 1782-1784
Francis Lightfoot Lee, 1775-1779
Henry Lee, 1786-1788
Richard Henry Lee, 1774-1780, 1784-1787
James Madison, 1780-1783, 1787-1788
James Mercer, 1779-1780
John F. Mercer, 1783-1784
James Monroe, 1783-1786
Thomas Nelson, Jr., 1775-1777, 1779
Mann Page, 1777
Edmund Pendleton, 1774-1775
Edmund Randolph, 1779, 1781-1782
Peyton Randolph, 1774-1775
Meriwether Smith, 1778-1781
John Walker, 1780
George Washington, 1774-1775
George Wythe, 1775-1776

Elected but did not serve—Gabriel Jones, John Blair

Sources and Acknowledgments

SOURCES AND ACKNOWLEDGMENTS

It has been the aim of this book, as far as possible, to let the 342 members of the Continental Congress tell their own story. Their decisions, as recorded in the *Journals;* their opinions, as expressed in the *Letters;* and their contacts with European nations, as revealed by the *Diplomatic Correspondence*—these are the three main sources.

Three of America's greatest historical scholars have contributed their knowledge and judgment as editors—Worthington Chauncey Ford, for the *Journals;* Edmund Cody Burnett, for the *Letters;* and Francis Wharton, for the *Diplomatic Correspondence.*

Considering that the Continental Congress had so much to do with creating the United States, it is noteworthy that some of this material was not made readily available until the eve of World War II. Although the *Diplomatic Correspondence* appeared in 1889, the publication of the *Journals* took from 1904 to 1937, and of the *Letters* from 1921 to 1936.

The material originally entered in the *Secret Journals* is found in these sources. Next to them in importance are the collected writings of the leaders who shaped the era of the Continental Congress—John and Samuel Adams, Benjamin Franklin, Alexander Hamilton, Richard Henry Lee, James Madison, James Monroe, Gouverneur Morris, Thomas Paine and George Washington. Force's *American Archives* and the Collections of the New York and Connecticut Historical Societies also have contributed items not found elsewhere.

The statistics in this book as to ages, occupations, education and war service of members of the Continental Congress owe largely to the *Biographical Directory* published by a later Congress. Edmund Cody Burnett's *Letters* have been the guide for the years of actual attendance of the members (often varying widely from the periods of election) as found in the Appendix.

Permission for the use of quotations has been given by Mr. Howard C. Myers, Jr., the Macmillan Company, Funk & Wagnalls Company, Houghton Mifflin Company, J. P. Lippincott Company, McRae Smith Company, G. P. Putnam's Sons, the Connecticut Historical Society, the Carnegie Institution of Washington, the Huntington Library of San Marino, the Library of Congress, the National Society of Colonial Dames of America, and the Martin Memorial Library of York, Pennsylvania.

The portrait section has gained from the use of reproductions which are credited with appreciation to Independence Hall, Philadelphia, The New York Historical Society and *Harper's Magazine.*

Acknowledgments are gratefully made to Dr. Malcolm G. Wyer and the librarians of the Denver Public Library, and to Mrs. Eulalia Chapman and assistants of the Denver Bibliographical Center. Thanks are due to the editors and production staff of Harper & Brothers for unfailing helpfulness throughout the preparation of the manuscript. In particular, the section of portraits is largely the achievement of Miss Marjorie Mulhall and Miss Florence Selby.

Finally, this book is indebted not only to its eighteenth-century sources but also to the more recent commentators on special subjects who are included in the following list:

ADAMS, CHARLES FRANCIS (editor). *Familiar Letters of John Adams and His Wife Abigail Adams*. Houghton, Boston, 1875.
——. *Studies Military and Diplomatic, 1775-1865*. Macmillan, New York, 1911.
ADAMS, JOHN. *Works*. 10 vols., Charles Francis Adams, editor. Boston, 1850-1856.
ADAMS, SAMUEL. *Writings*. 4 vols., Henry Alonzo Cushing, editor. Putnam, New York, 1907.
ALLEN, GARDNER WELD. *A Naval History of the American Revolution*. 2 vols. Houghton, Boston, 1913.
ANDREWS, CHARLES M. *The Colonial Background of the American Revolution*. Yale University Press, New Haven, 1931.
ARNOLD, ISAAC NEWTON. *Life of Benedict Arnold*. McClurg, Chicago, 1880.
BALCH, THOMAS W. *The French in America during the War of Independence*. 2 vols., Lippincott, Philadelphia, 1891-1895.
BARCK, OSCAR THEODORE JR. *New York City during the War for Independence*. Columbia University Press, New York, 1931.
Biographical Directory of the American Congress, 1774-1927. House Document No. 783, Sixty-ninth Congress, Washington, 1928.
BOUDINOT, ELIAS. *Boudinot's Journal*. Bourquin, Philadelphia, 1894.
BURKE, EDMUND. *Works*. 6 vols. Boston, 1839.
BURNETT, EDMUND CODY (editor). *Letters of Members of the Continental Congress*. 8 vols. Carnegie Institution, Washington, 1921-1936.
——. *The Continental Congress*. Macmillan, New York, 1941.
BURT, STRUTHERS. *Philadelphia, Holy Experiment*. Doubleday, New York, 1945.
CARRINGTON, H. B. *Battles of the American Revolution*. New York, 1876.
CHASE, EUGENE PARKER (editor and translator). *Our Revolutionary Forefathers: The Letters of François, Marquis de Barbé-Marbois*. Duffield, New York, 1929.
CHASTELLUX, MARQUIS DE. *Travels in North America in the Years 1780, 1781 and 1782*. 2 vols. Philadelphia, 1812.
CHATHAM, BURKE, AND ERSKINE. *Masterpieces of English Oratory*. Porter & Coates, Philadelphia, 1885.
CLARK, JANE. "Perfidy of Howe and the Convention Troops;" *American Historical Review*, XXXVII, 721-723, 1932.
DEANE, SILAS. *Correspondence*. Connecticut Historical Society, Collections, Vol. II, Hartford, 1870.
DRAKE, FRANCIS D. *Henry Knox, Life and Correspondence*. Boston, 1873.
DRINKWATER, JOHN. *Charles James Fox*. Cosmopolitan, New York, 1928.

FAY, BERNARD. *The Revolutionary Spirit in France and America.* Harcourt Brace, New York, 1927.

FISHER, GEORGE SIDNEY. *The Struggle for American Independence.* 2 vols. Lippincott, Philadelphia, 1908.

———. *The Evolution of the Constitution of the United States.* Lippincott, Philadelphia, 1910.

FITZGERALD, PERCY H. *The Life and Times of John Wilkes.* 2 vols. London, 1888.

FLICK, ALEXANDER C. *Loyalism in New York during the American Revolution.* Columbia University Press, New York, 1901.

FORCE, PETER. *American Archives.* 9 vols. New York, 1885.

FORD, WORTHINGTON CHAUNCEY (editor). *Journals of the Continental Congress.* 34 vols. Library of Congress, Washington, 1904-1937.

FRANKLIN, BENJAMIN. *Writings.* Albert Henry Smyth, editor. 10 vols. Macmillan, New York, 1905-1907.

GRAHAM, JAMES. *General Daniel Morgan of the Virginia Line.* New York, 1856.

GREENE, G. W. *Historical View of the American Revolution.* Boston, 1865.

———. *Life of General Greene.* 3 vols. New York, 1867-1871.

HAMILTON, ALEXANDER. *Writings.* 7 vols., John C. Hamilton, editor. New York, 1850.

HARLEY, LEWIS R. *The Life of Charles Thomson.* Jacobs, Philadelphia, 1900.

HATCH, LOUIS CLINTON. *The Administration of the American Revolutionary Army.* Longmans, New York, 1904.

JAY, JOHN. *Correspondence and Papers.* 4 vols., Henry P. Johnston, editor. Putnam, New York, 1890.

JEFFERSON, THOMAS. *Writings.* 10 vols., H. W. Washington, editor, New York, 1861.

KNOLLENBERG, BERNARD. *Washington and the Revolution.* Macmillan, New York, 1940.

LEE, RICHARD HENRY. *Letters.* 2 vols., James Curtis Ballagh, editor. Macmillan, New York, 1911.

LONG, JOHN CUTHBERT. *Mr. Pitt and America's Birthright.* Stokes, New York, 1940.

LOSSING, BENSON J. *Life of Schuyler.* 2 vols. New York, 1872.

LOWELL, EDWARD. *The Hessians and the other German Auxiliaries in the Revolutionary War.* Harper, New York, 1884.

MACLAY, EDGAR STANTON. *A History of American Privateers.* Appleton, New York, 1899.

MADISON, JAMES. *Writings.* 9 vols., Gaillard Hunt, editor. Putnam, New York, 1900-1910.

MERLANT, JOACHIM. *Soldiers and Sailors of France in the American War for Independence.* New York, 1920.

MILLER, JOHN C. *Sam Adams, Pioneer in Propaganda.* Little, Brown, Boston, 1936.

MONROE, JAMES. *Writings.* 7 vols., S. M. Hamilton, editor. Putnam, New York, 1898.

MORRIS, GOUVERNEUR. *Diary and Letters.* 2 vols., Anne Carey Morris, editor. Scribner, New York, 1888.

MUMBY, FRANK ARTHUR. *George III and the American Revolution.* Houghton, Boston, 1923.

NEVINS, ALLAN. *The American States During and After the Revolution.* Macmillan, New York, 1920.

NICKERSON, HOFFMAN. *The Turning Point of the Revolution.* Houghton, Boston, 1926.

PAINE, THOMAS. *Writings.* Random House (Carlton House), New York, 1934.

PALMER, JOHN A. *Life of Steuben.* Yale University Press, New Haven, 1937.

PROWELL, GEORGE R. *History of York County, Pennsylvania.* Chicago, 1907.

RAMSAY, DAVID. *The History of the American Revolution.* 2 vols. Philadelphia, 1789.

ROWLAND, KATE MASON. *Life of Charles Carroll.* Putnam, New York, 1898.

SANDERSON, JOHN. *Biography of the Signers of the Declaration of Independence.* 4 vols. Boston, 1823-1827.

SEARS, LORENZO. *John Hancock.* Little, Brown, Boston, 1912.

SPARKS, JARED. *Correspondence of the American Revolution.* 4 vols. Boston, 1853.

———. *Life of Gouverneur Morris.* 3 vols. Boston, 1832.

STEDMAN, CHARLES. *History of the Origin, Progress and Termination of the American War.* 2 vols. Dublin, 1794.

STEVENS, WILLIAM OLIVER. *Annapolis.* Dodd, Mead, New York, 1937.

STILLE, CHARLES J. *The Life and Times of John Dickinson.* (Published at request of Historical Society of Pennsylvania.) Lippincott, Philadelphia, 1891.

SULLIVAN, JOHN. *Letters and Papers.* Otis G. Hammond, editor. New York Historical Society Collections, XIII-XIV, New York, 1930.

TASWELL-LANGMEAD, THOMAS P. *English Constitutional History.* Boston, 1881.

TATUM, EDWARD H. (editor). *The American Journal of Ambrose Serle, Secretary to Lord Howe, 1776-1778.* Huntington Library, San Marino, 1940.

TREVELYAN, SIR GEORGE O. *The American Revolution.* 4 vols. Longmans, New York, 1899-1907.

UMBREIT, KENNETH. *The Founding Fathers.* Harper, New York, 1941.

VAN DOREN, CARL. *Benjamin Franklin.* Viking, New York, 1938.

———. *Secret History of the American Revolution.* Garden City Publishing Co., Garden City, 1941.

VAN TYNE, CLAUDE HALSTEAD. *The Loyalists in the American Revolution.* Macmillan, New York, 1922.

———. *The War of Independence.* Houghton, New York, 1929.

WALTHER, DANIEL. *Gouverneur Morris.* Funk, New York, 1934.

WALPOLE, HORACE. *Memoirs of the Reign of George III.* 6 vols. London, 1845.

WASHINGTON, GEORGE. *Writings.* 14 vols., Worthington Chauncey Ford, editor. Putnam, New York, 1889-1893.

———. *Writings.* 12 vols., Jared Sparks, editor. Boston, 1834-1837.

WHARTON, FRANCIS (editor). *Revolutionary Diplomatic Correspondence of the United States.* 6 vols. Library of Congress, Washington, 1889.

Chapter References

CHAPTER REFERENCES

Abbreviated titles have been used in the Chapter References, such as *Journals* and *Letters* and *Dipl. Cor.* for the three main sources—the *Journals of the Continental Congress*, the *Letters of Members of the Continental Congress*, and the *Revolutionary Diplomatic Correspondence of the United States*. Collected works, such as those of Jefferson, Franklin and Madison, are listed for purposes of brevity by the name only, followed by the volume and page—for instance, "John Adams, II, 369." Full titles of all references may be found in the foregoing list of sources.

CHAPTER 1

1. Chatham, Burke, Erskine: *Oratory*, 32
2. *Journals*, V, 509
3. *Letters*, I, 529
4. *Letters*, I, 527
5. *Amer. Arch.*, Fifth Series, II, 170
6. *Amer. Arch.*, Fourth Series, II, 240
7. Van Tyne: *Loyalists*, 89
8. Adams: *Familiar Letters*, 85
9. *Journals*, IV, 258
10. Gouverneur Morris (Sparks), I, 167
11. *Letters*, V, 381
12. Chatham, Burke, Erskine: *Oratory*, 32

CHAPTER 2

1. John Adams, II, 144
2. John Adams, X, 247
3. Chatham, Burke, Erskine: *Oratory*, 11
4. *Massachusetts Gazette*, Jan. 2, 1775

CHAPTER 3

1. John Adams, II, 369
2. John Adams, II, 370
3. John Adams, II, 353
4. *Conn. Historical*, II, 144
5. John Adams, II, 350
6. *Conn. Historical*, II, 145
7. John Adams, II, 356
8. *Conn. Historical*, II, 170
9. John Adams, II, 357
10. Stille: *John Dickinson*, 343
11. *Letters*, I, 9
12. *Conn. Historical*, II, 173
13. *Journals*, I, 15-24
14. *Journals*, I, 25
15. *Journals*, I, 25
16. Harley: *Charles Thomson*, 95
17. *Letters*, I, 27 and 59
18. John Adams, II, 360
19. *Conn. Historical*, II, 175
20. John Adams, II, 366-368

CHAPTER 4

1. John Adams, II, 370-374
2. John Adams, II, 383-385
3. *Conn. Historical*, II, 174
4. John Adams, II, 369
5. *Conn. Historical*, II, 174
6. Jefferson, I, 7
7. *Journals*, I, 31
8. *Letters*, I, 55
9. *Journals*, I, 39
10. John Adams, II, 387-390
11. *Journals*, I, 58

12. *Journals*, I, 67-72
13. Jefferson, I, 11
14. *Journals*, I, 89
15. *Journals*, I, 115-121
16. *Journals*, I, 105-113
17. *Journals*, I, 90-101
18. John Adams, II, 382
19. John Adams, II, 401
20. *Journals*, I, 75-80
21. *Journals*, I, 122

CHAPTER 5

1. *Journals*, I, 79
2. Jefferson, I, 9
3. Taswell-Langmead: *English Constitutional History*, 713
4. Sears: *John Hancock*, 198-199
5. *Conn. Historical*, II, 222
6. *Conn. Historical*, II, 227
7. *Letters*, I, 98
8. *Letters*, I, 114

9. Adams: *Familiar Letters*, 59
10. *Letters*, I, 112
11. Serle: *American Journal*, 35
12. *Letters*, I, 93
13. *Journals*, II, 89
14. R. H. Lee, I, 130
15. John Adams, II, 417-418
16. Adams: *Familiar Letters*, 70

CHAPTER 6

1. Adams: *Familiar Letters*, 67
2. Adams: *Familiar Letters*, 69
3. *Letters*, I, 138
4. *Letters*, I, 134
5. *Letters*, I, 128
6. Adams: *Familiar Letters*, 40
7. *Letters*, I, 156
8. *Letters*, I, 92
9. *Journals*, II, 111
10. *Journals*, II, 103
11. *Journals*, II, 204
12. *Journals*, II, 221
13. Adams: *Familiar Letters*, 64 and 75
14. *Letters*, I, 145
15. *Journals*, II, 225-234

16. *Journals*, II, 128-157
17. Jefferson, I, 11
18. *Journals*, II, 160
19. Jefferson, I, 11
20. *Letters*, I, 156
21. *Letters*, I, 158
22. *Journals*, II, 165
23. *Letters*, I, 162
24. *Journals*, II, 69
25. *Journals*, II, 110
26. *Journals*, II, 174
27. *Journals*, II, 177
28. *Journals*, II, 186
29. Jefferson, I, 203
30. *Journals*, II, 202
31. *Journals*, II, 187

CHAPTER 7

1. *Pennsylvania Ledger*, March 11, 1778
2. Adams: *Familiar Letters*, 83
3. John Adams, II, 422
4. John Adams, II, 423
5. John Adams, II, 360
6. John Adams, II, 423
7. *Journals*, III, 265
8. *Letters*, I, 169
9. *Letters*, I, 279
10. John Adams, I, 256
11. *Journals*, III, 273-274
12. *Amer. Arch.*, Fourth Series, III, 717
13. *Letters*, I, 235
14. John Adams, III, 7
15. *Journals*, III, 348
16. John Adams, III, 11-12
17. *Letters*, I, 225-226
18. *Journals*, III, 334
19. *Journals*, III, 319
20. John Adams, III, 21
21. *Letters*, I, 246

CHAPTER 8

1. Gouverneur Morris (Sparks), I, 72
2. *Conn. Historical*, II, 312
3. Adams: *Familiar Letters*, 126
4. *Letters*, I, 266
5. *Conn. Historical*, II, 315
6. *Journals*, III, 405
7. *Letters*, I, 263
8. *Journals*, III, 445
9. *Letters*, I, 310
10. *Letters*, I, 355
11. *Journals*, IV, 70
12. *Journals*, III, 409-412
13. *Journals*, IV, 19-20
14. *Journals*, IV, 21
15. *Journals*, IV, 146

CHAPTER 9

1. *Conn. Historical*, II, 340
2. *Letters*, I, 375-376
3. John Adams, II, 485-486
4. John Adams, III, 35
5. John Adams, III, 38
6. *Letters*, I, 401
7. *Journals*, IV, 49
8. *Journals*, IV, 149
9. Franklin, VI, 445-446
10. *Journals*, IV, 301
11. Washington (Sparks), III, 268
12. *Amer. Arch.*, Fourth Series, V, 1392
13. *Journals*, IV, 203-204
14. *Journals*, IV, 203-204
15. *Journals*, IV, 244
16. Samuel Adams, III, 250
17. John Adams, III, 31
18. *Journals*, IV, 230
19. *Letters*, I, 416
20. *Journals*, IV, 258

CHAPTER 10

1. *Letters*, I, 521n
2. Jefferson, I, 12-13
3. *Letters*, I, 420
4. *Amer. Arch.*, Fifth Series, I, 95
5. Van Tyne: *Loyalists*, 218
6. *Journals*, IV, 341
7. *Journals*, IV, 334
8. John Adams, III, 43

CHAPTER 10—(continued)

9. *Journals*, IV, 358
10. John Adams, III, 46
11. Adams: *Familiar Letters*, 173
12. *Letters*, I, 460
13. *Letters*, I, 460
14. *Amer. Arch.*, Fifth Series, I, 479

15. Lowell: *The Hessians in the Revolution*, 20
16. *Letters*, I, 465 and 467
17. *Letters*, I, 476
18. *Letters*, I, 455

CHAPTER 11

1. *Amer. Arch.*, Fourth Series, II, 443
2. Burke: *Works*, II, 14
3. R. H. Lee, I, 196
4. Burnett: *Continental Congress*, 171
5. *Letters*, I, 476-477
6. *Journals*, V, 428
7. John Adams, II, 514
8. John Adams, III, 52
9. *Journals*, V, 433
10. *Letters*, I, 497
11. R. H. Lee, I, 204

12. *Letters*, I, 489-490
13. John Adams, III, 65
14. Jefferson, I, 14-17
15. *Letters*, I, 508
16. Burnett: *Continental Congress*, 180-181
17. *Journals*, V, 464
18. John Adams, III, 54
19. John Adams, III, 54
20. Jefferson, I, 19
21. *Journals*, V, 515
22. *Letters*, I, 526

CHAPTER 12

1. *Letters*, II, 5
2. Van Tyne: *The War of Independence*, 341
3. *Letters*, II, 7
4. *Letters*, II, 13
5. Stille: *John Dickinson*, 202-203
6. Adams: *Familiar Letters*, 198
7. *Amer. Arch.*, Fourth Series, VI, 590
8. *Journals*, V, 602

9. *Amer. Arch.*, Fifth Series, I, 725
10. Serle: *American Journal*, 86
11. Serle: *American Journal*, 88
12. *Journals*, V, 575-589
13. *Letters*, II, 19
14. Burnett: *Continental Congress*, 219-220
15. Fisher: *Evolution of the Constitution*, 7-8
16. *Letters*, II, 23

CHAPTER 13

1. John Adams, III, 75-76
2. John Adams, III, 77-79
3. Serle: *American Journal*, xxiii, Preface
4. *Journals*, V, 765
5. *Journals*, V, 730

6. *Letters*, II, 72
7. *Journals*, V, 762-763
8. John Adams, III, 83
9. John Adams, III, 68-69
10. John Adams, III, 48
11. *Letters*, II, 32

CHAPTER 13—(continued)

12. John Adams, III, 16
13. John Adams, III, 69
14. Jefferson, I, 28-30
15. Jefferson, I, 30-35
16. Letters, II, 48
17. John Adams, X, 177
18. Letters, II, 118
19. John Adams, II, 492-493, 502
20. Journals, V, 837

21. Journals, VI, 917
22. Journals, VI, 980
23. Washington (Ford), V, 84
24. Journals, VI, 1019-1020
25. Washington (Ford), V, 82-83
26. Letters, II, 156
27. Letters, II, 214
28. Journals, VI, 1022, 1027

CHAPTER 14

1. Washington (Ford), V, 114
2. Journals, VI, 1032
3. Journals, VI, 1045
4. Journals, VI, 1053
5. Journals, VII, 277
6. Adams: Familiar Letters, 256
7. Letters, II, 178
8. Letters, II, 196, 256
9. John Adams, II, 433-434
10. Adams: Familiar Letters, 247, 261
11. Journals, VI, 1036
12. Letters, II, 257
13. Burnett: Continental Congress, 235
14. Letters, II, 260
15. Maryland Historical Magazine, Vol. 42, 21-23
16. Letters, II, 135
17. Letters, II, 344
18. Adams: Familiar Letters, 237

19. Letters, II, 149
20. Journals, VII, 106
21. Adams: Familiar Letters, 249, 251
22. Journals, VII, 122-123
23. Journals, VII, 123
24. Adams: Familiar Letters, 276
25. Journals, VII, 133
26. Journals, VII, 174, 189
27. Washington (Ford), V, 259
28. Washington (Ford), V, 285
29. Journals, VII, 180
30. Serle: American Journal, 167, 182, 200
31. Letters, II, 399
32. Adams: Familiar Letters, 292
33. Adams: Familiar Letters, 301, 304, 306
34. Letters, II, 446-447
35. Letters, II, 519-520
36. Letters, II, 508

CHAPTER 15

1. Prowell: History of York County, Pennsylvania, 289-298
2. Journals, VIII, 649
3. Journals, VIII, 599
4. Burnett: The Continental Congress, 250
5. Adams: Familiar Letters, 319
6. Journals, IX, 817
7. Journals, IX, 854

8. Journals, IX, 933
9. Journals, IX, 982
10. Letters, III, 5-9
11. Journals, X, 29-35
12. Clark: The Convention Troops and the Perfidy of Sir William Howe, American Historical Review, Vol. 37, 722-723

CHAPTER 15—(continued)

13. Van Doren: *Secret History of the American Revolution*, 275-276, 277, 294, 353
14. R. H. Lee, I, 410
15. *Letters*, II, 562
16. *Letters*, III, 63
17. *Journals*, X, 336, 390

18. *Letters*, II, 232
19. Walther: *Gouverneur Morris*, 31-32
20. *Letters*, III, 84, 85, 181
21. *Journals*, X, 253
22. Gouverneur Morris (Sparks), I, 167

CHAPTER 16

1. *Letters*, II, 263
2. Washington (Ford), VI, 353-354
3. Knollenberg: *Washington and the Revolution*
4. *Letters*, III, 29
5. *Letters*, III, 199
6. *Letters*, III, 184
7. Van Tyne: *The War of Independence*, 162-170
8. Chatham, Burke, Erskine: *Oratory*, 36
9. Van Tyne: *The War of Independence*, 144
10. Chatham, Burke, Erskine: *Oratory*, 45-47
11. *Journals*, X, 375
12. *Journals*, X, 375-379
13. Burnett: *Continental Congress*, 329

14. *Journals*, XI, 457
15. *Letters*, III, 224
16. *Journals*, XI, 474-481
17. Serle: *American Journal*, 263, 294
18. *Journals*, XI, 615
19. *Letters*, III, 303
20. Serle: *American Journal*, 296
21. *Letters*, III, 285
22. *Letters*, III, 317, 319
23. R. H. Lee, I, 421
24. *Letters*, III, 332
25. *Letters*, III, 329
26. *Journals*, XI, 699
27. *Letters*, III, 329
28. *Letters*, III, 363
29. *Letters*, III, 330
30. *Letters*, III, 510-511

CHAPTER 17

1. Van Tyne: *Loyalists*, 153-155
2. *Rivington's Gazette*, January 24, 1778
3. *Journals*, XI, 721
4. *Letters*, III, 382
5. *Journals*, VII, 92
6. Samuel Adams, IV, 61
7. *Journals*, XI, 801
8. *Letters*, III, 444
9. *Letters*, III, 420 and 453
10. *Journals*, XII, 1042-1048
11. *Journals*, XII, 1001
12. Samuel Adams, IV, 65

13. *Letters*, III, 395n
14. *Letters*, III, 394-395
15. John Adams, III, 448-449
16. *New York Journal*, October 26 and November 1, 1778
17. *Letters*, III, 507
18. *Letters*, III, 530
19. *Journals*, XII, 1205-1206
20. *Letters*, III, 535
21. *Letters*, III, 540
22. *Pennsylvania Packet*, January 2, 1779
23. *Journals*, XIII, 54

CHAPTER 18

1. *Letters*, IV, 60
2. *Letters*, IV, 221
3. *Journals*, XIV, 619-622
4. *Letters*, IV, 253
5. *Journals*, XIII, 13-15
6. *Journals*, XIII, 108
7. *Journals*, V, 702; XII, 946
8. *Letters*, IV, 328
9. *Journals*, XIII, 239-244
10. *Letters*, Preface to Vol. IV
11. *Letters*, IV, 39
12. Samuel Adams, IV, 118
13. R. H. Lee, II, 54
14. *Journals*, XIII, 455-457
15. R. H. Lee, II, 202
16. *Journals*, XIV, 536-537
17. *Letters*, IV, 135 and 177
18. *Journals*, XIV, 736-739
19. *Letters*, IV, 293-294
20. *Letters*, IV, 299
21. *Letters*, IV, 243
22. *Letters*, IV, 232
23. *Letters*, IV, 119
24. *Letters*, IV, 407
25. *Letters*, IV, 172 and 316

CHAPTER 19

1. *Letters*, IV, 426
2. R. H. Lee, II, 54-55
3. *Letters*, IV, 554
4. *Letters*, IV, 490 and 549
5. *Letters*, IV, 479
6. *Journals*, XII, 1048-1052
7. *Dipl. Cor.*, III, 44
8. *Dipl. Cor.*, II, 439-440
9. *Journals*, IX, 971
10. Serle: *American Journal*, 217
11. *Journals*, XIII, 25
12. *Journals*, XIV, 626
13. *Journals*, XIV, 649-657
14. *Journals*, XIV, 691
15. *Journals*, XIV, 674
16. Hamilton, I, 116-125
17. *Journals*, XV, 1052-1061
18. *Dipl. Cor.*, III, 156-157
19. *Letters*, IV, 116
20. *Dipl. Cor*, III, 267-268
21. *Dipl. Cor.*, III, 324-326
22. *Letters*, IV, 182
23. *Letters*, IV, 373
24. Hamilton, I, 83

CHAPTER 20

1. Madison, I, 59
2. *Letters*, V, 73
3. *Journals*, XV, 1377
4. Madison, I, 128
5. Washington (Ford), VIII, 304
6. *Dipl. Cor.*, III, 483-485
7. *Dipl. Cor.*, III, 485-486
8. Van Tyne: *Loyalists*, 182
9. *Journals*, XVI, 118
10. *Journals*, XVI, 150
11. *Dipl. Cor.*, III, 132 and 137
12. Maclay: *American Privateers*, viii preface
13. *Letters*, V, 182
14. *Journals*, XVI, 326
15. *Journals*, XVI, 387
16. *Letters*, V, 165 and 174
17. *Dipl. Cor.*, III, 683-684
18. *Letters*, V, 155
19. *Journals*, XVII, 516
20. *Dipl. Cor.*, III, 846-847
21. *Letters*, V, 281

CHAPTER 20—(continued)

22. Letters, V, 248
23. Journals, XVII, 555
24. Letters, V, 330
25. Letters, V, 312
26. Letters, V, 373
27. Letters, V, 404
28. Letters, V, 349

29. Letters, V, 571
30. Letters, V, 402
31. Letters, V, 420
32. Letters, V, 413 and 510
33. Letters, V, 527
34. Journals, XIX, 79

CHAPTER 21

1. Dipl. Cor., III, 610 and 640
2. Journals, XVII, 807
3. Journals, XVIII, 915
4. Letters, VI, 1
5. Pennsylvania Packet, March 3, 1781
6. Hamilton, I, 150
7. Adams: Familiar Letters, 207
8. Letters, V, 71
9. Hamilton, I, 157-158
10. Journals, XIX, 284
11. Letters, VI, 11
12. Dipl. Cor., IV, 105
13. Journals, XIX, 126
14. Washington (Sparks), VII, 400n
15. Letters, VI, 42
16. Letters, VI, 53
17. Letters, V, 477

18. Letters, VI, 14
19. Letters, VI, 83 and 86
20. Letters, VI, 88
21. Letters, VI, 15 and 83
22. Journals, XIX, 411-412
23. Journals, XIX, 112
24. Dipl. Cor., IV, 328-330
25. Dipl. Cor., IV, 434
26. Letters, VI, 146
27. Letters, VI, 38
28. Letters, VI, 195
29. Letters, VI, 207
30. Franklin, VIII, 333
31. Letters, VI, 239
32. Letters, VI, 241
33. Franklin, IX, 261
34. Letters, VI, 249
35. Letters, VI, 248n

CHAPTER 22

1. Dipl. Cor., IV, 726-727
2. Journals, XXI, 999-1003
3. Burnett: Continental Congress, 527
4. Letters, V, 546
5. Letters, VI, 264
6. Letters, VI, 304
7. Letters, IV, 118
8. Samuel Adams, IV, 238
9. Madison, I, 166
10. Letters, VI, 326
11. Journals, XXI, 1017

12. Letters, VI, 362
13. Letters, VI, 308
14. Letters, VI, 340
15. Madison, I, 252n
16. Madison, I, 249
17. Madison, I, 178n
18. Madison, I, 228 and 242
19. Journals, XXII, 290
20. Journals, XXIII, 545
21. Madison, I, 251-252n
22. Letters, VI, 411
23. Journals, XXIII, 791-792

CHAPTER 22—(continued)

24. *Letters*, VI, 348-350
25. Madison, I, 235 and 239
26. *Journals*, XXIII, 543

27. *Journals*, XXIII, 638
28. *Journals*, XXIII, 578
29. *Letters*, VII, 43

CHAPTER 23

1. *Letters*, VII, 79
2. *Letters*, VII, 118
3. Madison, I, 408n
4. Madison, I, 413-414
5. *Journals*, XXIV, 242
6. *Journals*, XXIV, 287-288
7. *Journals*, XXIV, 288-289
8. *Journals*, XXIV, 44
9. *Letters*, VII, 123
10. *Journals*, XXIV, 277-283
11. *Letters*, VII, 164
12. *Letters*, VII, 150
13. *Letters*, VII, 46
14. *Journals*, XXIV, 296-297
15. *Letters*, VII, 180
16. *Letters*, VII, 134
17. *Letters*, VII, 199

18. Madison, I, 483
19. *Letters*, VII, 203
20. *Letters*, VII, 193
21. *Letters*, VII, 213
22. *Letters*, VII, 215 and 235
23. *Letters*, VII, 266
24. *Letters*, VII, 343
25. *Journals*, XXV, 657
26. *Journals*, XXV, 697
27. *Letters*, VII, 347 and 350
28. *Letters*, VII, 370-371
29. *Letters*, VII, 292
30. Hamilton, I, 353
31. Washington (Ford), VIII, 331
32. Washington (Sparks), VII, 267
33. *Letters*, VII, 394

CHAPTER 24

1. *Letters*, VII, 472
2. *Letters*, VII, 451
3. *Letters*, VII, 498
4. Monroe, I, 23-24
5. *Letters*, VII, 6
6. Hamilton, II, 284-286
7. *Letters*, VII, 399
8. *Journals*, XXVI, 23
9. *Letters*, VII, 448
10. *Letters*, VII, 414
11. *Journals*, XXVI, 245
12. Jefferson, I, 163
13. Jefferson, I, 58
14. *Letters*, VII, 534

15. *Letters*, VII, 534
16. Monroe, I, 29
17. *Journals*, XXVII, 524
18. *Letters*, VII, 555
19. *Letters*, VII, 565
20. *Letters*, VII, 576
21. *Letters*, VII, 575 and 578
22. *Letters*, VII, 583
23. *Letters*, VIII, 850
24. *Letters*, VII, 593
25. *Letters*, VII, 591
26. Monroe, I, 46 and 50
27. R. H. Lee, II, 292
28. R. H. Lee, II, 303

CHAPTER 25

1. *Letters*, VIII, 15 and 25
2. *Journals*, XXVIII, 9
3. *Journals*, XXVIII, 86
4. *Journals*, XXVIII, 199
5. *Journals*, XXVIII, 84 and 105
6. *Journals*, XXVIII, 258
7. *Letters*, VIII, 81
8. *Letters*, VIII, 101n
9. *Letters*, VIII, 18
10. *Letters*, VIII, 209
11. Jay, III, 226
12. Gouverneur Morris (Anne Cary Morris), II, 428 and 526
13. *Letters*, VIII, 121
14. Monroe, I, 95 and 103
15. *Letters*, VIII, 92
16. *Letters*, VIII, 119
17. *Letters*, VIII, 129-130
18. R. H. Lee, II, 371
19. *Letters*, VIII, 141
20. *Journals*, XXIX, 632
21. *Letters*, VIII, 291
22. *Letters*, VIII, 240
23. *Letters*, VIII, 254
24. *Letters*, VIII, 264
25. *Letters*, VIII, 309
26. R. H. Lee, II, 368
27. Monroe, I, 145-146
28. *Journals*, XXXI, 783-784
29. Jefferson, I, 550
30. *Journals*, XXXII, 142
31. Monroe, I, 148
32. *Letters*, VIII, 412
33. *Journals*, XXX, 364-365
34. *Letters*, VIII, 315
35. *Letters*, VIII, 465
36. *Journals*, XXXI, 753-754
37. Washington (Ford), VIII, 334-335
38. Madison, II, 318
39. *Journals*, XXXI, 887

CHAPTER 26

1. *Journals*, XXXI, 985
2. *Letters*, VIII, 327-328
3. *Letters*, VIII, 369-370
4. *Letters*, VIII, 383
5. *Letters*, VIII, 471
6. *Letters*, VIII, 486 and 487
7. *Letters*, VIII, 511 and 516
8. Madison, II, 227
9. Madison, II, 262
10. *Journals*, XXXI, 480-481
11. *Letters*, VIII, 468-469
12. *Letters*, VIII, 475
13. *Journals*, XXXI, 679-680
14. *Journals*, XXXII, Preface vii
15. Madison, II, 314
16. *Journals*, XXXII, 73
17. Madison, II, 319
18. *Journals*, XXXII, 194 and 198
19. Monroe, I, 116
20. *Journals*, XXXII, 192-193
21. *Letters*, VIII, 601
22. *Letters*, VIII, 611
23. *Letters*, VIII, 570
24. *Letters*, VIII, 607
25. *Letters*, VIII, 619-620
26. *Letters*, VIII, 623-624
27. *Letters*, VIII, 602 and 614
28. *Letters*, VIII, 618
29. *Journals*, XXXII, 334-343
30. R. H. Lee, II, 423
31. Madison, V, 17
32. R. H. Lee, II, 448
33. *Journals*, XXXIII, 549

CHAPTER 27

1. *Journals*, XXXIII, 502
2. R. H. Lee, II, 240-242
3. *Letters*, VIII, 678
4. Madison, V, 76
5. *Letters*, VIII, 689
6. *Letters*, VIII, 764
7. *Letters*, VIII, 696
8. Madison, V, 100-104
9. *Letters*, VIII, 706-707
10. *Letters*, VIII, 722 and 729
11. *Journals*, XXXIV, 26
12. *Journals*, XXXIV, 194
13. *Letters*, VIII, 761
14. *Letters*, VIII, 768 and 784
15. *Journals*, XXXIV, 353
16. *Journals*, XXXIII, 732
17. *Letters*, VIII, 737
18. *Letters*, VIII, 743
19. Madison, V, 309
20. Madison, V, 246
21. *Journals*, XXXIV, 522
22. *Journals*, XXXIV, 543, 549 and 573
23. *Letters*, VIII, 802
24. *Letters*, VIII, 808
25. *Letters*, VIII, 810
26. Madison, V, 270
27. *Letters*, VIII, 815 and 817
28. *Letters*, VIII, 818
29. *Letters*, VIII, 827
30. *Letters*, VIII, 829
31. Statistics compiled from the *Biographical Directory of Congress*, 1774-1927.

Index

Adams, Abigail, 68, 73, 103, 134, 157, 163, 201, 207; describes Bunker Hill, 74, and high prices, 78, 186
Adams, Deacon Samuel, 18
Adams, John, as delegate, 18, 20, 36, 61, 67, 79, 100, 182, 199, 201, 215; on Continental Congress, 8, 38, 77, 82, 162; on entertainment, 28, 29, 32, 39, 55, 76, 196; on journey to first Congress, 30-32, 33; on delegates, 31, 39, 55-56, 68, 73, 91-93, 103, 113, 117, 163; on English guilt, 90; on military affairs, 94, 108, 139, 147, 206, 207, 216, 227; as diarist, 30, 54, 92, 157, 176; as father of Navy, 96-98; leads fight for Independence, 128, 129, 138-139, 144, 145, 151, 152-155, 157; notes of debates, 40-42, 45-46, 50-51, 119-120, 152-153, 182; commissioner in France, 224, 270, 306; negotiates loans in Netherlands, 290, 337, 415; negotiates peace with Britain, 334; minister to Britain, 90, 386; elected vice president of United States, 420, 421
Adams, Samuel, as delegate, 36, 39, 47, 67, 79, 92, 121, 196, 198, 200, 203, 211; as archrebel, 17-22, 24-27, 30, 33, 48, 61, 247; poverty of, 17, 18, 27, 29; puritanical codes, 22, 57, 257, 327; at Lexington, 64-65; in Deane-Lee controversy, 268-269; distrust of power, 126, 311, 314, 316; retires from Congress, 327-328
Addresses of Continental Congress: to People of Great Britain, 52-53; to Inhabitants of Quebec, 53-54; to St. Johns and Nova Scotia, 54; to East and West Florida, 54; to American Colonies, 54; to Inhabitants of Great Britain, 82; to Ireland, Jamaica and Canada, 82

Alamance, battle of the, 40
Albany Plan, 173
Alexandria, Va., 393
Allen, Ethan, 69-70
Alsop, John, 31, 36, 67; opposes Independence, 120, 163
American monarchy considered, 379, 401
American Revolution, causes of, 15, 17, 19-26, 43, 56; acceleration of, 100-101; economic background, 40, 43, 46, 56-57, 79, 119, 179-180; influence of merchants, 23, 34, 231; moderation of, 16, 17, 60, 101, 135-136, 281
American rights, 38, 43, 45-46, 51-52
American Turtle, first submarine, 103-105
André, Captain John, 237
Annapolis, as seat of Congress, 350, 355, 358-360
Annapolis Convention, 393-395
Arnold, General Benedict, 69, 96, 108, 180, 188; military politician, 69, 108, 203; at Saratoga, 211, 216-217; profiteer and traitor, 221, 273-275, 303; British officer, 329
Arnold, Jonathan, 355
Arnold, Peleg, 413, 414, 418
Armstrong, John, 266, 277, 287, 414
Armstrong, Major John, Jr., 349, 415
Asgill, Captain Charles, 329-330, 331
Association, Articles of, 11-12; debated and adopted, 56-57; effects of, 58-61, 86, 101, 119-120, 198, 211
Atrocities, charges of, 89, 111, 166, 195, 212, 320, 329-330, 334

Bacon's Rebellion, 90
Baldwin, Abraham, 398, 414; elected to new Congress, 417
Baltimore, seat of Congress, 191, 193-200; as seen by delegates, 195-196; hospitality of, 196

Baltimore and Ohio Railroad Company, 422
Baltimore Resolution, 203
Bank of England, 307
Bank of United States, 317, 326
Bartlett, Josiah, 94, 146, 174, 200
Beaumarchais, Caron de, 170, 253, 261, 417
Bedford, Gunning, Jr., 260, 368
Bemis Heights, battle of, 217
Bennington, battle of, 211
Benson, Egbert, 414
Berckel, Peter John van, Dutch minister, 355-356
Beresford, Richard, 363
Biddle, Edward, 36, 67
Biddle, Nicholas, 105, 147
Bill of Rights, 13, 411, 419
Bills of Credit, see Paper money
Bills of Exchange, 279, 290, 299, 319
Bingham, William, 401, 414
Blanchard, Jonathan, 369, 372
Bland, Richard, 36, 67
Bland, Theodorick, 353; elected to new Congress, 417
Blockade, British, 279-280
Blount, William, 398, 400-401
Board of Treasury, 210, 387
Board of War, 147, 179, 203, 210, 224
Boerum, Simon, 27, 36, 67
Bonaparte, Napoleon, 289
Bonvouloir, Achard, 116-117
Boston, as storm center of revolt, 15, 17-25, 27, 32; rumors of destruction, 47-49; loyalists of, 60
Boston, siege of, 105, 108, 127
Boston "Massacre," 24-25, 31
Boston Port Bill, 15, 25, 35, 48
Boston Tea Party, 15, 24
Botetourt, Lord, 133
Boudinot, Elias, 242, 323, 326; president of Congress, 335, 343, 350, 351, 355, 384; elected to new Congress, 417
Brandywine, battle of the, 208
Braxton, Carter, opposes Independence, 130-131, 146; signs Declaration, 164
Brehan, Madame de, 415-416
Bristol, England, 32
British Empire, 20, 310
Brooklyn Heights, retreat from, 178

Brown, John, 414
Brownson, Nathan, 200, 211
Bulloch, Archibald, 94
Bunker Hill, battle of, 74-75, 166
Burgoyne, General John, 206, 212; surrenders at Saratoga, 216-218; charges violation of Convention, 218-221
Burke, Edmund, 5, 62, 64, 144, 170, 230
Burke, Thomas, 197, 200, 202-203, 247, 263, 267, 288, 289, 293, 315, 327; accuses General Sullivan, 208; disciplined by Congress, 222-223; death of, 277
Burnett, Edmund Cody, historian, 214, 268
Bushnell, David, 103-105
Butler, Pierce, 398; elected to new Congress, 417
Byles, the Rev. Mather, 60
Byrd, William, 133

Cambridge, Mass., 89, 94
Cambridge, University of, 250
Camden, battle of, 303
Canada, addresses to, 53-54, 82; commissioners to, 123-124; invasion of, 96, 106-109, 123-124, 139, 141, 142, 166; plans for further invasions, 226, 257, 264; refugees, 376
Carleton, Sir Guy, 54, 108, 124, 180, 188, 329
Carlisle, Earl of, 236, 239
Carmichael, William, 276, 288
Carpenters' Hall, first meeting place of Congress, 33, 36, 55
Carrington, Edward, 400, 414
Carroll, Charles, of Carrollton, 123, 141, 211, 224, 230, 247, 251; advocate of Independence, 151; elected to new Congress, 417; director of Baltimore and Ohio Railroad Company, 422
Carroll, Daniel, 325; elected to new Congress, 417
Carroll, John, 123, 251
Caswell, Richard, 36, 67, 94, 134; governor of North Carolina, 200
Catherine the Great, 140, 218, 318
Catholic religion, 54, 123, 251
Caucus Club, 18, 35
Charles I, 16, 77

Charles V, Emperor, 11
Charles Edward, Prince, 7, 134
Charleston, S. C., 22, 27, 65; British repulse from, 166, 232; captured by British, 301
Charlestown, Mass., destrucion of, 74, 220
Chase, Jeremiah Townley, 369
Chase, Samuel, 36, 46, 67, 123, 141, 174; advocate of Independence, 151, 186-187, 211, 247; accused of profiteering, 258
Chatham, William Pitt, Earl of, 43, 64, 170, 230; addresses House of Lords, 4-6, 64, 231-232; death of, 232, 233
Cherokees, efforts to arouse, 140
Chittenden, Thomas T., 334
Church, Dr. Benjamin, appointed surgeon-general, 85-86; treason of, 98-99, 101
Cincinnati, Society of the, 378-379
Claims to South Sea, see Western Lands
Clark, Abraham, 327, 402, 414, 418; on Independence, 6, 165; on Constitution, 411
Clark, George Rogers, 309, 382
Clinton, George, 67; governor of New York, 216, 225, 277, 297, 412
Clinton, Sir Henry, 134, 166, 207, 218, 221, 240, 241, 254, 266, 274, 304, 322
Clymer, George, 78, 174, 193, 325, 327; elected Representative, 417
Collins, John, 248, 287; as governor of Rhode Island, 392
Committee of the States, 214, 368-370; collapse of, 371-372
Committees of Correspondence, 24, 25-26
Committees of Safety, Inspection, Observation, etc., 59-61, 76, 101, 198
Committees, standing: Marine, 97, 105; of Secret Correspondence, 109, 116-117, 123, 124; of Foreign Affairs, 224, 261, 279, 299, 314; of Finance, 122-123, 126; on Declaration of Independence, 145-146, 154; on Confederation, 146, 169; at Cambridge, 94; at Ticonderoga, 107; at New York, 125; at Philadelphia, 193; at Valley Forge, 224-225; at Morristown, 297-299, 301-

302; to confer with Lord Howe, 176-178; to consult with Luzerne, 293; for increasing powers of Congress, 300; to regulate commerce, 377
Commons, House of, 23, 29, 61-62, 64, 230, 241, 307
Confederation, 10-12; Galloway's plan, 50-51; New York plan, 84; former plans, 172-173; motion for, 144; committee appointed, 174-175
Confederation, Articles of, 10-12; reported by committee, 171; debated, 174-175, 181-187, 202-203, 213-214; adopted, 214, 217-218; delays in ratification, 226, 241, 262-264; ratification, 305, 309-310; weaknesses, 310-311; efforts to amend, 394, 399
Congregationalists, 40, 47
Connecticut, elects delegates, 26; instructions to delegates, 37; colonial government of, 40; westward claims of, 181; retains royal charter, 199; ratifies Constitution, 410
Constitution of United States, 12-13, 185, 400-401, 405-406; criticisms of, 407-409, 421, ratification of, 410-412, 413-415
Constitutional convention, 12, 185, 312, 395; called by Congress, 396; in session, 398-402, 405-406
Contee, Benjamin, 414
Continental Army, adopted by Congress, 71-72; first generals elected, 72-73; bounties and enlistments, 106, 179, 265; shortages of arms, 141, 169, 179; material odds against, 294-295, 319; politics played by officers, 203-204, 205, 216-217; discharge of unpaid soldiers, 324, 332, 348-349, 350; on peacetime basis, 368; strengthened for Shays' Rebellion, 390
Continental Congress, inception of, 25-26; elections, 26-27; instructions, 37-38; powers, 7-9, 37-38, 42, 59-61, 162, 197, 293, 297, 299, 300, 310-311, 312, 316, 379; petty business of, 6, 9, 98, 126, 156; long working hours, 8-9, 76, 103, 126, 257; addresses and petitions, 52-54, 80-83; journeys and entertainments, 28, 29, 30-33, 39, 55-56, 358; com-

pared to Parliament, 22, 29, 43, 59, 61,
86; Lord Chatham on, 5-6, 13-14;
urges states to form governments, 99,
136-138; financial problems of, 10, 77-
78, 122, 279-287, 290-293, 317, 319,
324-325, 387; military problems of, 69,
70, 72, 76-77, 83, 86, 94, 95-98, 106-
109, 141-142, 179-180, 203, 211-212,
223, 226, 254, 264-265, 292, 294, 301-
302, 304, 319-320, 326, 332; measures
directed at Loyalists, 111, 125, 132,
151-152, 280; flight to Baltimore, 190-
191; relations with Washington, 191-
192, 193-194, 205-206; repudiation of
Saratoga Convention, 221; regulations
for secrecy, 38, 98, 182, 213; absenteeism, 10, 187, 197, 199, 222, 229, 326,
363-364, 382-383, 395-396; factionalism, 149, 256, 258-259, 268-269, 276,
286, 288, 366-367; puritanism, 49, 57,
77, 202, 206, 257; sectionalism, 25-27,
31, 40, 71-72, 75, 94-95, 183-186, 199,
207, 266, 268, 286-287, 308, 311;
self-criticism, 10, 38, 225-226, 316,
372; fears of tyranny, 76, 77, 167, 182,
192, 194, 203, 214, 311, 378; as
scapegoat, 7, 190-191; success of, 7, 8,
161-162; solicited by aspiring seats of
government, 350-351, 373, 416; ap-
points executive officers, 314-315; pre-
pares for government under new
Constitution, 417-422
Continental Navy, founding of, 96-98;
results of, 147-148, 296
Conway Cabal, 227-229
Cornell, Ezekiel, 300, 301
Cornwallis, Earl of, 322-323
Counterfeiting, 278, 282
Cowpens, battle of the, 307
Coxe, Tench, 419
Crane, Stephen, 36, 67
Crown Point, 69, 166
Cushing, Thomas, 16, 36, 67, 70

Dana, Francis, 224, 234, 238; minister
to Russia, 314; returns to Congress,
360, 369
Dane, Nathan, 399, 401, 414; opponent
of Constitution, 405-406
Dauphin, celebration of birth, 336-337

Dawson, John, 419
Dayton, Jonathan, 398, 414
Deane, Silas, 36, 38, 47, 67, 70, 97, 108;
on journeys to Philadelphia, 31-33, 66;
on delegates, 33, 39; agent in France,
117-118, 170, 171, 256, 259, 417;
treason of, 328
Deane-Lee controversy, 256, 258-259, 268-
269, 270-271, 328
Declaration of Independence, 6, 11, 145,
146; debated and adopted, 154-156;
reception in England, 162; signers, 7,
29, 131, 163, 164-166; persecution of
signers, 165-166; see also Independence
Declaration of Rights, 51-52
Declaration of Thirteen United Colonies,
110
Declaration on Taking Arms, 80
De Hart, John, 36, 67
Delaware, elects delegates, 26; votes on
Independence, 3-4, 150, 153; colonial
government of, 40; ratifies Confederation, 262; at Annapolis Convention,
394; ratifies Constitution, 410
Delaware river, 189, 194; banks of, selected as site for new seat of government, 354
Delegates of Continental Congress, election of, 26-27; ages, 28, 249, 361; education, 29, 248, 249; occupations, 29,
200, 248; ability, 9, 89, 90; financial
status, 28-29; compensation, 10, 102-
103, 210; expenses, 10, 102, 210-211,
332-333; terms of service, 214, 313,
367-368; rotation of service, 199; nicknames, 8, 248, 276; invalidism, 93, 202,
221-222; plots to seize, 9, 161, 206;
pen portraits of, 31, 39, 55-56, 68, 73,
91-93
Depreciation of currency, 207, 278, 282-
286, 297-298, 302; see also Paper
money
D'Estaing, Comte, 241, 254, 255
Detroit, 95, 385
DeWitt, Charles, 369
Dickinson, John, 35, 36, 39, 55, 100, 109,
146; opponent of Independence, 7,
120, 128, 130, 131, 143, 145, 149,
152-154, 317; quarrels with John
Adams, 93, 120; pamphleteer, 53-54,

80-81, 113, 282-283; soldier, 163; advocate of Confederation, 173-174; country estate destroyed by enemy, 240; returns to Congress, 262, 267, 272, 276, 287; president of Pennsylvania Council, 351-353; at Annapolis Convention, 395; at Constitutional Convention, 398; defender of Constitution, 411
Dickinson College, 376
Diderot, Denis, 44
District of Columbia, 350
Dollar, Spanish milled, 10
Drayton, William Henry, 234, 247, 267, 270, 271, 275, 288
Duane, James, 31, 36, 40, 45, 47, 50-51, 67, 68, 123, 211, 234, 247, 264, 276, 287, 309, 313, 314, 316, 321, 327; opposes Independence, 120, 130, 137, 317; mayor of New York, 375, 384
Dublin, 32
Duché, the Rev. Jacob, 47-48, 67, apostasy of, 215-216
Duelling, 269, 367
Duer, William, 211, 248
Dunmore, Earl of, 111, 134
Dyer, Eliphalet, 32, 36, 67, 75, 94, 208, 211, 221, 247, 327, 384

East Florida, 54, 173
East India Company, 24
Eddy, Jonathan, 376
Eden, Sir Robert, 151, 236
Eden, William, 236, 239
Edinburgh, University of, 29, 250, 256
Edwards, Pierrepont, 414
Ellery, William, 225, 235, 327, 368, 374, 383, 384
Elmer, Jonathan, 200, 210, 327; elected to new Congress, 417
Ellsworth, Oliver, 293, 316, 347, 350, 351, 360; at Constitutional Convention, 398; elected to new Congress, 417
England, political grievances of, 62-64; crude new nobility, 64; popularity of war, 231; gains from American Revolution, 363; see also Great Britain and British Empire
Episcopalians, 40, 47, 251
Eton, 249
Eutaw Springs, battle of, 322

Falls of Potomac, selected as site for federal city, 354
Falmouth, destruction of, 111, 125
Fasting, humiliation and prayer, days of, 48-49, 191, 206, 223, 312
Fawkes, Guy, 17, 161
Federalists and Antifederalists, 410, 412
Fell, John, 272, 276, 287
Ferguson, Colonel Patrick, 307
Few, William, 398, 402, 414, 417
Fisher, Sidney George, historian, 172
Fitch, John, 413
FitzSimons, Thomas, 346; elected to new Congress, 417
Flag resolution of Congress, 206
Fleming, William, 288
Floyd, William, 67, 327, 343; elected to new Congress, 417
Folsom, Nathaniel, 36, 211, 215, 224, 247, 327
Forbes, James, 287, 297
Foreign adventurers, problem of, 204
Foreign alliances, 144, 149; committee appointed, 146-147; model treaty approved, 170-171
Foreign loans, 278, 279
Fort Pitt (Pittsburgh), proposed as seat as government, 354
Fort Washington, British capture of, 188
Forty-Five, the, 63, 134
Foster, Abiel, 417
Fourth of July, as national holiday, 6, 157, 206, 271-272, 300
Fox, Charles James, 5, 62, 230
France, financial aid of, 11, 197, 286, 319, 324, 337, 344, 346; arms supplied by, 116-118, 170-171, 253; treaties of alliance with, 234-235, 252, 267; military and naval aid of, 254-255, 264, 298, 299, 321-322, 324-325; warship presented to, 338
Franklin, Benjamin, 6, 57, 61, 104; as delegate, 67, 76, 78, 81, 91, 93, 94, 109, 115, 147; appointed postmaster-general, 85; on mission to Canada, 123-124, 141, 150; favors Independence, 145, 154; estrangement from son, 150; as commissioner and minister in France, 171, 198, 233, 270, 289, 299, 318-319, 322, 323; Philadelphia home pillaged

by enemy, 233, 240; offers plan for confederation, 85, 172-174; negotiates peace with Great Britain, 344; at Constitutional Convention, 398

Franklin, William, 33, 35, 150

Franklin (Tennessee), proposed state of, 382, 397, 413

Frederick the Great, 70, 141, 218

Freeman's Farm, battle of, 212

Frelinghuysen, Frederick, 355

French royal couple, portraits of, 369

Gadsden, Christopher, 22, 36, 39, 46, 56, 67, 97; resigns to serve own state, 199

Gage General Thomas 26, 64

Gale, Benjamin, 104

Galloway Joseph, 33-34, 35, 36, 39, 45, 47, 132; offers plan for colonial union, 48-51, 173; retires from Congress, 69; tells of plot to seize delegates, 206

Gallows humor of Congress, 131, 205

Gardiner, John, 420

Gardoqui, Diego de, 385, 394, 397

Gates, General Horatio, 108, 128, 349; elected major-general, 72; given "dictatorial" powers, 147, 180, 204; at Saratoga, 211, 216-217, 218; on Board of War, 224, 225, 227; appointed to command in South, 301; defeated at Camden, 303

Gates-Schuyler feud, 205, 216, 303

George II, 63, 173, 221

George III, 8, 19, 20, 114, 196, 218; petitions to, 70, 80; personal rule of, 23, 63, 64, 89, 110, 120, 128, 140, 144, 221, 232, 294, 307, 338; assailed in Declaration of Independence, 155-156, 170; considers abdication, 338-339

Georgetown, 350

Georgia, not represented in first Congress, 16, 27; colonial government of, 40; western land claims of, 181; invaded by British, 255, 282, 300; ratifies Constitution, 410; cession of western lands refused, 415

Gérard de Rayneval, Sieur Conrade Alexandre, given reception by Congress, 241-242; minister of France, 253, 260-261, 264, 267, 270, 286, 288

German mercenaries, 89, 120, 140, 141, 144, 148, 175, 194, 206, 232, 295, 325

Germantown, battle of, 212

Gerry, Elbridge, 10, 123, 131, 200, 211, 287, 290, 293, 359, 365, 379; advocate of Independence, 138, 150, 165; elected to new Congress, 417

Gibbon, Edward, 230

Gilman, Nicholas, 398, 414

Gladstone, William E., 407

Glasgow, University of, 250

Goldsborough, Robert, 36, 67

Gordon riots, 306-307

Gorham, Nathaniel, 346; president of Congress, 383, 389, 398

Grayson, William, 380-381, 384, 389, 393, 399, 402, 409, 411; elected to new Congress, 417

Great Britain, 9, 46, 52-53, 60-64, 82, 85, 109, 129, 131, 137, 230-233, 267, 278, 306-307, 330, 393, 415

Great Rebellion, 16

Greece, City-States of, 11

Greene, General Nathaniel, 188, 204; elected brigadier, 72; resigns as quartermaster-general, 301; commands in South, 304, 307, 320, 322

Griffin, Cyrus, 256, 293; president of Congress, 412, 414, 415

Guilford, battle of, 320

Gunpowder, shortage of, 70, 74, 78, 79

Gwinnett, Button, signer of Declaration, 7, 138, 367

Half pay, for officers, 265-266, 350

Halifax, Lord, 133

Halifax, Nova Scotia, 127, 204, 257

Hall, John, 67

Hall, Lyman, 67, 138, 200

Hamilton, Alexander, 19, 180, 208, 248, 258, 303; as delegate, 328, 345, 346, 351, 414; on finances, 284-285; on powers of Congress, 310-311; in defense of Congress, 361; on need for new constitution, 312; at Annapolis Convention, 395; advocate of Constitution, 411

Hancock, John, 9, 22, 56, 61, 66, 67, 255; at Lexington, 64-65; president of Congress, 72, 91, 93, 95, 121, 141, 200,

211, 215; resigns from Congress, 218; governor of Massachusetts, 327; declines presidency of Congress, 383

Hand, Edward, 369

Hanson, John, president of Congress, 326

Harding, Seth, 105, 148

Haring, John, 36, 402

Harlem Heights, combat of, 178

Harnett, Cornelius, 211, 222, 277, 288; death of, 277

Harrison, Benjamin, 36, 67, 81, 93, 94, 109, 119, 121, 147, 183, 186, 211; opposes Independence, 130, 146; governor of Virginia, 350, 360, 362

Hart, John, victim of man-hunt as signer of Declaration, 165

Hartford, Conn., 65

Hartford Convention, 311

Harvard College, 17, 18, 22, 29, 249

Harvie, John, 224

Hawkins, Benjamin, 351, 402; elected to new Congress, 417

Haynes, Captain Isaac, 330

Hazard, Jonathan J., 414

Henry, John, 225, 226, 247, 287, 309, 384; elected to new Congress, 417

Henry, Patrick, 9, 19, 22, 36, 48, 53, 61, 131, 144; as orator in Congress, 12, 41-42, 51, 67; resigns to serve own state, 199, 385; opposes Constitution, 411

Hessians, see German mercenaries

Hewes, Joseph, 36, 67, 68, 70, 103, 121, 140, 142, 161, 172, 174; member of Marine Committee, 97, 105, 275, 288; death of, 275

Heyward, Thomas, Jr., 211, 318

Higginson, Stephen, 346

Hillegas, Michael, 78, 210

Hiltzheimer, Jacob, 302

Holland, see Netherlands

Holten, Samuel, 239-240, 253, 287, 374, 402

Hooper, William, 36, 67, 191, 195, 196, 224

Hopkins, Esek, commodore of fleet, 105; dismissed, 148-149

Hopkins, John Burroughs, 105

Hopkins, Stephen, 36, 67, 97-98, 146, 184, 247, 327

Hopkinson, Francis, 153

Hortalez and Company, 170, 253, 283

Hosmer, Titus, 258

House, Mrs. Mary, 200

Houston, William C., 287, 297-298, 314

Houstoun, William, 369, 376, 377

Howe, Richard, Viscount, 105, 143; confers with American committee, 176-178; cool to American loyalists, 177, 280

Howe, Sir William, 127, 143, 147, 188, 207, 208, 212, 233, 236-237, 280

Huddy, Captain Josiah, 330, 332

Hudson river, 109

Huger, Daniel, 402, 414; elected to new Congress, 417

Humphreys, Charles, 36, 67; opposes Independence, 154, 174

Huntington, Benjamin, 414

Huntington, Samuel, 186-187, 248, 287; president of Congress, 289, 298, 302, 313

Illinois settlements, 309, 382, 404

Immigrants, colonial, 34

Impost, 280, 318-319, 333, 346, 370, 376-377, 387

Independence, 3-4, 6, 113, 115; motion for, 143-144; contest in Congress, 136-139, 143-146, 149, 152-154; contest in Colonies, 149-151; as means to an end, 139, 144-145; confirmed by Congress the following year, 233-234, 238; see also Declaration

Independence Day, see Fourth of July

Indian Affairs, departments of, 83; neutrality urged by Congress, 83-84, 140-141, 253

Indians, American, 9, 44, 90, 109, 140, 212, 232, 253, 267, 344, 386

Inns of Court, 29, 225, 249

Intolerable Acts, 15, 25, 47

Ireland, 82, 109, 173

Irvine, William, 414

Italian City-States, 11

Izard, Ralph, 328; elected to new Congress, 417

Jackson, Andrew, 308

James II, 17

Jamaica, 82
Jay, John, 36, 39, 46, 50, 67, 80, 100, 107, 108, 247; author of address, 52-53; opposes Independence, 130, 145; president of Congress, 259, 271, 275, 282, 285-286, 287; minister to Spain, 289, 299, 314; negotiates peace with Britain, 344; Secretary of Foreign Affairs, 355, 368, 373, 385, 394, 398
Jefferson, Thomas, 19, 44, 52; as delegate, 67, 80-81, 85; author of Declaration, 3, 6, 145-146, 154-156, 282; debates Confederation, 186-187; notes on debates, 149, 182-187; as leader in Virginia, 48-49, 61; resigns from Congress to serve own state, 198; returns to Congress, 360, 361; introduces decimal system, 366; advocates creation of public lands into new states, 364; minister to France, 369
Jenifer, Daniel of St. Thomas, 263, 273, 317
Johnson, Dr. Samuel, as British pamphleteer, 230
Johnson, Thomas, Jr., 36, 67, 80, 108
Johnson, William Samuel, 375, 377, 398, 417
Johnstone, George, 236, 239
Jones, John Paul, 105, 254, 275, 316
Jones, Joseph, 211, 309, 353
Jones, Noble Wymberly, 320
Jones, Willie, 309
Journals of Congress, 126, 156, 180, 256, 287, 347, 357, 372, 403, 406; votes of delegates published in, 213

Kalb, Johann (Baron De Kalb), 204, 303
Kean, John, 402
Kearny, Dyre, 402, 414
Kentucky, 397, 413
Kieth, Sir William, 172
King, Rufus, 361, 375, 379, 380, 383, 389, 394-395; at Constitutional Convention, 398; elected to new Congress, 417
King's College (Columbia), 29, 225, 249, 374
King's Mountain, battle of, 307
Kingston, N. Y., 350
Kinloch, Francis, 361

Kinsey, James, 36, 67
Kloster Seven, Convention of, 220-221
Knox, Henry, 94, 204; reports on Shays' Rebellion, 389
Kosciusko, Thaddeus, 204; at Saratoga, 217, 218

Lafayette, Marquis de, 204, 208, 228, 229, 255
Lake Champlain, 69, 109, 123, 180
Lake George, 123
Lancaster, seat of Congress for a day, 209
Langdon, John, 67, 107; at Constitutional Convention, 398; elected to new Congress, 417
Langdon, Woodbury, 276
Langworthy, Edward, 248, 260, 273
Laurens, Henry, 207, 208, 211, 213; president of Congress, 222, 228, 229, 234, 237, 247; resigns presidency, 259-260; remains as delegate, 264, 267, 269, 271, 275, 288; imprisoned in Tower by British, 290, 318, 329
Laurens, Colonel John, 318
Law, Richard, 211
Lee, Arthur, 61, 117; commissioner in France, 171, 256, 259, 270, 286, 314; delegate, 328-329, 335, 365; on Board of Treasury, 387
Lee, General Charles, 71, 72, 124-125; captivity of, 205-206
Lee, Ezra, 105
Lee, Francis Lightfoot, 93, 199, 211, 240, 259
Lee, Richard Henry, 10, 36, 39, 45, 48, 50, 52, 67, 97, 125, 128, 148, 203, 211, 222, 228, 235, 247, 270, 276; advocate of Independence, 143, 144, 165; president of Congress, 373, 380, 384; on Northwest Ordinance, 403-404; opponent of Constitution, 400, 408-412; elected to new Congress, 417
Lewis, Francis, 36, 67; ruined by enemy as signer of Declaration, 165; continues as delegate, 248, 287
Lexington, battle of, 64-66, 166
L'Hommedieu, Ezra, 354, 414
Liberty Boys, 23
Lincoln, General Benjamin, 301; Secretary of War, 315

Lind, John, British pamphleteer, 162
Livermore, Samuel, 321-322, 330; elected to new Congress, 417
Livingston, Philip, 31, 36, 67; death of, 239
Livingston, Robert R., 67, 107, 146, 293, 299, 300, 309; opposes Independence, 120, 130, 145; Secretary of Foreign Affairs, 315, 335, 355; advocate of Constitution, 412
Livingston, Walter, 387
Livingston, William, 36, 52, 67, 80, 107; resigns to serve own state, 199; at Constitutional Convention, 399
London, population of, 32; miseries of poor, 62; rioting in, 306-307
Long, Pierse, 377
Long Island, battle of, 175
Lords, House of, 4-5, 13, 231, 232
Lottery, 187, 196, 197, 279
Louis XVI, 170, 235, 271, 286, 294, 336-337
Lovell, James, 196, 200, 208, 211, 228, 238, 241, 247, 286, 287, 289, 303, 314, 317, 318, 327; French interpreter, 204; decodes British messages, 322
Low, Isaac, 36, 69
Loyalists, American, 8, 20, 27, 29, 99, 136, 252, 253; disarmed by Congress, 111, 125, 132; property appropriated, 280-281; effects of Association on, 60-62, 101, 198; rights upheld by Congress, 151-152; plundered by British, 195; uprisings of, 111, 134-135, 138, 152; snobbishness of, 132-133, 281; military service of, 180, 253, 295, 303, 307
Luzerne, Chevalier Anne C. de la, 284, 289, 293-294, 298, 300; influence on ratification of Confederation, 309; relations with Congress, 314-315, 319, 324; as Philadelphia host, 328; announces birth of Dauphin, 336-337; leavetaking, 369
Lynch, Thomas, Sr., 36, 39, 42, 46, 67; death of, 239
Lynch, Thomas, Jr., 94

McAdam, John, 133
McComb, Eleazer, 353

McClene, James, 287
McCrea, Jane, killed by Indians, 212
McDougall, Alexander, 22, 315, 349; first rebel to be imprisoned, 31
McHenry, James, 358, 360, 375
McIntosh, Lachlin, 367
McKean, Thomas, 3, 36, 67, 146, 153, 154, 180, 185, 238, 247, 260, 287, 293; president of Congress, 313, 320, 321, 322, 384
McPherson, James, British pamphleteer, 230
Madison, James, 19, 291, 309, 313, 328, 335, 337, 343, 346, 351-353, 393, 396, 399, 414, 415, 419; expenses as delegate, 10, 332-333; advocates more powers for Congress, 292, 389; notes of debates, 331, 332, 344-345; address to States, 348; in defense of Congress, 360; at Constitutional Convention, 399; advocate of Constitution, 411; elected to new Congress, 417
Madrid, 270
Magna Carta, 16
Maine, 111, 397, 413
Manifest Destiny, 397
Manning, the Rev. James, 392
Marbois, François, 284, 289
Marchant, Henry, 211, 242
Marine Corps, founding of, 97, 106
Marshall, John, 411
Martin, Governor Josiah, 134
Maryland, elects delegates, 26; colonial government of, 40; decides for Independence, 151; forms state government, 198, 199; opposes states with western claims, 186-187, 213; opposes Articles of Confederation, 241, 262-263; ratifies Confederation, 305, 309-310; ratifies Constitution, 410
Mason, George, 405, 411
Massachusetts, instructions to delegates, 37; elects delegates, 26, 64; punished by Intolerable Acts, 15, 25; colonial government of, 40; forms state government, 99; passes act regulating trade, 378; puts down Shays' Rebellion, 391; ratifies Constitution, 410
Mathews, John, 247, 256, 288, 301-302, 318, 319, 321; serves on committee at

Morristown, 297, 301-302; criticizes South, 311

Mease, James, 273

Members of Continental Congress, see Delegates

Mercer, John Francis, 345, 367, 372

Meredith, Samuel, 414

Meschianza, 236-237

Methodists, 251

Middleton, Arthur, 92, 211, 320, 327

Middleton, Henry, 36, 39, 67; president of Congress, 57

Mifflin, Thomas, 33, 36, 39, 67; serves as soldier, 73, 224; as delegate, 327; president of Congress, 357

Militia, 59, 178, 212, 351-352

Miller, Nathan, 392

Miralles, Juan, 385

Mississippi river, navigation of, 268, 270, 271, 286-288, 343, 394, 397

Mitchell, Nathaniel, 402, 414

Mitchell, Stephen Mix, 384

Monmouth, battle of, 240

Monroe, James, 19, 360, 361, 372, 375, 377, 379, 397; marriage of, 384-385

Montgomery, John, 339, 351, 353

Montgomery, Joseph, 325

Montgomery, General Richard, 72, 96, 107; killed at Quebec, 108

Montreal, 96, 107, 125, 166

Moore's Creek, combat of, 134-135, 138

Morgan, General Daniel, at Quebec, 108; at Saratoga, 211, 217, 218; victor of Cowpens, 307-308

Morris, Gouverneur, as delegate, 224, 225, 229, 234, 235-237, 247, 256, 264, 267, 276; wit and cynic, 49, 226; on Continental Congress, 10; on financial debacle, 278; financial adviser, 347, 366; at Constitutional Convention, 399; on Constitution, 407

Morris, Lewis, 67, 95

Morris, Robert, 56, 108, 109, 128-129, 239, 248, 258, 269; opposes Independence, 130, 146, 154, 163, 171, 198; on flight to Baltimore, 191; advocate of executive authority, 193, 195, 224; Superintendent of Finance, 315, 318, 322, 325, 346, 348, 362, 365; at Constitutional Convention, 399

Morristown, 194, 294

Morton, John, 36, 37; message of defiance, 68; votes for Independence, 154

Moultrie, Major William, 166

Mount Vernon, 393

Moustier, Comte de, 415-416

Muhlenberg, Frederick, 287

Mutiny, of Pennsylvania Line (1781), 304-305; threatens Congress in State House (1783), 351-353

Natural law, 43-45, 113

Navigation Acts, 19, 55

Nelson, Thomas, 93, 123, 146, 196

Netherlands, United Provinces of, 11, 56; negotiations for loans from, 290, 335, 337-338, 415; treaty of amity with, 355

Newark, 188

Newburgh addresses, 349

New England, 27, 40, 72, 75, 94, 199, 207, 213, 266, 268, 286-287, 311, 371

Newfoundland fishing rights, 257, 268, 270, 271, 286-288, 343

New Hampshire, elects delegates, 26; colonial government of, 40; takes lead in establishing own state government, 99, 191; ninth state to ratify Constitution, 410

New Jersey, elects delegates, 26; colonial government of, 40; loyalists of, 99, 100, 150, 194; admonished by committee of Congress, 100; decides for Independence, 150-151; forms state government, 171; legislature addressed by committee of Congress, 389; at Annapolis Convention, 394; ratifies Constitution, 410

New Model Army, as object lesson, 77, 136

New Orleans, 208

Newspaper critics of Congress, 259, 271, 272, 284

Newtown, battle of, 267

New York, elects delegates, 27; colonial government of, 40; proposes plan of union, 84; feudal traditions of, 31; loyalist faction of, 31, 111, 125, 168; delays acceptance of Independence, 3,

151, 163; at Annapolis Convention, 394; ratifies Constitution, 414

New York campaign (1776), 167-169, 178

New York City, visited by New England delegates, 30-32, 65-66; first bloodshed of Revolution, 40; greets Washington and Tryon, 73; celebrates Independence, 162; abandoned by American forces, 180; great fire of, 180; last seat of Continental Congress, 374-422; social life of, 374; offers City Hall as Council Chamber, 375, 418, 420; boarding houses of, 384; celebrates ratification of Constitution, 414; chosen as seat of new government under Constitution, 416

Niagara, 385

Nicholas, Robert Carter, 48

Nonexportation and nonimportation agreements, 23-24, 46, 56-57, 59; see also Association

Norfolk, destruction of, 111, 125, 134, 329

North, Frederick, Lord, 63, 79, 230, 233, 323, 338

North Carolina, elects delegates, 26; colonial government of, 40; battle of the Alamance, 40; loyalist uprising, 134-135; decides for Independence, 138; as battleground, 320; delays in ratifying Constitution, 415, 416

Nova Scotia, 54, 134, 173

Ohio Land Company, 402

Olympic Games, 272

Oratory, prejudice against, 12, 152, 185, 367

Osgood, Samuel, 365, 368, 387

Oswald, Richard, 339, 344

Otis, James, 19-22, 43, 44, 75, 113, 282

Otis, Samuel Alleyne, 412, 414, 418, 420

Oxford University, 250

Paca, William, 36, 67, 270, 327; governor of Maryland, 358

Paine, Ephraim, 367

Paine, Robert Treat, 16, 36, 67, 107

Paine, Thomas, author of Common Sense, 112-115; soldier and author of Crisis

papers, 188-189; secretary of Committee of Foreign Affairs, 224; resigns, 260-261; relieved from financial worries, 356

Paper money, 10, 77, 122-123, 141, 187, 196-197, 210, 272, 276, 278, 281-286, 289-290, 292, 296-297, 317-318

Paris, 306, 362

Parker, John, 414

Parker, Sir Peter, 134, 166

Parliament, 16, 23, 24, 25, 48, 52, 54, 56, 109, 128, 231-232; corruption of, 5, 19, 51, 61-62, 76; ignorance of American affairs, 22-23, 61

Peace with Great Britain, 320, 326, 338; provisional treaty of, 339; favorable terms of, 343; misgivings of Congress, 344-345; definitive treaty ratified by Congress, 362-364; ratified by Great Britain, 370

Peace commissioners, British (1776), 128-129, 136-137, 144, 176-178; (1778), 233, 236, 238-239

Peabody, Nathaniel, 277, 287, 297

Peale, Charles Willson, 92, 273

Peerage, British, under George III, 64, 133

Pell, Philip, 420

Pell's Point, combat of, 188

Pendleton, Edmund, 36, 67, 72

Penn, John, 269, 288, 327

Penn, William, 172

Pennsylvania, elects delegates, 26; first acts of revolt, 35; colonial government of, 40; loyalists of, 99; contests for Independence, 149, 150, 153, 154; forms state government, 150; defies Congress, 274; mutinies of state's troops, 304-305, 351-353; rebuked by Congress, 346, 388; at Annapolis Convention, 394; ratifies Constitution, 410

Pennsylvania Gazette, 122, 152

Pennsylvania Herald, 401

Pennsylvania Packet, 241, 260, 310

Pennsylvania, University of (College of Philadelphia), 29, 249

Pensacola, plan to capture, 207-208

Pensions, 266

Peters, Richard, 224, 328, 343, 348, 351

Pettit, Charles, 392, 393

Philadelphia, 3, 9, 14, 16, 26; welcomes first Continental Congress, 28-33; as seen by delegates, 32-33; population of, 32; boarding houses of, 39, 200-201; welcomes second Congress, 66; occupied by Howe, 208, 236-239; return of Congress (1778), 239-241; parade of French troops, 321-322; postwar social life, 328; angry departure of Congress, 353, 354; rejected as seat of Congress, 399, 416
Pierce, William, 402
Pinckney, Charles, 361, 389, 391-392, 398; at Constitutional Convention, 398
Pitt, William, see Chatham
Pitt, William, the younger, 363
Plessis, Chevalier du, 204
Poland, Partition of, 218
Politics, practical, 13, 18, 22, 34, 35, 47, 55, 75, 90, 200
Pomeroy, Seth, 72
Popular education, 381, 404
Ports, American, resolution to open, 85, 118-119, 129
Postal service, 26, 84
Presbyterians, 40, 47, 251
Preston, battle of, 178
Price regulation proposed, 197
Priestly, Joseph, 81
Princeton, as seat of Congress, 353, 357-372
Princeton, battle of, 194
Princeton College, 10, 29, 32, 165, 225, 249, 291, 383
Privateering, 128, 296
Profiteering, 196-197, 258, 272-273, 281; see also Speculation and high prices
Public Lands Ordinance (of 1785), 380-382; see also Northwest Ordinance
Pulaski, Count Casimir, 301
Putnam, General Israel, 72

Quakers, 28, 40, 47, 201, 251
Quartering Act, 25
Quebec, fortress of, 96; American defeat at, 108, 124
Quebec, Province of, 54, 173
Quebec Act, 54, 124, 251
Quincy, Dorothy, 65, 201
Quincy, Josiah, Sr., 123

Quincy, Josiah, Jr., 21
Quorum (under Confederation), 313, 362-363
Quotas assigned to States: of funds, 78, 182-183, 333, 346, 362, 409-410; of supplies, 292, 295, 299, 300; of troops, 295

Ramsey, David, 383
Ramsey, Nathaniel, 383
Randolph, Edmund, 277, 288, 316, 344, 405, 411
Randolph, Peyton, 61, 65; first president of Congress, 36, 57; death of, 239
Read, George, 36, 67, 76, 417; opposes Independence, 3, 120, 130, 153; signs Declaration, 164; at Constitutional Convention, 399; elected to new Congress, 417
Read, Jacob, 369-372, 380, 384
Reed, Joseph, 39, 224, 239, 247
Refugees, loyalist, 60, 134, 374
Reid, James R., 414, 420
Religious toleration, 47-48, 124, 251
Revere, Paul, 22; rides to Philadelphia, 25, 49; rides to Lexington, 65
Rhoads, Samuel, 36
Rhode Island, elects delegates, 26; colonial government of, 40; retains royal charter, 199; battleground of Franco-American forces against British, 255; French troops under Rochambeau arrive, 299-300; opposes Impost, 334, 370; sharply criticized, 370, 377, 415; not represented in Constitutional Convention, 399; does not ratify Constitution until long later, 412, 416
Rhode Island, College of (Brown), 334, 375
Riflemen, 66, 70-71, 77, 211, 217
Rivington's Gazette, 252
Roberdeau, Daniel, 210, 211, 216
Rochambeau, Comte de, 299, 321
Rodney, Caesar, 36, 38, 67, 92, 141, 272, 327; rides to Philadelphia, 4, 6, 153, 154
Rodney, Thomas, 310, 316
Root, Jesse, 248, 325
Ross, David, 414, 420
Ross, George, 36, 67

Royal governors, 26, 61, 99, 133, 151
Rumford, Count (Benjamin Thompson), 133
Rush, Benjamin, 92, 174, 184, 197, 227, 228, 354; advocate of Constitution, 408
Russia, 318
Russian mercenaries, British attempt to employ, 89, 140
Rutledge, Edward, 36, 39, 45, 50, 67, 91, 125; opposes Independence, 120, 130, 145; signs Declaration, 164; on Confederation, 174, 176, 187; retires to serve own state, 198, 320
Rutledge, John, 36, 39, 42, 80, 92, 100; governor of South Carolina, 207, 222; returns to Congress, 325, 346; at Constitutional Convention, 399

St. Clair, Arthur, as general, 206, 351; president of Congress, 395
St. George's Fields, "Massacre" of, 63
St. Johns, 54, 70, 173
Salomon, Haym, 332-333
Sandwich, Earl of, 5, 62
Saratoga, campaign, 211-212, 216-217; Convention of, 218; British violations anticipated by Washington and Congress, 219-221; charges of Burgoyne, 219; resolution of Congress, 221
Savannah, 65; captured by British, 255; Franco-American defeat, 300-301
Schureman, James, 402
Schuyler, Philip, as delegate, 67, 70, 83; as general, 72, 83, 107; rebuked by Congress, 205; returns as delegate, 297, 309; elected to new Congress, 417
Scotch-Irish population, 34, 40, 134-135, 150, 251
Scottish Highlanders, 134-135, 148
Scudder, Nathaniel, 243, 247, 277; killed in battle, 327
Seabury, Samuel, 60
Searle, James, 287, 315
Sedgwick, Theodore, 386, 414
Seney, Josiah, 414
Sergeant, Jonathan D., 196, 260
Serle, Ambrose, 69, 169, 177, 195, 206, 236-237, 251
Sharpe, William, 288, 318

Shays' Rebellion, 389-391; effect on Constitution, 391, 396
Sherman, Roger, 29, 31-32, 36, 57, 67, 92, 145, 147, 201, 243, 309, 321, 359, 384; at Constitutional Convention, 398, 401; elected to new Congress, 417
Six Nations, 253, 267
Slavery, 90, 155-156; as issue of Confederation, 182-183; of Northwest Ordinance, 404; of Constitution, 408
Smallpox, 108, 140
Smith, Adam, 22
Smith, James, 210
Smith, Melancton, 402, 412
Smith, Meriwether, 248, 264, 267, 274, 288
Smith, Richard, 36, 67, 123
South Carolina, elects delegates, 27; instructions to delegates, 37; colonial government of, 40; loyalists of, 99; opposes Association, 56; contest for Independence, 153, 154; overrun by British, 303-304; ratifies Constitution, 410
Spaight, Richard D., 367, 369, 377
Spain, 267, 279, 286, 289, 290, 344; danger of American war with, 397, 398
Speculation and high prices, 78, 207, 258, 272-273, 276-277, 317; see also Paper money, Profiteering
Spencer, Joseph, 72, 287
Stamp Act, 22, 23
Stamp Act Congress, 23, 38
Stark, General John, 211-212
State governments, 9, 99, 136-138, 171-172
State House (Independence Hall), 4, 67, 149, 161, 240, 241, 336, 351-353, 399
States' rights, 9, 202, 223, 370, 400
Steamboat, application to Congress for, 413
Steuben, "Baron von," 204, 238
Stockton, Richard, 153; imprisoned by British, 165, 205
Stone, Thomas, 67, 187, 360
Suffolk Resolves, 49-50, 51
Sullivan, John, as delegate, 36, 41; as general, 67, 204; defended by Washington, 208; defeats Indians and Tories,

267; returns to Congress, 304, 314, 327

Swann, John, 414

Sweden, treaty with, 335, 353

Swiss Confederation, 11, 184

Tarleton, Colonel Banastre, 307

Tarring and feathering, 22, 59

Taxation, colonial, 20, 23, 56; right retained by rebelling colonies, 77; jealously guarded by new states, 197; levied with reluctance, 278-279, 282; see also Impost, Paper money, Quotas

Taylor, George, 174

Tea Act, 24, 56

Tennessee, see Franklin

Thomas, John, 72

Thomson, Charles, early life of, 34; as Pennsylvania radical, 22, 35; secretary of Congress, 38, 57, 91, 121, 190, 250, 274, 315, 336, 355, 357, 371-372, 395, 401, 402, 403; summer place ruined by British, 240; on defeats in South, 304; during last days of Congress, 420-422

Thornton, Matthew, signs Declaration, 164; 196, 200

Tilghman, Matthew, 36, 67

Tilghman, Tench, 323

Tilton, James, 368

Ticonderoga, captured by Ethan Allen, 69-70; aid to American cause, 107, 108, 166; objective of Carleton, 180; captured by Burgoyne, 206

Tories, American, see Loyalists

Tories, British, 63

Townshend Acts, 23, 46

Trenton, as seat of Congress, 355, 372-373

Trenton, battle of, 194

Trumbull, John, 164

Tucker, Thomas T., 414

United States of America, named in Journals, 355-356

Valcour Island, battle of, 188

Valley Forge, 223-224, 225-226; as training school of army, 238

Van Dyke, Nicholas, 287, 320

Van Tyne, Claude H., historian, on Continental Congress, 8, 161

Varnum, James Mitchell, 303, 313, 315, 316

Vergennes, Comte de, 116, 170, 270, 297, 315, 331, 344

Vermont, 330, 334, 369, 397, 413

Virginia, elects delegates, 27; proposes committees of correspondence, 25, and general congress, 26; colonial government of, 40; loyalist uprising in, 111, 134; forms state government, 100, 171; urges Independence, 138, 143; repudiates approval of Impost, 335; cession of western lands accepted, 364; at Annapolis Convention, 394; ratifies Constitution, 411

Voting and representation, 41-42, 181, 183-184, 202, 213-214; under Confederation, 313; under Constitution, 401

Wadsworth, Jeremiah, 392, 419

Walton, George, 193, 320, 327, 376

War claims, 375-376

Ward, Artemas, 72

Ward, Samuel, 36, 42, 45, 67, 121; death of, 239

Warfare, eighteenth-century, tactics of, 70, 141; mercies and courtesies of, 89, 112, 166, 329

Warren, James, 139, 149, 279, 329

Warren, Joseph, 21, 49; killed at Bunker Hill, 74-75

Washington, George, as delegate, 36, 39, 43, 67, 68, 70; commander in chief, 71-72, 73, 75, 94, 95, 141-142; at siege of Boston, 105, 108, 127, 134; in New York campaign, 167-169, 175, 188; generalship of, 175, 189, 208, 212; political ability of, 228; personal leadership of, 9, 161, 190-192, 220-221, 223-224, 233, 274, 302, 349, 356-357; as unofficial executive, 191-192, 204-205, 264-265; given "dictatorial" powers by Congress, 193, 195, 223; pessimism of, 226, 266, 320; idolized by own generation, 227-228; statue ordered, 354; urges more powers for Congress, 293, 297, 356, 388-389;

visits Congress at Princeton, 353, 356; farewell address of, 357-358; western journey of, 380; at Constitutional Convention, 396; elected first president of United States, 419, 422

Washington, John Augustine, 75

Wayne, General Anthony, 240, 266, 305

Wesley, John, as British pamphleteer, 230-231, 306

West, William, 273

West Florida, 54, 173, 236, 344

West Indies, 46, 82, 133; arms smuggled from, 170

West Point, 274, 303, 368

Western lands, claims of states, 181, 202, 213, 262-264, 331; cessions of, 308-309, 333-334, 364; as source of income, 280, 333, 346, 364, 380-382; as prospective new states, 364; see also Public Lands Ordinance, Northwest Ordinance

Westward migration, 380, 397

Whigs, American, 63; British, 63-64

Whipple, Abraham, 105

Whipple, William, 125, 200, 258, 262, 267

Whitehaven, raid on, 254

White Plains, battle of, 188

Wilkes, John, 5, 61-63, 230, 306-307

Wilkinson, Colonel James, 216

William and Mary College, 29, 249

Williams, William, 185, 186, 211

Williamsburg, 22

Williamson, Hugh, 349, 414, 415; elected to new Congress, 417, 420

Willing, Thomas, 67, 123, 258, 269; opposed to Independence, 154

Wilson, James, 67, 95, 107, 115, 119, 147; opposes Independence, 130, 137, 145, 154; proposes open sessions of Congress, 182; debates Confederation, 183-184, 203; serves later terms in Congress, 247, 317, 327, 360; at Constitutional Convention, 399

Wingate, Paine, 412, 414

Wisner, Henry, 36, 67, 154

Witherspoon, John, 32, 39, 153, 196, 197, 247, 267, 291, 317, 327, 384; expenses of, 10; on British cowardice, 178; on American union, 243; saves gains of Saratoga, 218-221

Wolcott, Oliver, 118, 129, 200, 222, 235, 318, 327

Wooster, General David, 72, 107, 147

Writs of Assistance, 19

Wyoming Valley controversy, 84, 326, 413, 415

Wythe, George, 93, 100, 119; advocate of Independence, 149; at Constitutional Convention, 399

Yale College, 29, 249

Yates, Abraham, 402, 403, 414

York, as seat of Congress, 209-240; cramped quarters of, 210, 222

Yorktown campaign, 321-323

Zubly, John J., 94; opposes Independence, 130, 252